Fool of the Family

By the same author

Criticism and Biography

Sheridan Le Fanu and Victorian Ireland
James Joyce and Modern Literature
Ascendancy and Tradition
The Battle of the Books
Dissolute Characters
The Paper War of 1786–1788
From Burke to Beckett
The Pamphlet Debate on the Union
Ferocious Humanism

Poetry and Autobiography
(published under the name, Hugh Maxton)

The Noise of the Fields
Jubilee for Renegades
At the Protestant Museum
The Puzzle Tree Ascendant
The Engraved Passion
Swiftmail
Waking; an Irish Protestant Upbringing
Gubu Roi

Fool of the Family

A Life of J. M. Synge

W. J. Mc Cormack

NEW YORK UNIVERSITY PRESS
Washington Square, New York

First published in the U.S.A. in 2000 by
NEW YORK UNIVERSITY PRESS
Washington Square
New York, NY 10003

Library of Congress Cataloging-in-Publication Data
Mc Cormack, W. J.
Fool of the family : a life of J. M. Synge / W. J. Mc Cormack.
p. cm.
Includes bibliographical references and index.
ISBN 0–8147–5652–2 (alk. paper)
1. Synge, J. M. (John Millington), 1871–1909. 2. Dramatists, Irish—20th
century—Biography. I. Title.
PR5533.M36 2000
822'.912—dc21
[B]   00–034878

Typeset by Selwood Systems, Midsomer Norton

Set in Minion

Printed in Great Britain by
Butler & Tanner Ltd, Frome and London

Contents

Illustrations

For the Grenes of Clash

'Synge fashion we trust all well by the silence.'

Alec to Jack,
21 November 1859

Prologue

Thus saith Pharaoh, I will not give you straw.

Exodus 5:10

There were few smiles around the late-Victorian Irish dining table when children took biblical instruction. Hell outshone heaven. Among the countless biblical texts Mrs Synge expounded to her offspring, the Old Testament verses about the Israelites and their sufferings in exile featured prominently. Plagues of locusts, plagues of boils – the Lord inflicted much on his enemies. The Chosen People suffered also, and it was with them that Kathleen Synge identified. She had lost a father in the Great Irish Famine of 1845–7, a husband in the smallpox alarms of 1872. Her youngest and most famous son endured boils and abscesses in childhood. She spoke with authority about the seven lean years in Egypt.

Anyone turning to the task of writing that famous son's life will respond enviously to the tale of brickmakers deprived of just one basic ingredient. At least the people under Moses' leadership were still given mud, at least they could immerse themselves in tactile, sticky, but undeniable reality. The biographer – more particularly Synge's biographer – must search high and low for anecdote, casual self-revelation, recurrent personality trait. Not that there is any shortage of other material.

The straw which is available – abundant family correspondence in which young Johnnie is often passed over in silence, folkloric memory in rural Ireland, financial documentation, obscure biblical allusion – does not disappear in the alchemy of brickmaking or biography. Patiently gathered, it becomes a garland in which the enigmatic author of *The Playboy of the Western World* can be apprehended. As with the Children of Israel, so with the children of Kathleen Synge – it is often a story of land and religion, a story in which self-censorship and the destruction of personal papers also feature.

For Irish Protestants, even upper-middle-class ones like the Synges, there had never been a Promised Land. In the closing years of the nineteenth century, there was a palpable sense of gradual dispossession, paralleled by the momentous changes in European thinking about character and the unconscious, biology and history, order and political identity. Oscar Wilde, from a background somewhat similar to J. M. Synge's, turned crisis into comedy: in *The Importance of Being Earnest* (1895), we are assured that, while a severe chill usen't to be hereditary, 'I dare say it is now. Science is always making wonderful improvements in things.'

To grow up during these years, reading and thinking deeply, but saying little, was to run the gauntlet between rival views of human personality and its place in the scheme of things. Furthermore, the places where Synge successively lived – a widow's evangelical household, rented rooms in Paris, a primitive cottage on island or glenside, a nursing home turned hospice – did nothing to encourage bourgeois confidence in the self. There never was 'honey still for tea'. Dying at thirty-seven during the Edwardian 'Indian Summer', Synge crowded much into his last decade. Despite the exuberance of his drama, he steadfastly refused to exude 'character'. Only in death does he achieve definition. His short life, genteelly impoverished, is a long, rich story.

Previous versions cannot be ignored. It's worth noting how the conventional account of Synge's life, accepted as gospel until recently, unconsciously mimicked the Life of Christ. Obvious differences occur, but we have been told a tale of obscure childhood, temptation (in Paris rather than the desert), discovery of a mission (in the west of Ireland), triumphant entry into the capital (via the Abbey rather than the Temple), and ultimate rejection by the stiff-necked and uncircumcised of heart. Tragic death at thirty-something, and resurrection as a master of *theatrum mundi*.

The new life is considerably different, more detailed, less inspired. Genius is not assumed to have existed, unrecognised, from the start. A measure of incoherence is acknowledged, at least in the late-adolescent Synge, and a larger measure of folly in the last days. The great achievement is not *The Playboy of the Western World* but *The Well of the Saints*.

London
24 March 1999

BOOK ONE

Unfair Seedtime

CHAPTER 1

The Former Lives of J. M. Synge

From time to time in a fit of absent-mindedness nature raises up minds
which are more detached from life – a natural detachment, one innate
in the structure of sense or consciousness, which at once reveals itself
by a virginal manner of seeing, hearing or thinking.

T. E. Hulme[1]

The subject of this biography was an exception to rules. Even if the
magnificent drama which he gave to world theatre were to be left aside,
he would still emerge as a contradiction, a provoking enigma, a figure in
his lifetime more attractive than knowable. This is in keeping with a
certain family pattern which he repudiated and exemplified. Prior to the
sudden arrival of the plays on stage, the Synges – where they had any
reputation at all – were known as churchmen. 'Vir gravis admodum et
doctus' was said to be the family type in the eighteenth century, 'a man
of singular gravity and great learning'.

To understand Synge, one has to pay attention to the individuals –
some critics of the work, some relatives of the man – who have moulded
his reputation. In the mid-1970s, as Nicholas Grene was putting the
finishing touches to his study of *Riders to the Sea, The Playboy of the
Western World* and Synge's other plays, he rightly concluded that the
playwright was sufficiently well-known by then, even in the academic
industry, to be referred to simply by his surname. And so Grene's book
became *Synge: A Critical Study of the Plays* (1975). The clipped initials
(J.M.), their genteel expansion (John Millington), and the full baptismal
orotundity (Edmund John Millington), could all be dispensed with in
the public domain. The only two occasions on which I have been able to
trace even a fleeting reference to that initial 'Edmund' relate to a Christmas present the near-seven-year-old received from his elder brothers'
friend John Joly (1857–1933), and a teasing reference by one of the adult
Synge's German friends. Fifty-five years after his act of kindness, the same
Joly could report complacently to the dead dramatist's sister, 'I look at
the fine edition of Johnny's wonderful writings and can hardly believe

they are the work of the little fellow sitting at his dear Mother's knee . . .'[2] And so the enigma remained behind the now familiar surname, the man behind what Joyce saw as a 'harsh gargoyle face', a fool in the Parisian suburban woods of Clamart.[3]

Synge disliked his Christian names, preferring to use initials instead, even on legal documentation where the full citation was usually required.[4] This causes a minor technical problem for the biographer and his readers, because it is very difficult to settle on an agreed form of reference. It is hard to believe that a man known for his reticence, for keeping his own counsel, should be referred to as Johnnie – Synge came early to detest the notorious domesticity. At the same time, some theatregoers and students alike are still occasionally in a quandary about the famous surname. Does it rhyme with ring or with binge? Was he a Sing or a Singe? Commentators on the dramatist's origins take delight in telling how a member of the family had won royal commendation for his singing in the court of Henry VIII – *cognominatus quia canonicus fuit.*[5] The story at least settles the problem of pronunciation and, additionally, indicates the antiquity and dignity of the family's social position. It also, however, ties the Synges to an English line of association whereas the family has particularly distinguished itself in Ireland, through the Church, the theatre and (more recently) in physics and the sciences.[6] The tying of Synge to Ireland has become an accepted principle of interpretation: there is no reason for believing that what is a necessary interpretation is also a sufficient one. We shall look beyond Ireland, while rarely losing sight of it.

If Synge habitually minimised his name, from a very early date he appears also to have been the practitioner (or victim) of a disappearing act inside his family. To take one example from the year of 1888 – when he was neither child nor adult – we can scrutinise a complete file of almost weekly letters written by Mrs Kathleen Synge to her eldest son in South America. Johnnie figures in less than a third of these, usually as the victim of a cold or the recipient of an umbrella for Christmas. In her 'last letter of this old year', her youngest son is nowhere referred to.[7] Nor did Johnnie engage in his own correspondence with his brothers, when they were away from home. (And there were quite a lot of siblings – Robert Anthony (1858–1943), Edward (1859–1939), Annie Isabella (1863–1949), and Samuel (1867–1951) – among whom to get lost, deliberately or otherwise.) When Johnnie was ten, his second-eldest brother was settling in to the difficult business of being a land agent, and writing fairly regularly to his chum, Joly, a friend of the Synge family as a whole. Once again Johnnie rarely features, apart from an inquiry if 'he has brushed his hair' – that, and some tell-tale allusion to health and ill-health.[8] In 1888, it is virtually certain he never wrote to South America; for later periods, the possibility of papers having been destroyed cannot be discounted. On the contrary, it is a near certainty that such a purge took place, perhaps two or more purges. One way or another, he slips through a thicket of family papers like a fox downwind of the blood relatives. When Joly came to publish his memoirs long after *The Playboy of the Western World* had become a classic, he never thought to mention his many visits to the Synge household or the occasions in which he met and talked with the sickly boy.[9] Synge and rumours of Synge in the 1920s will require our attention later.

Being dead has been a central feature of Synge's literary identity. The first biography so-called was published as early as 1913, that is, just four years after the playwright's demise at the age of thirty-seven. It was dedicated to the pioneering literary historian Louis Cazamian, and to his wife who had written on Synge. The author, a young French drama critic and translator named Maurice Bourgeois, had not been given access to the great archive which remained in the family's possession. Yeats regarded Bourgeois' book as too drearily factual, and his hand is detectable behind Ezra Pound's savage review in *The Egoist*. Nevertheless, a few of the biographer's footnotes indicate that he had parleyed with some success with Edward Hutchinson Synge (1890–1957), a nephew (known as Hutchie) who plays a major, if ambiguous, role in the posthumous career of the dramatist. By 1936 at the latest, Hutchie was confined to Bloomfield, a mental hospital in Dublin.[10]

Synge himself had left his literary estate to Hutchie Synge and another nephew, Edward Stephens (1888–1955), who later became a busy and distinguished lawyer. In so doing he overlooked the abilities of other family members, notably his brother-in-law Harry Stephens. The nephews may have shared some of the testator's political and social views, but that did not guarantee their availability at moments when the estate required careful management. In any case, the executors were Edward Synge and Frank Stephens (Harry's elder son). When Synge died, Edward Stephens was only twenty years old, Hutchie Synge two years younger. Both nephews travelled in Europe on the strength of their inheritance, with Hutchie certainly back in Dublin for the Easter 1916 Rising (on which he reported to outlying relatives). In 1921 Edward Stephens accompanied Michael Collins to London for negotiations which led to the Anglo-Irish Treaty, the scandal of which can hardly be explained by his English wife's failure to pack a second pair of trousers.[11] This did not prevent him from playing an important role in the development of the constitutional arrangements put in place after the cessation of hostilities between Britain and Ireland and between conflicting parties in the Irish Civil War (1922). While it is impossible here to record the extent of Stephens's behind-the-scenes contribution to public life in the Irish Free State, one can trace a political 'legacy', stemming from J. M. Synge's treatment of Ireland and (in his last, unfinished play) of myth and history, and reaching into the 1920s if not later, a legacy of critical service.

Though Hutchie became incapacitated, he published a number of mathematical papers of long-term rather than immediate significance. He also set to work on a biography to supersede Bourgeois, nothing of which survives. There is evidence to suggest that he contemplated some augmentation of the official canon in the 1920s, if only by the release of selected correspondence. Maunsel of Dublin, publishers in 1910 of the *Works* in four volumes, proposed a larger edition early in 1923, the last volume to be a biography of which 'Mr Synge ... will not have the MS ready before September or October'.[12] Unfortunately, ill-health permanently disturbed these intentions. From 1930 onwards, his solicitor cousin Edward Stephens diligently maintained a commitment to their uncle's memory, accumulating something like three-quarters of a million words in a biographical dossier which swallowed family tradition, affectionate personal recollection, much accurate research, many shared philosophical attitudes – and a not negligible *auto*biographical aspect – to the point where a coherent life-story of John Synge became near invisible. This self-consuming dedication to the original project had been assisted by his becoming custodian of the relevant papers in 1939 on the death of Hutchie's father, the dramatist's second eldest brother. Frank Stephens remained aloof, despite the powers conferred on him by Synge's will.

In the meantime, the dramatist's youngest brother had published *Letters to My Daughter: Memories of J. M. Synge* (1932). Sam's exercise in seemingly disorganised reminiscence and exculpation, presented through a correspondence between a father and his child, none the less preserves some valuable detail. Though it is not a biography of the playwright – indeed drama is scarcely mentioned – the *Letters* constitute a limpid rewriting of the life as discrete moments of sentiment and gentlemanly conduct. It is a good source for anecdotes of a touching kind, very valuable to the biographer of a tight-lipped subject. But what if the correspondence had been fabricated by its author long after the child 'recipient' had become a mature adult?[13] While we know that Sam 'had much hesitation in publishing the book of memoirs', we need to inquire into his conscious motives in doing so at all, as well as into the unconsciously revealed desire to infantalise his brother's memory.[14] What significance can be read into Sam's decision to address his account of the dramatist to – effectively – a non-existent child? Like Christy Mahon in *The Playboy of the Western World*, Synge was worth shamming for and fighting over, especially when he could be reduced to an impotent malleable servant of other people's projections twenty or thirty years after his death.

At Harvard in the late 1930s, David H. Greene was writing a doctoral thesis on Synge's achievement as a writer. Meeting Edward Stephens in Dublin, he gradually took over some of the informal responsibilities of getting the best results of the lawyer's enterprise into shape and into print. Though Stephens died suddenly in 1955, Greene retained his collaborator's name on the title-page of *J. M. Synge, 1871–1909* (1959). This was indeed a life-story, but its coherence was won by oversimplifying aspects of the dramatist's religious background and political significance. Samuel Beckett, hardly anyone's idea of that 'general reader' beloved of publishers, found it 'very dull and cautious'.[15]

There were by now at least four biographies of the dramatist in existence, including the unpublished, unwieldy but valuable original dossier made by Stephens alone, and (less certainly) Hutchie's manuscript of 1923. Even if this latter never amounted to an extended narrative, the notebooks Hutchie kept while 'institutionalised' at Bloomfield, sketch out a life of his uncle. This was not a situation which could endure, though various legendary 'versions' of Synge continue to recruit followers. Thus we have Synge the paragon of Anglo-Irish nobility and (in the red corner) Synge 'the *colon* who refuses'.[16] Sometimes discussions of the dramatist resemble a Punch and Judy show, in which all parts are played by a travesty of the dramatist himself – as versioned in these legends.

With the transfer in 1968 of papers to the library of Trinity College, Dublin, and the growth of academic interest in Irish literature from the mid-1960s onwards, it was inevitable that Stephens's labours would be harvested a second time. So it was that Andrew Carpenter, of University College, Dublin, came to edit a judicious selection from the Stephens material, publishing it as *My Uncle John* (1974). Appearing with a foreword by Lilo Stephens (who failed to pack the second pair of trousers in 1921), this edited version of her late husband's work understandably preserved its original author's perspective, without any overt questioning of his methodology or memory.

Perhaps for that reason, little further biographical work was undertaken, though Ann Saddlemyer's two-volume edition of Synge's letters (1983–4) is accompanied by extensive annotation of a very high order. In an article published a few years later, Professor Saddlemyer came close to conceding the impossibility of anyone writing Synge's biography: 'the clue to this enigmatic, very private person whose self-confidence so astonished those who knew him, and whose craftsmanship resulted in such dazzlingly complete works of art, continues to elude us.'[17] David H. Greene, introducing his 1989 revised edition of the 1959 biography, reiterated his belief that a biographer should 'present the facts of Synge's life in such a way as to leave the reader free to form his own judgments . . .'[18] That particular judgement ignores the issue as to which facts the biographer deems relevant. There never was a time when Synge was unjudged: he was swaddled, cradled, coached, tutored, nursed and shrouded in judgement.

The same Introduction claimed that 'it is now possible, as it would not have been thirty years ago, to explain why Synge's literary remains passed into the wrong hands after his death, why some of his letters – how many we do not know – were destroyed, and why access to his papers was denied.' Yet the new revelations were as discreetly handled as the previous silences.[19] While the second version of Greene and Stephens materially improved on the first, in that it drew on Synge's then recently published correspondence, arguably Greene depended too heavily on the letters to Molly Allgood in assessing Synge's emotional life. A more balanced account of the quality and significance of the relationship between dying dramatist and brilliant pupil-actress, within a family tradition of which Synge himself was acutely aware, is now possible. This is but one further stage in a long process of adjusting critical focus on John Synge, a figure who often preferred to stay out of view or to discount the importance of his own presence.

From the outset he underwent a process of redesign at the hands of Yeats and others, with the result that the manner in which his major works were presented gave a particular colouration to his life (and death). Hardly had he been laid to rest in Mount Jerome Cemetery in Dublin, when plan and counter-plan were prepared for the dissemination of his legacy. The major result of these efforts was the four-volume *Works of J. M. Synge* of 1910. This posthumous collective edition is virtually unique in the annals of the Irish Literary Revival, promptly establishing a canon of the late author's work and, by the same token, excluding items deemed non-canonical or ephemeral. Simultaneously, it struck a blow for a native-based publishing industry committed to serving the exuberant literature then being produced by Irish men and women. Canonicity and cultural nationalism were mutually defining in the case of Synge's reputation, and the influence of the Maunsel edition can be traced through to the scholarly four volumes of *Collected Works*, edited by Ann Saddlemyer and Robin Skelton and appearing between 1962 and 1968.

There is also a critical history, a history of interpretations. On the title-pages of virtually all the book-length critical studies devoted to Synge, he is explicitly linked to Irish or Anglo-Irish literary contexts. For many readers, this may not seem out of the ordinary. The same readers would doubtless express surprise if Anton Chekhov (1860–1904) were presented in the same way, with pointed obligatory reference to Russian literary history. Surely both dramatists contributed to what became known as 'world theatre', with Synge honoured as early as 1923 with 'various Japanese translations', not to mention extensive circulation in Europe and America.[20] Indeed, their generation – which broadly is also that of August Strindberg (1849–1912) – gave rise to the very notion of world theatre. In relation to Synge, it may be that the fundamental interpretative concern of the biographers and many of the critics has been precisely with the question of national identity. Between (on the one hand) the tendency of Irish critics to regard Synge as clubbable, and (on the other) the too-loosely constellated features of 'world theatre', it must surely be possible to plot a third course.

In doing so, I hope I have not falsified the accounts of other writers on Synge, nor discounted the debts I have run up. If he was the detonating figure who provided the Abbey Theatre with a repertoire, a style, and some badly needed managerial ability, it is none the less important to see that coming together of the man and the movement as part of what Katharine Worth has called 'the Irish drama of Europe'. Far from being a kitchen-sink affair, Irish nationalism had its place in wider cultural and political developments which came to a head with the Great War. The contribution of small nations, lost provinces, and the territorial detritus of exhausted empires, to the great literary and artistic revolution known as modernism has often been noted. The decay of bourgeois confidence and the pervasive sense of historical crisis manifest themselves in Synge's work as in the early fiction of Thomas Mann and the sociological theories of Max Weber. Similarly, the 'New Woman' debates of the 1890s, which implicated Thomas Hardy, Bernard Shaw and many others, may be traced in Synge's plays from *In the Shadow of the Glen* (1903) to the unfinished *Deirdre of the Sorrows*. And it is only because Yeats insisted on positioning himself so close to Synge that we cannot fully make out other figures – for example, James Joyce, Ezra Pound, Arthur Symons, and Mrs Humphry Ward – who were on-stage.

On-stage or – too often – backstage were a striking number of women eclipsed in the same way. Synge's cousin Florence Ross plays the role of childhood sweetheart. Her friend Cherrie Matheson is first and foremost in a line of adult women of independent mind which includes the Americans Margaret Hardon and Agnes Tobin, and the English art historian Hope Rea. Some of Synge's friends aspired to be the New Woman; others chose more traditional roles. Only Molly Allgood, who is last in the line, can be said to have made her mark in the world of theatre and anger.

It is ironic that the world-theatre or universalising mode of criticism has found a congruence of God and man in the titular hero – if that's what Christy Mahon is – of *The Playboy of the Western World*.[21] Synge knew all about Christ, but his knowledge and his qualified scepticism should be read in an historically alert manner and not as a dogma of the Medes and the Persians. The recent 'cultural traditions' approach to Irish literary history has tended to classify everybody as under a binary system, with no exemptions permitted. This has had a disturbing and distorting impact on the history of ideas, reducing, as it must, theological nuance and complexity to the level of negative identification. (Maria Edgeworth – or Derek Mahon – must be a Protestant because s/he clearly is not a Catholic.) All writing is thus shown to be about religion in much the same way as all music can be treated as noise. The crudity of these procedures is nowhere more evident than in attempts to deal with the eminent (late) Victorians. Religion will feature in this account of J. M. Synge's life because the household he grew up in, the family tradition he inherited, and the (first) woman he loved were articulated to themselves and to the outer world in theological terms. It may seem at first glance that the codes of behaviour and standards of judgement emanating from this inheritance provided him with very little stimulus towards astringent thought or resolved action. But no simple model of Victorian Protestantism, or even of Irish Victorian Protestantism, will serve as summary of this background of Synge's, which was far more various and contrarious than a statement of allegiance (and then, in his case, disaffiliation) could comprehend.

As my citation of Mann and Weber – to whom André Gide might be added – should indicate, post-Protestantism is by no means a local Irish phenomenon. When Synge was dying in 1909, he received a letter from a friend in Canada, 'this prosaic, shapeless land where religious bigotry and abject utilitarianism of the worst kind seem to be perpetually fighting...'[22] The characteristic Modernist preoccupation with an epochal struggle between the past and the present may indeed find a particular register in the ethical predicaments and preoccupations of various post-

Protestants. Synge's literary career and spiritual crisis also reveal unexpected similarities with those of the Austrian poet, Rainer Maria Rilke (1875–1926), to whom I will advert from time to time.

Within this broadly conceived Western or European cultural nexus, I have opted not only to tell Synge's life-story anew but also occasionally to scrutinise the motives and objectives of previous biographies. If this dimension of the book occasionally manifests itself in knuckle-rapping, I suppose apologies are due to readers who prefer 'a round unvarnished tale'. But Synge – like Othello – is perpetually a contested figure: one cannot begin with a clearly delineated individual character and then proceed to write his biography because (to some degree at least) the character is produced, debated, questioned, redefined and reappropriated in the course of many acts of writing his life. From the moment that we encounter a written record of the child, Johnnie Synge, we are implicated in acts of possession and dispossession, through his early years of negotiated and – in his own subsequent reflections – renegotiated selfhood.

In a special sense, every Life is a plot behind which the biographer has been obliged to seek out the inexplicable, and to order the material of explanation. It does not follow that every detecting biographer has a crime to unfold; if there are skeletons in *this* cupboard, they are not of J. M. Synge's commission. But the proper ordering of his life-story will require more attention to domestic accountancy and legal documentation (in Chapter Four) than admirers of *The Aran Islands* or *The Tinker's Wedding* might reasonably expect. For related reasons, details of family history and even some passages of religious history are not to be found in the opening pages where straightforward chronology might insist they appear; on the contrary, *Fool of the Family* is ordered so as to reveal Synge's own encounter with the past, as a dramatic feature of his maturing experience and as a pressure upon a dramatist in the making. Among those encounters I discern an anxiety about health and heredity which, while it may cause a frisson in some readers, ultimately is clarified as unfounded fear, exacerbated by late-Victorian secrecy.

This biography is divided into five books. In the first, John Synge is gradually located amid the proliferating evidence that he did not count for very much in the family annals, though these in turn were to count quite a lot for him. In Book Two, he strikes out into the world, visiting Germany and France, reading Ibsen and Marx, associating (briefly and reluctantly) with Irish emigré politics in Paris, but seasonally returning to Dublin and Wicklow as if to nudge the pattern of his own life into the paradigm of exile and return. No strict chronology can be maintained in so complex a life as his, and so the third book, 'Return of the Native', commences with a lengthy account of his first great romantic passion, covers his travels in the west of Ireland, and takes the reader up to the production of the first two one-act plays of 1902. Book Four concentrates on the two great full-length dramas – *The Well of the Saints* (1905) and *The Playboy of the Western World* (1907) – and locates Molly Allgood (Synge's second and last love) exactly in the space between the two plays: it is entitled 'Contra Mundum' as an indication of the oppositional tendency displayed not only in the action of the plays but also in their author's determined resistance of popular opinion. The last section of *Fool of the Family* takes its title from the familiar room backstage where players waited for their cues to enter. The room was so coloured because green was thought a soothing contrast to the glare of the footlights; in various kinds of Irish lore, however, it has been a colour of superstitious ill-luck and, of course, of strident nationalist iconography. Synge dies in such a 'green room', or so it seems to this biographer. The Appendix provides material on the beliefs of a small religious group with which his family was loosely but suggestively associated. In a different perspective, new research into the fate of Synge's reputation in the twenty years or so following his death links him to the emergent cultural policy of the Irish Free State.

If the critical moments and movements of his life are conventional almost to a fault – difficult home-life, romantic infatuation, illness, public rejection, much-documented death – Synge's dramatic idiom is difficult to absorb into narrative and discursive prose. There is, for a start, rather a lot of cursing! While the language is recognisably English, its rhythms, lexical profusion and grammatical compaction immediately mark it off from the norms of Anglo-American speech. Much learned commentary has been devoted to assessing how it relates to Irish speech, both to Irish speech in English (what is called here Hiberno-English) and to Irish speech in Gaelic. For the moment, let us be content in saying that Synge's dramatic speech is utterly distinct from Synge's voice, as recorded in his letters – frankly, he was a poor letter-writer – and in the recollections of a few friends. While his characters proceed to fight or philander, their author has not only walked off-stage, he has left the building unnoticed, by a back door.

Fool of the Family derives its own title from Synge's attempts to find a name for the play we know as *The Playboy of the Western World*. If Synge in his generation felt isolated from the habits and values of his kinsfolk, if after his death his reputation and literary estate were occasionally at the mercy of individuals less than perfectly qualified to handle these matters, in the long run both the fool and the family are richly vindicated. There will be passages when the good sense of his nephew, Hutchie (acting as if he were a literary executor) must be questioned. In the end, and long after his death, Hutchie's mathematical studies bore fruit in a multiple-mirror telescope built by the University of Arizona.[23] His uncle, John Synge, possessed the patience to appreciate this delayed justice, had he lived long enough.

J. M. Synge remains in the end 'a meditative man', as Yeats described him in one of the greatest commemorative poems in the English language. For reasons of his own, Yeats wished to present Synge as an aristocrat, which was not accurate. But aloofness had been so long sustained by Synge as to have become second nature. It allowed him to mix easily with those who were neither his social equals nor his superiors, at times with persons virtually illiterate or at least unlikely to leave memoranda for biographers. Perhaps Synge was too shy to appear shy, an achievement only possible for someone of immense self-control. All of this amounts to a situation in which enlivening gossip, of the kind every Life requires, remains in short supply. The irony would not have been lost on him; to one inquirer for details of how the Abbey Theatre directors managed it, he retorted: 'Yeats looks after the stars, and I do the rest.'[24] He died, one year and one month and one day later, of – it is generally accepted – Hodgkin's disease.

He experienced ideas with great immediacy, though his reactions were often muffled, masked or delayed. He stored in his nervous system implications and nuances deriving from early acquaintances and explorations. His literary apprenticeship was conducted in a series of ill-chosen culs-de-sac – not all of them Parisian – yet there he forged a galloping high style, to be wondered at by all, once he turned to the open road. At the close of the nineteenth century, he began to write as if the dissociation of mind and emotion might be overcome in a small number of heroic works. The last of these eviscerates heroism, prophecy, and maybe even drama itself. It was perhaps a doomed undertaking, but the tracing of his endeavour has for me never been less than an act of homage.

CHAPTER 2

Fin-de-Siècle Beginnings

Degenerates are not always criminals, prostitutes, anarchists, and pronounced lunatics; they are often authors and artists.

Max Nordau[1]

When J. M. Synge was born, the nineteenth century had thirty years to
run. Optimism was buoyant upon the European surface of things. Trade
was flourishing; new markets were expanding in Africa, the Far East, and
the British colonies of the southern hemisphere; missionaries brought
spiritual Good News to augment the benefits of industrial capitalism.
Photography recorded exotic landscapes and advertised exportable goods.
With the benefit of this hindsight, the year 1871 can be refocused as
a moment connecting the aftermath of the Franco-Prussian War, the
prosperity of the Victorian United Kingdom, and the coming arms race
between Britain and Germany.

But the surface of things gave back only a superficial reflection of social
and cultural realities. Traditional patterns of living were already sharply
disrupted – by international mass-migration, by the concentration of
people into conurbations of unprecedented size, by rapid personal transport, by philosophical and scientific questionings which challenged such
'eternal' concepts as matter and spirit, time and space, character, morality
and order. *The Communist Manifesto* had appeared in the year of the
California gold-rush, 1848; Charles Darwin published *The Origin of
Species* in 1859 and followed it up with *The Descent of Man* in 1871 – the
year of Synge's birth. Friedrich Nietzsche's *The Birth of Tragedy* (1872)
and Sigmund Freud's *The Interpretation of Dreams* (1899) confirmed
the merely provisional or occasional sovereignty of consciousness and
deliberation in human affairs. On his first trip to Germany in 1893, Synge
caught a glimpse of Kaiser Wilhelm II who had dumped Bismarck as
chancellor two years earlier.[2] In the year of Synge's death (1909), Louis
Blériot flew across the English Channel for the first time, and a cinema
opened in Dublin.

At the beginning of the twentieth century, the British Empire covered one-fifth of the earth's land-surface. Ireland was placed ambiguously in this Empire, as a turbulent and discontented territory with a history of resistance and rebellion, but also as an integral part of the United Kingdom. It was a metropolitan colony. Viewed from a European perspective, empire seemed to be the preordained system of human government, but the first Russian Revolution was attempted as early as 1905 when Albert Einstein enunciated his special theory of relativity. *The Playboy of the Western World* had not yet been completed.

The Western world was on the move, but in Ireland debate seemed fixated on issues of an atavistic kind. The Literary Revival movement was concerned to re-establish values indiscriminately termed Celtic; Home Rule justified itself by pointing to the kind of parliamentary independence enjoyed by Ireland in the eighteenth century. The Gaelic League (1893) campaigned for restoration of the old language. Nationalist imitators of Baden-Powell's Boy Scouts (1908) adopted the jargon of heroic saga. Even in matters of land ownership, the socialism of a few like Michael Davitt was overshadowed by an undeclared alliance of British conservatives and Irish reformers happy to settle for a form of peasant-proprietorship. At no point in Synge's lifetime did armed nationalism seriously threaten to inaugurate a new polity. When his mother tidied out a storeroom at the top of their high terraced house in January 1901, the pistol she found was a relic of the Land War, not an omen of the next war.[3] Synge lived through an Indian summer of unusual and exhausting length – a summer with occasional localised storm-clouds (especially in Ulster), but without storms.

This image of Ireland is too simplified. It depends not only on the results of a century's research and exhortation by a succession of political thinkers and activists, but also on the absence of the kind of reflection so amply provided for France between 1848 and 1945 by Théodore Zeldin. Nevertheless, the apparent stability of the Kingdom should not obscure the relative newness of the arrangements enshrined in its constitution nor the nervousness displayed by opponents of Home Rule in 1886 and again in 1893. If the Union *tout court* was flawed by more than one major anomaly, simultaneously the notion of Ireland as some kind of natural unity began to collapse.

As a political tenet, nineteenth-century All-Irelandism differed markedly from the casualness of earlier assumptions. It had various origins – often conflicting in their implications – but the accelerated industrialisation of the Belfast area from about 1840 onwards introduced a distinction which was eventually to become an international frontier in

1921. A corollary development was the convergence of All-Irelandism with nationalist separatism, whether expressed through the cosy domestic metaphor of Home Rule or through more trenchant versions of politics. All-Ireland and Ulster were by now poles of conflicting loyalty. The tensions and ironies of these heady debates can be heard in Synge's work, transposed into various keys – quasi-primitivist in *The Aran Islands*, Celticist in *The Well of the Saints*, sexual-generational in *The Playboy*.

To the Irish Catholic majority (a minority within the United Kingdom) a new dawn was breaking as the nineteenth century drew to a close. As with any self-respecting dawn, an initial chill in the air was to be endured in the form of the old question of land ownership. It was not for nothing that local idiom described a well-off farmer as a *warm* man. To the Irish Protestant minority (part of a majority within the United Kingdom if the adherents of a state church can be said to believe anything) the same years were felt as crisis, as a threat to prosperity even if that prosperity was to a large extent the product of the same years. Irish Protestants felt the last decades of the century forcing their backs to the wall – a wall of their own industrious manufacture. When the premier journal of Irish Protestantism declared that 'the landmarks of society are in danger' the only remarkable feature of its anxiety was the retention of so rural a term as 'landmark'.[4]

The contradictoriness of all this is best caught in the German word, *Dämmerung*. At once dawn and dusk, *Dämmerung* will be evoked in the very title of Synge's first fully-completed play, *When the Moon Has Set*, with its double suggestion of an end to night and an end to light. That great testament of *fin-de-siècle* paranoia – Max Nordau's *Degeneration* (English translation, 1895) – opened with a fear-filled invocation of a 'Dusk of the Nations in which all suns and all stars are gradually waning, and mankind with all its institutions and creations is persisting in the midst of a dying world'.[5] This is the birth-dirge, or anthem, of a generation fated to fall in swathes during the savage harvests of 1914–18, with the premature losses of the preceding decade featuring as neglected omens, unread signs. Many of Synge's diversions of the 1890s are to be found in Nordau's listing and sifting of the age's cultural con-and-pro-fusion – Ibsenism, the term '*fin de siècle*' itself, insanity, mysticism, the pre-Raphaelites, Nietzsche.

As in Palestine on a more world-historical occasion, the year of Synge's birth saw the taking of a census. The population of all Ireland in 1871 was 5,412,377, which represented a decrease of 6.67 per cent in the preceding decade. Two years after Synge's death (i.e. in 1911), the figure stood at

4,390,219, confirming the pattern of sustained emigration and low fertility (mainly due to late marriage). The ratio of Catholics to members of the (Protestant) Church of Ireland is as significant as the drop in population: in 1871, Catholics accounted for 76.69 per cent and the Church of Ireland for 12.34 per cent of the total; by 1911, the figures had adjusted slightly to 73.86 per cent and 13.13 per cent respectively. Other denominations were duly counted, but the remaining 10–12 per cent (dissenting Protestants, for the very great part) were largely concentrated in Ulster, and did not impinge so markedly on social life in the south of Ireland.

The population of Dublin, including its suburbs, was a few hundred short of 330,000 when Synge was born. These suburbs were steadily expanding in the approved Victorian manner; among the building developments of the mid-century had been Synge Street, crossing the southern Circular Road at right angles just in time for George Bernard Shaw to be born there in 1856. The street's name reflected property ownership in a valuable development area, but did so precisely because the property had been sold (by the archdiocese of Dublin) in less than optimum financial circumstances. Indifferent to details of Synge family misfortunes in its midst, the city's population continued to rise.[6] The family did not keep pace. Victorian Dublin had little heavy industry, but produced consumer goods in great quantity – whiskey, stout, cigarettes, biscuits, etc. – and it was a major port for the sale of agricultural produce to Britain. Though it had not been a capital since 1800, it supported a vigorous newspaper industry, and was well endowed with national institutions – museums, art galleries, learned societies, universities, and so forth. Moderately prosperous, it 'housed' a teeming population of desperate slum-dwellers. Many of these lived in multiple occupation of what had been the eighteenth-century town mansions of gentry and noblemen. By European standards it was a pretty small place.

Down in the communal churchyard overlooking Schull harbour in west County Cork, a solid rectangular wall defines the last resting-place of Synge's maternal grandfather, the Rev. Dr Robert Traill (1793–1847). He had died of famine fever while ministering to his flock in 1847: scores of their humbler graves surround his, each marked by a stump of unhewn slate.[7] Traill's reputation was sanctified in a ballad, though his charitable labours involved no suspension of a fervent anti-Catholicism. In Schull of the 1990s, the sceptic Synge is remembered as having used for some romantic encounter a seat on the road beyond his grandfather's burial-place.[8] Harnessing the energy of theological conflict to the fear of recurring famine, W. B. Yeats's play, *The Countess Cathleen* (first produced 1899)

provided the Irish Literary Revival with an emotional charge polarised
between memory and desire.

Famine shaped the popular imagination for decades, acting as a traumatic point of reference behind the statistics. While no district in Ireland
is typical in this or in any other connection, population figures for
Wicklow (the county most intimately associated with the family and J.
M. Synge's work) are revealing:

1841	126,143	
1851	98,979	(−21.53%)
1861	86,479	(−12.3%)
1871	78,697	(−9.00%)
1881	70,386	(−10.56%)
1891	62,136	(−11.72%)
1901	60,824	(−2.11%)
1911	60,711	(−0.19%)[9]

No such decline of population took place unnoticed. Very quickly there
was established a public consciousness of the impact of famine, death,
internal migration, and emigration, on a rural community like that of
Wicklow. In addition to subsistence agriculture, the county's population
looked to scattered but substantial mining operations for a livelihood.
Grandfather John Synge (1788–1845) had owned an estate in east Wicklow,
including Glanmore Castle and Roundwood Park, with extensive lands
and quarries. Lead mining proceeded among desolate hills to the south.
Yet Glanmore was among 'the fair gems of the County Wicklow' in the
eyes of a young frequenter of clerical meetings there around 1830. But an
ex-navy man turned do-gooder, who lived on the edge of the estate as 'a
moral agent', wrote eloquently about ' "Nobody's People," as they are
emphatically called in this country, being either the tenants of little landlords, almost as poor as themselves, or cabin keepers by the roadside, who
are neglected to a proverb . . .'[10] John Synge was not an efficient manager
of property and the crash came in the first year of the Famine. With
fine dramatic timing he died as the bailiffs were taking possession of
Glanmore. In one version of the saga, his corpse was seized in the hope
of selling it for dissection, so infuriated were the agents of credit at the
disappearance of the family silver.[11]

Here lay the basis for a powerful identification: the decline of the
Synge family as landlords and the decline of the general community. That
Grandfather Traill might be best regarded as a self-sacrificing bigot, and
that the loss of Glanmore did not result from the Famine but from

mismanagement by an individual more concerned with the state of his soul, did nothing to mitigate its impact.[12] The estate passed to Francis Synge (died 1878), who succeeded in recovering (by purchase) the Glanmore portion in 1850, though only after the humiliation of living as a tenant of the courts in the Gothic pile he thought he had inherited as eldest son. Tradition speaks of a local blacksmith, friendly to the old family, who by pushing any unwelcome bidder against the wall, smothered prices.

Despite this partial recovery, J. M. Synge's father found himself a suddenly urbanised professional, whereas he had been brought up as the carefree youngest son of Glanmore and Roundwood.[13] As a married man he and his family lived for the most part in the south Dublin township of Rathmines. It was a new suburb which nevertheless served to buffer the injured susceptibilities of a displaced rural landlord family. The area was sufficiently undisturbed for corncrakes to take up summer residence in early May.[14] In the latter half of the century, growth of population in Rathmines 'was achieved without any decline in the area's status'. Its local government was not strikingly democratic; a historian of Victorian Dublin has written that 'at no stage were Catholics prominent in the life of Rathmines. They fell from 52% of the population in 1861 to 48% in the following decade and only recovered to 50% in 1891.'[15] The older Synge boys attended a small establishment, modelled on the English 'public school', simply called the Rathmines School. But Johnnie did not.

Born in April 1871, J. M. Synge grew up in a local atmosphere which encouraged the belief that the country's best interests and true identity lay with people like his family. Excursions to Uncle Francis's place in County Wicklow seemed to confirm that the older order stood, while also hinting that change and decay functioned with a divine indifference to class, privilege or inherited dignity. The county's 1891 population retained an 18.7 per cent minority attached to the Church of Ireland and so mirrored, as best a non-Ulster county could, the denominational oddity of suburban Rathmines. Extreme disproportions of religious affiliation could be found in adjoining electoral divisions: Togher in 1901 was 98 per cent Catholic; neighbouring Calary (which included the townland of Glasnamullen, long a part of the Synge estate) was 58 per cent Protestant.[16] The realities of Irish life – the development of a Catholic bourgeoisie in provincial towns, the introduction of local democracy in municipal affairs, the drifting apart of Ulster from the other provinces, the steady growth of national feeling, the equally steady growth of resentment against the land-ownership system, the increased power of the Protestant working class in distant Belfast – were filtered to the Synges through the stained glass of evangelical religion and Victorian plate-windows. Theirs was, in many senses, a semi-detached existence.

The amenities of bourgeois life were to hand, albeit in a structure which perpetuated some features of the *ancien régime.* Two universities catered for the youth of Ireland – an Elizabethan foundation of strongly Protestant hue, and a network of nineteenth-century colleges appealing mainly to Catholics. Medicine was similarly divided, both in terms of education for doctors and of hospital facilities for the sick. Catholicism might not debar a man [sic] from some high offices, but any combination of Catholicism and articulate national sentiment certainly did. In the congested public service, promotion was often more available to those – whether Catholic or Protestant by upbringing – who were prepared to serve overseas. All of these aspects of the society into which Synge was born were amplified in the tight circumstances of his own family – one brother became a medical missionary in China, another (trained as an engineer) spent some time as a rancher in Argentina, and a third negotiated between the gentry and their tenants as a land agent.

Though insurrection never occurred during Synge's lifetime, and politically motivated violence was rare, a perpetual vigilance characterised the upper classes. The assassination of Lord Frederick Cavendish in May 1882 caused great alarm, but there is something excessive in Ned Synge's determined confusion of the Invincibles' isolated murder of the Chief Secretary with the parliamentary campaign for Home Rule – 'it beats Russian [sic].'[17] Distrust of nationalist politics was more often blended with a dogged determination to find a niche in changing conditions. 'It is a wretched thing to be a professional man with no profession,' Johnnie's second eldest brother remarked of an acquaintance. 'What is a "Real Position" [?]', the same Ned Synge asked his friend John Joly with exasperation some time in 1882.[18] Things were evidently getting worse as Johnnie grew towards manhood. Referring to the family into which Ned married, Mrs Synge reported in 1888 that 'Arthur Price is looking for work but as yet, has not heard of any ... Eddy P[rice] sprained his back lifting & carrying heavy pipes which they were laying down ...'[19] If these were the scions of a Protestant Ascendancy, then how were the mighty fallen!

Though discreet, orchestrated lamentation played a part in the emotional economy of many respectable houses, the dominant experience was frustration. This was all the more terrible for its being experienced in the absence of that densely packed, throbbing, impersonal crush of human beings which typified the European city. Those zones of Dublin near-monopolised by the Protestant middle classes were proportionately narrow and familiar. Such intimacy verges on desolation. The depopulated glenside, half-shut-up mansion, and neglected shoreline – these sites of Synge's brooding drama are symbolic constructions which do not wholly exclude urban traces. The claustrophobia he powerfully evokes in 'The Oppression of the Hills' (published 1905) is a clutter of absences. Unmarried old women, a solitary man demented to the point that he strips himself naked under the ghastly weather – each figure is shadowed by a disappearance or non-appearance.

But this was only one side of a divided growing-up in *fin-de-siècle* Ireland. In settings which are contrapuntally haunted by revenants from the provinces, James Joyce (1882–1941) provides the specifically urban counterpart to Synge's images of rural desolation. Through sedate vacations at Greystones, the young Synge had known a solicitor whose wife later drove him from their Dublin home so she could consort with a horse-trainer; then she shot herself through the heart. What might have roused the Ibsenite in Joyce, only served as an unspeakable omen for an older Synge.[20] As contributors to the Irish Literary Revival (loosely defined), Joyce and Synge complement each other, stressing the same hemiplegia, a paralysis of the half-body, the half-state. Yeats sees this condition as a prelude to apocalypse, a battle between two civilisations which he sometimes identifies with England and Ireland, on other occasions with industrialism and tradition, and on others again with occultic antagonisms. Yeats will associate Synge with the Last Judgement, as if to recruit his dead friend to that apocalypse. On a 1914 lecture tour in America, he declared that Synge 'tasted all the bitterness of dying that he could reach out and find new beauty'.[21]

But for the moment, Synge for us is still alive, at work on those intensely evocative scenes which open his plays. It is worth rehearsing a few of their details – Pegeen drawing up her shopping-list in *The Playboy of the Western World*; Martin and Mary groping blindly past a ruined church in *The Well of the Saints*; the girls in *Riders to the Sea* anxious to know their mother is asleep so that they can additionally know their brother is really dead; Nora with her sham-dead husband in *In the Shadow of the Glen*. What is the balance between these sparse landscapes of Galway, Mayo and Wicklow and the tremulous appetite of the characters? It is not adequate to say that these are scenes full of longing and frustration – 'full' is the wrong word.

The sensations involved are at the same time plenitudes and phantasms of experience, at once full and vacant. They are like the amputee's missing limb, something clinically *gone* and yet equally *felt.* Synge's drama presents a surprisingly concentrated analysis of the whole anxious condition of the late-becoming-terminal Victorian age. The surgical analogy can be traced in individual plays – the absent body and tell-tale stocking in *Riders to the Sea*, the burning of Christy's leg in *The Playboy* – and (again) the blind visionaries of *The Well of the Saints* in their different ways dramatise it. Here the struggle between Darwinians and Marxists, or biologists and sociologists, for recognition as the paramount radical *avant-garde* briefly occupies common if contested ground. Synge read both Darwin and Marx; if his notes on Darwin are the more extensive, his (few) declarations of a socialist allegiance are clearer than any endorsement of biologism.

It is therefore ironic that, in his last days, Synge should have become dependent on the paramedical care of a Huxley, Margaret, kinswoman of the dreaded Thomas Henry Huxley (1825–95) whose coinage of the term 'agnostic' in 1869 was just one of his sins against the Holy Ghost. In this context, the physical body and social class repeatedly appear and disappear as points of reference in damp, crepuscular late Victorian Ireland. Sometimes they join forces and masquerade as the Nation; Yeats's Cuchulain will stride out of the dark as the apotheosis of that alliance, exposing and exploiting its constitutive parts. Synge generally avoids the synthetic in this sense, preferring – as in the opening pages of his great prose masterpiece, *The Aran Islands* (published 1907) – to leave his evidence open to the reader's interpretation:

This evening an old man came to see me, and said he had known a relative of mine who passed some time on this island forty-three years ago.

'I was standing under the pier-wall mending nets,' he said, 'when you came off the steamer, and I said to myself in that moment, if there is a man of the name of Synge left walking the world, it is that man yonder will be he.'[22]

Here is the urge towards a theory of biological identity which so attracts the nationalist. Yet the relative of forty-three years earlier had been run off the islands for mixing evangelical zeal with exploitative fishing of the sea-stock. Moreover, the percipient old man 'seems to have shut himself up in a world of individual conceits and theories, and to live aloof at his trade of net-mending, regarded by the other islanders with respect and half-ironical sympathy.' An eye for continuity or, at least, for inherited and defining traits, had been vouchsafed to a partial outcast. Alienation, an abstract term never found in Synge's lively plays, nevertheless features by name in his non-dramatic account of rural society.

He had an eye for just such individuals, especially among the tramps and vagrants of the Irish mainland. In the plays, their mood and outlook is not so much dramatised as evoked by characters musing upon their experience of the world beyond them. A detail extends unexpectedly into the exotic. In the first act of *The Playboy of the Western World*, Pegeen seizes on Christy Mahon's name – 'a kind of a quality name, the like of what you'd find on the great powers and potentates of France and Spain' – in a way neither of its components justifies. The name, Synge, on the other hand was to be found only among the gentry, among that rather ill-defined social group whom Irish countryside people used to refer to as 'the quality'. G. B. Shaw asserted in the *New Statesman* that 'The Playboy's real name was Synge ...'[23] By the Aran Islanders Synge, who drank whiskey with them and rode in their frail canvas-covered boats, was addressed conventionally in Gaelic as 'Duine Uasal' (literally, Noble Person, equivalent to the Hiberno-English, 'Your Honour'). In such loose terminology, the actuality of social class is masked, though in Christy's case Pegeen will deduce 'great people in your family ... with the little small feet you have'.[24]

Synge was an acute commentator on social change. In the more strictly literary texts, the exchanges between the human body and the language of class are significantly undertaken under cover of 'the darkness of the night' in 'a dark lonesome place' during 'a long night and with great darkness' – all these phrases from the opening minutes of *The Playboy*. Aran with its blinding storms of wind and salt water constitutes a similar photographer's darkroom in which images of the visible world of sup-position can be developed into intelligible negatives. The tension between object and image, the anxiety implicit in reading the latter as altering the former, contribute to a highly-charged stasis palpable in the first moments of every play by Synge. It is worth noting that the composer of these dramatic tableaux was also an accomplished composer of photographs.

Ignoring the highly specific settings of these plays, one might be for-given for recalling a mood of enchanted frustration in the initial chapters of novels by Thomas Hardy (1840–1928). Consider Eustacia Vye in *The Return of the Native* (1878), standing by the dammed-up pond. Both writers exploited a geographical and cultural region with which they had enjoyed a personal intimacy, but of the two only Hardy is commonly described as a regionalist. The tension in his Wessex novels between the local and universal turns repeatedly upon a tragic note. Tragedy is not absent from Synge's dramatic range; indeed, *Riders to the Sea* has been deemed veritably Greek in its generic perfection. Though it may be a unique masterpiece, *Riders to the Sea* is not a unique undertaking; there is also the unfinished *Deirdre of the Sorrows*. While the boisterous comedy of *The Playboy* and *The Tinker's Wedding* is unforgettable, a rigorous dramatic structure informs plays of both kinds, even to the point where tragedy and comedy are seen as related forms of drama, each appealing for redemption by the other, each casting its sardonic eye on the pretensions of the other.

There is, however, little evidence that Synge ever read much of Hardy's work; like Joyce (again) he had a small appetite for contemporary writing.[25] In the canonical plays, an elemental, sparse rural landscape (usually with water present or implied) serves the needs of both comedy and tragedy in their destabilised forms. By a striking contrast, Synge's first memorable impression of the outer world must have registered as he came down the granite steps of No. 4 Orwell Park, Dublin, seeing the big gates that closed off the suburban driveway, waving a chubby hand to Grandmamma next door, allowing Nurse to secure him in the perambulator. Yet it was less than a mile from Orwell Park that the tragi-farce of the solicitor's wife and the horse-trainer came to its sorry and noisy end, in a milieu where the professional Synges were obliged to live, move and have their being. 'The Mrs tells of some one coming home from Milltown the other night who got knocked on the head for his money. You ought to get some sort of defence for night work on those roads.'[26] Is this a world away from the glens and the treacherous tides of the drama? The nearness of the Dublin hills to the south reduces the appearance of distance, but only on a superficial scale. Orwell Park was an unfinished project, and so represented a kind of ruination common in nineteenth-century Ireland. Out of view in its sunken course, the River Dodder ran between the suburbs and the hills, with several abandoned mills and manufactories on its banks. Much of the inner city stank.

Yet to fix on localised emblems of adversity is to neglect a larger context of feeling in which Irish counties were no further from Paris than the Danube Bend or the Hanseatic ports. If Hardy is easier to relate to Eurocentric universalism than Synge, the reason may lie in the translation of Synge's region into an insurgent nation with all the claims of uniqueness, unparalleled distinction and so forth which power the separatist cause. It was not always so. Only after a riot or two did Irish cultural nationalism take Synge to its bosom. By then he was safely dead.

In *Hereditary Genius* (1869), Francis Galton announced that 'the sure operation of Darwin's law of natural selection' determined intellectual qualities in individual human beings as well as physical characteristics in species.[27] These pervasive theories – and pervasiveness was itself an important part of the theory, underpinning its universal, inescapable application – coloured the local struggles of particular European societies and states up to and including the Great War. The dream of Empire required the Contagious Diseases Acts (1864 etc.). Vast urban concentrations led to vice of a kind qualitatively different from the eighteenth-century milieu of Hogarth's *A Harlot's Progress*. Charles Baudelaire (1821–67) became the reluctant prophet of modernity, a condition not just of being new but of being momentary. The sprawling city with its shattered monuments and fetid canals was his 'homeland', the wellspring of what was called (almost euphemistically) 'precocious depravity'. In such visions of damnation, rather than in the pellucid essays of Matthew Arnold, was to be fulfilled the prediction that literature might replace religion as modern man's guiding star. Moral confusion was rife. Huxley the agnostic consulted mediums. Liverpool opened a Syphilis Museum in Paradise Street. Across the Irish Sea, the MP for Wicklow, W. J. Corbet, supported Parnell and preached Galton.[28]

Everywhere new, last-ditch religions sprang forth – Brethrenism, Christian Science, Jehovah's Witnesses, Mormonism, the Salvation Army, Theosophy. Anxious for revelation, most of these abandoned or confused the fine distinctions of post-Reformation theology. In an instance close to the Synge family, it is reported that the young Charles Stewart Parnell held views which were 'agnostic with an inclination ... towards the Plymouth Brethren'.[29] Such broad-church intolerance is best seen as a decline in the intellectual rigour which had once been the proud boast of Protestantism generally. Pietism gave way to a less discriminating 'religion of the heart'. Where systematic thinking persisted – as in Swedenborg's arcana which Blake, Emerson, Synge, and Yeats studied – it came back from the shades to reinscribe the future state in the present tense.

Prophecy had a central role in the particular version of Irish Protestantism to which Synge was exposed. But prophecy works backwards in relation to secular modernity, so that Baudelaire is succeeded by the propagation of texts predating his birth. In Arthur Schopenhauer's *World as Will and Idea* (1818), man must suffer because his Will – which is his misfortune – generates more needs and desires than can ever be fulfilled. Escape from Will is the only hope. While Schopenhauer (whom Synge read) personally had found consolation in oriental religion, neo-Schopenhauerians came closer to endorsing decadence. Synge's sojourns in Paris gave him a back-row seat at some of the rowdier sideshows of European civilisation entering crisis – the Dreyfus Affair, the Arms Race,

Alfred Jarry's *Ubu Roi*, the Race for Africa, Naturalism, Ibsenism, the brilliant spume of art which became known as Post-Impressionism.

In the Anglophone world, these epochal disturbances are disguised as an ordered, evolutionary (as opposed to revolutionary) culture. The English literary history into which Synge (like all his contemporaries) was obliged to fit was itself the product of ideological struggle in France. In 1903, Louis Cazamian reformulated Victorian English literature so successfully that ordinary readers remain happily unaware their beloved 'social problem novels' were crucially located in a French academic struggle against Marxism. Cazamian and his wife knew their Synge.[30] In time, Synge's mature work will impose a reordering of literary history, forcing London-based coteries of Literary Revivalism to return imaginatively and actually to Ireland. His earlier writings reveal the maelstrom of uncertainties, conflicts, and potentialities in which a young writer, dividing his time between Dublin and Paris, found himself at once floating and drowning.

Nor had the west of Ireland lain beyond the ken of all writers before Synge and his Irish colleagues. Under the auspices of the British Association, Oscar Wilde's father led a party of scientists to Aran in 1857. The English critic, Arthur Symons (1865–1945), reached the islands two years before Synge, and relatives of the syphilitic French novelist, Guy de Maupassant (1850–93) set foot in County Clare somewhat in advance of Yeats. As for Synge, one of the most striking features of his arrival in the west was his acceptance as a revenant, a latter-day version of his missionary uncle or another of the philologists who had been studying the Gaelic of Aran for decades. The allegedly primitive condition of the west of Ireland, its lying beyond the rim of civilisation, was increasingly a theme which placed it at the centre of discontented civilisation's concerns.

In another perspective, Ireland was centrally placed on the map of Western developments. Its emigrants constituted the largest recently arrived population group in the United States. Synge was not the only ghost on Aran; emigrants returned to die, and in the Mayo of 1905 he noted the influence of returned Irish Americans. The many-decades-long experience of transatlantic voyaging as the enactment of life and death, going away to earn livelihoods, returning to die in the natal spot, gave to the west of Ireland something of the air of a vast open-air seance. Synge's spiritualist interests do not derive from his friend Yeats's commitment to the world of faery; they precipitate from the dissolution of communities (including his own family) throughout the nineteenth century, from dissolution and from phantasmal resolution. In reciprocal fashion, his declared sympathy with socialism is partly a revulsion *against* society (as he knew it, mainly in Ireland) and partly a contribution to the recon-struction of some framing outlook or *Weltanschauung* in which spiritual, aesthetic, and ethical values might constellate. Nor are the hostile forces which Pegeen (in *The Playboy*) fears in her out-of the-way location restricted to this world; in a balanced phrase she declares that, with a potboy for company, she'd not fear either 'the loosèd khaki cut-throats, or the walking dead'.[31]

The visible world was a theatre in which spirits and fishermen, girls in red petticoats, tramps, corpses and scholars were equally accessible. In Wicklow, where the guerrilla aspects of the 1798 insurrection had been most intense, what Synge heard by the roadside often implicated his own inheritance. Persuaded to sketch out a commemorative play in 1904, he outraged colleagues with his irreverence. From the moment when the young adult Synge began to comment on his childhood, we find recurring approval of the primitive as a welcome alternative to conventional sophis-tication, breaking through the fourth wall of theatric pretence. This was no isolated idiosyncratic choice of terms on his part. Primitivism had an ancient history among the Greeks. Far more recently, the term had been applied to the art of Henri Rousseau (1844–1910), whose paintings had been initially ridiculed by his contemporaries in France. *War*, which he exhibited in the Louvre in 1894, marked a turning-point.

It would be easy to list a dozen major artists working in the twentieth century who sought to intoxicate their work with a primitivist quality. Let Béla Bartók, Paul Gauguin, Knut Hamsun, D. H. Lawrence, Pablo Picasso, Igor Stravinsky serve as examples. No Irish names are listed, though there are aspects of Yeats's work, where drama and politics meet, which qualify him for consideration. It is not the formal absence of the primitive from the Irish Literary Revival which is significant, rather its pervasive influence throughout the entire texture of the movement. The Irish intellectuals' revolt against England was not conducted on the basis of 'anything you can do we can do better' – as in Hungary's 'compromise' with Austria. It was a root and branch rejection of the metropolitan in favour of a purer, simpler, more traditional world view. This relied on an agrarian subsistence regime to be borne by others than those who advocated it.

On the whole, Synge did not advocate it. He was never at ease in England, though he had more contact with the place than has perhaps been recognised. He disagreed sharply with his land-agent brother at the end of the first Land War: in equally sharp remarks he tended to support the grazier-farmers during the second (1906–8).[32] He was at ease with fishermen and tramps but never mistook himself for one of them. Irony held him apart from the dreamy Yeatsian compact of nobleman and beggar. In a preface written in 1908 a few months before his death, he indicated his attitude to the primitivist programme in a sentence carefully constructed to avoid dogmatism – 'It may almost be said that before verse can be human again it must learn to be brutal.'[33] The caution of this, its delicate suggestion that brutality should be approached by a process akin to self-analysis – with therapy as its implied consequence – indicates a shrewd and sensitive awareness of realities in the field, the shop, and the slum. It is not that verse should change in the absence of other brutality; on the contrary, literature should be aligned with the condition of things. A context had been originally set by the Brothers Goncourt in a journal entry dated 3 September 1855:

Savagery is necessary every four or five hundred years in order to bring the world back to life. Otherwise the world would die of civilization. When bellies were full and men had lost the power of making love, hordes of barbarians six foot tall would sweep down upon them from the north. Now that there are no savages left, it is the workers who will do the job in fifty years or so. And they will call it the social revolution.[34]

Historians of ideas have yet to explore the avenues and drawing rooms of Irish Victorian opinion. The late novels of Sheridan Le Fanu (1814–73) and the early work of George Moore (1852–1933) might be taken as indicative studies of middle-class sensibility. And in that connection, a Flaubertian verdict of stupidity might well be justified. Published when Synge was sixteen, Moore's *A Drama in Muslin* (1887) exposed a world of fashion parades, marriage markets, and callous philistinism revolving round Dublin Castle, the official centre of administration in Ireland. Le Fanu's novels, obediently set in English locations to please his London publisher, reflected an enfeeblement of thought and action in the country house and a terminal febrile emotionalism in character.[35]

Where might a widow seeking to raise her children in Rathmines turn for moral enlightenment? The extent to which Kathleen Synge distrusted literature can be measured by her sons' very late encounter even with Dickens and Scott.[36] She took it upon herself spiritually to nurture her older children's friends, but what we can recover of her teaching only confirms the traditional view of her narrow-mindedness. When Bob and Ned, with their friend Jack Joly (and perhaps Harry Stephens who had also gone to school with them) had been clowning in the hallway one bright May evening, Joly – who was in his mid-twenties – unwisely used some expression she had '*never* heard used except by the common people on the road who know no better'.[37] Eight-year old Johnnie was safely in bed, excluded from the family chronicle as so often he will be in the future. But if it is conceded that tall straight-backed, dry-skinned Mrs Synge in her full black dress and white lace cap was too long committed to evangelical Christianity to contemplate any other point of reference, where might that bright but broody youngster on the thirteen granite steps look for alternative guidance?

CHAPTER 3

The Banality of Good

Four ducks on a pond,
A grass-bank beyond,
A blue sky of spring,
White clouds on the wing:
What a little thing
To remember for years –
To remember with tears!

William Allingham[1]

In spring 1871 Mrs John Hatch Synge (née Kathleen Traill, 1838–1908) was well advanced in her eighth pregnancy. Many years later, Samuel Synge recalled the occasion in the first of a series of letters designed to acquaint his own daughter Edith (born in 1904) with her uncle's life. 'I was moved out of my nursery and put to sleep in a little room with your Uncle Ned. I remember one night being somewhat alarmed before he came to bed because the old-fashioned candle had not been snuffed, and as it burned down it formed a red ball of glowing wick. The next day or soon afterwards I was told that I had got a little brother.'[2]

If this account of John Millington Synge's birth on 16 April 1871 had simply been addressed to a child, its tone might be understandable. Though Samuel Synge's letters to Edith were allegedly written between July 1914 and February 1926, their repetitive apologies are sustained in the published collection of 1932, when the recipient was twenty-seven. Their authenticity – though not their authorship – is gravely in doubt.[3] Though *Letters to My Daughter* contributes something to our knowledge of the dramatist's hidden childhood, it is more significant as the published embodiment of one side in his immediate family's make-up. Behind the hand-wringing explanations of an occasional alcoholic beverage, *Letters* represents a sustained attempt posthumously to lobotomise the author of *Riders to the Sea* and *The Aran Islands*, to tap his brain and drain his sap and generally rehabilitate a man who had never brought a blush to maiden's cheek.

This youngest child lost – as the Victorians put it – his father before his first birthday. According to the family archives, John Hatch Synge (Jack) contracted smallpox by visiting an infected neighbour who survived while he didn't. The crisis was short and fatal, with Jack Synge dying at home on 14 April.[4] He was buried on 16 April 1872, the first anniversary of Johnnie's birth. Thereafter birthdays were occasions of grief and remembrance. 'I pray that my dear little child never knowing an earthly father's tender love & care, may be more abundantly cared for by His heavenly father & drawn to know & love Him while he is still young.'[5] The widow was never convinced her prayers were answered. Not one to restrict spiritual vigilance to her own household, she worried also about her older sons' friends. Of Harry Stephens (1856–1935), who later married Annie Synge, she confided to another youth, 'he still seems to be groping in the dark'. The boys returned her concern by helping Sam with his homework.[6]

A widow who had married for love while still in her teens, Kathleen Synge was not always able to conceal the interconnections of erotic and spiritual need. Still innocent of Freudian interpretations, Victorian correspondence could be oddly suggestive even as it strove for positive clarity. Joly was scarcely twenty-one when the forty-year old woman wrote in anxious rapture:

My heart yearns over you, with an <u>intense longing</u> that you may be stirred up & quickened by God's spirit to <u>follow Jesus</u> more closely. My only relief is bearing you <u>often</u>, constantly in my heart in prayer asking our loving Saviour to <u>draw</u> your heart to Himself, to renew your mind day by day, to make you <u>long</u> after Him.[7] [original emphasis]

If the financially secure – though domestically insecure[8] – visitor to the Synge household received ambiguous written exhortations, to what degree of intense and physically intimate entreaty was its youngest son subjected? Johnnie is rarely mentioned in the family's correspondence, yet he was all the closer to the vortex of faith and self-denial. He who would later characterise his reading of Darwin's work in terms of its sanctioning both incest and parricide grew up under duress.

John Synge's recollections of childhood have been pieced together to form a so-called 'Autobiography' from which we learn that, till he was twenty-three, he never knew a man or woman who shared his opinions. His memories were reconstructed round a sequences of nurses who looked after him. As these numbered eight in as many years, we may perhaps conclude that the women involved were not happy in their position. Given that the head of the house had died a few days short of the child's first birthday, genteel economic hardship may have persuaded each nurse to seek a better-paid situation. Shortly afterwards, the widow moved her family to No. 4 Orwell Park in nearby Rathgar.[9] There the Synges formed part of an elaborate double-household in which Traill relatives in No. 3 came and went through a communicating door. It was an extended family in a strangely restrictive sense, a household in which the tenets of evangelical Protestantism governed every aspect of behaviour.

'I hear Johnnie has been & gone & got the chicken pock.' That was ten weeks before his ninth birthday. And nine months later, 'Johnnie was ill last night & they are uneasy about him.'[10] Perpetual ill-health, of a minor kind, interrupted the boy's education, though he attended a junior school in Upper Leeson Street, Dublin, and was enrolled later at what was known as the Bray School (later Aravon House) for some time. The kind of hero-worship endemic in such establishments led to early disillusion in Synge's case. 'One day the course of my class put me for a moment beside my temporary god, and before I could find a fit term of adulation he whispered an obscene banality . . .'[11] In any case, attacks of the croup, persistent coughs, bronchitis and other ailments led to the curtailment of school, a private tutor serving instead. Samuel Synge, who went to the trouble of recovering his brother's reports from Aravon, suggests that arithmetic was his best subject and that spelling was already identified as a difficulty.[12]

Rathgar was a suburb on the southern edge of Dublin, part of the township of Rathmines. Rathfarnham lay further south in the shadow of the hills which form an extensive border zone between counties Dublin and Wicklow. Newtown Villas had been built close to one of the ornamental arches which distinguished Edward Blackburne's place, Rathfarnham Castle:[13] it consisted of two semi-detached houses with an avenue and gate common to both; in 1871, fields surrounded the little development. Orwell Park was unambiguously suburban, though only four houses (plus the Presbyterian Manse) had been built at the time of the Synges' arrival. At the entrance, red iron gates declared the shared privacy of the road.

The River Dodder ran between these two childhood homes of the Synge boys; its banks provided extensive grounds for adventure. Quite how they mixed with or avoided 'the locals' is unclear. Edward, reporting a drunken Orangeman's indecent jokes in rural Donegal, allowed that they were 'nothing to the ones that are heard in the vicinity of the Dodder'.[14] Blackburne's woods lay to the south beyond the river. According to John Synge at twenty-something, the discovery that a wood near

Rathfarnham (which had been his idea of bliss) was 'a piece of artificially arranged planting on an artificial hillock' had led to his hating the neighbourhood thereafter.[15] On the same principles, he refused even as a young child to sit on the seats provided along the banks of the Dodder, insisting that his nurse walk on until a low branch or convenient stone presented itself. This objection to man-made things he later attributed to Sam, but in the same passage of the 'Autobiography', he related his own fervour as 'a worshipper of nature' to 'a very strong feeling for the colour of locality'. Expressing this in 'syllables of no meaning', he was reprimanded for using such 'gibberish'. Years later, walking the same river-bank with the poet Padraic Colum, he could tell him that birds built their nests in the quiet before dawn.[16]

The river was not a quarter of a mile from the house in Orwell Park, with open fields intervening. And for all of the Synge boys' contempt for manufactured benches on its banks, the Dodder was industrialised in its modest way, with mills and dye-works; notions of it as an unspoiled Wordsworthian stream are sentimental. Near a point, where Johnnie famously discovered a water-ousel's nest behind a waterfall, were cottages inhabited by saw-mill employees and their families.[17] The red iron gates of Orwell Park came down when a new road linked the area to Ranelagh, turning what had been a private road into a thoroughfare, but their function had never been purely symbolic. Whatever might be said about Rathfarnham, and Newtown Villas snuggling under the protection of Blackburne's Castle, the northern (or city-side) bank of the Dodder was steadily incorporated into modern and public life during John Synge's infancy and childhood. Transport was provided by the railway, later by trams. The Dublin and South-Eastern – affectionately known as the Slow and Easy – served the coast lying to the south of the capital, with a line looping through the genteel suburbs of Ranelagh and Milltown by means of which either the city or more distant Bray in County Wicklow might be reached. This was the line later used by Dan Rooney in Samuel Beckett's *All that Fall* (1957), the celestial railroad of Dublin's Protestant bourgeoisie.

At least part of the material now known as the 'Autobiography' was written in Paris, and some details elsewhere suggest that it was not without a fictional aspect.[18] Even in adult life, Synge needed to create distance between his upbringing and his maturity. When he wrote of seaside holidays and 'a vivid recollection of being caught in a heavy shower in the ladies' bathing place and bundled into a bathing box that was not empty!', it is unlikely that he had publication in mind. 'Little boys are rightly considered inoffensive but some of them who have unusual memories grow up with souvenirs that illustrate a celebrated line in Dante.'[19] The indirectness of this allusion is characteristic. His had been a passionate intelligence, long frustrated by domestic pressures in the home and the stifling expectations imposed by the upper middle class in which the Synges placed themselves. If he successfully transcended these restrictions in his literary career, it must be noted that less than six years were left to him when he began to publish his plays, and that the business of remoulding his reputation began as soon as he died in 1909.

The earliest surviving documentation of Johnnie Synge's childhood takes the form of a letter (carefully preserved) from his cousin Florence Ross (1870–1949), dated 8 March 1882. While it naturally reports more of her activities than his – she is taking German and drawing lessons, and minding her guinea-pig – it also alludes to a renewed outbreak of smallpox, the disease which had killed Johnnie's father ten years earlier.[20] A fuller account of their close childhood intimacy is to be found in a small notebook in which they jointly recorded their activities for the month of November 1882; he was eleven and she twelve:

CHAPTER I

A few words about Bird=nesting, and birds and Beasts in general.

Nov 6th 1882
We went to Mr. Blackburn's today for the purpose of finding a suitable place for putting bread for the Birds during the winter months. We were not very successful at first, but as we were sitting on the lime, we saw a bird in a holly=tree, and we went up to see what it was and when we reached the top of the bank, we saw something in the grass, and we found it was a squirrel it saw us and ran up a tree, and then we crept up behind a tree, and very soon we saw another, which the first began to chase round a tree, and then we saw a third which ran up another tree close at hand. We discovered that there were a great many birds about, and we thought we had found a very good place for putting the bread. We sat watching the birds for some time, and then went home feeling that we had succeeded very well for the first day. F. R.

– Nov 7th   Day 2
Come to the plantation of fir tree where we had seen the squirrels. It being a nasty day and the birds not coming down to any bread we threw so we ded [sic] not stay long. But we saw some very small birds with long tails that we had never seen

before that flew about the tops of the trees but we will find out and mention further on. J. S.

Nov 9   Day 3

We went up to Mr Blackburn's today in a hurry because we wanted to get there before Stewart and Mamma. ~~because we were afraid that Stewart would shoot the Squirrels with his catapult.~~ We went up to the fir plantation, without crossing the river, we went through a sort of thicket of trees and holly=bushes and we thought we had found a much better place for putting the bread than at the holly=bush. We put a lot of bread at the top of the bank close to the railings, just at the other side of the railings there are some bushes, which are filled with birds they were very tame and did not fly away when we were quite near them. As we were creeping along on our hands and knees not to frighten the birds, I came upon a bunch of rabit's [sic] fur we traced it, and a little further on we saw a skeleton of a little anamal [sic] we were not sure whether it was a squirrel or a Rabit [sic], but from the colour of the fur we think it must be a Rabit [sic], then we traced it further on and found more fur, some back=bone and a jaw bone with some teeth in it, and the skull and beak of a bird, we were looking about to find more things, and we saw some beautiful moss, in a kind of dell, and we mamed [sic] it Moss dell. There is a little arch of decayed wood, all covered with moss, though very nice, it was not half so pretty as the moss that gave the mane [sic] to the place. On a little further, there is a very damp bank, all over=grown with Hart's toung [sic] fern and we named its [sic] Fern grove. We had found out that the little long tailed birds mentioned in day 2 are long tailed Titts. F. R.

Nov. 10th   day 4.

We went up by the path, there were a lot of birds in the bushes on each side of the path, we saw one squirrel running along the bank of the stream, we crossed the river and went up the bank and fed the birds at the holly bush. there are six crossings to the river

1st Wall, because there is a wall near it

2nd Islands, because there is a patch of stone in the middle of the river.

3rd Lime, because there is a lime tree hanging over the river.

4th Waspsnest, because there is a wasps nest under the bank

5th Fir, because there is a fir tree over it.

6th Beach, because there is some sand and stones on one side of the river,

We then went up the river and found a bank of ferns wich [sic] we named uper [sic] fern grove. [not initialled but in Synge's hand]

Nov 11th   day 5

We went today to Mr Blackburns to find a hiding place in case Robert would come

there too [sic] shot [sic] the birds and then we would want some place to hide
from him so we went up the bank at the path side of the river to look for one, and
after looking for some time, we found one behind a holly bush which we named
Hawk hide, because we saw a hawk that day, then we fed the birds, there were no
birds at holly=bush, we walked along the bank, and came to some bushes where
there a [sic] lot of tits, we threw some bread, and then sat down on an old stump
to watch the birds eating it, some [sic] a dear little wren came down and hoped
[sic] quite close to us, we named these bushes tit grove. F. R.

Nov 13th   Day 6

the women gave us some beach [sic] nuts for our rabbits, and we saw a squirrel
running along the ground near the mounds and we saw another up near tit grove
and fed the birds there too J. S.

Nov 14th.   Day 7

We crossed by lime today and went up and fed the birds at the holly-bush and fir=
plantation and as we were walking along to tit grove we saw a dear little squirrel
up in a tree, we saw a Golden-crested wren and several Creepers. We saw another
squirrel when we were down making catapult balls, and cutting sticks to fight
Robert. F. R.

Nov 16th   Day 8

We went up and fed the birds at tit grove, and then crossed by beach and went up
the glen, we put some sticks in hawk=hide and went home. J. S.[21]

It is likely that Florence was the primary author of the journal, even
for those passages which are in Johnnie's hand. This pre-eminence of the
female role will persist in John Synge's life. His relations with women –
Cherrie Matheson, Valeska von Eicken, Margaret Hardon, Molly
Allgood – constituted a more powerful focus of energy and imagination
than any conventional 'male-bonding' friendship or commitment to a
larger collective identity. Declan Kiberd has argued in favour of Synge's
androgynous sympathies as evidenced particularly in *The Playboy of the
Western World.*[22]

The journal of November 1882 could be analysed in terms of those
entries in which the names of relatives occur. These are Florence's responsibility; if one were to compare Johnnie's own private notebooks and
diaries (even those which he kept when he was an undergraduate), the
usual absence of any member of his immediate family is striking. Even as
a child, he shied away. But the journal also engages in acts of territorial
possession, an undertaking which leads to a rash of misspellings to the

point where to name virtually becomes confused with maiming. The aggression in this is never external, or even overt. Words are taken over at whatever cost. Nevertheless, the names imposed on features of the Castle grounds ring with an unmistakably suburban tenor – Fern Grove leading to Upper Fern Grove. Thus while the children explored a territory which provided an alternative to parlour life in Orwell Park, they underlined the essentially bourgeois nature of the Synge household.

Mrs Synge positively liked the area, comparing it favourably to Monkstown where she had grown up with her widowed mother. 'I dont like Monkstown at all,' she confided emphatically to her eldest son. 'It is all houses & walls & roads & sea. No greenness or verdure or singing birds. I much prefer Rathgar.'[23] Conceding that there might be better company elsewhere, she never descended into nostalgic recollections of a lost or threatened social eminence. Instead, her rented semi-detached is refocused as a *rus in urbe*, a little bit of the countryside adjacent to the tram. But this view of Orwell Park – as nature green to the very door – was rather a view *from* Orwell Park, a view of the river and mountains to the south, obtained by turning one's back on the city and its tramlines.

The son of a dead barrister whose landed income had dwindled, young Synge was a tolerated intruder in a demesne under siege from middle-class housing. His two eldest brothers appear to have clung on to the family's earlier social connections, paying courtesy calls to the Truells of Clonmannon, near Glanmore, and spending holidays with the Traills of north Antrim.[24] As the youngest of the brood, John Synge was more closely tied to the maternal apron strings. If we think of children playing explorers, we tend to interpret their antics as the mapping out of new worlds which either are wholly imaginary or are hitherto unknown to them; but Johnnie Synge's recreation explored the old world of landlordly landscapes. The Edenesque elements in the journal which he kept with Florence opaquely acknowledge a fall which has already occurred even before their shared adventure had begun; by the addition of one day too many, a biblical time-table of seven days is marred; there are acts of naming which are less than transparent, there is a postponed acknowledgement of violence (Stewart Ross's catapult) reinforced by the later admission of a personal involvement in such violations – in the making of catapult ammunition. Finally, there is a cast of male and female, on the lip of puberty.

The social priorities and cultural values nurtured in this rewriting of J. M. Synge's origins and upbringing could be isolated in any of a hundred details. For example, a print showing 'Lord Alexander George Russell, and his Pony Emerald' (after Edwin Landseer) was one of six or seven cheap pictures which hung in the room shared by Sam and Johnnie in their childhood. A toy-boat incident, and others occurring on holidays at Greystones in County Wicklow, incite in their author a toy-language, or – worse – assumptions of a toy-intelligence in the recipient of the letters:

Our boats used generally to carry someone on board to sail them. Various things would do for men. A stone would do sometimes ... It was supposed to be a man and he was named 'Mr Wynne'. The Rev. Frederick R. Wynne had begun to come to Greystones in the summer and no slight was intended to him, rather the reverse, for although neither of us knew him personally in those days, we had every respect for him ...[25]

Such anxiety in establishing the perfect manners of a child who had died, a world-renowned dramatist, at the age of thirty-seven – just six years before the letter was supposedly written – fills the blank account of John Synge's emotional life in *Letters to My Daughter*. That Samuel Synge should have chosen to convey an image of his famous, long-dead brother to the Irish reading public by means of letters ostentatiously addressed to a girl aged between ten and twenty-two – without much adjustment of tone for her growing to woman's estate and intelligence – is itself a symptom of a trait tending towards refined infantilism.

Synge's childhood knew more than its share of emotional and intellectual crises. The journal of 1882 cannot be taken as a thoroughly personal statement, even in those paragraphs initialled by the eleven-year-old boy. Florence Ross's influence pervades the entire document. But just over a year later, Johnny commenced a record of his naturalist activities into which neither cousin nor brother is admitted. In the interval he fell victim to asthma, a condition sometimes thought psychosomatic in its unnamed causes.[26] Sam, just four years older, took to lecturing him on theological matters.[27] Secret writing, of the kind which a naturalist's diary can discretely absorb, provided some relief.

The study of nature was Johnnie Synge's solace. At first the new notebook is maintained in pencil, beginning in December 1883; ultimately it will also accommodate details of examination questions of the kind he faced in Trinity College, Dublin, ten years later. But the first portion of the notebook, up to about March 1886, is revealing for the subsequent over-writing in ink with which Synge emphasised some individual sentences among his descriptions and measurements of birds and other natural phenomena. These doubly-written passages are always brief and generally of the 'I saw a corncrake...' variety.[28] That is, the second writing asserts, or assists in constructing, a personal identity; the first person pronoun initiates these double-inscriptions with remarkable consistency. Synge's economical use of the same notebook over a ten-year period does not help in dating these inky details. Personality grew silently as the substance which threw inky shadows on the notebook.

Natural history has a respectable pedigree as the scientific indulgence of country gentlemen. It featured prominently among the enthusiasms of his brother's fellow pupils at Rathmines School. In the family, science has played a more complicated role over the years. Johnnie's ancestors included a non-Synge eighteenth-century bishop of Ossory: this was Hugh Hamilton (1729–1805), a Fellow of the Royal Society who published on conic sections in Latin and helped to found the Royal Irish Academy. Hamilton's granddaughter, Isabella, married John 'Pestalozzi' Synge. When Glanmore finally passed out of the family in the middle of the twentieth-century, a sundial designed by 'Pestalozzi' Synge was presented to John Lighton Synge and is now in the possession of his daughter, a professor of mathematics at New York University. Scientific commitment has also drawn members of the twentieth-century family to work in anthropology and botany, and to publish 'travel writings' of a very high order. Johnnie's early engagement with natural history is perhaps the first evidence of that later development, even if it were motivated by a need to escape as much as by a desire to explore.

Membership of the Dublin Naturalists' Field Club provided a rare occasion for social intercourse. In November 1886, he heard Dr McNab talking on the various locations where Coleoptera (beetles) are to be found – 'under stones in runing [sic] water, beside small water falls, under stones in the dry bed of a stream.'[29] These notes are carefully revised for grammatical completeness, even if spelling remains erratic. By the following January, Synge's records of a *Bombyx rubi* larva are replete with air temperatures, clock-times, and dates. On his sixteenth birthday, he simply noted night and day temperatures. By 2 June, an entry had extended to accommodate bits of scientific Latin alongside Irish place-names in a manner not unlike that of the Imagist poets:

Saw fox glove flowering at the Scalp. A larva beaten from sallow near Stepaside head pale green. The whole body green darker underneath the spinacular lines Dorsal line dark green, subdorsal and spinacular and a small interrupted line between them pale yellow getting almost white towards the head, the joining of several of the middle segments marked with a lighter yellow.[30]

Entries now tend to dispense with the first-person pronoun, being content
with 'saw two king fishers near the common' and similar terse reports.
The notebook writer is in charge of his material. A lengthy account of a
Field Club meeting on 22 November at which the entomologist, W. F. de
Vismes Kane, spoke on the life of James Tardy ends with young Synge
noting an observation of his own made at Greystones which complements
the evidence adduced by adult speakers.[31] As an indicator of the smallness
and closet-closeness of Anglo-Irish society, we might note that Ned Synge
in Cavan was on chatting terms with the Rev. Elias Tardy, eldest son of
the famous entomologist. Even at club meetings Johnnie still walked
within a narrow circle. He escaped from home only to find himself in an
echo chamber.[32]

Meetings at the Field Club were not restricted to empirical reports of
natural life. Just before Christmas, the anthropologist A. C. Haddon
lectured on 'the supposed Atlantis or submerged continent which he
proved never existed'.[33] The revolution in biology which Charles Darwin
had launched touched on a myriad of other disciplines, including the
study of mythology and the transmission of life beyond the known centres
of ancient civilisation in Europe and Asia. At this point Synge was sixteen,
and there is no evidence that he had run up against Darwin. His notes
are at times so unyielding as to indicate nothing more for Christmas Day
1887 than the information that he heard a 'wren singing' – two words for
a notable event in the Christian calendar. A notebook used between 1896
and 1898 claims that he was about fourteen when he encountered natural
selection, evolution, and the origin of species. If his memory is to be
trusted, that would date the discovery to 1885, when he was keeping his
first tolerably methodical notes. But, as we have seen, MS 4370 contains no
reference to Darwin; indeed some time in May–June 1886, he transcribed a
longish passage from Charles Waterton's *Wanderings in South America*, a
work – though useful in practical matters of taxidermy – which is, in
conceptual terms, light years away from evolution. Darwinism was a topic
Synge played hide-and-seek with in his private writings.

Haddon and Kane were pioneers in their field, men with international
reputations in the making. Young Synge's enthusiasm for such studies
was pursued in a household where the natural world was appreciated as
the handiwork of the Creator. His mother was very fond of birdsong and
the sight of wild flowers in the fields beyond Orwell Park, but she also
could write at tedious length about the shape of clouds as evidence of

God's goodness.[34] The beliefs she inculcated into all but one of her children provided little scope for independent modes of expression, let alone free thought. This mental condition, together with the young people's narrowly circumscribed field of behaviour, led to an enfeeblement of the very creed she aimed to instil in them. 'Sam is always on the watch for opportunities of doing good. He & I often talk about it. He says we are told to testify not to preach . . .' As for his sister Annie, the next-closest in age, even Mrs Synge found her hostility to symbolic interpretations of scripture alarmingly comprehensive: 'She is so matter of fact I think she never likes taking things in a spiritual sense unless they are palpably spiritual.' Science was not scorned or prohibited in the family, but it was treated as the occasion for ulterior interpretations. When Sam happily accepted an invitation to visit the astronomical observatory at Dunsink, he subjected his companion on the walk from Dublin to a lengthy account of the evangelical underground in Trinity College and its campaigns against scepticism and ritualism.[35]

Against this background, Johnnie's encounter with Darwin is described in terms derived from the religious practices from which he sought release. In a household where the Bible was taken literally as God's word on everything from ambition to zoology, the teenager fittingly turns to an alternative book:

It opened in my hands at a passage where he asks how can we explain the similarity between a man's hand and a bird's or bat's wings except by evolution. I flung the book aside and rushed out into the open air – it was summer and we were in the country – the sky seemed to have lost its blue and the grass its green. I lay down and writhed in an agony of doubt. My studies showed me the force of what I read, [and] the more I put it from me the more it rushed back with new instances and power. Till then I had never doubted and never conceived that a sane and wise man or boy could doubt. I had of course heard of atheists but as vague monsters that I was unable to realize. It seemed that I was become in a moment the playfellow of Judas. Incest and parricide were but a consequence of the idea that possessed me.[36]

Darwin himself had responded to his realisation that species were not immutable with a morally self-accusing extremism -'it is like confessing a murder'.[37] The greater particularity of Synge's fears deserves attention. The incident may have occurred in Wicklow – the family holidayed nowhere else in Ireland. But whether Greystones or Glanmore provided the immediate backdrop to the deconversion remains unclear; in either

case, of course, evangelical exclusivism pervaded the air now robbed of
its celestial blue. If his response to Darwin *circa* 1886 seems to lack something in dramatic timing – the author of *The Origin of Species* had died
four years earlier in patriarchal old age – his theatre of spiritual crisis was
impeccably chosen. No Irish county outside Ulster possessed a similar
concentration of Protestant inhabitants, and these included not only
landed families of the 'big house', but tenant farmers, cottagers, shopkeepers, tradesmen, and a small spillover population from Dublin to the
north. It was just possible, if one shut one's eyes to the newspapers and
closed one's ears to the angelus bells of rawly new Catholic chapels, to
imagine a community in which Protestantism and unbelief totalled the
options open to man or boy.

The retrospective which Synge provided on his confrontation with
Darwin has nothing to say about Irish Catholicism, a religious community sturdier in resistance to agnosticism and scientific explanation
than the Church into which he had been born. But he has a curiously
precise view of the consequences of unbelief – amounting virtually to the
sanctioning of incest and parricide. The lengthy passage of time between
the crisis and Synge's account of it discourages any identification of him
as a teenager experiencing sudden floods of illicit sexual desire and an
urge to slaughter his mother. The apprehensive response to Darwin
underlines the absence of any complex system of moral values in the
household, apart from blind faith. Being good required little more than
some consideration towards worm-bait and other fellow creatures. The
trouble was that Darwin's arguments about the fellowship of men, bats
and birds concluded in a doctrine which predicted survival of the fittest
only.

The dating of Synge's first encounter with these ideas is at once important and difficult, important particularly in seeking to establish how his
intellectual experience synchronises with sexual or medical timetables,
difficult because the writings taken as autobiographical derive from
various later periods of reflection. If we seek a more direct record of his
meeting Darwin, the focus shifts to the Continental *Wanderjahre*, c.1894–
5, and settles on two sources. These are: i) a notebook in which his reading
of such diverse authors as Matthew Arnold, Madame Blavatsky, Auguste
Comte, Darwin, G. W. F. Hegel, Karl Marx, Friedrich Nietzsche, Herbert
Spencer and Baruch Spinoza is detailed; and ii) the diary for
September/October 1895. As far as the notebook is concerned, the work
in question, however, is *The Descent of Man* and not *Origin of Species*.
Jottings on Marx and Morris (on socialism) suggest that Synge's interest

was at that point cultural and social rather than biological.[38]

Questions of sexuality and aesthetics, however, are not excluded. In fact his diary for the autumn of 1895 very suggestively records Darwin's name among others less renowned. On Friday 20 September, in domestic Kingstown, he began to read *The Ascent of Man* which Henry Drummond had published the previous year in direct if delayed response to Darwin's *Descent of Man* (1871). Here was a balanced argument between pro- and anti-Darwinian positions – without Darwin himself making an appearance.[39] Ten days later, Herbert Spencer's *Principles of Psychology* (1870–2) was 'done with'. The diarist was uncertain as to its title or subject and gave it as 'Physichology', suggesting an unease as to where body and mind meet or collide. The same day Synge turned to various reference books – probably in Trinity library – for articles on Goethe, Spencer and Darwin. Only then he 'Began the Origin of Species'.[40]

For the next day – Tuesday, 1 October 1895 – all that the diary records is 'tea on Killiney with the M.s [space] Darwin'. Nothing could be less indicative of a traumatic occasion. Killiney Hill lies south of Kingstown and remains a place of recreation, with light woodland, some open heath, an obelisk, and precipitous slopes down over the railway line, towards the sea. But who were these 'M' people with whom Synge picnicked that mid-autumn day? Given that it was a working day, a family excursion with Miller relatives seems unlikely, for Charlie Miller had his college duties to attend to. The other possible candidates were the Mathesons, a family of one son and four daughters ranging in age from twenty-eight to sixteen, who lived a few doors from the Synges in Crosthwaite Park East. In fact, Robert Matheson had just celebrated his sixteenth birthday the previous day; his sister, Cherrie, would be twenty-five on 12 October. John Synge, who was some months her junior, spent her birthday finishing Darwin's *Descent of Man*. Given the tense emotional and intellectual exchanges which would soon link them, the interweaving of Darwin's undermining of orthodox belief and apparent sanctioning of illicit sexuality with a virtually unique recording of Synge's social intercourse with Cherrie Matheson's family is worthy of note.

It is probable that Synge's crisis with Darwinism did not occur in childhood but in his mid-twenties.[41] Doubled responses recur in his mature discursive or reflective prose. The pattern was established early. As with the two reactions to Darwin, he provided in the notebooks of 1896–8 a different perspective on his childhood relationship with his cousin Florence Ross to that recorded in the Rathfarnham demesne or in the parlour of No. 4 Orwell Park. Writing fourteen years or more after the event, he refers to her as 'a girl of my own age who was our neighbour', 'my little friend' and 'my friend'. She is no longer presented as a cousin, a blood relative. He makes no reference to the formally composed and jointly authored journal of November 1882; perhaps from this we can conclude that it had remained in Florence's possession and was not available to him on the various occasions when he reflected on their friendship. Much of his adult's reflection focuses on their shared interests, and the close communion into which they were thrust when an aunt died in Orwell Park in the summer of 1882.[42] The period – Synge accurately puts it in the month of August – when the house remained in mourning behind drawn curtains – the two youngsters spent their time together in the woods near Rathfarnham: 'The sense of death seems to have been only strong enough to evoke the full luxury of the woods. I had never been so happy. It is a feeling like this makes all primitive people inclined to merry making at a funeral.'[43]

From this intimacy, there came inevitably a dreadful falling-off:

Our two families joined in a large country house in June where some Indian cousins of mine were coming to spend the later months with us. This June was absolutely delightful. I had my friend now under the same roof, and we were inseparable ... we wandered arm in arm about among the odours of the old-fashioned garden till it was quite dark watching the bats and moths. I loved her with a curious affection that I cannot pretend to analyse and I told her, with more virile authority than I since possess, that she was to be my wife. She was not displeased. My cousins arrived, a small boy and a girl of my own age. My friend threw [me] over completely, apparently without a shadow of regret, and became the bosom friend of her new companion, my accursed cousin. I was stunned with horror.[44]

The implication of terming Florence a 'friend' rather than a cousin takes on suggestive colouration here. She may well have regarded the newcomers as less 'family' than Johnnie Synge, and consequently had seen in the visitor from Argentina a more independent boyfriend. Given that the boys were twelve in the summer of 1883, sexual desire cannot have been very highly developed. Yet Synge in retrospect hedges memory in with words of accusation and exculpation. Early in the passage just quoted, he had scrupulously noted that the two of them 'were left in complete liberty and never abused it'. His narrative stated that 'we talked of sexual matters with an indifferent and sometimes amused frankness that was identical with the attitude of folk-tales', a remark which betrays an adult basis of comparison Synge acquired only years after the event. Finally, 'we clubbed our resources and bought a ten-shilling telescope, which led to trouble afterwards. This period was probably the happiest of my life.'[45]

The trouble remains unspecified. And the implicit diminution of 'virile authority' in the succeeding years is recorded as valid at the moment of autobiographical writing, a moment (evidently) when the prospect of marriage was closed off. Quite when Synge resolved never to marry, and why, is impossible to specify. But the evidence of his first completed play, with its ruthlessly plotted final wedding ceremony, and its repeated emphasis on 'cleanness', indicates a period of prolonged anxiety on the topic and a determination to solve on-stage what could not be contemplated in life.

The breach with Florence Ross was gradually healed, and indeed Synge later recorded details of his sentimental love for her – kissing the chair she had sat upon, and so forth. Natural history was inextricably related to his feelings for her – 'I remember telling – or intending to tell her – that each egg I found gave three distinct moments of rapture: the finding of the nest, the insertion of [the] egg successfully blown in my collection, and, lastly, the greatest, exhibiting it to her.'[46] But the paragraph immediately following the account of his showing eggs to Florence interrupts the recollection of childhood diseases and friendships to set up a longer-term perspective:

This ill health led to a curious resolution which has explained in some measure all my subsequent evolution. Without knowing, or, as far as I can remember, hearing anything about doctrines of heredity I surmised that unhealthy parents should have unhealthy children – my rabbit breeding may have put the idea into my head. Therefore, I said, I am unhealthy, and if I marry I will have unhealthy children. But I will never create beings to suffer as I am suffering, so I will never marry. I do not know how old I was when I came to this decision, but I was between thirteen and fifteen and it caused me horrible misery.[47]

If we now translate back from the terminology of 'my friend' to the actual cousinship which linked John and Florence, then the horrified response to Darwin which had been voiced in terms of a permitted incest becomes intelligible. The 'accursed cousin' from South America officially earns condemnation because he comes between Johnnie and Florence. But Johnnie, Florence and the young Traills were equally the grandchildren of Mrs Traill next door; it is really Johnnie who is her accursed cousin in the light of his (retrospectively reported) reading of Darwin, sanctioning an incest which would befoul her. Moreover, the logically flawed 'therefore ... I am unhealthy' may be illuminated, not so much by reference to rabbit-keeping but to an awareness (however indistinct) that he was the son of an unhealthy parent – his father, whom he could not remember.

Such anxieties are not uncommon in childhood, and the facts of Synge mortality were undeniable. The conventions of life – banality of expression among them – were bulwarks thrown against the facts of death. Within twelve months from Johnnie's birth, four of his grandfather's surviving children had died, with the survivors feeling that an era had closed. This feeling pervaded the years to come. We have already noted one of the influential casualties by anticipation. The Rev. Alexander Hamilton Synge (c.1821–72) had served briefly on the Aran Islands in the 1850s, departing for London's East End (en route for Ipswich) after a confrontation with local fishermen. Though his time on the Mile End Road was brief, it was not without significance. Describing a 'thorough' London fog to his youngest brother, the new arrival wrote of the city with a curious, leaden eloquence. 'We can scarcely discern the houses on the other side of the street. Yesterday the air was impregnated with little urchin voices in every direction shouting out bits of poetry for Nov. 5th ...'[48] Resolutely evangelical in his own open-air preaching, he was part of a migration of conscientious Anglican clergy who were taking up the East End as a cause. One result of this socially concerned movement was the idea of housing settlements, prompted by John Ruskin and Arnold Toynbee, and still expanding in the 1890s when the Passmore Edwards Settlement was established. Several of John Synge's friends stayed in this social-reformist institution in the early part of the new century. Synge himself took shelter under its protection in 1903.

Uncle Alec was by then long dead, and he would not have approved of the tendency towards liberalism and even unitarianism among some whose mission began in the East End. In his meagre publications can be found 'low church' doctrines which become significant later when the question of J. M. Synge's familiarity with Plymouth Brethren teaching arises.[49] There is a buried stream of continuity, linking Alec in Aran and Stepney with his sceptical nephew. If J. M. Synge cast himself ironically as the fool of the family, there is still room for both the fool and the family to be revisioned in the light of careful research.

Another influential casualty of 1872 – the Rev. Edward Synge in Australia – left money for the benefit of John Hatch Synge's three youngest sons. But Kathleen, suddenly widowed, was appointed administrator of the will because the named executor was still a minor.[50] Here was anguish piled upon anguish, even if the infant in his cradle was oblivious to the grim circumstances. By the end of the 1870s, the last male of that generation, Francis Synge of Glanmore, was also dead, leaving only two unmarried sisters. That was four years before the death of Aunt Anne Traill which led young John Synge and Florence Ross to experience 'the full luxury of the woods' at Rathfarnham.

While Victorian death-rates may astonish readers at the onset of the twenty-first century, the significant factor in Synge's childhood is to be identified in the household's response to death. Much of this could be said about any version of Christianity, but the evangelicalism of his upbringing dwelled on the degree to which the sinner might (even at the last moment) claim God's forgiveness through genuine repentance. In this regard the adult John Synge was right to remark that, though 'religion remained a difficulty and occasioned terror' for many years, the brand he was brought up in was not 'peculiarly Calvinist'.[51]

Calvinism, indeed, might have provided an intellectual framework in which a thoughtful youth could find meaning. Any version of Protestant dissent, rooted in dogged opposition to the Establishment, could have provided at least a degree of vigour and emotional engagement. But the plight of the Synges, as descendants of a once established episcopalian clerical élite, members also of a mildly embarrassed but still financially viable social élite, discouraged rigour or system. Even the notion of 'a good death' was too robust for the Protestant drawing rooms of Rathgar. The best to be aimed for was a polite passing. All too soon, J. M. Synge was documenting his own last struggle with death in a series of letters notable for their balance of realism and cheerfulness.

This image of John Synge's childhood has not paraded the available lists of dogs, rabbits and other pets which doubtless gave him great pleasure. The straw is not to hand for such brickmaking. While he wrote no connected narrative of his childhood and youth, Synge returned to his formative years as though they made up a drama possessed of its own unity, from which extraneous material had been purged. The brevity of his life imposes a peculiar pressure on his childhood, obliterating images of continuity and development. Florence Ross, for example, became a close friend of Edith Synge, recipient of the retrospectively dated letters: the two women went painting and sketching in the west of Ireland, finally untouched – or at least unscarred – by the more intense restrictions of their growing up. It was not John Synge's destiny to escape in this manner.

CHAPTER 4

The Encumbered Present

There is little sympathy felt in this world of rhetoric for the silent sufferings of the genteel poor, yet there is no class that deserves a more charitable commiseration.

Edmund Gosse[1]

Oscar Wilde observed that, while every great man attracts numerous disciples, it is always Judas who writes the biography. In this, as in so many other respects, Synge declines to fit the pattern. He has been more often the victim of the beloved disciple who, while faithfully sticking to his commission, glosses over difficulties which even a diligent observer would have pursued. There seems to be no reason for doubting Sam Synge's statement that he was born in Newtown Little (in the parish of Rathfarnham) in March 1867, and even less reason to doubt that the last child of the family duly followed at the same birthplace, in April 1871, and was christened in the parish church shortly afterwards.

However, Dublin street directories suggest that John Hatch Synge's migration from the city to the outer suburbs did not take place quite so smoothly as has been assumed. This uncertainty introduces other issues of a kind which – as in the notable case of John Butler Yeats, the poet's father – the scrupulous chronicler never fails to investigate nowadays.[2] These issues can be summarised in one word – money. But on a more sensitive graph of psycho-social registrations, we might substitute the word – security. Nothing in the Irish Literary Revival united its competing giants as much as a sensitivity about accepted belonging, a state of affairs which required genealogical authentication. Neither the English Romantic poets of a century earlier, nor the wider Modernist generation of which the Irish Revivalists formed a contentious part, could hold a candle to the zeal of the latter sub-platoon in their fight for social certification.

Synge, on the other hand, never acknowledged his first baptismal name (Edmund) and he sought consistently to evade his inherited names by signing himself, J. M. Synge. Who were these Synges in the 1870s? What was the nature or substance of their security? These questions will bear with urgency on Synge's entry on a career as dramatist. The Dublin directory for 1870 lists the father at No. 8 Dawson Street, business premises which he shared with one other barrister (John S. Collins), four charities (mainly attached to the Church of Ireland), and a firm of gun-makers called Trulock and Harris. His residence is given as Orwell Road Little, Rathgar, which may be assumed to be No. 3 Orwell Park, the residence of his mother-in-law, Mrs Traill, who is the listed ratepayer. It would seem from this evidence that, towards the end of 1869, Jack Synge was still unsure of establishing a permanent (nuclear) family home at Newtown Little and relied to some extent on his wife's family for support.

There is also a factor of inherited position. The extended Synge family had undergone several changes of fortune in the previous century, principally negative ones, in England. Alec Synge, son of the Rev. A. H. Synge, was in the bankruptcy courts in mid-1885, with consequences which jeopardised the family's association with Glanmore Castle. Robert Synge, as John Hatch Synge's eldest son, saw it as a personal mission to reverse the pattern in Ireland.[3] We need to take a look at the marriage settlement of J. M. Synge's parents.

John Hatch Synge (1823–72) had been the third son (by the first marriage) of John 'Pestalozzi' Synge (1788–1845) who, despite an attachment to the Brethren in Plymouth, took up residence in County Wicklow in the 1830s when his father died.[4] In the difficult economic conditions of the day, 'Pestalozzi' Synge found the estate unviable, and when he died on 29 April 1845 the bailiffs were in possession. Subsequently, Glanmore was put up for sale under the Encumbered Estates legislation and the heirs obliged to live as tenants of the courts, pending a resolution of the problem. Thus, when John Hatch Synge chose to marry Kathleen Traill in 1856, the family was in no very prosperous condition. As a younger son of a first marriage, he had taken the precaution of acquiring a profession, but there is little evidence that he was a successful (or even a notably competent) barrister. In later years, his widow described him – affectionately enough – as slow.[5] He did, however, possess some property – including up to eleven hundred acres of poor land in County Galway, demised to him the year before his marriage by the Lord Bishop of Tuam.[6]

Kathleen Traill, for her part, was the daughter of a widow who also had raised a numerous family. The memorial of marriage settlement delicately states that she was 'an infant under the age of twenty-one years that is to say of the age of seventeen years and upwards'.[7] At thirty-two, her husband-to-be was still only at the outset of his career, and both his parents were dead. Quite apart from an unpropitious financial situation and, without reference to the couple's origins in families of unbending evangelical zeal, it is clear that this was a love-match. But was it love in a hovel? John Hatch Synge's property lay principally in Galway land – 'the towns, hamlets and lands of Knockroe, Brackloon and Gurtagurnane'. A charge on these was duly vested in two trustees (the bridegroom's brother, the Rev. A. H. Synge, and a Donegal solicitor), as was a sum of £2,000 to be settled on Kathleen, subject to the life-interest of her mother and payable on the latter's death. As Mrs Anne Traill did not die until April 1890, while her daughter's husband died in April 1872, the arrangements of the marriage settlement turned out to be less supportive of the young widow and her family than anyone can have anticipated. On the other hand, old Mrs Traill and Kathleen Synge lived virtually under the same roof between 1872 and 1890 and their mutual support was perhaps all the greater for its informal nature.

In mid-January 1856, the couple had married in Dublin.[8] It has not been possible to establish where John Hatch Synge had lived as a bachelor. Kathleen was married out of her widowed mother's house at Montpelier Parade in Monkstown on the southern shore of Dublin Bay. At first the newlyweds lived in Hatch Street: Edward Stephens suggests 'first at No. 1, and afterwards at No. 4'.[9] The street bore the name of the bridegroom's grandmother, hardly an intimate relationship, though the uncommonness of the name may have increased an awareness of the link. The choice of Hatch Street was probably facilitated by the falling-in of leases; in 1864, John Hatch Synge and his brother Alec leased thirteen of the Hatch Street houses in what was most likely a renewal to the former leaseholder.[10] What is significant in these details is the married couple's reliance on inherited property for a residence and their movement out of it after a few years to a small development in the suburbs.[11]

Implicitly or otherwise, commentators on J. M. Synge's background have cast him as the beneficiary of oppression. Landlordism had acquired an opprobrious reputation in the course of the nineteenth century, with the Famine years providing a dramatic focus. The principal lessee of Brackloon until 1888 or 1889 was Charles W. Baylee, a member of the Church of Ireland whose brother was in holy orders. Baylee held close on two hundred and eighty acres of which nearly fifty was made up of water. The Synges' farm at Brackloon was thus both an economic and a recreational unit, providing a basis for agricultural activity with fishing and/or shooting facilities. As there appears to have been no dwelling on the farm – apart from a thatched 'herd's house' – we may take it that

Baylee held other property in the area. At one point in his skirmishes with Mrs Synge he was able to retreat to the family seat in County Clare, leaving his wife and children in north Galway. All in all, he was a tenant in a strictly legal sense only, and a middling gentleman in mode of living.[12]

In 1866 the Synge brothers granted a parcel of ground (10 perches in extent) near Leeson Street Bridge, Dublin, to the Grand Canal Company in return for a rent of 4s od per annum.[13] A second transaction which John Hatch Synge is known to have conducted between his Hatch Street business and his death turned on a very different kind of property. In 1869, he and his brother demised to William Sandford Pakenham of Harcourt Street, Dublin, a ninety-nine-year lease on No. 8 Ely Place, a vast house situated between the fashionable quarters of St Stephen's Green and Merrion Square: from this he derived an annual income of £129, though – as with the renewals in Hatch Street – there may have been a one-off cash payment also. This occurred after the removal to Newtown Little, and the contrast in architectural scales could hardly be more pronounced. The sum of £129 was a useful component in the annual income of a modestly successful professional man.[14]

What, then, of the exodus of John Hatch Synge from Hatch Street in the mid-1860s? No hard conclusions can be drawn, but the evidence indicates uneasy or contemplated mobility. At the beginning of 1868 he is listed as having shifted to Newtown Little, Rathfarnham, though by the time the 1870 directory is being prepared (late 1869, the year of the Ely Place leasing), his address is Orwell Road Little. Newtown Villas had been built as recently as late 1863, a cautious housing development of two rather old-fashioned semi-detached houses of two floors above basement, lying outside Rathmines township. If Sam Synge's claim to have been born there in March 1867 is to stand, then a decision to leave – if not an actual removal – had been contemplated, with Mrs Traill's Orwell Park address published in the 1870 directory.

It is, of course, possible to devise an explanation which does not rely on financial calculation. After Sam's birth in 1867, his mother would have sought her mother's support and company; this in turn might have led to discussion of uniting the two families, a decision which was (so to speak) advertised in the 1870 directory but not put into effect. In fact, Stephens tells us that 'shortly before Mr Synge's death, Mrs Traill had moved from Monkstown to No. 3 Orwell Park, a small house near Newtown Villas but on the opposite side of the river Dodder.'[15] Though the house was not small by Hatch Street standards – it is a semi-detached of three storeys with decent gardens front and rear – it lay in a new housing area without hereditary associations.[16] The sequence of events now looks like this: the Synges vacate Hatch Street for a small new house (in Newtown Villas) on the edge of Rathfarnham Castle demesne, Mrs Synge's mother zooms into No. 3 Orwell Park on the city side of the Dodder, and the Synges contemplate joining her in the same house, but in fact do not do so. Nothing in the family's fortunes after John Hatch Synge's death mitigates the suspicion that genteel hardship afflicted his household just as it did that of Yeats's father and Joyce's father.

Schooling was a crucial indicator in these matters. A distinguishing feature of Johnnie's education can only be expressed in negative terms – he did *not* go to Rathmines School. This was a small establishment, run by a patriarchal Dr Benson. Among the early entrants were the Matheson brothers – Charles Louis Matheson in 1863 and the Australian-born Robert three years later. Robert Synge enrolled in the same year as George Tyrrell did – but Tyrrell confounded the traditions of the place by converting to Catholicism, becoming a Jesuit, and being excommunicated for his 'modernist' views. (He died in the same year as J. M. Synge.) Ned Synge and Sam Synge were also educated here, together with some members of the Price family into which Ned would marry. John Joly and Henry Francis Colclough Stephens entered together in 1872: both later aspired to be the Synge boys' brother-in-law. Stephens was lucky, not only in marrying Annie Synge but also becoming the family lawyer.

Harry Stephens evidently had charm; he won the school's good conduct medal and played on the rugby first XV in 1876. Later he was to make his fortune with Fred Sutton & Co.: two sons of Sutton's were also Rathmines pupils, entering in 1876 along with C. A. H. Tuthill. Three boys named Frizell(e) entered between 1873 and 1883, with addresses in County Wicklow: property owned by their family played a major part in Johnnie Synge's discovery of his rural background, and one of their number was a medical doctor at Annamoe where a succession of obscure dispensary officers contributed to the shadowy social links between the grandeur of Glanmore and the facts of annual holiday rentings.[17] At the school, William Hume Frizell distinguished himself by winning the Wilson Medal for English Literature, editing the school magazine, and lecturing his fellow pupils on the birds of County Wicklow – in all, doing the things a future great dramatist might be expected to have done.[18] All of these names, most of these individuals, played an important part in shaping a milieu from which John Synge was – for whatever reasons – excluded.

The explanation for his non-enrolment in the school where his brothers all matured may lie in his own fragile health, or in the further eroded finances of the family at the beginning of the 1880s. The effects included a sense of difference, which often afflicts the youngest child in a large family, but which in this case was intensified by the awareness that his brothers' circle consolidated itself and prospered in their early careers while things at home in Orwell Park did not. Charles Matheson married Elinor Tuthill in 1877 or thereabouts. Johnnie Synge later ardently sought to marry Matheson's niece, Cherrie, and failed. Young Charles James Edward Sutton was admitted a solicitor in 1884, joining his father's firm; he later became a member of Arthur Guinness's board of directors, and was eventually managing director. Harry Stephens, who became Johnnie's brother-in-law in 1884, flourished as an increasingly important partner in the firm of solicitors who acted for the city's leading employer (especially of Protestants). That this good fortune stemmed from a jealous defence of alcohol when the brewery was engaged in its most intensive expansion added irony in a household where even mild stimulants were forbidden. But the great brewing family also staffed the evangelical movement – when Cherrie Matheson finally married, the officiating cleric was R. Wyndham Guinness, rector of Rathdrum.

The Dublin Protestant professional class constituted a small, intricate world. In a variety of ways, Johnnie was kept outside of its charmed – not always charming – circle. The older Synge boys had already embarked on their education by the time their father died, whereas he was brought up in altered circumstances. His hatred of business success, perhaps cultivated as a rationalisation but inherited by his nephew John Lighton Synge, did not stifle a natural talent for sympathetic management when he became a director of the Abbey Theatre. In the difficult 1880s, management threatened to replace proprietorship. Shortly after taking up his post as a landlord's agent in Cavan, Ned Synge reported various gestures of social equality made by his employers, 'just as I was going into Church the Pratts drove up. They brought me into there [sic] seat ... After church I drove home with the Pratts & had lunch & a walk with them. I dined with them at 8 ocl ...' This was all very gratifying, even if three months earlier Ned Synge was active in the north of England evidently collecting rents due to him in his own right.[19] On the basis of this double career as agent and landowner, he was able to report at the beginning of 1882 that he was 'not at all pinched for cash': 'I am comparatively affluent ... although I am a distressed agent.' Yet two-and-a-half years later, when he finally took his degree examinations, he had to borrow Harry Stephens's dress suit.[20] As the decade brought increasing conflict between landlords and tenants, the role of the small landowner as someone else's agent became even more embarrassing. The family expended time and ink exploring and deploring its condition, to the near exclusion of more intimate responsibilities. While Johnnie was very young, nobody thought much about him, apart from loving him, worrying about his health, and – it gradually emerged – praying with some desperation to save his soul.

When Johnnie was seventeen, his mother wrote to her eldest son, Robert, in Argentina, 'I see no spiritual life in my poor Johnnie.' She also recalled the physical anxiety of his coming: 'I was so dreadfully delicate and he, poor child, was the same.'[21] The difficulties certainly had not ended in April 1872 with John Hatch Synge's death. On the contrary, Sam's *Letters to My Daughter* specifies with more than his usual precision that the family left Newtown Villas 'in the spring of '72' – that is, immediately after the funeral. The children had already been moved out when their father's illness (smallpox) was diagnosed as potentially terminal – most likely to their grandmother in nearby Orwell Park. It was not unusual for families of the Synges' standing to take accommodation on short or medium-term leases, even when they owned property elsewhere: in the present case, this arrangement facilitated a rapid regrouping of an extended Synge–Traill family.

While it is clear that old Mrs Traill encouraged such multiple occupation – for example, Florence Ross spent a prolonged period with the Synges after her mother's death, and Annie Synge went with her husband Harry Stephens to share No. 3 after their marriage – there is also evidence of penny-pinching, at least on the Synge side of the communicating door. On the issue of genteel hardship, victims are prone to maintain a genteel silence. *Letters to My Daughter* reports numerous acts of kindness and generosity which the younger children enjoyed. Early in September 1881, a surviving Synge relative took Annie, Sam and young Johnnie (he was ten) to the Zoological Gardens in the Phoenix Park on the north-western margin of the city. 'Our old Aunt Jane was very good about taking us to places of this kind.'[22] In the same year, Henry Joly (or 'Guy' as John Joly's brother was known) had given Sam Synge five bantam hens, a gift he duly recorded in his diary, together with a book given by his school-friend, Richard Sealy. Writing to his daughter from Bray in County Wicklow near the close of the Irish War of Independence forty years later, Sam cited the childhood diary in eternally grateful acknowledgement.[23]

This was a long-standing relationship the Synge boys found difficult to articulate. 'I do not reenclose the money, but I do not want to keep it. I consider that the value of presents is not for the worth – I would far rather get some small present from you, such a one as I would give you, than a sum of money that I do not want and do not like to take ... I have nearly all the money that you forced me to take at Christmas last ...'[24] At no point did the little mortifications and charities of the Orwell Park household reach the scale of embarrassment which intermittently afflicted the home-life of W. B. Yeats and James Joyce as children. Lacking the mental insulation, which John B. Yeats found in unworldly artistic ambition and John Joyce found in alcohol, J. M. Synge's mentors made up in sensitivity to hardship what they lacked in experience of it.

A conflated passage in the 'Autobiography' at once records and distorts his encounter with urban poverty:

I studied the arabs of the streets ... I remember coming out of St Patrick's Sunday after Sunday, strained almost to torture by the music, and walking out through the slums of Harold's Cross as the lamps were being lit. Hordes of wild children used to play round the cathedral of St Patrick and I remember there was something appalling – a proximity of emotions as conflicting as the perversions of the Black Mass – in coming out suddenly from the white harmonies of the Passion according to St Matthew among this blasphemy of childhood. The boys and girls were always in groups by themselves, for the utterly wild boy seems to regard a woman with the instinct of barbarians. I often stood for hours in a shadow to watch their manoeuvres and extraordinarily passionate quarrels ...[25]

There is much of aesthetic and even anthropological interest here – the relationship between music and intense experience, the concept of the barbarian. But the social geography of the scene has become confused. Slums did not greatly characterise Harold's Cross, a lower-middle-class district lying between the Grand Canal and the north-west frontier of Rathgar. They did greatly characterise the immediate environs of the cathedral and the route (Clanbrassil Street) by which young Synge would have walked home from St Patrick's. Among the squalid streets of the cathedral district, Dublin's bird-fanciers carried on their street-trading. In May 1881, Sam Synge sold a pigeon for eight pence at Patrick's Close; we know this because he chose to tell his daughter, and the incident was not an isolated one nor of a kind which excluded his brother.[26] J. M. Synge's self-portrayal, as a music student transfixed for hours on his way home from Sunday service, is less convincing than a recoverable image of a younger Synge standing around with his pigeons for sale amid the pell-mell of the cathedral precincts.

While the younger children looked to Aunt Jane for treats, their elder brothers were already adults. Having qualified as an engineer, Robert worked for some time for the Hull, Barnsley and West Riding Junction Railway, based in an office in Hull and engaged in tunnelling operations. All that could be said in favour of this occupation was that it avoided the middle-class routine of office hours in London. The embarrassment of his social position was neatly caught in his student project-work – a survey of the lost Synge estate at Glanmore.[27] During the summer of 1883, it was decided that he should emigrate to Argentina where some of his relatives had already blazed a trail. From 1877 onwards it became technically possible to export refrigerated beef back to Europe. The political and military triumphs of General Roca in 1880–81 tempted many to settle there. The Traills had been involved in ranching since 1868, and the proposition for Robert was that he should somehow come into the business, an arrangement which he was to find irksome. Among the Wicklow gentry, enterprise emigration was not unknown – the Tighes of Ashford were also on the move.[28]

With Robert's imminent departure, for some years at least, the family finances needed adjustment. By two separate agreements, mother and son gave each other £2,000. Robert's assignment to Kathleen was absolute, and was based on the will of Francis Synge of Glanmore (died 1878) and its provision for the heirs of his late brother, John Hatch Synge. Her counterbalancing action provided a charge of £2,000 on the Galway properties in Robert's favour. These transactions are of interest for several reasons, not least in their featuring Henry Francis Stephens for the first time acting as solicitor for Mrs Synge. But there were further stages to the business: in December 1883, she raised a loan of £150 from the Commissioners of Public Works for improvement of the lands in Galway, and in the first half of the next month, she entered into a complicated arrangement with Conway Edward Dobbs, a relative who lived in Fitzwilliam Square, perhaps the best address in town. Under this, Dobbs paid Robert Synge £1,977 10s 0d in return for the charge on the Galway properties. Finally, it was stipulated that the matter cited was to have priority over two earlier dealings, involving substantial sums. The best interpretation of these incomplete data would present the departure of Robert for Argentina as the occasion for utilising the Galway lands to raise money, but suggest that the hard cash element had to be provided by an obliging and financially secure relative (Dobbs) who had – probably – already assisted somehow to the tune of £850 and £1,500 in the years immediately following John Hatch Synge's death.[29] At the time of the latest Dobbs subvention, Johnnie was silently approaching his thirteenth birthday.

Dating from this time or a little later, a family photograph was taken, probably by John Joly, later a pioneer of colour photography. The background is a studio mirage of elaborate vegetation in a high wrought-iron conservatory. Robert and Ned stand to the rear, one moustached, the other with sideboards, men in the world but not of it. Annie looks away from the camera, bashful or disapproving; her hand rests on the shoulder of her brother, Sam. Seated in the foreground, Kathleen Synge dominates the picture, her mouth firmer than any of the young men's, dressed in the attire of a Victorian widow but blooming still. In tweed knickerbockers, Johnnie rests his elbow on her chair, his head on his hand. There is just the suggestion of a controlled teenage yawn.

Robert's South America experiences were not happy. He disagreed with his Traill uncles about the price of cattle, and entered into fractious correspondence on the topic. In March 1888, his mother had to advance £40 to pay the interest which he owed his maternal grandmother.[30] She tried to mediate between her son and her brothers on the cattle question. Robert complained about the 'religio sentimental fashion' in which she viewed his business affairs; she in turn worried about his spiritual life.[31] Meanwhile Annie, who had just turned twenty-one, had two suitors. One was Harry Stephens. The loser was her brother Ned's friend, John Joly, wealthy and academically brilliant, who would shortly, at the age of thirty-one, be appointed to a Trinity professorship. Stephens, Joly, Ned and Robert Synge had all been friendly as youths; their families knew each other not only in Rathmines School but from holidays in Wicklow also.[32]

As with her parents, Annie's was a love-match in which financial calculation evidently played no part. Harry was said to be 'such a wild young fellow, such high spirits, so good', a tripartite judgement which steadily rescues him from any serious imputation of impropriety.[33] Yet Harry's background deserves attention, given the role he will play in J. M. Synge's life and death. His solicitor father, Henry Colclough Stephens, was related by marriage to the family of Lafcadio Hearn (1850–1904), an exotic writer in whom JMS took a certain pride of very distant connection. The Stephenses and some of the Hearns had shared No. 48 Lower Gardiner Street with a doctor; the Hearns had artistic leanings, and generally an air of potential bohemianism had hung over their arrangements.[34]

Under the marriage settlement, Kathleen Synge provided a £2,000 charge upon the Galway holdings she had inherited at her husband's death, and Annie herself assigned £500 to the trustees of the settlement, this coming from benefits left her in the will of a deceased relative.[35] The 'towns, hamlets and lands of Knockroe, Brackloon and Gurtagurnane' once again served to provide security – as much social as financial – as the basis for insurance of Harry Stephens's life.[36] After the wedding in January 1884, timed to allow Robert to be present, the newly married couple moved in with Grandmother Traill in No. 3, and so added a further dimension to the complex double household in Orwell Park. There continues to be little reference to Johnnie.

One of the trustees of Annie's marriage settlement had been her brother Ned, giving his address as the Cabra Estate Office, Kingscourt, County Cavan.[37] At twenty-five, he was already embarked upon a career which embroiled him in the turbulence of what amounted to a small-scale rural war. In the course of this, his youngest brother would dissent from the family's solidarity with landlordism. Just one year later, Ned was set to marry, in keeping with a pattern of relatively early marriages among male Synges: indeed, he was seven years younger than his father had been on his marriage to Kathleen Traill. This pattern sets in stark relief John Synge's youthful determination never to marry, and the pathos of his finally dying before he could wed his beloved Molly Allgood. It signals a vitality which he presumed not to find in his own blood. He was to be exceptional. Even Sam, when posted to the Chinese mission fields, could confide: 'There were strong reasons for my marrying at any early date, some of which I have told the mother.'[38] Sam's English wife, Mary Harmar (they married in 1897 and she died 1939), had been a medical student in Dublin; the couple met in the Eye and Ear Infirmary, Molesworth Street, whose superintendent was later to play a crucial role in caring for John Synge. Miss Harmar's father had made his money in Sheffield steel. By staying single, John Synge stood outside a burgeoning circle.

The marriage of Ned and Ellen Frances Price (1861–1933) in Greystones Church of Ireland on 11 September 1885 demonstrated the practical effects of the evangelicals congregating for long summer retreats in the little County Wicklow village. Suitable partnerships were established among the young people, leading to the perpetuation of holy living. The narrow religious base of this did not exclude a degree of interdenominational mixing – as between strict Protestants, of course. Catholicism was unthinkable in social terms, unspeakable in terms of intermarriage. Kathleen Synge's family found itself more attached to its present theological position than to its inherited social position.

Something of the paradox of this emerges from the Synge–Price marriage settlement. While Mrs Synge put up £1,500, charged yet again on the Galway properties, Ned's contribution was based on Nos. 50–56 Camden Street, Dublin, the lands of which had come through a fee-farm grant of

1838 from the Archbishop of Dublin to 'John Synge deceased'.[39] In Ned's case, the inheritance upon which he founded the marriage settlement came from ecclesiastical sources in a manner which recalled those grave and learned Synge bishops the nineteenth century was markedly failing to produce, in consequence of the Church's financial difficulties.

The years between late 1883 and 1885 saw three of Johnnie's siblings embarked on life's highway. The episodes with Florence Ross, the telescope and 'trouble later' had occurred a year or so before, and his promotion to long trousers followed promptly. It was an introduction to adolescence characterised by a peculiar rhythm of development-and-no-change. Sam was a student but lived at home. Annie had married, but she was living next door. Ned had married, but Nellie his wife had belonged to the pre-existing small band who worshipped together in Greystones. Robert had departed for Argentina but remained in the pocket of Uncle Robert Traill. While it is true Johnnie was too young to know much if anything about marriage settlements and indentures of release, it does not follow that he was untouched by altering financial arrangements within the family. In fact, as one of the heirs of John Hatch Synge, he too was possessed of some real property even while he lacked the legal independence to do anything with it.

This problem persisted. When J. M. Synge came of age on 16 April 1892 he was nearing the end of his undergraduate studies at Trinity College, Dublin. His early passion for natural history gave way gradually to the study of ancient monuments and other human remains which he found in his field excursions in the south Dublin countryside. In both regards, he was obliged by circumstance to pursue his enthusiasms either alone or in the company of adults. Education at home deprived him of 'peer-group' company. The mixture of subjects he studied in Trinity was not to grip him with anything like the same enthusiasm; instead, music became the principal means through which his maturity was shaped. The details of these engagements will be examined in due course but, in order to understand how the family fortunes and misfortunes bore upon him, we have to note in advance how his first foreign travel – to Germany in 1893, in pursuit of a musical career – was facilitated by his mother's willingness to finance a project of which she personally disapproved.

The need for her continued support implies either that Johnnie could not raise money on his inherited property, even to the small extent required for immediate purposes, or that he accepted the logic of his class which insisted securities were not to be frittered away for short-term advantage. There is no evidence to suggest that his differences with the family on matters of religion, science, and music extended to economics or the ethics of personal independence. On the other hand, what evidence is accessible strongly suggests that his room for manoeuvre, as the beneficiary of inherited leases or properties, was strictly limited: for the time being at least, everything was 'tied up'. Ned, the second eldest of the male Synges, possessed properties in both Ireland and England, but evidently was not disposed to 'float' a younger brother with little or no commitment to earning a regular salary. He may have offered Johnnie a job in his office, but that was hardly calculated to promote independence.

There were other forms of income, however slight, which could be occasionally tapped. In the middle of 1896, an exchange of £800 was agreed between J. M. Synge and Kathleen Louisa Fitzgerald, a widow with an address in Leamington, Warwickshire, in consequence of which she demised to him Nos. 53 and 54 Upper Mount Street, Dublin.[40] The first half of 1896 had been spent in France and Italy, the latter half in Ireland. Though the division of his year conformed to something like a pattern for this period of his life, the date of mortgage indicates that the Mount Street business was one of the first things he turned to on his return to Dublin in the summer of 1896. The same properties feature in a reconveyance of April 1908 by which Synge transferred all his interest in the Mount Street houses to Marcus Lingard, for whom no address or further particular is provided.[41]

When she was editing his letters, Professor Saddlemyer came upon the draft of a letter from Synge to Fred Sutton & Co., the Dublin firm of solicitors in which Harry Stephens was a partner. Written on the back of an early version of his essay, 'A Landlord's Garden in County Wicklow', this sought to confirm the division of a sum of £1,530 – 'giving Miss Fitzgerald as you say about £50 – provided of course that the arrangements you are making do not interfere with the pro payment of the interest due to me'.[42] In whatever circumstances or subject to whatever conditions, two houses in Mount Street belonged to J. M. Synge through the years of his Abbey Theatre fame.

Upper Mount Street lies at the eastern extreme of a zone within the city's limits where John Hatch and his heirs had property – Camden Street, Ely Place, Hatch Street, Leeson Street Bridge. Apart from the concentration in Hatch Street itself, which originated with the Wide Streets Commissions, this 'portfolio' does not contain an orderly block of property. Transmission down through several generations had led to the break-up of what had been a very substantial inheritance.[43] If these street names appear remote from the dramatic world for which Synge is remembered, they occur tellingly in other classics of Modernist Irish literature. All of Joyce's fiction is based on a street map of Dublin where the vestiges of Synge property can now be identified. The undergraduates of *A Portrait of the Artist* conduct their highfalutin debates round the corner from Hatch Street; Harcourt Street and Mount Street feature in Stephen Dedalus's confessions. Had Joyce known of Synge's residual properties he might have been less inclined to accept the playwright's self-characterisation as tramp or tramper. But the Joyces were too well-known as having come down in the world to point the finger at others.

No local and dynastic rationale explains two transactions of the 1890s in which J. M. Synge was involved, for the property in question lay in the midlands. The first was a mortgage made between Charles Ignatius O'Beirne on the one part and Synge on the other, dated 18 August 1892. Synge had turned twenty-one the previous April and was now legally entitled to conduct his own affairs. But less than six years later, under an indenture of release and surrender, he conveyed to his brother-in-law Harry Stephens (whose company also handled JMS's business affairs) a complex property lavishly described in the public memorial:

the lands hereditments and premises comprised in ... the Malt House and Park adjoining thereto with the gardens and two small houses in Nunnery Lane and the houses and plots of ground whereon Patrick and Bartholomew Finlay formerly dwelt with the privilege of the passages to said gardens in the manner as heretofore possessed by William Roache of Athlone Merchant and also the house formerly in the possession of Darby Naughton and John Greenham all which said premises are situate lying and being in the Connaught side of the town of Athlone and County of Roscommon being the premises formerly known as Thomas Dillons plot ... now in the occupation of Patrick Kelly Henry Perry and Patrick Lennon and which are familiarly known as Shannon View and Nunnery Lane...[44]

Grubby details of Athlone tenements can be cited to prove what implacable critics of the Literary Revivalists know on first principles – that the Gregorys, Synges and Yeatses were alien extortionists. On the other – less heavy – hand, the same details suggest the very mixed fortunes of *soi-disant* Anglo-Irish families. Undoubtedly the Synges had come to Ireland as part of a comprehensive English colonising movement, in which the Church played its part. But the descendants of these ecclesiastical conquistadors included many who were, if not 'passing rich on forty pounds a year', certainly no better off than Doyle, the Kingstown provisioner, in Joyce's short story, 'After the Race'.[45] As for the other side of Synge's family, the Traills had never been part of the English enterprise. Norwegian in origin, they had spread through Orkney into Scotland and thence to Ulster, building a house in 1789.[46] Just as one of the Synges voted against the Union in 1800, so one of the Traills had joined the Volunteer movement of an earlier decade. When financial detail bothered the late Victorians, these variegated ancestries were prone to interpretation as a burden, even a guilty one.

John Synge's immediate family could only have been described as 'the genteel poor' if that phrase is loosely interpreted. Uneasily incorporated into the professional classes, they were – to be more exact – impoverished gentry, for whom decay in the material domain was balanced by changes in the spiritual. Shifts in Irish religious affairs placed young Synge at a vantage point from which he could contemplate the ironies of political realignment and contagion as they emerged in the middle of the century and after. It was rarely if ever a comfortable vantage point.

CHAPTER 5

Grey Stones and Plymouth Brethren

Rock of Ages, cleft for me . . .[1]

On 13 April 1996 – which would have been Samuel Beckett's ninetieth birthday – I decided to renew my acquaintance with some of the places J. M. Synge had known as a child, places in County Wicklow. Driving through the little hilly village of Delgany – where Edith Synge, recipient of *Letters to My Daughter* had lived until her death – I was surprised to see large banners across the sedate tree-lined approach road: SAVE DELGANY. Living in London, I was out of touch with local environmental passions. Delgany was in danger of being bulldozed into a dual-carriageway. Parking on Church Street in Greystones – where Synge's parents had initially met in the early 1850s – I wound down my Volkswagen window the better to hear a gospel preacher in full flight. God was still love. What's more He would be healing people that night at eight o'clock outside the Hungry Monk restaurant. The face-painted testifying preacher was still in his teens. His accent bespoke an Ulster origin. The guitars strummed, the public-address system oscillated. He sang of freedom – a term little used by the evangelicals of Synge's day. A passer-by said it was all a bit embarrassing. The last two Mohicans in County Wicklow clanked past me, their noserings glinting in late-winter light. At that moment Greystones was being beaten by Dungannon, a mighty force in Ulster rugby. At least something was rationally explained.

Despite the sprawling force of Dublin's vulgarity, Greystones remains the anomaly it was created to be. Virtually invented by the railway system, it became the watering-hole and bolt-hole of generations bred up in southern Irish Protestantism. Developed by two enterprising families of humble standing – the Doyles and the Evans – the place had little or no history for those who took their summer holidays there in the final decades of Victoria's reign: to them, it was like a comfortable pioneer settlement on the edge of wilderness. Houses cropped up, a street emerged, public amenities were provided in a pattern not very different from that pushing westward in contemporary America. As recently as the mid-1960s, it stood on a road not taken.

John Ferrar, in the 1790s, put the matter in perspective when he wrote: 'on coming out of Delgany church ... we could see the herring boats at sea.' The insurrection of 1798 briefly discouraged interest in Wicklow, though industrious travellers in the new century were soon assessing its potential for development.[2] It is only in the 1820s that we begin to get a measure of the place – still 'a little wild headland' – as a human habitation with seven families engaged in fishing. A decade later, it was 'the small fishing hamlet called the Greystones', though a school had sprung up in the interval.[3] What changed the place was the extension in 1855–6 of the railway southward from Bray, in a tunnelling operation overseen by Kingdom Brunel himself. Bray became the resort of Dublin's Catholics, a place of quasi-permanent residence for the Joyce family in the late 1880s: older than James Joyce, the teenage Synge mooched through predominantly Protestant groups of holiday-makers in Greystones unaware of the infant heresiarch asleep in No. 1 Martello Terrace, Bray.

The fact that Jack Synge and Kathleen Traill had met in Greystones is testimony to the area's appeal to evangelical Protestants in the pre-railway era. The Synges' stronghold at Glanmore lay only a few miles inland, and the La Touche family – who controlled Delgany – were astute patrons of evangelical religion. The 1851 census records twenty households (ninety-three persons) in Greystones; ten years later these had risen to fifty-five households of more than two hundred and thirty persons. A church was erected in 1857 for local members of the Church of Ireland – largely at the expense of the La Touches – but it was not formally consecrated until 1864. A Catholic chapel opened close by in Black Lion in 1867, though allegedly there were only four inhabitants of that persuasion.[4]

In the year of Synge's birth, Greystones had a population of 355, a figure swollen in the summer by visitors (like the Synges) from Dublin. In addition to the mechanical convenience of the railway, revivalism in the 1850s boosted Greystones. Quite apart from the emergence of new meeting-houses and sects (notably the Brethren in both Open and Exclusive forms[5]), the major Protestant denominations experienced a sudden and (to many) alarming efflorescence of conversion, hysterical prostration, testifying, and clamorous fears of damnation. Though Wicklow was remote from the epicentre of the Revival in Ulster, the tiny Presbyterian community in Kilpeddar had links with Scotland and thus with the Scots–Ulster religious community. Although no Presbyterian church building existed in Greystones before July 1887, 'meetings' had been held in the intriguingly named Coffee Palace (later Ardrigh House) throughout the 1860s and 1870s.[6] This presence, together with delay in consecrating the Church of Ireland's premises, contributed to a pan-Protestant society. Edward Stephen Daunt, the long-reigning (1882–1928) rector of Greystones, was recognised as 'a man of great brotherliness and evangelical spirit' who had lent the Church of Ireland's school to the Presbyterians during the construction of their own church. Meanwhile, the Catholic community was growing: St Killian's at Black Lion was enlarged in 1886. The present building was erected in 1907.

Wicklow had its strong Protestant tradition, and Greystones during Synge's childhood there boasted of an Orange Hall and a Masonic Hall.[7] The Easter Monday vestry meeting of 1886 – in effect an annual general meeting of the Church of Ireland congregation – voted unanimously against Home Rule, as if to underline a No Surrender outlook on political developments.[8] Despite the reputation of evangelicals for dour living, social activity flourished. At Tinnapark Hall, once the home of the Clark family who had been the Scottish backbone of Kilpeddar Presbyterianism, concerts famed throughout the area were held, at which the police from Newtownmountkennedy used to sing. While staying at Greystones, Johnnie and his Aunt Jane attended an evening concert on Friday 12 August 1887, an event distinguished by 'great singing and clapping', the combination being a feature of the way hymns were treated at revivalist gatherings.[9] Nothing quite so neatly encapsulates the intimacy of Protestant evangelicalism and loyalty to the United Kingdom than the participation of Royal Irish Constabulary (RIC) songsters in such gatherings. On the other hand, similar occasions were enlivened by regular recitations of an essay on 'Love' by Art Byrne. Gaelic surnames and RIC choirs signal different orientations among the Greystones faithful. These events took place while the young James Owen Hannay (1865–1950) – later known as the novelist George A. Birmingham – was curate at Delgany. That dates them to a period including the years 1888–92, the closing phase or aftermath of the Land War when a government inquiry into charges made against Charles Stewart Parnell exposed the forged documents on which his alleged complicity in murder had been based. In Wicklow, he was a local hero or devil incarnate, depending on your point of view. Aunt Jane, who had often dandled 'The Chief' on her knees at Glanmore, piously wished she had choked him in infancy. Johnnie was to be in some ways Parnell's literary twin.

Hannay's recollections of his years in Delgany and Greystones under-line the extent to which the Synges were cut off from a new wave of thought and feeling in the Protestant community. It is perhaps irrelevant to note that the curate was in the habit of boxing with his rector, smoking a pipe, and plotting a novel about a socialist-clergyman. Hannay also met T. W. Rolleston (1857–1920), a resident of the area, poet, critic and translator of Gaelic poetry; Rolleston presented the young curate with a copy of W. B. Yeats's *The Wanderings of Oisin* (1889), introduced him to the writings of Standish James O'Grady (1846–1928) and encouraged his latent enthusiasm for contemporary literature. Hannay married Ada Wynne, daughter of the clergyman towards whom Sam Synge was so deferential; his rector was John Joseph Robinson, who had moved from the shadow of Glanmore to take up the Delgany post. The Synges, by contrast, had little or no contact with the cultural life of their time; the notion of a boxing curate would have struck Mrs Synge as quite improper.[10] If she ever knew that the Reverend Hannay also played cricket with the local Catholic curate (Father Walter Hurley) in matches which saw occasional performances from two future Irish revolutionaries – Erskine Childers and his cousin, Robert Barton – she might have done more to prevent Johnnie from later visiting the Bartons at Glendalough House.[11] Twenty years after the world-renowned dramatist died, his bro-ther's discreet attempts at biography were passed round in Glendalough House, in a circle which included David Robinson, friend of Constance Markievicz and legendary hero of Anglo-Irish gentry Republicanism.

Between the autumn of 1888 and that of 1892, J. M. Synge was an under-graduate in Trinity, though still a fixture (as the Dublin custom was) in his mother's home. His second eldest brother, Ned, was active as a land agent evicting tenants on the far side of Ireland in County Mayo.[12] Robert was in Argentina enjoying (despite himself) the boom decade which was to end with the Barings Bank Crisis of 1890. Sam was acquiring the medical degree he needed for missionary work in China, though he found time to get up a few songs suitable for picnics – 'Don't Judge a Man by His Coat', for example. One trip to Lough Dan on 3 August 1892 saw the Synges take tea with some of the Childers family.[13] But a change in the household management was imminent, with holidays at Greystones soon to be replaced by a more isolated stay at Castle Kevin, a largeish house further south and set among the inland hills of the county. Edward Stephens regarded the seaside resort as particularly associated with the experiences of Synge's childhood and youth, and the summers in Castle

Kevin as part of his adult life. But this is perhaps to draw too absolute a line of division between the two phases of Synge's maturing. Greystones continued to feature in his recreational life.

From the mid-1870s, when he was still virtually an infant, the family regularly spent several months there. Sam's *Letters to My Daughter* emphasise the primitive condition of the place in their early years, a topic on which he can be relied. 'There were very few houses in Greystones ... along Church lane there were no houses. Along Church Road very few houses and, of course, no road on either side of the railway between the station and the bridge ... no police station, and no other place of worship but the church, which was much smaller than it is now.'[14] To a degree, this suggests social as well as denominational exclusivity.

John Joly, school friend of the older Synge boys, plied their mother with suitable reading at Greystones, even if she could only take it up 'when Johnnie went to bed and all the others were out'.[15] Johnnie needed careful looking after. When he and his mother arrived by train in June 1879, a heavy shower detained them at the station: his brother Bob and Eddie Price took turns in carrying him rolled up in a shawl to Trafalgar House where the family were staying.[16]

Susceptibilities were easily offended. That summer, jolly John Joly gave offence by describing a Protestant charity as 'the Home for Old Maids'. This prompted Mrs Synge to insist that it was 'just as much for "old matrons", if they are in need'. Susceptibilities recovered: her letter turns casually from rebuke to the acknowledgement of a good-sized trout, safely arrived from County Mayo: when Ned Synge stepped out of Enniscoe House – the grim Georgian mansion of his Pratt employers – he enjoyed briefly a grand view of Lough Conn with its abundant trout.[17] It was a perspective, however compromised by the status of a land agent, his youngest brother never experienced.

Visitors from Dublin rented houses some of which were speculatively built for the holiday market by Greystones entrepreneurs – Trafalgar was not one of these. On 28 June 1881, the family took over a new house called Menlo, owned by a Mr Flynn who lived with his wife in a cottage nearby. During the next two months, Johnnie had a first dip in the sea, his frail health having postponed this childhood initiation. He and Sam walked to Little Sugar Loaf mountain, and the family were entertained to afternoon tea by John Joly in the Glen of the Downs, a beauty spot on the western edge of the La Touche demesne. By 30 August everyone was back in Orwell Park, and the school year began.[18]

Johnnie's pre-university education remains something of a mystery, given that he was withheld from Rathmines. He certainly attended Mr Harrick's Classical and English School in Upper Leeson Street, Dublin, for upwards of a year, *circa* 1881. This was a prep school, despite its grandiose name. After Mr Harrick's, his attendance at the Bray School was intermittent at best, and it is usually said that he was educated at home by a private tutor. Mrs Synge recorded that, in the autumn of 1887, a Mr Cooper commenced in this capacity.[19] It is likely that this was one of two Coopers on the staff of the Rathmines School in the mid-1880s.

The following year, Mrs Synge took her youngest children to the Isle of Man. Julia Macleod, Kathleen's eldest sister-in-law, had lived at Glanmore Castle during the years of its insolvency. After her marriage to a seafarer of limited social standing, the couple had settled at Douglas, a holiday resort to which Greystones could not compare. The 1882 summer holiday, which began with a very rough boat-crossing, was to be cut short by news from Dublin. While it lasted, it gave the Synges insight into the behaviour of a lower class which was – officially at least – loyally Protestant. Ned, hard at work in Cavan, tended to discount the attractions of a Manx holiday – 'seems to be very crowded with tourists & summer people. Rather too full to be comfortable I should think like after dinner at Glendalough.'[20] As that last remark testifies, even the recesses of mountainous County Wicklow were falling before the suburban herd. According to Edward Stephens, Johnnie (who was eleven) 'found that in his aunt's house [on the Isle of Man], he felt at home'.[21] That is to say, the indifference of the trippers to the truths of the Gospel confirmed in the family a confident assumption of their own spiritually privileged, minority status. Given the nephew-biographer's personal ecumenism and political liberalism, it is striking that he should insist: 'John's creed suffered profound changes as years passed, but this assumption remained unshaken.' Early in August a telegram recalled Kathleen and her children to Dublin, as her sister was gravely ill; on 23 August Anne Traill (long deaf as a result of scarletina) died in No. 3 Orwell Park. Johnnie's woodland idyll with Florence Ross followed directly.

The absence of 'the Mrs.' and Johnnie had given Ned an opportunity to advance his courtship of Nellie Price. Plotting with Joly, he arranged to use a cottage in Greystones without previously revealing his intention of being there – the cottage was to be rented in Joly's name. 'The old Prices' – that is, Nellie's parents – 'dont appreciate my company'. But there were complications in such an arrangement, notably in the tendency to drink in the family from whom the two young men proposed to rent.

'I expect one of us will have to keep watch with a revolver against a nightly attack from the Doyles. He is highly vicious when drunk.' These high spirits were damped down by Aunt Traill's death and the sudden return of the holiday-makers from the Isle of Man. But while the idyll was yet a possibility, Ned revealed an unsuspected capacity for mischief in which Aunt Jane Dobbs might connive because the location of the cottage would allow her to 'drop in & have a weed on her way to the coffee [house]'.[22] Quite how liberated this cigarette-smoking aunt was is difficult to determine. But when, the following month, Ned spent an evening with his employers in Cabra Castle, he reported to Joly that 'Aunt Jane would have had great fun ... Every one was drunk more or less.'[23]

As far as Johnnie was concerned, there was no repetition of the Isle of Man experiment. Mrs Synge may have heard of her second son's manoeuvres during her absence. Mrs Price, for her part, was not above intercepting correspondence between her daughter and the Synge boy when it was conducted surreptitiously through the agency of his aunt, Harriet Dobbs.[24] After 1882, Greystones was preferred either for its greater decorum or its cheapness or both. The holiday of 1883 was based on Dromont, closer to Delgany than Greystones, but the amenities of the seaside were readily at hand. Due to her mother's illness, Florence Ross had been more or less absorbed into the family, and some Traill children returned from Argentina helped to swell but hardly to diversify the company. Holidays were, at this period, generally regarded as a way of reuniting families rather than of exploring new horizons. Among the adults were Edmund and Robert Traill, and Robert Synge who was on the point of embarking for South America. This was the summer of 'the accursed cousin' who came between Johnnie and Florence. When in October Ned Synge expressed the hope that 'Greystones is quiet again now the intruders have all departed' he was in all likelihood pointedly referring to cousins rather than summer trippers from Dublin.[25] But John Synge's retrospective account of the crisis suggests 'an old fashioned garden' as the scene of disenchantment rather than the brand-new facilities of Greystones. Houses in Delgany (like Dromont) were older; further inland lay Glanmore Castle and Roundwood Park, long – but no longer – strongholds of the Synge family. A trip to Aunt Editha was always a feasible proposition, and from there a covert visit to Roundwood (lost at the end of 1850) might be possible for adventurous children. One way or another, the accursed cousin inflicted his wound on John Synge's pride in a property to which the family could make no proprietorial claim. Adolescent disenchantment re-enacted ancestral loss.

Although such matters were virtually unmentionable, the sexual urge was strong among the Synges and among those whom they married. In this light, Johnnie's decision never to marry, allegedly made when he was about fourteen, is remarkable. But the family's willingness to take to wife and (usually) to beget led occasionally to ironic conclusions. Francis Synge, having recovered Glanmore in 1850, had married Editha Jane Truell, a wealthy young woman from Clonmannon House, between Delgany and Newrath in 1861. While the two lived and reigned in the Castle, Kathleen Synge and her children regarded 'Uncle Francis and Aunt Editha . . . as the most important people in their circle'. But in 1878, when things were going well on the estate and Johnnie's elder brothers were frequent guests, Uncle Francis died. His widow lost no time in remarrying in 1879, and Glanmore effectively became the preserve of Theodore Webber Gardiner (1838–1919), a retired British Army officer and member of the Exclusive Brethren.[26] Shifts of a similar kind had taken place a few miles to the south when, on coming of age, C. S. Parnell found Avondale to be effectively controlled by a zealous member of the Brethren, G. V. Wigram.[27] County Wicklow, of which J. M. Synge was virtually a native, has often been – to revert to its own dialect – 'sniving with Dippers'.

In symbolic details like the intrusion of Gardiner and Wigram, the traditional link between landed property and Irish episcopalianism was formally broken, just as the Synges had ceased to hold their patrimony. 'Noblesse oblige' allowed the picnic lunch of the Girls' Friendly Society (Delgany and Killiskey parishes) to take place on the lawns of Glanmore in July 1891, thirty-eight of these young women arriving under the Gothic shadows in 'two large drags, a wagonette and a car'.[28] The breach with the family's eighteenth-century self-image involved leachings of one religious position into or through another. Major Gardiner may have been an Exclusive Brother, whose possession of the Castle irked the descendants of its founder, but Brethrenism in its Open form seeps round the immediate domestic life of J. M. Synge. Even when he died in 1909, an alarm went out among his literary friends that 'Synge's executor is a Plymouth Brother and that he regards Synge's writing with grave disapproval.'[29]

Squeezed between the indifferent masses on the Isle of Man and the new Exclusivism in Glanmore, Mrs Synge's choice of holiday location for her younger children was limited. Greystones was becoming more like Douglas, though hurdy-gurdies and amusement arcades lay in the dark future. It served as a regular place of retreat from Synge's fourth summer to his twenty-first year and, even after his mother had begun to rent Castle Kevin for lengthy periods, it continued to feature on his itineraries.

In 1884, several years before her decision to alter the pattern of their summers, Mrs Synge took the children to Rathdown House in Greystones for more than three months; once again, the extended family of Traills, Stephenses and Rosses reassembled. The Dobbses had a house called Knockdolian at which Sam occasionally stayed, and Charlie Miller visited from time to time. Though Florence Ross's father was a minister of the gospel, the company reflected only in dim miniature the tradition of *vir gravis admodum et doctus* which had been exemplified in the Synges' line of eighteenth-century bishops. Willie Ross was a doctor, Cathcart Dobbs an engineer, Mary Harman's father a businessman in steel, Harry Stephens a solicitor, the Traill brothers ranchers briefly returned from foreign parts.

In 1885, Prospect House was the new base for the summer excursion: the sequence of four Greystones houses in the course of four holidays – Menlo, Dromont, Rathdown, and now Prospect – was further evidence of discontinuity, mere year-by-year security, professional engagement and relaxation rather than sustained vocation in the world. Sam, in a burst of recollection allegedly written during the Irish Civil War of 1922, added six or so further addresses, if anything less respectable – '3 Bethel Terrace (the terrace otherwise known as Mattie Doyle's cottages)'.[30] Here is no continuing city, or even summer, residence.

There was a great deal of moth-collecting and other naturalist activity on Johnnie's part, for Greystones was adjacent to the countryside without being dangerously rural. Its pastoral suggestiveness was not lost on local preachers. Here was a village founded – like the Christian Church itself – upon a rock. When on Sunday 26 June 1887, Mrs Synge attended an afternoon 'rock service' she was participating in an open-air liturgical exploitation of the founding pun (Petrus = a rock, as well as Saint Peter's name) of Christianity. The livelihood of local people still depended, as had that of many among Christ's original disciples, upon fishing. If too many in the surrounding district adhered to the errors of Rome, Greystones was a citadel from which truth would go forth and do battle.

One well-documented instance of this warfare occurred in the summer of 1887. Nellie and Ned were due to join the family, taking a holiday from the Pratt estate office near Kingscourt in Cavan. But Ned had an appointment to keep with Aunt Editha at Glanmore when decisions would be reached about evicting tenants from a cottage on the former Synge property. A decree of ejectment for non-payment of rent had been obtained against Hugh Carey, who lived on a small farm in the townland of Aghowle (pronounced, 'a howl') about two miles south of the Castle. Ned arrived in Greystones on Friday 15 July, and consulted his mother on the matter before calling on the Gardiners the following Wednesday. 'Mrs Synge's faith in Providence prevented her from feeling any anxiety about Edward's personal safety when he was discharging his duty ...' and in any case she held strong scriptural views on the sanctity of private property.[31]

Thus fortified, the holidaying agent for Cabra Castle set out to finalise arrangements for the eviction. But on 20 July, Major Gardiner of the Exclusive Brethren made it a condition of his approval for the action that his wife should sanction it. The Land War had subsided and, as a native of the county whose parental home at Clonmannon lay only a few miles away, she was reluctant to take the final step. Ned Synge persuaded her that he could devise a fail-safe plan. This included some details of significance for his younger brother, then only sixteen years old.

Part of Aunt Editha's reluctance to evict lay in her awareness that Carey lived with two sisters, one of whom was bedridden. Unimpressed by the message of *Dombey and Son*, Ned countered successfully with arguments about setting examples. On 22 July, the sub-sherriff for the county was to take possession of the cottage at so early a time of day that little resistance would be possible. To back up this legal procedure, Ned arranged to meet even earlier on that Friday morning two 'emergency men' at Tomriland crossroads. These were 'temporary tenants' who hired themselves out to evicting landlords to prevent illegal re-entry by the former occupants. Tomriland lay on the other side of Aghowle from Glanmore, and thus a pincer movement was designed: it was also a townland where Mrs Synge and J. M. Synge would subsequently holiday in 1902, his *annus mirabilis*.

Things went smoothly. Some time after eight in the morning, the Careys were evicted; only later when news spread did local opposition voice itself in a protest meeting. Mrs Synge recorded events on the coast a few miles away from the action: 'Very warm day. Ned went off early to evict Carey. I sat by the sea on a point of rock – full tide, nice breeze, lovely air. Then went to Bayswater and saw Mamma. After dinner went to South Shore. Annie and Florence painted and we sat with them. Nellie went to meet Ned. Johnnie played tennis.'[32]

The protest was reported the following day in the *Freeman's Journal*, a Dublin paper of nationalist sympathies. Carey was 'the mainstay of two aged sisters, one of whom is an imbecile'. The villains were sub-sheriff Davidson and 'Mr Synge the agent from County Cavan'. The meeting, addressed by several local men of consequence including Garrett Byrne, MP for West Wicklow, passed a vote of thanks to Mr Hutton, a Protestant neighbour of Carey's who provided emergency accommodation.[33] One way or another, the honour of the Synges of Wicklow was but slightly tarnished: Ned was linked to Cavan, fellow-Protestants gave succour, and Greystones was bathed in warm balmy air. Ned Synge ordered his men to prostrate the cottage, making it 'an uninhabitable ruin'.

Eviction violated bonds of a fundamental, almost sacred kind, between a family and its place of being. The large-scale evictions which occurred all over Ireland – except, largely, the north-east – quickly came to symbolise the heartlessness of landlords. J. M. Synge's appreciation of the profound emotional and psychic violence of eviction will find expression in *The Aran Islands*. At one level, however, the conventional image of a well-to-do owning class callously dispossessing a hard-pressed occupying class is misleading. Without discounting the violence of eviction as such, one has to note in the Synges and many small-scale landowning families the insecurity of their own residential base. Traills and Synges lived in rented accommodation – by choice, to be sure, and economically astute choice at that. Their holidays – luxury though it must have seemed to onlooking small farmers in the Wicklow hills – depended on the state of the market. In 1888, Kathleen Synge wanted to take Prospect House for July and August. But 'Uncle Cathcart ... says a great many of the houses are taken already.'[34] Her plans involved Aunt Jane Synge's willingness to pay her share and, in a remoter way, on Baylee (of Mount Baylee) paying some of his arrears.

In the event, she got Prospect House, but accommodation for Harry and Annie still had to be found. James Price, Ned's father-in-law, rented out cottages, and on occasion even reduced the considerable rent. In the end, the Stephenses took a place with 'a sitting room & two bedrooms for £7:0:0 a month'.[35] The relationship between landlord and tenant in Victorian Ireland was not simply that of the Haves and the Have-Nots. Involving more than economic competition, it provoked a kind of jealousy, a projection of desire and resentment in which the closeness of the tenant to his hearth mocked the leaseholder's concern with gold prices, bonds, and the seasonality of fashion. The tenant in reply invoked a feudal demonology to characterise what was often in practice a heavily mortgaged middle class.

Edward Stephens, recounting the Carey episode, waxes satirical at his uncle's and grandmother's expense. Writing long after the landlord system had ceased to be a cause of social unrest, and after nationalism had produced an Irish Free State within the British dominions, he could afford to invest his rhetoric in Hugh Carey's plight. Mrs Synge's god was 'the Great Landlord of the earth' whose scheme included 'the eviction of the first man and his wife from the Garden of Eden'. J. M. Synge, as a tennis-playing teenager at the time, was not unaware of the moral implications of his brother's profession and his mother's theology. Later, he wrote a poem about a 'mergency man in which his own sympathies are displayed. But the incident of 1887 occurred before conventional family members could escape the economic priorities of a land system in which they retained only a vestigial or vicarious role. Synge's politics, while it will employ the terms of nationalist and even socialist protest, never acquires the name of action.

Not that the Protestant community in Greystones saw itself as above mundane issues of the day. On the contrary, it claimed leadership in social and economic affairs. The state of the harbour constantly gave cause for concern, to the extent that W. L. Jackson, Secretary to the Treasury, met a delegation in November 1889 to discuss the development of facilities in the village. Among those who briefed him were Cathcart Dobbs, husband of Harriet Traill (Mrs Synge's sister), and James Price, Ned Synge's father-in-law.[36] But with Ned away in Cavan and Mayo, Robert stock-farming in Argentina, Sam and Johnnie tied up with their studies, there was no adult male of the Synge line to serve on such committees. The death of Jack Synge in 1872 cast its shadow towards the end of the century with an unrelieved intensity.

After Disestablishment in 1869, the influence of local church patrons was diminished. Rectors like the brotherly E. S. Daunt were now salaried, not unlike men in the other lesser professions. On Sunday 10 July 1887, Mrs Synge and her unmarried sister-in-law Jane attended morning service not in the church of her birth but with the Presbyterians.[37] While Greystones provided evangelical support for Kathleen Synge in the 1880s, it also presaged an end to the hereditary dignities she had married into thirty years earlier. There was another way. It lay not in the direction of Methodism (originally a reformist movement within the Church) nor of Presbyterianism with its predominantly Ulster following. It lay – to be crudely topographical – at the end of a short journey one might make from Greystones west to Roundwood and then north towards Enniskerry, a distance in all of perhaps twenty miles. There, under aristocratic patronage, a young Church of Ireland cleric – John Nelson Darby (1800–82) – had broken with the Establishment *circa* 1830 and contributed to the setting-up of what had become known as the Plymouth Brethren.

Though neither Kathleen Synge nor any of her children ever formally embraced the discipline of the Brethren, the sect was everywhere about them, forming a backdrop of salvationist drama in muslin. Editha Truell had inherited strong Brethren (and homoeopathic) views from her mother, declaring on occasion, 'I hate allopathy and the Church of England.'[38] Her second husband's advanced notions prevented them from praying (or indeed, eating) with anyone they were not convinced of as being already saved. What did Brethren believe, and how do such beliefs impinge on the life of J. M. Synge? *The Protestant Dictionary* isolates a number of points of relevance. For example, 'their peculiarities are largely determined by their system of "unfulfilled" prophecy, which leads them to regard some portions of the New Testament, especially the Sermon on the Mount, as intended for the guidance, not of Christians, but of the "remnant" of pious Jews destined to appear after the secret coming of the Saviour for the "saints".' This has been used to argue that Brethren dismiss good works, though the evidence which most closely concerns us will not wholly confirm the diagnosis – their record during the Great Famine was good. At the same time, however, the social condition of Irish Protestants reflected an isolationism which, in Brethren theology, found an exotic language. 'An overwhelming majority through all their sections have believed in the "Secret Rapture" … whereby believers would be withdrawn from a world destined to the judgment of "the Great Tribulation".'[39] The Dublin-based literary critic William Magee (who wrote under the pseudonym John Eglinton), deployed such terms in *Two Essays on the Remnant* (1895).

For the late-Victorian Synges, the most important centre of Brethren fervour was the family of Robert E. Matheson with one of whose daughters, Cherrie, John Synge fell rapturously in love. In the small and introverted world of genteel evangelicalism, a Matheson girl was evidently regarded as 'a good catch'. Only half in jest, Ned Synge had teased his friend Joly (a wealthy young man in his own right) on hearing the news that 'you have lost Miss Matheson of the £300 a year'.[40] In January 1888, when none of these righteous minds was in storm-swept Greystones, Annie Synge (Mrs Harry Stephens) was visited in Orwell Park by Mrs Matheson, with news about Ivon Price's engagement 'to one of the Miss Dillon's where he was a tutor'. Eagerly disapproving of such gossip Mrs Synge duly informed her son in Argentina.[41] The Mathesons were on visiting terms, despite their sect's reputation for self-containment. They lived on Crosthwaite Park West in Kingstown, a prosperous middle-class seaside suburb on Dublin Bay. In October 1890, Mrs Synge moved (with John) into No. 9, preparatory to her getting a lease on No. 31 Crosthwaite Park West – an end-of-terrace house just three doors away. The prolonged affair between Johnnie and Cherrie – unconsummated, of course – gives Greystones a significance in the most traumatic relationship of Synge's emotional life. Mrs Synge did not disapprove of the alliance her son desired; on the contrary, her sympathies lay with Cherrie who felt unable to marry a man who did not share her faith.

In addition to the usual discourses of evangelical Protestantism, Brethren doctrine was committed to a wholly lay religious community, or – to put the matter in a better order – it insisted on the sanctity of all who believed and were saved and, consequently, on their ability to undertake the tasks reserved for ordained clergy in formal churches. This rejection of ordination, likewise of territory or quasi-territorial bases for the sanctified community – the parish, the glebe, the circuit – combined with an intense concentration of spiritual energy on the present, on the immediate relationship of the soul with God. Land and history were alike discounted, so the Brethren came to resemble a private limited liability company subject only to its own, often truculent and fractious, decisions.

The Brethren have had a bad press, denounced as manipulators of adolescent emotionalism or (from within the larger community of believers generally) as spiritual tyrants. Edmund Gosse's autobiography, *Father and Son* (1907), came too late to assist Synge in his struggle with the same foe. Edward Stephens had little time for them, describing Editha Truell and her mother as people who 'while they retained the manners and prejudices of their family, had lost its culture', a phrase which echoes all too clearly his earlier, broader condemnation of 'the landlord class' which 'had retained all its self-esteem, some of its education, but very little of its moneyed influence'.[42] Kathleen Synge's household was invited to visit Glanmore Castle under Editha and the Major's suzerainty during the summer of 1889, but the invitation came second-hand, from relatives who in turn had rented the place from the Gardiners. Emily Frances Synge (1835–1905), a cousin returned from England, was most likely the welcoming tenant; certainly she was among the party who greeted Florence Ross, Johnnie and his mother when they arrived at the hall door on Tuesday 13 August. On the Friday, Florence and Mrs Synge travelled back to Greystones by the early train, leaving Johnnie to enjoy what had been his late uncle's demesne.[43] Stephens emphasises the importance of the Glanmore interlude for his uncle, his sensitivity to the collapsing estate and the imminent dispersal of its 'treasures', and argues (reasonably enough) that the essay 'A Landlord's Garden in County Wicklow' derives from the experience.[44] The concluding words of 'Vita Vecchia' (an abandoned work in prose and verse) echo this week-long return to the family seat, while suppressing the death of its Synge master.

Whether in Orwell Park or any of the numerous summer houses in

Greystones, Johnnie Synge was throughout the 1880s the locus of a vigorous if loving warfare. In the autumn after his outing to Glanmore, his
mother enlisted the aid of John Dowse, curate in Zion, the church where
she worshipped while living in Orwell Park. Johnnie had been attending
Dowse's bible classes throughout 1887. On 17 September 1889, the Reverend Dowse called to the Synge house and, after a preliminary discussion
with the mother in the drawing room, took John aside for a soulful
exchange in the parlour.[45] The eighteen-year-old held his sceptical ground,
but the incident was only the culmination of a sustained pressurising of
his attitude and behaviour. The issues were never reducible to matters of
belief but permeated every fibre and cell of thought, word, and deed.

Mary King has written tellingly on Mrs Synge's attitude towards language and its implications for her son's concept of literature, quoting
Stephens's account of the household:

His mother had made language one of the special subjects of her religious instruction. She taught that to refer to God in any but a strictly religious manner was a
sinful taking in vain of the Holy Name, that to use expletive oaths or curses was a
breach of St James's injunction 'Let your yea be yea; and your nay, nay', and that
to exaggerate was to lie. Mrs Synge sought divine aid in confining within the closest
limits the already restricted speech of the Victorian period, praying fervently, 'Set
a watch O Lord, upon our lips.' So strict was her rule that it almost paralysed
language as an expression of feeling.[46]

Disapproval of the theatre, of anything frivolous in the way of entertainment, naturally accompanied this linguistic doctrine. The act of
reading should be confined to the study of scripture which was literally
true in each and every detail. Secular schooling was hardly compatible
with such teaching, and as Mrs Synge's circumstances became more
pinched with the years so the education of her sons aimed for greater and
greater conformity with the Lord. Richard Chenevix Trench's *English
Past and Present* (1855), which John Synge brought to Greystones in the
summer of 1888, may have escaped his mother's eye. Her last son was
about to go up to Trinity in the autumn, her daughter was expecting a
second child; she herself was now fifty. From being virtually a child-
bride, Kathleen Traill had been transformed into the widowed ageing
mother of a sceptical teenager. As late as April 1898, Mrs Synge was still
holidaying in Greystones, recovering in fact from a bout of influenza:
John Synge, on his return from Paris, took the opportunity to renew a
proposal of marriage which was rejected. Within two weeks he had

departed by train for the west of Ireland on what was to be a journey of momentous literary significance.

There has been much celebration of this change of heart, change of direction, as if Synge had unilaterally and unambiguously quit the kingdom of God for the kingdom (or even, in very recent discourse, socialist republic) of Ireland. Yeats will be the first to be found guilty on this count, with critics Daniel Corkery and Declan Kiberd answering to lesser charges. It was in Rathdown House, Greystones, in the summer of 1884 that thirteen-year-old Johnnie heard his first cousin, Eugenia, describe the Aran Islands.[47] Yeats's too famous injunction of December 1896 – 'Go to the Aran Islands. Live there as if you were one of the people themselves; express a life that has never found expression'[48] – takes no more account of the Synge family's western experience as landowners and churchmen than it does of all the forms of expression which emanated from sources other than Yeats's circle. In addition, somewhere in Synge's home were preserved the letters which Alec had written to his brother Jack, describing his western hopes and disappointments, a correspondence which circles round the cryptic remark serving as epigraph to the present book – 'we trust all well by the silence'.

The promotion of Synge as socialist, while it is justified in the strict sense by a number of authenticated remarks, has more recently merged with the discourse known as post-colonial theory. In this latter light, the figures of Cathcart Dobbs, Charles Louis Matheson and James Price, interfiled with Florence Ross and Kathleen Traill, become vulnerable to retrospective abuse. If Anglo-Irish barons offer at least a whiff of romance to the myths of post-history, Protestant professionals like those just listed contribute nothing, neither to the growing confidence of a national middle class nor to the emergent Anglo-Irish Revival – or so the modish theory goes. It is true that the Greystones 'rock service' gave rise to no musical innovation such as Aaron Copland or Charles Ives wove and unwove out of the civic culture of Puritan America. But these Irish figures on the beach at dusk, or figures entering the church portals, are far from being *désengagé* pensioners from life. A striking number of the men were engineers, or had taken engineering degrees – Cathcart Dobbs, J. C. Mahon (Joly's father-in-law), James Price, Bob Synge. If neither Florence nor Cherrie is remembered today as a painter, it is clear that J. M. Synge would not have become the dramatist now celebrated without their existence, their effort, their sacrifice.

During the War of Independence, C. L. Matheson's body was brought from loyalist Belfast (where he had become City Recorder) for burial near

Greystones: despite the British patriotism he had recommended in an 1874 student debate, Cherrie Matheson's uncle was buried in the south – in the graveyard where Samuel Beckett's parents also rest. Perhaps there is a moral in that. In 1921 Southern Ireland was not magically turned into the hegemonic domain of the Exclusive Fianna, populated only by Catholics in belief and nationalists in practice; variety persisted, even within what might be thought of as the Catholic/Nationalist monolith. By the same token, it would be a crude misrepresentation to cast Synge's departure for Aran as the act of a man going native, finding his roots, leaving his mission post for an authentic life with 'the people'. By May 1898, he had learned not only how to escape but also how to reflect. Greystones and Inis Meáin came in time to interpret each other.

In 1888, however, Synge's rather intermittent education as a gentleman promised no such insight. At the Bray School, he had acquired no permanent friends, the equivalents in his age-group of Jack Joly and Harry Stephens, the latter by now his brother-in-law. Ned's health seemed to be deteriorating; Robert's prospects were dimmed by misunderstandings with his Traill sponsors in business; Sam was so unrelievedly good and kind that he merited constant mention in despatches, and Annie's first child next door in No. 3 Orwell Park warranted equal attention. But Johnnie? 'He hates to be asked to go any where or do any thing for *me*. He had to get a basket of eggs left at 44 Harcourt Street yesterday for me, & he made such a fuss.'[49] In addition to exercising the constitutional privileges of an ordinary teenager, John also worried his mother on spiritual grounds. 'He is very reserved & shut up on the subject, & if I say anything to him he never answers me...'[50]

Better-off relatives underwrote Sam's clerical education but were unlikely to do the same for a sullen agnostic with little aptitude for a useful profession. Yet there clearly was a strong bond of active affection between Kathleen and her youngest. Twice in 1888, she penned extensive accounts of his accomplishments. A tutor had proposed that he take an honours degree in literature, a course which was not ultimately adopted. Kathleen was proud to declare that 'Johnnie certainly is the literary man of the family', even if she measured that fact by clock-time devoted to reading and the cost of second-hand books. She concluded that he took after her father, the translator of Josephus – 'he was a very literary man.'[51]

This praise was followed up with an account of Ned's success at Glanmore. He took in £50, and 'sent away over £40 because they did not bring their full rents!' One of Aunt Editha's tenants observed that 'it would take a Synge to do that'. Down in Galway, two tenants in particular remained troublesome. James McDonagh was in arrears, while Charles Baylee had cited his mother's chronic illness as an obstacle to Mrs Synge's collecting their rent. When McDonagh paid £50 on account and demanded a reduction, it was tacitly acknowledged in the family that the farm he occupied was not worth what it once was.[52] Privately his contribution to Mrs Synge's budget was translated into upholstery - 'When that sofa was last covered when we were in Newtown, we sent it to a shop to be done & it cost £6. I remember how horrified I was.'[53] Now a tradesman had declared the springs beyond repair. Baylee, for his part, had only advanced £20 in the previous six months, having retreated to the impressive address of Mount Baylee in County Clare, and left a wife and some children on the rented farm.[54]

Ned was worryingly thin. Kathleen Synge's letters to South America so thoroughly interweave themes of economic and sentimental woe, religious and domestic piety that it is sometimes hard to distinguish between dear Nellie and the dear Lord, between tenants and fellow sinners. Yet when the calculating McDonagh and the ingenious Baylee held their fire, she could sketch for Robert in Argentina a quite humorous if contradictory account of mother and son at their music: 'Johnnie & I practise every day. He is improving in keeping time, but I have great work with him. When he comes to a *rest* he scampers away as if there was none, & leaves me behind him. Of course he has no ear for time. But by dint of patience & perseverance I hope I shall knock it into him.'[55]

Kathleen Synge did not believe in leaving matters quietly in the hands of her son, the professional land agent. While Ned was staying in Dublin to be with Nellie during her confinement, his mother plotted to meet him in St Stephen's Green and to talk over the McDonagh business. Rain drove them into the Museum where they 'had a quiet chat for about an hour'. In the next street, Nellie was within days of giving birth to her first child, after an unusually prolonged Victorian illness. (The arrival of a daughter brought a period of great nervous tension to an end.) As McDonagh had refused a 30 per cent reduction, he evidently intended to take his case before the land court. On the bright side, Ned reported that the other tenant, Reilly, had paid up; this led to a tolerably happy muddle of words – 'I am keeping with my above water thank God!' Not for the last time, she acknowledged Aunt Jane's kindness to Sam in meeting some of his fees.[56]

The day Kathleen wrote this chequer-board letter of sacred and profane anxieties was 16 April 1888, Johnnie's seventeenth birthday. Beyond the family circle, he had scarcely met a soul, let alone a free spirit of his own age. His communion was with things rather than people, things of nature admittedly. Her fears about his spiritual state have already been noted. But the larger discourse in which these find their place reveals an unstable code of decorum and expression even if it does so only in the privacy of a mother's letter to her distant son.

I got so dreadfully hot that Sam had to carry my mantle & even without it I was roasting & my face as red as fire & I got very hungry & weak so that I had to put on speed & go as fast as I could or I felt should never get home ... This is Johnnie's birth day. I can hardly fancy he is 17. I have been looking back to the time he was born. I was so dreadfully delicate & he poor child was the same. How much mercy has been shown to him in his wonderful restoration to health, & oh! that I could see him showing in his life that he has a due sense of all the mercy vouchsafed to him. I see no sign of spiritual life in my poor Johnnie. There may be some, but it is not visible to my eyes. He is very reserved & shut up ...[57]

Kathleen's casual shifting from redness of face to deadness of soul would have struck Somerville and Ross (the final arbiters of Anglo-Irish taste) as unspeakably vulgar. To them, the enthusiastic boarding houses of Greystones were happily unknown. In time J. M. Synge would eclipse the *Experiences of an Irish R.M.* in the annals of Irish comic writing. And ultimately, his mother's pathetic tenacity may yet be recognised in Samuel Beckett's Winnie (*Happy Days*) or less sympathetically his Miss Fitt (*All that Fall*). But John Synge's immediate problem was to get into, and then get out of, Trinity College, Dublin.

CHAPTER 6

The Stay-at-Home Student

Our academic class has worked against imagination and character, against the mover and sustainer of manhood; and eternity is putting forth its flaming fingers to bring its work to nothing.

W. B. Yeats[1]

In the autumn of 1888, Johnnie ceased to be a schoolboy and became a student. Trinity College, Dublin, an Elizabethan foundation of traditionally Protestant loyalties, housed itself in frosty eighteenth-century architecture. His mother had paid the entrance fee of £15 (in June), by calling in the compound interest due to her on money held in trust by Uncle Robert Traill, a resource she had not tapped since Annie's marriage four years earlier. In the west, Baylee played cat-and-mouse with his lease, but departed from Brackloon some time in 1889. James D. McDonagh, however, survived all of the Synges' efforts to dislodge him.[2] Rents were severely reduced. Kathleen Synge told Lissie Traill that her income was 'likely to diminish considerably'.[3] Though Synge's college record has been analysed on numerous occasions, little attention has been paid to the oddity of a declared agnostic following courses specifically designed for divinity students. Did financial advantage play a part in the choice? Perhaps relatives were expected to assume that, in time, he too would follow in the footsteps of the Master.

As a Junior Freshman, Johnnie was listed among 171 students newly come on the college books. The total number of undergraduates for the year was 810, a veritable mob in the eyes of a privately tutored youth from an introspective home. But Synge's comrades included no name which now leaps forward as a breaker of moulds or a leader of revolutions. The Calendar of 1888–9 records a typical intake of typically middle-class Irish lads, Protestant in the vast majority of cases.[4] At least for three or four months this advance in his education brought little change in his routine. Under the college's lackadaisical regulations, students were required to attend lectures in only one of the three terms, credit for the other two being obtainable simply by passing the appropriate examinations.

Dublin-born students did not usually take rooms in college. By this arrangement, Johnnie continued to live at home with his mother at Rathgar, devoting much of his time to music. He attended lectures by William Smyth M'Cay in mathematics, and by T. K. Abbott (the college librarian and professor of Hebrew) in classics. Though the curriculum provided a grounding in subjects upon which a diligent student might build a reputation, Synge had become fascinated by antiquities, especially the stone monuments plentiful in south County Dublin where he took leisurely walks.

In addition to its general educational and social role, Trinity served as a training school for young men about to take holy orders. As befitted a family who had given the Church of Ireland several distinguished cler- gymen, the Synges had well-established ties there. Kathleen Synge's cousin, Anthony Traill, was a lay Fellow since 1865 who ultimately was elected Provost. This was a link of some value to a Junior Freshman with genuine if alarmingly unfocused intellectual powers. More ambiguous was the family's friendship with Charlie Miller, manager of the college office, and as such a wholly non-academic functionary on Trinity's tiny administrative staff. Miller was solidly of the Church of Ireland, a respect- able middle-class man. But his position somehow indicates a slippage in the ranks of the Synges and their kin, from secure reliance on land- ownership and investment to a need for salaried income – vulgarly a job – however respectable an employer the college might be.[5] J. H. Synge had taken up the law as a barrister, the most highly regarded of the professions in Protestant Ireland. Miller stood distinctly lower down the social order. Lower again was Marshall – he is never graced with a Christian name in the family records. Joseph Marshall was head porter, carrier of the college mace, a man raised on the Glanmore estates who owed his job to Wicklow zealotry and the strong preference of Trinity for Protestant appointees among its liveried menials.

It has been customary to regard Synge as a nondescript undergraduate, scraping by on the minimum of study and opting for private reading whenever permissible.[6] This assumption, viable enough if the notebooks and diaries were the sum total of available evidence, overlooks the issue of the college's condition and its relation to his own spheres of engage- ment. Since the beginning of the 1880s, Irish university education had undergone several major reorganisations. In 1880, the establishment of the Royal University of Ireland provided a new and more dignified frame- work in which the Queen's Colleges of Cork and Galway functioned; two years later, the Catholic University was reconstituted as University

College, Dublin, and took its place under the mantle of the Royal University. These changes, together with the independent development of the original Queen's College in Belfast, emphasised the gradually self-isolating condition of Trinity. Yet if Synge's college was drifting towards the margins of contemporary Irish cultural debate, it had among its closest neighbours in the city centre the Royal Irish Academy of Music where he spent a good deal of his time. A visit to the Academy in Westland Row brought him into the vicinity, if not behind the railings, of Trinity. Through the external factor of his musical studies, Synge may even have had more contact with Trinity than many of those among his contemporaries who opted for the mode of private reading. He called on Anthony Traill in his study, he saluted Charlie Miller through the office window, he nodded to Marshall in Front Square.

While historians of the RIAM are understandably keen to emphasise the extent of Synge's commitment to music, the surviving evidence does not include enough to warrant laments for a lost composer.[7] But a note should be added on the non-sectarian nature of the Academy. While Dublin remained self-consciously divided into Catholic and Protestant camps, it brought together members of the two larger religious groups. A Catholic bishop featured among the Vice-Presidents, where other institutions often emblazoned the name of a Church of Ireland prelate. Friends for the future met here, among them Edith Oldham (died 1950). The governors included George Cree, whose son later befriended Synge in Paris. Oldham, who later married another of his Paris friends, the Celticist Richard Irvine Best (1872–1959), was a 'professor' together with the exotic figures of Signor Michele Esposito (1855–1929) and the cellist Henri Bast (1856–1907) who had played under Wagner, Liszt and Brahms. The Academy was perhaps more universal than the university.

During Synge's lifetime, cultural debate would shift markedly, with his own contribution being far from negligible. The study of Gaelic literature, whether through scholarly editions of texts or popularising translations, was to give spirit to the political movement which eventually brought a large measure of independence to the country. But in 1888 that Celticist endeavour did not yet possess the influence it came to wield early in the new century. W. B. Yeats had not published *The Wanderings of Oisin;* that pioneering visionary poem followed some four months later. One cultural historian of Ireland has gone so far as to argue, in effect, that music pioneered a renaissance in the 1880s which literature then appropriated.[8] In this light Synge's devotion to the violin and Schubert places him in a vanguard, later outmanouevred by Yeats and company in a struggle which was at least in part political. While this may be somewhat unfair to Yeats, Synge's dexterity in realigning with the new theatrical movement is evidence of more than passive literary genius.

Sam was already taking his divinity courses in Trinity, attending lectures from Cousin Anthony Traill and Dr Thomas Maguire. His dealings with each differed markedly. In practice, Traill was easy-going on doctrinal matters; he had never taken orders himself, and yet sat on committees which administered the Church of Ireland. When Ned decided to apply for a post as District Receiver, Traill obligingly wrote to two of the appointing judges.[9] Maguire was quite a different character. Charged with teaching New Testament Greek to the aspirant clergy, he was a Catholic, one of the very few of that persuasion to achieve Fellowship in Trinity before Irish independence. The opportunity to rescue a soul from the dark tyranny of Rome was not to be lost. Mrs Synge approved, and Sam's efforts featured in her weekly letter to Robert, whom fate had stranded among the 'dark' population of Latin America. Maguire 'is quite ready to talk about religion to Sam, but told him that he had not changed his opinions ... He told Sam [that Catholics] took their belief not from the Bible but from the tradition handed down through the Church. He has his Greek Testament & discusses words in it with Sam, but when he does not take it as ["]the only true Guide" the light becomes darkness to him ... He has lent Sam a little book on "Good Works" to read & that will lead to further talks. I was looking up the passages about the traditions [in] Mark 7 & Isaiah 29. They are very strong & clear to eyes that can see. Sam intends to show them to him.'[10] Following on this conspiracy between his mother and brother, John Synge kept his own counsel in all matters. Next year, Maguire was murdered.

James Joyce, in *A Portrait of the Artist as a Young Man*, describes Trinity as that 'dull stone set in a cumbrous ring'.[11] The phrase is coloured – or dulled – by the fictional nature of the narrative, but it conveys a tolerably accurate impression of the outsider's view. Joyce, though no ally of the Celticists, would have had less time for the distinguished scholars upon whom Trinity relied for its reputation in the final decades of the nineteenth century. Improbable though it may seem in the light of subsequent prejudices, the college distinguished itself in the social sciences – with John Kells Ingram and J. P. Mahaffy being the best known to the outside world. But this was a period of transition; more precisely, it was the early stage of a period of transition, the stage often mistaken for stasis. The term 'social sciences' was virtually unknown in Ireland, and the uncertainty of the period can be gauged in the departure for New Zealand in 1886 of a young man called Hutchinson Macaulay Posnett who had written on the Ricardan theory of rent.[12] At the time of Synge's connection with the college, Trinity was on the point of being trumped in a new game of cards; its old academic strengths were of diminishing relevance since the Disestablishment of the Church of Ireland in 1869; its new strengths were not only unrecognised but were imminently to be superseded by the yoking together of Celticism and militant nationalism.

Despite all the calendars might say, Synge's Trinity was virtually that of a pre-Disestablishment era. The degree he read for was shaped by the former needs of the Church of Ireland, as a Protestant missionary force in a predominantly Catholic land. Even his academic study of the Gaelic language was determined less by cultural than by evangelical interests, and his principal instructor, James Goodman, was a country rector half-timing as university teacher. Later, in Paris, Synge would find a close friend in Richard Best, a contemporary at Trinity and subsequently a leading Gaelic scholar. But there is no evidence that the shy youth from Orwell Park knew his future friend when they were undergraduates together; on the contrary, it is clear the two were introduced by a third Irish exile. Some time in the autumn of 1897, Stephen MacKenna recommended 'one of the most charming chaps that exist – a jewel of a man with great knowledge and reading and real *uncantified* culture.' During the years at Trinity, Kathleen's youngest made no acquaintance with charm.[13]

If the social sciences were not yet visible as a coherent element in the syllabus, there were other areas of study open to the Junior Freshman. The Erasmus Smith Professor of Modern History at the time of Synge's entry was J. W. Barlow, whose successor after 1893 was John Bagnell Bury. While Synge privately read historical works, he never studied history formally. Neither Barlow nor Bury could have appealed to the Synge family, the former having decidedly liberal views on damnation and the latter regarding all theological questions as so much hooey. Though Synge had taken the brave step of not accompanying his family to any church service on Christmas Day 1888, the course of study he had just commenced conformed to the pattern of clerical education already embarked upon by his brother Sam.[14] Financial calculation should not be ruled out as an undeclared motive.

Sam was due to graduate as a BA in 1891. He was however also pursuing other courses in preparation for his missionary work abroad, taking the Divinity Testimonial in 1891 and his medical degree in 1895. Thus while the brothers were simultaneously students, Johnnie was paradoxically thrown back to a greater extent upon home resources, as Sam was progressively required to attend clinical lectures and to work in hospitals.[15] In October 1890, Kathleen Synge moved with her two youngest sons from Orwell Park, Rathgar, to the port and seaside resort of Kingstown on the southern shores of Dublin Bay. The move was initiated by her son-in-law, Harry Stephens, who had decided that the new and fashionable suburb would provide him with a social circle in which his business as a lawyer and his recreational life might flourish to an extent evidently not possible in Rathgar. Though Stephens outwardly conformed to his mother-in-law's religious notions, one cannot but suspect that he was attempting to escape from her too-neighbourly love. Life in Orwell Park, with the widow Synge's family in No. 4 and the Stephens family in No. 3, must surely have been irksome for an active and outward-looking solicitor. If there was any substance behind these conjectures of disloyalty, then Harry Stephens failed in his rebellion, for a communicating door between Nos. 29 and 31 Crosthwaite Park West soon reproduced in Kingstown the symbiotic double-household into which he had married.[16] From the point of view of a Trinity undergraduate, the notable difference in the Kingstown arrangements was the greater accessibility to a railway service into and out from the city. This made travel to lectures easier, but it also eliminated any possible argument in favour of living in college rooms. Sam and Johnnie were his mother's sole companions in Crosthwaite Park, as Aunt Jane (who offered to rent two rooms and so defray some of the expenses) in practice lived with the Stephenses.[17]

By 7 December, John had sustained his crucial break from one collective family practice, choosing on that frosty Sunday to go walking on Three Rock while his mother and brother attended service in their new local church.[18] The relative nearness of these lowish hills to his former home in Rathgar should not be taken to endorse any desire to move back behind the gates of Orwell Park. In the following year, he began to keep a notebook in which he recorded some of the instruction he received in Trinity and in the Academy of Music. Very early, there are extracts from Shakespeare, Spenser and other major English authors, evidently demonstrating the varied use of certain words. For example, the second act of *I Henry IV* and the first book of *The Faerie Queene* are quoted to illustrate the word 'purchase'. His coverage of Edward Dowden's lectures in February 1889 includes an aside to the effect that 'In no case can we exactly copy nature, there must be some thing reflex in art.'[19] By the end of the year, however, he has adopted the practice of maintaining an alphabetical list of words which is – so to speak – interfiled with longer lecture notes. The list derives from R. C. Trench's *On the Study of Words* (1851) in which the liberal Protestant Archbishop of Dublin and effective founder of the *Oxford English Dictionary* project commented methodically on the etymologies of many seemingly unremarkable terms in the language. Though Synge's notes amount often to little more than a transcription of Trench's printed commentary, the selection which the future playwright makes has its own interest. Of 'ascendency' – that word so often associated with his own social origins in 'the Anglo-Irish Protestant Ascendancy' – he noted cryptically that it 'shows belief in astrology'. A little later he dwells on the word 'idiot', recording that it signified

a private man, contradistinguished from one clothed with office and taking his share in the management of Public affairs. In this its primary use it is occasionally used in English: thus Jeremy Taylor – 'humility is a duty in great ones, as well as in idiots['] Thence it soon signafied [sic] a rude intellectually unexercised person; this secondary sense becoming witness to a conviction in the Greek mind of the indispensableness [sic] of public life, even to the right development of the mind. This pushed further gives our tertiary meaning – an imbecile.[20]

In *The Playboy of the Western World* – which first set out under the title, 'The Fool of the Family' – Old Mahon declares his son to be a 'dribbling idiot' not to be confused with 'a likely man'.[21] While no interpretation of the play should reduce to an autobiographical anxiety, the evidence suggests that the playwright confidently consulted his notebooks in elaborating the exchange of insults and blows between Christy Mahon and his 'da'. The notebooks and diaries reveal not Johnnie Synge their author, but J. M. Synge their subsequent reader.

On one occasion at least, Synge was subjected to gentle inquiry about his difficulties with spelling: his interrogator was John Kells Ingram.[22] It is unlikely that as a Trinity Freshman he was aware that Ingram, who became President of the Royal Irish Academy in 1892, was the English-language translator of Auguste Comte (1798–1857). Ingram, the most distinguished (if also discreet) scholar at work in Trinity, was thus one of the means by which Comtean positivism was mediated to the British and Irish public. Dowden's celebration of the Elizabethans should thus be read not simply as a statement of what F. R. Leavis will much later regard as obvious, natural, and vital: the emphasis on 'positive concrete fact' might equally be taken as a passing acknowledgement of Ingram's influence within the confines of Trinity's intellectual community.

During the week ending Friday 18 March 1892, Synge bought a sixpenny diary, and began promptly to make businesslike entries, a practice he maintained with gradually decreasing efficiency for just over a decade. He was due to sit his Senior Sophister (or final year) examinations at Trinity, and much of the little Collins Pocket Diary which he used is filled with details of his day-to-day reading. There was, of course, a parallel engagement in studies at the Academy of Music; indeed, on 16 March he was awarded a scholarship in counterpoint, and a cash prize of £3 0s 0d. In the course of writing his daily chronicle, Synge managed to misspell Joseph Haydn's surname and the word 'schoolarship'.[23]

The following day – St Patrick's Day – he went walking in the hills of south County Dublin, no great distance from his suburban home in Kingstown. But in his diary, he resorted for the first time to a macaronic form of making entries: 'Finished the 4th chapter of Genesis with Gray. Perambulavi. Senex agricola, super Baile corus terram esse [?] "kind" dixit.' Young men are prone to believe that their secrets are under scrutiny, and Synge may have been experimenting with a means of frustrating his mother's intrusive gaze into his diary by mixing English, Gaelic and Latin in a follow-up to the placid account of his progress in biblical studies. On the other hand, one should not assume that Kathleen Synge, whose father had translated Josephus's *Jewish Wars*, was ignorant of basic Latin. In the event, the macaronics only tell us that, in the course of this walk, an old farmer near Ballycorus addressed the youth as 'kind'.[24] It is an idiom that occurs in his earliest attempts at a drama set among countryfolk.

The smelting tower at Ballycorus rose into the view from Dublin's southern suburbs like a relic from archaic times, yet lead from the Wicklow mines had been processed there in mid-century, and there had been a glint of silver on the eve of the Great Famine. Synge's reading wove contrasting elements and vestiges together. Edward Gibbon's *Decline and Fall* alternated with *The Children of Lir*, not to mention Goethe's *Egmont* and Fénélon's *Télémaque* which he read slowly in their original German and French. Whereas the Gaelic legend recorded a dispersion of people metamorphosed as swans from Ireland into the surrounding inhospitable seas, in Gibbon's twenty-fifth chapter, 'he looks at Irish theory of the Milesian colony, and denies that Scotland was peopled from Erin.'[25] Even in the reading which departed from the diet approved at home, Synge frequently fell on the earlier side of a significant shift in opinion or style. It does not follow that he was at all comfortable in repeatedly being typecast by changing fashion as a young man with middle-aged tastes;

the discomfort of this was to contribute to his finding himself rather than simply finding his bearings.

The more strictly literary side of his study also looked backwards. Goethe's prose tragedy (written between 1775 and 1787) contributed further patterns of contradiction or dramatic contrast, being a play in which the political and the individual aspects of man are interwoven, partly through Goethe's notion of the 'daemonic'. Two further aspects made it additionally attractive to the youth who should have been persisting in his biblical studies – its historical setting in the Netherlands during the clash of Catholic and Protestant forces at the time of the Counter-Reformation, and its use by Beethoven as the basis for a famous overture. As for Fénélon, the Archbishop of Cambrai had been renowned for the liberal attitude he adopted towards those converts to Catholicism who were his especial charge; his *Télémaque* (1699) negotiated with equal suavity between classical and post-Renaissance sensibilities.

John Synge reached his twenty-first birthday on 16 April 1892. It was Easter Saturday, that lull in church ceremonial between the tragedy of Good Friday and the comic resolution of Sunday morning, a day not so much of solemnity but of empty dullness in Irish Protestant households. He spent a good deal of the day walking – alone, as far as we can tell. Taking a long route by the Phoenix Park and the riverside villages of Lucan (where he saw swallows) and Leixlip, he paused to examine a very ruined old church about a mile on the Dublin side of Maynooth. In his diary, which was for the most part laconic and sparse in detail, he drew a little sketch of the archway, enough to prove that he was no draughtsman. At Maynooth, the castle struck him as the finest ruin he had ever seen, and indeed even today the sturdy remains of the Fitzgerald stronghold are impressive. At some point in the day he took time off from these antiquarian pursuits to read the latest number of the *Review of Reviews*.[26]

Living at home and preparing for his final examinations at Trinity, Synge was on the brink of adulthood. The absence of any family celebration to mark his coming of age may partly be explained by reference to Easter, but parties were not Mrs Synge's preferred way of giving thanks. Nor would she have been pleased to know what her youngest son was reading and thinking on the happiest day in the Christian calendar. He dipped into Thomas Carlyle's essay on the German romantic writer Novalis (Friedrich von Hardenberg, 1772–1801) whose unfinished novel – Novalis died even younger than Synge was to die – typifies a high romantic faith in the transforming power of art. Then his mind strayed back to the walking expedition of the previous day:

The striking contrast that I saw yesterday between the barren desolate country lying along the road from Leixlip to Maynooth, and the overcrowded wretchedness of Dublin, confirms my opinion that much good might be done by building artisan cottages in the country and supplying free railway passes to and from town to the workers who might take them.[27]

The urban poverty of Dublin was notorious, and it was particularly evident in the vicinity of St Patrick's Cathedral through whose 'liberties' Synge walked on his way to the Phoenix Park beyond the Liffey. The desolation he observed further west requires more comment. The great house of this area was Carton, home of the dukes of Leinster whose Fitzgerald kin had built Maynooth Castle centuries earlier. The demesne straddled the border of counties Dublin and Kildare, appearing to symbolise the ideal rural retreat of everything and everybody implicit in the term, Georgian Dublin. Yet the tenement buildings near the cathedral were Georgian also, and probably older – outward and visible signs of an inward fall from grace which had overtaken a class to whom the Synges believed themselves (once) attached.

On Easter Monday he walked to the Scalp, a short rock-strewn valley just north of Enniskerry on the Dublin–Wicklow border. The estate pertaining to the village was Powerscourt, and it was under the patronage of a Lady Powerscourt that the religious movement subsequently known as the Plymouth Brethren had first quickened into life. Synge had complicated interests in the Brethren. Some of his forebears had cleaved to the Brethren's puritanical code, and – more pressingly – Cherrie Matheson came from a well-to-do Dublin family of that persuasion. Moreover, the branch of the Synges who had 'fellow-travelled' with the Brethren once owned Glanmore Castle, a substantial property in County Wicklow to the south and east of Powerscourt. Thus, while the naturalist in John Synge marvelled at the geological extravagance of the Scalp and observed its bird life and flora with care, there were contending implications on the southern horizon. The conical peak of Sugar Loaf which dominates the landscape with an almost oriental elegance blocked off any view of Glanmore and its rugged uplands, towards which the larger and grander Powerscourt estate languidly extended. These walking expeditions of the young Synge's have been taken as evidence of a precocious identification with the rural Irish landscape. In fact, they were typical pastime activities of his class. Rathmines pupils published numerous travels in rural Ireland – for example 'A Walk to Lough Bray' or the more adventurous 'Story of Lugnaquilla' with its account of rival lovers amid the dangers of

1798.[28] Synge's development as a youth was not a matter of a deeply individuated originality; it was a process of finding on his own the fairly conventional paths of exploration which his brothers and their school-friends trod together.

The Devil's Glen, a steep and twisting gully linking Glanmore to the mountain road, had provided the most unorthodox of rebels in 1798 with a hide-out. On the second to last day of March, Synge had begun to read Richard Musgrave's highly partisan account of the United Irishmen rebellion, balancing this bulky intake with a less demanding diet of Charles Lamb's essays. He finished Musgrave – in which he had especially noted the foundation of Maynooth College in 1795 – on Wednesday 20 April 1892. Throughout the intervening weeks, he attended to the reading required for his BA finals and also kept up his musical studies. *Memoirs of the Different Rebellions in Ireland* had been first published in 1801; in the excited atmosphere built up after the insurrection of 1798 and the debates leading to the Union between Great Britain and Ireland in 1800, it had come to occupy a prominent position in the library of political and historiographical controversy. Musgrave was a true-blue loyalist whose object in writing was to vindicate the government's behaviour before, during and after the events of 1798. At this level, John Synge's recourse to the *Memoirs* was unremarkable, for in staunch Unionist households it was regarded as having something of the authority of the Bible – a comparison Kathleen Synge would not have tolerated.

Quite apart from the diaries, there is one other source of information on Synge's reading of Musgrave's *Memoirs*. In what has come to be known as Notebook 30, he wrote a series of highly cryptic references, especially to the appendices of Sir Richard's narrative. These occur at the back of the notebook, and written upside down, together with a brief 'Comment on Nietzsche', notes on Richard Mant's *History of the Church of Ireland* (1840), Louis Petit de Julleville's *Histoire de Théâtre en France* (1880), Thomas Paine's *Age of Reason* (1793), and on the state of Belfast in 1792. Nothing more palpably conveys this student's highly secretive and syn-thetic mode of thinking than these fourteen (undated) leaves – even if they represent a second reading of Musgrave, undertaken some years after he had left Trinity.[29]

The centenary of the United Irishmen's rebellion was approaching, and with it a heightened awareness of conflicting interpretations, surviving memories, local animosities pickled in folklore. The business of reading Irish history involved its own 'double-entry' accountancy. What appeared as a debit in one context turned up as a credit elsewhere. While Musgrave denounced French influence, United Irishmen conspiracy, and the disloyalty of an overwhelmingly Catholic peasantry, he was also obliged to disclose evidence of well-born, even aristocratic Irish Protestants in the leadership of the 1798 insurrection. One of these was Lord Edward Fitzgerald, whose family owned Carton near Maynooth. For Synge, reading Musgrave in the days before and after his walk of Easter Saturday 1892, it was possible to conclude that the social decay evident both in Georgian Dublin and in the countryside near Maynooth resulted in part at least from the failure of Irish radicalism just under one hundred years earlier.

Unlike W. B. Yeats, Synge never evolved, nor was he possessed by, a philosophy of history. Neither did he elaborate a distinctive political position in the manner of the young James Joyce. In an autobiographical piece which remained unpublished in his lifetime, he wrote, 'Soon after I had relinquished the Kingdom of God I began to take a real interest in the kingdom of Ireland. My politics went round from a vigorous and unreasoning loyalty to a temperate Nationalism. Everything Irish became sacred ...'[30] Even this has to be read with a wary attention to Syngean irony, for there is little evidence that he had ever found the Kingdom of God. Moreover, the tension between *temperate* nationalism and the *sacredness* of all things Irish is a dramatic device no reader should discount. His reading of Irish history led to more than one experiment in play-writing.

The most enduring evidence of this influence survives in the several versions of a play called *When the Moon Has Set*, the background to which has earned its own chapter in Synge's biography. Far briefer, and yet more immediately revealing of his talent and temperament, are two fragments which have been edited together under the title 'Bride and Kathleen: a Play of '98'.[31] In this projected play two women, taking refuge together from the violence of the insurrection in counties Wexford and Wicklow and its suppression, discover that they come from opposite sides of the conflict, the one Catholic, the other Protestant. (At this point Synge's four pages of dialogue terminate.) But the irony of victims learning their own codes of mutual victimisation is closer to the reversals of *The Playboy of the Western World* and *The Well of the Saints* than anything in the never-abandoned *When the Moon Has Set* – and this despite the historical dimension which both the fragments and the last-named play have in common. If we are to see the possibility of a 'reading of history' in Synge's reading of Musgrave's *Memoirs* and other histories of Ireland, then what is implicit is an awareness of comic discordance, of anomaly as structural elaboration, and of unsuspected or suppressed conflicts (between the sexes, or between women) behind the more famous contestations of male history.[32] For in Musgrave, the displaced Protestant leaders of insurrection are not confined to some romantic subset of the aristocracy and landlord classes, they include Joseph Holt – 'a low fellow, without any kind of principle and a notorious robber' – who maintained his followers in the Devil's Glen, that picturesque defile on the edge of the Synge estate later beloved of tourists. Yet for years Holt had held from Francis Synge (later MP) an appointment as deputy overseer of roads for a portion of the route from Roundwood towards Dublin, a route John Synge was to learn in travelling it by bicycle.[33]

In June 1892, he sat Trinity examinations in Hebrew and Irish, even winning a £4 prize in the latter.[34] Later that summer, Synge sought his holiday relaxation in Castle Kevin, a sizeable house south of Glanmore. Here was a Wicklow close to the action of Musgrave and further from the pulpits of Greystones. The feudal manor of Castle Kevin had associations with the see of Glendalough and thus with the world of Celtic Christianity before 'the foreigners' – Vikings first, then Normans – arrived on Irish shores. It suggested links between Synge's own experience of family and orthodoxy on the one hand and, on the other, a world of little monasteries, of nature poetry, and of pre-schismatic harmony.[35] On Friday 20 July, he cycled into Wicklow, the rest of the party travelling by rail and road. The journey took him up on to the most easterly edge of the Wicklow Mountains and along the brim of desolate bogland. Houses were few, their inhabitants perhaps fewer, such was the extent of human withdrawal and ruination. The once established Church of Ireland maintained outposts at Calary and Derrylossary. The biblical name of Elijah (Sutton) was invoked orally where an isolated signboard named the Mountain Side Tavern.[36] (Back in Dublin, brother-in-law Harry was working his way up through the legal firm of Fred Sutton, which had roots in the same vicinity.) Though the congregations in a few churches sustained themselves into the twentieth century, the county population was declining in absolute numbers; to a shrewd observer, the fate of the minority could not be better than that of the upland community as a whole.

Territoriality is a concept at once vital and fatal in Synge's imaginative world. As the descendant of landowners, he was aware of changes which had come over Irish society in the decades following the mid-century famine. As youngest son, he was made aware of a need to complement the once-automatic reliance on landed inheritance with some suitable mode of life and with a livelihood in keeping with the delicate status of his family. He was never to content himself with a connoisseur's appreciation of landscape. As the 'refusnik' inheritor of a religious outlook (sometimes called territorialism) which had depended on civil authority, he was above all sensitive to a myriad complex relations between the physical land under his feet and the historical situation of the individual and his inheritance. Edward Stephens, favourite nephew and family chronicler, believed that he shared many of the playwright's attitudes to such matters. Even in Andrew Carpenter's edited version, Stephens lingers over details of geology, land reclamation, boulders with the incised markings of pagan times, birdsong, even a cloud of flies – and family history. 'John had come to stay in the district with which his family had ... been associated' for over a century.[37] Without the seemingly eternal beauty of the yellow gorse bushes and the elusive fragrance of heather, this territory still made claims upon John Synge – or vice versa.

Castle Kevin was one of the summer places which Mrs Synge rented in the area during the 1890s, and the pattern of these annual excursions took him closer to the landscape of Musgrave's violent and retributive history. Linked to the nearby townland of Tomriland were the violent deaths of John Beaghan, Thomas Hatton and others, including the husband of Mary Waddock who was murdered 'with much cruelty' on 14 July 1798. These names – all Protestants as Musgrave insisted, except John Waddock ('a papist') – were ritually inscribed in appendices of the Memoirs, the reading of which Synge noted in his diary.[38] Young Synge's access to the events of 1798 did not depend exclusively on printed history.

Though his immediate family no longer held land there, Wicklow featured in an informal or oral tradition which preserved details best left uncommitted to paper. For example, Musgrave recorded a rebel attack in May 1798 on the home at Drumeen of a Mr Hugo who was 'noted for his zeal, activity and courage'. Without citing sources, Stephens provided a less bland summary: 'It was said that Mr Hugo used to shoot, against the back of the garden wall, anyone he took to be a United Irishman. The story goes that [the reverend] Mr. [Ambrose] Weekes one morning wrote him a note asking that he would postpone shooting rebels until the afternoon as he hoped to call over with his gun.'[39]

It is not possible to establish exactly when Stephens added this colourful detail to his portrayal of the historical background against which he saw John Synge's genius emerging. The absence of any cited source suggests reliance on family lore, and the existence of such guilty knowledge – relating specifically to Wicklow in the eighteenth century – undeniably played a part in Synge's first extended effort at drama. Charles Weekes (1867–1946), a kinsman of the murderous Weekes, popped up as a Dublin man of letters in the 1890s; later, as a lawman, he advised Synge's publisher on contractual matters. Recollection pervaded the Irish *fin de siècle*, as the centenaries of great events loomed and the security of landed families declined. Here again, the presence of family papers in the house where Synge lived provided a stimulus to reflection. But the availability of Castle Kevin in 1892 resulted from recent political disturbance.

Parnell had died suddenly less than a year earlier on 6 October 1891. Johnnie had spent much of that autumn with his brother Edward who, in his capacity as land agent, was attempting to collect rents near Kingscourt in County Cavan. While the death of Parnell had registered most forcibly in the area of constitutional politics – the practicality of Home Rule dying with him – it also marked an end to a particular phase of agitation about the ownership and occupation of Irish land. The years 1879–82 had witnessed a veritable Land War, which in 1886 had been transformed subtly into what was known as the Plan of Campaign whereby withheld rents were collected by the Irish leadership pending some ultimate agreement as to amounts morally due. In the course of the prolonged struggle between landlordism and tenantry, the tactic of 'boycotting' had become widespread.[40] The constabulary were powerless to break this negative resistance, and it was a hardy individual who rushed in where the RIC feared to tread. Castle Kevin had been a 'boycotted' house, uninhabited for years except during certain summers when it was available for rent.

Wicklow provides the dramatic setting of three plays – *In the Shadow of the Glen* (first performed October 1903), *The Well of the Saints* (February 1905), and *The Tinker's Wedding* (published 1907) – or four, if you count the problematic *When the Moon Has Set*. For this alone, Synge's first adult encounter with the area deserves close attention. Strictly speaking, we should say that he was familiar and concerned with the mountainous parts of east Wicklow only, for the county is divided in several ways which deprive it of any unified character.[41] The area in question runs roughly from Sugar Loaf Mountain, the Long Hill, and Glencullen on its northern frontier as far south and west as Aughavannagh. It includes much bogland, the secluded valleys of Glendalough and Glenmalure, the tiny villages of Roundwood, Laragh, Annamoe, Greenane and Ballinaclash, with the more substantial 'towns' of Rathdrum and Aughrim. The eastern border-line is effectively the main road which now links Dublin to Wexford, and the westerly boundary is high, virtually uninhabitable, mountain. That Joseph Holt had been able to hide out in the Devil's Glen, less than thirty miles from Dublin Castle, indicates how inaccessible the county was even at the beginning of the nineteenth century. Some of the routes travelled by Synge (and later by Beckett) form part of what is still known as the Military Road, in tribute to its origin in the campaign to suppress rebellion and prevent its recurrence.

Castle Kevin occupied a site of multiple historical associations. A solid three-storey eighteenth-century mansion, in the 1890s it was owned by the Frizell family who, during the period of boycotting, had left it in the care of a local farmer, Harry Harding.[42] As is so often the case with Irish country houses, the name is not restricted to a single building. In Stephens's re-creation of Synge's arrival by bicycle on the afternoon of 20 July 1892:

Soon after passing the mill, John came to 'the red bank', a waste bit of land in the angle between the main road, bending round Tomriland Hill, and a by-road, dropping away on the right to Castle Kevin. Across the bog he could see the square green mound where the old manorial castle of the archbishops of Dublin had stood, and near him, on his left, the great circular mound where, the people said, Cromwell's cannon had been placed for the attack by which the castle had been finally destroyed. After crossing the sudden hump of a small stone bridge, his road joined the road round the town opposite the gate of Castle Kevin.[43]

Stephens gives us a castle (finally destroyed) and a house both called Castle Kevin. Likewise young Synge has 'his road', though knowledge of the area depends on what 'the people' said. The 'road round the town' must be glossed by Carpenter as 'a local name for the largely disused road which circled the townland of Castle Kevin'; it is, in fact, a metalled laneway hardly wide enough for two horses to pass. A gappy-ness in language gradually becomes evident, as the reader learns that Castle Kevin is not a castle but a house named after a castle which is neither wholly destroyed nor fully accessible. The Synges' first residence there did not pass without a reminder of the house's moral reputation; betimes a police-man or two would patrol the avenue but, if anything, the family were preferred by the local community to the owners who still provoked hos-tility. Anonymous lines chalked on a door celebrated in doggerel the absence of the Frizells; Synge later adapted these for his own purposes, in acknowledgement of a constitutional inadequacy in names, curses, and language at large.[44] Summer tenants in a boycotted house possessed it in analogous manner; and when one of these tenants later chose as the central figures of dramatic action the restless tramp, the blind roadside beggar, and tinkers who steal tins rather than make them, the question of territory and its occupations should not be ignored.

Synge had been reading G. T. Stokes's *Ireland and the Celtic Church* (1888) prior to his arrival at Castle Kevin, and persisted into the latter part of July. From the notebook dating to 1889, we know that he had already discovered in Stokes an account of Ireland's national saint, according to which Patrick had landed 'at the mouth of the Vartry (Having no mission from the Pope) which locality was most suitable to their flat-bottomed boats. The neighbourhood of Wicklow as far as the 3 Rock was inhabited by the Cualanni (whence Glencullen) till the 13th cent. whent [sic] they were expelled by the O'Byrnes and O'Tooles.'[45] At eighteen Synge was still piecing together fragments of information, mingled with a casual reassurance of Patrick's non-Roman credentials, and a topography which has for its northern frontier, the Three Rock hills he could see from the Dublin suburbs. In Trench he had come across the notion that the word 'pagan' came from the Latin *pagus*, a village, adding that 'Pagani were countrymen as opposed to townsmen.' Together, Stokes's Wicklow-invading Patrick and the essential paganism of country life might be read as the fundamental details of *The Well of the Saints*. In the 1889 notebook the two fragments of learning remained discrete. By 1892, Synge had four thoughtful years behind him, and a greater confidence in approaching the physical remains of history.

On Friday 22 July, he went to inspect 'old Castle Kevin', once the stronghold of Norman archbishops in their confrontation with the Gaelic chiefs of Wicklow. But he also commenced reading Robertson's *History of Scotland*, while keeping in touch with Horace's *Satires*. He was, at least in his own eyes, balancing local and universal matters as when, on 28 July, he read in *Diarmuid and Grainne* and in the *Iliad*. Ancient epic was followed by modern prose fiction. The next day he finished Thackeray's *The Newcomes* and began Standish O'Grady's *Red Hugh's Captivity* (1889), a historical romance which comes to its happy ending in Glenmalure, a long and desolate valley lying some distance to the west of Castle Kevin.[46] His interest in fiction was conventional; August saw him digest three novels by Walter Scott and three by George Eliot. In September, he felt more confident to go on extended walking trips, southwards to Avoca, or over the mountains to Glendalough. But by the middle of the month, summer vacations were over. On 15 September, he walked to Greystones and then rode – perhaps having had his bicycle mended – on to the house in Crosthwaite Park which continued to be home. All in all, Synge's first residence at Castle Kevin had amounted to just under two months. There had been much fishing, but now there were examinations to be faced.[47]

Music and Gibbon's *Decline and Fall* held his attention back in Kingstown. He found time to see Beerbohm Tree in *Hamlet* in the Gaiety, at a cost of 1s 6d. But a list of books read in 1892 makes no reference to English literature, as if it merely provided relaxation or a distraction from more serious reading. Until late October, the diary is unrevealing of any concentrated effort towards passing his examinations in Trinity, and even then music takes priority. Nevertheless, he completed his finals six weeks later. On 15 December, 'he was given what was known as a gentleman's or pass degree, and the college authorities must have thought that a gentleman was all he was capable of becoming'.[48]

Despite this low-key assessment by his nephew and biographer, Synge's academic achievement was not just that of a young man acquiring a certificate of social respectability. The tally of results over four years is sufficiently uneven to deserve consideration.[49] It is true that in his first year he had attended only the minimum of lectures in science (i.e. mathematics, etc.) to keep his terms; in classics he exceeded the minimum number by just one. His highest score that year was eight out of ten in a Euclid viva test, and in his Senior Freshman year this fell to seven. In his finals, he scored ten out of ten in one of two ethics papers. His performance in English composition never rose above seven (Hilary term, 1892), and more frequently came to rest well below this level. The range of subjects was wide, and he veered from one to another without any revelation of profundity but, equally, without serious dereliction. If Synge's record in Trinity indicates the behaviour of a conventional gentleman, then the parallel commitment to music went a good way towards jeopardising this status, at least in his mother's eyes. On 15 December 1892, a wet and windy day, she did not travel into Dublin to see Johnnie 'commenced' as a Trinity graduate: his sister Annie and cousin Florence occupied the two seats allocated to parents.[50]

BOOK TWO

The Wander Years

CHAPTER 7

Escaping Home Rule in Germany (1893–4)

> If we possessed a perfect pedigree of mankind, a genealogical arrange-
> ment of the races of man would afford the best classification of the
> various languages now spoken throughout the world; and if all extinct
> languages, and all intermediary and slowly changing dialects, had to be
> included, such an arrangement would, I think, be the only possible one.
>
> Charles Darwin[1]

Finally graduated from Trinity College, John was able to devote the opening months of 1893 to more important things. He had joined a private Instrumental Club, based at the Academy of Music, where he heard Haydn, Mozart, Beethoven, Schubert, and even a little Wagner (the *Tannhäuser* march) between February and May.[2] His energies were divided between violin practice and composition, the preparation of established classical/romantic works for public performance and the slow putting-together of his own first endeavours to write music. The composer whom principally he was required to rehearse was Franz Schubert (1797–1828), that astonishingly prolific and short-lived genius for whom the writing of songs and sonatas had been at times a daily routine. January saw him doggedly engaged with Schubert's music.[3] He dutifully read in Grove's *Dictionary*, and analysed various movements of Schubert's compositions. He continued to take long walks in the south Dublin hills, beyond which Wicklow lay close to hand and foot. Towards the end of the month, he showed the composer Robert Stewart (1825–94) what he had written of a sonata in G minor, and was able to play it through by 9 February.[4]

The next day, 10 February, Synge participated in one of Werner's pupils' concerts in which the well-known ballet music from *Rosamunde* featured. But the Schubert he was rehearsing also included the less familiar three sonatas for violin and piano, posthumously published works derivative of Mozart and scarcely central to Schubert's achievement. In these the task of music-making was divided between two instruments, two artists, a situation in which John felt more at ease than amid the throng of an orchestra. Later in the year,[5] he played through the sonata in D (op. post. 137 no. 1) with a visitor from England, Mary Helena Synge (born 1840), the sympathetic distant cousin through whose good offices he was shortly able to get out of Dublin and travel first to London and then on to Germany. Mary Synge was a professional pianist whose religious views gave blessedly little offence to Kathleen Synge.

The first of the three sonatinas (as they were long termed) had been composed when Schubert was only nineteen, and in it he maintained a close balance between piano and violin. John and Mary Synge's performance was a private affair, and their family relationship (though remote enough in terms of blood kinship) added a further stratum to the composer's harmonies. Like many lonely children in upper-middle-class Victorian homes, he knew the bitter-sweet intimacy of cousinly rapport. Here was a woman, more than fifty years of age, his late father's cousin and English by residence, a woman whose career proved that Irish church history was not the only backdrop to his future existence. The bishops were not the only nests of distinction in the Synge family tree. Artists and scientists might be found camouflaged by its Victorian rectitude.

Mary Synge's presence in Kingstown gave the Stephens family an opportunity to throw a party. In all, seventeen people gathered on the evening of 28 March 1893, including the Mathesons from 25 Crosthwaite Park, the Rowlands from nearby *Rus-in-Urbe*, the Millers of Glenageary whose number included Charles Miller from the office in Trinity, and the Synges from next door. Mrs Synge was able to participate because she 'knew that none of them would sing any worldly songs'.[6]

Mary Synge had ambitions for a public concert in Dublin, and recruited John to her cause. The Antient Concert Rooms were booked for 17 April with young Synge acting as steward, and a friend, Louis Buchanan (from the Instrumental Club), as conductor. In addition to Mary's piano repertoire, the small audience – the night was, in the words of a sympathetic *Irish Times* reviewer, 'unfavourable' – heard solos from Werner and Bast, and some songs by Miss St John Kearney who may be the original of the 'Kathleen Kearney' so disliked by Molly Bloom in Joyce's *Ulysses*.[7] Mary Synge was sufficiently orthodox in her beliefs to propose Sunday morning attendance at Monkstown Church, when Warburton Rooke (an Academy professor) played the organ. John complied, equally pleased by her professional musicianship, her dexterity in handling his mother, and her own striking personality.[8] Stephens remembered her violent movements, spiky white hair, and aggressive laughter. The RIAM declined her offer of a public lecture. In the spring of 1893, John Synge seized the opportunity provided by his English relative and shook the dust of Irish bishoprics off his feet – temporarily, at least.

His musical concerns did not stop him reading. On New Year's Day – a Sunday – he got through Tennyson's 'Enoch Arden etc'.[9] His tight-fingered record-keeping indicates that music was frowned on as a Sabbath activity, though what Kathleen Synge thought of the recently dead laureate's verse-tale of female bigamy and revenant remorse lies beyond inquiry. Tennyson's sensational poems skiffled between prurience and probity with great technical skill. The diary retreated to the opacity of Gaelic to record how he sent (or more likely delivered) a poem to 'sogart [sic] na leabhair [sic]' – that is, Father Matthew Russell, editor of the *Irish Monthly*.[10] He had reached the fourteenth canto of Dante's *Inferno* by 5 January. But before the end of the month, Synge had embarked on a far less predictable programme of reading.

Isaac Taylor the Younger (1787–1865) had been an engraver, author and inventor. Synge's diaries indicate his considerable interest in the Englishman's quasi-philosophical work, which embraced linguistics and theology. Whether he was aware of the biblical illustrations (praised by D. G. Rossetti) which Taylor had published as a young man cannot be established. Certainly Synge began to read the essay 'Ultimate Civilization' in the last week of January 1893.[11] Nothing explains how he came upon this work; perhaps he had heard of the author's lucid opposition to religious enthusiasm and fanaticism; perhaps his immersion in Trench's *On the Study of Words* had led him back to Taylor's *Elements of Thought* (1822) with its alphabetical list of the principal terms 'relating to the nature and operations of the intellectual powers'. In the first three months of 1893, Synge was pursuing his first truly independent inquiry.

And yet, Synge's access to Taylor had its domestic aspect. During the 1840s, Kathleen Synge's father, Robert Traill, had been doggedly working on a translation of Flavius Josephus's *Bellum Judaicum* (AD 75–9). Famine was raging in Ireland, nowhere more virulently than in Cork where Traill succumbed to fever as a consequence of his efforts on behalf of parishioners in 1847. The task of completing his edition fell to Isaac Taylor, a more liberal man than Traill at least in his attitudes to Christians attached to churches other than his own. The diaries do not disclose whether Synge also read his grandfather's translation of Josephus, but it is implausible to suppose that he neglected it while turning to its co-editor's later opinions. 'My family is not ignoble, but is descended from those who bore the priesthood from its first institution.'[12]

Robert Traill exactly fitted Edmund Gosse's description of 'stout Protestants, gallant "Down-with-the-Pope" men from County Antrim'.[13] So *The Jewish Wars* had been an apt choice of text for the Ulsterman to devote his life to; written by a pious Pharisee scholar and administrator, it advanced an implied rationale for acceptance of the imperial yoke. Traill's railing against Roman Catholicism, his inveterate evangelical zeal, may be read as characteristic of that Protestantism which has long characterised the north of Ireland; attachment to the Union with Britain followed automatically from his sense of insecurity in his mission. 'It occurred to me on one occasion to be under the necessity of having two bodies of police armed for my protection.' That was fifty years earlier than the Castle Kevin experience of his daughter and grandson over whom a vigilant local policeman watched in the summer of 1892. Thus protected, John Synge had read Musgrave's *Irish Rebellions*, a work very different from *The Jewish Wars* yet sharing its acknowledgement of the imperial necessity.

The title essay of *Ultimate Civilization* has much to say on the relationship between personal illness and 'national pestilence', with the objective of qualifying the view that 'a fever in a family comes no doubt by "the visitation of God" '. Even if the consequences were properly hedged round with professions of religious concern, the moral of the argument thrust responsibility upon a component which – in the Synge family circle – was palpably missing. In both domestic and national crises, 'it is true (conditionally true) that if the master of the family drains and ventilates the house, and reforms the personal habits of his children and servants, then the "visitation" will not occur: and so the pestilence (the limits of human preventive means being always religiously kept in view).'[14] Followed promptly by a rebuke to fat landlords who complain about the mere 3 per cent which they gain from cottagers on their estates, these essays of Taylor's were not comfortable reading. J. H. Synge had died – like many others – in the smallpox epidemic of 1872–3. But there had been no need for him to die; he had contracted the fatal disease only through a casual visit to neighbours, not a typical activity for the generally unsociable Synge parents. (Had he really died of smallpox? Such a question might well have struck the child given to brooding on his own unhealthy condition.)

We cannot establish what else Synge may have read by Isaac Taylor: his notes and diaries are too laconic to be accepted as evidence of a comprehensive kind. The whole drift of Taylor's work, even dating back to the period before he had taken over Grandfather Traill's responsibilities for Josephus, undermined the certainties upon which the widowed Kathleen Synge built her household. For example, the second section of *Fanaticism* (1833) explained with alarming complacency that 'every term, whether popular or scientific ... is more or less indeterminable, and is liable to many loose and improper extensions ... This disadvantage – the irredeemable grievance of intellectual philosophy ... is besides much aggravated by the changing fashions of speech ...' From this Taylor promptly concluded that 'Men speak not entirely as they think; but as they think and hear ...'[15] In effect, he acknowledged a dialectical relationship between speaking and hearing which tended to set a discount on the supremacy of deliberate thought.

Later in the same book, Taylor's treatment of conventional symbology drew on the dangerous topic of geological science: 'The rugged surface of our globe, such as it is seen among the Alps or Andes, imposes awe, as if those stupendous piles of primeval rock, capped with the snows of thousands of winters, were the very symbols of protracted unchanging duration – or of eternity itself; and yet is it not true that the huge masses owe their stern grandeur and their lofty pride to terrible powers of commotion? – these mountains were upheaved when our world was in her fit of boisterous frenzy – when convulsions shook her centre. Instead then of regarding the now motionless forms as emblems of repose, we should deem them rather the relics and the portents too of confusion.'[16]

For a hill-walker such as John Synge, with an elder brother farming under the shadow of these now unstable Andes, Taylor's pursuit of fanaticism as the enemy of true Christianity had taken a decidedly personal turn. The author might concede that the influence of religious motives upon the lowest ranks in society was 'decidedly favourable to public order'. But if Synge joined him in declaring that 'none now call this capital political truth in question, but [the privileged] few', then fat years of consolation in Orwell Park and Crosthwaite Park had been as soon swallowed by lean years consumed in self-question.[17]

There is little difficulty in relating Synge's reading of Taylor to his family's response to the political events of the day. His mother's diary records that on the evening of 28 February 1893, he canvassed for an Anti-Home Rule – that is, Unionist – petition.[18] This activity had been prompted by the Prime Minister's introduction of the Second Home Rule Bill earlier in the month, since when a commission had reported on those Irish estates where tenants had been recently evicted by – among many –

Edward Synge. Thus when Taylor's denunciation of those who brutalised the helot class concluded that 'None now deny this first axiom of political science – that religion is the bond of peace; none deny it, we say, but the Planter and his Patron', it seemed that Grandfather Traill's co-editor prophetically condemned the fanaticism of Kathleen Traill and her son, the land agent, who insisted on interpreting the Land War and the campaign for Home Rule in terms of a racial/theological struggle.[19]

As early as 1885, Synge's brother had been active as an agent, and in 1887 his services had been employed to dispossess tenants on the Glanmore estate in Wicklow in an incident reported in the *Freeman's Journal*. According to the dramatist's nephew, 'when Synge argued with his mother over the rights of the tenants and the injustice of evicting them, her answer was, "What would become of us if our tenants in Galway stopped paying their rents?" To this he could find no answer . . .'[20] though it might be said in mitigation that he was still in his teens when the sweet chestnut of Self-interest vs. Charity was frankly posed. Nothing occurring between 1885 and 1893 made Taylor more palatable.

Darwinism had not failed to evolve since the appearance of *On the Origin of Species* in 1859. *The Descent of Man*, published in the year of Synge's birth, took the argument into ever more sensitive areas. Social Darwinism, the dominant factor in the cultural scene of the 1890s, had become allied to positivism; Auguste Comte had been an early supporter of Darwin and, in return, 'heredity' and 'environment' were transferred to what had been a philosophical outlook valuing deliberate and rational choice as a basis for human action.[21] John Kells Ingram, as Comte's discreet advocate in Trinity College, Dublin, sat on the substitutes' bench while the great contest of late Victorian controversy played on.

Francis Galton, a cousin of Darwin, had published *Hereditary Genius*: a work combining historical and statistical material in abundance. The families whose successive generations of distinguished progeny were discussed included the Taylors of Ongar of whom the most recent was the author of *Ultimate Civilization*. In Galton's words – republished in 1892 – 'this family is remarkable for the universality with which its members have been pervaded with a restless literary talent, evangelical disposition, and an artistic taste', a phrase equally applicable to the Synges.[22] But the broad diagnosis of clerical families was not good – 'as regards health, the constitution of most of the divines was remarkably bad'. Worse again, 'the children of very religious parents occasionally turn out extremely badly'.[23] Kathleen Synge had long been tormented both by her youngest son's irreligion and by his asthma. Galton laid the blame squarely on the mode of thinking and living in pious households. Later, Synge himself observed that 'in the middle classes the gifted son of a family is always the poorest – usually a writer or artist with no sense for speculation – and in a family of peasants, where the average comfort is just over penury, the gifted son sinks also, and is soon a tramp on the roadside.'[24] The blatant special pleading of this observation should not disguise the extent to which Synge's thought takes up themes from mid-to-late Victorian controversy. The first traces of this personal credo can be traced to efforts at Wicklow-dialect writing undertaken in Germany.

Germany was the locus of the most intense interest in Social Darwinism during a period which included Synge's visits of 1893/4. The new doctrines fuelled an ideological Cold War which burst into flames in August 1914. Synge's catching sight of the new Emperor, Wilhelm, on 1 September 1893 has the symbolic force of a futuristic vision, as the strange violence of his last, unfinished play will reveal. Though Synge's Germany is generally thought of in terms of riverside inns and Bavarian slopes, a world of small, richly-worked effects, it was in practice an imperial regime, under-going rapid industrialisation, and rapacious in its appetites. The year 1893 saw the foundation of the Gaelic League, a fusion of German scholarship with Irish nationalism and disenchanted Protestantism.

If Galton had been a prophet of 1890s political conflict, he had not neglected an Irish dimension. Commencing with some lofty anxieties about the quality of offspring from families of various kinds, Galton declares that 'there is a vastly larger number of capabilities in every living being, than ever find expression, and for every *patent* element there are countless *latent* ones'. This could get political, without much delay: 'Let, however, by virtue of the more rapid propagation of one class of electors, say of an Irish population, the numerical strength of the weaker party be supposed to gradually increase, until the minority becomes the majority, then there will be a sudden reversal or revolution of the political equi-librium, and the character of the borough or nation, as evidenced by its corporative acts, will be entirely changed.'[25]

Written or at least published in 1869, these views were reissued in the year of Synge's graduation. The Fenian Rising had led to the Represen-tation of the People (Ireland) Act which enfranchised lodgers. With the election of November 1868 bringing W. E. Gladstone and the Liberals to power, the last chapter of Galton's *Hereditary Genius* touched on issues which were to remain central in Anglo-Irish political debate for close on half a century. By 1869, the Church of Ireland had been disestablished. Successive Land Acts eroded the once substantial well being of families like the Synges. The Anti-Home Rule petition which John Synge assisted in distributing on 28 February 1893 stemmed from initiatives reaching back to the Home Government Association of 1870: titanic struggles followed in 1886 and now again in 1893.

At some point, Synge's interest in German philosophy and politics led him to read the early chapters of Marx's *Das Kapital*, and to compose a brief paragraph on Nietzsche. These are difficult to date, yet suggest an appetite for difficult reading which has been largely neglected. More local issues are guaranteed no more certain attention. Commentators on Synge's literary achievement have not paused long to consider the implications of his participation in the Anti-Home Rule campaign. But so strong has been the presupposition that the author of *The Playboy of the Western World* was essentially committed to a non-metropolitan, even separatist, aesthetic programme that the fact of his opposing Home Rule – in what may have been a token gesture – has become unthinkable. In the mid-1890s, writing in French to an unknown correspondent, he was to suggest that 'the first effect of Home Rule in Ireland would be a war or at least a great social conflict between Protestants and Catholics'.[26]

Synge's compliance with the household's opposition to Home Rule must be interpreted in the light of his previous divergence from family codes of behaviour and belief. Post-nationalists may take comfort in the notion that he complied precisely because it was a matter of less importance to him, intellectually and morally, than a pretence of religious devotion or an abandonment of artistic vocation. It is also significant that Synge departed for Germany less than six months after the Anti-Home Rule canvass and while the issue was still being hotly debated throughout the United Kingdom. Despite the death of Parnell and Gladstone's defeat (March 1894), Home Rule continued to dominate public affairs. The House of Lords' rejection of Gladstone's bill (in September 1893) spelled the end of a distinctive phase of English liberal interest in Ireland. Synge contrived to be on the Continent during much of this turmoil.

With the death of Gladstonian liberalism, Ireland became an awkward rather than an urgent question in constitutional debate, not only Ireland as second island in the kingdom but Ireland as 'represented' in Britain by Liverpudlian voters and West End comedians like Oscar Wilde and Bernard Shaw. By 1893 Galton was proving the permanence of human fingerprints in another of those advances of knowledge which were to bring about the ambiguous sciences of criminology and eugenics. Synge's mature work will be seen to be not wholly indifferent to forensic developments.[27] Amidst these, old corruption endured. On the great stage of parliamentary action, the existing system of representation survived 1893 by the decision of hereditary peers. The virtually unnatural 'sport' (Galton's term) of Irish majorities had been avoided. Some weeks or months after he arrived in Oberwerth, Synge wrote to his mother in such a way as led to her noting in her diary, 'I had a long letter from poor Johnnie. He has a bad cold. Curious letter attributing his unsociableness to his narrow upbringing and warning me!'[28] The letter does not appear to have survived.

There were other motivations for his visit to Germany, additional to the need to escape from Crosthwaite Park and perhaps also from the Home Rule debate. Nor did familiarity with Schubert's chamber music account for all of Synge's accomplishments in German culture. Along with the Schubert sonatas for piano and violin which Synge was rehearsing early in 1893, he studied the 'Eroica' Symphony, and read Richard Wagner's essay on Beethoven in an English-language edition which included passages from Arthur Schopenhauer's philosophical writings. Beethoven, however, was not just another composer, another string so to speak to the young would-be violinist's bow. Unlike the music played with Cousin Mary Synge, the Beethoven symphony had uttered itself from new experience, from the disillusion and exhilaration of a turbulence which had transformed distinctions between art and politics, between the spiritual and the physical. The 'Eroica' investigated what Goethe had called the 'daemonic' in mankind. Synge would invoke Beethoven on Aran in 1898.

Wagner's essay – originally issued in the year before Synge's birth and published in an English translation in 1880 – begins with a brief account of the 'Eroica', through which he distinguishes between Goethe and Beethoven as great artists. By such a comparison the composer must remain an inscrutable mystery – unless Schopenhauer is consulted. For *The World as Will and Idea* (1818; 1883–6 in English translation) provides Wagner with a paradox – only music (which defies conceptualisation) can provide insight into reality. Trinity College had not prepared Synge for such notions, yet his diary indicates clearly that he read steadily both the essay (which is not long) and the excerpts from Schopenhauer which appear as supplements. Wagner advances an eloquent vision of the great man as saint – 'he continuously falls from the paradise of his inner harmony into a hell of fearfully discordant existence, and this discord again he can only resolve harmoniously as an artist.'[29] Some discussion of a string quartet follows, but the rest is a celebration of Beethoven as a thoroughly *German* composer – it also celebrates the Prussian victory over France.

Schopenhauer had been keen to show that perceptible pictures could be apprehended by the intellect, even though these had no link with bodily presences. 'Luckily a familiar phenomenon disposes of every doubt in this direction: the *dream* ... Our capacity for representation whilst dreaming is immeasurably superior to our imaginative faculty.'[30] Synge has left no comment on his reading, but the final pages of the Wagner/Schopenhauer volume to which he applied himself between 6 and 11 April 1893 discuss the relationship between dreams and insanity, the appearance (in dreams) of the dead who are not acknowledged as dead, and non-musical topics. On Aran five years later, Synge would dream of Dreyfus, the victim of anti-Semite prejudices.

Considered in the abstract, his reading appears widely, even wildly, diverse. Though utterly different in tone and philosophical implication, Schopenhauer's texts had one feature in common with Isaac Taylor's which Synge was simultaneously reading – modern invention as a topic of intellectual interest. Photography, which Synge later excelled at, pre-occupied both. There is nothing in Taylor, however, to parallel the German's discussion of sexuality as a philosophical crux. For that, you had to turn to Galton.

Such explosive themes may have been detected by Kathleen Synge even when she commenced her opposition to Johnnie's musical studies. Had she picked up an erotic dimension in his absorption in music? Perhaps this is to attribute an over-sophisticated response to a woman whose yardstick was decorous Victorian conformity wherever a strict evangelical faith required no break with middle-class convention. Yet domesticity is a notorious bolt-hole for abashed eroticism, no less so in an Ireland innocent of Freudian reports from the couch. However we regard the dynamics of Synge's departure to a household of unknown, cultured German women, his taking on of Wagner and Schopenhauer constituted a first step towards (near)-contemporary culture, towards the lively (and deadly) issues which would define Modernism.

Synge's commitment to German culture required lessons in the language from Aemilius Wespendorff, who taught in the Rathmines School. Though he had never been a pupil there, his mother was aware that a group holiday to the Black Forest region had taken place in July 1888, reported with a reassuring emphasis on religious devotions in the school magazine. On the basis of such credentials, later in 1893, John Synge duly left Ireland for Germany, accompanied by Cousin Mary, and in doing so he not only developed his obsession with music but also broadened his experience of Protestantism as a social phenomenon. He may have contemplated enrolling in a music college in London, for Mary had sent him the regulations of a scholarship scheme some time before 6 May.[31] His stay in Germany confirmed a strong interest in certain authors – notably Goethe – but also saw a decline in his commitment to music as a possible vocation. Mary Synge's contacts led him to board with a family named Von Eicken at Oberwerth on the Rhine. The two cousins stayed for two months, after which Mary returned to London but John decided to stay on. The conventionally Protestant Von Eicken household took his literary and musical ambitions in its stride, providing an ideal bridge between the religious conformism of his mother's home and the cultural realm he was struggling to enter. On the very day of his arrival – 29 July 1893 – he began to record his expenditure on concerts, exhibitions, and the like. This uncharacteristic attention to money-matters was almost certainly prompted by demands from 'the mother' that he should be economical on his first foreign excursion. His accounts list 'Bierman's Concert' on 8 August, a drive to Höhn castle on 21 August, and the purchase of some books (no details) on 13 September. They are the kind of record designed for public inspection and parental approval. On 30 July, however, in a separate diary he had recourse to elementary Gaelic in order to inscribe its secret significance. It was 'Lá Bhalesca' – that is 'the day of Valeska', she being one of the orphaned Von Eicken sisters who ran the guest-house.[32]

Oberwerth lies a short distance from Koblenz on the left bank of the Rhine, a small island community in a region of hills, cataracts, and vineyards. Despite its seclusion, it had its own colourful scandals when Synge arrived. A baron, virtually landlord of the town, lived next door to the six Von Eicken sisters. When he abandoned his wife for the usual reasons, she aimlessly streeled about the place by herself. Synge later remembered her as 'a faded poor creature'.[33] As orphans of an army officer, his hostesses were also abandoned, though in better circumstances. Synge's sympathy for women was uncanny. His susceptibility to female charm never deserted him, bringing much anguish and exhilaration.

Germany brought modest opportunities for both. Though Valeska von Eicken was seven years older than Synge, she was among the youngest of her family. Like Cherrie Matheson, she was an uncomplicated Protestant believer with a more than casual interest in the arts. Valeska decided to call him 'Holy Moses' in tribute to a mild oath he was fond of using. She became his 'Gorse', named after the bright, sharp yellow bush which lined the roadsides of his beloved Wicklow. Neither was quite able to behave naturally in such a relationship: attracted to her, he nevertheless told her all about Cherrie who was accordingly renamed 'The Holy One'. Valeska agreed to help him with his German. Though he remained on good terms with the whole family, he characteristically selected one woman with whom to build a special, half-phantasmic relationship.

With an increasing command of the language, Synge attended a performance of Goethe's verse-play, *Iphigenie auf Tauris*, on 30 October. Homesickness, unwelcome proposals of marriage endured by the heroine, the conflict between morality and barbarous custom – all of these themes in the play can be identified somewhere or other within Synge's own small circle of experience. The next month, he saw *Die Jungfrau von Orleans*, another German Romantic verse-drama. Though based on Joan of Arc's well-known career, Schiller's play has Johanna's intolerant and narrowly religious father play a sorry role in the action.

This summer holiday, rolling now into the Rhineland's lovely autumn, had extended Synge's knowledge of the world, but also encouraged a tendency to interpret it in terms of what he had known all too long. He had wanted to pursue a musical career, and the German accounts certainly record the purchase of music paper, and the repeated hiring of a piano. The diary for 1893 contains a goodly body of work apparently on original musical compositions, but it is a *pocket* diary and nothing develops beyond notes. While at Oberwerth, he kept up violin lessons, but there is a discernible lack of commitment. Music in Kingstown, or even Dublin where everyone knew your business, was an admirably abstract art, its relationship with the emotions intense but inscrutable except to sympathetic musicians. In the Von Eicken household, it proved easier to talk about the emotions than he could have expected. Besides, Synge paid little or no attention to contemporary music in Germany. Any seriously aspiring composer would have had views on Wagner or Brahms. More to the point was Richard Strauss whose music autobiographies (such as the 'Sinfonia Domestica' of 1904) battle heroically with problems of art and expression Synge himself was tentatively exploring. Wagner's essay on Beethoven had featured on his preparatory reading list for the German trip, and while at Würzburg, he played piano transcriptions of passages from *Tannhäuser*.[34] And there his exploration of the century's dominant musical innovator ended.

Though he had written bluntly complaining about the narrowness of his upbringing, and the pleasure he had found in new friends, Kathleen Synge authorised a further extension of the visit. Some time in February 1894, a sizeable sum of money arrived from home and he subsequently moved to Würzburg where he continued to study violin and piano. On 7

February 1894, his little account book records simply *Werther*, Goethe's phenomenally successful novel of 1774. The part played by characters of opposing temperaments, the intensity of feeling, and (ultimately) the suicide of the hero may have encouraged him in the strange compositions in prose and verse where women similarly contrasted in mood and outlook buffet the unsteady soul of narrator/diarist/musician.

Würzburg not only extended Synge's acquaintance with foreign ways, it allowed him to put Oberwerth into perspective. Though his letters to Valeska have not been located, rough drafts reveal some progress in dispassionately assessing his own emotions. He had been 'terribly sentimental for a few weeks'. One letter to her had been 'foolish, ridiculous, and tasteless', but (he went on) the obligation to write 'sensible and well-behaved letters to Ireland' half-justified his self-indulgence.[35] At Oberwerth he had lived with a family of 'cloistered maidens' (their own description) who ran a guest-house which apparently catered mainly for women – 'eighteen ladies in the place', he mischievously informed his worried mother. In Würzburg, however, he took his meals at the Railway Hotel, while lodging with a Frau Susser doubtless recommended by his pious Rhine-maidens. At table he regularly met a young German doctor who asked ludicrous questions about the size of Belfast. Synge responded by feeding his acquaintance with even more absurd questions. He wanted to know the exact number of insane men, then insane women, and finally insane children in Würzburg. While this retaliation was explained to Valeska as comic parody, the substantial topic of Synge's inquiries – insanity – was a matter of concern with him. Relating the whole episode to the Von Eickens, Synge oddly prefaced it with the remark, 'The company at table is slightly more Irish ...'[36]

Mixing with students, he began to feel that his own education had been inadequate and he contemplated graduate study in a German university. An American, Robert Peers, intrigued him on the question of English spelling reform on phonetic lines, but Würzburg did not produce any significant new friend. Problems of etiquette arose, as when he considered calling on a young woman whom he had met in Oberwerth; this may have been Nellie Wrighton, a music student like Synge. He expected 'news from the beloved island' in seeking out this new arrival, but the island might be Oberwerth or Ireland. Escaping from Ireland was one thing, escaping from upper-middle-class rectitude was quite another. Despite vine-covered hills and 'Teutonic' castles, Germany never quite ceased to remind him of home. While he was at Würzburg, the Von Eickens were expecting another guest from Ireland, a woman. Somewhere in the circle, there had been a 'Titi' Fenwick, a friend of theirs since childhood. Two of the Von Eicken sisters had evidently taught at Redhill in Surrey, not far from Edward M. Synge, the etching cousin whom Synge came to know well and to like.[37] These names, which are never more than names, underline the pre-existing links between the former convent on the Rhine and the Unionist-Protestant background in which Synge had spent his life to date. He had only reached Germany thanks to a cousin's support.

Oberwerth followed him to Paris in which he took up seasonal residence for several years. During his first French sojourn in 1895, the ever helpful Valeska wrote advising him very conservatively on the question of friendship. His choice had perhaps not been 'the correct one'; he had perhaps chosen people who were too young, 'too often there appears between such people a different feeling called "Love" '. Her circle had already provided him with contacts in the French capital, notably with a Breton student, Albert Cugnier, whom he had met in Oberwerth. Cugnier and his mother featured in the unobtrusively Protestant circles where Synge first put down roots in France.

But Wicklow had followed Synge to Germany also. In a notebook, he composed too many poor poems derivative of Wordsworth, one of them even called 'Prelude' though blessedly shorter than the Lake Poet's. As his biographers Greene and Stephens have noted, the only piece of real interest in these lispings is 'Ballad of a Pauper', the title provided by a latter-day editor:

> 'Good evenin Misther niver more
> My face you'll see again
> I'm so filled full of emptiness
> So drownded with the rain
>
> 'That I'm jist goin' to the House
> Jist goin' to be a pauper
> To axe her gracious Majesty
> For a life of meal and torper.'
>
> 'Why ragged bones twere better choose
> A schoolin in Glencree
> Where you'd be taught a dacent thrade
> With duds and eating free.'
>
> 'There's none goes there but them as steals
> I'm honester nor you,

I niver stole a staavin thef
As yous are proud to do!'

'This but the course of equity
We work for laws and right.'
'Och Misther Horney spake the thruth
Your jobbers all for might!

'Well looked here young double phrase
If words are your desire,' –
'Its food I want great dunder head
Its cloths and meat and fire.'

'Hold your whist you graceless imp
And let me say my say –'
'It's I thats faged wid waitin for't
I'm wastin night and day.'

'If you adopt the pauper thrade
They pay with public gold
For all your keep till daddy Nick
Upon your life grab hold.

'But if you my advice will heed
And just some thrifle steal
In some six years of strict Glencree
You'll quite a rouser feel.'

'By Jabs I niver had beleeved
It was a Horney spoke
Your comin nice and easy on
Wid us young thinkin folk!

'Its deuced stiff a cove must steal
To grow an honest man
But Gob I'll do't if you think
It is the best I can!'[38]

This may well be Synge's first literary use of dialect, the only rival claimant being his earliest attempts at dialogue for *When the Moon Has Set* (see Chapters 8 and 10). Both works relate specifically to County Wicklow, and while both are aesthetically wretched they contain suggestions of autobiographical material. At a technical level, it must strike every reader that the poem – never prepared for publication by Synge – fails to distinguish sufficiently between the two speakers. But part of the flaw becomes itself a theme. Both speakers are enmeshed in Wicklow dialect so that the man contemplating the Poor House sounds much the same as the young son of a Big House. If the pauper is desperate, it is the other who advises crime as a means of access to Glencree Reformatory (where the food is better, and one can learn a trade). Here, in a crude form, is the germ of Synge's most intimately conceived dogma – that tramps and artistically inclined sons of the gentry are soul-brothers under the rags and gaiters.

Synge understood this as an existential truth; he signed hundreds of love-letters to Molly Allgood as 'Tramp' or 'Tramper'. But he also recognised it as a historical or sociological truth. The play draws extensively on Synge family history, of a kind often thought better left unexamined. And the 'Ballad of a Pauper' touches on the same theme of wealth acquired or transmitted by dubious means. In the fourth stanza, the poor man declares himself 'honester nor you' – 'nor' is the common dialect substitute for 'than' in Wicklow – and proceeds to make a collective judgement about 'yous' who are proud to steal. The next stanza effects a rapid exchange between the two, in which the pauper appears to identify his interlocutor as 'Mister Horney'. (Synge's editor informs us that 'horney' was Dublin slang for 'policeman'.) But a re-presentation of the stanza, eliminating dialect for the moment, would produce this –

> ' 'Tis but the course of equity;
> We work for laws and right.'
> 'O Mister Harney spoke the truth –
> You're jobbers all for might!'

In this 'translation' into a more standard English, the first speaker makes a case for the universal applicability of law and justice. The second scornfully rejects this, citing Mr Harney's observation that the previous speaker's people are 'jobbers' concerned only with power. If this clarifies the basis of disagreement between the two – one advocating universal law, the other relying on a truth which identifies special 'interest' at work – it also eliminates the anachronistic Dublin policeman and introduces a wholly recognisable folklore authority: that of the Harneys in Glenmalure. This well-known Wicklow family, and their farmstead, feature in local history from the late eighteenth century onwards. They feature also in the recreational activities of Synge's older relatives.

Synge's sojourn in Germany in 1893/4 produced the first tangible evidence of an interest in local speech and the intertwined fates of vagrants and inheritors of 'might'. He may have been spurred on by discussions with Robert Peers about pronunciation and reformed spelling. His work on a play-sketch about a young Irish landlord who returns from abroad and marries a young woman from a cottage on the family estate is dated '23.4.94 Würzburg'. Written in German, the piece mixes themes from Goethe and Maria Edgeworth. The decision not to use his native language reflects uncertainty as to the play's bearing on his own identity and past. Ever careful to compartmentalise his jottings, the diary indicates that Synge was reading a play by Ibsen rather than working on one of his own.[39] Ibsen, whom he studied extensively in German translation, had to be held at a distance from anything recognisably Irish or personal.

Dialect exercises, anxiety about inherited rights, reform of spelling to deal with 'fossilised' etymologies, wicked barons – these may seem totally separate concerns of a young man as yet without any concerted view of the world and his role in it. Yet Darwin's revolutionary publication in 1859 had presented a comprehensive view of reality in which morally discrete issues collapse into classification. The 'Ballad of a Pauper' is a Darwinian dialogue on issues of survival, morality, and language. Synge's reading of Isaac Taylor the previous year, in the run-up to his German departure, is of a piece with these emerging concerns, especially in its condemnation of 'the few, whose enormous usurpations are of a kind that can be secured only by imposing brutalizing degradations upon the helot class ...'[40] But, between Taylor's day and the Neo-Darwinism of 1894, moral indignation had been killed off by news of the dinosaur's extinction.

While Synge boarded in Würzburg, he returned to the Von Eickens for a week's holiday in March 1894. Having worked on his play project, he began to pack up for the long return journey to Ireland. The baron of Oberwerth may have prompted something of the plot – he subsequently took up with one of his farm girls and 'kept her' in Koblenz. Early in June Synge took farewell of his 'cloistered maidens', and in mid-month reached Dublin. These warm last weeks on the Continent are largely undocumented, and may have been taken up with some of the casual countryside tramping which was later woven by Yeats into an image of Synge as wandering minstrel. Valeska wrote on 25 June commiserating with him about the absence of his 'Holy One' from damp Ireland, and inquiring whether he had tackled his family about returning to postgraduate study in Germany. Implicit was the rejection of music as a career, with languages substituted as the focus of his intellectual life. To German, he would quickly add French and Italian, with colloquial Gaelic as a more intimate and creative element.

The summer of 1894 he spent with his mother at Castle Kevin. Country pastimes during July and August were heavily coloured by Cherrie Matheson's eventual presence for a fortnight as Mrs Synge's guest and Florence Ross's companion. The advice of 'Gorse' on love and friendship was put to the test more rapidly than Synge in Oberwerth could have imagined likely. Having spent October back in Dublin, he departed again for Koblenz and nearby Oberwerth, dedicated now to improving his linguistic fluency. Christmas passed joyfully among the cloistered maidens, and armed with Von Eicken introductions he set out for Paris on 1 January 1895. Though he spent more time in France, and returned more frequently, interacting with exile Irish groups and individual writers, it is arguable that Germany provided the decisive impulse for his literary development.

CHAPTER 8

Dämmerung; or, Wicklow Revisited

Sweet vale of polyglotts and pony carriages,
Barren, alas! in concerts, balls, and marriages!
Sweet vale! where prophecy and tea abound
But dulcimers and fiddles never sound![1]

The Darwinian shudder behind 'Ballad of a Pauper' had repercussions. The priggish moral resolution with which he proposed to bring to a climax the play sketched in Würzburg, did not survive. Instead, he began to work unsteadily but sustainedly on a dramatic project which, while it took in a small measure of dialect, also examined the possibility of ethics in the gentleman's library. It is natural that the first completed play by a dramatist of Synge's genius should excite attention. Even cognoscenti, who know he made his stage debut with the one-act *In the Shadow of the Glen* in October 1903, have wondered how so assured a script could be delivered by unknown hands. While he was not unknown to W. B. Yeats and Augusta Gregory, they had been adamant two years earlier in rejecting a two-act play by Synge set in County Wicklow.[2]

Their adamance in 1901 gives rise to suspicion. Suspicion is further justified by the inconsistent way in which *When the Moon Has Set* is treated by latter-day editors. From the biographical point of view, the question can be formulated in two ways – when did Synge begin work on this play, and what (if any) were its sources? These issues bring together in a unique manner Synge's commitment to drama and his awareness of family history. The standard modern edition of his plays dates the conflate one-act version, which it prefers over other options, to 1900–1903. But the editor also accepts that 'letters of 1906 and 1907 ... echo early drafts of his first completed play, *When the Moon Has Set*, begun in notebook jottings when he first embarked on his journey to the continent'.[3] This would indicate the latter half of 1893 as the time when he became pre-occupied with a theme which remained with him for at least thirteen years. He got to work as soon as he was out of Ireland; more suggestively, he was, by coming of age, enabled to know the material facts of his inheritance, social and substantial. The period hummed with discussion of eviction, tenant proprietorship, and the anxieties of property. The play deals with a young man's inheritance of a country house, resulting from his uncle's death but interrupted by a deranged victim of the uncle's earlier behaviour. There is much business with lost wills, and a good deal of innuendo about illicit sexual relations between master and housemaid.

Summer holidays in the Wicklow countryside, as distinct from Greystones, had commenced after his twenty-first birthday. Synge was now in touch with local people living close to what had been family estates fifty years earlier. These contacts fanned outwards from Castle Kevin as he explored by bicycle and on foot. An early acquaintance was Mrs Rochford, who lived in a low thatched cottage on the hill behind the Castle. Known as Mavourneen from her use of that Gaelic term of endearment, she remembered the Famine of the 1840s. Synge wrote her nickname in a stricter orthography than others did, as if to signal a greater degree of sympathy.[4] Willie and Lissie Belton, Protestants whom Mrs Synge employed in menial capacities, were also close to hand.

Oral tradition has played a vital role in Anglo-Irish literature, acting as a bridge between two languages (Gaelic and English) and between different social groups (landlords and their tenants, residents and visitors to a given district). Through the Beltons and others, Synge augmented his bookish sense of the area. G. T. Stokes's accounts of the pre-Reformation Church explained the ruins near the Castle gate, but the lore of cottagers came closer to home. Honest Jack Tar, a tramp said to be a hundred years old, reminisced about the good times at Roundwood Park: 'I never went there but Mrs Synge offered me a glass of whiskey.'[5]

As holiday-makers, the Synges found themselves at once the audience and the material of these performances. According to Stephens, his grandmother heard of the house through Emily Synge who had taken nearby Uplands after her return from England in 1881. Synges owned land – little more than shooting facilities – in Ballinacorbeg and Tomriland. But there were other links. The elder Synge boys had been at Rathmines School with some of the Frizell boys when Land War evictions had taken place here. Though depredations had occurred after the Frizells fled Castle Kevin, these ceased when a local farmer, Harry Harding, was given management of the place. Even still, the house was boycotted when Mrs Synge agreed to rent it in July 1892. It scarcely needed folk wisdom to prove the liveliness of recent history as it might bear upon the new occupants.[6]

The Frizell family had transmitted the property at Castle Kevin through several generations, though not without legal argument. In 1892 the owner was the Rev. Charles William Frizell, with an address in Belfast; he it was who had fled during the disturbances of the previous decade. His grandfather had made a will in which he referred to 'Mr William Weeks' holding in Castle Kevin'. (This was a son of the Rev. Ambrose Weekes who had carefully cleaned his gun in 1798 before shooting rebels in Thomas Hugo's garden.[7]) Frizell had purchased Castle Kevin in 1789; earlier, 'Charles John Bentinck granted the said Estates to Luke Gavan and John Hatch'.[8] Little of this surfaced when the diplomatic Harry Stephens was negotiating on his mother-in-law's behalf. Nevertheless, local memory ran deep and clear. Mr Weekes's murderous activities were recalled by a schoolboy in 1938, who could point out one victim's grave 'in a white thorn bush in the field over the road to the right of the castle'.[9]

The decision to rent Castle Kevin stemmed from long-standing links between the owners of the house and the Synge family, which reached back to John Hatch, the dramatist's great-great-grandfather. On the one hand, the evidence merely confirms that 'Anglo-Ireland' was a small community, that everybody who mattered knew everybody else, and that this was true in 'church' circles such as linked the Synges, the Traills, and C. W. Frizell. On the other, the same evidence incorporates the death-dealing Reverend Weekes, albeit at a goodly distance in time. Such distances tend to be discounted in oral tradition, where a grave is preserved 'in a white thorn bush'. Synge heard many tales of his ancestors in Wicklow, intermingled with accounts of the famine and the rebellion of 1798. The tone adopted by his informants might be complaisant, even flattering, but the burden of their recitations was sometimes disturbing.

In fact, rural Wicklow (like Greystones before it) proved vulnerable to popular intrusion. In a notebook used at various times, Synge commenced a vignette of summer Sundays on the bridge at Annamoe, the little village which served Castle Kevin and Uplands. The picnic parties which had passed southward in the morning towards Glendalough returned 'in a condition [of] bestial drunkenness':

All the afternoon the ~~steady industrious~~ peasants who have laboured all the week among the sweet scents of the earth stand in rows upon the bridge and watch ~~with happy eyes~~ the procession of riotous women and young men that drives ~~on homeward~~ wildly to the city. The smell of the limes is blown across them, every moment some exquisite change in the ~~water~~ light upon the hills fills the stream with ~~blue and green designs~~ beauty yet these peasants stand with delated [sic] nostrils and pursed lips sucking the sad delirium of from the pageants of disease. Man is not made fashioned as are the swine and stars.[10]

The desperate search for aesthetic effect in nature, the insistent recognition of socially reprobated disease, a more specific focus on women – these features of the crude vignette recur in Synge's pre-mature writings. In the 1890s and early in the new century, when he was perfecting his idiom and outlook with painfully slow deliberation, the county his family had been so closely associated with fell victim to the tourist's bicycle and the organised excursion.

Wicklow's anomalous condition has sometimes been explained by the conjunction of close proximity to the capital with difficult and dangerous terrain in the form of mountains, tarns, and steep glens. Ribbons of cultivation ran through otherwise impenetrable barrenness. The houses of gentry nestled on river-banks near Enniskerry and, beyond Calary Bog, near Roundwood, Ashford and Rathdrum. Their estates were often secondary to other economic resources, professional or inherited. 'A low, straggling house of grey stone with a porch – quite unlike the usual kind of Irish house . . .' was how one of these Wicklow residences was described by Constance Gore-Booth, during the later Troubles, 'a sun-trap, in the midst of the bleakest mountain scenery'.[11]

The plaiting of prosperity and desolation in a twisted, vivid landscape was mirrored in the county's folklore where past and present could also intertwine. Synge published an article in *The Shanachie* (a quarterly magazine edited by Joseph Hone) entitled 'The People of the Glens', a collage of Wicklow impressions gained on different occasions, separated perhaps by years. Though he disguised the name of his informant, he published the man's account of the family's history:

'There are two branches of the Synges in the County Wicklow,' he said, and then he went on to tell me fragments of folk-lore connected with my forefathers. How a lady used to ride through Roundwood 'on a curious beast' to visit an uncle of hers in Roundwood Park, and how she married one of the Synges and got her weight in gold – eight stone of gold – as her dowry: stories that referred to events which took place more than a hundred years ago.[12]

Elements in this reminiscence certainly cleave closer to a pattern of folkloric story-telling than to historical narrative; the business of a woman's weight being equalled in gold occurs in a story Synge recorded on his first visit to the Aran Islands in 1898. But others unmistakably relate the fortunes of the house which Uncle Francis had been unable to recover in the post-Famine buying-back of his property in 1850.

The earlier history of Roundwood Park was even less reassuring. In the 1760s, the place belonged to John Hatch and his wife Barbara Synge (born 1731): their two daughters (Dorothy, died 1836 aged sixty-nine; and Elizabeth, 1766–1809) married their cousins, 'the brothers Francis and Samuel Synge, sons of their mother's brother Edward Synge D.D. ... Francis Synge and his bride [Elizabeth Hatch] moved to Co. Wicklow soon after their marriage in 1786 to live on the estate at Roundwood ...'[13] In this way, the family historian only confirms what the man on the roads had told John Synge – that Elizabeth Hatch was well provided for when she married Francis Synge.

Though 'The People of the Glens' was published as late as 1907, Nicholas Grene has calculated that the encounter between Synge and his informant occurred in the mountain village of Aughavannagh on 24 August 1901, and that the informant was eighty-two-year-old Patrick Kehoe (not Cavanagh, as the published essay has him name himself). Certainly, Synge spent that summer at Castle Kevin with his mother, returning to Dublin by bicycle on 6 September with his Stephens nephews.[14] His prompt departure a week later for Lady Gregory's country house at Coole Park in Galway is remarkable, for the play which she and Yeats rejected on that occasion was based on the same material which Patrick Kehoe – carrying an empty gallon can – had recited by the roadside.

The encounter with Kehoe confirmed sources which Synge had been working on, perhaps for as long as eight years. If it is not possible to identify exactly what these were, it is easy to state what they contained – an account of how Synge property in Wicklow descended from the eighteenth-century businessman and MP, John Hatch, and (more obscurely) how these had been acquired in the first place. The recent decision of Kathleen Synge to rent Castle Kevin had brought the family into touch with yet another of Hatch's properties; the fact that the solicitor was also her son-in-law increases the likelihood that the connection featured in conversation. Having rented the place over an eleven-year period, she and her son (aged thirty in 1901) were not unaware of its history.

John Hatch, sometime MP for Swords, County Dublin, was the son of the Temple family's factotum in Ireland, the latter much despised by Jonathan Swift. Stephens's manuscript biography of his uncle records basic details of how John Hatch came to be involved in the Roundwood properties. Some time around 1750, he and an 'old cousin' called Samuel M'Cracken acquired a house there, which they held for Luke Gardiner, a tenant of the Temple estate, also a major political figure and entrepreneur. Advancing in years, M'Cracken proposed to a grand-niece of Henry Hatch's but, if for no other reason than that she was very young, nothing resulted.

Throughout the 1760s, M'Cracken made a series of wills in which John Hatch featured as beneficiary. But in August 1769, a crisis arose from an illicit relationship between the old caretaker/proprietor of Roundwood and a young local woman, a servant in the house. M'Cracken consulted Hatch in Dublin, and was advised to complain at the Wicklow assizes about threats to his life. On Sunday 6 August, M'Cracken went to Derry-lossary Church, 'dined at home, read prayers to his family in the Evening went to bed about 9 o'clock and was found Dead on the floor of his bed Chamber next morning with his brains blown about and a Discharged Pistol by his side ...'[15]

Ibsen could not have asked for more – a brooding landscape, a brooding religion, a discharged gun. But the suicide (if such it was) did not result in a simple execution of the will in favour of Hatch. An unwitnessed will was discovered, and the proposed beneficiary of this second will (William Stewart, a nephew) eventually forged – or was believed to have forged – a third in the hope of giving effect to the second.[16] Meanwhile, John Hatch prospered. Then, in 1797, he resigned his directorship in the Royal Canal Company and resolved to deliver 'his' seat in the Irish Commons to his son-in-law, Francis Synge, who also became a director of the Company.[17]

While details from the 1770s obscure the exact nature of M'Cracken's household, and while his state of mind cannot be known, even as he had confessed his affair to Hatch, what is certain is that Hatch and his wife (Barbara Synge) owned Roundwood by the beginning of the decade. The uncle whom Elizabeth Hatch (wife of Francis Synge MP) visited can only have been a M'Cracken. Within a few days of his going to submit *When the Moon Has Set* to Yeats and Lady Gregory at Coole Park, the aspiring dramatist had run into a family ghost in folk-tale guise. And as late as the 1990s, Wicklow folklore could link the Synges to Thomas Hugo, the rapacious yeoman captain of 1798, by supposing a marriage into M'Cracken's extended family.[18]

While it is unlikely that the facts of M'Cracken's sad existence up on the mountain will ever be fully established, access to such documentation is highly suggestive. There can be no doubt that Stephens learned of these papers through his father, the solicitor who had handled the affairs of his mother-in-law Mrs Synge since 1883. In 1898 J. M. Synge conveyed to Stephens the web of town properties in Athlone already described in

Chapter Four. The evidence strongly argues that the solicitor described to the aspiring dramatist the circumstances in which the family had acquired properties which it had, by the 1880s and '90s, either lost or upon which it based marriage settlements. In short, Harry Stephens told Synge the story of Sam M'Cracken's death and the acquisition of Roundwood Park by John Hatch. It is immaterial whether the information was imparted through professional advice of a client or while the two reloaded shotguns during a weekend's sport on the mountain where M'Cracken died. Or to be more exact, it is precisely the relationship between formal advice and words spoken under a tree's protective shelter which characterised the protestant subset of the Irish middle classes. It was thus they muddled through, clad in tweed and – some of them at least – sadly in need.

We could even speculate as to the day on which Harry began to impart tidings of this doleful inheritance. Was it during January 1890 when, at his mother-in-law's behest, he took the eighteen-year-old aside and warned him against a career in music?[19] That would seem too early. Was it the night in August 1897 – later written up in 'An Autumn Night in the Hills'[20] – when the two men walked to the head of Glenmalure to collect a gun-dog wounded in an accident? Nicholas Grene has shown how the house in which the dog was looked after had played its part in the tumultuous events of 1798 as a hold-out position for the Protestant rebel, Joseph Holt.[21] This pioneer guerrilla leader had impudently kept winter quarters in the Devil's Glen, the romantic defile which leads up from one Synge property, Glanmore, towards the other – Roundwood Park. Evidence would suggest that the low-born Holt enjoyed some degree of protection from the Synges. The loneliness of Glenmalure, 'the fears of haunting and enchantment associated with desolate places, the danger of madness' ... carried over from 'An Autumn Night in the Hills' to In the Shadow of the Glen.[22] The political role of the house in 1798 was suppressed in the drama and the element of madness, feared or endured in the present, dispersed into other texts. The proprietors of this old mountain home were the Harneys to whom Synge had alluded in the ballad written at Oberwerth or Würzburg.

Like many ordinary Victorian families, the Synges knew madness as a distant kinsman, the unwanted child of ferocious repression or the orphan of medical negligence. Young Hutchie Synge underwent some prolonged childhood disturbance in the spring of 1897, when his mother was expecting her third child. During this period, the Cavan household moved en bloc to stay with Kathleen Synge, in contrast to the remote confinement

Nellie had endured during her first pregnancy nine years earlier. According to Hutchie, the folks in Crosthwaite Park 'were rather fond of saying people were mad'. Under the thin disguise of initials, he recorded some uncertainty about how 'W.D.' and 'R.T.' were viewed in this regard. Hutchie was inclined to associate JMS with his own mental condition, even to suppose a degree of identity between them. This tendency ran to excess, as when the nephew in adult years confided that JMS had 'held very odd and altogether ridiculous views upon me, believing me to be a changeling whom the happenings of his own life had somehow or other brought into existence . . . a sort of double being.' So there was a tale of ancestral despair in M'Cracken, the fear of madness in Synge himself, and the not unusual disturbances of an extended household briefly locked in upon itself for a pregnancy traumatic for at least one member of the family. All of this circulated round some occasion when Harry, in his bluff yet calculating businessman's way, told his brother-in-law about the family's past and present transactions in land and self-advancement.[23]

But no particular occasion is required, for the general circumstances were propitious to a gradual divulgence or to Synge's piecing together his history from diverse sources. Patrick Kehoe, on the roadside at Aughavannagh, had told stories not only to J. M. Synge but to an MP whose name Synge omitted from the published essay. William Joseph Corbet (born 1825), however, was not only a Parnellite who had sat for the county from 1880 to '92, he was a local historian, an energetic writer on the subject of insanity in Ireland and (to a lesser extent) its connection with sexuality.[24] Something of the eighteenth-century and Victorian Synges was bound to have been known to such an authority, and the suppression of Corbet's name cannot be judged merely a matter of decorum. The politics of 'killing Home Rule with kindness', as the process of reform was sometimes called, engendered an ambiguous balancing of termination and renewal. In the politician Michael Davitt's deliberately exaggerated phrase, 'the fall of feudal Ireland' could be sold to the former landlord class as a price they might be wise to pay as protection against the greater dangers of separatism. In 1902, some eighteenth-century Hatch rentals were found in the library at Glanmore, probably by Robert Synge who was trying to re-establish the family name there.[25]

Synge caught the bitter-sweet quality of these years in 'A Landlord's Garden in County Wicklow', written some time after the summer of 1901. Lithely entwining a meditation on the gentry's decline with a tale of stolen apples, the essay is a set-piece performance in his work, not unlike Maurya's final speech in *Riders to the Sea* though attentive to very different social realities. But the original act of depredation involved a young man who broke in to steal cherries, rather than apples, and one draft was called 'The Garden of the Dead'. The alterations which Synge made in these respects serve no function comparable to preserving the privacy of the Harneys. On the contrary, a political context is admitted in the published title of the piece, and the ironic-Edenesque possibilities of a garden break-in are hinted at by the specification of apples. Though now the two protagonists are young men of the same age, one the author and the other a thief, 'A Landlord's Garden' recalls the partnership in naturalist writing with Florence Ross in 1882.

As it happened, 1901 was to be the Synges' last summer at Castle Kevin. Since 1892 they had spent seven summers in the Frizell house, finding alternative accommodation in the Annamoe district when it was not available. One of these, Avonmore (once the home of the murderous rector, Ambrose Weekes), they shared with Harry Harding's family and, less amiably, with a mildly deranged lodger. 'These are the robbers,' John Drought greeted the family one summer on their arrival, 'they've been in gaol for a year.'[26] John Synge did not wholly dismiss this view of his ancestry. So the sad celebrant of 'A Landlord's Garden' was well qualified to narrate his guardianship of the apples and his discovery of an exact equal in the intruder – 'by sheer weight I brought him down at my feet, and an armful of masonry along with him. I caught him by the neck and tried to ask his name, but found we were too breathless to speak.'[27]

Synge ran into difficulties in trying to publish his Wicklow essays. As a title, 'The Garden of the Dead' may have compounded the problem. 'A Landlord's Garden in County Wicklow', on the other hand, was calculated to reawaken names which readers of the *Manchester Guardian* in 1907 would not wholly have forgotten – the association of Wicklow with land-lords rather than peasants, tinkers and fishermen, and in particular with one landlord who had died back in 1891. Charles Stewart Parnell's presence and absence broods over Synge's work a decade before James Joyce took on the task of transforming 'the Chief' into a symbol of the betrayed artist, and several decades before Yeats extended the process by celebrating him as a Gothic hero. As in Oscar Wilde's anonymous and decisively radical journalism of the 1880s, Synge's writings generally decline to give a name to this pervasive spirit. The exception occurs in Part Two of *The Aran Islands*. Synge has reached the city of Galway on his way back from the islands. 'It was the eve of the Parnell celebration in Dublin, and the town was full of excursionists ... A wild crowd was on the platform, surging round the train in every stage of intoxication ... The whole spirit of the west of Ireland, with its strange wildness and reserve, seemed moving in this single train to pay a last homage to the dead statesman of the east.'[28] 'Aunt Jane, who had often dandled ... Parnell on her lap at Glanmore, used to say years afterwards that she wished she had choked him in infancy.'[29] The Chief, however, had been dead for eight years when this incident occurred.

Mary King has been the only critic to suggest a connection between the anachronistic Parnell of *The Aran Islands* and *When the Moon Has Set*, the anomaly among Synge's plays, when she writes of 'social, political and religious guilt and fears of illegitimacy'.[30] To appreciate her argument, one should perhaps look back at the famous parable of the master and bondsman in *The Phenomenology of Spirit* (1807), fortified in knowing that Synge had read some Hegel also. By demonstrating how the Master depends on the Bondsman for his consciousness, the parable works to establish negativity and irony as motive forces in human self-creation. Mediation is a more relevant concept to the matter in hand. What is at issue is not Synge's philosophy, a system of personal beliefs against which his practice might be checked, but rather the already-existent practices of his writing, especially as they emerge into view with his first completed play. In particular, we need to scrutinise his dramatic (and so, mediated) presentation of social living and his explicit relating of biography to the art of writing.

In the notebook from which the vignette of peasants and picnickers has been quoted, Synge also worked on a three-act version of his play. What is recorded there amounts to a fairly full sketch of Act One – though the characters are simply (A) and (B) – and a less developed outline of Act Three – blank pages stand in for the middle portion. (A), who is a mouthpiece of Synge's, addresses (B), a nun in whom he invests romantically, employed to care for an old man dying off-stage:

There is no [one] in the house under seventy except ourselves   there are no girls or children in the district ... My family is dead   the country is dead. The turf bogs are stripped and the timber is cut down...[31]

Given Synge's difficulties with his mother's religion, what is remarkable in this early version is its retention of Christianity, not only as the justifying context of the nursing nun's profession, but also as (A)'s point of reference:

You are like people who live in a church and look out at the hills and river through quaintly stained rose windows   What you see is beautiful   you are sheltered from the rain and winds   every morning you see Christ appearing in the East. But there is another world the real world which we [learn?] to look at with white light and in it we have rain and wind and snow but we see all things . . . I wont send my soul to the workhouse while I have power to sustain it.[32]

This last detail of contemporary social realism serves to link the observations of economic ruination (turf and timber supplies exhausted) and the play's plot – of inheritance – in an unexpected convergence of religious and political themes:

(A): . . . I am celebate [sic] for another – liberty and for freedom of mind and body. Am I free? I have only changed the absolute monarchy of Christ for a democracy that sometimes ends in mob Rule in which the poet and saint in me is sometimes hardly treated. My only objection to absolute monarchy in real politics is that the monarch is likely to be a fool or [word illegible] a good monarch was perpetual would grant the greatest possible liberty to his people therefore as Christ has perpetual tenure I ought to welcome his authority. I dont, –
(B): He is dead.
(A): What a life he has had. I suppose It is a good thing that this Anglo-Irish aristocracy is dying out. They were neither human nor divine.[33]

At this point (B) 'hums middle theme of Chopin's Dead March'!

A great deal of work lay ahead before this impossible script achieved anything like a dramatic form. But Synge not only eliminated absurd props like an illustrated volume of Rabelais, he introduced the theme of biography as such and the historical outline of his own family's arrival in Glanmore and Roundwood. By the time we reach a version of the play sufficiently competent to be assimilated in what is now a two-act project, the first speaker is reading from a manuscript: 'Biography, even autobiography, cannot give this revelation, for the deeds of a man's lifetime are impersonal and abstract, might have been done by anyone, while art is the expression of the abstract beauty of the person . . .'[34]

It is a cumbrous dramatic moment set in an 'Old family library', and perhaps the play never recovers from its excess of literary self-reference. The characters, however, have acquired names. A slip of paper is discovered by the speaker (Sister Eileen) and her cousin (Colm Sweeny, the younger), and this in turn leads to the discovery of a box and – after a shooting and an interval between two acts to allow for convalescence – the reading of an undramatically long letter written by Colm Sweeny, the elder:

If you love a woman subdue her. You will not love a woman it is not lawful to love. No man of our blood has ever been unlawful. If you live in the country live with the country, and find a woman who will understand with you the mysteries of growth and life. Let her know as you will know the two twilights and the quietness of the night. Neglect nothing, for God is in the earth and not above it. In the wet elm leaves trailing in the lanes in autumn, in the deserted currents of the streams, and in the breaking out of the sap, there are joys that collect all the joy that is in religion and art . . . Be careful of my books. The dress and the rings were made for a woman I once hoped to marry. She was poor. She died afterwards, and her brother became crazy. He would have shot me but some vow restrained him. He thought I had wronged her . . .[35]

Little of this makes sense until one negatives it. Indeed the text begins this essential task for itself. No one has been unlawful, yet someone felt it right to shoot the innocent. Constrained from so doing, the outraged figure shoots a namesake of the man who has wronged his sister. Though old Sweeny implies that no wrong was done his beloved in the past, in the latter-day dramatis personae, Bride (aptly named though not legally married) is pregnant. The old story of Sam M'Cracken's love of a local woman, an affair provoking feelings of guilt and the use of a gun, is now distributed among two generations and several characters. It is rec- ognisably M'Cracken's story, down to such details as the delayed discovery of documents. While there is a great deal more in *When the Moon Has Set* which links the play to contemporary experiences of Synge's – among them the wicked baron of Oberwerth – underpinning the story are the eighteenth-century themes of inheritance, *mésalliance*, derangement and gun-play.

Critics of Synge's drama find it an embarrassing first contribution to world theatre, especially in its reliance on internally quoted texts, some in French. That it shares broad characteristics with Synge's last (unfinished) play, *Deirdre*, gives it additional interest. Yet as a product of his early years, in which he later invested a sick man's time and a good measure of emotional energy, it uniquely debates the relationship between (auto)biography and literature. *When the Moon Has Set* also combines the gentleman's library with the speech of servants and the passing exist- ence of persons confined to the roads or the county asylum. This gulf has been visualised in images of castles and cabins, big houses and mud hovels. Daniel J. Casey duly reinscribes Irish-America's stereotypical view of pre-independent Ireland not only by casting Synge into a family which had 'the wherewithal to carry on in true Ascendancy style' but also by pointing to 'intermarriage with the Hatches, who were land barons of standing'.[36] If John Hatch came to own swathes of property by the end of the eighteenth century, it was not by inheritance, but through the relentless pursuit of business. Of the 4,000-odd acres in Wicklow, the bulk was mountainside and bog.

It is pointless to charge John Hatch with high crimes and misdemeanours; the influence he exerted on Synge arose not out of proven wrongdoing but from the altered susceptibilities of an intervening full century. These were less accentuated in the dramatist's older brothers and mother. Even in *When the Moon Has Set*, where the family legacy is more thoroughly pried into than elsewhere, there is an unmistakable tone of special pleading. If 'the deeds of a man's lifetime are impersonal and abstract, might have been done by anyone', then the irregularities of the M'Cracken and Hatch cousins are amenable to a retrospective aesthetic. The art of the writer gives rise to 'the expression of the abstract beauty of the person'. This is little more than a crude statement of the anti-ethical philosophy of Walter Pater, though it is subtly attached to questions of inherited rather than personal guilt.

At another level, it is a paradoxical inscription of religious antinomianism, and this into a play determined on an extravagantly 'pagan' conclusion. For if extreme evangelicalism insisted on salvation by faith rather than works, then breaches of the Ten Commandments (law or *nomos*) could be laid aside, as if they had never occurred. Sister Eileen's reading from an aesthetic manuscript breaks off at exactly the point where the role of the writer is about to be considered. In the course of the play, there is much – too much – discussion of art, musical form, and literature. But the critic Mary King has pinpointed where the play picks up Friedrich Nietzsche's *The Birth of Tragedy* (1872) – 'whoever gives himself up entirely to the impression of a symphony seems to see all the possible events of life and the world take place in himself.'[37] The point is not well taken by the dramatist himself. 'The writer ...' – as Eileen had been about to discover at the opening of the play – disappears without comment. One reading of this immature, but highly revealing, play would be to see it as Synge's attempt to reconcile his position as a family heir at the secondary level (a youngest son, where Colm Sweeny is a nephew) with his individual desire for a specific sexual alliance. But in the course of tracing such a reading, we have uncovered the persistence, even pervasiveness, of the theme of property in all its Burkean inertia and with an additional codicil of delayed contamination.

An old man at Glanmore whom Stephens remembered 'often saw the master drive eight hundred pounds' worth of horses up to the door under the one whip'.[38] The master in question was Uncle Francis who had been obliged to buy back his own inheritance. There is no doubt that the young boys who had worked the estate and lived half wild in collective bothies saw the Synges as people of inexhaustible wealth, nor can one exaggerate the poverty of the urban poor and the displaced vagrants of the post-Famine countryside. In 'A Landlord's Garden in County Wicklow', Synge composed a disheartened lament for a class to which he has been invariably assigned by critics and biographers. His disagreements with Kathleen Synge and with his brothers have never been denied, but there remains a dimension to his analysis which deserves emphasis. When (A), in one of the several versions of *When the Moon Has Set*, observes, 'I suppose it is a good thing that this aristocracy is dying out. They were neither human nor divine',[39] we find that Synge had cancelled the specifying term Anglo-Irish. To be neither human nor divine, on the other hand, is hardly the conduct of a gentleman.

CHAPTER 9

French Leave
(1896–1903)

Murthering Irish. His image, wandering, he met. I mine. I met a fool i'
the forest.

James Joyce[1]

On New Year's Day 1895, despite a bad cough, Synge travelled by train out
of Germany to the French capital, home of the Folies and the Moulin
Rouge, equipped with introductions by the pious, cheerful Von Eickens.
Paris became a constant point of reference for seven years, while he did
not return to Oberwerth till within a few months of his death in 1909. He
chose to wander for a high proportion of his adult years, trying Koblenz,
Paris, London, Florence, and Rome. Always a product of coastal Wicklow
and suburban Dublin, he was sometimes a transient in his own home.

He had a broken experience of what happened around him. The Continent, the nation, the family, the ego bubbled and boiled over; he simply
moved from one back room to another. Ireland had gone through the
excitements of Parnell's fall in the early 1890s; between 1894 and 1899
France was riven by the Dreyfus Affair; Britain for the last portion of the
decade was preoccupied by the wars in South Africa. These events did
not pass him by, nor did he ignore them; he saw more than he admitted,
and he did not neglect politics even while he remained silent. In this,
indirect way, he was a true modern.

In some respects he mirrored the family's experience. Apart from Ned,
safely married among the Greystones Prices, who had transformed the
Synges' landowning past into a tolerably lucrative agency for others in
the present, Kathleen's sons each sought to fit in by moving around the
globe. Robert came and went, with the Argentine as polar opposite to
Kingstown. He worked land under the Southern Cross, which provided
a surrogate dignity in the face of losses in Wicklow and Galway. While
John was intermittently in Paris and Wicklow, Sam became the first
Church of Ireland minister ordained for the Church Missionary Society's

foreign fields. He left London on 23 October 1896 to take up his duties at Fu-Ning in southern China. Being on opposite sides of the world came to be the dominant relation between Synge and the brother he had been closest to as a child.

In evident breach of CMS rules, Sam married Mary Harmar the following April, having originally met her in the Molesworth Street Infirmary, Dublin, when both were studying medicine. Some energy went into explaining the apparent haste of a wedding 'so early . . . that a letter from the society in reply to our letters could not be received'.[2] The family propensity for early marriage did not fail Sam, even *in terris infidelibus*. From the bay-windows of Crosthwaite Park, the local demographic picture was of steady emigration, abandoned homesteads, late marriage and much adult celibacy. In the starkest contrast, the province of Fu-Kien was bigger by far than Ireland, with a population of more than twenty million. Much of the work involved what Sam termed 'itinerating', journeys through the Chinese countryside spreading the good news and treating disease, preaching God's love and amputating occasional limbs. The missionary not only left his home to labour in foreign fields, but endured risks which were no less real for their being taken in the name of a disguised imperialism. The Boxer Rising of 1898 was about to break on the Europeans scattered throughout China, and in May a boy was found in Fu-Chow with his throat cut and one leg missing. The CMS magazine coolly reported that a Chinese man 'was arrested at Nang-Wo, and under torture confessed that he was an accomplice to the crime'.[3] That brought an end to the suspicion directed at the missionaries, at least for a time.

During the early years of Sam's sojourn in China, the team were responsible for between seventy and eighty hospital beds, with about 700 patients and some 10,000 out-patients. Support from home was essential, both in guaranteeing supplies and in consolidating morale. In the early months of 1897, Mrs Synge collected six guineas. Under the leadership of Miss E. E. Yeates, the Dalkey 'Time and Talents' group put together aid-parcels. A Mrs Matheson, who was probably Mrs Synge's neighbour in Kingstown, featured more frequently as a donor.[4] Sam was emphatic in regarding the mission as an Irish enterprise, no less so than his Catholic counterparts in the western territories of the United States when they set up colonising associations.[5] A boat which Dr and Mrs Synge used for a rare local holiday was named the T. C. D. [as for Trinity College, Dublin], yet the Scottish Dr Mackenzie could chide Dublin readers of *Mercy and Truth* bluntly enough: 'it is not becoming to call this a T. C. D. hospital in its present condition. We hope that Irish surgeons and medical students will under-take to help this institution, which is probably the worst C. M. S. hospital in China.'[6] Alluding to the British introduction of Indian opium to China earlier in the nineteenth century, he remarked that 'a country which helped to place a yoke, grievous to be borne, on the people of this land ought certainly, through its mission agents, to see that each mission station is provided with an opium refuge ... Surely some of our Irish supporters are willing to contribute the necessary funds.'[7]

In due course John Synge would write a full-length play on the themes of pious itineracy and unheard-of cures. *The Well of the Saints* did not see the light of day until 1905, whereas early 1897 – the first months of his brother's sojourn in China – saw the future dramatist reluctantly entan-gled with Irish nationalist agitators in Paris. Having moved there at the beginning of 1895, he gradually saw the French capital as a possible second home. Though he sometimes stayed at the Hôtel Corneille, from the outset he sought to integrate himself into French domestic life. At first he lodged with the Arbeau family at 94 rue Lafayette in the tenth district. In the same month, he joined the Société Fraternelle d'Etudiants Protestants. The Von Eickens provided an introduction to Jean Monnier, an ordained minister and a professor in the faculty of Protestant theology of the university. Pastor Monnier signed Synge's Carte d'Entrée for the Society's 'Club' in rue de Vaugirard on 4 April, though the period of membership was given as the year from November to November 1894/5. Synge may have met the author of *La Descente aux enfers. Etude de pensée religieuse, d'art et de littérature* (1905) through the Cugniers, a Breton Protestant family whose acquaintance he made during the earliest phase of his first Paris sojourn – at the Von Eickens' request, Albert Cugnier had organised Synge's first accommodation in Paris.[8] His arrival in the city of Baudelaire was watched over by believers, devout Protestants. He was approaching his twenty-fourth birthday.

The first Paris residence lasted from 2 January to 28 June 1895. A legacy of £500, under the will of Aunt Jane who died in February, provided for semi-independent life, though he still relied on subs from home. On 24 March 1895, he wrote a morbid poem of more than one hundred lines about Saint Kevin, the fiercely misogynist patron of Glendalough.[9] At the beginning of the new month, he moved to 2 rue Léopold-Robert, slowly establishing himself in better accommodation. The back of his Carte d'Entrée carries the pencilled note: 'association pour la prop. des langues étrangères, rue Serpente'. Mystery surrounds the survival of this relic among *James Joyce*'s effects, as Synge and Joyce did not meet until several years after the expiry of the *carte*.[10] The teaching of English was a way of making a few francs which both young men pursued in Paris, and Synge may have used his old card to scribble a useful address for the new arrival from Dublin. That interpretation involves Synge's retaining some interest in, or even connection with, the Société Fraternelle d'Étudiants Protestants more than five years after his initial arrival.

In late April 1895, he enrolled at the Sorbonne for courses in modern French literature with Auguste Emile Faguet (1847–1916) and in medieval literature with Louis Petit de Julleville (1841–1901). Music was to be superseded by literature as the object of study. Yet it was language as such which held Synge's attention. He commenced work in general and comparative phonetics with Paul Passy (1859–1940) at the École Pratiques des Hautes-Études, and took private lessons in French conversation with Thérèse Beydon who in turn was keen to learn English from him. De Julleville had published an enormous quantity of material, covering topics from the history of Greece and French medieval comedy to the contemporary theatrical repertoire. The medieval source which Synge drew on for *The Well of the Saints* was a favourite topic of de Julleville's, whose work lent a shape to his intellectual development.[11]

All of this suggests a determined young man putting down roots in a new culture and in the most modern city in Europe. Yet old patterns, if not allegiances, were reasserting themselves. Beydon, an art teacher in a girls' school, was devoutly Protestant. Synge and she became fast friends after they began to exchange lessons on 3 June, yet his first sustained rebellion against regular church attendance followed in the summer of 1895 on his return to Wicklow and Castle Kevin. There were specific domestic irritations which may have prompted revolt, as well as the broader influence of foreign travel. Mrs Synge had rented Duff House, a farmhouse wonderfully placed close to Lough Dan. It was, however, owned by Catholics, and she was reluctant to invite Robert Synge's fiancée for fear that the beds might have fleas!

According to Stephens, Thérèse Beydon sympathised with feminism and interested herself in political matters.[12] In particular, she was concerned with efforts to organise the nursing profession, and her influence can be traced in Synge's various immature writings about nurses, including the nun/nurse of *When the Moon Has Set*. Paris offered a broad range of ideological options, and on Saturday 18 June he sampled revolutionary anarchism at a lecture by Sébastien Faure (1858–1942), author of *Le Douleur Universelle* (1892). Despite his own cultivated taste for dolour, Synge judged the event 'Très intéressant, mais fou' (very interesting but daft), with the *fou* underlined three times. Nevertheless, he wrote up the occasion for the *Dublin Daily Express*, which Maurice Bourgeois regarded as 'mere reporting, and not very good'.[13]

Quite how the Étudiants Protestants at 46 rue de Vaugirard reacted to their Irish visitor's interest in anarchism we shall never know. The 'Club' served as the focus of Synge's activities in Paris from 5 April until the end of his first Parisian residence. His diary and other records preserve little but names – Otto Boehrig, Albert Cugnier and his mother, Morik Dalmigere, Edward P. Denny, William R. Gourlay – and there is no suggestion of any liturgical activity, bible-reading or hymn-singing. Synge preserved his membership card, as if it encapsulated some rite of passage. The diversity of backgrounds – German, Breton, Irish, Scottish and so forth – suggests that the Club provided a social base for visitors (male only?) in a city better known for Catholicism and paganism. Only Denny, a shadowy figure of whom little is known, appears to have been a fellow Irishman; his name hints at a connection with the Dennys of Tralee Castle in County Kerry, whose most renowned representative was Sir Edward Denny (4th baronet, 1796–1889), a leading light among the early Plymouth Brethren, a writer of hymns and poems. It was the younger Denny who introduced Thérèse Beydon to Synge, and the two men kept in touch until 1898.

Other contacts in Paris had been set up by the Von Eickens. The young visitor was securely placed among respectable, even pious households on some of which he made social calls. From 1 April, he had been lodging with the Peter family in the fourteenth district. Whereas the Arbeau establishment had been cramped and uncomfortable – Arbeau, a cook, made extra cash by selling tooth-powder, while his wife made hats with Synge's occasional help – he kept in touch with the Peters, staying with them on a second visit and corresponding with Madame Peter when he was back in Wicklow. Life in Paris gave rise to various snatches of family legend at home – how he sat on a dish of butter, lacking a table to put it on, how he took a bottle of frozen milk into his bed to thaw it out for breakfast, and so forth.[14] Synge observed that the real benefit of living in Paris was that one could wear dirty clothes, the reaction of a gentleman no longer possessing any country estate on which to potter about in a briar-torn jacket.

At the end of June Synge carefully assembled certificates of attendance at the various courses he had followed, and prepared to return to Ireland for the summer vacation. He had been on visiting terms with Passy, evidently getting from him a list of addresses of others whom he might contact. The date of his departure followed directly after the completion of twice-weekly classes in phonetics. In a letter of farewell – written because he was too shy to speak to his teacher in front of others – he wrote: 'si vous désiriez quelque information à propos du Celtique ou de notre accent je vous prie de vous adresser à moi.'[15] As Synge's knowledge of contemporary or vernacular Gaelic was very limited – he would not reach Aran for another three years – the last part of his letter may reveal an interest in the phonetics of his own 'Anglo-Irish' speech, in this case the language of one too shy to speak. While in Paris, he had kept in close touch with home. Kathleen wrote as regularly to him as she did to Sam in more distant China. In return, Johnnie dutifully corresponded with his mother, resorting to a telegram in early February when some money had failed to turn up from Kingstown. In April, home funds provided £15 to meet his quarterly expenses at the Sorbonne. None of these letters survive, and Sam's later transcription of his mother's diary for the period omits all reference to the eight/nine weeks of May and June 1895.

The company he kept on his second excursion to Paris was very different to the safe milieu of the Société Fraternelle. The next year saw Synge passing to and fro through the city, first to Italy, then back to Ireland, and returning to France in late October. His base between 3 January and 3 February 1896 was a hotel beside the Odéon Théâtre, and during this period he began lessons in Italian. The Corneille was worlds away from the Société Fraternelle. Between the Paris of safe 'digs' and the Paris which his mother dreaded, Synge found accommodation, not, as has been alleged, in the hotel's attic, but *en pension* on a lower floor. The hotel had featured in George du Maurier's 1894 novel *Trilby*, and Miss Trilby had Irish blood. Though the resemblance would have shocked Kathleen Synge, Trilby's grandfather had been a medical doctor in holy orders, like her son Sam.[16] The Corneille was well known in different Irish circles as the base for John O'Leary (1830–1907), Fenian prisoner of the British and exile in France (till 1885), whose *Recollections* appeared in 1896. Here, according to an introduction Yeats wrote for *The Well of the Saints*, Yeats met Synge in 1899. Synge's more reliable diary gives 21 December 1896, though it misspells Yeats's name.[17] Maurice Bourgeois oddly proposed March 1898 as the date when the two met, perhaps to create a dramatic timetable in which Synge takes Yeats's too famous advice – 'Give up Paris' – and arrives on the Aran Islands in less than three months.[18] The truth moved rather more slowly.

Indicating that Paris as yet had no monopoly on his affections, Synge commenced Italian lessons with a Dr Meli, planning a two-month trip to Italy. His inspiration in this connection came from Cherrie Matheson, the neighbour in Kingstown to whom he would soon propose marriage. For the interim, he stayed on at the Corneille, and in preferring this arrangement to his previous reliance on private digs he gradually escaped into the larger life of the French capital, with its flotsam population, its venerable buildings, and its art treasures.

February 3 saw him installed in another hotel, this time in Rome, though after a few days he moved into lodgings on the via Aureliana. This short, quiet street lay halfway between the main railway station and the Borghese Gardens where he walked in less rigidly formalised urban parkland than that of Paris. His contacts in Italy had been set up by Cherrie. His landlord, a Count Polloni, provided language lessons, and the Collegio Romano courses in literature. He mixed in student circles, and tried his hand at journalism.[19] Riots prompted by Italy's defeat at the hands of the Ethiopians led to the fall of the government in March. As ever, first-hand evidence of Synge's feelings is very scarce. He kept his diary, laconic as ever, in German. He sent some kind of coded account of events to his Dublin-based Italian teacher, who was connected with the Academy of Music. A covering note ended: 'La prego di non mostrarlo a nessuno' (I ask you not to show it to anyone). Whatever he sent has not been recovered.[20] A letter to Thérèse Beydon outlined his movements, complained of American and English visitors, but said little more. The phrase 'avec l'aide de mon amie irlandaise j'ai trouvé cette maison ...' might suggest that Cherrie was in Rome at the same time, but more likely records a letter of introduction.[21] Protestant Kingstown was discreetly steering his exploration of the eternal city.

After Rome came Florence, 'quelque chose de [s]plendide, la ville [,] la ville les tableaux, les statues, tous charmants' as he enthused to Beydon.[22] While Synge's initial excursions to the Continent appear superficial, the effect is generated more by his own understated reactions than by any external measure. In addition to developing his considerable linguistic skills, he was absorbing the cultural history of western Europe, first in the Louvre, and now in the galleries and museums of Rome and Florence. As a student in Dublin, he had enjoyed very limited exposure to European art. His family was not attentive to painting or sculpture, and they had had reservations about his earlier commitment to music as a career. With Goethe's Letters from Italy as a too-ostentatious guide, he explored new perspectives on literature and life. On 26 February, he bought a copy of Petrarch, some of whose sonnets he would later render into a distinctive Hiberno-English literary idiom. On 3 March, he ventured to the Vatican and actually saw the Pope, spiritual and temporal head of that depraved

Church his mother was forever deploring.[23] And, as before, he read.

Though Italy played a relatively unimportant role in Synge's maturing, it features strongly in his nephew's biography. Though Synge had written in a notebook of how a scene in the Roman Campagna with an old man and a girl had formed for him 'a synthetic excitement of all my experience in Italy', the would-be biographer strove to inflate this limited aesthetic epiphany into a process of spiritual maturation.[24] What Synge as a subject of biography clearly needed was synthesis, unification of being – a self. For this reason, the translations of Petrarch are utilised to explain Synge's relations with the Plymouth 'Brother', Cherrie Matheson, though in Italy he was in contact with other women to whom he was able to express his heterodox views with greater ease. The first of these was an American named Capps whom he met in his Rome lodgings. At Florence, he made friends with Hope Rea, an English art historian, and Maria Zdanowska, a Polish student of sculpture. May was given over to the Pitti and Uffizi galleries, and conversations on religion during trips to Fiesole, and his plan was to return to Paris at the end of the month. Back this time in the Hôtel l'Univers (rue Gay-Lussac) by 3 June, Synge followed up his conversations with Capps, Rea, and Zdanowska by proposing marriage to Cherrie Matheson. His letter of 9 June led to one of rejection, both of which have disappeared. Synge's prolonged 'first love' deserves the closest attention, but for the moment the remainder of June 1896 had to be disposed of in Paris. He fell victim to a heavy cold, resumed his earlier routines, and set out for Kingstown and Wicklow.[25]

This was the last summer he spent with Sam, who had been ordained on 21 May, before the latter's departure in October for several years on the Chinese missions. The family had taken first Avonmore and then Castle Kevin, and he passed July, August and half of September with sundry members of the Synge–Stephens household in their Wicklow retreats. On Sunday 19 July, the newly reverend Samuel Synge preached at Laragh, but John absented himself from this proud occasion in their mother's life. Harry Stephens's occasional trips to his Dublin office left the horse and trap free for Synge to use, driving his sister and her children about the district. He and Harry fished Kelly's Lake.

The elements of a future dialectic were visible, though they would not develop into the happy, personal synthesis devised by Stephens who – as it happens – disliked Cherrie Matheson.[26] On the surface, it looked as if young John Synge was dividing his time sensibly between cultural holidays on the Continent and gentlemanly recreations in the Wicklow uplands. In due course, he would no doubt 'settle down' and finance the sustaining of this pattern through a respectable profession having, perhaps, sown a few wild oats. This was certainly the view of Hutchie Synge, who wrote of the Crosthwaite Park circle: 'at the time he [John Synge] does not seem to have had any desire to move out of it into what one might call an artistic circle.'[27] In November 1896, Kathleen Synge received a letter from 'poor Johnnie . . . he says he has gone back to Paris to study socialism and he wants to do good.' Sam's cautious editing – Synge's letter is lost – resorts to initials: 'A says he is so changeable and takes up with so many things he may get disgusted with it . . .' 'A' was probably cousin Anthony Traill. Unknown to Sam Synge and Edward Stephens at the time, their changeable kinsman was reading Karl Marx.

Yeats introduced Synge to Maud Gonne, the beautiful English colonel's daughter turned Irish firebrand, on 27 December. Two days later he resumed lodgings with the Peter family in the rue Léopold-Robert. The New Year of 1897 inaugurated L'Association irlandaise; Synge with Yeats waited on Maud Gonne whose Paris home sheltered this latest conspiracy. Though he appears to have assisted in drawing up a list of potential members, his reservations were evident by mid-March when Gonne agreed that his name should not be published in reports of meetings. St Patrick's Day (17 March) was sufficiently exceptional to allow him to attend a wreath-laying ceremony at the statue of Lazare Hoche, the French general whose revolutionary expedition to Ireland in December 1796 came to grief in stormy seas: Synge was among those who dined that night at Gonne's.[28] On 6 April 1897, he resigned. To judge from a draft of his letter to Gonne, he declined to 'get mixed up with a revolutionary and semi-military movement', insisting, however, that he wished 'to work in my own way for the cause of Ireland'.[29]

The letter does more than register his disagreement with 'physical force' nationalism. It suggests that he was already contemplating (if not actually writing) the play which we know as *When the Moon Has Set*. The musical motif which runs through successive drafts may owe something to the example of Michele Esposito, whose cantata 'Deirdre' was first performed in 1897. Synge's nervous, clumsy, highly-charged 'prentice work deals with the traumatic discoveries which a young Irishman, returning from Paris, makes in Wicklow. Certainly the Kingstown household was worried by his trend of thought. His mother had tackled him about becoming 'a rebel', but he sought again to reassure her by arguing that Ireland would 'come to her own in years to come when socialistic ideas spread in England . . .'[30]

Despite his differences with L'Association, Synge's new friends in Paris were recruited from the camouflaged ranks of Irish nationalist exiles. James Arthur Cree (died 1906) had qualified as a doctor in Dublin in 1892, the year of Synge's own graduation from Trinity College, and settled with his wife in Paris in 1895. Ann Saddlemyer has proposed Cree as the intermediary through whom Synge met both Stephen MacKenna and Yeats, though D. J. O'Donoghue also claimed the latter honour. Perhaps friendship with Cree had come initially through Samuel Synge's medical colleagues, or through George Cree's role in the Royal Irish Academy of Music, for in that way the disparity between the safely Protestant circle in which Synge moved during his first Paris sojourn and the nationalist circle of 1897 would be explained. Cree's family remained in Dublin, and Synge frequently ran errands for them as he moved to and fro. A pacifist as well as a nationalist, Cree was the nephew of George Coffey, Keeper of Irish Antiquities in the National Museum. As a friend, he certainly extended Synge's range of acquaintances even if, as a doctor, his advice proved useless.

By far the most important of the Parisian exiles whom Synge met was Stephen MacKenna (1872–1934), Liverpool-born journalist and later the dedicated translator of the third-century philosopher, Plotinus. A sturdier nationalist than Cree, MacKenna and Synge shared a chronic shortage of day-to-day funds. Competitive penury was a matter of pride; Yeats, in one of his tributes to Synge, describes him as 'even poorer than myself' at the time of their first meeting.[31]

Pathetically little of his Paris experiences can be recovered. The political involvement did not last, and MacKenna recorded with precision that 'Synge gently hated Miss Gonne' specifically for the lies she found it necessary to tell in advancing her cause. The penury did last, however, despite Aunt Jane's legacy and the bits of property in Athlone and in Mount Street. 'Synge lives on what MacKenna lends him, and MacKenna lives on what Synge pays him back' or so the anonymous legend has it. Though nothing is known of any friendship between Synge and Richard Irvine Best during their undergraduate days in Trinity, it was probably Best who brought the two middle-class paupers together in Paris. Best and MacKenna occupied adjacent apartments in the rue d'Assas: they were an odd pair, the one an Ulster Presbyterian studying Celtic, the other writing for an English Catholic magazine and preparing to be the great mediator of Neoplatonism. MacKenna rescued another Parisian down-and-out, an Armenian doctor, Michael Elmassian, whom he met destitute on the embankment, and all four – Best, Elmassian, MacKenna and Synge – chopped and changed accommodation. In practice, Best was comfortably off, and Synge was not without resources even if he could not convert them into ready cash. Elmassian died in 1913, director of a bacteriological institute in Paraguay.

MacKenna was already the translator of Thomas à Kempis's *Imitation of Christ*, a late-medieval work of piety which has appealed to Catholic and Protestant alike in Ireland. Though about thirty English-language editions had appeared over the centuries, MacKenna's version was published in Dublin in 1893. Synge had been reading a translation in November 1896 while staying at the Corneille; later he considered rendering the entire text into an Anglo-Irish literary dialect, but did not live to begin this puzzling work. Eclectic in more matters than the average mind can grasp, MacKenna was reading Lafcadio Hearn (1850–1904), the Greek-born orientalist of Irish background with whose family Synge liked to claim kinship through Harry Stephens. Hearn was perhaps in turn related to 'that excellent observer Hearne' whom Charles Darwin commended in the final volume of *The Descent of Man* (1871).[32]

These were footloose individuals, for whom Paris was a rite of passage and Ireland a loosely defined common heritage. In addition to MacKenna, there was Arthur Lynch on whom Synge often depended for supper. Arthur Alfred Lynch (1861–1934) – later 'the notorious Colonel Lynch' – had been born in Australia, the son of an engineer from County Clare and a Scottish mother. Once in Europe, he married an Anglican parson's daughter, and supported himself as Paris correspondent for the *Daily Mail* until 1899, when he decided to 'cover' the Boer War. Equipped with a camera, he travelled to South Africa and quickly joined the anti-British forces. Dublin Castle believed that 'no man of such importance in a revolutionary sense' visited Ireland from the mid-1880s till about 1893, a reputation acquired despite Lynch's 'good Eng. accent'.[33] But in the Paris of Synge's day he and his wife lived in rooms over James Whistler's former studio, and his recollections stress the Irish circle's occupation of what had really ceased to be La Bohème. With the casualness of a future doctor, he commented on his friend's appearance – his large head and a voice 'of a peculiar husky flatness'.[34]

Despite or because of his commitment to the Boers, Lynch was elected MP for Galway City in 1901 on a paper campaign which stressed the need for industrial and agricultural development in Ireland, and the expansion of technical education. Found guilty of high treason in 1903, he was condemned to death, though by June 1902 he was back in the relative safety of the rue Chaptal in Paris. Colonel Lynch later qualified as a doctor in London; he had been pardoned in 1907, the year in which he featured (unnamed) in the opening scene of *The Playboy* – 'fighting for the Boers, the like of the man beyond, was judged to be hanged, quartered, and drawn'.[35] Synge's continuing interest in Lynch's career took him well beyond the circle of Thérèse Beydon and Jean Monnier.

From Lynch and MacKenna we have an account of the one incident in Synge's external Paris existence which provides insight into his personality at this period. In April 1897, shortly after his resignation from Gonne's Association irlandaise, Synge and his friends were sitting at the Café Harcourt near the corner of the rue Champollion, while students and others were protesting against Turkish oppression of the Greeks. Given that MacKenna would shortly enlist for Greece, that Elmassian as an Armenian had no reason to be indifferent, and that Lynch was allegedly a member of the Irish Republican Brotherhood, these lookers-on cannot be written off as passive observers. In Lynch's recollection, the group has taken to the café terrace for the better protection of the weaker sex: 'I saw Synge standing pale and trembling. I put this down to nervousness at the time. He said nothing. It was only months afterwards that I learned that he had been struck on the head by one of the police, and the blow had been so violent as almost to have knocked him senseless ... he uttered no complaint, but had held himself together with desperate force, so as not to cause pain to the ladies.'[36]

Yet Synge never affiliated himself with La Bohème or the Rive Gauche. According to MacKenna, in his memoir of those days, Synge 'never sought but rather avoided the society of painters' and the aspect of French life typified by the boulevards of Paris – the cafés, the casual encounters, the *demi-monde* – 'was utterly repugnant to him [while] the Moulin Rouge he thought absurd and hateful.'[37] In contrast, April 1897 saw him attend a lecture by Anatole Le Braz which fired shy young John Synge with enough enthusiasm to approach the speaker afterwards. The Celtic Brittany of which Le Braz spoke could be interpreted as a middle ground between Paris and Ireland, or rather between the unseen hinterlands of western seaboards.[38] The plodding exercises for teachers in the Sorbonne, and the steadying role of his friend Best among the more volatile Irish exiles, all began to fall into a pattern.

Synge in this amorphous group looked different to every observer. To MacKenna he was 'most intensely Nationalist' whose hatred of England somehow led him to take part in the reception of Paul Kruger, President of the self-styled Boer Republic, in Paris.[39] Yet Lynch, whose credentials as an Irish MP condemned to death for fighting in the Boer cause are undeniable, thought Synge 'only mildly Nationalist': 'I cannot speak with certainty on this point, for although he was a visitor at our house, I seem to have no recollection of having ever discussed politics with him, and it is from Mrs Lynch that I have had the suggestion that Synge was critical rather in respect to our means than to our ultimate aim.'[40] Here too MacKenna concurs: '[Synge] tolerated my political activities, intense in desire though petty in effect, only because he knew that I never uttered the modish lie . . .'[41] For what it is worth, of the three – Lynch, MacKenna and Synge – only Synge was actually Irish by birth and upbringing.

There was a larger exile community in Paris than the Irish nationalist circle. The city had become a home-from-home for refugees of various kinds. English aesthetes and intellectuals like Arthur Symons had come in a new wave after the arrest of Oscar Wilde in 1895; following his release from prison two years later, Wilde moved to France, staying first in Berneval, and later in Paris where he died in 1900. Synge had no traceable, or even half-likely, contact with these sexual escapees from Victorian England – though Wilde was an Irish writer and had been (briefly) a student at Trinity College. Predictably the young diarist from Kingstown makes no reference to his notorious fellow Dubliner, and Wilde had no reason to notice someone who had scarcely taken the lid off an ink-bottle. Yet Best, who was a little vain with his golden hair and boyish pink complexion, reported an incident in a café when 'Oscar Wilde looked at me'.[42]

Wilde had spent part of his childhood in Mayo. The divisions between the Rive Gauche and the west of Ireland can be pressed too far. The France to which Synge retired each year had its own perspective on Ireland; indeed, cultural interchanges between the two countries were and are more complex than bald summary could indicate. The ambassadors who shuttled from Paris to Aran included Devonshire-born Arthur Symons. With Yeats and others, Symons had set out from Cashla Bay, County Galway, in Tom Joyce's hooker – a distinctive west of Ireland seafaring sailboat – in August 1896. The avant-garde magazine, *The Savoy* brought Verlaine, the Aran Islands, and Nietzsche before the English public as though this were a natural coalition in the face of pompous and brutal authority. French leave might be taken in Connacht. Symons's best remembered work, *The Symbolist Movement in Literature* (1899), was avidly read in Dublin and its author 'became a sort of god of the younger college set'.[43] The nearest the two dramatists come to meeting is in the claim that Synge persuaded Albert Cugnier 'to write a French translation of Oscar Wilde's *Intentions*', a volume of critico-philosophical essays and dialogues, 'which he actually helped him with. Whether the translation was published or not we cannot say . . .'[44]

Although we know comparatively little of the Parisian lives led by Wilde, Beardsley, and other transient exiles, their names conjure up the 1890s *demi-monde* of bars, brothels, cafés and cheap hotels.[45] MacKenna insists that the Moulin Rouge was hateful to Synge, yet the diaries suggest that he nevertheless had been there – on 9 April 1898. The previous month he had been 'Au cabaret des Noctambules'.[46] Entries noting, with characteristic terseness, 'la robe verte' have been the subject of occasional speculation – might they encode meetings with an unnameable woman of the night?[47] The biographies deriving from Stephens's dossier tend to assume that these entries simply record a meeting (conversation, meal, drink, etc.) with one of the women who befriended him in Paris – the American art student, Margaret Hardon. On the other hand, his visit to the Moulin Rouge had followed after a dinner with 'les Beydons', a diary entry which links pious Thérèse Beydon to the nightclubs (at least in his mind) but which also indicates that Synge visited her *en famille*. A *robe verte* is not easily pinned down as a signifier of excursions into the *demi-monde*. But a green robe – wedding dress, by context – will also feature in *When the Moon Has Set*, and green connotes far more than it might denote as a code for Margaret or Thérèse.

Green was the national colour of Ireland, allegedly in tribute to the freshness of its verdure, and also a colour associated by Wilde with superstition. In France, it was the colour of absinthe and of decadence. 'La langue verte' was the idiolect of pornography. What these various readings share is a context of subversion, of resistance to formal codes and authorities. If 'la robe verte' in the diaries does not just refer to Margaret Hardon, and does not refer to illicit sex, it might still allude to the *demi-monde*, to the *café-concerts* where *diseuses* like the famous Yvette Guilbert (1867–1944) and the less-celebrated May Belfort performed. Guilbert was exceptional in her thinness, heightened by her long black gloves, and set off by her distinctive green dress. Belfort was Irish and lesbian. Both singers included English material – for example, 'Linger Longer, Loo' – in their repertoire, and both featured in Toulouse-Lautrec's albums of the late 1890s.[48] The 'robe verte' or 'gants noirs' were trademarks of Guilbert's cabaret art, and the painter intensified their metonymic significance by allowing the gloves to become subjects of portrayal in their own right, disembodied items of clothing caught in the act of masquerading as limbs.

Elegance and the grotesque, body and amputation, the exotic and the parochial – half-a-dozen such pairings of the extreme surrounded Synge in Paris, albeit at a distance, on a broad circumference to which he never refers. Wilde (6' 3"), Lautrec (4' 11") and Guilbert (the ugliest woman in the world, said Oscar) were sketched in an 1898 café by Ricardo Opisso. But remote things provoked intimate recognitions. The entire spiritual milieu of the Parisian 'Bohème' derived not from Czech-speaking Bohemia, but from the gypsies (cf. Synge's tinkers) who formed part of its early population.[49] There were links between Parisian care-freedom and Irish subsistence. Synge's later equation of the beggar and the artist did not spring from nowhere.

Late April and May 1898 saw Lautrec (1864–1901) featured in a London exhibition which included at least four 'portraits' of May Belfort and three pictures of scenes at the Moulin Rouge. But Synge was safely at home in Kingstown by 23 April, having travelled through London before the opening at the Goupil Gallery on 30 April. It may seem impossible to link these scandalous *objets d'art* – mere posters, some of them – to the sublimity of *Riders to the Sea* or *Deirdre of the Sorrows*. Yet the role of physical objects, including items of human clothing – a green dress, stockings, 'a piece of a grey thread and a sharp needle', red petticoats, 'sorrow like a shoe that is worn out and muddy', a riot-provoking shift – in Synge's drama and the drama of Synge's career cannot be exaggerated.[50] It may seem – again – impossible to link the counting of stitches in an Aran cottage to the high jinks of the Moulin Rouge. W. B. Yeats found a place for another *diseuse* of the 1890s, Loïe Fuller, in 'Nineteen Hundred and Nineteen', a poem committed to investigating the violent consequences for a culture in failing to see links between high and low, disease and health, peace and degeneration. Perhaps the dwarfish and deformed Lautrec exercised his own profound influence on the Olympians of Coole Park. The *soi-disant* Anglo-Irish Ascendancy from which Gregory, Synge and Yeats hailed was itself in a state of degeneracy, loyal neither to nation nor Empire, resentfully bewitched by the power each claimed for itself. Synge's fondness for Paris, his locating himself close to (but never quite in) La Bohème, and his impartial silence on matters of conduct, formed the basis from which he viewed a collapsing world.

On his return to Dublin in the late spring of 1897, he met (probably for the first time) his nephew, E. H. Synge. Hutchie was then almost seven years of age and – according to his own later but qualified judgement – already experiencing behavioural difficulties. 'I cried a great deal in those years, but my mind was never clouded in the slightest.' Back from Paris, having undergone a year of bruising emotional experience, Synge (again according to Hutchie) acquired an interest in the occult which was prompted by his nephew's condition or behaviour. What lies behind these fifty-year-old recollections is, I believe, less Synge's interest in the occult (though he did borrow books from MacKenna) than in alienation *per se*. What Hutchie confused was his own existence with the birth of his brother, which did indeed occur about a month before Synge's arrival home from the Continent. Hutchie's tears 'in those years' were eloquent and moving evidence of the human mind's exposure to forces beyond its control, yet which also appeared to arise from within. Anxieties stemming from an awareness of Darwin's theories of evolution and 'the survival of the fittest' sought nervously to translate themselves into paradoxes about the sanity of a man who wrongly believes himself mad. Sudden references to the then-current term 'alienation' were not solely based on self-exam- ination, though Synge's own bodily health gave cause for concern in not unrelated ways.[51] Hutchie's account of his uncle, fragmentary and surviving only in typescript copies made after his death, hints at an alternative view of Synge's French exile.

The years in Paris, or rather the regular half-years, not only proclaimed a rational determination to cut loose from inherited traditions re-enacted daily in family rituals. They became the young man's means of dealing with his inability to fit into conventional domestic life. This inability was not simply intellectual but, in a convenient euphemism, behavioural. Synge was indirectly encouraged to keep at a distance, even to the extent of being financed in pursuits his mother could not morally endorse. Only when he was recognised as a master of world theatre could his wanderings be depicted as a form of apprenticeship.

The latter part of 1897 was dominated by the first of what was to prove a life-long, or life-short, series of treatments in the Mount Street Nursing Home. Early summer in Dublin allowed him to develop his association with Yeats and even Maud Gonne; they met in the Contemporary Club, a debating shop where some leading ideas of the emergent Irish Literary Revival were teased out. His initial contact with the club was more likely through Edith Oldham who taught in the Academy – her father was the club's founding father – or John F. Taylor (1850–1902), a contemporary at Trinity. 'The well-known Irish orator' was an advocate of the Gaelic language whose personality none the less impressed James Joyce.[52] At this time Synge also met George William Russell, the mystic painter and poet who used the signature A E: the two attended Dublin's Theosophical Club.

Change was in the air. A 'Feis Cheoil' (or music festival) held in May was written up by C. H. Oldham in Maud Gonne's *L'Irlande Libre*.[53] The lapidary style of diary-keeping which Synge now practised led him to record the first baton-charge he had ever witnessed at home with the words 'To town – evening.' Protesters against the Queen's Jubilee, led by the socialist James Connolly (1868–1916), had tried to stage a mock funeral of John Bull.[54] Dublin was imitating Paris.

Wicklow brought relief. Part of its charm lay in its predictability – the same streams to be fished, the same stars to be gazed at during the same late-evening conversations. To MacKenna, Synge confided that the family's occasional guests made him long for 'a breath of the wickedness of Paris'.[55] Yet holidays were not uninterrupted exercises in pious sleep-walking. The summer was divided between two houses close to the des-erted-but-not-empty mansion of C. S. Parnell, who had died in 1891. Harry Stephens disliked staying in Casino, a steward's house; 'his visits, which created a sense of unrest in the family party, were not long.' Monthly rental for one accommodation, and then another, underlined the tem-porary nature of this tranquillity. Seizing a piece of green silk which Mrs Synge used for a dinner-table decoration, her grandchildren ran about shouting 'Who Fears to Speak of '98?' It was a nervous season.[56]

Synge's badly swollen glands prevented any rapid escape to Paris. His hair fell out, and surgery was recommended. 'Some members of the family attributed [his symptoms] to distress of mind about his sad love affair' with Cherrie Matheson. MacKenna supplied lists of books for him to read, but the uncertainty continued until finally admission to the nursing home could not be avoided. As a patient, he immersed himself in Spinoza's *Ethics*, went under the knife on Saturday 11 December 1897, and returned home for Christmas with a scarf round his scarred neck.[57] Edward Stephens, who was just turned nine, decided this was another nationalist emblem, like the table-silk; his accusation that Uncle John had been away in gaol supplied the Christmas dinner-table with a badly needed laugh.

As in Orwell Park, the Synge and Stephens households in Crosthwaite Park were linked by a 'cross-door' between the adjoining houses. The grandchildren came for religious instruction round Mrs Synge's table every Sunday morning for an hour. It is from the period immediately after Synge's first operation that his nephew recalled her insistence on the literal truth of the Bible and the horrors of damnation. 'Some people will reject Christ's offer of salvation and will be lost for ever,' she advised the nine-year-old, his brother, and asthmatic sister. As she admitted to Robert in Argentina, 'Johnnie ... is very impatient to be off.' On 19 January 1898, he was off – via London where he saw Hope Rea (whom his mother disapproved of, sight unseen) and Yeats – back to Paris.[58]

The diaries continue in their economical fashion, rarely giving more than a detail of reading, a place visited, neither exceptional in most cases. But the single word, 'Ecrit', also emerges, a translinguistic admission of Synge's attempts to write. By the time he returned to Dublin in late April he was (in Ann Saddlemyer's view) half in love with the American Margaret Hardon. He began to compile the strange fragmentary dossiers of prose-and-poem, 'Vita Vecchia' and 'Etude Morbide', the ostentatiously foreign titles of which are exercises in projection and distancing. What is striking in all these texts is the absence of a father. According to Alan Price, editor of Synge's prose, the origins of the 'Etude' can be traced back to 1897, and certainly to Paris. The earliest version opens with references to a young man on the Boulevard Saint Michel in May – the month Synge usually quit France for Ireland. Much of the morbidity of the 'Etude' arises from the absence or near-absence of Self.

Unlike the 1897 version, 'Etude' at its fullest is written in the first person because Synge cast it as an imaginary diary – the subtitle, echoing Walter Pater, is 'An Imaginary Portrait'. The contradiction between a diary and a portrait, the one centred on Self and the other on the Other, is pervasive. The Diarist is located between two women – the Chouska and the Celliniani – who address contrasting sides of his uneasy personality. 'A man with two friends of different tendencies is developed in opposite ways neither of which is really his own.'[59] Geographical locations complicate the pattern further – 'When I am here I do not think without a shudder of the books of Baudelaire or Huysmans. Among heather I experience things that are divine, yet I know not how I should express them.'[60]

The third-person narrative of the 1897 'Etude' records an ideal liaison:

She was not clothed like the women of the streets, and in her face there was a surprising joy without trace of provocation. He went out and joined her and they went down the boulevard with her arm in his. Till that night he had never made advances or casual acquaintance on the ways but in this woman he saw the presence that had filled his dreams and he had not force to quit her.[61]

This is no more to be trusted as autobiographical than any other 'prentice work; what it reveals is wish-unfulfilment rather than braggart confession. The passage might be read as a rewriting, in comparatively non-decadent terms, of poems by Baudelaire – 'A une passante' (from the *Tableaux Parisiens*) for example. The young man is dogged by dreams and nightmares, and the woman's double soon emerges. In a later version of the 'Etude', sexual material is divided between the two named women, one of whom is associated with green cloth. This figure – on other evidence identified by Stephens as Margaret Hardon – dies unexpectedly, only to have her essence somehow re-established in the surviving woman who had been her opposite. Perhaps it comes as no surprise that the Diarist muses on the paradoxes of insanity:

Nov. 30. A man is mad who believes that he has a disease which he is really without. Suppose he believes himself insane. Is he mad? If so his conviction is well founded and he is so far sane. Is he sane? Then he believes delusively that he [is] mad: therefore he is mad. Are these the uses of adversity?[62]

The entry for the next day records readings in the work of Herbert Spencer. A few days later, the Diarist writes:

My brain by some horrible decadence is grown a register for appalling things, and my almost preternatural destiny throws such things continually about me. In the newspapers I read of men who have gone mad and slain their kindred; in reviews I find analysis of nerve decay; if I go among the streets I fall in with wretched beings on the brink of total alienation.[63]

These sentiments are attached to, and detached from, their author. They constitute emotions of which he is capable but which he experiences only as imaginary emotions. Yet to imagine 'the brink of total alienation' is to some degree to have reached it, to have approached it in, or for, one's self. Two themes protrude from the doughy prose with painful clarity – the fear of a disease somehow related to insanity; and the recognition of other people some of whom have killed their kindred. The logic of the Diarist in relation to madness and disease is faulty in the extreme. Or rather, his knowledge of human folly is inadequate, for it is not uncommon for people to believe they are ill when they are tolerably well. Hypochondriacs do it every day of the week. But if the illness were linked causally to some form of madness, then at least the Diarist's anxiety would be understandable, despite his evident reluctance to specify any such illness – a congenital condition, perhaps. The two themes had come together before, in Synge's response to Darwin.

While the sexual and philosophical aspects of the 'Étude' naturally attract attention to themselves, the formal profession of the Diarist should not be ignored. Like Synge in the year or so immediately after graduation, he is committed to the vocation of music. But whereas Synge had suffered agonies of apprehension during his brief foray into public performance, the Diarist 'had an absolute success' – at least on one occasion. Ten years later, as he lies awaiting the surgeon's knife, Synge will urge W. B. Yeats not rashly to print 'a morbid thing about a mad fiddler in Paris' – this is it, or at least one version of it.[64] As Mary King has demonstrated, the musical analogies of *When the Moon Has Set* run back into the prose pseudo-fictions of the 1890s. Seen in that cultural context, they link Synge's initial literary efforts to the Symbolist movement, both French and English. The analogies seek awkwardly to enact Théophile Gautier's doctrine of transposition, or earnestly to recommend Walter Pater's borrowed programme of artistic *Anders-streben* – whereby the arts mutually enrich each other in a breakdown of trivial, external boundaries.[65] Gautier (1811–72) and Pater (1839–94) lie beyond the declared frame of reference in the 'Etude'. But Baudelaire and Huysmans, even more trenchant anti-naturalists, are prominently invoked.

Writing in the *Fortnightly Review*, Arthur Symons in his role as obituarist of Aubrey Beardsley extended the practice of giving the graphic arts a shove in their aspiration to the condition of music. That was in May 1898, a week or two before Synge departed from Dublin for the Aran Islands – to which Symons had been an early visitor with Yeats in August 1896. All in all, Synge's preoccupation with the figure of the musician is of a piece with the 1890s' Aesthetic/Decadent movement in the arts generally.[66] Yet, before moving to Paris from Koblenz, he had more or less abandoned music as a possible career. Music, of course, was in as great a turmoil of imminent transformation as any of the arts; the solemnities of Brahms were soon to give way to Mahler, Richard Strauss and Schoenberg. There was as much to fear in music as there was in literalism.

During 1898, the most important event of Synge's life took him to Aran for the first time. The earlier part of the year had been spent in Paris, and the late summer in County Wicklow with his mother and other members of the family. On 18 November he took over Richard Best's rooms at 90 rue d'Assas, which became his permanent address in Paris until, in the spring of 1903, he gave up the pattern of thus dividing his time. Synge's Paris was a relatively small place, mainly lying within the V and VI *arrondissements*, with the Luxembourg Gardens at its centre. From the Hôtel Corneille to the Etudiants Protestants on the rue Vaugirard was a walk of five minutes, past No. 8 where Knut Hamsun stayed in 1895: the apartment on the rue d'Assas (in a building no longer standing) lay perhaps five or eight minutes further away, beyond the Senate building. Only when he once stayed in the rue des Martyrs premises of some nationalist associates did he stray towards northern Paris and Montmartre, a district of 'lorettes' (prostitutes) ironically named from the church dedicated to Notre Dame de Lorette under whose shadow he slept that night.

Though the attraction of Aran deserves close attention in another chapter, and Cherrie Matheson's rejection of marriage cannot be ignored as a motivation sending him westward, foreign residence continued to appeal. Illness, theatre business, and a belief in Molly Allgood's love for him curtailed his travels abroad from 1905 onwards. The Yeatsian notion of Synge as a 'rooted man' is sentimental. The diary structure of the 'Etude' suggests that he wrote portions of it in Paris, Wicklow and Brittany, though only Paris can be confidently identified. His visit to Brittany in April 1899 confirmed his interest in the Celtic margins as an imaginative canvas on which he might work.

Although travel, movement, restlessness play a large part in Synge's vision of life, his own excursions hither and thither are less important than might first appear to be the case. The evidence of works both published and (until recently) unpublished confirm this view. His pre-dramatic writings – notably the 'Etude', 'Vita Vecchia', and an abortive novel about nurses – do not attach themselves to places in any significant or revealing way. The editor of his prose was inclined to date the 'Etude' initially to 1897–8, but preferred to publish a text he dated to 1899, itself 'partly revised, probably in 1907'. The entry 'Nov. 19', which uniquely specifies a day of the week ('A Sunday of delicious rain ...'), could be solemnly dated to 1895, 1901, or 1907. By this last date, of course, Synge had given up his Paris excursions; he was tied to Ireland and the Abbey Theatre, hoping to marry Molly. However, any attempt to correlate dates and places in the 'Etude' with Synge's movements breaks down on particular details; for example, the entry recording the Diarist's journey to Finisterre (in Brittany where Synge was in 1899) cannot be reconciled with either Sunday 19 November in 1895 or 1901.

In practice, the word 'Finisterre' is to be read allegorically as 'the end of the earth', an extremity, a reformulation in topographical terms of that restless despair which smoulders throughout the early writings. They are both fictitious and confessional, to be compared perhaps to the heartbroken cries of a doll for the absent ventriloquist. The other minor work, 'Vita Vecchia', contributes to the same paradox. There is no reason why we can't treat either of these two strange compilations as the later; they relate to each other less in sequence and more in complementarity. One uses the form of a diary; the other links fourteen poems by means of a prose narrative. Neither can be authoritatively dated, but both relate to

Synge's alternations between France and Ireland, between one woman friend and another, between music and literature.

'Vita Vecchia' [The Old Life] echoes in its title Dante's *Vita Nuova*. Whereas the Italian master traced the spiritual understanding derived from carnal desire, the Irish epigone does little more than imitate occasionally the outward shape of sonnet-and-prose. The intimacy and formality of the early Renaissance city is replaced by a scattered set of locations, the tenderness of Dante's affections by abrupt and coy locutions – 'this second person that I dreamed of'. Inevitably the 'Vita' has been read as disguised autobiography, even though Synge is not known ever to have set foot in Venice where much of the 'action' occurs. He had read Ruskin's *Stones of Venice*, and made unremarkable notes; more suggestively, these occur alongside three gnomic utterances about Dante which he may have transcribed rather than thought up for himself. Part of Ruskin's project was the construction of a 'Protestant' Renaissance and pre-Renaissance.[67]

Hutchie Synge believed that 'A young girl of the Roman Catholic Church' in the first sentence of the 'Vita Vecchia' is Cherrie Matheson, even though Cherrie was devotedly attached to the Plymouth Brethren. The account of a musical performance for the beloved, interrupted by children, exactly echoes an incident recorded by Stephens when he disturbed his uncle and Cherrie in Castle Kevin. Cherrie is undoubtedly present, but she is refracted, incomplete, desired, and so absent also. Loss, or intervening anxiety, holds the writer apart. A reference to a High Mass celebrated in Rome 'for the princes that had been killed in the Abyssinian war' would appear to date itself to 1895 or 1896, when the Italians invaded with disastrous consequences for themselves. Synge was in Rome in March 1896 and witnessed public protests at the conduct of the war. This recasting of Cherrie Matheson as a Catholic goes some way towards clarifying her contribution to *When the Moon Has Set*, where Sister Eileen obliges the hero – as no woman does in the 'Vita' – by marrying him.[68]

Sexuality pervades the 'Vita', alongside less predictable thoughts on fertility. One of the fourteen poems affirms childlessness:

> Cold, joyless I will live, though clean,
> Nor, by my marriage, mould to earth
> Young lives to see what I have seen,
> To curse – as I have cursed – their birth.[69]

On the condition of men, the Writer speaks of 'the offspring we have borne in travail darker than a woman's ...' And elsewhere in the thousand or so words making up the 'Vita', he writes: 'I am haunted by the briefness of my world ...' The possibility of fatherhood is not dismissed, though the achievement is considered more as a release than a fulfilment:

This person that I am now will not be next year, and the child that I was twenty years ago has perished and left no trace but the scars upon my body and my mind. If I should beget a child who resembles me he would be a more real survival of my childhood than I am. His body would have passed out of my body as directly, in a certain sense, as my present body has passed out of the body of my childhood. He would have fair hair and skin as I had, not the dark hair and sallow skin that I have...[70]

Synge's disturbed state at this period is not only deduced from the suspect process of reading literary constructs for biographical purposes. His nephew Hutchie believed that, in the church where Mass for the dead at Adowa was celebrated, Synge saw 'a woman kneeling ... who reminded him of the person whose letter he had been awaiting'. This shock led to the writing of a poem Hutchie quotes as:

> I heard low music wail
> Woe-wanton, wed to fear
> Heard chords to cleave and quail
> Quelled by terror sheer
> Like unto thine that form
> Far under mine that woe
> My terror's rage and storm
> Stern gods had died to know.[71]

The Italian woman's grief and presumed bereavement becomes an object-ive correlative for the young man's inexpressible loss in not hearing from his beloved. The fact that Cherrie Matheson did, in time, write – though to shatter Synge's hopes – is further substantiated by Hutchie's notebook. For he claims, again with every evidence of accuracy despite his own legal status as a certified person, that Harry Stephens had been instrumental both in consulting the Matheson family's wishes and in relaying or con-firming the bad news to Rome.

Too much of Synge's writing from the Paris period involves indulgence of, or submission to, reading. Close to the end of the 'Vita Vecchia' manuscript as it survives, Synge writes: 'I used to lie in the evening while my nurse sat in her white veil by the window with the twilight on the hills behind her and read out old books from my uncle's library.'[72] As reading displaced writing, so Ireland repeatedly drew Synge back from Paris. The long summer of 1899 was spent once again in Castle Kevin, but on this occasion Mrs Synge had other young guests, notably Sam's sister-in-law Edie Harmar (1870–1963) and Edie's friend, Madeleine Kerr, both from the London suburb of Norwood. There were mild visionary experiences. One evening Madeleine came across Synge apparently transfixed in the porch of the house, gazing with a ghastly appearance into the mist. Sexual tension was in the air, not eased by the arrival of letters from Margaret Hardon, the American in Paris. Young Edward Stephens gadded from one cottage of Protestant neighbours to another, warned never to mix with tinkers or the like. His uncle was planning a second trip to Aran.

'Johnnie went early to town and got his money from Harry [Stephens] ... rode over to Robert to say good bye.'[73] Synge's funds were managed by his non-pious brother-in-law, while the head of the family still deserved a valedictory salute. By early November 1899, he was back in Paris, avoiding the family's Christmas and continuing with the 'Étude', probably with the 'Vita' also. In spring 1900, Cherrie Matheson was returning to Ireland from the South of France where she had wintered. On 1 May, when she and her father attended the opening of the Salon, they caught sight of Synge. In her recollections, she noted 'the glimpse I had of him ... in his Capuchin cloak, with his head turned towards the man he was with speaking rapidly all the time.'[74] The anguish caused by her rejection of him may be discerned in the 'Vita' where the Writer reports of the Lady:

One night I went back to the town where she lodged, and went to look upon her door. As I passed she came into her window, and looked down on me with no sign of recognition. I went back to Ireland into the heart of the hills.[75]

The early-Renaissance world of Dante's 'Vita Nuova' is not easily rebuilt in late-Victorian Kingstown. But by 1900, the twenty-nine-year-old Synge had moved closer to establishing an equilibrium between some of the forces which he sought to arrange in neat doubles, symmetries, and transpositions. During a visit to Paris in April 1900, Augusta Gregory encouraged him to maintain his interest in Aran, even suggesting Jack Yeats – the poet's younger brother, shortly Ireland's premier painter – as an illustrator of Synge's writings on the islands. Money remained a problem, despite the publication of a few articles. Mrs Synge expressed her worries to Sam in China. Her youngest son was included in the Castle Kevin party because 'it is only fair to give him some benefit of the money I would spend on him if he was at home' all year instead of scraping in his Paris rooms for six months at a time.[76]

CHAPTER 10

'Give Me the Sun'

Ibsen – a woman-soul, who had taken man's form for power's sake.

Frances Lord[1]

Travel never took Synge beyond thoughts of Ireland, which followed him everywhere. Nevertheless, the quality of intensity with which he was identified – first as an Anglo-Irishman bent on slandering the rest of the population, then as the very genius of the place – has obscured the degree to which Synge lacked identity. Being abroad did not always take him away from domestic influences, but it did provide him with a code through which anxious or bumptious inquiries could be more objectively conducted. Reading, especially the reading of foreign literature, became a species of autobiography for Synge. Such a practice was peculiarly suited to a man building a reputation for silence or at least reticence, but it also tolerated self-deception at some low level.

At the risk of caricature, Jan Setterquist's *Ibsen and the Beginnings of Anglo-Irish Drama* (1951) could be summarised as the recognition of Nora in *A Doll's House* (English translation 1880) in the Nora of *In the Shadow of the Glen* (1903). Even the decisive alteration of setting between the plays, from comfortable bourgeois home to isolated mountain cottage, was of a piece with Synge's own development, his preference for eloquent risk-taking over established security. Though Setterquist did not limit himself to the consideration of Synge alone, his insight was limited by an incomplete awareness of the work preceding the world-renowned plays. He was writing prior to the publication of Stephens' and Greene's biography (1959) and the making available of the manuscript sources.

We can be quite certain as to where and when Synge read Ibsen. In addition to the London furore orchestrated by Ibsen's translator William Archer and Bernard Shaw, there was 'a regular Ibsen boom' in Germany at the end of the 1880s.[2] While Synge was in Oberwerth, and absorbing the Von Eickens' happy negotiations between confessional Protestantism and artistic pastimes, he read *The Pillars of Society*, *A Doll's House*, *Peer Gynt* and *Rosmersholm*. His diary names the plays in German. As he was saturating himself in the language and had little access to books in English, we can conclude that he used German translations. Or, to be precise, if he had been reading Ibsen in English, then he postponed any record of the fact until he got away from home for the first time.

If he had any knowledge of Ibsen's life, he would have noticed a parallel between his own disengagement from domestic piety and young Henrik's refusal to follow his parents into a secession from the Norwegian State Church: indeed, both men simply reject inherited belief. An awareness of this precedent stimulated no early pronouncement by Synge about Ibsen. His most public comment did not come until fame and notoriety had contended for possession of him; in the Preface to *The Playboy of the Western World* he dismissed 'Ibsen and Zola dealing with the reality of life in joyless and pallid words'.[3]

No explicit mention of *Ghosts* can be traced.[4] Two German translations of Ibsen's startling drama had appeared, in 1884 and 1893, the earlier running to three editions. George Moore's *Impressions and Opinions* (1891) contains a long and favourable account of a reading presented in a Paris theatre, the details of which may have struck Synge as uncomfortably familiar when he saw the same production in March 1898.[5] A reading by the same company had taken place in Berlin in 1894. Synge was by no means the only writer to respond nervously to *Ghosts*. Arthur Symons attempted his own version of a 'bad blood in the family' play. Like Synge's journeywork in *When the Moon Has Set*, Symons's *Barbara Roscorla's Child* gave its author more pains than it was worth.[6]

In many ways, it would have been more surprising if Synge had not been affected by Ibsen's work. In William Archer and Edmund Gosse, he had advocates few non-English authors have been blessed with. Irish contemporaries as different as James Joyce, Edward Martyn, George Moore, and the redoubtable Shaw all responded positively. 'The Quintessence of Ibsenism' was published as a reaction (in part) to the débâcle of Parnell's involvement in the O'Shea divorce case and then of his sudden death.[7] No unanimity between Martyn and Joyce, or Shaw and Joyce, can be assumed, even on the Ibsen question. But commentators have tended to stress the adaptation of Ibsen's concerns to Irish circumstances rather than to perceive the underlying similarity of milieu. In the nineteenth century, Norway and Ireland had each experienced a peculiarly suffocating relationship with its powerful neighbour. While Ireland persisted as a distinctive society within the officially United Kingdom, Norway after 1814 was united with Sweden under the Crown while maintaining a degree of local self-government. Each endured a form of what has been called internal colonialism. Each also witnessed the development of a middle class, unlovingly highlighted in the drama of Ibsen but more often denied in the work of his Irish followers and their colleagues.[8] As many of the writers who came to be regarded as the Irish Literary Movement had emerged from the denominational minority, one might also cite the common Protestant legacy of the two cultural traditions.

Joyce's preoccupation with Ibsen is readily traced in the essay 'Drama and Life' (1900), and the quasi-fictional account of an episode from his university career in *Stephen Hero*. Like Synge in the Preface to *The Playboy*, Joyce associates Ibsen with Zola. In a more original fashion he also salutes Ibsen as Dante's heir: 'Here and not in Shakespeare and Goethe was the successor to the first poet of the Europeans, here, as only to such purpose in Dante, a human personality had been found united with an artistic manner which was itself almost a natural phenomenon: and the spirit of the time united one more readily with the Norwegian than with the Florentine.'[9]

Joyce follows the same line (but not necessarily the same argument) as Synge himself, whose 'Vita Vecchia' overlaps with the Ibsenite themes of the 'prentice-or-journeyman play, *When the Moon Has Set*. Many years later Joyce wrote an 'Epilogue to Ibsen's *Ghosts*', which tabulates the possible sources of initial guilt, real or imagined.

> Reck not to whom the blame is laid,
> Y. M. C. A., V. D., T. B.[10]

In 1904 or 1934, the argument was not solely about 'decadence' or 'the French disease' or impaired sexuality: it concerned the perpetuation of human culture. Dedalus, in *Stephen Hero*, invoked Francis Bacon in this connection – 'The care of posterity, he quoted, is greatest in them that have no posterity.'[11] Between the immediate post-Reformation of Bacon's day and the modernity of Joyce's, the prohibition on begetting had altered in its form from traditional clerical celibacy to a sterility either personal or social. The demographic crisis of the mid-nineteenth century in Ireland was working itself out in cultural terms in the generation of Shaw, Wilde and their immediate successors. It was particularly acute among the inheritors (or non-inheritors) of the Anglo-Irish Big House.

Nothing of this latter factor can be detected in *In the Shadow of the Glen*, Synge's Nora-play, where issues of formal ideological attachment are carefully kept offstage – little, that is, except the biblical allusion in the play's title. But if one returns to Synge's never-abandoned manuscript of *When the Moon Has Set*, then social and sectarian differences are everywhere implicit, together with the Ibsenite theme of domination by the past. 'We sail', Ibsen observed, 'with a corpse in the cargo.' Whether or not he had Bram Stoker's *Dracula* in mind at that moment, Ibsen would soon have noted the recurrence of a restless cadaver in several of Synge's plays – Dan Burke in *In the Shadow of the Glen*, 'a power of young men floating round' in *Riders to the Sea*, twice-murdered Old Mahon in *The Playboy*, and (a special case) the living and the dead Colm Sweenys of *When the Moon Has Set*. For all its aesthetic bankruptcy and inflationary rhetoric, *When the Moon Has Set* remains a highly negotiable document. Because it acknowledges autobiographical, dramatic and historical registers of signification, meaning can be found in any one of these, only to be challenged by the claims of some other one of these registers. We are perpetually exhorted to exchange our tuppence of insight for some other equally debased coinage.

But, just as followers of Jan Setterquist have been disadvantaged by his initial lack of access to Synge's early work, so celebrants of Synge's transformation of 'joyless and pallid words' studiously neglect *Ghosts*, for the first production of which Ibsen had to rely on amateurs in Chicago. It was not any drabness of style which discouraged Norwegian and Swedish theatres from producing the new play: on the contrary, the subject-matter alone was lurid enough to provoke the Nordic equivalent of Abbey Theatre riots. There is a direct echo of Ibsen's theme in *Ghosts* to be heard in a doctor's remark on the crowds who broke up the first productions of *The Playboy of the Western World* in 1907 – 'It is all I can do to keep myself from jumping up on a seat and pointing out among the howling men in the pit those whom I am treating for venereal diseases.'[12]

Though translators admit the near impossibility of rendering the provincial Norwegian idiom of some characters, they testify to the liveliness of Ibsen's dialogue and imagery. Only the poet Geoffrey Hill has made a sustained effort to create an English fully adequate to the original.[13] Synge's access to the plays depended on more dogged translations, German rather than English. As with his study of Isaac Taylor, there is something touchingly outdated in Synge's programme of dramatic reading. However, his distaste in 1907 for problem plays is too promptly declared to be above suspicion. *When the Moon Has Set* is equally impulsive in revealing its familiarity with *Ghosts*. The relationship between the plays involves both imitation and revulsion, and results in an 'un-writing' of the dense Norwegian tragedy.

Though Synge's first sustained attempt at play-writing is little enhanced by a comparison with Ibsen's rain-sodden drama, some half-formulated notions about his inner life are clarified. Both plays centre on a young man of artistic inclinations who has returned from Paris to a family house in the provinces. Each play is anxiously concerned with inheritance, and in each the young man's sexual interests are aroused. Housemaids are remarked upon for their developed figures, and both of these have fathers of doubtful moral probity. But striking differences in the disposition of the characters within this plot deserve scrutiny.

Such an examination could begin with what we could call the atmospherics, or 'statics', of the work. Both plays juxtapose water and fire, elemental symbols against which the leading male is judged. In *Ghosts* rain falls perpetually, and yet a newly built orphanage is destroyed by fire. In the opening scene of *When the Moon Has Set*, the young man Colm Sweeny comes in drenched from the back-roads of Wicklow; he finds the housemaid attempting to light a fire with damp turf.[14] Finally, each play tracks a gradual improvement in the weather, from snow to a rainstorm which marks the end of spring, or from rain to the sunshine longed for in the dark fjiords of rural Norway. Each play concludes – in starkly contrasting ways – with a ritualised invocation of the sun.

The servant Bride's attempt to light a wet fire is the most successful symbolic detail in Synge's otherwise cumbersome play. Additionally, it serves here as a means of discriminating between the arrangement of characters in the two plays. In *Ghosts* Osvald Alving flirts with, and then desperately proposes marriage to, his mother's housemaid Regina. In *When the Moon Has Set*, the equivalent female role is divided between Sister Eileen, a nun of unspecified but implicitly Catholic loyalties, and the resourceful Bride. Colm Sweeny salutes Eileen's physical attractiveness – 'you are infinitely beautiful, and you have done a great action' – but it is Bride who is observed to be *enceinte*, that is, pregnant.[15] The discourse of sexuality is associated with Eileen, while its biology is alive and kicking in the unmarried Bride. This compartmentalising of the verbal and the procreative turns on an assumption of guilt; Eileen has to be persuaded (at great length!) that physical love is permissible, and this is facilitated in a mime-show transfer of its consequences on to a menial thoughtfully named Bride (from Gaelic, Bríde) as if in anticipation of her eventual legitimation in marriage.

A similar discretion marks Synge's treatment of the male characters and their inheritance. Ibsen's Osvald has long been away, his father is long dead. Colm Sweeny, however, has returned not to a parental home but to his uncle's (and namesake's) house. Each discovers a guilty inheritance.

But whereas Ibsen's third act is 'so appallingly tragic that the emotions it excites prevent the meaning of the play from being seized and discussed', Synge's denouement is little better than the 'vermouth of the last musical comedy'. Between these pungent phrases *When the Moon Has Set* effects its escape, between, that is, Shaw's tribute to Ibsen and Synge's own fatuous denunciation of contemporary theatre.[16]

Before looking at the conclusion to the two plays, we should remind ourselves of some details in the terms through which Colm Sweeny the Younger inherits from his namesake. As with the replication of Ibsen's Regina as *two* characters, in Synge's play so there is an excess of explanation about the past. Sister Eileen tells Colm that, long ago, his uncle had wanted to marry a woman called Mary Costello 'although she was beneath him, [and] when it was all arranged she broke it off because he did not believe in God'. Though now confined at the local asylum in conditions of deranged beggary, this woman was – in Bride's version of the past – 'a Costello from the old Castilian family, and it's fine people they were at one time ...'[17] While the belief that certain Irish names connote a lost aristocratic dignity is familiar, the telling feature in Synge's plot is the implicit contradiction between Eileen's account of the bride's reasons for not marrying and Bride's account. There is no little irony in the contrast between the Costellos' reputed origins and the general silence which surrounds the background of the Sweenys. Those who possess property lack pedigree, while those who walk the roads in misery are robed in legend. Nor were these Costellos just an invention of thirty-year-old Synge: on 9 August 1901 Kathleen Synge, who was staying with JMS at Castle Kevin, noted in her diary, 'Old Costello dead.' Wicklow deaths of this period, and what might be regarded as a 'copycat' death of one of them in particular, will powerfully motivate Synge's first mature work in 1902.

The relationship between breeding and beggary takes one further form – that of patronage. From 1839 until his death, 'Pestalozzi' Synge of Glanmore Castle sat on the Board of Guardians for the Poor Law union of Rathdrum. Later, a Dr John Hatch was appointed Dispensary Officer within the union, responsible for a district which included a primitive industrial community. In J. M. Synge's constantly changing play-plot, a descendant of the once noble Costellos is lodged 'below in the Asylum'. Conditions in which lunatics were kept in Rathdrum – ten men and twenty-three women in 1901 – were labelled a scandal in the local press.[18] Orphanage in Ibsen, asylum in Synge, institutions of coercive charity – perhaps masking guilt among the patrons – play a significant off-stage role in the drama.

In the two-act version of Synge's play, documents are found through which the dead Colm Sweeny (the Elder) provided a further variant of his relations with Mary Costello. Instructing his heir, he had written:

If you love a woman subdue her. You will not love a woman it is not lawful to love. No man of our blood has ever been unlawful ... Be careful of my books. The dress and the rings were made for a woman I once hoped to marry. She was poor. She died afterwards, and her brother became crazy. He would have shot me but some vow restrained him. He thought I had wronged her ...'[19]

The mixture of Nietzsche and pantheism which runs through these cited documents does not make any dramatic sense, but it allows for a further perspective on the elder Sweeny's affair of twenty years earlier. The emphatic negatives are too prominent to be taken at face value. Sweeny clearly felt that he had done wrong by the woman. Insufficient belief in the deity offers no adequate explanation of what that wrong had been.

In the curious isolation of its many versions, *When the Moon Has Set* is unable to articulate its obsessions. Mary King has written of its 'downgrading of language' and its concomitant interest in music as non-representational art.[20] Colm Sweeny, the would-be artist of Paris, will finally be united to Sister Eileen, not so much as a consequence of his subduing her resistance to sexuality but as a result of his being cleared of any inherited guilt. The force of this – as a biographical datum rather than as an achieved dramatic effect – becomes obvious when the conclusion of *Ghosts* is invoked. One might note some ghostly details hovering in the wings of Synge's own play. Colm Sweeny's letter to his friend in Paris includes an account of the rural Irish landscape – 'One morning after rain spectres of pale green and yellow and pink seemed to be looking out between the trees.'[21] More melodramatically, the one-act version thrusts the deranged Mary Costello on-stage; wondering whose death had required the bow of black crepe in Eileen's hands, she proclaims, 'I was afeard it was my little children – for if I was never married your honour, and have no children I do be thinking it's alive they must be if I never had them itself ... I do see them sometimes when my head's bad and I do be falling into my sleep ... There are five children ...'[22]

The speech of Mary Costello and Bride, though it is still a crude dramatic idiom, gives notice of Synge's latent power as a writer of 'peasant' dialogue. In this too he may be following Ibsen, for *Ghosts* also has its higher and lower registers of speech.[23] But Mary's contradictory words about children she never had cannot be relegated to the kind of nonsense a denizen of the asylum might conjure up. The poem of Synge's, written some time in 1896 or '97, and quoted in part as a component of the 'Vita Vecchia', in its entirety reads:

> I curse my bearing, childhood, youth [;]
> I curse the sea, sun, mountains, moon,
> I curse my learning, search for truth,
> I curse the dawning, night, and noon.
>
> Cold, joyless I will live, though clean,
> Nor, by my marriage, mould to earth
> Young lives to see what I have seen,
> To curse – as I have cursed – their birth.[24]

Within the proto-autobiographical context of 'Vita Vecchia', this rejection of marriage by a speaker who insists that he is 'clean' leads to the refusal to beget children whose birth he has already cursed. But if the poet/speaker has cursed the son/sun, his alter ego in *When the Moon Has Set* virtually worships it. To Sister Eileen, accoutred in a dress made twenty years earlier for Mary Costello, Colm Sweeny declares, 'In the name of the Summer, and the Sun, and the Whole World, I wed you as my wife.'[25] The two-act version has prepared Gaelic-speaking members of its audience for this heliotropism by naming the Sweeny house, Kilgreine, that is, the Wood (or perhaps, Church) of the Sun.

Returning to *Ghosts*, we are suddenly confronted with a very different conclusive apostrophe to the sun. At the end of Act One, Mrs Alving has been shocked to overhear her son chat up the housemaid, just as his father had done years earlier in a liaison which led to the birth of this young maid. (Osvald and Regina are half-siblings, and must be told so, an undertaking made difficult by Osvald's inexplicable suggestion that he might marry her.) In Act Two, Osvald confesses that he is ill, not with any ordinary illness but one which a cynical French doctor had glossed with the phrase, 'The sins of the fathers are visited on the children.' At the end of this act, an orphanage designed to commemorate Osvald's father catches fire, bringing to a hasty conclusion dialogue in which the elder (dead) Alving's dissipation, Mrs Alving's covert free-thinking, and her earlier love for Pastor Manders have been partly exposed. Now the final act sees Osvald press his confession further. He begs his mother to poison him before idiocy should ultimately overwhelm him. In a repetition of the accelerated pace which has closed the preceding acts, he is gripped by a renewed attack which leaves him murmuring senselessly: 'Mother, give me the sun ... The sun ... the sun ...' And, repeatedly amid his mother's screams, 'The sun ... the sun ...'[26]

Osvald is now in the grips of inherited, tertiary syphilis, a revelation on-stage so disturbing that it 'prevent[s] the meaning of the play from being seized and discussed'. How does the young Synge read this denouement? If we pore over the ancestral traces of Hatch and M'Cracken, it is not simply out of a duty to family history. For *When the Moon Has Set* not only draws on the business of Samuel M'Cracken's missing or contested will in the 1760s, with attendant gunfire; it also picks up the far more urgent matter of Ibsen's exposure of adultery and venereal infection in the contemporary middle-class home. Much-travelled Ibsen, at the age of sixty, was not unaware of the pervasiveness of syphilis in French society – in 1887, a commission was appointed to check its deadly advance, accounting for up to 14 per cent of deaths by the end of the century.[27] Inexperienced Johnnie Synge feared rather than knew its presence.

At the level of a general cultural diagnosis, one can argue that the two divergent perspectives have a point of intersection in the notion of generational anxiety, from which the past (along one line of perspective) appears dubious in the legitimacy it confers, and the future (along the other) depends upon a present which is dumbly tense. In politics as in literature, the great Irish generation of the late Victorian, the Edwardian and Georgian periods was remarkable for its declining to procreate – Michael Collins, C. S. Parnell, the Pearse brothers, Horace Plunkett, G. B. Shaw, J. M. Synge, Jack Yeats leave no heirs; Oscar Wilde and Augusta Gregory are in their different ways robbed of their sons; in middle age W. B. Yeats enters fatherhood only when that terminal phase has done its worst.

At this level, one can read *When the Moon Has Set* in both cultural and biographical terms, as signalling a crisis of continuity which is too stridently and abstractly resolved in Colm and Eileen's marriage under the sun, or as disclosing (in the very act of closing off) a profound uncertainty about the dramatist's personal identity within his own family. For, like Osvald Alving, John Synge was almost a posthumous child of a father who died suddenly; in Colm Sweeny, he seeks to translate paternity into the more remote relationships of uncle and nephew, counterbalancing that with marriage to a cousin whom he also calls 'Sister'. For all that Sister Eileen's religiosity echoes Cherrie Matheson's, the bonding of cousins recalls young Johnnie Synge's love of Florence Ross. There is a direct reference to 'days ... spent in the woods between [a] death and a funeral'.[28] Through cousinly love recurs the incestuous liberty Synge feared might stem from a reading of Charles Darwin.

The solution to one problem becomes the next problem, and the windy rhetoric of Colm and Eileen's heliocentric union discloses its own irresolutions. Relying heavily on musical analogies, Colm announces that 'from our harmonized discord, new notes will arise', as sexless a progeny as one could imagine. Initially congratulated on her new inarticulacy – 'You cannot tell me why you have changed. That is your glory' – Eileen is finally defined in terms of a verbal activity conventionally regarded as passive. She is 'the reader of the saints'.[29] Is this last phrase a nod in the direction of Cherrie Matheson?

On the surface, the answer is no. Sister Eileen is one who reads the lives of the Catholic saints. The seemingly 'pagan', sun-invoking marriage imagery echoes Francis of Assisi's early hymn, 'Il cantico della creature', thus allowing the happy couple to have it both ways, overcoming the nun's Catholic beliefs but repeating her devotional texts.[30] But, subliminally, the quarrel between her and Colm goes under the same ground as that which preoccupied Synge and his neighbour, the Plymouth 'sister'. There are identifiable allusions to other women in Synge's life, Florence Ross and Margaret Hardon particularly, as befits a play cut and pasted from various autobiographical writings. Yet Cherrie Matheson is the benign ghost of *When the Moon Has Set*; witnesses to this are her cousins *Eileen* and Vera (who campaigned on behalf of nurses).[31]

The non-idiomatic phrase 'under the same ground' was used in order to reinforce the notion of something under the threshold of consciousness. Biographers are not meant to play tricks with language unless, perhaps, they aim to highlight a feature of their subject's own linguistic behaviour. And while J. M. Synge will be quickly famed for the strongly idiomatic quality of his drama, he also used dislocations of idiom. Eileen, acceding to Colm's marriage plans, says, 'I seem to be in a dream *that is wider than I am*' (emphasis added).[32] Apart from a risible aspect, the phrase alerts us to other deviations which cannot be explained in terms of a character's idiolect.

One of these – which will recur in a later play – focuses exactly on questions of setting. In Saddlemyer's conflate edition of *When the Moon Has Set*, the scene is given as 'A country house in the east of Ireland, late spring or early summer at the turn of the century'. This is oddly evasive. The 'east of Ireland' has none of the connotative fluency of 'the west of Ireland' for – speaking of Synge's period – we find in the geographical east a mixture of metropolitan and rural societies, impoverished and prosperous economies, all of which stand in contrast to the west, which is characteristically poor, non-urban, and distanced from power. Moreover, the eastern counties had a higher proportion of non-Catholics in the population, Wicklow being a striking case in point.

Readers or audiences of the play are thus faced with a complicated problem of orientation. Lacking any agreed canonical form, even lacking a clearly authorised title, it haunts the student of Synge's life and work. Is the play, as many have concluded without absurdity, set in a Wicklow house such as Castle Kevin? Is it, as others may suppose with equal reason, set in a Wicklow house such as Glanmore? Glanmore was, in its odd way, still a family property, occupied till c.1903 by Mrs Gardiner, and then repossessed by Robert Synge. Castle Kevin is more on a scale of the play's Kilgreine; it, however, had never been more than a rented summer house. In so far as the two-act version implicates M'Cracken and Hatch's activities as precursors of the Synge interest in the county, then it alludes to Roundwood Park, a property which was gone after the Great Famine.

The play then is not so much located in an unspecified or imaginary place, as it is dislocated from several which can be specified through historical and biographical research. Iris Murdoch's *The Unicorn* (1963) makes a revealing comparison. Anyone who knows County Clare will recognise that her novel is set on the edge of the Burren, that unique and unmistakable limestone plateau which serves as background to Yeats's play, *The Dreaming of the Bones* (1917) and part of Shaw's *Back to Methuselah* (1921). But there is nothing in the novel which declares that setting. The novel as read is not set in Clare; the novel as discussed may well be set there, depending on who does the discussing.

Textually *When the Moon Has Set* has been displaced from the larger collection of notebooks and drafts which accommodated Synge's non-dramatic early writing, including 'Étude morbide' and 'Vita Vecchia'. That is, it has been abstracted out from the brooding, melancholic prose-verse *mélanges* to become a rebuttal of that Ibsen play which had shockingly revealed itself as familiar with Synge's Parisian morbidity. (As late as 1912, Yeats encountered confident rumours that Synge had died as a consequence of his Parisian decadence.) Property and propriety, the grounds of a gentleman's being, were no longer solid inheritances. The whole thrust of Synge's endeavour with his never-abandoned script was to reverse the nineteenth century, not simply in a plot which restores a country house and its 'paternal' acres to a nominal reincarnation of the late owner, but in stage business and sentimental fustian which attempts to re-enchant what has been thoroughly dis-enchanted or de-sacralised in the previous hundred years or more.

And here the sub-version of *Ghosts* by and in *When the Moon Has Set* becomes again undeniable in yet one further highly significant detail. When the surviving members of the Alving family briefly contemplate what is essentially an incestuous alliance between Osvald and Regina as a solution to the young man's terrible problem, there is some effective business in Act Two with a lamp and a half-bottle of champagne. In the final act, all is clear and Regina gazes bitterly at another bottle, unopened, never to celebrate her integration into the Alving family – of which she is a half-product. Synge's two-act *When the Moon Has Set* requires the soon-to-be-legitimised heir to heat wine for himself and his (bride) Sister Eileen. In an excess of revived life, it boils over on the turf and Eileen spills more of it on Colm's wordy manuscript. Whether as communion or wedding, the sacramental sharing/mingling of wine/blood seeks to reverse the catastrophe of Osvald and Regina.

There remains the difficult problem of dates: a Wicklow death of August 1901 interacts with uncalendared Continental themes. One hard (English) fact emerges: Synge saw 'When We Awaken from Among the Dead', as he wrongly called it, in London. He met Yeats the same evening. The following day (Tuesday 27 January 1903), his diary cryptically notes: 'Wicklow Play'. While this might refer to *In the Shadow of the Glen*, he had already shown an advanced version of it to Lady Gregory the previous autumn. The cautious 'place-naming' of what he was working on in Handel Street, Bloomsbury, suggests a more intractable problem than the Nora-play. He was *en route* for Paris intending to give up his rooms there. Before he left, however, he worked on what the diary unhelpfully calls 'Aughavanna Play', which may be the same thing.[33] Synge finished a one-act version of *When the Moon Has Set* on 23 May 1903, by which time he was back in Ireland. Late January in London is the moment when his never-abandoned project comes closest to an acknowledgement of Ibsen's presence.

BOOK THREE

Return of the Native

CHAPTER 11

First Love?

The Lord protect us from the saints of God!

J. M. Synge[1]

From the November 1882 journal which Synge kept with Florence Ross to the grim letters of 1909 written from his deathbed, a relationship with women played a crucial but often inscrutable role in his emotional and imaginative life. The particular intensity and narrowness of his dialogue with women can hardly be replicated in another case. Bernard Shaw retained his virginity with equal tenacity, but Shaw lacked the streak of sentimentalism one finds in Synge's relationship with Molly Allgood (1887–1952).

A distinctive characteristic of Synge's attitude towards women is that each brought to him, or elicited in him, an ideological classification which he then problematised. Even Florence had become bothersome in that she came to prefer a cousin other than the cousin whom her friend Johnnie had always been: the incest to which Darwinism allegedly prompted him thus became possible at least in the form of jealousy. Valeska von Eicken represented a viable combination – of music and Protestantism – which had previously been set at odds. Molly challenged the same domestic rules by combining the theatre in her professional and Catholicism in her confessional life. Between the cousin and the Catholic on Synge's list of *amours*, there came Cherrie Matheson (1870–1940), to whom he proposed marriage on more than one occasion.

When the Synges moved in October 1890 from Orwell Park to Crosthwaite Park West, the Mathesons were their near neighbours. The transfer had been negotiated during the previous summer which had been spent (as usual) in Greystones. If anything, the closeness of habitation which had deeply marked the years in Rathgar was to be intensified in Kingstown despite the greater social bustle of the resort town. Not only were Synge's grandmother, sister, brother-in-law and nephews immediately next door, but the family of the young woman to whom he became passionately attached lived just three doors away in No. 25. While the move had been mooted by Harry Stephens in his search for a residential base with social *éclat*, it was suggestively duplicated in the ranks of the Church of Ireland clergy. John Dowse who, as a curate at Zion Road in Rathgar, had earnestly tried to awaken faith in the eighteen-year-old Johnnie was transferred as rector of St Paul's (Glenageary) shortly before the family migration.

The Mathesons were stalwarts of the Brethren, Cherrie's father having converted with such decision as to require the breaking of his fiddle-bow.[2] Synge's agonised desire to marry her involved claims upon his identity which were simultaneously emotional, familial, political, and spiritual. Perhaps the desire arose from a scarcely mappable zone between them, a psychic space where those claims were welcomed as confirming a sub-jectivity otherwise in doubt. Beyond the facts of the matter in its historical and personal context, this relationship has been puzzling to modern readers of Synge for the added reason that they know little or nothing about the precise beliefs and practices of the group to which Cherrie adhered. If the Brethren are not taken seriously today by anyone but themselves, the proposition has to be rewritten for late Victorian times. *Then*, no one took the Brethren more seriously than their critics (see the Appendix, pp. 431–6).

The Brethren have produced some unlikely offspring – the black magi-cian Aleister Crowley and Major-General Orde Wingate of the 'Chindits' are two of the least likely. For most readers of literature today, the Brethren are familiar only through the pages of Edmund Gosse's autobiography – at once numbing and brilliant – with its account of a personal liberation from the dominance of Brethren teaching. *Father and Son* did not appear until 1907 by which point Synge had fought his own good fight without its aid. That Philip Henry Gosse (the solidly English and middle-class Father) had been a distinguished biologist and a faithful attender at Brethren meetings, does not diminish the extent to which his outlook mirrored Kathleen Synge's. Indeed, as a young woman his wife had worked as a governess in an Irish aristocratic household.[3] Despite the nickname of Plymouth Brethren, these saints originated in Ireland; and among the founders, Synges had been discreetly prominent. Not many great playwrights had a grandfather who took the chair when a religion was founded, a point upon which Yeats can only have been jealous.[4] The 'affair' between Cherrie and JMS cannot be regarded only as an episode in late-Victorian suburban morals and manners; it hummed with historical implication and ironised desire.

Synge himself remained mute on the subject. The nearest to commentary on the Brethren is a terse series of notes headed 'marks of primitive religion':

1) No priests proper
2) No temples
3) Spirits not gods are recognised. Names general not proper.
4) The rites are magical rather than propitiatory.

These arose from his reading of James Frazer's *The Golden Bough*, but their aptness (especially nos. 1 and 2, and the observation about names) to the topic of Plymouth Brethren is striking. Synge's recourse to Frazer is in part a search for explanations of the contemporary and urban as well as an inquiry into ancient rites and exotic locations.[5] Primitivism did not always require a natural backdrop: Paris could serve as well as Tahiti. But, in his scrutable behaviour, he avoided the topic of deviant religious conviction by adopting a sceptical stance towards all such convictions, especially established or socially approved ones.

Clergy with whom the Synges mixed socially or parochially formed alliances beyond the membership of the Church. F. R. Wynne, to whom Sam Synge was so anxious to be polite, associated with the evangelical Merrion Hall, Dublin.[6] A 'special series of children's services' held in the Zion schoolroom in May/June 1885 used the American evangelist Sankey's hymn-book to augment the official (and staider) hymnal; these were the intensely indoctrinating sessions to which Kathleen Synge despatched Johnnie – then still only fourteen.[7] The manner in which leading members of the original Brethren maintained their Church attachment, together with the practice of some ordained clergy fraternising with Brethren in 'non-denominational' activities, suggest that only a flimsy veil divided the formal allegiances of Cherrie Matheson and JMS. As the daughter of a leading Brother, she was perfectly well aware of the Synge contribution to the foundation of her own allegiance.

In the 1920s Hutchie (to whom Synge left half his estate) went to the trouble of recovering from Cherrie Matheson the letters which his uncle had written to her. These were documents of the highest significance for anyone attempting to understand Synge's development; we may assume that in addition to being affectionate letters they also touched on the ideological differences which contributed to Cherrie's refusal of his proposals. Hutchie, however, became increasingly demanding in his own correspondence with Mrs Houghton – her husband advised her to break off communications altogether – and in a fit of distraction destroyed the letters she had sent. The result is that any consideration of Synge's successive relationships with Cherrie Matheson and Molly Allgood is hamstrung by the total absence of the files on the one part and the (apparently) total preservation of half on the other.[8]

We know enough of Cherrie to establish that she was a cheerful and personable young woman, cultured in a high suburban way. Greene and Stephens would have us believe that she was short and plump, while Ronald Ayling (relying on the testimony of her daughter in old age) speaks of 'a slim girl with delicate sensitive features' as shown in a photograph taken in the year John Synge first proposed to her. Her hair was golden-brown, her eyes grey-green.[9] Vivacity of character, attested to by all (male) commentators, is evident in the one piece of documentary evidence which has come down to us. In July 1924, Cherrie (Matheson) Houghton published a memoir, 'John Synge as I Knew Him', in the *Irish Statesman*. She sketched, as young women of her class sometimes did, but she had the distinction of exhibiting work in Paris. None of this suggests an exclusivist shunning of the world. Her father, Robert Edwin Matheson (1845–1926, knighted in 1907) held a post in the Irish civil service, and published statistical reports arising from his work. Dull though it sounds, *Varieties and Synonymes of Surnames and Christian Names in Ireland* (1901) demonstrates his acquaintance with the Gaelic language.[10] From the Office of the General Registrar he had also written a pamphlet, *Observation Regarding the Potato Disease in Ireland in 1890*, indicating a concern with one of the great recurring fears of late-nineteenth-century Ireland – famine and depopulation.[11] While the distinctly 'low' evangelical fundamentalism of the Brethren (including the Open ones) cannot be denied, the Matheson household was not marked by rigid philistine or anti-intellectual views of the world. Cherrie's father may have been more 'liberal' than Synge's mother.

Cherie Marie Louise Matheson bore Christian names which encoded her grandmother's Francophone background in Protestant Switzerland. Familiarised as 'Cherrie', she has come to be regarded as a transparency, despite Ayling's 1964 article. Consequently, it is not surprising to find that a divergence of opinion about Synge's relationship with her quickly emerges, once the attempt is made to set down the evidence as it survives from both sides. Stephens's account, as presented in *My Uncle John*, begins in the summer of 1894 when Mrs Synge was planning the annual holiday at Castle Kevin. Since the death of Agnes Ross (née Traill) in 1891, Florence Ross was living with her aunt; consequently Mrs Synge encouraged Florence to bring a friend with her to County Wicklow. The girls were keen sketchers, and the rural landscape was an ideal subject. Synge himself had returned from Germany in June, and Stephens (with pardonable economy) presents a *mis en scène* in which Johnnie and Cherrie meet during this summer vacation. He allows that they had known each other earlier, but now 'gradually she had taken possession of his imagination and he had begun to worship her from a distance'.[12] This account passes over the significance of the domestic concert which JMS and his cousin Mary had given in March 1893, to which the Mathesons had been invited. While Mrs Synge was hostile to her son's musical ambitions, and Mr Matheson had foresworn fiddle-playing, her household did not preclude music-playing in the company of suitable neighbours – a semi-grand piano stood in the upper front room. It seems certain that the Schubert concert saw JMS and Cherrie together, even if he was separated from her in his role as co-star with Mary.[13]

At the end of July 1894 Cherrie joined the Synges at Castle Kevin. He was twenty-three, a graduate recently returned from sojourn abroad. Born on 12 October 1870, she was nearly a year older but, by Victorian convention, unable to take any kind of initiative in her personal affairs. Details derive from Stephens's observation and later recollection of events. All three – the lover, the beloved, and the future chronicler – lived within a few doors of each other. As Stephens was a child of five during the early manoeuvres, his testimony must be weighed carefully. An incident in the Castle Kevin drawing room highlights the difficulty. When Stephens interrupted JMS and Cherrie, 'he soon stopped playing [the violin] and went away, leaving me feeling that I had been in the wrong – but I do not remember any reproof.'[14] The account of 1894, written long after the event, is open to the suspicion of misunderstanding. 'John occupied his time as he would have done if she had not come.' Conversations between them took place in Florence's presence, as they walked at evening in the fields. 'His devotion to her deepened, but none of the family noticed it because [they] were never alone together and never made themselves remarkable in any way.'[15] A few days after this incident, when Synge drove Cherrie to the railway station in the Castle Kevin phaeton, he was alone with her. Indeed, one of the less remarked-upon features of Mrs Synge's extended family circle was the latitude with which young people of both sexes were allowed to spend time together unsupervised. This had been the case even when Synge was in his early teens, and the growing popularity of the bicycle facilitated one-to-one contacts.

September and October were devoted to preparations for a return to Germany. An unstated feature of Synge's annual movements between

Ireland and the Continent was the avoidance of Christmas at home, whenever possible.[16] This can hardly have been his principal concern as he readied himself to leave behind Kingstown and Cherrie Matheson. The decision to travel does not indicate any determination to prosecute his relationship with her; on the contrary it took him back to the Von Eicken sisters, music, and a sketch about gypsy life in which he acted. On 1 January 1895, he set out for Paris and a new variation on the theme of exile. Back in Ireland for the summer; he resumed contact with his young neighbour, though it seems that four months elapsed before the two were able to spend any extended time together.

In Stephens's words, Synge 'had established the precedent of going out with her alone, but it was not easy to follow it up by arranging another meeting quickly'.[17] Robert Synge was home from Argentina, and the domestic mood attuned to his reconciliation of prosperity with devout convention. The picnic on Killiney (if it included the Mathesons) gives little evidence of obstacles being placed in the way of the two young people. Subsequent meetings between John and Cherrie are more significant – the opening of a Sketching Club exhibition on Saturday 16 November 1895 (a dark evening with a new moon) and a casual visit to the National Gallery two weeks later. In these details lies further confirmation of a cultural tolerance not usually associated with the Brethren, even if Corot (whom Synge commended to her) was a solidly middle-class point of reference in late-Victorian taste.[18] Ayling's conversations and correspondence with Cherrie Matheson's descendants in South Africa have indicated that she, and not Synge, may have taken the initiative in their visiting the Sketching Club. It is even possible that his decision to spend time in Paris was encouraged by her familiarity with the Salon where she had exhibited water-colour paintings on more than one occasion in the 1890s – she had studied under Percy French.[19]

For his part, Synge responded by remaining at home for Christmas 1895, and throughout December he and Cherrie went for several walks together.[20] They discussed questions of religious belief, and she lent him books which she judged might bring him round at least to a point of view accepted in his own household, if not to that pertaining among the Brethren. It was during this passage of courtship that he studied John Ruskin's *Stones of Venice* (1851–3). Though its author combined a socialistic critique of modern society with a version of Christian piety, Synge was generally little interested in such a cultural synthesis. For the moment, Ruskin acted as a mediator between lover and beloved. But the gulf between them was graphically demonstrated on successive Sundays before and after Christmas: on 22 December, he wrote to Cherrie returning the books, and on 29 December they walked together until 'it was time for her to go with her father to the Plymouth Brethren's meeting house, and then he set out alone for the Smelting Chimney on the hill above Ballycorus'.[21]

Synge's alternative to the meeting-house was neither the parish church nor unalloyed nature; it was in its odd way a monument to the decay of an old and small-scale industrial layer of rural south Dublin. Stephens is invaluable on such details, for he came to share many of his uncle's interests in the Irish landscape, and appreciated the value of a place-name laconically entered in a diary. Sam Synge, while attentive to family gatherings and acts of kindness, is virtually silent on JMS's relationship with women. But it does not necessarily follow that Stephens is right in his biographical detail even though, after 1939, he had unimpeded access to Synge's notebooks and drafts.[22] Ayling, responding no doubt to suggestions made by Cherrie's daughter, is of opinion that she was scarcely aware of the intense degree of John Synge's feelings for her, until he proposed in writing. *My Uncle John*, on the other hand, reads the 'affair' with Cherrie through the scratched lens of literary experiment. In doing so, it ventures into its own hall of mirrors.

For example, Stephens holds that the 'plan for a play', outlined in German in April–May 1894 while Synge was living in Würzburg, reflects something of his love for Cherrie Matheson. Indeed, he refers to it 'as an imaginary version of their love affair'.[23] More is involved here than critical naiveté. For we must ask if there is any evidence of a 'love-affair' in 1894. Stephens's circular argument revolves round a fictitious name which appears in the diary for 10 December 1895 – 'Continued writing Sir John and Scherma'.[24] But the play-sketch of the previous April makes no reference to any character-names; the hero's beloved is the daughter of a widow (unlike Cherrie), and the only promising complications appear to involve the unexpected confrontation of brothers, and the rage of the hero's sister who discovers him resolved to marry beneath their social level.[25]

Certainly Scherma was a code-name used by Synge in his diaries to refer to Cherrie – the word is a lightly disguised compound of bits from her Christian and maiden names. While he was in Italy, he received a 'Letter from Scherma!!!!!' on the day before his twenty-fifth birthday. If the exclamation marks in his diary signal his great excitement, nothing survives to justify in any specific way Stephens's view that 'Cherrie's letter had given him hope'.[26] What evidence there is, suggests that her part in the trip to Rome extended no further than an initial introduction to people who might provide accommodation. A draft letter of *circa* 23 February 1896 *might* be read to imply that Cherrie was simultaneously with Synge in Rome, though not in the same lodgings.[27]

To be even more precise, we are left with nothing more than the signification of excitement – let us concede that it was indeed joyful excitement – on one side alone. Cherrie's brief published memoir may omit all references to rejected proposals of marriage because it was not seemly for a married woman to publicise such matters, but her silence on the topic of her own emotional commitment is consistent with the surviving documentation – to suggest powerfully that such commitment was not intense or passionate on her part. Hutchie Synge's rather shaky evidence tends to confirm this; Cherrie's letters (which Stephens allegedly wished to destroy after 1909) 'were all merely friendly letters which might have been shown to anyone'. Indeed, Cherrie showed Hutchie the other side of the correspondence, having sent him Synge's letters to her from South Africa in the 1920s. All but one item – Cherrie's first letter to Johnnie, preserved 'as a specimen of her style and penmanship' – was destroyed by Hutchie on two occasions, separated by up to ten years.[28]

In implicating Cherrie, Stephens's readings of the Würzburg fragments, 'Etude Morbide' and 'Vita Vecchia', and even *Riders to the Sea*, do more than advance an untenable notion of literature; they trace sexual emotion or eroticism within a two-way movement between author and text. But the early works – *not* including *Riders* – do rather less and do it more intensively; these 'pre-mature' writings seek to anchor the sexual within the textual, at once specifying and disguising a supposed, or merely formal, outside referent. Before coming to any conclusions of a theoretical kind, we should press ahead with an account of the evidence as it stands.

Cherrie's own 'John Synge As I Knew Him' immediately complicates such an undertaking. Having married and emigrated in 1902, she only saw JMS on one subsequent occasion, during a trip home in 1904. Her memoir, published twenty years later, was described by W. B. Yeats (to whom she had evidently sent it) as 'rather lacking in the personal touch'. His remark may hint at an intimacy known by him to have been greater than she had revealed or – alternatively and more plausibly – it may be recognised as a characteristic put-down effected by a rival friend of Synge's.[29] Nevertheless, she recorded that, during her return visit, she and JMS 'talked a little about *Dana* (a very short-lived but delightful paper).

He said it was too good to get a paying circulation in Ireland, that Ireland was too remote from the world of thought.'[30]

If this was not a personal touch in her memoir, it certainly prompted a guilty reaction in Yeats who – condescending to Cherrie as everyone else has done – wondered publicly why he hadn't edited out her reference to the magazine founded by Fred Ryan and John Eglinton.[31] Running from May 1904 to April 1905, *Dana* was distinctly antagonistic to nationalist and clericalist visions of Ireland, and Eglinton in particular was hostile to the mythological spin put upon Irish culture by the Literary Revivalists. That Synge should approve of its radicalism is not wholly surprising; that he and one of 'the saints' should agree on the matter is yet further evidence, if such were needed, that Cherrie Matheson was no dumb 'Brother'.

In tracing her relationship with JMS from the middle of 1896 until her marriage, we should bear in mind this new perspective on her own range of interests and abilities. Stephens is right in emphasising a high degree of internalised emotion in the Continental wanderer. 'By dwelling continually on the image of his "Holy One" he had convinced himself that on the successful development of his relationship with her all his future happiness must depend.' In this mood, he wrote on 9 June 1896 from Paris proposing marriage. Her refusal duly arrived on 17 June, and two days later Mrs Synge confided in her diary, 'I got a *sad sad* letter from my poor Johnnie from Paris.'[32] Neither of these letters has survived.

In making his proposal of marriage, JMS cannot have been unaware of other developments occurring in the family at the same time. His brother had been ordained a deacon the previous month.[33] By calculation or otherwise, he might rely on their mother for support in his quest for Cherrie's hand. While Sam made a direct compact with the Almighty by becoming His servant, poor Johnnie proposed a vicarious arrangement by which he would marry one 'holier than thou', while retaining his own scepticism in compensation. Harry Stephens had acted as a go-between on at least one occasion. His son's account probably derives from what his mother, Annie Stephens (née Synge) told him afterwards.[34]

My Uncle John proceeds with a synthesis of report and supposition which cannot now be challenged. Safely ensconced in their holiday retreat, mother and son had a heart-to-heart conversation on his dilemma. 'She could understand Cherrie's difficulties perfectly. In spite of all his study he had not become self-supporting and there seemed no likelihood of his being able to support a wife. His mother knew that if John married he would not bring up children "in the nurture and admonition of the Lord" and she asked herself: "How can two walk together unless they be agreed?" ' The order of these difficulties is noteworthy, even if it cannot be assigned either to Mrs Synge or to Stephens. First, Synge was not able to support a wife; second, he continued in unbelief. 'She had told [Synge] that, when staying at Castle Kevin, she had been misled as to his beliefs by his attending church.'[35] From this we deduce that she too had gone to the Church of Ireland at Derrylossary in the summer of 1894, despite her Brethrenish affiliation in Kingstown and Greystones. We cannot say whether she and John stood, sat, and kneeled side by side within the enclosed 'horsebox' pew; we cannot recover the harmony of their fingers meeting on the open pages of a church hymnal they shared. We can rely on the divergence of minds.

On the point of fact, Stephens may be trusted absolutely, for he and his parents helped to fill the Synge pews. This was in the parish church where Sam performed his earliest duties after ordination in 1896, the incumbency of which he took up in 1923 after his years in foreign missions.[36] Ayling, on the other hand, stresses that Cherrie Matheson's final choice of husband showed little evidence of caution or calculation. Ten years younger than her, Kenneth Hobart Houghton tended to support the Boer cause during the South African wars, took a relatively poorly paid teaching post in the Cape, and espoused anti-racial views which made him increasingly disillusioned with his adopted homeland.[37]

We return therefore to the problem of missing evidence. If, as we are led to believe, Cherrie's side of the correspondence was destroyed by Hutchie Synge, it is highly improbable that Stephens ever had direct access to her letter rejecting marriage. According to Hutchie's testimony, the packet of letters at that time lay in the Ned Synge household, and the suggestion that it be destroyed was rejected, temporarily. No doubt family tradition had its view on the matter, filtered to Stephens through his mother. What can be ascertained is that Synge's family were unable or unwilling to provide the income which would have overcome one of these obstacles. The youngest son must dine alone.

The summer of 1896 saw the Synges shift from one County Wicklow residence to another. First of all they had stayed in Avonmore, the farmhouse occupied by the Frizells' manager, Harry Harding and his family, but which had been the home in 1798 of the gun-cleaning Rev. Ambrose Weekes. Then, on Wednesday 29 July, Mrs Synge and her two youngest sons moved into their familiar base at Castle Kevin. The Stephenses joined them on 1 August, and the enlarged party stayed till the middle of September. This was one of the longest Wicklow holidays, Synge and his brother-in-law Harry Stephens spending a good deal of time together fishing at Kelly's Lake and other spots well known to them.

Once back in Crosthwaite Park a meeting with Cherrie was inevitable. When they bumped into each other on 25 September, she greeted him pleasantly. Five days later she came to tea in No. 31, an occasion on which Synge showed off his photographs. Pressing what he thought to be a new advantage, he took her to St Patrick's Cathedral to sit for an hour in what Cherrie described more than twenty years later as 'the beauty of the dear old place'.[38] Perhaps that sentimental response was precisely what Synge hoped for; he can hardly have hoped to impress her with his church attendance in Dublin. Yet, just as his forebears had presided at early meetings of the Brethren, so too had Synges occupied the cathedral stalls as dignitaries of the Established Church. Less than two weeks later, the couple visited Dublin's other Protestant cathedral, Christ Church; later in the same day they went to the National Museum in Kildare Street, a public place in which it was none the less possible to talk undisturbed.

Determined to justify his lack of religious commitment, he brought the 'Holy One' to lofty places of worship, neither of which can have appealed to a faithful adherent of the anti-clerical Brethren. Perhaps he intended a history lesson, in which the architectural and liturgical features of the buildings could then be placed in context with reference to the exhibits in the Museum. His reading of Dante, Karl Marx and William Morris during this period of renewed – but undeclared – courtship would have facilitated a lecture on the transformation of the medieval Christian hegemony into modern capitalism. Synge knew the poverty of the cathedral precincts, and the splendour of the buildings visited by the couple was a direct and recent consequence of ostentatious patronage by Dublin's premier industrial dynasty, the Guinnesses.[39] What's more, Harry Stephens's firm acted as legal agents for the brewery. The juxtaposition of squalor in St Patrick's Street with conspicuous reinvestment in St Patrick's Cathedral, appealed to his ironic humour.

At this point readers may well have voted for Cherrie's view of things and written off her bumptious lover with his endless self-justification and display of learning. Nevertheless, for him the attempt to reach an understanding was 'a terrible experience'. Stephens, who as a seven-year-old was either at school or at home in Crosthwaite Park, relies on family tradition, and on Synge's laconic diaries when these became available to him after 1939. On the one hand, he holds that Synge thought 'her decision had been based on her doctrinal beliefs rather than on personal feelings', intimating that Synge was mistaken in this; on the other, 'the more [Synge] tried to explain himself the more she relied on evangelical doctrine'.[40] As with most events, Cherrie Matheson's rejection of Synge sprang from multiple causes; sometimes one cause was stated so as to avoid the offence which another might give. But her response involved her religious beliefs, her worldly expectations of a husband, and her personal – let us frankly say, *sexual* – affections which had not been won.

This lopsided affair was woven into everything which he did during the mid-to-late 1890s. Though he left Dublin for Paris on 26 October 1896, his relationship with Cherrie had externalised itself to a degree which had not been the case in early summer. Sam had also left home, bound for China and the mission field. The departure of the two of them was a heavy burden for Kathleen, especially as Florence Ross had joined her brother the previous year in Tonga, to assist in his medical career. Mrs Synge was now approaching sixty. With all her own brood fled the nest – except the cuckoo, who arrived each early summer from Paris – she concentrated on the religious instruction of her grandchildren next door.

'The sorrow about poor Johnnie is the worst kind of sorrow,' she wrote, falling into a melancholy idiom half biblical and half Hiberno-English. We will hear it, more finely tuned, in her son's plays. Despite her decision, Cherrie frequented Synge's home – 'he saw her in the parlour on her way down.'[41] While Johnnie was packing his bags for Paris, both women were shocked by his openness in speaking about Hope Rea, 'the modern sceptic' in his mother's words, who was 'so thick with him'. Having picked up a second instalment of this chronicle at Brindisi, Sam steamed on towards the Red Sea. 'May God, the God of love and pity have mercy on his blindness and unbelief.'[42] Mrs Matheson was devoted to the conversion of the French: in November, Aunt Harriet Traill and his mother took part in a meeting in support of the MacCall mission in Paris, whereas Johnnie had visited James Cree's mother in Dublin to collect odds and ends for his exiled doctor friend. 'He says he has gone back to Paris to study socialism and he wants to do good, and for that possibility he is giving up everything. He says he is not selfish but quite the reverse, in fact he writes the most utter folly.'[43]

Synge was staying in the Hôtel Corneille. It was there that he met Yeats on 21 December. Momentous consequences duly followed, much to the gratification of the older man. Back in Ireland for the summer of 1897, Synge first began to display the symptoms of a disease – diagnosed in 1907 as Hodgkin's, or lymphatic sarcoma – which would kill him twelve years later. Though *My Uncle John* provides no details, he was also in touch with Cherrie. Her published recollections are occasionally faulty as to dates, a matter in which Yeats plainly declined to assist her. But her reconstruction of Synge's talk clearly indicates a relaxation in the differences between them.

He said: 'It is very amusing to me coming back to Ireland to find myself looked upon as a Pariah, because I don't go to church and am not orthodox, while in Paris amongst the students I am looked upon as a saint, simply because I don't do the things they do, and many come to me as a sort of Father Confessor and wish they could be like me.'[44]

The term 'saint' bandied between one of the saints and the author of *The Well of the Saints* displays a humour which had not been present at the Museum conference of 1896. Synge's political radicalism, which was certainly augmented by his Paris experiences, sharpened his historical awareness. In the memoir of 1924, Cherrie stated that 'he told me he was immensely proud that his grandfather was one of the "Twelve Righteous Men", having refused a peerage at the time of the Union.'

It was not his grandfather, but his great-grandfather (Francis Synge, briefly MP for Swords) who had opposed the Union of Ireland and Britain in 1800. Proud of this ancestry, Synge was not only revealing a sense of the family's historical role in the late eighteenth century but also participating in the revision of Irish historical sympathies which crystallised in the centenary of the 1798 rebellion. Anti-unionists in 1800 had included not only liberal luminaries such as Henry Grattan but also the Orange Lodges and the bulk of commercial prosperity in Dublin city. But just as the Literary Revival of Yeats, Gregory, Synge, and Joyce has been homogenised in recent years for touristic consumption – softening the political and aesthetic differences of fair-minded individuals who rarely spoke well of each other – so, at the time of the Literary Revival, was the stormy decade of revolution, rebellion and union revised in retrospect. Synge's efforts at a play about events in 1798 came to nothing in 1904. His sardonic suggestion that two women of different denominational loyalties might have preferred rape separately at the hands of soldiery or rebels to each other's safe company, did not fit the model propagated by Yeats and others for the 1898 commemorations.

In the spring of 1898, Kathleen Synge suffered an attack of influenza, with the result that when Synge arrived home to Kingstown on 23 April the house was empty. She was recuperating in Greystones, and had sent away her servants. The opportunity for another approach to Cherrie presented itself. Another Museum conference was arranged, and with no more positive result than before. He appealed his case two days later, called to No. 25 to be interviewed by mother and daughter. Mrs Matheson 'rated him soundly for pressing a rejected proposal of marriage when he was not earning enough money to support himself'.[45] The whole episode was ill-judged. If there had to be an appeal beyond the young woman's own judgement, Victorian convention demanded that her father be approached by the hopeful suitor.

Synge can only have felt that he had made a fool of himself. On Monday 9 May, he took the morning train to Galway, *en route* for the Aran Islands. He had never previously been to the county from which his mother derived much of her income, on which he still depended. He had little or no knowledge of the countryside beyond counties Dublin and Wicklow, and was far less well acquainted with the diversity of rural society than his brother Ned had been at the same age. Though he had dwelt beside the Rhine and the Seine, and had looked into the Roman Tiber, he had never crossed the Shannon. And yet, just as he felt foolish in Kingstown, he may have felt that he had already made the fateful choice between Heaven and Connacht.

Stephens gives the impression that a final breach with Cherrie Matheson and the discovery of the western seaboard were closely connected events. Her memoir makes it clear that this was not exactly the case:

he was walking with me one evening in Dublin and I remember him saying: 'I am a poor man, but I feel if I live I shall be rich; I feel there is that in me which will be of value to the world.' At this time he was writing a good deal, and shortly afterwards went to the Aran Islands. After that I only saw him a few times. Once after his return from Aran he said: 'Oh, I wish you could go there, you would love the Island people.'[46]

It is more than likely that the evening walk was that on which he renewed his proposal in April 1898, in which case her recollection strongly suggests that ill-health also featured in the considerations to be weighed – 'if I live I shall be rich'. But it is equally clear that the two were in touch after his return from the west. Given that he travelled from Aran to Lady Gregory's Coole Park for a few days, leaving for Dublin on 29 June and joining his mother in Castle Kevin on 2 July, such a meeting could have occurred in the four days intervening. Were this the case, then both parties had remarkably recovered from the embarrassing interview with Mrs Matheson. Alternatively, John and Cherrie did not meet until after he had returned from the family holiday in County Wicklow, that is, on 2 September at the earliest. Apart from a poem in a Trinity College magazine, and some reports from Paris which appeared anonymously in the *Irish Times*, Synge had published nothing. In November, the *New Ireland Review* carried 'A Story from Innishmaan'.[47] This was a modest start in the business of earning a living, but it was doubtless brought to Cherrie Matheson's attention.

On 14 November 1898 Synge returned to Paris by way of London. Four days later, he took over a room at No. 90 rue d'Assas, not far from the Hôtel Corneille. This remained his permanent address in France until March 1903. Near the close of her memoir, Cherrie, though vague about dates, describes a conversation with him which occurred after her engagement to Houghton. 'During one little chat we had I remember him saying: "You know I am getting quite swell; I have a little house of my own now in Paris." '[48] In this we may detect either Synge's gentle teasing of his property-conscious 'Holy One', or her softened recollection of an interview which was at the time less playful. In either case, the little chat in question must have taken place after Synge had taken over the rooms in the rue d'Assas and had returned to Dublin. The earliest date for this meeting falls between 8 May and 1 June 1899 (when he left Dublin for Castle Kevin). This period was dominated by the first production of Yeats's *The Countess Cathleen*, which Synge attended on 12 May. Consequently, Cherrie is still on-stage in Synge's life even as the theatrical movement for which he will provide the supreme justification was coming into being.

On the basis of precious little, Synge was mixing with the pioneers of a cultural movement which would make an impact across Europe, America, and eventually the entire world; one minute chastised by Mrs Matheson, another addressed by Lady Gregory in terms of warm respect. In the midst of this or even later, he answered a question of Cherrie's about his new acquaintance, Yeats. 'I remember asking him if he was a friend of his – he smiled one of his rare illuminating smiles and said: "You know he is far removed from me, but I think it would not be presumption in me to say he is my friend." He spoke also of Lady Gregory, and told me I should read her plays, that I would love them.'[49]

Now this is at once crucial and confusing. Given that Cherrie Houghton sent her memoir from South Africa to Ireland through Yeats, her report of Synge's highly judicious assessment of his relationship with the poet, and the distance between them, deserves respect. But Lady Gregory had not taken up play-writing much before 1901/2, when *Cathleen ni Houlihan* was written.[50] From this, it follows that the conversation absorbed into Cherrie's memoir occurred as late as the year of her marriage, or – to indulge another alternative – even later, in 1904, when she returned briefly from South Africa. With *In the Shadow of the Glen* produced in October 1903 and *Riders to the Sea* in February 1904, this would keep Cherrie Houghton still on-stage when her rejected lover had established himself as the great original of the Irish theatre. In her modest and yet revealing way, she made this clear when she recorded Synge's approval of the anti-Yeatsean *Dana* (first issue May 1904), an attitude from which she saw no need to dissociate herself. By then, his two one-act plays had been performed in London (26 March).[51] *The Well of the Saints* – his masterpiece reconciling conjugal love and renunciation of the world in favour of an intellectual vision – had been under way since late the previous year. It was completed by mid-June, whereupon he fled from Dublin to Kerry. He had been recently in the company of a most unpredictable saint.

In Thomas Mann's great novel, *Doctor Faustus* (1947), the ill-fated hero, Adrian Leverkühn, is a composer who strikes a bargain with the Devil in order to perfect his art. He is reported by the narrator as acutely and soullessly defining love as 'an amazing and always somewhat unnatural alteration in the relation between the I and the not-I'.[52] Between the Synge of 1904 and the ageing German novelist, there lay two cataclysms of unprecedented destruction. Yet Mann was only four years younger than Synge; his first novel *Buddenbrooks* (1901) was published on the eve of the Irish dramatist's self-discovery and self-denial. It tells a story of patrician bourgeois decline not unlike that which marked the Synges off from the more rackety bohemians of the Irish Literary Revival.

In a suppressed line originally intended for the play we know as *When the Moon Has Set*, Synge had invoked the German Romantic concept of the daemonic to dismiss the Anglo-Irish upper classes as neither human nor divine. As employed by Goethe to characterise Napoleon or the 'world-historical' individual, the daemonic named a near indescribable quality or power: 'It resembled chance, for it evolved no consequences: it was like Providence, for it hinted at connection. All that limits us, it seemed to penetrate; it seemed to sport at will with the necessary elements of our existence; it contracted time and expanded space. In the impossible alone did it appear to find pleasure, while it rejected the possible with contempt.'[53]

Synge read Goethe's autobiography though, as with most of his reading, we have little indication of his response to particular passages. He is closer in spirit to his contemporary, Mann, whose extraordinary story 'Tonio Kröger' ends with the protagonist seeking to convey the profound agony and yet the necessity of being rejected by other artists because he is a bourgeois and being rejected by his bourgeois family because he is an artist. Cherrie Houghton's recollection of Synge's self-presentation returns – 'It is very amusing to ... find myself looked upon as a Pariah, because I don't go to church and am not orthodox, while in Paris ... I am looked upon as a saint.'[54]

The modern 'daemonic' names a subordinacy of self, an incompleteness doubled in ironic compensation. If, in these late conversations with Cherrie Matheson, Synge was successful in effecting even a momentary self-presentation, then the credit should be divided between them. The inwardness of his attempted projection towards her had gradually been given articulation, as much through her refusal to marry him, as through her maintaining dialogue with him. The nurturing of unspoken emotion, the misunderstanding of gesture as response, the tortuous exchange, the repeated calamitous appeal: these stages of the lovers' artifice conclude in the possibility of dramatic release. The discovery of Cherrie Matheson, even when she has become Mrs Kenneth Houghton, still engaged in Synge's self-creation, eclipses any question of her ever being engaged to him. In this mediated sense, she makes the drama possible.

It is pretty certain that sex, in the form longed for by avid biographers, did not raise its lovely head. It may be that she did not love him in anything like the sense that he loved her. Her steady influence was not so much emotional as intellectual if, from the realm of the intellect, we can silently remove all religious questions. Her positive engagement in the arts, albeit in a distinctly amateur fashion, was unmatched in his own family. Not reciprocating his devotion, she made him capable of friendship and trust. As a personal achievement, that is quite impressive, especially among the deeply conventional Brethren.

Irish evangelicalism, laden with biblical allusions, runs like an underground railway beneath the famous names of texts and authors. In keeping with this, symmetry of relationship (as with Cherrie and Johnnie) is of more interest to the alert literary imagination than balance and reciprocation. Samuel Beckett, whose mother prayed Kathleen-like for her son, writes parodically about 'a Miss Farren of Ringaskiddy, who loved a Father Fitt of Ballinclashet, who in all sincerity was bound to acknowledge a certain vocation for a Mrs West of Passage, who loved Neary'.[55] Ballinclashet is Syngean, almost to the last 't'. Shortly after this passage, the Neary in question will travesty the sublime final moment of *Riders to the Sea* and simultaneously unveil its biblical source when he pronounces: 'My grove on Grand Parade ... is wiped as a man wipeth a plate, wiping it and turning it upside down.'[56] The tragicomic muse, which will be Synge's *forte* in the theatre, is neatly encapsulated in Beckett's tribute.

Synge's canon opens in what seems the pure tragic modality, without the hint of a joke. In the sublime final moment of *Riders to the Sea*, Maurya performs the Catholic priestly rite of sprinkling Holy Water on the clothes of her drowned but unrecovered son, which are lying across the feet of another son, also drowned. (An old man inquires of no one in particular if there are nails for the coffin. There are not.) She then stretches the clothes of the absent son beside the body of the present son, and from the cup in which she has kept the water sprinkles the last drops. Her two daughters speak. Then:

MAURYA [*puts the empty cup mouth downwards on the table, and lays her hands together on* BARTLEY's *feet.*] They're all together this time, and the end is come. May the Almighty God have mercy on Bartley's soul, and on Michael's soul, and on the souls of Sheamus and Patch, and Stephen and Shawn [*bending her head*] ... and may He have mercy on my soul, Nora, and on the soul of everyone is left living in the world. [*She pauses, and the keen rises a little more loudly from the women, then sinks away. Continuing.*] Michael has a clean burial in the far north, by the grace of the Almighty God. Bartley will have a fine coffin out of the white boards, and a deep grave surely ... What more can we want than that? No man at all can be living for ever, and we must be satisfied.[57]

Few in the first-night audience in the Molesworth Hall on 25 February 1904 could have placed that down-turned cup among the Old Testament prophets. If there were Brethren present – and the idea is unlikely, though the venue was a parish hall – they would have recalled 2 Kings 21:13: 'And I will stretch over Jerusalem the line of Samaria, and the plummet of the house of Ahab: and I will wipe Jerusalem as a man wipeth a dish, wiping it, and turning it upside down.'

In its profoundly sombre way, *Riders to the Sea* does accommodate jokes. There is an awkward lack of nails for coffin-building. More sub-liminally or sub-textually, there is the outrage of a lay woman usurping the priestly function, and the further outrage of the Catholic peasant mumming a scene from the ultra-Protestant prophetic tradition. But only a saint like Cherrie would get the joke. As only a bargainer against belief could have written lines of such faith.

CHAPTER 12

Dreaming of Captain Dreyfus
on Inis Meáin

... we talked of Parnell, of the county families, of mysticism, the analogy
of that old Biblical distinction of body, soul, and spirit with the sym-
bolical realities of the lamp, the wick, and the flame, and all the time I
was obsessed by the vague, persistent remembrance of those vanishing
islands, which wavered somewhere in the depths of my consciousness.

Arthur Symons[1]

When W. B. Yeats and his companions arrived on Inismore in August
1896, they were greeted by 'a strange being' with 'a curiously beast-like
stealthiness and animation ... a crazy man, bare-footed and blear-eyed,
who held out his hand, and sang out ... "Give me a penny, sir! Give me a
penny, sir!" ' Visitors to such a place inevitably forged an image of their
first encounter. For days Arthur Symons toured the island religiously,
noting 'a holy well, its thorn tree hung with votive ribbons.' In the course
of the same year, the two men attended the opening of Alfred Jarry's
absurdist play, *Ubu Roi*. Yeats made little or nothing of it. Symons,
however, approved its recognition of 'the brutality out of which we have
achieved civilisation'.[2] Aran revealed the underside or obverse of the same
coinage, in its ability to manipulate verbally the world outside. A visiting
Danish philologist, an islander assured him, had spoken 'all the languages,
the Proosy and the Roosy, and the Span and the Grig'.[3]

Synge's decision to visit the Aran Islands is conventionally taken as one
of the most momentous in the history of the Irish Literary Revival. From
it came his greatest prose work, *The Aran Islands* (1907), the germ of
several plays, and an example of commitment to the Gaelic-speaking west
which many would commend and some would follow. The Abbey Theatre
would have been unthinkable without his decision and his annual vis-
itations. Yet the practice of analysing an event in terms of what are
uncritically judged its consequences can be held up to unusually critical
scrutiny in this case. It is true that Synge visited the islands annually from

1898 to 1902, that he set *Riders to the Sea* there, and found the plot of *The Playboy* there. But it is equally true that he spent parts of long summers only, no more than four to six weeks at a time. The cultural significance of his example cannot now be exaggerated, though one might say that some who followed did exaggerate it.

'In the curve of a rocky field, some little way in from the road', Symons recalled 'a young woman, wearing a blue bodice, a red petticoat, and a gray shawl, carrying a tin pail on her head, with that . . . slow and formal grace, of Eastern women who have carried pitchers from the well.' Just as this landscape of mainland Galway prefigures what the travellers will see on Aran, so does the Englishman's aesthetic perspective on costume anticipate Synge's presentation of the islanders in the early pages of his own book. The vignette appeared in *The Savoy* of October 1896; two months later, Synge was allegedly directed to Aran because Symons would always be a better critic of French literature. Both men keenly observed the tiny itinerant population with – 'a company of tinkers . . . trail past, huddled like crouching beasts on their little, rough, open carts, driving a herd of donkeys before them . . .'[4]

Paris, and not just Yeats in Paris, assisted in Synge's decision. The Sorbonne and satellite colleges had played an important part in his development, and on 18 February 1898 he began attending lectures by d'Arbois de Jubainville in which the professor of Celtic at the Collège de France compared ancient Irish and Greek civilisations.[5] Building on his comparative study of philology with Paul Passy, Synge found an approach to questions of dramatic genre (tragedy) and archaic heroism quite different to conventional Aristotelian theories. It had been almost two years earlier that Yeats had delivered his 'Go west, young man' injunction; it was only after listening to de Jubainville that Synge did so.

Many reasons drove him to the Dublin railway station on 9 May 1898. Despair at his rejection in No. 25 Crosthwaite Park may have been one of them. Recollection of Yeats's subsequently trumpeted advice may have been another. The first serves too neatly the biographer's desire for a smooth narrative of cause and effect; the second explanation has been challenged on the grounds that Yeats is no reliable narrator, even of dates.[6] Apart from negligible poems, there was a substantial body of prose (and factual) literature about Aran; we know that Synge had long been acquainted with William Stokes's life of George Petrie (1868) in which Ireland's western isles were written up.

There was also a family connection. Addressing a letter with grand simplicity from 'Galway Bay' in March 1852, the Rev. A. H. Synge had directed his younger brother (father of JMS) to forward 'some of the old parchment leases lying in the loft in the [Glanmore Castle] stable yard rotting'.[7] These vestiges of landlordism were to be used as 'labels for the fish baskets'. Officially, he had upheld the Established Church in the Aran Islands, a vigorously eccentric figure whose distinctive gait an islander would recognise in J. M. Synge more than forty years later. Less officially, he tried to augment his living through the purchase of a largeish boat, and to set himself up in opposition to the fishermen of Galway. It had not taken long for the struggle over anchors and nets, shadowily inscribed on writs and injunctions, to be decided in the locals' favour.[8]

Thereafter, Uncle Alec was a fisher for souls in London and Suffolk. Touchy on the question of working-class encroachment upon his ancient East End parish, he was capable of insights which anticipate his nephew's talent in describing extreme weather and its concealed human elements. 'We have a thorough London Nov[ember] fog on today. We can scarcely discern the houses on the other side of the street. Yesterday the air was impregnated with little urchin voices in every direction shouting out bits of poetry for Nov. 5th & no end of firing off squibs all the evening.'[9]

An obituarist in the *Suffolk Mercury* remembered the late rector of St Peter's, Ipswich, for his 'far from men-pleasing method of advancing what he believed to be the truth'; compare this with Yeats in 1907 writing of the nephew: 'he judges us by himself.'[10] Nor should the rapid decamping from Aran to London be regarded as transcending worlds – while Alec Synge was attached to Trinity Church, in the London parish of Stepney and living on Mile End Road, he came across a clergyman who 'was long ago curate at Anamo [and] 7 Churches . . . Young Stopford Brooke is his curate . . .'[11] The dispersal of Irish clerical families ensured that J. M. Synge had his London contacts in the 1880s and '90s; Isabel Synge, the Ipswich rector's daughter, who lived at suburban Blackheath, south-east of London, was an early recipient of *The Aran Islands* when her first cousin eventually published it in 1907. Apologising for not yet having included her Vanbrugh Park home in his London itineraries, Synge expressed the earnest hope that she would like his book about Aran:

I think – I hope – you are wrong in saying that the Island people attacked him. I have always heard both from the islanders, and Aunt Jane, long ago, that it was the Claddagh fishermen in Galway who did so. They thought his trawl was destroying the spawn of the fish, and it seems they were not altogether mistaken as trawling is not allowed now within three miles of the shore. The old people who remember Uncle Alec so well are of course dying off, but I . . . was shown fruit trees in the parson [sic] garden that he had I think brought from Glanmore. They say he was extraordinarily [sic] powerful and could pull in the guy-yard [?] of his boat single-handed – a job that usually took two men. He made an [sic] sort of avenue also down to the parson's house and carted away the earth himself in a sort of wheel barrow that he used to yoke himself into with a leather strap.[12]

This wealth of remembered detail, garnered during May and June 1898 in the aftermath of Cherrie Matheson's rejection, stands in contrast to the laconic note of an islander's recognition of a distinctive Synge 'walk' to be found in the book's opening pages. Alec Synge's Herculean efforts are in the last analysis less remarkable than his determination to farm the seas commercially and to plant the island with saplings from an encumbered Wicklow estate. If eccentricity and entrepreneurial desperation are alike edited out of the nephew's published text, it certainly does not follow that he went to Aran in search of a personal 'cure', a means of sifting out the dross of recent experience from the pure materials of art. Interpretation is frustrated by a massive lack of evidence – just one letter by Synge survives from the year in question. Once he reached Aran, he felt intensely jealous of those who had got there before him. No one can make 'a fit place of a place every one visits'.[13]

Early in 1897, when both men had been in Paris, the literary Yeats was researching a mystical novel, *The Speckled Bird*, designed to bring its central characters from the Aran Islands to the French capital. The political Yeats strove to involve Synge in Maud Gonne's circle; affiliates included Margaret Stokes, artist, scholar and something of an expert on Aran matters. By April Synge was already laying down the terms of his courteous disengagement from Left Bank Irish nationalism.[14] Despite his differences with the 'revolutionary and semi-military movement' he believed Gonne to be contriving, he not only stayed in touch with Yeats (a desk militarist, at worst) but also remained close to MacKenna. The great scandal in France, where opinion was polarised between anti-Semitic nationalists and the supporters of Captain Alfred Dreyfus, conditioned discussion of every kind. Gonne was a fervent supporter of the Right and – since 1887 – the lover of Lucien Millevoye (a follower of General Boulanger). Yeats remained a more cautious commentator on French politics and racial issues. But it is fair to conclude that the Irish emigré circle in which Synge found himself occasionally embroiled during his Parisian sojourns aligned to the radical right wing of French attitudes.

Between 20 and 22 January 1898, he had stayed over in London *en route* from Dublin to Paris. Yeats invited him to Woburn Buildings in

Bloomsbury; no record survives of this encounter. On Inismore later in the year, Synge and Lady Gregory observed each other's presence but, never having been formally introduced, did not speak. On 21 June, Yeats wrote from Coole Park: 'Lady Gregory asks me to ask you here for a day or two, when you are on your way back to civilization. We can then talk about Aran & your work there.'[15] From this it is clear that Synge had already planned to write about the island, perhaps in contrasting parallel to Yeats's novel-in-progress, and Yeats was responding to an earlier letter – now lost – from Synge. In Galway Synge also trod in his father's footsteps as the late proprietor of those 'towns, hamlets and lands of Knockroe, Brackloon and Gurtagurnane' which still yielded a modest income.

The gathering at Coole in late June provides a useful focus for a consideration of Synge's state of mind at the time of his first visit to Aran. Like his distinguished fellow guest, he was familiar with Paris and London – more at ease in Paris than Yeats because he spoke the language, less so in London. The poet's oscillations between masturbation and drug-taking probably went unnoticed at Coole, yet Roy Foster has spotted a constant 'prickle of mutual suspicion' which on Synge's side could flair up into fastidious distaste for Yeats's mode of living.[16] Gregory's piety and Yeats's love-lornness may have conjured up Cherrie; the reasons for his being in the west were mixed.

Though Yeats had tucked his feet under her ladyship's dining table two years earlier, Synge enjoyed the better claim to that privilege. When he visited Edward Martyn at nearby Tullyra Castle, his family's name carried with it a legend older than any enjoyed by a Gregory or a Yeats, even if none could rival the ancient dignities of the Martyns, Norman settlers of pre-Reformation times. While he was no scholar in the academic sense, he was long acquainted with the antiquarian-cum-archaeological tradition of Irish self-definition for which the primitive redoubts of the west and south-west held a special fascination. Legendary saints clustered in these remote locations more thickly than at the meetings of Brethren at Greystones or Kingstown. In 1870 an anonymous pamphlet recorded *A Visit to the Aran-More of St Enda* – this was probably written by George Coffey, uncle of James Cree. The barrister Oliver J. Burke's *South Isles of Aran* (1887) struck a more contemporary note. While not failing to acknowledge the plethora of early Christian remains, he added for good value that the kind of potatoes eaten there were called 'the Protestants'. As if to test this blasphemy, Henry Truell, of the Wicklow family which hated the Established Church and orthodox medicine, travelled to Aran with the Royal Society of Antiquaries in July 1895.[17]

Commenting on litigation in 1886 between the islanders and their landlords – Miss Digby of Landenstown in Kildare, and the Hon. Thomas Kenelm Digby St Lawrence – Burke indicates that the latter were represented by 'Mr Stephens'. The islands, storm-girt in the poet's eye, were being drawn into the processes of modern disputation and improvement. In 1891 a road had been thrown across the main island by Chief Secretary A. J. 'Bloody' Balfour. As Synge indicated in the early pages of his book, scholars had long grazed the harsh pasture of the islanders' language. These processes were intimately if ironically linked. To philologists of the German school, the west was witnessing the last stand of a language imperilled by industrialisation and the inroads of imperial languages, English and French in particular. While the islanders might declare that 'there are very few rich men now in the world who are not studying the Gaelic', their audible speech was becoming a signifier of untold wealth.

Synge recorded his first impressions of Aran in diary French -'Dans le batteau à Arranmore à Hôtel'. This is not so much the alienation of the Parisian-based tourist as it is the irony of the future dramatist.[18] On the other hand, that figure of Mr Stephens in O. J. Burke's account of 1886/7 litigation between landlords and tenants on the islands deserves a second glance. Years later, Harry Stephens was involved in negotiations whereby holdings of Lord Ardilaun were transferred to the Congested Districts Board for division among Aran islanders. That was in 1908, but the earlier landlords' use of a Mr Stephens would suggest that Harry's family had been involved with Aran land for twenty years.[19] Synge's diary entry for 10 May 1898, however, is complicated by very different material of the same period, preserved in a notebook:

If a man could be supposed to come with a fully educated perception of music, yet quite ignorant of it and hear for the first time let us say Lamoureux's Orchestra in a late symphony of Beethoven I doubt his brain would ever recover from the shock. If a man could come with a full power of appreciation and stand for the first time before a woman – a woman perhaps who was very beautiful – what would he suffer? If a man grew up knowing nothing of death or decay and found suddenly a corpse in his path what would he suffer? Some such emotion was in me the day I looked first on these magnificent waves towering in dazzling white and green before the cliff.[20]

Shock is the key term. Synge had turned back to face the sea rather than the rocky fields about which his brother-in-law argued some time or other. And if he knew nothing of Harry's activities twelve years earlier, he knew of Uncle Alec's, both spiritual and commercial. The succession of traumatic confrontations which he imagines – Beethoven, a woman, a corpse – may chart an ideal decadence but it does not really conclude or find reversal in unmediated nature. The notebook-keeper has already landed and, whether from the cliff-top (Hamlet-like) or from a safer and lower point, he contemplates the Atlantic waves as the necessary veil protecting him from recent history.

Nietzsche published *The Birth of Tragedy* in the year of Jack Synge's death (1872). It seems unlikely that the author of *Riders to the Sea*, having read *Zarathustra*, omitted to read the shorter, more focused work. There the Apollonian and Dionysiac moods had been contrasted in terms which are strikingly echoed in Synge's notebooks – 'moved by the urge to talk of music in Apollonian similitudes, he must first comprehend the whole range of nature, including himself, as the eternal source of volition, desire, appetite. But, to the extent that he interprets music through images, he is dwelling on the still sea of Apollonian contemplation, no matter how turbulently all that he beholds through the musical medium may surge about him.'[21]

Synge's arrival on Aran on 10 May 1898 led to an aesthetic and philo-sophical crisis. As early as 1894/5, he had been reading Hegel and Marx: about what he called Transfigured Realism, he wrote that it 'simply asserts objective existence as separate from and independent of subjective exist-ence. But it asserts neither that any one mode of this existence is in reality that which it seems, nor that the connexions among its modes are objectively what they seem.'[22] That was the stuff his German and French travels were made on: now reality and seeming washed through each other on an Irish western shore. Apart from Wicklow, Synge had no great experience of the rural landscape. 'I have seen nothing so desolate,' he wrote in the opening paragraphs of the book which took more than eight years to reach print.[23] He had lived by the Rhine, and had seen the Alps in travelling to or back from Rome. These were guidebook visions, no matter how warmly he responded. He came to the Atlantic abruptly. Yeats may have been ringing in his ears. Mrs Matheson may have been ringing in his ears. But neither exhortation nor rebuke provides an adequate motive. Synge's encounter with Aran in May 1898 can only be measured against the doubling of exhortation into rebuke, that is, against an over-determined imperative.

He put up in the Atlantic Hotel, where Symons had stayed two summers earlier. This was a two-storeyed public house in the village of Kilronan, until recently a line of three whitewashed cottages but elevated to hotel status in its own eyes by occasional parties of bicycling priests on holiday from the mainland. The kitchen served as the landlady's bedroom. On the day of his arrival, he sought instruction in Gaelic and was recommended to Máirtín Ó Conghaile (anglicised as Martin Conneely). The half-blind old man had acted as guide to Sir William Wilde and others in mid-century, and Synge recognised a link with George Petrie whose books he had read 'years since when I was first touched with antiquarian passion'.[24] In fact, the old man had saluted him in Gaelic by the roadside though the island was bilingual. Now Máirtín climbed the rickety stairs to introduce himself. His previous association with British, German and Irish scholars provides a bridge between Synge's undergraduate learning of Gaelic and his presence on the island. Máirtín is described affectionately in *The Aran Islands* as witty and companionable; his disability is ascribed to an accident in mid-life – 'he had fallen over a cliff, and since then he had had little eyesight, and a trembling of his hands and head.'[25]

Among Máirtín's stories of the fairies was one in which the fate of a stolen child was conveyed to distressed humanity by silent mimicry, 'Then a dummy came and made signs of hammering nails in a coffin.'[26] Though Synge's official purpose in going to Aran had apparently been linguistic, and so related to the senses through sound and hearing, what is immediately conveyed both in the notebook kept at the time and in *The Aran Islands* is the crucial role of sight. As a symptom of his inadequate assimilation, Synge is reminded of 'the country near Rome' but this is momentary, an effect of conventional framing imposed on a more diverse scene. That evening another old man called 'and said he had known a relative of mine who passed some time on this island forty-three years ago'. When he went down to the kitchen-cum-public-bar, two men from Inis Meáin had arrived to stay overnight, obliged to do so by the bad weather or some other adverse circumstance. These in effect introduce him to the middle island, 'where Gaelic is more generally used, and the life is perhaps the most primitive that is left in Europe'. Though they are 'a simpler and perhaps a more interesting type than the people here', they also talk about 'the Book of Kells, and other ancient MSS, with the names of which they seemed familiar'.[27] His decision to move across to the middle island is based on a wish to improve his Gaelic, but it neatly takes him from a community where his family history is known into one where scholarship (however oddly conceived) is respected.

Before the journey by *curach* (a canoe covered with tarred canvas) brings him to the less bilingual island, Synge records his last day on Aranmor in a string of incidents and stories involving 'the Catholic theology of the fairies', 'the druids', 'wild mythology', 'many long prayers and sermons in Irish', and other highly-charged topics of belief. Sexual material is intermixed with this, as when 'old Máirtín took a freak of earthly humour and began telling what he would have done if he could have come in there when he was a young man and a young girl along with him'. The blind man also recited Gaelic poetry 'with an exquisite purity of intonation that brought tears to my eyes though I understood but little of the meaning'. These performances had taken place in a dry-stone hut of early Christian origin, virtually underground.[28]

That was on 23 May. The next day Synge left for Inis Meáin, but wrote in the published account, 'when we set off it was a brilliant morning in April ...' The May-to-April adjustment may have been made to accommodate the changeable weather for readers unlikely to associate May with storms. But it is also a piece of Apollonian self-editing, part of a sustained process of mediation between material and author, author and reader. Synge's final day on Aranmor, before moving to the middle island, had concluded (in his account of it) with Máirtín's subterranean sexual fantasies and poetic recital. Having come out into the sunlight, and passed a slated house where the schoolmistress lived ('Ah, master,' he said, 'wouldn't it be fine to be in there, and to be kissing her?') the two men walked several miles. Then at Teampall an Cheathrar Álainn (the church of the four beautiful persons) yet another old man told Synge of a miraculous cure effected at the well nearby, and gave him the basis for *The Well of the Saints*. In the Aran folk narrative, the person who receives his sight is a boy from Sligo, whereas Synge in his play will exclude children to concentrate on two ageing beggars.

The final recorded exchange with his Aranmore guide introduces Máirtín's successor, an old Inis Meáin man who walks on two sticks and talks of the fairies. 'Did you ever hear what it is,' Máirtín asks, 'goes on four legs when it is young, and on two legs after that, and on three legs when it does be old?'

I gave him the answer.

'Ah, master,' he said, 'you're a cute one, and the blessing of God be on you. Well, I'm on three legs this minute, but the old man beyond is back on four; I don't know if I'm better than the way he is; he's got his sight and I'm only an old dark man.'[29]

Synge's first spell in Aran ends in his answering the riddle of the sphinx.

*

This shapely configuration of a fortnight on the dark edge of Europe must be modified to accommodate less primitive matters. At the hotel, he and another visitor named Redmond struck up an acquaintance which led to his acquiring a camera. The hand-held Lancaster was awkward to handle, and Kilronan had no facilities for inspecting or treating his plates. These were carefully packed up for development in Castle Kevin by Frank Stephens.[30] Photography was a hobby pursued by many in the Crosthwaite Park circle, including the Mathesons. It provided Synge with a means of focusing his impressions of Aran, obliging him to select images, and to interpret the 'negatives' as a stage towards understanding.

Though he often benefited from the courtesy of Catholic clergy either visiting the island or (as with Father Farragher) ministering to the community, his contacts with the rector were slight. After four days, he introduced himself to the priest. The next two days were devoted to Maupassant's *Une Vie*, and then on 20 May he took his usual lesson in Gaelic, finished *Madame Bovary*, and went 'to the cliffs and to Mr Kilbride'.[31] William Kilbride died in the winter of 1898/9, and with him a tradition of proselytising going back to the days of Uncle Alec. Synge was informed by an islander friend that the rector's boat had been torn loose by a storm after his death and broken up on the rocks.[32]

Stephens's interpretation of his uncle's encounter with Aran has the effect of distracting attention from the society Synge had temporarily left behind in travelling west. It is in many ways an admirable précis of official Literary Revival beliefs, stressing the beneficial access to folklore and traditional symbolism which urbanisation was destroying. It is undeniable that 'the stories that John heard in Aran provided him with plots for his [drama]', but questionable in the extreme that this resulted 'because they were free from disputations . . .'[33] Some significance lies in his use of French to record events which took place through the medium of Gaelic. On 28 May he heard a 'Histoire des fées par P.D.', that is a history of the fairies, from Pat Dirane. These Francophone entries indicate a refusal to use English while he was actively improving his Gaelic. When, on 26 May, he noted 'Ecrit à Miss Hardon etc. tour de l'isle avec Mourteen' he linked the French and Gaelic worlds more indiscriminately. This was in keeping with everything he heard round about him. Miracles and evictions, murder, factory-fishing, and bilingual gossip all reached him on the same breeze.

Fishing was crucial to the islanders' survival. As Synge conceded in the introduction to his book, Kilronan was undergoing rapid change during the years of his annual visits, 1898–1902. The industry was developed by the Congested Districts Board so that 'it has now very little to distinguish it from any fishing village on the west coast of Ireland'. It was more advanced than some mainland areas. Father Farragher was active in the Aran Co-operative Fishing Society (modelled on an initiative taken on the Isle of Man). Seven Arklow boats, 'subsidised to make an experimental fishing at the Aran Islands', joined five other craft to constitute a small fleet. In April 1892 an ice-hulk was set up at Kilronan pier, where six thousand mackerel were processed in the first catch. More than seventy thousand were iced in a day, 'sent by steamer to Galway, and railed by special train to Dublin for shipment to England'. Autumn catches were cured for sale in the United States.[34] Just as the influences directing Synge to Aran included both Robert Matheson and W. B. Yeats, so the society which confronted him manifested subsistence and development, the primitive and the entrepreneurial. Uncle Alec had not been so wrong after all.

From 24 May to 9 June 1898, he stayed on Inis Meáin. Of the journey from island to more remote island, he wrote, 'It gave me a moment of exquisite satisfaction to find myself moving away from civilization in this rude canvas canoe of a model that has served primitive races since men first went on the sea.'[35] His use of the term 'moment' is repeated within consecutive sentences to characterise the thrill of going to sea and the business of checking in to a government-sponsored industrial project. In a notebook used at various times in his career, he contrasted Nietzsche with Walter Pater:

Nietzsche fails by seeking the sur-humain and thus yoking life and joy to a hypothesis in time
A truer morality would find everything in the instant – compare perhaps Pater noting that his views were city views not cosmic –[36]

This cryptic jotting appears close to reading-notes on Louis Petit de Julleville's *Théâtre en France* (1880) from which Synge derived further ideas for *The Well of the Saints*. His preference for the instant, rather than the passing, of time is no casual whim. Nor should his search for a 'truer morality' than Nietzsche's lead one to conclude that he was immune to the German's radical influence. As the paralleling of *The Aran Islands* with notebook entries eloquently testifies, Synge felt turbulence keenly.

'Every article on these islands has an almost personal character, which gives this simple life, where all art is unknown, something of the artistic beauty of medieval life.'[37] But whereas *The Aran Islands* will follow this up with an account of female dress equally cerebral, the notebook reveals a greater impact:

What has guided the women of grey-brown western Ireland to clothe them[selves] in red? The island without this simple red relief would be a nightmare fit to drive one to murder in order to gloat a while on the fresh red flow of blood...[38]

Or again, less melodramatically:

All the unoccupied women have thrown their shawls or petticoats over their heads and come down to sit in beautiful groups along the sea-wall and watch what goes on. Excitement is added by the arrival of the Indian meal sent as relief, and the Irish runs round me faster than I can understand ... I am so much a stranger I cannot dare under the attention I excite to gaze as I would wish at a beautiful oval face that looks from a brown shawl near me...[39]

These expressions of mental excitation were evidently stimulated during Synge's first week or two in the islands. They form part of the turbulence recorded after his giddy contemplation of the ocean at the cliff's foot. Linking such passages to Synge's interest in Nietzsche might seem excessive were it not for the distinctly foreign reading matter he had stuffed in his luggage – works by Flaubert, Loti, Swedenborg, Maupassant and the thirteenth-century *chante-fable*, 'Aucassin et Nicolette'. The last two, sharing a shelf in the Atlantic Hotel's draughty upper room, make up an odd pair – a medieval romance about frustrated love between young persons of the nobility, and a tough tale by France's most unrelenting realist. 'Aucassin et Nicolette' may have gotten into the luggage as a sentimental gesture towards Cherrie Matheson, though what really stood between John and Cherrie was Cherrie, not some tyrannical law of caste or race or even religion. Flaubert and Maupassant may have appealed because they stood for the country he had left behind, but they also represented a side of French culture which he had never approached personally or stylistically. The reading list was a mistake, like a guest list compiled by numbers, odd numbers more than evens.

   He dutifully read *Madame Bovary*, or part of it, in French, perched on some outcrop of granite or hunched beside a candle in a fisherman's cottage. He dutifully learned Gaelic from his new guide on Inis Meáin, Máirtín Mac Donncha (Michael in *The Aran Islands*). Pat Dirane, the old man he had heard so much of on Aranmor, was an accomplished traditional storyteller whose recitation about the Lady O'Conor included details of a woman's weight in gold similar to those he would hear of Elizabeth Synge three years later in Wicklow. Synge was well aware of how central motifs in folk-tale surface in slightly different forms in different parts of the world, and appreciated the strong element of ritual in Dirane's art. His closing phrase is given as 'That is my story', which exactly renders the Gaelic formulaic, 'Sé mo scéal'. Synge published a version of 'The Lady O'Conor' in the *New Ireland Review* of November 1898. From Dirane he heard the essential details of what became *In the Shadow of the Glen*, a tale of a husband shamming death to test his unfaithful wife, though the story veers decisively towards the wife's part in Synge's dramatisation.

One prompt assessment of his journey westward rests on his discovery of plots for drama. Accounts of the boy cured near Teampall an Cheathrair Álainn, and Dirane's version of the well-known folk-tale, 'The Faithful Wife', both noted by Synge in his first weeks on the islands, led to two of the plays which made his name. Before he left on 25 June, he attended a funeral which provided the atmosphere for *Riders to the Sea* and heard often about 'a Connaught man who killed his father with the blow of a spade when he was in passion, and then fled to this island and threw himself on the mercy of some of the natives with whom he was said to be related'.[40] How a writer adapts his material is just as important as its discovery. With Synge, the question is more complicated because our information about these stories is restricted to his own account in *The Aran Islands*, a book crafted no less carefully than his plays.

For example, an old man's story of the Connacht parricide fits into Synge's book alongside two different kinds of material – Dirane's recitation (which has its affinities with Shakespeare's *Cymbeline*) and accounts of events so recent that Synge himself observed them.[41] Thus the origins of *The Playboy of the Western World* are discovered by the reader midway between folklore and history. An immediate comparison of the storyteller's protagonist and Synge's Christy Mahon reveals a shift in family relationships – the Connacht man relied on the support of kinsmen on the islands, whereas Christy is wholly unknown and unconnected in the remote mainland area to which he has fled from the south. Blood relationship between characters in *The Playboy* will be important – it impedes the marriage of Pegeen Mike and her miserable cousin, Seán Keogh – but it does not affect the official moral dilemma of the play – whether a man confessing to murder should be accommodated in a house.

This attitude towards kinship and culpability is significant, given his brother-in-law's later activities. The sharpest pages of Part One of *The Aran Islands* are devoted to evictions carried out on Inis Meáin on 11 June 1898. 'Two recent attempts . . . came to nothing, for each time a sudden storm rose, by, it is said, the power of a native witch, when the steamer was approaching, and made it impossible to land.' Tim Robinson provides a summary history of evictions in 1884, 1886, and in January and May 1898. The January attempt failed due to strong local resistance, while that of May had indeed been frustrated by storms.[42] Synge's placing of the evictions suggests an urge to absorb contemporary affairs into the fabric of ritual and tradition.

The crisis had arisen because one islander had 'sold his honour' by agreeing to act as bailiff for the authorities enforcing the property rights of Henrietta Eliza Guinness and Geraldine Digby St Lawrence. Prices had recently fallen, and the plight of those islanders in arrears with their rent was acute. There had also been an outbreak of flu, which contributed to the general depression to which Synge responded sympathetically. He had witnessed police baton-charges in Paris and Dublin the previous year, and had quarrelled earlier with his land-agent brother about the Carey evictions on Glanmore in Wicklow. Moreover, the strong suspicion arises that he well knew his brother-in-law of fourteen years' standing was a partner in the legal firm advising the Misses Guinness and St Lawrence. His clerical uncle's reputation as an interloper who had tried to profit from traditional fishing grounds was still lively.

The evicting party of armed policemen travelled with 'a low rabble, who had been brought to act as drivers by the sheriff'. In addition, there was a doctor, a relieving officer, and an individual from Kilronan who was to identify the cottages of defaulting tenants. Though Synge records with little emotion the injuries suffered by animals in the rough conditions of island farming, and coolly approves the courage of men risking death on the sea, he responds to the 'mechanical police, with the commonplace agents and sheriffs' with undisguised wrath. He inveighs against 'the newer types of humanity' who represent 'aptly enough the civilisation for which the homes of the island were to be desecrated'. The sight of beds and kitchen utensils thrown out of what are little more than hovels moved him deeply, as did 'the wild imprecations' of an evicted woman who belonged to 'one of the most primitive families on the island'.[43]

During this discourse, the people become 'natives', a term strictly accurate but smacking more of the anthropologist's classification than the onlooker's sympathy. Emotion itself becomes classified, disposed in the written composition, and when some young men seek Synge's advice about setting a bull loose on the evicting party, he counsels against it. The writing of *The Aran Islands* is best appreciated not in terms of expression, as generally understood, but restraint. T. S. Eliot's critique of Words-worthian romanticism (emotion recollected in tranquillity, etc.) is apt here: strictly speaking, Eliot insisted, poetry is not emotion as such, nor is tranquillity involved, if properly understood. Instead, he insisted that 'the only way of expressing emotion in the form of art is by finding an "objective correlative"; in other words, a set of objects, a situation, a chain of events which shall be the formula of that *particular* emotion.'[44] Before congratulating Synge on anticipating Eliot in this connection, we should note that it was Nietzsche, in *The Birth of Tragedy*, who had originally conceived of 'the objective correlative'. When we moderns attend a Greek tragic play, the words of the heroes' speeches do not measure up to their actions, 'the myth, we might say, never finds an adequate objective correlative in the spoken word'.[45] Synge's decisive contribution to world theatre will not so much be a dramatic idiom (though that is fine) nor a complex negotiation between tragedy and comedy (though that too is fine) but it will involve a strikingly direct and subtle use of stage properties. Synge's 'props' are always in dialogue with his characters; they represent that reticence or decorum which he has chosen to flout in his char-acterisation. Such objective correlatives he came to understand on Aran.

But the islands lay westward of a larger island to which he had to return. On the steamer he spotted 'Gregory' but still did not speak. As a preparation for meeting both her and Yeats, he read *John Sherman*, a very short novella by Yeats set in a distinctly middle-class small town west of Ireland milieu. Hardly a representative choice, but a shrewd one, given Yeats's tendency to promote himself on the social ladder.[46] At Coole Park, on his way back to Dublin, Synge found himself in effect recruited to a movement. He was becoming an object of interest to impresarios, some of them ridiculous, others sublime. The aftermath of this terrifying exhil-aration was two months (2 July–2 September 1898) at Castle Kevin. He bicycled, walked and, much to his mother's distress, talked to tramps who remembered the whiskey distributed by earlier Synges.[47]

His return to Paris on 18 November led directly into his taking over Richard Best's flat in the rue d'Assas. Walter Pater's *Imaginary Portraits* (1887) prompted him to persevere with a disguised self-portrait in words. Within it he placed images, or rather silhouettes in stark outline, of several women. Burdened with extraordinary names – 'the Celliniani' and 'the Chouska' – these contrivances provide no clear framework for the narrator's own personality. The Parisian writings learn nothing from the experience of Aran, though they confirm the traumatised state of their author. One undertaking which has resisted scrutiny was a novel, under way by 12 January 1899, with the provisional title, 'Insight on the Path'. Nothing but diary entries of the curtest kind survive.[48] In April he paid a fortnight's visit to Brittany, a Celtic periphery within the French state. Letters to his mother arrived on 6 and 15 April: yet Synge's published correspondence includes not a single item for the year 1899. Back in Paris, he had further conversations and excursions with the American Margaret Hardon to whom he had written from Aran. A high degree of mutual misunderstanding ensued. On 9 May 1899, he returned to Crosthwaite Park.

Stephens alludes to 'a number of reasons' why Mrs Synge had so very early decided her summer plans, but specifies none. Robert Synge's activities in seeking to recover Glanmore for their branch of the family may have played their part. The Stephenses were not able to leave Dublin early, so she had recruited Edie Harmar (Sam Synge's sister-in-law) and her friend Madeleine Kerr as companions. John automatically was part of any Wicklow party. While the summer passed pleasantly, it brought contrasting moments of distress. On 12 June, Synge received a letter from Paris in which Hardon diplomatically annihilated any notion of romance or marriage – 'When I was in London I went to a palmist and she told me I was to marry a military man ...' Synge's sensible reply written the following day must also be listed among the missing.[49]

If Margaret Hardon had stimulated his interest in dreams and omens, Edie Harmar alarmed him. Asleep in a Castle Kevin bedroom, she thought herself awake with a hand-mirror by her side. A voice invited her to look and see: in a four-stage vision, she saw a girlfriend and the dead body of her brother, then she saw Synge leaning on his bicycle and talking eagerly; next she saw him smoking a pipe outside a cottage; finally, 'she lifted the mirror and saw in it a vision of John praying in a church'. Informed of this next morning, Synge recognised an Aran cottage and a German pipe he had used the previous summer. When Edie described the scene in which Synge prayed in church, he replied fervently, 'If you believe in prayer, pray that this may never happen.'[50]

Right at the close of his Wicklow sojourn, he read one of the classics of Irish satire, Maria Edgeworth's brief and comic novel, *Castle Rackrent* (1800), following it up with her more didactic *The Absentee* (1812). A few weeks earlier, he had been one of a group who drove over to Tiglin and Glanmore with Edie and Madeleine. In Stephens's view, his Uncle John 'joined the party because he loved the Devil's Glen and the woods and enjoyed showing the family home to friends'. This may well have been the case, but his subsequent reading of Edgeworth's ironic treatment of 'the big house' can only have served to point up pseudo-Gothic pretensions in the Castle. There was also Aunt Editha's 'peculiar cordiality which, to the time of her death, almost led her relations to forget the harm that she had done'. That *The Absentee* featured a Wicklow villa (the La Touche house near Delgany) also associated with evangelical piety, registered with the temporary resident in Castle Kevin.[51]

Summer in Aran is not always bright and sunny. An ocean of unmeasurable power sweeps over it without rest. But contrast rather than constant weather of any kind is the characteristic island experience:

A week of sweeping fogs has passed over and given me a strange sense of exile and desolation. I walk round the island nearly every day, yet I can see nothing anywhere but a mass of wet rock, a strip of surf and then a tumult of waves.

The slaty limestone has grown black with the water that is dripping on it, and wherever I turn there is the same grey obsession twining and wreathing itself among the narrow fields, and the same wail from the wind that shrieks and whistles in the loose rubble of the walls.[52]

Though very shortly 'it has cleared and the sun is shining . . .' the contrast here is between the internal and external. On his way to the west in September 1899, Synge stopped in Galway to meet Michael (Máirtín Mac Donncha, his island friend of the previous year) who had taken work on the mainland. Part Two of *The Aran Islands* opens with a displaced islander, a second Gaelic-speaking labourer, and Synge himself lying on a beach near Galway City for hours, arguing mildly and looking at women bathing. Even at this early point, the book signals its unwillingness to become a manual of primitivist sentiment or back-to-the-soil politics. As Synge knew, there wasn't enough soil on Aran.

From 12 September to 7 October he was on Inis Meáin, with only a few days spent on the bigger island. When 'a young and beautiful woman' leaned across his knees the better to see some photographs, Synge 'felt more than ever the strange simplicity of the island life'. This was hardly the stuff of primal bonding, and Synge in his written account of the incident goes out of his way to present photography as a complex mediation between himself and the islanders. His pictures from the previous year's visit were scrutinised till everyone was identified, 'even those who only showed a hand or a leg'. But when he produced others 'showing fairs in Rathdrum or Aughrim, men cutting turf on the hills, or other scenes of inland life', he describes these Wicklow images as 'fragments', comparable (by implication) with the leg or the arm in his Aran pictures.[53]

By further implication, he was able to give only a fragmentary or at best incomplete account of the islands and islanders, not because of any deficiency in him as a writer but because the whole (meaning a total reality) would be intolerable. One central aspect of human reality – death – especially defies representation. When, in the autumn of 1899, Synge recognised that 'this year I see a darker side of life in the islands' he was doing more than admitting the late season of his arrival. Weather obliterated and transformed the landscape; emigration took sons and sent back remittances; languages played leap-frog with each other so that Máirtín Mac Donncha was obliged to write home in English, being the only one among them who could read or write in Gaelic. Synge, who came to learn, found himself translating his tutor's letter for the household.

Palmistry in London and mild visions in Castle Kevin paled before 'this world of inarticulate power'. Synge keenly felt the extent of his exposure, not just socially but (in a Parisian term) existentially. On the night of Monday/Tuesday 25/26 September 1899, he dreamed of Alfred Dreyfus, the disgraced (and wholly innocent) French officer who had been a victim of rampant anti-Semitism. Found guilty of treason, Dreyfus had been banished to Devil's Island, off French Guiana, three years earlier. On 19 September, he was finally pardoned by presidential decree. Within a week news had reached Synge on Inis Meáin, presumably through a letter from France. Synge's own loyalties were undergoing a radical transformation and, in a far colder climate, he was prone to fear that he too had been cast out. 'If anything serious should happen to me I might die here and be nailed in my box, and shoved down into a wet crevice in the graveyard before anyone could know it on the mainland.'[54] This fear, not without a nod towards the old morbidity of the 'Étude', is followed up with a description of a child (not old enough to have a name) who eats cold potatoes and drinks very strong tea. He, unlike Synge, 'seems in perfect health', a dexterously placed youngster with an adult diet. Released from Devil's Island, Dreyfus did not make it into *The Aran Islands*.

Synge's fear of dying stands in stark contrast to his treatment of the topic in his first notebook relating to the 1898 visit. At sea in a curragh he had speculated:

What a difference to die here with the fresh sea saltiness in my hair than to struggle in soiled sheets and thick stifling blankets with a smell of my own illness in my nostril and a half-paid death tender [?] at my side till my long death battle will be fought out.

This passage did not find its way in to his book, and the musings on death in Part Two must seem positively healthy compared with the initial Keatsian desire. *The Aran Islands* tends to displace the Aran Islands. This is partly due to the paucity of information about Synge's life there, and not due to any post-modernist scepticism on the topic generally of knowledge about the past. Synge's literary activity does not displace or deny the real world: on the contrary it seeks to indicate, however indirectly and by way of formal arrangement, what is too often 'inarticulate power'. His reports of great talk among the islanders about war should not be read as evidence of an indigenous interest in violence, nor even as a massive curiosity about the outside world. They are part of a network of dialogues, negotiations, and exchanges in which the unimaginable or the ineffable is raised by way of questioning.

This dialogic view of culture emerges during the second visit. The sense of 'shock' is still present from the earliest moments of Synge's first encounter with the Aran landscape, but now the focus of attention is on human interactivity:

In some ways these men and women seem strangely far away from me. They have the same emotions that I have, and the animals have, yet I cannot talk to them when there is much to say, more than to the dog that whinges beside me in a mountain fog.

There is hardly an hour I am with them that I do not feel the shock of some inconceivable idea, and then again the shock of some vague emotion that is familiar to them and to me. On some days I feel this island as a perfect home and resting place; on other days I feel that I am a waif among the people. I can feel more with them than they can feel with me, and while I wander among them, they like me sometimes, and laugh at me sometimes, yet never know what I am doing.[56]

To Synge's development while visiting the islands, 1899 provided its fair share. Not only had he improved his vernacular Gaelic but, with his apparently sturdy physique, he had been accepted among the rowers who took their frail craft between the islands. This required courage, all the more so in one who accepted an old islander's theory of fear: ' "A man who is not afraid of the sea will soon be drownded," he said, "for he will be going out on a day he shouldn't. But we do be afraid of the sea, and we do only be drownded now and again." ' A thrilling curagh voyage then follows, with Synge taking the last seat in the boat. After an Odyssean struggle to keep control against 'magnificently brilliant waves ... rolling down on us at right angles' a crisis passed and 'we regained our course and rowed violently for a few yards...'[57]

Time on Inis Meáin moved almost as unexpectedly as the raging sea. Part Two of *The Aran Islands* conveys this by a contrast between its generally undated and undatable events and a calendar-exact commemoration invoked in its final pages. The myths and legends of Part One are replaced or represented by an expanded moment, a boundless present. But the second visit is also rigorously brought to a close with a return to the mainland, and an encounter with soldiers and a crowd of Parnellites at Ballinasloe, County Galway. Here the Franco-Jewish victim of Synge's dream acquires a local Anglo-Irish name, albeit in death. On the overloaded night-train, Synge found himself beside a young girl to whom he pointed out features of the countryside as they approached Dublin at dawn. 'Oh it's lovely, but I can't see it,' she exclaimed, obliging in her anticipation of *The Well of the Saints*. Round her, obscene songs and drunken merriment ruled. The last words in Synge's account of his 1899 visit to Aran virtually carry him to the rail terminus in Dublin. 'The whole spirit of the west of Ireland, with its strange wildness and reserve, seemed moving in this single train to pay a last homage to the dead statesman of the east.'[58]

The statesman was the Wicklow landowner, Parnell, who had died eight years earlier on 8 October 1891. The prelude to his death in Brighton had been a tumult of unprecedented bitterness and vituperation. The 'split' – a political response to basically private and domestic issues – survived 'the Chief', and indeed in one form or another remains high on the agenda of Irish nationalist organisations. By 1899 the kind of politics Parnell had stood for – a shrewd mixture of liberal reform on the land issue, a strong dose of nationalism presented as Home Rule, and a not unimportant display of stiff upper lip – was in abeyance, perhaps for good. Yet Synge refers to encountering his wild fellow travellers on 'the eve of the Parnell *celebration*' (author's emphasis). In miniature, he anticipates the cultic exploitation of a dead hero which will characterise Yeats's treatment of Parnell in the 1930s. The politics of *The Aran Islands* is complicated by this external incident, itself thematised oddly through the substitution of 'celebration' where 'commemoration' might be expected. Whereas Part One had focused on eviction as a symptom not only of landlord greed but also of bureaucratic process, and the body of Part Two had included discussion of language as a subject of revivalist activity, these final paragraphs of Part Two locate politics off the islands entirely.

Autumn arrival became a standard aspect of Synge's relationship with the islands, and for some years he moved according to a regular pattern between Dublin (spring–summer), Wicklow (summer), Aran (autumn), and Paris (winter–spring). In Paris he read and wrote, with little to show for it. In Dublin, he lived at home with his mother, and with his Stephens in-laws next door, working in his own room and visiting friends in the city, but essentially purposeless. Wicklow brought a temporary re-attachment to landscapes of the past, and allowed for some outdoor activity fitting for one of his class: walking, shooting and fishing, with cycling added as a gesture of modern independence. But it was in Aran that the inert elements of his chemistry began to interact. The trauma of May 1898 had led into more articulate and controlled emotional experiences.

Thus 1900 provided a month's residence on Inis Meáin which, however, he was now able to reach directly by steamer. Máirtín Mac Donncha was back living at home with his mother, his job at the mills in Galway having failed to suit him. The opportunities for further integration were excellent, and Synge's command of Gaelic had continued to expand. But the third part of *The Aran Islands* opens in Paris, or with a reference to receiving a letter from 'Michael' in Paris, and the entire text of this penultimate section of the book is punctuated with foreign allusions – to Paris, America, Bavaria, Dieppe, Greece, Poland, New York, not to mention places on the Irish mainland including Donegal, Dublin, Galway, and Wicklow. The conflict of modernisation and primitivistic impulses, best seen in John Eglinton's criticism but evident already in his *Literary Ideals in Ireland* (1899), is denoted in *The Aran Islands* through a short-hand of place-names.

As with the previous part, the dating of incidents to particular days is difficult, and no diary for 1900 survives. One Sunday Synge and Máirtín went rabbit-shooting, assisted by a ferret. A second gun, for the Mac Donncha household appears to have possessed one, had been thought-fully left by a priest for Synge's explicit use:

We put the ferret down in a crevice between two bare sheets of rock, and waited. In a few minutes ... a rabbit shot up straight into the air from the crevice at our feet and set off for a wall that was a few feet away. I threw up the gun and fired.

'Bhuail tú é,' screamed Michael ...

If I had done badly I think I should have had to leave the islands. The people

would have despised me. A 'duine uasal' who cannot shoot seems to these descendants of hunters a fallen type who is worse than an apostate.[59]

If the book can be taken as a tolerably accurate record of events, year
by year, then it was in mid-autumn 1900 that Synge found in Aran a means
whereby the definition of his personality could be advanced without an
obligation to deny or pretend. By his skill with the sporting rifle he is
confirmed as a gentleman, but the confirming term ('duine uasal') is that
of a language historically alien to the Irish gentry. A stern non-believer of
Protestant stock, he escapes the label 'apostate' by accepting the Catholic
priest's gun and using it effectively. The language of the passage negotiates
lithely between the idiom of leisured recreation ('I threw up the gun')
and that of island marginality ('Bhuail tú é').

The issue of identity dominates Synge's account of his third trip to
Aran. The string of foreign place-names form an outer cordon round his
inquiries. Other crucial markers are established through commentary on
the women of Inis Meáin and specifically on a woman mourning. 'The
women of this island are before conventionality, and share some of the
liberal features that are thought peculiar to the women of Paris and New
York ... The direct sexual instincts are not weak on the island, but they
are so subordinated to the instincts of the family that they rarely lead to
irregularity...'[60] In his private notebooks, however, this 'Paris and New
York' passage is found among comments on the second (1899) visit; these
make no mention of New York (which Synge never visited) but London
which he passed through several times a year. Moreover, immediately
above the manuscript passage just quoted we read, 'One woman also has
interested me in a way that binds me more than ever to the islands.'[61]
Nothing of this *deshabillé* emotion gets into the printed text. Instead, *The
Aran Islands* proceeds to consider woman in relation to identifying the
dead.

A sequence of recent drownings (all of men) is related which, in due
course, will provide material for a powerful and poignant moment in
Riders to the Sea:

Now a man has been washed ashore in Donegal with one pampooty on him, and
a striped shirt with a purse in one of the pockets, and a box for tobacco.

For three days the people here have been trying to fix his identity...

Later in the evening, when I was sitting in one of the cottages, the sister of the
dead man came in through the rain with her infant, and there was a long talk
about the rumours that had come in. She pieced together all she could remember

about his clothes ... and the same for his tobacco box, and his stocking ...

'Ah!' she said, 'it's Mike sure enough, and please God they'll give him a decent burial.' [62]

The ability of people living in subsistence conditions to reason foren-sically is acknowledged, while Synge's dramatisation of the scene will be based precisely on introducing the object itself on-stage: the stocking (part merely of rumoured report here) which becomes an objective cor-relative of bereavement and mourning. His own identity as a Gaelic-speaking gentleman who kills (rabbits) proceeds within the same cultural economy as the identification of the missing fisherman as dead. Other details of September/October 1900 provide confirmation of these pro-cesses. He noted that names on the island were conferred relatively late, that Christian names accumulated through the linking of an individual's baptismal name with that of his or her father or mother – for example, Seán Pheigín was Seán the son of Peggy – and that surnames were avoided by various additional means such as the invocation of trades or appear-ance (Seán Rua = Red Seán: Máire an iascaire = Mary, daughter of the fisher). He was familiar with some of this from his extensive knowledge of Wicklow, a county where many people called Byrne or O'Byrne carry nicknames. He also noted that 'If an islander's name is enough to dis-tinguish him it is used by itself, and I know one man who is spoken of as Éamonn. There may be other Edmunds on the island, but if so they have probably good nicknames or epithets of their own.' [63] Eamonn/Edmund was his own detested first baptismal name, which he omitted even from his signature on legal agreements.

On Saturday 13 October, Synge prepared to leave on the steamer for Galway. The weather was deteriorating, and the arrival of the inward vessel was in doubt for much of the day. He and Máirtín spent hours wandering aimlessly, keeping an eye on the horizon. After some time the boat arrived, and (though Synge's narrative is less than clear) in due course it set sail for Aranmor, the main island of the group where Synge had first disembarked. There, uncertainty about conditions at sea arose once more, and Synge betook himself to a low public house in Kilronan, a place of excessive drinking, poor whiskey, and a reputation for sending drunken customers out on to the dangerous seas.

But the captain had received instructions by telegram to remain over-night. As a result, Synge with difficulty got his bags off the steamer and headed to the Atlantic Hotel. There he learned that the old man who had looked him up on his first arrival was working as a watchman on the pier, and so he struggled back in the storm. A figure with a lantern 'remembered me at once when I hailed him and told him who I was'. This very tentative confirmation of identity – the old man remembered, but only after he was told – leads into an extended account of Synge's clerical relative, Alec Synge of forty years earlier, whose gait the old man had recognised in young Synge as soon as he had arrived in May 1898.

This personal reminiscence serves to confirm an identity in J. M. Synge which had been undermined by the old man's ability to remember him only when reminded. The figure now recalled is not the missionary who got run off the islands for exploitative fishing and anti-Catholic proselytising. On the contrary, he has become a dispenser of alcohol and preserver of the Gaelic language. In conversation in the watchman's hut on Kilronan pier, in fact a shack of corrugated iron thrown up by a building contractor, the old man extended his tribute by linking Uncle Alec to sailors who pretend to know Greek and encounters in New York with women quarrelling in Gaelic. This Synge is transformed into a protective influence who has watched over the Aran cabin-boy across the globe, and who has returned (as JMS) when the cabin-boy has himself returned as aged watchman. Implicitly, it is time for the younger man to sail the seas.

Several details suggest that Synge intended 1900 to be the last of his occasional, seasonal visits. The elaborate weaving between the biological determinism of the opening pages of The Aran Islands and the historical continuity indicated in the closing pages of Part Three is given particular focus in the declaration to Máirtín Mac Donncha that he 'was going back to Paris in a few days to sell [his] books and [his] bed, and that then [he] was coming back to grow as strong and simple as they were among the islands of the west'.[64] That was in October 1900. In practice, Synge did not decide to quit the rue d'Assas until late 1902, retaining his apartment till March. He returned to Aran on two occasions, from 21 September to 19 October 1901, and from 14 October to 8 November 1902.

The first of these visits is duly acknowledged in The Aran Islands in a Part Four largely given over to the transcription of stories and poems. But by the summer of 1901, Synge had already put together the manuscript of Parts One to Three, and shown it to Lady Gregory. It was her suggestion that the book would benefit from the inclusion of more folklore. When Yeats applauded the project, but complained about 'one or two passages towards the end' as being 'too personal', he was referring to the three-part Aran Islands and the resurrected A. H. Synge.[65] Synge made no attempt to incorporate his 1902 trip into a manuscript which was accumulating letters of rejection with depressing frequency.

Whether in the three- or four-part version, *The Aran Islands* was a wholly unexpected accomplishment for a young man whose literary endeavours to date were best left in obscurity. Sympathy for the islanders in their primitive conditions did not blind Synge to the essentially transitional period they were living through – a time of primitive canoes and factory fishing. Irony pervades the book, but as a means of advising the reader of what is valuably omitted, of what is still in the realm of 'inarticulate power'. Publishers found it puzzling, despite Yeats's support and the interest in primitive society generated by the writings of J. G. Frazer, Andrew Lang and others. Lang's *Myth, Ritual and Religion* had appeared in 1887, the second edition of *The Golden Bough* in 1900.

The book remains a testimony to Synge's unclassifiable intellect and imagination. Though he lapses occasionally into the jargon of primitivism, he is never taken in. His interest in folklore remains essentially aesthetic, even when he obeys Gregory's injunction and fills out a fourth (final) part with transcriptions and commentary. His views on the Gaelic League and language-revivalism, more implicit than explicit but still unmistakable, made *The Aran Islands* an awkward gospel. In the end the book was issued jointly by Elkin Mathews in London and by Maunsel & Co. in Dublin. Officially published in 1907, the first edition of *The Aran Islands* does survive in a few copies bearing the date 1906. Yeats was influential, of course. But the backbone of the new Dublin company was a less public figure, Joseph Hone, who shortly translated Daniel Halévy's biography of Nietzsche into English.

CHAPTER 13

Travelling at Nightfall

Cantabit vacuus coram latrone viator.

Juvenal[1]

The Atlantic seaboard's impact on the would-be writer can hardly be overestimated. He himself spoke of it in terms of shock, of creative trauma. But the transformation of a Parisian scribbler into a major world dramatist is not quite so simply explained. Synge may well have been changed utterly by the first visit of May 1898, but that in itself did not make him a writer. The stark contrast between the safely decadent and pseudo-Dantean experiments of the 'Vita Vecchia' and the confident, rhythmic speeches of the one-act plays is effected by more than simply the discovery of a dramatic landscape in the west of Ireland.

Before Synge was a writer he was a traveller. Even as a boy, he undertook lengthy excursions from his successive Dublin homes out into the hills to the south of the city. His enthusiasms – natural history and antiquities – required the sturdy constitution of a walker, and Synge was both walker and bicyclist. From coastal Greystones he ventured into the interior of Wicklow, and family excursions encouraged further explorations of a vast area upland which had once belonged to his ancestors. Though he went to Germany as a music student and to Paris as an aspirant writer, travel could always seduce him from his desk. The Roman Campagna, Bavaria, Brittany – he had a better than average familiarity with European landscape. Yet the journeys which finally counted were those undertaken at home. In lines close to a Gaelic original, Synge versed the paradox:

> Some go to game, or pray in Rome
> I travel for my turning home[.][2]

Synge travelled elsewhere in Ireland before he reached Aran. And even after he had discovered the islands which provided him with so much material for dramatic setting and plot, he maintained a daunting programme of walks and bicycle trips – in counties Wicklow, Mayo, and Kerry, notably. These were all desolate places, but they differed in their desolation and in their relationship to Synge. Wicklow, after all, was the county of his childhood, oddly balancing the evangelical laager of Greystones with the emptiness of Glenmalure, and with the lost ancestral pile of Glanmore Castle lying in between. Kerry was Gaelic-speaking, the Blasket Islands especially so. And whereas both Wicklow and Kerry were mountainous, Mayo was characterised by extensive flat bogs as well as mountains: it had been the birthplace of the Land League (founded in 1879 by Michael Davitt), a 'Congested District' in the eyes of bureaucracy. But the parts of Mayo which Synge focused on – the district surrounding Belmullet – had a complex recent history. Refugees from east Ulster had arrived in 1795, following the Battle of the Diamond: these would have been Catholics, with perhaps a very small number of non-Orange Protestants. The area had been written up by the evangelical Caesar Otway in the 1820s and after, and as late as 1851 there were plans for an Erris Fishing Settlement and Converts' Employment Society.[3]

Synge first travelled to Kerry in August 1903. He toured Mayo with Jack Yeats in the summer of 1905. But Wicklow had been in his blood since infancy, and not a year passed without his returning to what might have been his native county. Consequently it would be impossible to list his excursions, to name the places, and to the correlate the dates. Wicklow walked in Synge wherever he went. And it plays a crucial role in the transformation – less sudden than it might seem – of the despairing dreamer into master dramatist. Leaving aside the terse diary entries, and the longer but no less reserved fragments in notebooks, we can put together an account of his published writings on Wicklow without difficulty.

'An Autumn Night in the Hills' was published in *The Gael* (New York) in April 1903; 'The Oppression of the Hills' on 15 February 1905 in the *Manchester Guardian*; 'The Vagrants of Wicklow' in *The Shanachie* (Dublin) in the autumn of 1906; 'The People of the Glens' in *The Shanachie* (Spring 1907); 'At a Wicklow Fair' on 9 May 1907 in the *Manchester Guardian*; 'A Landlord's Garden in County Wicklow' in the *Manchester Guardian* on 1 July 1907; 'On the Road' in the *Manchester Guardian* of 10 December 1908; and 'Glencree' in Volume IV of the *Works* of 1910 (without its final paragraph). These eight sombre prose articles, amounting to a psychopathology of County Wicklow, appeared in print during a seven-year period essentially defined by Synge's explosive career as dramatist. They were never collected during his lifetime, though he did devote time in his last weeks to arranging them and linking them to his writings on Kerry, hoping for a book to complement *The Aran Islands.*

But in order of composition, they are far more difficult to tabulate. 'Glencree' – written in the present tense – unambiguously dates to the summer of 1907, when Synge and Molly took adjacent cottages in this precipitous area to the west of Enniskerry. During this period, he was making notes on Wicklow almost on a daily basis.[4] 'A Landlord's Garden', in many ways the most reflective of the Wicklow essays, is said by the editor to have been 'written some time after 1903', this judgement based perhaps on references to a Kerry cliff-path – Synge went to Kerry in August–September 1903 (drafts of his letters appear on the obverse sides of several sheets of the manuscript). 'At a Wicklow Fair' is – as Edward Stephens acknowledged – a composite picture rather than a unified work, and he assigned it with some caution to 1902–3. In short, the Wicklow material accumulates in the very early years of the new century, though some of it takes years to find its way into print. If Stephens's view, that some of these pieces date back to 1898, is considered, an even longer time-span between writing and publication is possible.

Despite Synge's lifelong familiarity with Wicklow, the business of writing about the county cannot be traced back earlier than the famous trip to Aran in 1898. But, whereas *The Aran Islands* emerged as a sustained and carefully structured narrative meditation, the Wicklow writings remained discrete and fragmentary. In 'People and Places' – a latter-day composite piece assembled for the *Collected Works* of 1966 – we find traces of Synge's orientalist inquiries. Writing about a tramp who was in the habit of sleeping rough, he proceeds:

As he sleeps by Lough Bray and the nightjar burrs and snipe drum over his head and the grouse crow, and heather whispers round him, he hears in their voices the chant of singers in dark chambers of Japan and the clamour of tambourines and [the] flying limbs of dancers he knew in Algeria...[5]

Holiday-making at the end of the Irish Victorian era involved a search for rest without an admission that rest was needed. The professional classes worked frantically, but pretended they were gentlemen of leisure. Their ladies could take no paid employment, and very few of them obtained advanced education, but they slaved none the less in bearing children, maintaining homes and bringing up the surviving children. To holiday in Ireland was to travel without the effort of extended locomotion. Certain days became emblazoned on the memory, images of well-deserved personal quietude, mirages of social stability. There were of course disturbing anomalies. The last Sunday in the last July of the nineteenth century was a 'very fine day, very warm' in Annamoe. Most of the Synge and Stephens family had been to church, though Harry and John stayed at the house. In the afternoon, Mrs Synge sat in a field nearby and read to Claire, her granddaughter. Harry was bustling with his sons, prior to setting off for Kingstown and the office. Mrs Synge 'read from L[ife] of Faith out under hay cock. Hay began to smoke, we had to pull down the cocks.'[6]

The big houses were not set to burn for another twenty years or more, but the end was nigh. The Gardiners had got into the habit of living in a smaller place than Glanmore, and renting out the Castle whenever they could. In July, Mrs Synge drove over to Tiglin (the Gardiners' retreat within the estate) to see her late brother-in-law's widow, 'went down by the castle' on the way home so as to catch a glimpse of the old place. Four days later, J. M. Synge and his sister Annie Stephens drove over with her children only to find their hostess going out. Nothing abashed, the Gardiners came for tea at Castle Kevin before the month ended. Editha Gardiner (previously Mrs Francis Synge, and née Truell) sold off some plate at the end of the year, end of the century. Returned from Argentina, Robert was so put out by this, he sped into Dublin to inquire about buying some of it back, almost in mimicry of his late uncle's efforts to buy back the entire Wicklow estates at the end of the Famine.[7]

The following summer the Synges again visited Tiglin one evening. When Dr Truell and Mrs Rolleston left, tea was taken. (Henry Truell and T. W. Rolleston had been on Aran in July 1895 as part of the Royal Society of Antiquities expedition.) But these recreations did not appeal to Harry Stephens or young J. M. Synge who preferred to play makeshift golf.[8] Other guests included Rosie Calthrop, an Englishwoman with whom Synge struck up an easy yet conventional intimacy in the course of two years. In 1901, the family was back once more in Castle Kevin. Their summers now constituted a sort of ritualised travel. While Kathleen and her guests stayed for the most part within the grounds of the rented house, or took circular walks round its outer defences and out as far as the friendly cottages of humble but Protestant neighbours, Synge himself cycled or walked further afield and within a similar pattern. Unexpected incursions included the arrival of some Frizells on 18 June, while Kathleen and others were out. The visitors-cum-owners took the opportunity to go all over the house as if to underline the Synges' position as tolerated, paying holiday-makers. Three days later, when Synge and Rosie Calthrop cycled from Annamoe to the reservoir at Roundwood, they were marking the boundaries of the old Synge property, now partly flooded and dammed to provide a water supply for Dublin.

Kerry was suggested as an alternative to Wicklow by Robert Synge, who had been fishing there during the summer of 1903. JMS stayed with the Harris family at Mountain Stage, a point on the Kenmare peninsula overlooking deep water in Dingle Bay. The English spoken in Ireland's most south-westerly county was rapidly uttered, inflected with Gaelic constructions and images. The bicycle was his passport to the high passes and vertiginous descents of the great peninsulas which stick defiantly out into the Atlantic. Once, a near calamitous encounter with an angry bull was avoided only by the bicyclist's sheer downhill speed.

The three weeks, 28 August to 19 September, which Synge spent with Philly Harris in 1903 substituted for the Aran visits of the previous five years. Edward Stephens was inclined to assign important early work on 'The Fool of Farnham' (as the infant *Playboy* was known to its author) to these autumn days in Kerry. Certainly, phrases which Synge heard in or about the semi-official shop/cottage he stayed in at Ballyferriter did sterling work when transposed to the mouths of the Mayo loiterers in another semi-official shop, Michael James Flaherty's licensed premises. But Kerry as a setting for drama never won Synge's heart. He did, however, support the notion of a Gaelic-speaking theatre which would foster links between the Abbey and the Gaeltacht (that part of Ireland where Gaelic is/was the vernacular). Indeed, Declan Kiberd has gone so far as to suggest that 'the possibility of employing him as the director of a subsidiary Gaelic theatre' influenced the decision to bring him in as an Abbey director.[9]

He returned to Kerry for the month of August 1904, and for a complicated visit involving a fortnight in the Blasket Islands in August–September 1905. As far as regularity is concerned he was settling into an Aran pattern. While he struggled with writing *The Playboy* in the autumn of 1906, he again put up with Philly Harris (25 August to 12 September). Recovering from the mental stress of *The Playboy* riots yet also slipping into terminal illness, Synge tried Kerry again as a retreat in October 1907, but stayed only four days, assailed by asthma. During these four expeditions, his response to his surroundings was very different from that stimulated by Aran or more slowly released by Wicklow.

In Kerry, Synge was free of the broody melancholy which Wicklow all too readily engendered. But he never encountered any equivalent to the traumatic urgency of the cliffs near Kilronan. On a Sunday morning, he walked out towards Dunquin. He lay for a long time on the side of a magnificently wild road –

where I could see the Blasket Islands and the end of Dunmore Head, the most westerly point of Europe. It was a grey day with a curious silence on the sea and sky and no sign of life anywhere, except the sail of one curagh – or niavogue, as they are called here – that was sailing in from the islands. Now and then a cart passed me filled with old people and children, who saluted me in Irish . . .'[10]

This is about as Apollonian as you can get on the Atlantic seaboard. Even when conditions are difficult, Synge's language manifests confidence in its similes: 'the road seemed to fall away under us, like the wall of a house.'[11] A ten-mile journey on foot during a wet night is undertaken without complaint, despite 'the sloughs of water and piles of stones on the roadway'. Between 13 and 27 August, Synge was on the Great Blasket, staying with Seán Keane (known as the King). He was once again much taken by the women of the remoter parts of Ireland, their characteristic harmony of dignity and directness. The King's daughter ministered efficiently and courteously to his needs, in a dwelling so small that the guest and the King slept in bunk-like beds in a room no bigger than a railway compartment, only to be joined in the middle of the night by a twenty-year-old who clambered over his father to the wall-side of the bed.

Describing two weeks in the Keane household, Synge paid repeated attention to ways of looking and to his own place in the visual area of the kitchen. Neighbours came to stare at him with curiosity. He showed a group of young women his photographs of Aran and Wicklow. A scene first acted out in Aran was replayed when the 'Little Hostess' drew close to him in order to study the pictures properly: she 'was especially taken with two or three that had babies or children in their foreground; and as she put her hands on my shoulders, and leaned over to look at them, with the confidence that is so usual in these places, I could see that she had her full share of the passion for children which is powerful in all women who are permanently and profoundly attractive.'[12]

The three articles which make up 'In West Kerry' were published in *The Shanachie* during 1907. As with the more deliberately planned *Aran Islands*, an incident is carefully framed in relation to other material. Miss Keane's interest in children is followed by a curious moment when Synge allows the islanders to see a photograph of statues in the Luxembourg Gardens ('naked people standing about in their skins'). The second and third stages of a thematic movement in this domestic sinfonietta are prefaced by one which only in retrospect takes on its full significance:

The little hostess set about getting my breakfast, but before it was ready she partly rinsed the dough out of a pan where she had been kneading bread, poured some water into it, and put it on a chair near the door. Then she hunted about the edges of the rafters till she found a piece of soap, which she put on the back of a chair with a towel, and told me I might wash my face. I did so as well as I was able, in the middle of the people, and dried myself with the towel, which was the one used by the whole family.[13]

Notwithstanding this awkward modesty, Synge fits into the Blasket household. A further instance of his domestic adjustment occurs in an incident which is reflected in *The Playboy*. Some of the islanders were having their hair cut in the King's parlour, and the little hostess inquired if Synge wished to shave:

I told her I would, so she got me some water in the potato-dish and put it on a chair; then her sister got me a little piece of broken looking-glass and put it on a nail near the door, where there was some light. I set to work, and as I stood with my back to the people I could catch a score of eyes in the glass, watching me intently.[14]

All in all, Kerry was a roaring success. Early on during his visit to the Blaskets, Synge was assured that, 'there has been no one drowned on this island ... for forty years'. Later he wrote of 'the singularly brilliant liveliness one meets everywhere in Kerry'.[15] His published account includes a few odd details – the little hostess's habit of combing her hair, a story about a woman dead and long buried from whose hair her missing money is disinterred, and a grotesque moment when he encountered a sick child in a sack by the fireside who emerged 'and began looking at me with a heavy stare'.[16] Yet he never mistook himself for a gamekeeper turned poacher, a gentleman gone native. 'I know even while I was there I was an interloper only, a refugee in a garden between four seas.'[17]

This being the case, why did he travel so persistently? In a scribbled note probably datable to 1895, Synge observed: 'the permanent scenery of the Inferno and Purgatorio is that of travel.'[18] This characteristically unsustained analysis promises more insight into his personal beliefs, and even into his personality, than the too-often-cited self-characterisation advanced in one of his Wicklow pieces: 'In the middle classes the gifted son of a family is always the poorest – usually a writer or artist with no sense for speculation – and in a family of peasants, where the average comfort is just over penury, the gifted son sinks also, and is soon a tramp on the roadside.'[19]

Synge's most thorough integration of writing and travel arose through a proposition he initially resisted. The English poet, John Masefield (1878–1967), whom he had met in Yeats's London circle, was active in stimulating interest in Synge's work and generally trying to boost his meagre income. The *Manchester Guardian* of the day was a campaigning liberal newspaper, edited by a benign patriarch, C. P. Scott. While the manuscript of *The Aran Islands* was still doing the rounds of English publishers, Scott wrote inviting Synge to contribute a series of articles on the west of Ireland. Though the area under the care of the Congested Districts Board (1890) included virtually the entire western seaboard and huge tracts of inland Connacht, Synge was certain exactly where he wished to travel: Galway, Mayo, and Donegal. He was less happy about the overtones of the proposal, recognising that Scott (like many well-intentioned Britishers since) equated benevolence towards Ireland with an unthinking acceptance of nationalist complaints and remedies. Towards the end of May 1905, he none the less presented himself to a CDB official in Dublin. While a political agenda undoubtedly existed, Scott was willing to let Synge 'give the readers a sympathetic understanding [of] the way their life is lived & to let the political lesson emerge out of that'.[20]

He was grateful for the opportunity to earn money, though he had reservations about 'lifting the rags from my mother country for to tickle the sentiments of Manchester'.[21] In writing to MacKenna, Synge had been able to enclose his two one-act plays (*Riders* and *In the Shadow of the Glen*) published by Elkin Mathews on 8 May. It had been a long and complicated negotiation between playwright and publisher, with various impresarios lending a hand. While Mathews had declined to include *The Tinker's Wedding*, and had failed to act in the matter of *The Aran Islands*, he proved generous with royalties.[22] Masefield had been helpful here, but his main contribution to the new venture does not appear to have been settled until the last minute: the participation of Jack Yeats, the poet's younger brother, as illustrator of Synge's reports for the *Guardian*.

Though the two men were aware of each other's work, they do not seem to have known each other personally, at least not to any degree. Jack Yeats didn't even know where Synge lived. Their collaboration has become a myth of Irish cultural nationalism, despite the writer's reiterated protestations. Part of their success lay in the brilliant combination of the word and image, but part also stems from several (often mutually exclusive) statements of political virtue. For Arthur Lynch and Stephen MacKenna in the 1920s, Synge was a solid Irish nationalist, give or take a scruple or two. For Bruce Arnold today, Synge held views which 'wavered between socialism and communism'.[23] In practice, the twelve articles which appeared between 10 June and 26 July 1905 focused a good deal of attention on the impact of state-sponsored 'relief works' providing employment and on the emergence of a new class or subclass in the western counties.

The venture took them first to south Connemara, west of Galway City, well known to Synge from his earlier embarkations for Aran. He noted the Galway to Clifden railway line, which his brother's brother-in-law had built. But 'one's first feeling as one comes back among these people ... is a dread of any reform that would tend to lessen their individuality rather than any very real hope of improving their well-being.' Yet again, he admires the young women – 'magnificently built'.[24] Inquiries about fishing elicit a complaint about 'the shopkeepers [who] would rather have the people idle, so that they can get them for a shilling a day' as casual sellers of turf. Describing the impact of state-sponsored public works, Synge concentrated on the role of 'the ganger' or overseer of the workmen 'swaggering among them and directing their work'. Local men and women forced by circumstance into these schemes have a 'hang-dog dejection that would be enough to make any casual passer mistake them for a band of convicts'.[25] At Dinish Island, in western Connemara, however, the two travellers encountered a voluble ferryman who restored their faith in Irish manhood and independence, though he had worked in New Orleans, and Manchester, and Newcastle-on-Tyne. The Congested Districts Board comes in for some pointed criticism, notably for neglecting industries like kelp-making in favour of 'a few canonised industries, such as horse-breeding'.[26]

The journey from Connemara to North Mayo exemplified one of the most irritating features of the Irish transport system. Once Synge and Yeats had completed their business on the Galway coast, they found themselves obliged to take a train back along James Price's line to Galway and then on to Athlone in the midlands, to transfer to another line for Ballina. (This problem has been eliminated under Independence by the elimination of the Clifden line.) Once settled into Deehan's Royal Hotel at Belmullet, Synge dutifully wrote to thank his mother for cigarettes, a fresh pair of pyjamas and £6. Kathleen Synge was holidaying at a new Wicklow location, Greenanemore House, close to the setting of *The Well of the Saints*.[27]

In the west Mayo town of Belmullet, Synge and Jack Yeats watched the bonfires and the high jinks traditionally enacted on St John's Eve. Flaming sods were thrown into the night sky, snakes of burning hay-rope were tossed to and fro among drinkers and singers and dancers. Amid all the antics of the carnival crowd a little girl, enthralled and frightened by the scene, clutched Synge's hand and 'stood close in his shadow until the fiery games were done'.[28] In 1907, Synge composed 'Danny', a narrative poem which shocked John Masefield in its (for him) revelation of the poet's desperate struggle with death. The violent incident, casually rhymed, was based on a murder which had taken place on the Belmullet–Bangorerris road in late 1881. A rate-collector named O'Malley had been murdered, and a large coffin-shaped stone erected as mock-memorial or ironic tribute to the dead.[29] It was also in Belmullet that the *Guardian*'s investigators encountered the embodiment of shopkeeper rapaciousness. Yeats drew Mrs Jordan in her wire-framed spectacles eloquently presenting unpaid accounts to a shawl-clad woman: Synge noted that she was the local kelp-buyer, against which kind of monopoly he reserved his severest criticism. Yeats's sketch was not included in the series, but appeared after Synge's death in *Life in the West of Ireland*, one of the means by which the cultural-nationalist myth advanced.

The west was a complicated place, less amenable to generalisation than the *Guardian*'s editor supposed. Land was being acquired by big farmers, to the detriment of many poorer families. Returned Americans brought money but sowed discontent and flaunted a tastelessness the fastidious Synge disliked. Emigration affected every aspect of life. At the jetty north of Belmullet over a hundred men were waiting to embark for Scotland as seasonal labourers: the boat was owned by Jack Yeats's Pollexfen relatives. A note of defensiveness enters Synge's commentary: 'A great deal has been said of the curse of the absentee landlord; but in reality the small landlord, who lived on his property, and knew how much money every tenant possessed, was a far greater evil.'[30] Childhood memories of Baylee and MacDonagh, the difficulty of extracting rents from the boggy acres of Brackloon, Gurtagurnane, and Knockroe still lingered.

While his articles for the *Manchester Guardian* pinpointed instances of social malaise, they followed no party line. His unguarded opinions were reserved for private consumption. 'There are sides of all that western life [,] the groggy-patriot-publican-general shop-man who is married to the priest's half sister and second cousin once-removed of the dispensary doctor, that are horrible and awful.' Not content with his condemnation of 'rampant double-chinned vulgarity', Synge pressed home the political analysis: 'This is the type that is running the present United Irish League anti-grazier campaign while they're swindling the people themselves in a dozen ways and then buying out their holdings and packing off whole families to America.'[31]

It is possible to assign this unambiguous detestation of William O'Brien's political initiatives to Synge's socialism, but only the detestation is unambiguous. While Michael Davitt's schemes for land nationalisation might seem to have anticipated the dangers of private accumulation in O'Brien's, there is no evidence that Synge gave much thought to Davitt and, in any case, he was strongly opposed to state intervention on issues of unemployment. The League's opposition to 'big farmers' and graziers offended Synge's lingering attachment to the landlord system, and while he recognised the historical redundancy of landlordism he disliked what was taking its place. For the moment, he retained a degree of radicalism in urban matters, as his comments on housing and overcrowding testify. But rural Ireland was a different matter.

The question came to a head two years later when a Dublin audience rioted over *The Playboy*. To MacKenna he wrote once again, complaining of 'the scurility [sic], and ignorance and treachery' of 'the middle class Irish Catholic'. Amid this accumulating bile, Synge managed to declare his 'wildest admiration for the Irish Peasants'. But by 1907 the issue between peasantry and middle class had been well and truly decided against the peasant. By then Synge's enthusiasm was already becoming a sentimental attachment to the past. The fisheries and lace-making factories of the Congested Districts Board were not simply relieving distress, they were altering social relations of many kinds. And his own (rather vulgar) insistence on physiognomy in denouncing 'an ungodly ruck of fat-faced, sweaty-headed, swine ... in Dublin, and Kingstown, and alas in all the country towns' indicates how social change in Ireland in the earliest years of the century was conspiring with his own declining physical energy to embitter a comic genius.[32]

In the aftermath of the *Playboy* riots, Synge wrote (but never published) an open letter in which the same physiological abuse occurs – 'what is senile and slobbering in the doctrine of the Gaelic League ... now we are passing England in the hysteria of old women's talk ... This delirium will not last ...'[33] But in 1905, things had not gone quite so far. On the Great Blasket, it was possible (just about) to forget the growth of a bourgeoisie and other lamentable developments. Synge's travels in Ireland were not only exploratory, they involved a leaving-behind, a temporary release from the constrictions of Protestant Kingstown and the irritations of a predominantly Catholic new middle class.

Belmullet stands at the upper end of the Mullet peninsula in the barony of Erris, one of the most remote, windswept areas in Ireland. This was to be the setting for *The Playboy of the Western World* to which Christy Mahon has fled from a potato field in the south where, he believes in fear and trembling, he slew his father. In one of Synge's earliest sketches, the summit of Christy's integration into his newly adopted community is reached when he 'is being elected county councillor'. This dates from September 1904, when the Abbey Theatre was in preliminary rehearsal of *The Well of the Saints*. To Lady Gregory he confided misgivings about Padraic Colum, who found the play 'unsatisfactory because the Saint is a Protestant'. The tensions of a social group finding itself to be a minority rather than an elite were breaking through the practised manners of urbane sang-froid. Synge's plans for another visit to Aran were frustrated by an outbreak of smallpox in Kilronan. He half connived in the helplessness of stricken islanders – 'it is so impossible to help them'. Other influences redirected him from Aran; 'My people want me not to go at all' no doubt recalling J. H. Synge's succumbing to the same disease in 1872.[34] Travel mapped histories, alterations in social power; it had a potential of its own – to turn emblematical.

Though his brief notes on Dante probably derive from reading some unidentified secondary source or commentary, they are worth citing. 'The permanent scenery of the Inferno and Purgatorio is that of travel,' Synge had written. Above this on the same page, we read: 'What Dante yearns after is the permanence of justice in civil society.' These two remarks are linked by the notion of permanence. In the non-celestial realms, there is permanent transiency; in the celestial realm there should be something akin to social justice, infinitely raised and transformed into the divine. But on the next page, Synge has written, 'Light in general is his special and chosen source of beauty.' The sequence of observations, transcribed if not conceived by Synge, is itself suggestive. There is purgatorial process which may be symbolised in travel; there is a paradisal state or condition for which justice is an apt if inadequate symbol because it can only be aspired to, and not 'processed'. There is an aesthetic, specific to this aspiration – 'light in general' or (as we might say) vision.[35]

The socialist interpreters of Synge may wish to know that the notes on Dante and social justice are followed by notes on Karl Marx. But these are as quickly succeeded by equally brief notes on Madame Blavatsky, and on the great edition of William Blake published by Yeats and Edwin Ellis in 1893. Travel was never mere relaxation for Synge. The money was useful – the *Manchester Guardian* paid £25 4s od – 'more than I've ever had yet'.[36] Writing to W. B. Yeats from the Great Blasket in August, Synge looked back on Mayo with some aversion. The 'patriot publican' as a type depressed him. With Jack Yeats, he toyed with ideas for a collaborative book about 'Irish types', but illness intervened. Nevertheless, the project fits in with Synge's ethnographical interests, from the photographs of Browne and Haddon to the wider-ranging inquiries of Frazer. If the Irish can be classified as various types, what type does the classifying Synge belong to? Bruce Arnold goes against received opinion when he suggests that, after the *Manchester Guardian* commission, the two men simply parted.[37]

CHAPTER 14

A Month in the County:
August 1901

He lived there in the unsayable lights.

Seamus Heaney[1]

The Castle Kevin holiday began early in the summer of 1901. Shortly after its conclusion, Synge stayed with Yeats at Coole Park. Under Lady Gregory's patronage, he was acquiring a place in the counsels of a new cultural movement. The fourth visit to Aran followed directly on 21 September. This was not to be the *annus mirabilis*, yet more obscure events of August 1901 would influence the shape of his career as a dramatist. This was to be a moment of apprehension rather than action. At the end of June, he was admittedly involved in a Sunday scuffle. But in the most formally organised of his Wicklow pieces, he dwelt on the atmospherics of that occasion, not its dynamics. 'There was a dead pear-tree, and just inside the gate, as one came back to it, a large fuchsia filled with empty nests.'[2] The tone of the essay is ironic in its hesitant identification of the fruit trees with biblical Eden, owing as much to the Russian example of Turgenev as to the 'Big House' tradition of Maria Edgeworth. Ireland was on the eve.

Still distant Paris intruded. On the great Orange festival of 12 July, Synge rode to Wicklow town (where an Orange Lodge quietly prospered) to post off his rent for the apartment in the rue d'Assas. A week later, Harry Harding came over from Avonmore House to chat about Walter Frizell and his affairs. The summer hotted up. July passed amid languid bicycle trips with Rosie Calthrop and conversations with a missionary on furlough called Miss Barry, both guests of Kathleen Synge's.

The month of August was laden with omens. The weather for harvesting was broken. Earlier, there had been trouble when soul-brothers of the Brethren had been gratuitously attacked in Camolin. This north Wexford village had become song-famous as a flashpoint of sectarian conflict in 1798. The newspapers reported pious commemoration of the rebellion, even three years after the centenary. The night before Rosie Calthrop was due to leave, she casually ran her hand over young Edward Stephens's hair as they sat in the firelight. He would 'have been covered with shame if anyone in the hall, when she said good-bye next morning, had suspected the truth . . .'[3] On the following day, Friday 9 August, while Mrs Synge was at Miss Belton's, a great storm broke from the south, casting the entire district into sodden darkness. Kathleen noted in her diary, 'Old Costello dead.' On Sunday, she wrote 'Funeral of Mr Costello'. Only the appearance of this surname in *When the Moon Has Set* gives significance to these meagre entries – that, and the breach of church practice in holding a funeral on Sunday. Who was Old Costello, and why did Mrs Synge record his passing? No report of his death appears in the *Wicklow Newsletter*, a Protestant-oriented weekly paper, nor in the more popular *Wicklow People*. From official records it can be established that James Costello of Laragh House, a former coachman, died on 9 August 1901, aged seventy-seven. Cause of death was 'general debility', no medical attendant was present. Costello, who could read but not write, was born in King's County. He and his wife were members of the Church of Ireland and, in the census of 1901, their occupation was listed as 'interest of money'. The Costellos appear to have lived, not actually in Laragh House, but in some smaller dwelling in the grounds. In 1901, the house was owned by Erskine Booth.

The Booths were related by marriage to the Bartons and the Childers. In the stretch of land running from Laragh to Annamoe – uncharacteristically gentle for Wicklow – the houses of these recent gentry families prospered inwardly. Robert Caesar Childers (1838–76), an English orientalist, had married Anna Maria Henrietta Barton of Glendalough House, whose sister Georgina Susanna Arabel (died 1868) married George Booth (died 1892) of Laragh House. One of Childers's brothers married a Matheson widow, though the networking here remains uncertain. What is certain is that the area comprised a finely-membraned local society, some of whom supported James Costello.

An Easter Vestry meeting for the parish (nominally Derrylossary) included Willie Belton, J. E. W. Booth, H. C. Childers, one of the Colemans of Tomriland, and Harry Harding – a vertical cross-section of the Church of Ireland in transition. If the Beltons were (to put it crudely) the worker bees of the Vestry, the Colemans of Tomriland were a cut above them. Tomriland was a solid but low farmhouse; an obscure Thomas Synge, perhaps a drop-out from his class, had occupied it in the 1850s.[4] Tomriland was part of the Gardiners' Glanmore property. From the solid possession of land, such families were now looking towards alternative visions of belonging. Synge's *The Well of the Saints* exploits a different side of this turn-of-the-century transition, its Celticist response to the militant nationalism soon to flower among the Barton and Childers cousins.

After the unusual business of a sabbath funeral, Kathleen spoke to 'Mrs Barton at Church door'. In fact, both the Bartons and the Archers were present, clearly an event of some moral consequence. Given that the deceased was semi-literate, his place in the Protestant community of Annamoe may well have depended on his earlier conversion from Catholicism. The saintly example of a humble sinner who chose to walk in the Lord's path earned Costello that ostentatious 'Mr' in Mrs Synge's diary. A new rector, appointed in June or July, chose to preach on 'Jesus wept over the city' – at least, that is how Luke 19:41 is inaccurately rendered in the diary. Even if the text relates a moment in Christ's Entry into Jerusalem, itself a stage in the last days before His arrest and crucifixion, the Rev. Meredith Halligan's choice of it makes more sense in the context of what goes immediately before. To the least pleasing of his servants, the nobleman of Jesus's parable had austerely said, 'Wherefore then gavest not thou my money into the bank, that at my coming I might have required mine own with usury?' (Luke 19:23). Usury, that is, the 'interest of money'.[5]

A few days later Mrs Synge, who was versed in prophecy, noted 'the house dismantled', evidently referring to the aftermath of Costello's death. 'We had a chat with Mrs Byrne.' As both a deranged male Costello and a Mrs Byrne feature prominently in *When the Moon Has Set*, another stage in the hidden evolution of that ghost-drama is discernible here. Several houses were passing through change and decay – Tomriland up for auction in the course of the month, Laragh House evidently empty, and another – greater than these – to have its political relics sold off as little more than curios.

Some miles to the south-west of Laragh, up in more mountainous territory, another kind of odd death occurred within a week. John Winterbottom, who farmed thirty acres of bad land in Sheeanamore (a place of legendary desolation in post-Famine times), supported a bad-tempered wife and three children by taking casual jobs at harvest-time. On Thursday 15 August, he had been employed by Mrs Byrne of Ballinagappogue to help at hay-ricking. Partly paralysed on his right side, he was none the less fit to work, and to drink occasionally throughout the day. Towards evening he was close to being incapacitated, though his employer refused to arrange for a horse-and-cart to bring him home.

Hence it was that Winterbottom, having knelt pathetically at the side of the road, disappeared into the hills, stripped naked and walked five miles through a dark and rainy night. This had also been the day of the Arklow races, which Synge attended, walking (or perhaps bicycling) home to Castle Kevin in the heavy rain.

Winterbottom's clothes were found near Mrs Byrne's gate when his wife went in search of him the next day. All but a penny of his pitiful earnings was gone from his pocket. A party of police assembled to locate him, and the body was found a week later, on Thursday 22 August, some five miles from where the clothes had been piled. On 24 August, Synge passed two policemen on the road near Aughavannagh carrying a coffin on an ass-and-cart. Making inquiries from an elderly local man, Patrick Kehoe, he was told of 'a poor fellow below reaping in the glen, and in the evening he had two glasses of whisky with some other lads. Then some excitement took him, and he threw off his clothes and ran away into the hills … In the morning they found his naked foot-marks on some mud half a mile above the road … when they found his body … [it was] near eaten by the crows.'[6] So much Synge incorporated into his essay, 'The Oppression of the Hills', which he published years later in the *Manchester Guardian*. He omitted the description (preserved in his notes) of the victim as 'a poor weak minded sort of a creature'.

Between the disappearance of Winterbottom – like James Costello, a Protestant of the dependent classes – and the discovery of his body, a third dead man claimed the headlines, albeit a decade after the demise. On Saturday 17 August, a local paper carried a long (and mildly satirical) article about the auction of the late Charles Stewart Parnell's furniture and household effects, the property itself having been bought by a Mr T. Boylan whose stated intention was 'to facilitate the family in redeeming the Avondale Estate if possible within … two years'.[7] The Chief's brother was reduced to bidding for the repossession of family knick-knacks and items of sentimental value. He was facilitated by others at the auction who deferred to him even against their own interests. In this fashion, the recovery of Glanmore Castle by Uncle Francis Synge after the Famine was re-enacted in miniature at Avondale, some fifty years later.

According to Synge's subsequent essay, Patrick Kehoe was following the two policemen who were 'driving an ass-cart with a coffin on it', Winterbottom's coffin. Their meeting on the 24th was also the occasion when Synge was regaled with an account of his ancestors in Wicklow, the two branches of the Synge family, and the wealth of the Roundwood heiress as well as the unreliability of the Parnellite MP, William Corbet, on matters of local history. Then, on the last day of the month, Winterbottom's mysterious death was extensively covered in both the *Wicklow People* and the *Wicklow Newsletter*, with details of the inquest held in Aughavannagh, close to Parnell's hunting lodge. The coroner's jury included one Patrick Kehoe, and the inquest had been held on the 24th, the day Synge and Kehoe met.

To complete this selective chronicle, note a lengthy (and again disrespectful) newspaper report of an attack in Camolin on a wooden hut erected by the Evangelistic and Missionary Alliance. Three preachers gave evidence of the threats made to them and the damage sustained to their property. Though the incident had occurred in late June, the ten defendants only appeared in court at the end of August, just in time for their case to run alongside the inquest into Winterbottom's death and the sale of Parnell's *lares et penates*. No reference to James Costello ever appeared in the papers. Mrs Synge may have felt a shaking of her Wicklow Protestant foundations. But as in Christ's parable of the ten talents, there were paradoxical rewards – the fall of Avondale had knocked Home Rule on the head.

Synge in the month of August 1901 remains inscrutable. Nevertheless, in addition to the Costello/Byrne presence both at the sabbath funeral and in *When the Moon Has Set*, it was another Mrs Byrne who left Winterbottom callously unprovided for. And John Winterbottom becomes Patch Darcy in *In the Shadow of the Glen*, an absent figure, a dead man whose skill at herding sheep – creating order and preserving life – had been legendary. The one-act play was still less than a project in Synge's mind, to be tackled the following summer in Wicklow when the Synge/Stephens family rented a smaller house than Castle Kevin for their holidays. But a longer play, the one we call *When the Moon Has Set*, was ready in some form or other to be shown to Lady Gregory and Yeats at Coole in September 1901. The day after the party had left Castle Kevin for Kingstown, the *Wicklow People* returned to the unsolved mystery of Winterbottom's death, five miles from where he had stripped off his clothes. 'A plentiful crop of rumours ... exist over the case ... Many consider it doubtful whether he accomplished the strange journey of himself.'[8]

The case was certainly strange, one of the jurors remarking that 'much blame could be attached to some one'. But it was not unique. Less than a year later, the body of John Doyle of Ballard, who had been missing for thirteen weeks, was found in the Black Banks district of Glenmalure. This

was far closer to the Synges' Wicklow stamping-ground than Aughavannagh. 'Beside the remains were some of the deceased's clothes, packed
as he had taken them off, and the boots were also similarly arranged.'[9]
The appropriate biblical text for this occasion is in the second to last
chapter of St John's Gospel, where the clothes in which the body of Christ
had been entombed are described in the light of the resurrection: 'the
napkin ... not lying with the linen clothes, but wrapped together in a
place by itself' (John 20:7). An inquest had been held at Laragh on 13 May
1902. Synge did not get back from Paris until 17 May, and did not travel
down to Wicklow before 17 June at the earliest. The year 1902 was to prove
something of an *annus mirabilis*, with the summer resulting in drafts of
both *In the Shadow of the Glen* and *Riders to the Sea*. The former play is
set in a Glenmalure cottage, close to the Black Banks.

Though the year 1901 cannot offer anything so durable as these one-
act plays, the drama commenced in 1902 would have been impossible
but for the events of August 1901. Nicholas Grene's case in favour of
Winterbottom as Patch Darcy's 'original' is secure, even though the dramatic appropriation converts a semi-paralytic 'poor weak minded sort of
a creature' into a good shepherd – 'the third day they found Darcy' – albeit
a dead one. Indeed, it may be even stronger than previously recognised,
if the possibility is permitted that Synge attended the inquest at the
Aughavannagh Hotel. After all, he saw the policemen, he spoke to one of
the jurymen. For one of his class, it would have been easy to sit at the
back of the room, while District Inspector Otter and Dr O'Gorman of
Aughrim got on with the grim business.

No diary for 1901 has been traced. Nor does Synge avert to the inquest
in any of the essays. He does, however, go to the trouble of dividing his
recollections of 24 August between two essays – 'The Oppression of the
Hills' (published 1905) and 'The People of the Glens' (1907). The first
includes the account of Winterbottom's death (neither the teller nor the
dead man is named), the second has 'Cavanagh' regale Synge with his
own family history. This discreet separation of recent calamity among the
humble and meek from the annals of 'all that has happened in three-score
years to the families of Wicklow' may simply be the result of Synge's later
sorting out of notes for journalism. But the resurrection of Winterbottom
as Patch Darcy only follows after a second naked death, that of John Doyle
in May 1902. Dying in Glenmalure, and haling from Ballard (less than a
mile from Laragh), Doyle was virtually a neighbour of the Synges' hosts
at Tomriland and Castle Kevin.

In the 1890s, Sigmund Freud spent an Alpine holiday which was interrupted by 'Katharina', who spontaneously brought her case to him. Writing up his notes, he elaborated on what he called 'the auxiliary moment', a psychic event (perhaps innocuous in itself) which reactivates an earlier (and repressed) experience and brings together two or more divided groups of emotion.[10] Without suggesting a 'Freudian' interpretation of Synge or his work, I think his encounter with the deaths of Winterbottom and Doyle, or rather the literary textual work elaborated from these deaths, can be regarded as similar in structure.

Winterbottom's death did not immediately prompt Patch Darcy. What happened in Synge's mind, and it happened 'off-the-page', was the sundering of Patrick Kehoe's discourse of August 1901 into two bodies of material. Winterbottom occupies one, and the acknowledgement of him as 'a sort of half innocent' is never transferred from notebook to printed page. Synge family history occupies another and, in suggestive parallel with the 'sanitising' of Winterbottom, the originating moment of Sam M'Cracken's death in 1769 remains mute. This constitutes the first stage of a crucial development in Synge's becoming a dramatist.

Then, at the 'auxiliary moment' of John Doyle's death in May 1902, the psychic significance of Kehoe's dual discourse is transformed. *When the Moon Has Set* is charged with the business of rewriting the eighteenth-century origins of the Wicklow Synges (including Tom Synge of Tomriland) and Hatches (including Dr John Hatch of Rathdrum Asylum and Laragh Castle). *In the Shadow of the Glen* converts the semi-paralytic in the manner already described. The circumstantial evidence to support the role of this 'auxiliary moment' in 1902 involves Willie Coleman as Synge's informant on the skills of mountain herdsmen (and not of Winterbottom specifically) but it also embraces the wider pattern of mortality and disposal in August 1901, the break-up of Parnell's Avondale, the death of the mysterious Costello, and the shades of Hatches in Larah and Synges in Castle Kevin, Glanmore, Roundwood and Tomriland.

Given the short distance between John Doyle's home in Ballard and Coleman's in Tomriland, and the mere month or so between Doyle's death and Synge's arrival in Tomriland, it seems reasonable to conclude that it was the Glenmalure corpse which prompted *In the Shadow of the Glen*, even if the uncanny detail of Mrs Winterbottom's identifying her husband through a distinctive black thread in a flitter of shirt is picked up in the play:

TRAMP (*moving uneasily*): Maybe if you'd a piece of a grey thread and a sharp needle – there's great safety in a needle, lady of the house – I'd be putting a little stitch here and there in my old coat, the time I'll be praying for his soul, and it going up naked to the saints of God."

CHAPTER 15

The Year 1902
and the One-Act Plays

The visual is essentially pornographic, which is to say that it has its end
in rapt, mindless fascination; thinking about its attributes becomes an
adjunct of that, if it is unwilling to betray its object.

Fredric Jameson[1]

During a storm in 1888, a great tree was blown down in front of Glendalough House, near Annamoe. Though the proprietor, John Barton, was
a staunch unionist, he gave permission to his famous neighbour Charles
Stewart Parnell to test his portable sawmill on the fallen giant. For Barton's
seven-year-old son, lifted up by his nurse to see the Uncrowned King of
Ireland with his latest mechanical gadget, this was a moment remembered
almost as world-historical. That sight, or so the legend runs, made of the
Big House scion a 1920s republican. No such event dates the transformation of young and gauche Johnnie Synge into the resolute J. M.
Synge, dramatist. But if we look for a process of change rather than a
single all-consuming metamorphosis, then the year 1902 is our focus and
the scene of action lies not far from Annamoe.

The opening of the year, however, found Synge still lodged in the rue
d'Assas (or Rude Asses, as his nephew Edward misheard it). Reading
fiction – Hardy's *Tess* and Meredith's *Diana of the Crossways* – he came
up with a neat if obvious formula: 'English novelists give us their work in
plaster, French novelists in marble.'[2] Two days later, he heard from Fisher
Unwin's office in London – *The Aran Islands* had not yet found a publisher.
His health continued badly. On Wednesday 22 January 1902, his French
physician (named Périer or Peirier) recommended a course of hypo-
dermic injections which Synge duly commenced at the end of the week.
This was no secret consultation, for he promptly informed his mother
that the *médecin* wanted to tackle the glandular condition, and she sent
money for this purpose. By 8 February, Johnnie was 'something better'
but Kathleen remained uneasy. His diary suggests that a different regime

of injections began on 12 February, though he was well enough to visit friends at Clamant and attend De Jubainville's lectures.[3] To Lady Gregory, he spoke of flu lasting 'for nearly two months off and on' which he had been able to do nothing about. He was writing, however, and recording the fact with bilingual self-regard – 'Ecrit "Waysides of Wicklow" '.[4] In March he sent off the resulting article and in April got it back. In the meantime, efforts at verse-drama preoccupied him.

He redirected the Aran manuscript, hoping for a better reception with Alfred Nutt, a publisher with strong Celtic interests. For most of the year, Nutt agonised over the matter, then came to a negative decision. On St Patrick's Day (17 March), Synge was able to buy copies of *L'Européen* containing his piece on De Jubainville, and a week later received twenty-seven francs in payment. When the great scholar had asked for assistance with the pronunciation of modern Gaelic, Synge obliged but confessed himself (in an oddly chosen metaphor) 'a blind guide'. In April, his head was aching 'mightily' but on 19 April he had the honour of dining at the home of De Jubainville with whom he had struck up a warm and valuable friendship.[5]

Politically, in Ireland it was a year of hope and well-intentioned initiatives, particularly on the question of landlord/tenant relations. In Kingstown, things proceeded with the usual minor anxieties and successes that typify middle-class life of the period. Annie Price, a relative through Ned Synge's marriage but more significant as one of the Greystones faithful, was in hospital. Robert, who had reclaimed something of the family's stake in Glanmore, was actively collecting what rents were still due under the gradually eroding landlord-tenant system. In April, he consulted Henry Swanzy (a former Rathmines pupil, like the elder Synges) about his eyes. It was high time to plan the summer vacation.

Tomriland was a plain two-storey house with three dormer windows to its forty-foot length. The Coleman family were still in possession though the 130 or so acres 'with house and offices' had been put up for auction in August 1901.[6] In April 1902, Mrs Synge learned that the summer rent on Castle Kevin was to be increased, and so arranged to take this humbler abode which had yet the respectability of Protestant ownership. Eva Matheson had made some inquiries, perhaps with a view to sharing accommodation elsewhere in Wicklow. The family mood was sombre, for in China Sam's wife had suffered a miscarriage. Only an exhibition of paintings by Laura Stephens brightened the scene. Synge had returned from Paris on 17 May, to be told of the summer arrangements. For the best part of a day he retreated to his room, then disappeared for the evening.

During this period, her youngest was making a little progress in publishing short critical articles, 'Le Mouvement intellectuel irlandais' in *L'Européen* and a review of Lady Gregory's *Cuchulain of Muirthemne* in the *Speaker* (London). He wrote to Stephen MacKenna (who married on 11 June), declaring himself 'bankrupter than ever', complaining bitterly if briefly about social change ('the "near-Dublin" people surtout. I won't repeat what I said last year') and longing for outer-suburban Paris. 'Clamart has been verdant and perfumed and melodious beyond describing. Agonisingly beautiful.'[7]

If Ann Saddlemyer is right in dating Synge's earliest surviving letter to MacKenna to 12 June 1902, then it appears that JMS travelled ahead of his family to Tomriland on Tuesday 17 June. Certainly he planned 'to come up every week for a day in T. C. D. library' to pursue his scholarly work on Old Irish. Yeats wrote from Coole Park on 6 July praising the *Speaker* review ('most excellent') and urging further journalism ('it would be a great advantage to you to have a few good articles to show') but making no reference whatever to plays Synge might be engaged on. Given that Kathleen and her retinue were not to arrive in Wicklow till 21 July, he had over four weeks of solitude in the modest farmhouse.

On that date, delayed perhaps by ill-health, she travelled down to Tomriland, by the crossroads where Ned Synge had joined the evicting party to unhouse Hugh Carey and his sisters. After just one night, John moved into the room over the kitchen because his mother declared she could not sleep there. Asthma assailed him, to the point where Kathleen even confided in her usually matter-of-fact diary that she was 'very sorry'.[8] Though she had been responsible for the change of accommodation, and so aggravated her son's asthma, she may also have unwittingly laid the scene for the infamous listening through floorboards by which Synge picked up the chit-chat of domestic servants in the kitchen below. He had been, his *Playboy* Preface declared, at work on *In the Shadow of the Glen*.[9] This can scarcely have registered with the other guests, though his typewriter was audible throughout much of the small house. He remained unwell until 25 July, but made excursions of various kinds, to Cousin Emily at Uplands and to the fair at Aughrim ten or so miles south of Tomriland on 30 July. He sat occasionally in a geranium-strangled porch with a view across an untidy vegetable plot towards Glanmore, reading casually or feeding to his nephews unconventional opinions of the Boer War. 'What were the English doing in South Africa but driving poor farmers out of their homes?' Before leaving the area in early September, the party visited Castle Kevin for tea.[10]

The day he returned to Dublin, 'The Old and the New in Ireland' appeared in *The Academy and Literature* (London), a largely optimistic piece harmonising with the progressive mood of the day. But alongside his draft, Synge had made jottings of a more regretful kind. Whereas the article announced that 'religious questions, also, are beginning to put less restriction on Irish culture', unpublished notes expressed the matter less positively and less fluently – 'Few knew that the old form of protest to which a certain passage of Erasmus may well be applied was beginning to lose hold on an increasing share of the upper classes, and that with this release a new culture was beginning...' If this could be taken as a pompous deployment of 'In Praise of Folly' to neutralise what Synge disliked in Irish Protestantism, a parallel passage revealed a greater sense of loss:

Few of us, perhaps, are quite conscious of the revolution in dress and architecture that is going on in County Dublin and the districts round it. In a few years, in fifteen or twenty at the most, the generation of old women who still look out in admirably picturesque clothes from the doors of many cottages will have passed away. The round bonnet with white frills that frames the face, with frilled-in-shawls, the old world curtsy and many decorous modes which linger with these women will be unknown...[11]

These lines of nostalgia do not simply lament the passing of tradition; Synge specifies the distinctive costume of Wicklow cottagers associated with the great estates of Protestant planters, the Wingfields of Powerscourt, the Howards, and even (on a smaller scale), La Touches and Synges. If he does not, even in the privacy of Notebook 30, identify these women as dependents of a now eclipsed Protestant ascendancy, this is in keeping with his half-citation of Erasmus. For what had caught his attention in the Dutch theologian was a use of 'evangelical' which did not collapse directly into 'Protestant'. Then, after a few pages on the inadequacies of French Symbolism, Synge abruptly returns to the theme and writes tersely, 'Journalism may be literary, literature is always scriptural.'[12]

The epigram fits Synge's various occupations in the summer of 1902. He had placed literary-journalist work in the French and British press, and retired ungraciously to the Kingstown bedroom and the 'upper room' at Tomriland. But when did he stoop to eavesdropping on the servants below; and is this somehow the aural equivalent of voyeurism as alleged after his death? If the practice began before 21 July, and if he was sharing the house with its owners, then his unwitting victims may have been local girls, Protestant or Catholic. He may, of course, have been alone in the house: but it is unlikely that a farming family would move out for a total of two months at the height of a busy summer.

If the infamous incident occurred after 21 July, then the servants on whom he eavesdropped were not daughters of Erin as represented in the iconography of Gaelic-Catholic rural nationalism. They were his mother's domestics. Both Florence Massey and Ellen the cook were products of a Dublin Protestant orphanage. Massey had been with the family for over a year.[13] In this latter case, which remains less than fully proven, the scriptural allusion in the title of *In the Shadow of the Glen* derives properly if ironically from the after-hours chit-chat of city-born Protestant orphans (cf. 'Yea, though I walk through the valley of the shadow of death, I will fear no evil: for thou art with me; thy rod and thy staff they comfort me', Psalm 23: 4.) Even the ambiguity of Mrs Synge's staff is apt.

In the Stephens recollections, Ellen was a stout girl with a loud voice, who bantered with the farmhands as they passed the kitchen door. The shrunken floorboards, which allowed her richness of phrase to float up to the listening guest, equally failed to stop a torrent descending on her when Synge in play threw a garden watering can (which he used as a bathroom jug) at an intrusive nephew.[14] If he had managed to grasp a few weeks alone before his mother arrived, the interlude had been substantial. Apart from the nephews, his mother's party included Edie Harmar, Sam's sister-in-law.

The interconnection of various projects – articles, plays, including (by anticipation) *The Playboy of the Western World* of 1907 – demonstrates the manner in which Synge's imagination found coherence during 1902. On 15 August of the previous year, he had taken himself to the races at Arklow. These sporting contests provide an arena, transferred to the west coast of Ireland, in which the sham-murderer Christy will genuinely triumph. On the same day as the races, miles inland near Macreddin, John Winterbottom tipsy (but also, it may have been, mentally retarded) went missing. In the summer of 1902 – on the anniversary, as it were, of these events – Synge worked on *In the Shadow of the Glen* in which a tramp recounts how, when he 'was coming from the races beyond' on a dark rainy night he heard 'a thing talking – queer talk, you wouldn't believe at all, and you out of your dreams'. With ironic biblical exactitude, the body of a missing man, the tramp recalls, was found on 'the third day'.[15] This deliberate dovetailing of his own return from the races, an obscure farmer's death in the hills, and an emerging dramatic character's

self-positioning has been deemed 'a literalist strain in Synge's imagin-
ation'. But, with its anti-resurrection on the third day, it is an ironised
Christian literalism, an inversion or subversion of his mother's creed.
And John Doyle's death of May 1902 contributed also.

The *annus mirabilis* advanced without any publicly visible triumph.
The Aran Islands was an accomplished, if not a published, fact. Willie
Coleman of Tomriland provided an eloquent run of eulogistic terms
praising the acuity of mountainy shepherds in recognising even a new-
born lamb from their own flock as the sheep grazed in common across
thousands of rough acres. This found its way into 'At a Wicklow Fair', an
essay arising from Synge's dawn walk to Aughrim on 30 July but not
published until May 1907 in the *Manchester Guardian*, and also into the
speech of the tramp in *In the Shadow of the Glen*. For one of these sharp-
eyed rustics is Patch Darcy, the missing man of that play.

The same essay contains the germ of *The Tinker's Wedding*, an awkward
customer among Synge's plays, a two-acter (never popular with critics)
which treats sustained and happy fornication among the untouchables of
rural Ireland. But it was drafts of the one-act plays which Synge chose to
show Yeats and Gregory in October, while pausing at Coole Park *en route*
for Inis Oírr. Having reached the islands, he abandoned his diary for the
rest of the year. Other forms of writing supplanted his intermittent daily
entries. Encouraged by the discussions at Coole, he went to see four short
plays in English and Gaelic at the Camden Street Hall in Dublin. The
experience further persuaded him to align himself with the Irish theatre
movement and, ultimately, to abandon Paris.[16]

Looking back from a newly privileged position in the Irish Free State,
Synge's nephew recreated the summer of 1902 in arcadian terms – hay-
making and phrase-making about hay-making, bicycling trips together,
refreshment from hidden springs, and uncle-ish promises about visiting
a public house. Synge entrusted the business of taking dictation to
Edward, or so the latter avers. Though largely play, it allowed the listening
guest to speak aloud the colourful phrases he had heard so that the boy
could tap them out slowly on the typewriter.[17] In such little pretences is the
great drama made possible. But the arcadian perspective on Edwardian
Wicklow is only part of the plot.

Synge's last visit to the Aran Islands – three weeks in late October
stretching into November – added little or nothing to his account of the
west. He had already learned all that it had to teach. Some time in
November at Lady Gregory's instigation he met James Joyce, even more
unknown than Synge himself. At a dinner party on Monday 3 November

A studio-style portrait of the widowed Kathleen Synge and her family, from right to left: Samuel, Annie (later Mrs Harry Stephens), Robert, Edward and seated in the foreground, the young J. M. Synge. Probably taken by John Joly, later a Fellow of the Royal Society, and a pioneer of colour photography.

Bethel Terrace, one of the several holiday houses rented by the Synges in Greystones, County Wicklow.

Tomiland House, County Wicklow, where Synge worked on *Riders to the Sea* and *In the Shadow of the Glen*.

The reading room of the Association des Etudiants Protestants, Paris,
looking towards the Luxembourg Gardens.

Aran women awaiting the steamer. A photograph taken by J. M. Synge.

Edward Hutchinson Synge (1890–1957), the dramatist's nephew, and one
of his literary trustees.

at the Nassau Hotel, Joyce was introduced to John B. Yeats, the painter father, but it is impossible that Synge was present on the same occasion, being still on Inis Oírr.[18] Whenever it was the two young men met, the event extended Synge's range of acquaintance beyond the exiles of Paris and the Protestants of Ireland, to include the sharpest literary intellect in Catholic Ireland. Just before Christmas, both Synge and Yeats were in London; it is clear that, by 21 December, *Riders to the Sea* took precedence as the one-acter with which Synge would make his debut. The summer in Wicklow had given substance in dramatic form to many ideas, some of them initially conceived in the Aran Islands four years earlier.[19]

Little of Synge's early work on *Riders to the Sea* has survived. This factor has contributed to the play's reputation as an unsullied gem, undiminished by any clutter of dross around it. This is ironic, given that the play relentlessly exposes the way in which human life is worn down, ruthlessly consigned to decay and death. Its aspiration to be unalloyed tragedy, though flawed in Joyce's Aristotelian eyes, discourages trivial or inessential comment. Oliver Gogarty reports an incident in the Nassau Hotel to indicate how the play was sanctified, while also conveying the puzzlement this caused:

Maud Gonne sat on the opposite side of the table. Synge was at one end by Lady Gregory. Patrick Colum sat next to me. Suddenly Yeats exclaimed in admiration of a scene he was reading:
   'Aeschylus!'
   'Who does he mean?' Colum whispered, amazed.
   'Synge, who is like Aeschylus.'
   'But who is Aeschylus?'
   'The man who is like Synge.'[20]

Part of the spell woven by *Riders to the Sea* had the effect of 'verifying' a relationship between its island setting and its theatrical debut in Molesworth Street, a relationship which quickly rose to the status of national myth. That is, the cultural heart of Ireland was to be found in the west, or (even better) in the western islands lying to the west of Ireland, while its cultural efflorescence was firmly rooted in the (provincial) east-coast metropolis. Experience and expression were radically separate but, by the same token, the nation in question achieved a kind of formal unity by bringing its margins into an articulate circle – the west articulated by the east, the east enthralled by images of the west.

Several factors complicate this convenient notion. First, Synge did not work on some magically accessible native 'experience', which he somehow transferred to the Dublin stage. There were complex processes of mediation which even he may not have remained fully aware of. The missing fisherman of *Riders* is identified by the familiarity his sister has with his clothing, his stockings: 'It's the second one of the third pair I knitted, and I put up three score stitches, and I dropped four of them.' This intimacy cancels the yearned-for postponement of identification based on the common cloth used in the man's shirt – 'aren't there great rolls of it in the shops of Galway, and isn't it many another man may have a shirt of it as well as Michael himself?'[21] The detail about stockings echoes the mathematical formulae used by all prudent housekeeping mothers, including Kathleen Synge. But the contrast between mass-produced goods and the fateful home-knitted stocking indicates Synge's craft in dramatising overlapping modes of production which touched even the most isolated households, shoreline and suburban. So, too, harsh experience and book-based learning are interwoven. For example, a poignant moment at the end of the play very likely derives from Synge's reading of an American account of Famine conditions in the 1840s. This is the moment where the mother (Maurya) acknowledges that her most recently drowned son (Bartley) 'will have a fine coffin out of the white boards' which she had bought intending to bury another son whose body remains off-stage 'in the far north'.

In keeping with the displacement across history, a crucial place of initiation for the players was not the western isles but the Dublin slums. Asenath Nicholson (1792–1855), born Asenath Hatch in Vermont, travelled extensively in Ireland, recording her experiences in two powerful and detailed books. In the second of these, *Annals of the Famine in Ireland* (1851), this intensely Protestant author recounted her experiences on the western seaboard among the starving population and the various agencies set up to alleviate their suffering. In several important instances, her movements anticipate Synge's fifty odd years later, not only in that they visited the same places (Erris, for example, in Mayo, which will provide Synge with a setting for *The Playboy of the Western World*) but also in that they were aware of the complexities of Protestant reaction to a crisis occurring in an essentially Catholic society. Nicholson wrote positively of the Plymouth Brethren in this unlikely context: 'They were very active in the Famine, working efficiently ... and the Sabbath-school in which Christ and only Christ was taught was numerously attended by the poor, who were fed and clothed, not as a bribe, but as an act of Christian charity, due to the poor.'[22]

But it was on 28 November 1847, while she was based at Achill Sound, that she recorded the incident taken up in *Riders to the Sea*:

a fisherman's widow called in who had been twenty miles, to 'prove', as she said, her husband, who had been washed ashore and buried without a coffin; she bought a white coffin and took it to the spot with her own hands, she dug him from his grave, and proved him by a leather button she had sewed upon some part of his clothes.[23]

If Synge read this – and echoes of Nicholson in *The Playboy* surely confirm that he did – it must have struck him for its reworking of classic motifs: the right to proper burial in Sophocles' *Antigone* and in Plutarch's *Life of Phocion*. In the first of these, a sister buries her brother, in the second a widow her husband. In *Riders to the Sea*, a sister identifies her brother through his clothes, and a mother has bought white boards for a coffin. *White* boards, in the context of 1847 when coffins were recycled by means of a trapdoor bottom, are unused boards, a priceless commodity. Synge retains their purity for the poignant ending of his play. But he undercuts potential sublimity by having Maurya neglect to provide nails for the coffin-maker. In both play and source, the widow has *bought* the necessary wood for a decent burial. There were also Wicklow sources for part of the detail. John Winterbottom was identifiable from 'a shirt button sewn with black [not white] thread on a small piece of shirt left on the body' by the crows.[24]

Winterbottom links the two one-act plays of 1902, the strange manner of his death apostrophised in *In the Shadow of the Glen*, the forensic business of identification through clothing dramatised in *Riders to the Sea*. This poignant detail of Irish rural life was unknown to the audience who gathered on the evening of 8 October 1903 at the Molesworth Hall, behind St Anne's Church in Dawson Street. It is unlikely the anonymous writer in that morning's *Irish Independent* knew it either, when he denounced with prescience a play based on ideas drawn from 'the gaiety of Paris'. With Yeats's *The King's Threshold*, *In the Shadow of the Glen* ran for three nights, and provoked great hostility in nationalist quarters, notably in the *United Irishman*. Its editor, Arthur Griffith, presumably had forgotten the non-sectarian ideas of Wolfe Tone, founder of the United Irishmen, ideas largely drawn from the gaiety of republican Paris in the 1790s. Mrs Synge took consolation in the fact that her son's debut occurred in a Protestant church hall, a fact which also weighed with Griffith. Opposition to Synge took root in October 1903, and not enough was done by the inexperienced management of the amateur company to clear the soil. Nevertheless, the decision to press ahead with the second one-act play in February 1904 fully justified itself. Public reaction to *Riders* was mixed, but the family reaction was decidedly negative. Synge absented himself after the opening night (25 February), the victim of an abscessed tooth and high temperature. Rosie Calthrop, who was staying in the house and with whom he had taken long walks and cycle rides in the immediately preceding days, attended none of the performances.[25]

Cross-allusion between the two plays occurs subliminally. The drowned fisherman of *Riders to the Sea* has his east-coast doppelgänger in Patch Darcy of *In the Shadow of the Glen*. Synge commonly thought in terms of reciprocities: mental illness in rural Ireland was compared with urban life. 'We hear every day of the horrors of overcrowding, yet these desolate dwellings on the hill with here an old widow dying far away from her friend and there a single woman with all the whims of over-wrought virginity have perhaps a more utter, if higher sort of misery.'[26] In life the old widow was a Wicklow woman, whom Synge and Harry Stephens knew well from their sporting expeditions in the mountains.

The production history of *Riders* also complicates any notion of it as an unmediated re-enactment of the west of Ireland in Dublin. In February 1903, four 'premier' readings of the play were led by the dramatist himself, not in the Molesworth Hall, Dublin, but in the London flats of Augusta Gregory and W. B. Yeats. The audiences were not those who would riot (and then recant) at their own perceived representation in Abbey Street, Dublin, but rather G. K. Chesterton, John Masefield, Pamela Colman Smith, Arthur Symons and others in English letters with whom Yeats associated.[27] Symons was no passive spectator. Calculating that periodical publication before the play's conversion into a book would bring in more money for its author who (he rightly gathered) 'would find that useful', he set about interesting the *Fortnightly* and the *Monthly Review* in Synge's text. To no avail, however. *Riders to the Sea* did find its way into print first through a magazine, but Yeats's *Samhain* of October 1903 was the vehicle and the Molesworth Hall stage premier followed four months later.

Though *Riders to the Sea* looks least likely among Synge's plays to reveal a hidden dimension, the circumstances of its first staging brought out an ironic relation between the austere, desolate primitivism of its setting and the higgledy-piggledy condition of the city. The director, encouraged by Synge, decided that the *caoin* (or *caoineadh*, 'keen' in Hiberno-English, or lament) should be rendered authentically. Someone had heard of an Aran woman living near Gardiner Street, a slum area where once Luke

Gardiner had developed fine Georgian town-houses. Máire Nic Shiubh-laigh and another (unnamed) player asked this woman to sing a trad-itional lament, intending to pick up the rudiments much as one might learn to hum a tune after a visit to the music-hall.

The woman, whose name they never learned, spoke no English though she lived with her married daughter in those overcrowded conditions Synge had linked to Wicklow misery. The room, home to an entire family, had served as a drawing room for the house's original occupants, with a massive marble fireplace almost filling one wall. The floor was rotting away. Dressed in shawl and red petticoat, the old islander sang the *cao-ineadh*, her eyes closed, arms outstretched, head thrown back, swaying backwards and forwards. As Nic Shiubhlaigh recalled years later,

It was strangely moving to see this old figure standing at the window of a crumbling tenement, looking over a city street, singing. She seemed to forget we were there. She sang:
'Tá sé imighthe uaim! [He is gone from me]
Go deo! Go deo! Go deo!' [Forever, forever, forever][28]

The death of a son, which Maurya laments in Synge's island-set one-act play, is transposed in this pre-production scene into the death of a lan-guage, the unwilling movement of individuals from seaboard to slum tenement, from the primitive to the degenerate without any intermediate stage of 'civilisation'.

The one-act plays of 1902, which were successfully completed, do not constitute an isolated group. Links between them and experiments which did not flourish reveal Synge's involvement with his family history. Asenath Nicholson's contribution to *Riders to the Sea* suggests that death in that play is not a monopoly of the sea's; it has textual roots in the Famine of the 1840s in which the playwright's grandfather (Robert Traill) died in West Cork. In Synge's diary for late January and February 1903, there are references to a further play, while in a notebook used in the same year, we find a fragment of dialogue involving a character called Bartley. The setting – 'street in country town in South of Ireland' – is unlike that in which we found the Bartley of *Riders*. Nothing in Synge's drama repeats this apparent concern with urban or semi-urban life. Not much can be gleaned from the few dozen lines of dialogue, except a preoccupation with hair-combing and a wedding which will not take place tomorrow. One of the two women, however, is Barbara, an unusual name in rural Ireland.[29]

Barbara is therefore an enigma. In the Aran notebook where Synge confided that 'one woman ... has interested me in a way that binds me more than ever', one page carries words written both 'right-way-up' and 'upside down'. In a hand which I do not believe is Synge's, the following address appears

> Barbara Conneely
> South Island
> Arran
> Ireland

Then Synge has turned the notebook on its head and written:

Prose???????
The aim of literature is to make the impossible seem inevitable (????!) or to make the inevitable seem impossible.[30]

This is one of his less impressive epigrams. The highlighting of 'Prose' as a particular form or genre in which this 'aim' is pursued is worthy of note, but the relationship of the 'aim' to the address remains characteristically unstated. Barbara Conneely was a young woman whom Synge knew, who took instruction in lace-making from one of the industries encouraged by the Congested Districts Board: she wrote to him on several occasions, with news of her progress. But he would never have spelled 'Arran' in that fashion, and would have no need to add 'Ireland'. This leaves the intriguing possibility that Barbara Conneely wrote her own address in his notebook, using a conventionally full form. What we are left with is a Barbara whose address uniquely appears in the notebook.

The name also occurs in the Synge family tree, notably in the instance of John Hatch's Barbara Synge (born 1731) whose daughters married Synge brothers and brought the family into Wicklow. As Nicholas Grene has established, on 24 August 1901 J. M. Synge had listened to folk-tale versions of this family history while he stood in the village of Aughavannagh. Another Barbara Synge had drowned at Syngefield in 1792 aged two, daughter of Francis Synge MP. Far closer to home, however was the death of yet another infant Barbara Synge in October 1901, the daughter of Robert Synge and his wife Mamie Blakiston.[31] J. M. Synge was in Dublin at the time, passing from Inis Meáin to London with the manuscript of

The Aran Islands. When Ann Saddlemyer published the Barbara fragment under the hesitant heading 'Aughavanna Play <?>', she worked by a process of elimination.[32] But Aughavannagh has nothing deserving the name 'street' – it is a mountain roadside with a scattering of houses, a classic Irish 'dispersed village'. Nor is Aughavannagh in any obvious sense (of 1903) in the south of Ireland. References to Mary's fine hair link the fragment to *The Well of the Saints* while details of covert surveillance resemble the background to *When the Moon Has Set*, both set in Wicklow. What the unnamed fragment reveals, I believe, is Synge's awareness of his ancestor's name and his tentative transfer of erotic frustration from the social level of the family to that of latter-day country people. 'Barbara' may also encode the decadent theme of death which he was slowly transforming from morbidity into dramatic closure.

The day Synge landed in the Aran Islands for the last time, his mother consulted W. M. A. Wright. Neither she nor her son were in improving health. While he was on Inis Oírr, he wrote requesting a supply of medicine which, loving and perplexed as ever, she sent on to his desolate fisherman's cot. He lived at a distance from her, even when he could not pull himself away from home. She would 'sigh over John's perversity and the long delay there seemed to be in the answering of her prayers', yet she dutifully packed up his manuscripts and despatched them to Yeats when her wayward son requested such favours. Though he might fulminate about the burden of *amor matris* to his friend MacKenna, he resolutely defended his mother's integrity in the face of Yeatsian cynicism.[33] Meanwhile, on 13 November, Alfred Nutt wrote from London declining to publish *The Aran Islands* on the grounds that it would not reach a large enough audience to be commercially viable.

Back in October 1900, some busybody had reported to Kathleen Synge that Cherrie Matheson had been spotted on a tram with 'a young man' whom the lynx-eyed Edward Stephens later identified as a maths master in his school. 'It seems so soon after she was thinking of marrying Uncle John.'[34] Yet links between the three houses on Crosthwaite Park remained affable in the aftermath of Synge's rejection as suitor. Connie Matheson came to tea with Mrs Synge, sometimes Mrs Synge called uninvited on Mrs Matheson and vice versa. When Annie Stephens held a party for thirty children in January 1899, Robert Matheson operated the phonograph.

But for Synge himself, relations with the Mathesons were naturally strained. On one occasion when Mrs Synge and her servant Mary Brien set out from Kingstown to Castle Kevin, taking the train as far as Greystones, they saw Cherrie and her sister Winnie 'up on a bank as [they] passed on beyond Delgany, spoke to them'.[35] Synge had opted to travel by bicycle, avoiding the evangelical laagers of the coastline. Now, at the end of 1902, Cherrie was marrying Kenneth Arthur Hobart Houghton, whose home at Montpelier Place (Blackrock) was cheek by jowl with the house from which Kathleen Traill had set out to marry Jack Synge in 1856. The wedding took place on 25 November, with Annie Stephens and her elder son Frank among 'the great number' who attended at Monkstown parish church (the Brethren could not conduct weddings themselves). The celebrant was the Rev. R. Wyndham Guinness, rector of Rathdrum.

With Cherrie's departure into matrimony and the Cape Province, a particularly tense and protracted episode in Synge's development came to a close. He never wholly abandoned *When the Moon Has Set* in which he struggled to convert Cherrie into a dramatic character by converting her into an unconvincing nun. But the claustrophobic web of domestic religion and family history, sexuality and convention had been lifted from his shoulders. On Christmas Day, his mother wrote up her diary during the afternoon. 'John in his room writing, it is very quiet – all the Stephens family at church. John and I are to dine with them.'[36]

The great one-act plays can be assigned to 1902, even if details are traceable earlier or later. They spring from the pattern of the year, with modest accommodation in Tomriland, a final visit to the Aran Islands, and a decisive change in Cherrie Matheson's bearing upon his emotional life. Synge's literary career had begun to move when, in December 1901, Yeats decided to assist in finding a publisher for *The Aran Islands*, despite 'one or two passages towards the end too personal'.[37] A recognition that Synge's talent lay in prose (dramatic or otherwise) led to the quiet abandonment of verse-plays and narratives interspersed with poems.

The achievement can even be related to his reading of fiction in January and his encounter with Joyce in November. Anticipating *Dubliners* by several years, both *Riders to the Sea* and *In the Shadow of the Glen* possess qualities admired or feared in Joyce's short stories – an unblinking attention to death and deep-rooted unhappiness, a sardonic but generous humour, aesthetic patience in allowing implication to emerge at its own pace, their native city's uneasy awareness of rural Ireland. This is said with no intention to discount the plays' theatricality, their serene yet taut dramatic structures. None the less, their author may be better understood as a contemporary of Joyce rather than as a disciple of Yeats. By the end of 1902, even his last, unfinished drama had been embarked upon: while on Aran he had commenced a translation of 'Oidhe Chloinne Uisnigh', the Gaelic saga material which provided the basis for *Deirdre of the Sorrows*.[38] At this date, not a word of his had been uttered on the public stage. The Abbey Theatre lay hidden in the future. But the strong foundations were all in place.

It is not premature, therefore, to ask – what lies at the centre of this achievement, what thematic preoccupation or structuring symbolic action? The answer at its simplest is, I feel, *concealment*. A more elaborate or theoretically acute answer might point to the recurrence of the absent (dead) figure, at least in Synge's early work – Michael in *Riders to the Sea* has been drowned in the far north; Patch Darcy in *In the Shadow of the Glen* has been eaten by crows; both the elder Sweeny and the deranged Costello in *When the Moon Has Set* mightily affect the action by remaining off-stage. Even the few dozen words constituting the 'Barbara' fragment conjure up a quizzical version of the same basic problem – 'What is it he'd look at if it wouldn't be a thing you can see?' – in terms midway between Bishop Berkeley and Samuel Beckett.[39]

To counterbalance this preoccupation, Synge had become a proficient photographer. He had obtained his first camera from a fellow resident in the Atlantic Hotel, Kilronan, during his 1898 visit to the Aran Islands. Not only did he take many photographs of the islanders (and, less frequently, of island scenes), he showed photographs of Wicklow and other places to the Aran islanders on his return. Among the many prompts directing him towards Aran one should not neglect the ethnographical work of Charles Robert Browne and Alfred Cort Haddon, published in the *Proceedings of the Royal Irish Academy* with photographic illustrations.[40] Synge had encountered Haddon as a lecturer to the Dublin Naturalists' Field Club. While his own photographs of Aran sometimes look like attempts to 'deconstruct' the rigidly formal record-keeping of the ethnographers, he would have noted with interest their observation that 'the range of distinctness of the vision is astonishing' among the islanders, some of whom could see a small sailing boat twenty miles out to sea before the doctor from the mainland could spot it with his binoculars.[41] As a photographer who also developed his pictures from plates, and as one with a keen interest in painting, Synge chose deliberately when he found himself through literature, the visible literature of stage-drama. While the pervasive concern with blindness-as-vision in *The Well of the Saints* is entirely in harmony with these more isolated figurations, it is also useful to consult Synge's best-known work, *The Playboy of the Western World*, and its sources.

'Often', during Synge's earliest days on the Aran Islands in May 1898, he heard the story of a Connacht man 'who killed his father with the blow of a spade'. Too often attention has concentrated either on the patricidal aspect of the incident which becomes central in his riot-provoking play of 1907 or on the islanders' alleged propensity for protecting criminals. Between the Freudian and the populist interpretations, the means of concealment goes unnoticed. But the story told by a unnamed old man was only one of Synge's sources. The other, more widely publicised, story was also of crime: Synge's blending of them constitutes a fine instance of artistic development from crudely cut materials.

When the remorseful Connacht man reached the safety of remote stony Aran, the islanders hid him in a hole beneath the great slabs and boulders which cover so much of its uncultivated surface. Synge was shown the exact spot and, understanding that the murderer had relatives on the island, he appreciated the motives of sympathy which kinship substantiated. His own panicky fear in the autumn of 1899 that he might die and be 'shoved down into a wet crevice' inverts this protective concealment, suggesting a fearful identification with the Connacht man. The murderer's identity (a topic Synge does not touch on) is now known: he was a native of Callow, born about 1838, the son of a poor farmer named Ó Máille (in English, O'Malley or Maley). In the heel of the hunt, Ó Máille escaped to America, and revisited Galway years later as a ship's captain.[42]

The second source also involves an American dimension, but the Irish focus is Achill, County Mayo. Since the 1830s, the island had been a stronghold of Protestant (Church of Ireland) proselytising, in a broad missionary movement to which the Rev. A. H. Synge had made his own contribution. Mrs Agnes MacDonnell, a leading member of the mission community, was attacked in her island home and left for dead, horribly defaced and mutilated. Having been hidden (in a hole, under a kitchen dresser) by relatives including a female cousin, a local man was charged with the crime, convicted and gaoled for life. The motive for James Lynchehaun's crime has never been fully established; vengeance, perhaps involving a sexual subplot, was at work. On 7 September 1902, the prisoner escaped from Maryborough Gaol, eventually reached the United States, and featured in an extraordinary extradition case first in Indianapolis and later in the Supreme Court. When Synge visited Mayo in September 1904, the story was everywhere spoken of.[43]

Later, when The Playboy controversy broke, he half admitted that Lynchehaun and 'the Aran case' (of Ó Máille) had contributed to his play.[44] The element of unfinished murder links Lynchehaun and Synge's Christy

Mahon; the island locations of Achill and Aran link Lynchehaun and Ó Máille and Christy. Perhaps to protect his sources on Inis Meáin, Synge changed the location for his play to the Mayo mainland coast. He retained Ó Máille's patricide but allows it to emerge as unsuccessful. In a symmetrical move, he also retained Lynchehaun's helpful cousin and her dresser, and related Pegeen as cousin not of the murderer but of her local, low-spirited suitor. What Synge comprehensively omits is the sectarian dimension in Mrs Agnes MacDonnell's life.

If Synge conceals the proselytising nature of the community in which Mrs MacDonnell lived, the real-life plots he exploited also feature concealment as part of the hero/villain's credentials. For it is only through a ritual of successful evasion of authority, effected through self-concealment or the generosity of others, that he moves slowly from police files into folkloric reputation. Between the absent characters of the one-act plays and the farcical tragedy of *The Playboy* lies Synge's greatest achievement. In *The Well of the Saints*, concealment is raised to a philosophical, visionary level. It is to be the high point of Synge's career. Not only had he assimilated the story of a miraculous well on Aran the waters of which, borne to Wicklow, inaugurate the play; he had also noted the French medieval fable of beggars who choose blindness over physical sight.

CHAPTER 16

Too Many Impresarios

Synge said: 'Now the elder of us two should be in command on this trip.'

Jack Yeats[1]

Aestheticism, primitivism, mysticism – these cults of the day informed the pilgrimage of Yeats and Symons to the west of Ireland in summer 1896. As his career gathered strength, the Irish poet brooked no rivals. Recognising that he himself was always likely to cleave more intimately to the mystical than to the primitive, he quickly saw in Synge exactly the man to head off Arthur Symons who, as a potential orientalist of the western world, had noted acutely, 'I have perceived the insidious danger of idealism ever since I came into these ascetic regions.'[2] Directing Synge towards the Aran Islands, and casting the Englishman as a critic of Symbolism, Yeats was himself moved to adopt a more concessive attitude towards the harsh, impoverished landscape of Clare-Galway and its irreducible physicality. The Literary Revival took a decisive turn when Synge went to Aran in 1898, a turn-away from coterie London and hashish, towards the 'folk'. But it is arguable that the crucial moves were fought out in *The Savoy* two years earlier, and that Synge never embraced folkish ideologies.

Power ebbed and flowed throughout the Irish *fin-de-siècle* years. Parnell dominated parliament and fell; Wilde dominated the West End and fell. There were Parnellites and anti-Parnellites; there were sexual refugees in Paris and Dieppe. The Catholic Church felt the impact of the political crisis as both a demonstration of its grip on the public realm, and as a fissure dividing some individual clergy from the bishops. Unionists were revolted by the display of ecclesiastical power, and for quite different reasons they revolted against democratic authority. James Connolly stood for election as a socialist in the municipal contests behind James Joyce's 'Ivy Day in the Committee Room' (set in autumn 1902). Literature was part and parcel of this to-and-fro struggle between those who had fallen and those who were prevented from rising.

Personal devotion or servitude was more typical of the period than ideological commitment. Artists no less than politicians sought to wield power over others. Joyce spoke of 'the gratefully oppressed'. Denis Donoghue's brilliant essay on Yeats devotes twenty pages to 'a kind of power' though the piece might be better entitled 'every kind of power'.[3] Synge had been signed up as a useful researcher, a man who could do missionary work in the west, collecting folklore and brushing up his Gaelic. Even when he gave evidence of a quite different genius, Yeats treated Synge as a recruit, albeit to the officers' mess rather than the ranks of the foot-scholars.

Yeats still had a base in London, and it was at Woburn Buildings on 12 January 1903 that Synge met John Masefield, the English poet with whom he shared a love of travel. Synge had lodgings in No. 4, Handel Street; Masefield was staying nearby. In letters dutifully sent back to Kingstown, lack of money contended with breeding. 'Board-Residence places abound in this neighbourhood and are fairly respectable and cheap, but I don't think [I] could stand that sort of thing now.' For fourteen shillings a week, he had bed and breakfast in a house of apartments, though the bill came to about £2 when extras were included. 'The only drawback is that there is a door into the next room where an individual groans and giggles to himself as if he was off his head.'[4]

Mrs Ward required payment in advance. Cul-de-sac Handel Street lies in an area being developed at the time by Mrs Humphry Ward, Stopford Brooke and other 'post-Anglican' philanthropists. Though the issue defies proof beyond all reasonable doubt, the strong suspicion exists that Synge's accommodation was provided through the agencies then developing the Passmore Edwards Settlement in nearby Tavistock Place. Hard-up but respectable, he took time to notice the suffering of others. 'The unemployed walk about London in dreary endless procession every day with collecting boxes.'[5] Having differed with his family about the Boer War, he did not hesitate to see misery in the streets as the afterlife of bellicose triumphalism. London for Synge in 1903 was not unlike Dublin in 1904 for the author of *Ulysses*, a place of dismal routine, pointless activity, and uncanny weather. 'Roads and pathways sheeted in thin ice so that every body had to creep along in single file in the gutter where there was a sort of grip.'[6] The fogs Uncle Alec had reported still shrouded the imperial capital. It was here that he hoped to finish *The Aran Islands*, free from the distractions of Dublin and the pressures of home life. London publishers, however, were not easily persuaded. In addition, Ireland continued to exercise its influence, not only through Yeats but through Lady Gregory who arrived ten days after Synge. Of those he met in London, Pamela Colman Smith, who ran an extraordinary magazine called *The Green Sheaf*, published 'A Dream of Innismaan' in 1903.

Yeats and Synge were never to throw their lot in with the cultural nationalists, represented to various degrees by Maud Gonne, Arthur Griffith and Patrick Pearse. Literature might be allied to nationality, but the last word lay with literature. Furthermore, for reasons of inherited prejudice as well as intellectual independence, they were unsympathetic to the popular Catholicism of the Irish majority. Consequently, London and Paris remained points of reference, even of strategic orientation. The dynamic of these formative years lay exactly in unresolved tension, potential movement between rootedness and restlessness. Much later, Samuel Beckett locates and dislocates the exhilarating frustration of Jack Yeats's landscapes and cityscapes as 'the being in the street when it happens in the room, the being in the room when it happens in the street, the turning to gaze from land to sea, from sea to land...'[7]

South of County Galway, on the edge of an even sparser, harsher landscape, Count Florimond de Basterot (1836–1904) occupied Durras House for parts of each year. His great-grandfather had inherited the place from an Irish wife.[8] A cousin of Guy de Maupassant, an inveterate traveller and amateur anthropologist, de Basterot provided the occasion for notables in the district to strike sparks off the flint of his Gallic hardness. The world was in urgent need of regeneration. As a step to that end, Gregory took Yeats aside in the estate office of the Frenchman's small seaboard country residence; the Irish theatre movement was born on premises where Ned Synge would have been quite at home.[9] In 1898, while he was on Aran, Synge received an invitation from Yeats to stop off at Coole Park on his way back to Dublin. Widowed, conscientious, troubled by the relentless devaluation of her inheritance, Augusta, Lady Gregory was gradually asserting herself as the focal point of the cultural moment. Since the summer of 1897, theatre had been uppermost on the agenda. Synge stayed with her from 27 to 29 June 1898, before resuming his journey eastwards to Kingstown and Castle Kevin. On 28 June, he and his hostess had called on Edward Martyn at Tullyra Castle.

Doors were opening in unexpected places to reveal unlikely collaborators. Martyn was a devout Catholic of the oldest Norman stock in Ireland, an ill-tempered celibate and patron of church music. The 'Big Houses' of the Gregorys, the Martyns and the Moores were a motley collection, in terms both of architecture and social position. Synge's access, at least to some of them, came not through ancestral links with Galway, but through his Parisian encounter with Yeats. Though Gregory saw in him a social equal who also shared her evangelical training (she remaining faithful, he in stolid revolt), Synge's symbolic role at this moment was that of vanishing mediator. He had ceased to be a landowner, he had not become an artist. He was at home in Coole precisely because he was homeless. Like Yeats he concerned himself with the traditions of the poor, but he never pretended to be in search of a creed or a way of life.

Before leaving Coole, Synge borrowed some unpublished articles. Ann Saddlemyer has suggested these were writings on folklore which later appeared under Yeats's name in the *New Ireland Review*. He wrote back from Crosthwaite Park on 1 July to describe a colourful, talkative acquaintance he had made on the train. 'One night he sang a song in Moate and a friend of his heard the words in Athenry.'[10] The rudiments of Synge's future might be detected even in these sparse details of folkloristic investigation and extravagant behaviour observed in 'modernised' contexts. Gregory respected Synge and backed him, despite his remarkable inability to suppress total honesty in favour of courtesy. When he got hold of her prose retelling of the Cuchulain saga, he wrote from Paris:

'Au fond' I am a somewhat quibbling spirit and I never expect to enjoy a book that I have heard praised beforehand, but in this case I have been altogether carried away. I had no idea the book was going to be so great.[11]

Nor was she the only victim of his frank exactitude. Reviewing *Cuchulain of Muirthemne* in the *Speaker* a few months later, he went out of his way to tell the public that Yeats's claim on Gregory's behalf – she had discovered the peasant idiom into which she rendered the ancient story – could not stand. Douglas Hyde had used it earlier in his *Love Songs of Connacht*. Yeats himself, the review continued, had done likewise in some articles on folklore. As these were very probably the articles lent him at Coole, in which Gregory had played a greater creative role than Yeats ever acknowledged, Synge's independence of mind outstripped his gratitude. His general account of 'the intellectual movement that has been taking place in Ireland for the last twenty years' opts for a theoretical term then still carrying a high nervous charge – it was the result of 'an evolution [sic] rather than of a merely personal idea'.[12]

This review was written while he was still based in the rue d'Assas. The decision to leave Paris was not the result simply of Synge's absorption by

Yeats and the faerie lure of rural Ireland. Of all Synge's Paris acquaintances, the most important ultimately was Joyce whose attitude remained at once critical and admiring. Nine years younger, but many years more precocious, the future author of *Ulysses* and *Finnegans Wake* (then planning to be a medical student) had met Synge in Dublin in December 1902 through Augusta Gregory. Yeats almost succeeded in bringing them together again in London in January 1903 when all concerned were bothering the editors of magazines in which they might publish. As reported by Richard Ellmann, Synge wrote back to his mother that 'This week Joyce – on his way back to Paris – [is] going to them all so I will not go round for a few days as it is better not to have too many Irish men turning up at once.'[13]

The ease with which he uses Joyce's name in writing to Kathleen suggests a rapport which can hardly have pleased his mother, if he had given her any details of his new friend's habits and beliefs. The gentlemanly code of employing surnames as an indication of equality anticipates (oddly in this case) the latter-day academic practice of citing the literary results of blood, sweat and tears simply as 'Yeats' or 'Joyce'. Synge clearly saw something in the younger, ill-dressed, aggressively lapsed Catholic which no one else in the family would have cared for. According to one of Joyce's earliest biographers, the two met 'seven or eight times' in Paris, to eat cheap lunch in the rue Saint-André-des-Arts.[14] It was never to be Synge's practice to put himself in the hands of a patron or promoter. On the contrary, he kept a distance some resented between himself and even his closest colleagues. But his range of associates was wide, transcending the notorious Irish categories of religious background and class affiliation.

While knocking on doors in London, he had been pleased to chat with George R. Sims (1847–1913), editor of *Men and Women*. A close acquaintance of Edward M. Synge of Byfleet (the painter and engraver), Sims also knew the 'Alecks' – descendants of Synge of Aran, Stepney and Ipswich. Quite a friend of the family, in every respect except finding work for JMS. It was in the course of reporting to Kingstown how Sims had described a Doreen Synge (born 1893) – unknown to his caller – 'as the most interesting member of the family' that Synge dropped Joyce's name. In Paris, Joyce stayed at the Hôtel Corneille, very likely at Synge's suggestion, during the course of the younger man's endeavours to set up as a medical student. Fortunately, neither stuck to his Parisian undertakings. Joyce later claimed to have been the first reader of *Riders to the Sea*, the two men sitting down to lunch over it.[15] That encounter took place some time in the spring of 1903, when Synge was disposing of his flat, at which point – according to Joyce – Synge had already written four plays, 'all in one act'.

Joyce spoke of Synge's drama, making no reference to poetry or prose fiction. Yet we know that Stephen MacKenna had seen reams of verse, and it is unlikely that Synge would have talked to Joyce about the one literary genre the latter was not then concerned with. In *Stephen Hero*, on which Joyce was working in 1904/5, Dante's *Vita Nuova* is alluded to; it is used later in *Giacomo Joyce*. Quite apart from differences of literary genre, Synge's 'Vita Vecchia' stood in contrast to his drama in its palpable struggle with autobiographical material. In this regard the two would-be writers were on common ground, though Joyce occupied it more confidently. An Italian critic has described how 'division' or 'explanation in prose' is imposed in Dante's *Vita Nuova* as a method of setting up a restructuring of categorical frames or levels, while at the same time aesthetic order is achieved by what Joyce termed the 'coordinating power of the intellect'.[16] This amply states the inadequacies of 'Vita Vecchia' and the new-life rhetoric of *When the Moon Has Set*. Did Synge show Joyce his prose-and-verse experiment in Dantean aesthetic self-making, alongside the four plays in one act?

Though Joyce was a critical supporter of Synge, and provided an intellectual link to the Catholic middle classes at home, he could also be a damned nuisance. On the evening of 20 June 1904 – four days after his unplanned assignation with Nora Barnacle – Joyce turned up drunk at the National Theatre Society's (pre-Abbey) premises in Camden Street, Dublin. Ten days earlier, he had been present when Synge told the company about his new play, *The Well of the Saints*. Whereas *In the Shadow of the Glen* had only hinted at an aesthetic of self-making, the new play's protagonist articulates a virtual politics (of rights) by which the blind seer marks himself off from the mass of people. Ellmann suspected that Joyce's drunkenness was part-prompted by Synge's creativity, which the younger man was not yet able to match. So, on 20 June, he collapsed incontinently in the passageway between the street and the dingy hall, to be discovered by Vera Esposito (one of the actresses) and her Russian mother. Within a day or two Joyce resumed work on *Stephen Hero*, which did not see the light of day for another forty years.[17] In the Espositos, Synge found a useful bridge between his Academy of Music training and his theatre involvement.

The Abbey (when it finally emerged) constituted a collective entrepreneurial unit in itself, with Synge acting as a highly effective, but discreet, partner. Joyce had no part in the new enterprise, regarding it as irredeemably provincial and folksy. The personalities of this busy period in Irish literary life were drawing up lines of communication and division. But those who were allies in formal terms did not always see eye to eye. Synge's remark to MacKenna that, for the theatre's good management, 'Yeats looks after the stars, and I do the rest', catches the difference between two personalities, but masks the extent to which the Abbey made Synge. Without the theatre conceived in de Basterot's estate office, *Riders to the Sea* might have remained a desk-manuscript, an entry in the annals of the Molesworth Hall. Strictly speaking, we should not assign Synge's first two plays to 'the Abbey' (always a loose term), because the Irish National Theatre Society did not move to Abbey Street until October 1904. The complex financial and professional negotiations which brought the Society to the Mechanics' Institution (in Abbey Street) did not directly involve Synge.[18]

In August 1904, Joyce had printed a longish poem, 'The Holy Office', all copies of which were destroyed when he could not pay the printer. In it he satirised most of Dublin's self-proclaimed literati. Synge was not exempted – 'he who sober all the day / Mixes a naggin in his play'. But the identities of Joyce's victims merge into one another rather like figures in the 'Circe' episode of *Ulysses* or those who ebb and flow throughout *Finnegans Wake*. Editors have confidently named 'John Eglinton', also known as Stiff Breeches, in connection with certain lines:

> him who will his hat unfix
> Neither to malt nor crucifix
> But show to all that poor-dressed be
> His high Castilian courtesy –[19]

Synge like Eglinton came of Protestant stock (unlikely, then, to bow to a Catholic emblem) and was (as already noted in the poem) modest in his drinking. As his full and legal name suggests, William Kirkpatrick Magee (1868–1961) was born a Presbyterian. So 'high Castilian courtesy' seems adrift from both men – until one recalls that the Costello family in Synge's *When the Moon has Set* pride themselves on such origins. If Joyce does pick up a Syngean allusion here (and pinpoints it as disguised self-allusion), then it can be only as a result of Synge's having shown him his play-in-progress in Paris in the spring of 1903. And that in turn would explain Joyce's otherwise remarkable claim that he had seen *four* one-act manuscripts.

The company's exodus from the hall behind Camden Street to a former mortuary in Abbey Street was made possible by Annie Horniman (1860–1937), a colleague of Yeats's in the Order of the Golden Dawn and the daughter of an English tea-merchant and Liberal Member of Parliament. As a female Croesus with occult powers, she exercised more power in what was becoming the Abbey Theatre than anyone that band of inspired amateurs had previously encountered. The consequences included a form of professionalisation which made it possible for Molly Allgood, shortly to become Synge's beloved, to be a full-time actress. One of Horniman's earliest moves in Synge's direction was to cast his horoscope. The result smacks more of canny research than inspiration – 'you should be able to learn languages pretty easily ... tragic stories please you ...' But there were also predictions which came home to roost. 'Strange unexpected events will turn up in your love affairs & spoil them ... I think you are unlikely to marry...' As an astral comrade, she loyally declared that Yeats's influence 'has been excellent for both of you', a view calculated to buttress the Yeatsian theory of how Synge found Aran and its tragic stories. That was in May 1904, just before the formal contract by which Horniman funded the new theatre was signed.[20] Among the inflated male egos of the Irish Revivalists, the Englishwoman was closer to being an impresario than anyone else Synge had to deal with. She had a hold over Yeats, she was free to transfer her patronage to Manchester (with important consequences for Molly), she was a boss. Synge, doing more than his share of the work as a director of the company, remained politely independent.

During his visit to Dublin in the autumn of 1904, the American John Quinn (1870–1924) dined with Yeats and Lady Gregory at the Nassau Hotel, a place favoured by Yeats for intermittent residence in the city of his birth. Afterwards, he walked over to Camden Street where he met Douglas Hyde and Synge; they watched rehearsals of Gregory's *Kincora* and a performance of Yeats's *Pot of Broth*. Then 'the whole crowd' marched back to the hotel where most of them stayed till one in the morning. There is no indication whether Synge joined in the late-night conviviality. But he certainly took part in some decorous high jinks which Quinn reported to the journalist Frederick John Gregg (1864–1927), an old school-friend of Yeats's. On a Sunday evening – probably 30 October – having dined at the Yeats family house in Dundrum, Quinn and Synge travelled by side-car to Rathgar Avenue, one of those suburban roads which Synge as a boy had used in his comings and goings between Orwell Park and the cathedral environs. They reached the small abode of George W. Russell about eleven o'clock:

It was a gray, moonlight night, and he interested me by telling me all the way stories of his tramps through the country in Germany and how he loved the nights and the quiet and how many and many a night he had slept out under a hedge or in a farmer's house or in a hay loft ... He was in college with John F. Taylor, the well known Irish orator. Synge's name beginning with S and Taylor's with T, they both sat together three or four years in Trinity. Synge told me wonderful tales of Taylor's intensity and eloquence and earnestness. Taylor was an older man than Synge when they were in college, because he got a late start. Taylor, Synge told me, had been a clerk in a shop or store in his early days.

This is a rare account of Synge off duty, when reticence has been laid aside in favour of more sociable instincts. Yet the effect is rather to confirm what has always been suspected – that Synge liked simple pursuits and mixed easily with people from humble backgrounds. Quinn was a successful New York lawyer, but his parents had been immigrants from rural Ireland. The company who gathered at Russell's stimulated this side of his personality. In addition to the bearded host, there was Padraic Colum, Oliver Gogarty, 'a young man named Joyce', Maud Gonne, Susan Mitchell and several young women whose names have not been preserved. There was no drink, but much smoking of cigars and cigarettes. Amid stacks of unframed pictures, people sat on the floor. Red-haired Mitchell recited parodies of Yeats's poems and Gonne capped these with an imitation of her erstwhile lover in his most soulful mood. The men, including Synge, told stories in the best Dublin style. According to a fragmentary diary of Quinn's, others included Constance Gore-Booth and her Polish artist husband, Casimir Markievicz. Russell himself regaled his guests with an account of Yeats at a seance, so overwhelmed by the spirit presences that he ended up on the floor reciting the first lines of Milton's *Paradise Lost* as if it were a prayer. The party broke up at one in the morning, with Synge and Quinn driving into Dublin together.[21] Quinn was staying in the Shelburne Hotel, on the north side of St Stephen's Green. Synge, however, had moved earlier that month into lodgings with a Mrs Stewart, at 15 Maxwell Road, close to Russell's house on Rathgar Avenue. So his purpose in accompanying Quinn in the early hours was evidently to continue the conversation, and little more.

Synge had arrived. On Monday 31 October, rehearsals began in the new Abbey Theatre. He and Quinn were duly in attendance. In December, *Samhain* published *In the Shadow of the Glen* while Quinn's publication of it in the United States protected Synge's American copyright. After Christmas, the Abbey was officially opened (27 December), and Synge's

one-acter was revived on the second evening of the theatre's public existence. There was no doubting the skilful organisation of the movement of
which Yeats was the most recognisable and self-promoted leader: theatre
and print went hand in hand to advance the name of J. M. Synge as its
latest prodigy. Having given up his *pied-à-terre* in the rue d'Assas the
previous year, Synge was never to see Paris again.

Dramatist and company had assisted at each other's postponed debut.
February 1905 marked Synge's real success with a three-act play, *The Well
of the Saints*. Spring and summer were given over to controversy in the
newspapers, the publication in London and New York of three plays,
negotiations with German and Czech translators, and a month-long tour
of the west of Ireland with Jack Yeats. It was only in mid-September –
seven months after *The Well of the Saints* – that Synge became involved
in the inner workings of the theatre, when he attended a five-day-long
policy meeting with W. B. Yeats at Coole Park. On 22 September 1905 the
Society voted to become a limited liability company, with Synge as a
director together with Gregory and Yeats. In addition, he, George Russell
and Fred Ryan (of *Dana*) were appointed to draw up the new company's
rules, a trio which might be regarded as 'the left wing' of the Abbey.

Terry Eagleton has done much to resuscitate Ryan's reputation, or
rather to lay the foundations for it. As with Ellmann's vaster endeavour
on Joyce's behalf, Synge loses out. The point revolves round Synge's
attitude to *Dana*, which Ryan edited with that other unclassifiable 'non
Yeatsian' 'W. K. Magee'. Eagleton spots Synge's opinion of June 1904 that
there was 'no hope' for the magazine, and is right in diagnosing this as
hostility, not mere pessimism. But the following year, *Dana* rallied to his
defence, specifically defence of *The Well of the Saints*. If Mary King is
right – she usually is – in reading that play as a Nietzschean proclamation,
then within a year Synge had moved closer to the sympathies of Magee
('John Eglinton') who wrote about Nietzsche in *Dana* just as Havelock
Ellis had done in *The Savoy*. In later years, Cherrie Matheson recalled the
magazine her suitor cordially damned in 1904 as one they had read
together with some enthusiasm.[22]

By 1906, Synge had certainly come to appreciate Ryan's ability as a
committee man. The two shared a critical opinion of the Gaelic League,
and both supported the suffragette movement. But they met when they
were about to part – Ryan (the younger by three years) anxious to assist
radical politics in Egypt, Synge increasingly tied to his own island by
affection and chronic ill-health. If *Dana* under Ryan's co-editorship supported Synge morally and critically, it had in James Joyce the sole con-

tributor who extracted money from 'Stiff Breeches'. No socialist underground should be identified here, even if Joyce, Ryan, and Synge all declared themselves to one degree or another. The three – four if you count Magee – were united by what they disliked rather than in any worked-out philosophy of either art or politics. Synge held very decided political views, sharpened by his tours of the west with Jack Yeats in June 1905; they meet Ryan's in a detestation of middle-class greed, Joyce's in that regard and also in a suspicion of the clergy, Magee's in a complicated anxiety about modernity. In the end, the two creative writers, Synge and Joyce, leave the other two in the margins of their journalism.

The two men held much in common, including a profound respect for the classics (better informed in Joyce's case), a love of music (more formally developed in Synge), and a natural talent for languages. Both were temporarily enthralled by a need to rewrite autobiography as something else. Joyce associated Synge with Wicklow rather than the west, and this underscores the likelihood of his having seen *When the Moon Has Set* in manuscript almost two years after it had been rejected by Yeats and Gregory. Joyce can hardly have failed to recognise Ibsen as its adopted progenitor; later he complained that the last act of *The Playboy* derived from *The Master Builder*. As a supporter, Joyce was never uncritical. But he brought to that role his huge contempt for pettiness in Irish public opinion and for bombast among the Revivalists. His principal service lay years ahead, when he sought permission from Synge's executors to have an Italian translation of *Riders to the Sea* performed in Trieste. So brief was J. M. Synge's career that his early supporters virtually walked by his coffin, impresarios and pall-bearers at the same time.

But Yeats accepted no walk-on part. Part of his power as cultural commissar lay in a wide network of contacts in Dublin, London, and Paris. Disqualified from any simple-minded commitment to Ireland, yet possessed of valuable credentials in Irish-America, he could recruit from strength while giving the appearance of isolation and unworldly competence. His long relationship with Ezra Pound, poet and translator, is a case which bears upon Synge and his legacy.

Pound had reached Europe shortly before Synge's death. In the winter of 1913, Yeats and he took a small house in rural Sussex and there evolved many of the doctrines of that version of literary modernism which later provided a glove for the fist of totalitarianism. The project was seen by Pound as an attempt to set up a poetic 'unfounded order', also referred to as the Brothers Minor. This was not wholly a facetious endeavour, for all that it shared terms promiscuously with the Brothers of the Common

Life (associated with Thomas à Kempis), with the more familiar Franciscans, and with the nineteenth-century aesthetic Nazarines. Even before 1913 the foe was identified as democracy, popular opinion, the rule of the mob (as they saw it). Synge's death, following on or from his conflict with the public over *The Playboy*, provided an occasion for outrage. Yeats stimulated Pound to contribute a pseudonymous diatribe to *The Egoist* in February 1914.

Pound, or rather 'Bastien von Helmholz', took the opportunity to double-damn 'a democracy of commentators', and to reserve exclusively to artists the sacred business of judging art.[23] In egging the American into the defence of his dead friend, Yeats presumably suppressed memories of Synge's repeated emphasis on 'democracy' in the management of the Abbey Theatre. Pound chose Edmund Gosse as the 'static man' to be scornfully contrasted with the dynamic type exemplified in Synge – this in ignorance (one supposes) of the extent to which both Gosse and Synge were in revolt against Victorian literalist fundamentalism. In the *New Age* of February 1915, Pound persisted in his campaign by extreme methods: 'When Ireland turned against Synge's genius it ceased, quite simply, to exist' to which the poet James Stephens replied from Paris by deploring how mistakenly Pound wrote about Synge – and Joyce, and Lawrence![24]

Even earlier, 'John Synge' does not feature among the names flung about by Pound in his efforts to establish Imagism. Annie Horniman was sufficiently intrigued by the term to publish a letter in *T. P.'s Weekly* requesting a definition. The facetious editorial reply pointed to Paris as well-spring of the movement, though Synge wrote speeches which could double as exemplary Imagist poems – 'nothing left of a man who was a great rower and fisher, but a bit of an old shirt and a plain stocking' ... 'my own fingers will be making a tent for me, spreading out my hairs and they knotted with the rain ...'[25] Nationalists have striven occasionally to relate Synge's images of dazzling gorse, grey rain, and white hair to Early Irish literature – that is, to the formally strict poetry of pre-Norman times, associated with the Celtic Church and hence innocent of foreign influence. If there is truth in this attenuated tradition, then a crucial turn was taken in the movement of this poetry between Gaelic and English. For it is in the course of translation that sky, leaf, and deer's cry acquire the synthesis of clarity and strangeness, unmediated presence and irrecoverable naturalness for which the literature-as-translation – or second nature – is renowned.

The precepts of Imagism insisted that nature could provide fully adequate symbols for poetry, and that direct 'treatment' of a thing was all-important. Behind this, Schopenhauer has been detected: he described how one who 'gives the whole power of his mind to ... the quiet contemplation of the natural object actually present, whether a landscape, a tree, a mountain, a building, or whatever it may be; inasmuch as he loses himself in this object' gains knowledge of a higher, Ideal, order.[26] Synge's contribution to a movement which never acknowledged him was the ironic dividend of his early reading. Schopenhauer's ideal absence of mediation becomes the Irish writer's disappearing act.

But, in tension with this, Pound's belief that poets should read in a foreign language to learn new rhythms indicates a reliance on distance or even alienation at the heart of ideal Imagism.[27] Synge's drawing on the rhythm and syntax of Gaelic and Hiberno-English, and of utilising dramatic irony to offset didacticism, offered less doctrinaire models. Pound's friendship with Desmond FitzGerald (later an Irish Free State minister) serves to underline once again the absence of Synge from Imagism's pantheon of strange gods. The movement provoked violent reactions and even more violent developments. One writer in *The Egoist* of June 1915 reached proudly for the conflicting notions of sacrament, to illustrate the gulf between Victorian poets ('Protestants ... [t]he sacrament is incomplete) and her own brand of Imagism ('Catholic ... believe in Transubstantiation').[28] Joyce's *Portrait of the Artist as a Young Man*, running alongside, added point to this use of sectarian difference as a metaphor for divisive energies at work under well-polished couplet or haiku. Some proponents of the movement promptly moved further – to Vorticism and *Blast*. No one in these hand-to-hand exchanges recalled Martin Doul in *The Well of the Saints*, who well knew the efficacy of transforming superhuman powers, or the ominous, unseen 'strange fighters' of Synge's last and uncompleted play.

A certain, uncharacteristically generous devotion to Synge's work persisted in Joyce even after the dramatist's death. On 12 July 1909, Joyce sought permission from the publishers to stage his translation – with Nicolo Vidacovich (1875–1935, a Triestine lawyer) – of *Riders to the Sea*.[29] Less than a month later, he wrote to his brother Stannie reporting at length a conversation with Gogarty who had been Synge's roadside medical adviser. While the letter charts a grudging reconciliation between the originals of 'Buck Mulligan' and 'Stephen Dedalus', it concludes with several postscripts, two of them medical in import – 'Arthur Symons has G. P. I.!' and 'Synge is said to have been syphilitic, poor man.'[30]

Unabashedly spreading this (inaccurate) report, Joyce sought the executors' permission for a production in Italian of *Riders to the Sea*. Ned

Synge replied promptly enough on 23 August 1909 from Mellifont Rectory, near Drogheda, where he was a guest. At this place of retreat, a gardener practised his own Syngean imagery: 'the apples were as long as your hand'.[31] But, even with such a chorus under the window, it proved impossible for Ned to reach agreement with Joyce, a situation which was to recur in the Synge family's response to inquiries about their famous kinsman's work. Joyce took the business very seriously, visiting the theatre to inspect costumes and seeking a musical notation for the 'keening' (lament) as delivered in Abbey productions. By 2 September, he was inclined to let Ned go 'to the Wicklow quarter of hell', to which Dantean fate he also assigned JMS.[32]

BOOK FOUR

Contra Mundum

CHAPTER 17

A Tragic Miracle, 1905

After an energetic attempt to focus on the sun, we have, by way of remedy almost, dark spots before our eyes when we turn away. Conversely, the luminous images of the Sophoclean heroes – those Apollonian masks – are the necessary productions of a deep look into the horror of nature; luminous spots, as it were, designed to cure an eye hurt by the ghastly night.

Friedrich Nietzsche[1]

With the conclusive events of 1902 – the last visit to Aran, the marriage of Cherrie Matheson – Synge had also embarked on the real business of his all too brief life, the writing of plays. His mother's home remained his home, whenever he was not away in Paris, London, or Kerry. Her household continued in its Siamese-twintimacy with the Stephenses next door, but guests who came to stay put up with Annie and Harry rather than Mrs Synge. Isabella Hamilton, whose connection with the family reached back to 'Pestalozzi' Synge's first wife, arrived on 1 June 1901. In September of the following year, Cousin Mary Synge who had negotiated Synge's escape to Germany, returned also to stay on the Stephens side of the party wall. Sam remained in the mission-fields of China. Ned, now almost as prone to illness as his youngest brother, lost weight, regained it in hospital, worried himself unwell again, worried about the health of his elder son. On the bright side, Robert had extricated himself from South America to set about a restoration of the Synges at Glanmore. In May and June 1903, he and JMS spent a good deal of time together, with the latter making at least two excursions to the Castle. Dead rats were reported in the newly reacquired family seat.[2]

Kathleen took Tomriland once again, but Synge remained in Crosthwaite Park for most of the summer, anxious about the onset of asthma and working on his new play, *The Well of the Saints*. Conscious of Glanmore, Mrs Synge noted her social encounters with a higher class than the Edges or even the Hardings: 'Met Tom Barton and D. Childers.'[3] In the same year, Erskine Childers published *The Riddle of the Sands*, a novel of imperial derring-do about German preparations for a Great War which, in due course, helped to turn its author into an Irish republican. While the Bartons and Childerses of Annamoe were moving imperceptibly towards gentry-nationalism, Robert Synge was rebuilding Jericho.

On 12 November 1902 Synge's cousin, Anthony Traill, took part in a debate at the College Theological Society. The auditor spoke on 'The Church of Ireland and the Celt'. Traill's contribution drew a scornful reply from Ambrose Coleman, a Dominican friar for whom the Senior Fellow embodied prejudice and privilege of a kind associated with Trinity in the eyes of the Catholic majority. Since Disestablishment (1869), a movement had grown within the Church of Ireland, to emphasise its unbroken links with the (allegedly non-Roman) mission which brought Christianity to Ireland in the fifth century. No longer a handmaiden of the State, the Church claimed honour as the direct descendent of the Celtic Church. According to this line of thought, the corruptions rooted out at the Reformation had been introduced after the Norman invasions. Modern Anglican Protestantism was the ancient faith of Patrick, Columba, and Bridget.

Though it retuned the harsh opportunism of the Church's policy towards Gaelic, the Celtic movement had its greatest impact in terms of art and architecture.[4] Whereas parish-church building in the early nineteenth century had settled for a square-tower-plus-nave, based on an English model, later experiments included Romanesque features of a distinctly pre-Norman Irish variety. Ballinatone in Wicklow (mentioned in *The Well of the Saints*) exemplifies the first tendency, Sandford in south Dublin the second. The High Cross, which had stubbornly survived in humble graveyards of mixed occupation, was revived as a symbol of austere, insular Protestant continuity. Translations of ancient Gaelic hymns were gradually introduced into the church hymnal. Celtic patriotism became a middle ground between nationalism (increasingly indistinguishable from Catholic middle-class aspirations) and imperialism (increasingly aggressive.) Mrs Cecil Alexander's rendering of what is known as Patrick's Breastplate ('I bind unto myself to-day') is only the best known of the Celtic elements in the evolving Disestablished church liturgy.

Synge's new play took up the theme. But in the ecclesiastical arena everything aspired to the condition of polemic. Arguments about the early Celtic Church thrived – Heinrich Zimmer of Berlin, who had preceded Synge on Aran, had written a short study translated into English in 1902. Stokes, whom Synge had read as a student in Trinity, had published a

more accessible work in 1888.[5] The middle road between Catholic nationalism and British imperialism was strewn with the *disjecta membris* of
scholars. As a youth exploring the countryside round Castle Kevin, Synge
had sought direction in books of Irish church history. While he found
the fundamentalism of his mother and brothers intellectually unaccept-
able, and was impressed by the arguments of Darwin and others, Synge's
long attachment to Cherrie Matheson and his slighter association with
Pastor Monnier and the Société Fraternelle d'Étudiants Protestants suggests that issues of belief had not been cast off like worn-out or too-small
clothing. In a notebook used during his first visit to Aran in 1898, he
recalled how, as a youth living in Dublin or holidaying in Wicklow, he
'used to wander many miles to seek the vestige of some tiny church
gloating on its few fragments with more joy than [he] felt at Rouen or
Amiens'.[6] The tone of famishment is unmistakable.

At Aghowl in County Wicklow, where Hugh Carey and his unfortunate
sisters were evicted by Ned Synge, there is an unusually long building of
the Romanesque type, with a remarkable doorway showing the influence
of sixth-century Syrian architecture. This is just such a 'ruined doorway
of church with bushes beside it' which Synge specifies in the stage directions at the opening of Act One.[7] But the most extensive network of
such buildings lay further north at Glendalough, known colloquially as
the Seven Churches. Here, before the Viking raids, a Celtic university had
flourished; in Synge's time, the ruins (including one known popularly as
Kevin's Kitchen) were visited more by tourists than pilgrims or scholars.
These were the intruders whom he had deplored as they thronged over
the bridge at Annamoe.

Early Christian architecture had attracted his attention on Aran also.
On the islands, these sites tended to mark the habitation of hermits or
the survival of very small communities in an Atlantic version of the
'desert' monasteries of North African Christianity. Teampall an Cheathrair Álainn, on Inis Mór, took its name from four saints celebrated for
their spiritual beauty and said to be buried in the same tomb. One of
them, Fursu or Fursey, founded monasteries in East Anglia and France,
and wrote a visionary work about Heaven and Hell which contributed to
the European genre now known through Dante's *Divine Comedy*. Synge
began to appreciate that the geographical insularity of Ireland had not
inhibited a rich commerce of ideas and images. Those who thought that
In the Shadow of the Glen derived in some vulgar way from the gaiety of
Paris knew little of cultural history and the transmission of histories,
legendary and otherwise. Whereas the spokespersons for Irish uniqueness

and purity constituted themselves as a broad movement, it was the comparativist or pan-culturalist who was cast into solitude. In this context, *The Well of the Saints* is a riposte to the Griffithite attack on Synge's earlier Wicklow play.

But there is a characteristic Syngean difference. The hermit or outcast is represented in the play by a couple, man *and* woman, and in admitting woman into the representation of cultural dialectics Synge further irritated the Jansenist puritans of latter-day Irish nationalism. Sex, as they suspected, was at the heart of his work. Mary, in *The Well of the Saints*, is described as 'the beautiful dark woman of Ballinatone', a daringly local tribute.[8] In a draft letter to MacKenna, Synge had linked protracted celibacy with the increase in certified madness, and compared the French and Irish stage's contribution to their nations' apprehension of sexuality. 'I have as you know', he wrote, 'perambulated a good deal of Ireland in my thirty [years] and if I were [to] tell, which Heaven forbid, all the sex-horrors I have seen I could a tale unfold that would wither up your blood.'[9]

In one regard, Synge's enemies were right. The plot of his new play did come from France. In 1921 its source was identified as the late-fifteenth-century *Moralité de l'Aveugle et du boiteux* written by André de la Vigne.[10] This was a farcical companion piece to a play about Saint Martin, the renowned patron of beggars. Synge came across it in Petit de Julleville's *Histoire de théâtre en France au moyen-age*, where the beggars are a cripple and a blind man (one acting as the eyes/legs of the other). Among the many transformations of this crude material is the role of male and female as mutually supportive. With this went a greatly increased emphasis on blindness/vision as the play's central theme.

The centrality of the play to Synge's work can be gauged from the overlapping of preliminary drafts with work on both *When the Moon Has Set* (early 1903) and *The Playboy of the Western World* (May 1904).[11] (At this point, *The Playboy* was evolving under the title, 'The Fool of Farnham', which indicated a greater affinity with the beggars than the ultimately completed play retained.) Six drafts of Act One survive, from *circa* spring 1903, one entitled 'When the Blind See'. Act Two also survives in six drafts from a similar date, with one called 'The Crossroads of Grianan'. Greenane, in County Wicklow, provides the setting for Acts One and Three; Synge renders the place-name in such a way as to bring out its links with the sun (Gaelic *griain* = the sun), and in doing so links the new play back to *When the Moon Has Set* with its focal house at Kilgreine (an invented place-name meaning the wood of, or church of, the sun). Synge worked on *The Well of the Saints* over a prolonged period; after its controversial first production on 4–11 February 1905, he took it on his tour of the Congested Districts with Jack Yeats (3 June–3 July) even though a theatre edition had been published by Maunsel & Co. (Dublin) during the Abbey's week-long run. Further alterations to the third act were made in the spring of 1908, which did not get into print until 1932 when Hutchie Synge was instrumental in having a new collection of the plays published by Allen & Unwin in London.

The tale of a miraculous cure at the Church of the Four Beauties, heard in May 1898, finds a sardonic distortion in the opening act of *The Well of the Saints*:

TIMMY: Did you ever hear tell of a place across a bit of the sea, where there is an island, and the grave of the four beautiful saints?

MARY DOUL: I've heard people have walked round from the west and they speaking of that.

TIMMY [*impressively*]: There's a green ferny well, I'm told, behind of that place, and if you put a drop of the water out of it, on the eyes of a blind man, you'll make him see as well as any person is walking the world.

MARTIN DOUL [*with excitement*]: Is that the truth, Timmy? I'm thinking you're telling a lie.[12]

This is not only a debased presentation of the ancient mystery; it is also a travesty of its geography. Whereas Christianity came from Palestine via Roman Britain, in Synge's play its miraculous powers reach Wicklow from the west – a place of shams or playboys, as we shall discover. Indeed, Synge exploits this oddity for the sake of a private joke. Yeats had set out for Aran from Cashla Bay in Galway; in *The Well of the Saints*, the miracle-worker boasts of 'the power of the water I'm after bringing in a little curagh into Cashla Bay' as if transporting the place itself across the island of Ireland. The saint is a dangerous combination of Yeatsian mage and Christian (or Plymouth) Brother. In his stern injunction to the locals, he warns against 'the words of women and smiths'. Here Synge ironically invokes Patrick's Breastplate, not in the placid version absorbed by the church hymnal, but in the text rendered by the scholarly Whitley Stokes and others, invoking God's power 'against spells of women and smiths and wizards'.[13]

Holy wells, with a potential for what György Lukács called the 'tragic miracle', were as common in Wicklow as in the west. One is to be found in the townland of Glasnamullen, a part of the Synge estates located in the parish where J. N. Darby had launched the 'Saints' in the 1830s. Such frish-frash origins, with debased Victorian schism repeating (as farce) the fundamentalism of Celtic Christianity, are entirely in tune with Synge's dramatic mood.[14] The first act is an ironic exposition of cheap miracles marketed by an ascetic sales brute. Bride, a minor character, pointedly inquires, 'Did you watch him moving his hands?' as if the Saint were a thimble rigger at the Arklow races, or a pre-Christian wizard.[15] The cure offered to Martin and Mary Doul (= DALL, the Gaelic word for blind) is restoration of their sight. By extension, the miracle might as well be national independence or seats in heaven, the first promised by Parnell's sexless successors and the second by the drunken priest of *The Tinker's Wedding*. In the wretched outcome, the beggars are deeply disillusioned by each other: Martin does not possess the splendid features his once-blind woman had taken pride in, nor does she have the 'eyes would make the saints, if they were dark awhile and seeing again, fall down out of the sky' he had doted on. Instead, Martin is cruelly spun in an inverted blind-man's-buff, misrecognising all now that he can see. Mary has 'a dirty twist' of hair on her head, and 'there isn't two eyes in any starving sow, isn't finer than the eyes you were calling blue like the sea'.[16]

The second act finds Martin compelled to work for a living in the forge of Timmy the Smith, who had introduced Saint and beggar to each other. Whereas first curtain-rise had found them making rushlights (so those who had their sight might see!) at the roadside, the beggars are now drawn down into a world of toil and care. A note of imminent change is signalled in the watering of Timmy's eyes, caused by smoke from his fire. Martin and Mary are apart for much of the act, this occasioned by the necessity of work – off-stage, Mary picks nettles for the Widow O'Flinn – and in turn occasioning talk between Martin and young Molly Byrne, the beauty whom he had mistaken for his wife in the first moments of restored sight. Synge worked long at the love-scene (one-sided) between Martin and Molly: it possesses biographical interest because of his intense love of Molly Allgood, who casually joined the Abbey Company in the weeks running up to rehearsals of *The Well* and who got a walk-on part in the first production. Molly Byrne, to confuse things, was played by Sally, Molly Allgood's sister.

The second act closes with a double development – first, Martin's ill-starred attempt to seduce Molly and, just as he is exposed in this folly, the waning of his sight. Synge magnificently redeems the moment from any accusation of contrived sentiment by having Mary Doul enter, her sight all too keen, and discover her man's infidelity. Martin is now thoroughly alone. Blind once more, he reverts to the power of words. These are now execrations more appropriate to the Saint, and debased visions of the afterlife:

MARTIN DOUL [*stands a moment with his hand to his eyes*]: And that's the last thing I'm to set my sight on in the life of the world, the villainy of a woman and the bloody strength of a man. Oh, God, pity a poor blind fellow the way I am this day with no strength in me to do hurt to them at all. [*He begins groping about for a moment, then stops.*] Yet if I've no strength in me I've a voice left for my prayers, and may God blight them this day, and my own soul the same hour with them, the way I'll see them after, Molly Byrne and Timmy the smith, the two of them on a high bed, and they screeching in hell ... It'll be a grand thing that time to look on the two of them; and they twisting and roaring out, and twisting and roaring again, one day and the next day, and each day always and ever. It's not blind I'll be that time, and it won't be hell to me I'm thinking, but the like of Heaven itself, and it's fine care I'll be taking the Lord Almighty doesn't know.[17]

The last phrase well illustrates Synge's awareness of the problems faced by a dramatist simultaneously concerned with abstract ideas and with extremes of feeling. Alan Price associated *The Well of the Saints* with a type of play – he couldn't put a name on it – which included Ibsen's *The Wild Duck* (1884) and Chekhov's *The Three Sisters* (1901) – 'the kind that, barely tickled by the comic spirit and mainly unpurged by purely tragic exaltation, deals searchingly with serious issues, and, unblurred by morbidity, reflects, with some compassion, a melancholy vision of the human condition.'[18] The extremity of Martin Doul's curse upon Molly and her coaxing lover borders on frenzy, but the final phrase pulls the speech back into conscious exaggeration.

In Synge's preliminary work on Act Three, Martin was the first on-stage. But he soon chose Mary Doul to open the business, blind now also and alone. Having spoken in soliloquy, she remains still as Martin gropes his way on-stage, unaware (at least at first) of her presence. His language has modified, not in its intentions but in its use of idiom: 'Ten thousand devils mend the soul of Molly Byrne ...'[19] and Mary nods in silent approval. A reconciliation is gradually established between the two, the result of a sustained but finely modulated bout of ironic 'flyting' between them. Nothing in Synge so touchingly anticipates *Waiting for Godot* than the opening of this final act of *The Well of the Saints*, both for its use of stasis (inaction moved by words) and for its palpable implication of worlds beyond the empty roadside of the stage directions. If *The Aran Islands* had channelled inarticulate power into a prose of steady description and eloquent meditation, then *The Well of the Saints* goes further with a negative metaphysics in which the spiritual or transcendental is indicated purely by the manifest inadequacy, triviality, incoherence of the material.

Thus, when the Saint returns to the district and the possibility of a second miracle arises, he is presented as an even more crass and brutish functionary than he was in Act One. The blind beggars hide behind some briars, comically anxious about their visibility. Mary insists, 'I'll go in first, I'm the big one, and I'm easy to see.' Martin replies in the best tradition of male superiority, 'It's easy heard you are ...' Words are no reliable defence against the imposition of serial curses, and no curse can now guarantee protection against the Saint:

MARTIN DOUL: What way would I find a big terrible word, and I shook with the fear, and if I did itself, who'd know rightly if it's good words or bad would save us this day from himself?[20]

Taken in conjunction with the close of Act Two, this tense moment in the third act surely reflects Synge's memory of Psalm 139:

If I ascend up into heaven, thou art there; if I make my bed in hell, behold, thou art there.

If I take the wings of the morning, and dwell in the uttermost parts of the sea;

Even there shall thy hand lead me, and thy right hand shall hold me. If I say, Surely the darkness shall cover me; even the night shall be light about me.

Yea, the darkness hideth not from thee; but the night shineth as the day: the darkness and the light are both alike to thee.

For thou hast possessed my reins: thou hast covered me in my mother's womb.

The Bible pervades Synge's work, and his debt to the rhythms of the King James version has been long acknowledged. Oscar Wilde's parables in prose had explored a line of typological subversion which Synge had developed in *In the Shadow of the Glen* and now in *The Well of the Saints* also. But in any biographical context the Bible is held aloft by Kathleen Synge. In June 1905, several months after the play's first production, Mrs Synge spent some time holidaying in Greenanemore House – until then the tiny village of Greenane had not featured in the Synges' Wicklow gazetteer. The extraordinary proliferation of local place-names which are invoked in *The Well of the Saints* has been analysed as the careful marking-off of dramatic territory from family territory.[21] There are traces of extraneous, or at least bonus, material in the play. Martin refers to 'the night they killed the old fellow going home with his gold ... and threw down his corpse into the bog'. And later he advises his wife cruelly enough that 'if it was yourself you seen, you'd be running round in a short while like the old screeching madwoman is running round in the glen'.[22] Perhaps the first of these contributes to a folkloric background of remotely remembered incidents, and the second is an undeclared endorsement of Nietzsche's view of the self as an unbearable reality, best masked or veiled. But to invoke Nietzsche is not to shun Kathleen Synge, for her youngest son was struggling to make sense of a post-Protestant a-theology just as the author of *Zarathustra* had done.

The climax of the final act is reached when Martin stretches forth his hand ostensibly to confirm-by-touching the water-can of the Saint, but instead dashes it to the ground. Saint and villagers – those two mutually supporting pillars of the 'community' – turn on Martin and Mary, driving them away for good. Martin Doul's final speech of defiance and justification emphasises the politics of *The Well of the Saints* by stating the claims of the imagination in terms of rights:

MARTIN DOUL: We're going surely, for if it's a right some of you have to be working and sweating the like of Timmy the smith, and a right some of you have to be fasting and praying and talking holy talk the like of yourself, I'm thinking it's a good right ourselves have to be sitting blind, hearing a soft wind turning round the little leaves of the spring and feeling the sun, and we not tormenting our souls with the sight of the grey days, and the holy men, and the dirty feet is trampling the world.[23]

Yet this clarion call to the self, and the self's partner in blind beggary, cannot be taken as a triumphant life-enhancing victory. The play leaves the audience in no doubt about the future. Timmy, who has brought the Saint into the action at the outset, now dismisses his beneficiaries:

There's a power of deep rivers with floods in them where you do have to be lepping the stones and you going to the south, so I'm thinking the two of them will be drowned together in a short while, surely.[24]

Reaction began in advance of the premiere on 4 February 1905. Arthur Griffith published 'The Messenger' by Maurice Joy, in the issue of the

United Irishman in circulation throughout January, just to show that he knew a feeble play before he saw a strong one. The theatre's architect felt obliged to advise the director of Synge's play that all sorts of quasi-imaginary remarks in the script about the birth of monstrosities must be cut before opening night. An audience which would 'crowd to hear *The Geisha* and the other musical comedies full of eroticism', Willie Fay responded, 'will not be affronted when they hear two or three people on our stage speaking after their kind ... Have you read Shakespear lately?'[25]

The *Freeman's Journal* was hostile; Martin Doul, for whom 'religion is only a decayed mythology', particularly gave offence. As for Synge, he 'is as preoccupied with the sex problem as any of the London school of problem playwrights'. On the front page of the *United Irishman* (11 February), Griffith accused Synge first of borrowing from an English novelist (he meant Wilkie Collins) and then concluded by condemning the entire national theatre movement for alternating 'a decadent wail with a Calvinist groan'. Even the *Irish Times* found something to dislike – the scenery devised by Pamela Colman Smith. George Moore came to the rescue with a mischievous paean of praise in which Synge's name was linked to Oscar Wilde. It little mattered that the English press was favourable.[26]

It is difficult to see how *The Well of the Saints* can be reduced to a problem play about sex, but there can be no doubt as to the gravity of the situation Synge found himself in. Twice in less than two years, he had given offence to an alliance of forces – Catholic piety and nationalist introversion – marching confidently on the future. In Belfast, where opinions are often happily divided, a reviewer could allude to 'Mr Synge's madness' before proceeding to congratulate him ironically on at last writing 'a play without corpses'. This pathological emphasis is all the more remarkable because L. J. M'Quilland had sensitive things to say about the set. The Abbey itself was no safe sanctuary: Lady Gregory quizzed Synge about his absence from the Friday performance – 'What happened to you last night? We thought you have committed suicide.'[27]

While Joseph Holloway cannot be trusted to catch the nuances of aristocratic speech, Gregory's remarks illustrate the potential for disagreement or at least misunderstanding within the Abbey. Already, by 1903 or 1904, profound differences were evident between Yeats and Synge, especially where social class was involved. Maire Garvey (died 1946), for example, inspired the poet to observe that actresses of her background 'have not sensitive bodies, they have a bad instrument to work with'.[28] The potential for a clash of ideologies existed within the theatre movement, not simply because some members of the company would eventually defect (in January 1908), but because Synge's themes distilled the anxieties of the age. *The Playboy of the Western World*, on which Synge had been fully engaged already, was to confirm the point.

In March 1905, while he was settling again at Crosthwaite Park and taking some comfort from Moore's spirited defence of *The Well of the Saints*, he received a letter from a hotel in remote Belmullet describing the colourful characters its author – a Breton enthusiast for all things Irish – met on the Mayo bog roads and mountain tracks. This was Henri Lebeau who remains one of the more shadowy figures in Synge's correspondence file, disappearing finally to a teaching post in South America. In what was to be celebrated as the playboy's refuge from justice, Lebeau met men 'all so violent against the British(!) although so little different in features and type from those Irish soldiers who are to be seen in Cairo' in the king's armed forces.[29]

Lebeau's refusal to allow love of Ireland to cloud his judgement of social realities almost equalled Synge's own blend of patriotism and dispassion. Together with the Breton writer, Anatole Le Braz, he spent the late winter and early spring of 1905 in the west of Ireland, having evidently met Synge and Frank Fay on his way through Dublin. Fuelled with a copy of 'The Oppression of the Hills', Synge's most intimately claustrophobic evocation of Wicklow, Lebeau wrote on *The Well of the Saints* in the *Revue de l'art dramatique* (15 April 1905).

As a friend, Lebeau is remarkable for his late arrival into a cast of trusted acquaintances most of whom had known Synge before the troubles over *The Well of the Saints*. He fitted in with the travelling cosmopolitanism of Synge's Parisian friends, having already been in Greece, and published an account of the monks on Mount Athos.[30] MacKenna and Lynch had soldiered abroad, one earning a death sentence. Seen amid this company, Synge's annual visits to the Aran Islands between 1898 and 1902 are little more than holidaymaking. Theatre provided as many risks as any journey by curagh between the islands. In these careers – Lynch excepted – restless cosmopolitanism combined with a pronounced distaste for urban or industrial society. *The Well of the Saints* had concealed a little of that theme among its more obvious execrations – it is 'the rabble' whom Martin denounces in a curiously urban image of Greenane's tiny population.

Lebeau's outlook can be further deduced from his staying at the Passmore Edwards Settlement in London, after he left Ireland in May 1905. This philanthropic institution, in Tavistock Place, he described as 'a society of young men with whom I have opportunity [sic] of exchanging ideas and learning a lot of things about English politics and life'.[31] Its activities included children's recreation schools and other attractions for the neighbouring poor.[32] Philanthropy and its poor relative, Social Engineering, were among the topics which bred disagreement in Ireland. Synge's well-informed, unsentimental but none the less subjective views on vagrancy were balanced by an endorsement of the institutional provisions of German and Swiss authorities. 'The Tramp' appeared in the March 1905 issue of *Dana*, above the signature of Laura Stephens, a minor painter and remote member of the extended Synge/Stephens family.

There was still some chance of Lebeau joining the expedition to the Congested Districts, which Synge was planning with Jack Yeats. In the event nothing came of this.[33] In May Synge and his eldest brother, Robert, went fishing for a week in Donegal, while the Breton party visited Rathmullan and Carrick in the same county. Though Synge's holiday was marked by bouts of feverish cold, he did not return to Kingstown but travelled further south to Annamoe to stay with his English cousin, the painter from Byfleet in Surrey, who had inherited Cousin Emily's property at Uplands. (A Cambridge graduate, Edward M. Synge had retired in 1901 to devote his time to art.) Lebeau was so taken by the scenery and society that, when he republished an article on *The Well of the Saints* in *Dana*, he signed himself 'A Lover of the West'.[34]

But *Dana* was dying after a year's intellectual success and financial failure, having been edited from May 1904 to April 1905 by the unlikely team of Fred Ryan and W. K. Magee. Synge had praised it to Cherrie Matheson, returned from South Africa as Mrs Houghton in 1904. 'He said it was too good to get a paying circulation in Ireland, that Ireland was too remote from the world of thought.' That view was almost certainly expressed before Lebeau's article had appeared in the closing issue (which carried a further article principally on Synge's position in Irish cultural debate[35]). Synge had promised to write something for *Dana* in its first few months – the matter is even recorded in *Ulysses* – but nothing has been identified among the very few unsigned items in its pages. According to George Moore in *Hail and Farewell*, an article on Anatole France was duly submitted, only to distress Magee with its 'incorrect' writing.[36] Though fragments of such an article are to be found among Synge's surviving papers, it cannot be confidently accepted that Synge had provided final copy and had it rejected. In May and June 1904, he had been in touch with Richard Best (who, like Magee, worked in the National Library), both seeking material on which to base a 'puff' of *Dana* in the London press and promising 'the stuff for Dana, but I fear it wont be brilliant'.[37]

The end of 1905 found Lebeau in Cambridge. He wrote to Synge in cryptic style:

I wonder whether in Kingstown or romantic Wicklow you sometimes regret my being over the way: as for myself, I must avow that since you left me I miss ... [in the original] I won't say something, which would be unpolite [sic], but you and something else. No doubt you brought away the young girl with the walk of a queen.[38]

Here was one positive consequence of *The Well of the Saints*, the walk-on actress, Molly Allgood, who became the inspiration for Synge's two great-est female parts (Pegeen in *The Playboy* and Deirdre in the final play). Here indeed was a transfiguring, head-turning newcomer into his life, compared with whom Lebeau was a temporary acquaintance. Yet Lebeau's correspondence with Synge reveals much that is left in silence by more local observers in Ireland.

The irrepressible Breton resumed globe-trotting. Somewhere between Rangoon and Calcutta, he paused to write at length on his travels. The disgraceful behaviour of three 'scoundrels of the lowest type of Eng-lishman which is met in the Colonies' was forgotten with the arrival of 'a message of relief and sympathy' from Synge. Lebeau was ever willing to be anti-English. A 'remarkable faculty for making everything everywhere alike, and levelling all to a nauseous state of average mediocrity' char-acterised the English for him. On the other hand, 'inquiries both in America and the Colonies left ... so little hope as to the permanence of any genuine Irish feeling.' Back home, the Irish were (he feared) 'a little too much "English" ...', too conformist, even to the point where he half-longed for Synge's fanatical enemies at least to save the country from dullness.[39]

Clearly a high degree of common ground existed between them, even if Lebeau oversimplified Synge's complicated view of Irish society. The Breton's anti-English bias was partly a distaste for modern standardisation and 'dumbing-down'. Both he and Synge were sceptics in religion, reform-ers in politics. When the next upsurge of anti-Synge animosity broke over *The Playboy* in January 1907, Lebeau was on his way home to France. From Paris, he deplored the 'Dublin bourgeois and ascendancy ladies' in the Abbey stalls whose shouting only confirmed the general accuracy of Synge's depiction of Irish society. He also expressed regret at news of his friend's renewed glandular trouble.[40]

That summer, Lebeau proposed a shared holiday on the French coast. For various reasons, including the need for surgery in September, this project never materialised. Synge had resisted a proposal that the two should share a room, and Lebeau quickly reassured him that 'if there is any inconvenience for either in such an arrangement, I will either continue to sleep here at my friend's, while you occupy the room for yourself, or else hire another room for me in the same village.'[41] Lebeau was entering a period of depression or emotional disturbance, and his letters tend towards the effusive. 'I felt for you more and more as we were living together a little more closely among the fine Wicklow scenery.' His strange English, with its fluent immediacy and syntactic distance, is never easy to interpret. In mid-to-late September he despatched a postcard to the invalid Synge: 'I have thought of you very much on the day of the operation.'[42]

The correspondence lapsed temporarily, with Synge confined to a nursing home for most of September, and then committed to a convalescent holiday in rainy Kerry. He wrote on Sunday 24 November from Dublin a 'long and so interesting and candid letter', from which Lebeau learned about his imminent marriage. On the same day, Synge had written to Molly Allgood, worrying about a tour to America, insisting that he trusted her 'very fully (to be good)' and letting her know that, with a boat's siren heard in Kingstown harbour, he 'got hollow again at the sound of it'.[43] If this was the first the Breton wanderer had learned of wedding plans, he took three months to reply. In his eventual response to Synge's 'candour', he admitted to having suffered an unspecified 'disappointment' the previous summer, paid tribute to 'the fidelity you showed me in your friendship', frankly inquired about a job in Trinity College, and sent regards to a string of Irish friends – John Eglinton, Richard Best, AE (George Russell), and George Moore among them. He hoped he might soon be introduced to Synge's wife.[44]

Certainly, the summer of 1905 had restored France to Synge. Back in 1899, he had written about Le Braz in the *Dublin Daily Express*, and touched again on topics close to the Breton's research in a piece in the *Freeman's Journal* (22 March 1900), 'A Celtic Theatre'. The arrival of Le Braz, his wife and young Lebeau provided a fillip after the difficulties of *The Well of the Saints* and renewed controversy over *In the Shadow of the Glen*. But Synge was gradually disenchanted by his native land. 'I envy you Paris,' he wrote to MacKenna on the last day of May.[45] Molly, however, made Dublin seem like both ends of a rainbow.

One interpretation of Synge's greatest play would see it as the product of his reading of Schopenhauer. This is not to insist that Synge possessed a philosophical mind – his intelligence operated in other ways, his reading never sustained or systematic. To that extent he admired Molly's insouciance. But Schopenhauer not only preached renunciation of the Will, he 'had a notion of transfiguration, through art'.[46] Artists from the German-speaking world founded a tragic vision on the soiled coat-tails of Schopenhauerian denial, notably Thomas Mann in *Buddenbrooks* (1901) and 'Tonio Kröger' (1903), and Gustav Mahler in – say – the Third Symphony (1896).

The silences of Mahler match the quietudes of Martin and Mary Doul, shredding rushes by the roadside in Act One. Into this comes the Saint's clamorous offer to restore their Will, those lost senses which will (when restored) bind them to the treadmill of labour and disillusion. The renunciation, which Martin's dashing of the can of holy water from the Saint's hands enacts, leads to a transfiguration of the beggars' world. With this intensified vision, death comes nearer. The approximation between Martin's new sense of nature – 'a soft wind turning round the little leaves' – and the imminent doctrines of poetic Imagism indicates how Synge's dramatic language might be related to contemporary cultural developments outside Ireland. But, in biographical terms, a striking feature of the play thrown into relief by a brief excursion into Schopenhauerian readings is its identification of futile desire with the name Molly.

CHAPTER 18

Enter Molly, Centre-Stage

May she be granted beauty and yet not
Beauty to make a stranger's eye distraught...

W. B. Yeats[1]

John Synge met Mary Allgood (1887–1952), who acted under the name
Maire O'Neill, during rehearsals for *The Well of the Saints*. Chaperoned
by her grandmother, she was just turning eighteen. Hers was a heart-
breaking prettiness more dangerous than classic beauty, and she had a
combination of virginal Irish innocence and strong 'come-hither' well
calculated to drive men mad.[2] The exact moment of her meeting Synge
goes unrecorded. Her birthday, 12 January, fell less than a month before
the play's opening night. In one sense, her role did not demand real acting:
she was part of a hostile 'rabble', mocking the visionary poet/beggars. In
Synge's next play, she played a role Dubliners revolted at.

In Elizabeth Coxhead's affectionate account of the Allgoods, an element
of calculation in their personalities is admitted. Theatre promised a way
out of the unhappy domestic mess of the Allgood family and, for Molly's
sister Sally at least, provided a ladder of social advance. She aligned herself
with Lady Gregory. Molly can only have moved more slowly, despite an
impetuous temperament. As aspiring actress and siren, she had to infil-
trate the Abbey gradually. By the spring of 1906 the younger Allgood was
Synge's Molly, 'a very determined young woman' sixteen years his junior.
The secession of Máire Nic Shiubhlaigh and others from the Abbey to
form the Theatre of Ireland resulted in the promotion of 'bit-players' like
Molly to the security of a contract and twenty-five shillings a week.[3] Her
success was not professional only. For the three years remaining to Synge,
she occupied the centre of his imaginative and nervous life. Pegeen Mike
in *The Playboy* and the title role of *Deirdre* were written expressly for her,
together with casual poems and four hundred letters. It was their intention to marry, though his ill-health proved insurmountable. In this stormy
pact, the silent Synge found a private voice. Questions about his personality, politely deflected by the lonely child, austere bachelor and dedi-

cated dramatist, find answers in the love-duet of Molly and her 'Old Tramp'. Whereas Mrs Houghton wrapped her account of him in the language of neighbourly friendship, the Synge Molly knew emerges as a passionate, even desperate man, voluble in his almost daily correspondence and unguarded in his ardour.

From the outset, it was an 'office love-affair' with all its advantages and trials. In February 1906 Dossie Wright, an actor whom Synge cast as chief rival for Molly's affections, was surprised to find the invariably proper director sitting with an arm half-enclosing the young girl. By mid-March, he was travelling with the players outside Dublin so as to spend more time with her. He worked his passage, sometimes travelling ahead 'doing the hack advance work alone fagging round with the little books to reporters and booksellers'.[4] The relationship bloomed under English skies. In Liverpool, where the company played in late April, he drew Molly's attention to his age, as a factor to be borne in mind in her assessment of him as a lover. (He had turned thirty-five on 16 April.) At Whitley Bay, north of Newcastle-on-Tyne, they enjoyed a 'smoky backyard kind of sun'. More than a year later, he would specify Glencree in Wicklow as the site of their 'first flirtations', which would suggest a spring or early summer tryst.[5]

During an extended British tour, 'Cardiff complications' (as Synge discreetly termed them) arose. Disapproval was registered at the highest level. Annie Horniman, who held the theatre's purse-strings, protested at the restlessness inspired in Synge by 'three months of one girl on his knee'. That was in July 1906, when the company had returned after six weeks. Lady Gregory complained about the impact that her fellow director's behaviour might have on discipline in the Abbey. With characteristic bluntness, she told Yeats that Synge was 'quite useless'.[6] Six months later, his masterpiece *The Playboy of the Western World* made the international reputations of both theatre and leading actress.

It was not roses, roses all the way. Synge's first datable letter to Molly carries a scribbled 'Idiotic' in her hand. The letter seems unremarkable, but a reference to Balbriggan served as an oblique inquiry about her keeping company with Wright, who had relatives in the town. 'Changeling' – his favourite term of endearment – catches everything he worshipped and feared in her: a capacity to transform his loneliness into ecstasy of love or (as often) agony of doubt. Most of the letters are written from Glendalough House, in Glenageary, to which he moved with his mother on 9 July 1906. As he had briefly rented rooms alone in Rathgar, the more or less simultaneous inauguration of the love-correspondence with his return to the maternal home deserves attention.

At the Abbey, boundaries of class, religion, and age were violated, together with the protocols of professional conduct. Molly was the daughter of a household which had only one thing in common with Kathleen Synge's – it too lacked a *pater familias*. George Allgood (c. 1855–94) had been a humourless member of the Orange Order, a compositor in the Dublin print trade. His wife, Margaret (née Harold, c. 1860–1928), came from a second-hand furniture shop in the city's northside; No. 37 Mary Street lay in a not quite respectable quarter. At some point during the family's gyrations at the bottom end of the social scale, they lived above a huntin'-and-fishin' tackle shop on Essex Quay, run by the uncle and namesake of the very minor poet, Charles Weekes, who later became legal adviser to Synge's publishers.[7] Dublin was a small place, where even the poor could rub shoulders with literati. There were claims of French or even Danish contributions to the Allgood/Harold pedigree, but the truth was less exotic. The mixture of ardent Protestantism in the father and regular Mass-attendance in the mother made for an unhappy upbringing. After Allgood's death in 1894, Molly was despatched to a Protestant orphanage from which she ran away.

Synge and Sally Allgood (1883–1950) had already collaborated in one bold initiative: on 11 May 1904, they both signed the Irish National Theatre Company's formal letter accepting Annie Horniman's offer to secure permanent premises in Abbey Street. This step towards professionalisation laid the grounds for the codes of behaviour which he and Molly Allgood were to treat with intermittent disrespect two years later. Professionalisation also affected the place of women in the Company, as Yeats complained after some months – 'Miss Allgood has some objectionable trick of voice, certain sounds that she gets wrong . . .' Criticising two other actresses for lacking 'sensitive bodies', he made no bones about the class element in these differences.[8] When Molly Allgood arrived, she was walking into a backstage drama where her 'wildness' was likely to be thought vulgar, whatever talents she might additionally possess.

Synge himself was not immune to this view of his beloved. 'I heard accidentally of your walking arm in arm with Wright at Longford.' But more insecurity on his part than flirtatiousness on hers is revealed in these early letters. The story about Dossie Wright 'came out at a moment and in a way that was peculiarly painful and humiliating to me'. Untrained in the tactile gestures and casual playfulness of ordinary people, Synge found his young love difficult to understand. A master-dramatist, he was incapable personally of acting a role. Nor was he acute in self-understanding, at least not at the outset of the affair. Offered the plausible excuse that Molly had been leaning on the actor's shoulder because of a sprained ankle, Synge considered that 'a trifle compared with what you have made me suffer ... I have had a lot of trouble and lonesomeness in my life, changling, and for God's sake dont disappoint me now.'[9]

Disagreement worked as a kind of unofficial currency between them, not negotiable with others, but valuable in testing each other's resources. Molly and he spent a great deal of their free time walking the roads of south County Dublin and the glens leading into Wicklow. While he was 'rather amused' at the prospect of meeting Sam on furlough from China, and did not 'mind him a bit', the business of introducing Molly to the other Synges was a protracted one.[10] A decent suburban compromise between the bustling quayside world of junk-shops and the *rus-in-urbe* retreats of former gentry was needed. Glendalough House abutted on to open ground, where smaller dwellings were soon to rise. But uphill from Mrs Synge's rather grandly named semi, her daughter lived at Silchester House, a monument to Harry Stephens's professional success. Sometimes Synge waited in Annie Stephens's garden 'near the post hour, sitting on a dark seat ... under a chestnut-tree ...' These were the insatiable days of early love, when he craved her letters – 'what are those few lines for a very starving man?' While Yeats and Gregory worried about the impact of Molly on company discipline, their fellow director's correspondence might have raised even greater fears for the intellectual rigour all three demanded in the theatre.

A family dinner party on 17 August provoked Synge to assert his independence of his relatives' veneration of success in life. 'They are rich and I am poor, and they are religious and I'm as you know,' he confided to Molly. Now that he had a changeling of his own he was less desolate, while continuing to bemoan his standing as 'a poor relation ... a paying guest'. Things weren't much easier for Molly who left home after a row with Sally, doubtless centred on the young girl's serious involvement with a director of the company they worked for. The lovers were prepared for domestic upheavals, hoping for domestic bliss together. Yet Synge's language veers into the safe waters of affectionate encouragement.

they understand no success that does not bring a nice house, and servants, and good dinners. You're not like that are you? I wish we could keep each other company all these evenings. It is miserable that we must both be lonesome and so much apart. I hope you'll read steadily when I'm away. I hate to preach at you or schoolmaster you, – I like you so perfectly as you are.[11]

And there the relationship finds an odd equipoise, which does not last. Later in the month, Synge took himself off to Kerry to stay with the Harris family. With touching confidence, he described a honeymoon couple on the train. 'The good lady's wedding ring was too tight for her and her finger was puffed up double its size ... Unless they look out she'll lose her finger.' Staying in the same house was 'an old tramper' who remembered the Famine, a great storyteller in Gaelic who complained that the loss of his teeth impaired his art and who slept naked in the kitchen under a tattered coat. Such colourful details enlivened his long article on West Kerry, published in *The Shanachie* in 1907, but to an eighteen-year-old girl they carried a more intimate piquancy. He recommended *Arthur*, evidently some version of the Camelot legends of adulterous chivalry. When he had to stay in London, he 'always kept some book like "Arthur" on my hands and found it a great plan for keeping myself up ... in ugly surroundings'.[12]

Molly in Dublin was not letting the grass grow under her feet. She had inspected some flats in the Coombe, a poor district close to St Patrick's Cathedral where efforts were being made by Margaret Huxley and others to renew run-down housing stock. While Synge implied that marriage might be possible within four or five months, he advised Molly against talking about any plans to set up together. Her sister Peggy and brother-in-law Tom Callender, with whom she was staying after the flight from Mary Street, may also have been thinking of a flat in the Coombe, likewise one of the Fay brothers.

Even down in Kerry Synge, working now on *The Playboy*, was interrupted by headaches and 'a sort of asthma'. He had planned to set the opening scene in a field where Christy Mahon and his 'da' fight, but during the long process of refinement the plot through its three acts is played out in a single domestic interior. Changes of title also occurred during which the all-too-revealing 'Fool of the Family' was abandoned.[13] By early September, 'an ailment brought on by the damp, and unsuitable food' gave him such intense pain that he nearly fainted. He had already written to Willie Fay 'on the teeth question' in the hope that he would 'devise something'. Synge was unusually anxious about unauthorised reading of his letters – by postmen or inquisitive landladies – and these casual phrases may conceal a need to raise funds for expensive dental work. Anxiety about Molly's keeping company also bothered him. 'You seem determined that I am never to TRUST you.'[14] Her crisp response to one of these plaintive letters from Kerry is summarised in her annotation at the top – 'reconcile'. Apart from a few such phrases, her side of the voluminous correspondence has totally disappeared, though it must have amounted to hundreds of letters, short notes for the most part. In 1971, the editor of *Letters to Molly* ventured the opinion that, 'always protective', Synge had 'apparently destroyed them before entering Elpis Nursing Home for the last time'. This is only one possible explanation for their disappearance.[15]

Back in Glendalough House, he recovered from the afflictions which had befallen him in Kerry. He and Molly met Agnes Tobin (1864–1939), an American patron of the arts from whose translations of Petrarch Synge himself drew better inspiration. Devising a timetable of snatched, covert meetings with Molly, he confessed himself 'sick and tired of this sort of thing', and declared they should make themselves 'official' and defy gossip. Though he even considered dropping in on Mrs Allgood unannounced, there is no evidence that the critical encounter with his intended mother-in-law ever took place. Before September was over, however, squabbles with Molly, renewed anxiety about his health – 'Surely you wouldn't like to worry me into consumption' – and the 'continual, deadly strain' of finishing *The Playboy* began to take their toll.[16]

The Abbey had more than one problematic love-match on its hands. Willie Fay and Brigit O'Dempsey wanted to get married, and were prepared to falsify the bride's age on the paperwork. When the company toured, there had been some misinformed view that Scottish law might smile on their plans. Brigit stayed in Glasgow with relatives of the Allgoods, 'but her talk of love matters shocked them' – so they threw her out. This Synge heard privately, not from Molly but from her older sister, Sally (or so he told Lady Gregory). Synge pleaded for Gregory's silence, ostensibly to protect Fay but perhaps also to conceal from Molly how much he knew about the ways of setting up a wedding. He had even persuaded Fay to see a Catholic priest in Dublin, who had been sympathetic, and he suggested another in London who might have been willing to help the couple.[17] This went far beyond anything known of his plans with Molly.

Sundays provided the best chance of a meeting and an excursion to the north Wicklow hills. Often she took the train to Glenageary, where he waited on the platform with two tickets for the further journey south to Bray. This postponed the question of Molly setting foot inside Glendalough House. Sam Synge, who was about to return with his family to China, was duly told of his brother's involvement with Molly – 'he seems quite pleased'. But nothing further was done to introduce the actress to the reverend doctor. On 16 October, Synge was still hoping to have some further word with Sam but 'the days slip by and I never see him alone'. Nothing was falling into place: 'I am very bothered with my play again now, the Second Act has got out of joint in some way, and now its all in a mess. Dont be uneasy changling, everything is going on all right I think, I will go and see your mother soon. I dont much like the job so I keep putting it off.' This was too much for Molly who pencilled furiously across the top:

you may stop your letters if you like. I dont care if I never heard from you or saw you again so there! & please dont let thoughts of me come into your head when you are writing your play. It would be dreadful if your speeches were upset I dont care a 'rap' for the theatre or anyone in it the pantomime season is coming on & I can easily get a shop; in fact I shall go out this afternoon & apply for one.

M. Allgood.[18]

Synge had forgotten to sign his name.

Molly's stormy responses cannot have lasted long. The day after this incident there had been trouble in the theatre about her unpunctuality, which provided a cause for the two to join forces. But John's intention of speaking to Sam had still not come off. 'He is extremely busy, of course, these few days bidding farewell to all his friends.'[19] Relations between the brothers were cordial but hardly intimate: one was a missionary, the other a confirmed sceptic. In addition, one was troubled by recurring illness, the other a doctor. Quite what John's own mission was in seeking, hesitantly, to speak alone to Sam cannot be determined. It is possible that the lovers considered asking Sam to marry them, a move which would have done something to reconcile the family to a baptized Catholic. More likely, however, is the intention simply to tell Sam quite how serious the relationship was – and in this John signally missed every opportunity.

Meanwhile, conditions at the Abbey still required the keeping up of appearances. One Friday evening, John was delayed by a garrulous theatregoer while he watched Molly depart on her own. Then the two men followed her, with Synge exclaiming like Wemmick in *Great Expectations*, 'There's Miss A. going home alone.' Deliberately or otherwise, Molly turned into a chemist's shop and closed the door on her pursuers. 'You hardly know, my own changling, how entirely you've got hold of your old Tramp by the heart.'[20] How were they to evolve some means of making this intense, unstable relationship work? On several occasions, Synge suggested that Molly write about her own experience – 'say about your life in the convent school'. Or, even better:

Suppose you and I write a play together! Wouldn't that be great! You could supply the actual stage experience and I'll supply the fundamental ideas. Then you can write all the men's parts – I know you like men – and I'll write all the female's. We'll do a play at once about life in Switzer's [department store] – with an Act II laid in Miss Fluke's – Then we hire the Abbey and stage it ourselves and make our fortunes and live happily ever after. Now I'm going to bed as that's settled.[21]

Many an untrue word is spoken in jest. His planning amounted to little more than studied neglect of the barriers which stood between them. Often Synge was at home with his mother while Molly trod the boards. The theatre itself was a divisive issue, scarcely respectable in the eyes of Kathleen Synge and her conventional offspring. When John read newspaper compliments paid to Molly, he might have 'tears of pleasure in my eyes to the wonder of my family', but his lover's talents were not likely to reconcile the two sides of his existence.

He still had not told Sam about 'Ourselves'. Business led him seemingly to neglect Molly at the theatre. A four-hour walk was planned, but rain stopped play. At last John got round to confronting Sam and showed him Molly's photograph. Sam beamed and said, 'Thats a *very nice* face.' The same evening he departed for China, never to see his youngest brother again.[22] Yet something of Sam Synge's tone is mimicked in John's letters to his nineteen-year-old beloved, a desire to please which sacrifices his customary rigour for occasional condescension and the suspension of intelligence. Molly's responses are not simply those of a younger and healthier person impatient with fussiness: they register anger at his inability to acknowledge her mental world. If class and education complicated these misalignments of the two lovers, money posed less of a problem – he had no more spare cash than she had.

When Willie Fay and Brigit O'Dempsey finally married in October 1906, John declared that he would give Fay a copy of *The Well of the Saints* because of 'the smallness of my subscription' to the Company's formal presentation.[23] This was while he was finishing the greatest money-spinner the Irish theatre would produce for many years. Tied to his mother's purse-strings as youngest son, as practitioner of no lucrative profession, John Synge became the symbolic terminal point for a process of financial decline which has been traced steadily from the heyday of Francis Synge MP, through Famine and Land War to suburban adequacy.

Glendalough House had no electric light. Mary Tyndal, the housekeeper, could feed her bachelor care on eight shillings and sixpence per week. On a typical day he consumed four fresh eggs, two chops, 'and cabbage, and marmalade and everything I want' – hardly a gentleman's diet, but mighty economical. His eating habits were admittedly bohemian, yet his places of rendezvous with Molly were usually Dublin cafés of a conventional kind. These frugal ways of living depended on a small domestic staff, maintained not out of his income but his mother's. While proud of Mrs Tyndal's 'knacky' management of the budget, Synge could loftily complain of 'a bungle the servants made about not airing my night garments'.[24]

Molly's introduction to this anomalous establishment had to be effected diplomatically. No longer tempted to intercept the post by lurking in his sister's garden, thirty-five-year-old Synge appears to have engaged the tacit support of Mary Tyndal. Her intervention was nerve-racking, especially when Molly neglected to write. Inside the church-hall decorum of Glendalough House, an old woman, her ill son, and a shrewd house-keeper turned their different attentions to the front door when the postman knocked:

I hammered on the floor with my stick for the servant and told her to get me my letter, but she said there was none for me. I turned over then in my bed and said to myself that now I had better try and die quickly as my little changeling had turned against me or something terrible had happened. These disappointments I need not say are very bad for me. Why do you torture me? Little soul I did not know till these days how utterly I am wrapped up in you.[25]

Some agreement, however, had been reached that Molly would visit Glen-dalough House. Perhaps the fact that liberal-minded Florence Ross had arrived on 15 November, to stay for several months, opened up an oppor-tunity. However, as an unwelcome consequence, Annie, Edward, and Robert with their families were constantly in and out of the house. On Saturday the 17th, John took so ill that Alfred Parsons, his regular doctor now, was summoned from Dublin. On the Tuesday afternoon, he wrote to Molly with renewed directions – including a sketch-map – and enclosed for her benefit the letter just quoted which he had written (but not posted) the previous day. Amid all the visiting relatives, he could not bring her upstairs to his room (though he was an ill man, bedridden) and 'down-stairs, we'd have to face the whole crowd'. Molly had been prepared to travel out alone from Dublin and present herself at Glendalough House, but John put her off. Like the chat with Sam, a step forward had been diverted. On Thursday, he was still half-hopeful of her unannounced arrival, trying 'to keep the coast clear' that he might see her quietly in the dining room. A grown man feted in his chosen artistic realm, he was skulking in window embrasures to snatch a few minutes with the woman he loved – in his own home.[26] As far as his mother was concerned, Molly was 'a great friend' of his, whose photograph he produced. 'That is as far as I can go till I am stronger[.] I am thoroughly sick of this state of affairs [.W]e must end it and makes ourselves public.'[27]

Molly duly arrived on the day this unconvincing resolution was made, wearing a solemn long coat and spectacles. The circumstances were awkward. Florence Ross had drawn yet more relatives to the house, this time Edward M. Synge of Byfleet, the etcher. John's closer family – his brothers and sister – lived so close that they too had to call once again. The room where John and Molly were able to meet was needed for a tea-party and so he had to let her 'trot off' back to Dublin, while worrying that she might have got on the wrong train and headed away from Dublin by mistake. However, the die was cast; Molly had crossed Mrs Synge's doorstep, albeit to what served as a temporary waiting-room. The brief encounter allowed for serious reflection. 'It is curious what a little thing checks the flow of the emotions,' he wrote to her the next day.[28]

The events of October/November 1906 added up to a minor crisis. The decision to tell Sam something or everything about relations between them had not been executed. Instead, Molly had been obliged to cut her own ice among John's relatives. John had waited passively for her to arrive in Glenageary, yet he was sufficiently mobile the next day to travel into Dublin. She met him off the train and then he had to wait two hours to see Parsons in his Fitzwilliam Street rooms. He liked her (in spite of her hat) more than he could say: 'But to get to the point. The doctor says I've got on very well, but I've a very slight irritation on one lung still, so it is well for me to be careful, and he advises me to put off *Playboy* and to go to England for a fortnight. So, dear heart, I think I'll go for your sake as much as for my own.'[29]

Letters of this kind read as if written between partners who have long ago settled into a steady understanding of each other, a balanced meeting of each other's well-adjusted needs. But the case of John and Molly was far different. For convalescence, he looked not to a retreat where Molly might have uncluttered access to his heart, but to Edward M. Synge's well-appointed and comfortable house in Surrey. The cousins had known each other since early in 1902, sharing an interest in France and in art. It was a world to which Molly could not follow. The check in emotion is not only traceable in those oddly restrained expressions of John's – 'I liked you (in spite of your hat) more than I am going to say' – but also in the way family is preferred over the outer commitments.

Synge did not depart for England until a week had passed. Edward M. Synge had to be introduced to old John Yeats, while the Abbey arranged a reading of the *Playboy*-in-progress at the Nassau Hotel during which the author was chronically hoarse. Kathleen ventured the shy opinion that Molly seemed 'very bright' and suggested a second visit. Despite this progress, John resolved that, when he went to England – but only then – he would write back to his mother 'and tell her all. I am afraid I might say something too violent if we talked it over at first as I loose [sic] my temper so easily.'[30] Molly and he met on the Wednesday evening; she was in sombre mood and, whatever transpired, John retired home to compose two letters the following day, each more pathetic than the other. He had only slept an hour-and-a-half that night.

The first was wild enough – 'My life is in your hands, now, as well as my honour. You will very soon send me into my grave if you do not act like a woman who loves . . .' The second was more chillingly precise – 'You must know as well as I do the low scurrilous thoughts medical students and their like have when they dangle after actresses . . .'[31] Neither lover was in a settled frame of mind, Molly irked by the endless discretions of Glendalough House and John racked by the knowledge – all too evident in his friend Joyce – of what men-about-Dublin wanted with women as lively as Molly. His virginity shines through or, at the least, his physically unconsummated love. In the wake of medical consultations all too grave in their implications, he speaks of death from dishonoured love. A post-script to the later letter reports more cheerful feelings, though her power over his life and death is confirmed. It is high time to go to England.

Wintersells Farm, in Byfleet to the west of London, lay beyond Molly's reach. From the boat, he wrote in the now established formula of admonishment and supplication. She should avoid cigarettes and forgive him for being hard on her. 'Do let us be wise and open.' The boat pitched and rolled, preventing him from completing a sentence, but the letter ended 'Yours tenderly and forever' – a rare display of sensitivity in Synge's signing-off. He had been so long out of the habit of expressing emotion, indeed of experiencing emotion which was reciprocated, that he was so to speak homeless, an unaccommodated man. Edward Synge's old house was 'very nicely furnished in a quiet artistic way'. Edward was keen to

show off his pictures and John frankly confessed to Molly that he wanted
to be given some of these. Writing proved difficult: Edward tended to fuss
round the table 'checking the flow of my emotions', as John phrased it in
quotation marks. (He was quoting himself.) Mild recriminations shuttled
in the mail between Dublin and Surrey – what would Molly have thought
if he, John Synge, had gone off 'to spend the evening with say a ballet-
girl'? If the Abbey collapsed, then they would have to spend part of their
year in England. And 'as my wife you will have more chance than you
would have by yourself' of getting parts in 'the intellectual plays at the
Court or elsewhere'.[32] Yet his obsession with the obstreperous 'medicals'
obscures a more intimate anxiety about his own health.

While she was abjured to give up the companionship the stage offered,
he found in her all the company he needed. He had been 'infinitely lonely
though [he] was so used to it in a way'. The mood of Wintersells was balm
to his bruised feelings and troubled body. In the library where he sat with
Jones (the dog) between four in the afternoon and dinner at seven, he
dipped into books or dreamed about his 'changeling'. The quietude and
amplitude which Synge longed for during this interlude pointed towards
a future – 'I wish we could make ourselves a beautiful home like this . . .
My next play must be quite different from the P.Boy . . . something quiet
and stately and restrained . . .' But it also implicated a retrospect, with
almost liturgical undertones – to 'think about all one has done or left
undone . . .' These visions merged in a scaled-down version of his present
surroundings: 'our own little abode . . . books that are not common and
pictures that are not common and I'll have a little wife who is altogether
unheard-of(!).' From this slip, John rescued himself awkwardly by
explaining that Molly as little wife would be 'unlike anyone that has ever
been'. They would be 'well away from all good commonplace people'.[33]

Wintersells brought him into contact with members of his extended
family. Edward Synge's sisters – one a hospital nurse, the other a professional writer – travelled down from London on 3 December to meet
their nearly famous Irish cousin. John had always been intrigued by
nurses; their vocation reassured him of his security in the world. The
other, Margaret Bertha Synge (1861–1939), had just published A Short
History of Social Life in England. All in all, the English Synges were useful
and kindly folk. It was hard to strike the right balance with Molly. She
was never out of his mind, and he declared he loved her as the very breath
of his soul. But she accused him of regarding her as silly or sentimental,
and he rocked backwards and forwards between lecturing her and indul-
ging in something not far from baby-talk.[34]

Though the house at Byfleet exuded comfort, its owner was not the secure master of English reality whom Synge covertly envied. Host resembled guest in ways both instinctively recognised. For years, Edward had been employed in 'a laborious profession' as land agent on Lord Boyne's estate at Weybridge, before making a break to take up etching. His health was marked by a 'constitutional weakness', and throughout the greater part of his life he suffered from chronic illness. Both men were contemplating marriage, but more as a buttress against loneliness than as a full-blooded embrace of life. When he died four years after JMS, Edward was commemorated for his 'truly heroic patience in most trying circumstances'.[35] To visit Byfleet had been to gaze into a mirror.

Near rural Wintersells, work had already begun on a motor-racing track (Brooklands). When a woman was murdered half a mile away, Synge was inclined to blame 'a lot of cut-throats' employed on the site. *The Playboy*, on which he was engaged, vividly evoked an isolated district with discharged soldiers or 'khaki cut-throats' ranging through it by day and night. Though Synge consistently personified himself as Molly's Tramp, restless humanity unsettled him. He longed for married life with Molly as his wife. Despite the late season and some cold, if glorious days, he often sat out in a greenhouse, fiddling with *The Playboy* and dreaming 'pleasant little dreams but nothing remarkable' about her. On Friday 7 December, he finally posted a letter to his mother. He postponed writing to Lady Gregory at Molly's unexplained request.

Kathleen Synge replied after nearly a week, 'quite a nice letter for a first go off', but cautious about the couple's financial prospects. The great issue of marriage, however disguised, had been brought to the fountainhead, and some further waters of balm were offered in return. Kathleen's deep concern for her errant, sceptical, and impractical son could not be disguised. Sam and she would never meet in this world again. Though marriage into the Catholic lower orders promised to bring her pain, she conceded that it might be a good thing if it made Johnnie happier – and kept him near at hand. The discretion with which he had tiptoed round his own emotional life was well registered in his mother's conviction that the friend he had walked with so often, whom he had met so regularly on the platform at Glenageary station, was a man. But his showing her a photo of Molly – the one which had delighted Sam – and the constant flow of letters to the house when he was ill had begun to unconvince her. Now, from distant Byfleet, her youngest son had announced a desire to keep company in Mary Street, Dublin, perhaps to take an Abbey actress for wife. And Kathleen accepted, as best she could, that it was the right thing for Johnnie to do.[36]

But Molly, for whatever reason, was stalling. The Abbey directors were not yet to be informed of any firm plans. John was now keen to press ahead with a commitment to love, and recanted an earlier opinion that 'the love of a man of 35 was a very, or at least a rather different thing from that of a man of 25'. If he had said this in Liverpool back in April, then he had been mistaken. Now he felt 'all the flood of fullness, and freshness and tenderness' that he thought he had left behind. With this phrase, John comes as near to a libidinous surge as anywhere in the correspondence. At the end of 1906, it is clear that their love had not been consummated, though he acknowledged a degree of sexual excitement (and thus the prospect of consummation) he had hitherto discounted.[37]

In many important respects, the correspondence of two further years does little to advance the relationship. Lacking everything which Molly wrote – apart from barbed annotations on a very few letters from John – we see only one side of the tennis court on which they played out their tempestuous affair. In contrast, suburban ritual is fully documented. The year ended with John spending Christmas Day at Silchester House, though not before he had agonised over the accursed *Playboy*. The mental leap from Michael James Flaherty's lonely pub in Mayo to the crisp linen of Silchester House was one Synge had to make in the course of a few minutes' walk up Adelaide Road, past St Paul's Church where he had not celebrated Christ's nativity. Ten members of the family sat down at Annie Stephens's table – five Stephenses, John and his mother, Florence Ross, and two unidentified souls. Ever motherly in her attention to his health and comfort, Kathleen gave him gloves and socks. Loyal Florence had a book for him. The nephews, Frank and Ned Stephens, had bought a tin of cigarettes. John in turn gave the favourite nephews, the unremarked niece and loyal Florence, spare books which he already owned and didn't want.

Two days later, he had not yet made contact with Molly whose Christmas remains unrecorded, spent no doubt with her mother and one or more of her sisters in a very different Dublin. After 'two hard days' on *The Playboy*, John was reading Agnes Tobin's Petrarch, and was in a mood to encourage Molly's cultural development. He would teach her Italian so that she could read the great love poetry of Dante and Petrarch – the poetry also of loss, separation, and death. Her tastes were different from his, but in no ways inferior. In the National Gallery of Ireland, a few days earlier, she had preferred the Dutch paintings to the Italian ones. They shared with each other a profound joy in love which 'the ordinary run of people' could not quite grasp, but 'the worst of it is that we have the same openness to profound pain ...' And he added hastily, 'of mind I mean'. Pain of the body had been threaded through their first year, with some squabbling and evasion. He ended with a hope: 'please Heaven we shall have a few years of divine love and life together and that is all I suppose any one need expect.'[38]

Throughout this demanding courtship, Molly kept up her career at the Abbey unable (where John often was able) to conduct her business from home. Her advance in the company was firmly based on talent rather than on the influence of her lover among the directors. Within a short period, she was challenging her sister for leading roles. Synge's contribution to this, the part of Pegeen Mike in his new play, proved crucial. But it took its place in a developing repertoire which revealed Molly Allgood (or, rather, Máire O'Neill) as an actress of considerable power and maturity, given her age.

On Saturday 19 January 1907, the Abbey revived *In the Shadow of the Glen*, with Molly in the part of Nora Burke. The tramp was played by Willie Fay. Few dramatic texts more touchingly dealt with the condition of womanhood in Ireland. But in the wake of *The Well of the Saints*, interpretations of the one-acter were more varied and subtle. Molly and Máire Nic Shiubhlaigh (Mary Walker) differed in their approach to the role. Maurice Bourgeois, who translated several of Synge's plays into French and wrote the first biography (1913), preferred the original production of 1903, where Nic Shiubhlaigh had revealed in Nora a 'poetic desire for something new or exciting which may relieve the oppression of solitude'. In the revival, Molly opted for 'the love-yearning of the woman who knows the world sexually'. According to one actor, there was organised opposition in the audience to hiss the new production.[39] No letter of Synge's commenting on the incident has survived. But Bourgeois' emphasis raises issues which go to the heart of the uncertainty surrounding Molly and John's love-affair. The hissing was a prelude to the more frenzied disruption of Synge's new play, to follow a week later. If, as his remarks of December 1906 on the difference between a lover of thirty-five and one ten years younger suggest, he had not consummated his love of Molly physically, the issue focuses intensely on Molly's sexual history. A good actress can play a part well beyond her actual experience. But the recurrent rows about 'medicals' and other low fellows indicate that he was consciously uncertain of her sexual history.

A revival of Nora was child's play compared to the debut of Pegeen

Mike whose wooing will take place on-stage amid boasts of murder and threats of torture. Directors and players alike knew that *The Playboy of the Western World* would take them into new territory. At home, it was impossible wholly to ignore Synge's imminent premiere. As a visitor, Florence Ross arranged for a small party including Frank Stephens and one of the Traills – perhaps the 'accursed cousin' of 1883 – to attend the theatre. Mrs Synge found it disturbing to have the young people out after midnight, and at so worldly an entertainment. John was conducting rehearsals and, in his spare time, looking for a flat. Negotiations were in progress to recruit a new business manager, with John acting on behalf of the authors – notably Lady Gregory and himself. Given the long gestation of *The Playboy*, the serious illness of its author in October, and the ding-dong tenor of his relations with Molly, it is striking how effectively Synge functioned.[40]

One last-minute change of mind put Synge not only at the centre of the firing-line, but put him there alone. It was the practice to play 'curtain-raisers', so that the audience would be familiar with something on the bill before they got to grips with a new production. A decision had been made that Yeats's *The Pot of Broth* would usher in *The Playboy* and, according to Joseph Holloway, playbills had been printed featuring these two items. But Lady Gregory manoeuvred to have *Riders to the Sea* substituted as the opener, thereby making Synge the only playwright on whom the audience might call whether in delight or protest. A week earlier, *In the Shadow of the Glen* – with Molly playing the restless 'widow' – had provoked hisses. Though Yeats had come greatly to dislike his *Pot*, Gregory's motives were not charitable; in her homely-rural idiom, she felt that 'Synge should not set fire' to Yeats's property in order 'to roast his own pig'.[41]

Early rehearsals bypassed Pegeen Mike to allow Molly to attend the hospital. On Saturday 26 January 1907, Lady Gregory and Synge interviewed Ben Iden Payne, an Englishman whom they decided to appoint as theatre manager. That evening, the curtain went up before first a murmurous, then a noisy audience. During the third act, the noise grew so loud that the final speeches were virtually inaudible. Synge slept little that night. Next day, badgered by a headache, he wrote to congratulate Molly on her performance. He had been unable to get away from Gregory after the opening night, even to talk to its leading lady, his fiancée. But she had 'played wonderfully', everybody had been delighted. A man sitting behind Synge had declared, 'What a beautiful girl!' Then at length, he acknowledged how he was 'wrapped up' in her. 'You are my whole world ... you that is, and the little shiny new moon ...'[42]

The moon had long been a favourite image of Synge's, a conventional light under which lovers meet. It also measures the female cycle. The last-minute choice of *Riders to the Sea* as curtain-raiser fed a line of parody in his letter to Molly: 'Its four fine plays I have though it was a hard birth I had with everyone of them and they coming to the world.' The tragedy of his one-acter prompted a moment of self-characterisation as aged and bereaved and resigned to death. One Abbey veteran has suggested that the first-night production had veered towards a tragic rather than comic interpretation of the *The Playboy*, insisting that it was 'played seriously, almost sombrely'.[43] The rows demanded that the newspapers be written to and *esprit de corps* maintained in the theatre. Synge was seeing so little of Molly he thought letter-writing might have to be resumed. A walk together, a union as when the letters adopt the idiom of the plays, that would be wonderful – 'when we are out again in the twilight with ourselves only, and the little shiney new moon sinking on the hills.'[44]

Though *The Playboy*, and its attendant rioters, had a prolonged influence on Irish public opinion, conditioning the tone in which Church and culture, bourgeois and bohemian, nationalist and non-political citizen spoke to each other, the row also impacted severely on Synge's private life and especially on his relations with Molly. The real crisis had broken in October. Yet Synge's decline in health was predictably linked to the rows of early 1907. He was wheezy and hoarse when Florence departed on 5 February, irritable at the thought of less amiable (Dobbs) relatives arriving the next day. News from the Abbey came as from a great distance – even news of Molly's salary rise. She had written diligently, and her unsubtle appeal for a loan did not fall on deaf ears. He in turn had errands in Dublin, in search of newspapers for his Czech and German translators, and for Henri Lebeau. The doctor was in almost daily attendance.

Molly visited on Sunday, 10 February, and he thought her 'a little god-send . . . so pretty, and so kindly, and so clever, and so sensible, and such a baby, and so fond of the world'. She confided in him, or gave him some anodyne account of her doings, and as a result he could regard as funny what previously he feared were 'terrible secrets'.[45] Her little notes became more frequent, while his attitude shifted towards brotherly affection. An inherent liking for 'good ordinary people' blossomed in a longish letter to a fruit salesman, who had responded to *The Playboy* by sending samples of his own writing. Recurrent bouts of severe pain were half-explained as the pangs of love:

This morning I have been in terrible pain, – with the ailment I had in Kerry, –

since four o'clock. At eight I thought I heard the post[man] pass without coming here, and I gave myself up for lost, and I broke out into a cold sweat of misery all over; I thought you had only written me one line in two days instead of two letters every day as you did...⁴⁶

Yeats had called but Synge had been unable to see him. Then his mother fell ill and took to her bed. Molly continued to alarm him with her 'adventures' yet also maintained a supply of reading – Stevenson's *Master of Ballantrae*, among other things. He conceded that she had a right to move round in the world, but urged her never to consider flying to 'some sooty ornamental water in some filthy town'. This totally opaque exhortation he signed off 'Yours as always, J. M. Synge', perhaps in playful formality.⁴⁷

He was writing for *The Shanachie*, edited by Joseph Hone, a director of the firm, Maunsel & Co. 'The People of the Glens' was published in the Spring 1907 issue. Even further from the public eye, on the last day of February, John reported to Molly on the doctor's view of his improving condition. If the fever continued to abate, he might go downstairs. But the fever blew up again – 'so I am in *our* room still'. With this last emphasis, he sought to bind her to his privacy, while the *Playboy* riots echoed across Ireland and beyond.

CHAPTER 19

Edwardian Winter, 1907

The time of this patrician art is a sacred one, in contrast to the mere
empty, homogenous time of, say, the Playboy riots.

Terry Eagleton[1]

Synge's play opened on Saturday 26 January 1907 before an audience
primed for trouble. The Abbey had recently gone through various
changes – foreign sponsorship, professionalisation, defection – which
found expression in the row about to break on the ailing playwright's
head. One instance of a new sophistication allowed for publication of the
play in advance of its production. Unlike the printing of the one-acters in
magazines such as *Samhain*, Synge's two completed three-act plays were
published as independent books. He wrote a preface to *The Playboy*, dated
21 January 1907, just five days short of the opening night. Though he pre-
cautiously defended the play's language by recording that 'the wildest
sayings and ideas in this play are tame indeed compared with the fancies
one may hear in any little hillside cabin in Geelsala, or Carraroe, or Dingle
Bay', everyone connected with the forthcoming premiere was aware that
offence might likely be taken.[2] On cue, the London-based *Speaker* carried
an article, 'The Irish National Theatre' by Ellen Duncan, as an introduction
to what proved to be a memorable week or two of controversy.

Holloway, the theatre's architect and loyal first-nighter, was banned
from dropping in on rehearsals, yet throughout the month Yeats expressed
little or no interest in the new play. By 21 January he was in London, while
Synge completed his Preface. Several days earlier, one of the extras told
Holloway that there would be an organised opposition to hiss the new
play. Willie Fay wanted to delete a violent moment in the third act, and
both Yeats and Lady Gregory were worried by the proliferation of exotic
oaths and casual invocations of the Almighty. But, as Fay admitted, they
'might as well have tried to move the Hill of Howth as move Synge'.[3] He did
consent to the temporary omission of a blasphemous conceit involving
mutton breast-fed by the Widow Quin. As the organised opposition
clearly had inside information on the play – which was also in preparation

for the printer – offence might easily be taken at words not used on-stage, words never spoken in the hearing of the offended.

Offence was taken with little delay. The first-nighters were generally appreciative, but they did not write Monday morning's papers. Rioting then took place, in the strict sense that the police had to be called to quell rowdy members of the audience. The trouble occurred in two separate 'theatres' of action – the building itself, and the newspapers. Only in an incidental way did it spill on to the streets of Dublin. Despite the limited scale of the action, the *Playboy* riots have a place in the growing violence of the city. Within a few years, the Lock-out of 1913 (with the attendant brutal suppression of workers) and, of course, the Easter Rising of 1916 would turn the streets into a political theatre. Though *The Playboy* occasioned conflict in Edwardian Ireland, Yeats – with more courage than generosity – was responsible for souring relations between the various touchy constituencies who made up the Irish public.

In his Preface, Synge had shown a historical sensitivity to the country's temper; only 'for a few years more', he wrote, would 'we have a popular imagination that is fiery and magnificent, and tender'. This offered an opportunity not given 'to writers in places where the springtime of the local life has been forgotten, and the harvest is a memory only, and the straw has been turned into bricks'.[4] Early biblical instruction had returned to him, with ironic aptness. Controversy over *In the Shadow of the Glen* and *The Well of the Saints* had done little to sweeten his temper. Máire Nic Shiubhlaigh held that he had retaliated with *The Playboy*, settling scores with the small minds (now personified in Shawneen Keogh) who had assailed him on earlier occasions.

Riders to the Sea was listened to attentively, and it seemed for a moment that Lady Gregory's strategy had worked. The sublime aspect of Synge had been restored to the audience's attention. When the curtain rose again, the scene was familiar enough – a country kitchen in the west of Ireland, albeit in a home doubling up as public house. The set had been designed by Willie Fay, the director who also played young Christy Mahon. Brightness was unobtrusively achieved against the lime-washed walls of the set: off-stage lay the source of that brightness, the sea, inexorable taker of lives in the one-act play just seen. Thus, while the tragedy of *Riders* reassured the audience, the contrast in mood within the same social setting threatened promptly to offend them. Molly Allgood, under her stage-name Máire O'Neill, was alone on-stage, listing the items for her trousseau. The first act went reasonably well. Perhaps battle had not been joined.

Act One of *The Playboy* makes elaborate comic use of question-and-answer. Christy has taken refuge in the pub where Pegeen Mike stands in for her frequently drunk father, Michael James Flaherty. The locals, alerted to a stranger's arrival, are curious to know what has driven him to their remote corner of Mayo. But remote though this may be, it is criss-crossed by 'the harvest boys with their tongues red for drink, and the ten tinkers is camped in the east glen, and the thousand militia ...' This is Pegeen speaking, and her reputation as 'a fine, hardy girl would knock the head of any two men in the place' is not disputed. Inside the kitchen Christy, unknown and unimpressive, comes to represent these violent floating populations, while the locals speculate about what guilty offence had driven him so far into hiding. The dialogue/interrogation builds up to an unflattering image of contemporary Ireland:

MICHAEL: If you'd come in better hours, you'd have seen 'Licensed for the Sale of Beer and Spirits, to be consumed on the Premises,' written in white letters above the door, and what would the polis want spying on me, and not a decent house within four miles, the way every living Christian is a bona fide saving one widow alone?

CHRISTY [*with relief*]: It's a safe house so. [*He goes over to the fire, sighing and moaning. Then he sits down putting his glass beside him and begins gnawing a turnip, too miserable to feel the others staring at him with curiosity.*]

MICHAEL [*going after him*]: Is it yourself is fearing the polis? You're wanting, maybe?

CHRISTY: There's many wanting.

MICHAEL: Many surely, with the broken harvest and the ended wars. [*He picks up some stockings etc. that are near the fire, and carries them away furtively.*] It should be larceny, I'm thinking?

CHRISTY [*dolefully*]: I had it in my mind it was a different word and a bigger.

PEGEEN: That's a queer lad! Were you never slapped at school, young fellow, that you don't know the name of your deed?

CHRISTY [*bashfully*]: I'm slow at learning, a middling scholar only.

MICHAEL: If you're a dunce itself, you'd have a right to know that larceny's robbing and stealing. Is it for the like of that you're wanting?

CHRISTY [*with a flash of family pride*]: And I the son of a strong farmer [*with a sudden qualm*], God rest his soul, could have bought up the whole of your old house a while since from the butt of his tail-pocket and not have missed the weight of it gone.

The dialogue proceeds to focus on who Christy may have killed, if his crime is a bigger one than larceny:

MICHAEL [*to* CHRISTY, *mysteriously*]: Was it bailiffs?

CHRISTY: The divil a one.

MICHAEL: Agents?

CHRISTY: The divil a one.

MICHAEL: Landlords?

CHRISTY [*peevishly*]: Ah, not at all, I'm saying. You'd see the like of them stories on any little paper of a Munster town. But I'm not calling to mind any person, gentle, simple, judge or jury, did the like of me.

By now, the weak-willed Christy has a certain command over his audience of locals, though they are distracted from murder into issues of counterfeiting money (at this moment, he is counterfeiting drama). They then consider bigamy (widespread 'among the holy Luthers of the preaching North'), or enlistment in foreign armies (here a nod towards Synge's Paris friend, Arthur Lynch, or to Maud Gonne's husband, 'was judged to be hanged, quartered and drawn'). But Pegeen brings the interrogation back to the point when she denies Christy's suggestion of lying:

PEGEEN [*in mock rage*]: Not speaking the truth, is it? Would you have me knock the head of you with the butt of the broom?

CHRISTY [*twisting round on her with a sharp cry of horror*]: Don't strike me … I killed my poor father, Tuesday was a week, for doing the like of that.[5]

So, the truth (as Christy believed it to be) was out. The crime was parricide, and it had been committed in a manner very close to that threatened on him by Pegeen – he had hit his father with a loy (a dedicated turf-spade) 'on the ridge of his skull'. But the intimacy of Christy's crime and the locals' fantasies reached out to entangle the Abbey audience. They represented an Irish public which Synge in turn represented as given over to violent crime; or – worse – as fascinated by the prospect of violent crime, the chance to meet a man who had performed the ultimate outrage of cancelling his procreator. Synge's audience (or jury) invested much in western life, from which they refined a new mythology, that of the noble Gaelic-speaking peasant. If *Riders* could be accepted as enhancing that view, despite a suspicion of paganism, then the modern licensed premises of Mr Flaherty with its knowing gossip about California and the Boer Wars began to look like a deliberate insult. 'This is not the West' rang throughout the week.

Despite the hint of Greek resignation in Maurya's final speech, and the ambiguous time-setting of *The Well*, Synge's previous plays had never challenged the happy assumption that the Irish were unanimously Catholic. On the whole, this was achieved by neglecting all possibility of religious difference. *The Playboy*, in contrast, opens with a prominent reference to the Pope, whose dispensation is required before Pegeen and Shawn Keogh can marry. Quite why they need a dispensation is never explained in the play – though the programme lists them as cousins, that is, related within the tables of consanguinity so closely that incest or *mésalliance* must be officially discounted. Actually, the programmes in January 1907 were misleading on this detail, suggesting (by the order in which names were listed) that Shawneen Keogh was cousin to the Widow Quin rather than to Pegeen. Synge was to be dogged by minor blunders.

The dialogue does not clear up the point about a need for papal dispensation, so the question arises: Is one of the intended happy couple a non-Catholic, undeclared in the play, in need of a sympathetic priest or pontiff if s/he is to take the sacrament of marriage? When Pegeen is suddenly roused to fury by the Widow Quin, the sacraments feature scandalously in her response:

PEGEEN [*with noisy scorn*]: It's true the Lord God formed you to contrive indeed! Doesn't the world know you reared a black ram at your own breast, so that the Lord Bishop of Connaught felt the elements of a Christian, and he eating it after in a kidney stew?[6]

'Elements' here is more than comic phraseology – the elements in Catholic theology were the bread and wine which, sacramentally, become the body and blood of Christ. Pegeen, in effect, accuses her neighbour of gastronomic black magic with a bishop for victim. (She also killed her man – husband, rather than father – by hitting him with a worn pick.) Even if the 'black ram' conceit was suppressed that first night in the hope of a happier reception, the audience had much to worry about, during Act One of what was billed as a comedy.

Máire Nic Shiubhlaigh was sitting in the pit. There were murmurs from the stalls and parts of the gallery during Act Two. 'Before the curtain fell it was obvious that there was going to be some sort of trouble. Faint calls and ejaculations like "Oh, no!! Take it off!" came from various parts of the house and the atmosphere grew taut.'[7] According to Mary Maguire (later Mrs Colum), the man who began the hissing in the pit was Francis Sheehy-Skeffington, 'and he was certainly neither narrow-minded nor anti-Abbey Theater'.[8] Evidence from Maguire and other witnesses suggests strongly that the full outburst was prompted by the use of the word 'shift', which occurs prominently in Act Three but is earlier used in the second act. The second act is dominated by Christy's growing popularity with the local girls, who bring him gifts as a tribute due to a man who killed his 'da', and who find him with a looking-glass hidden behind his back. The detonating word is used by Pegeen, in her role as shop-keeper/publican, once more locked in verbal battle with the Widow Quin:

PEGEEN: . . . And what is it you're wanting, Widow Quin?

WIDOW QUIN [*insolently*]: A penn'orth of starch.

PEGEEN [*breaking out*]: And you without a white shift or a shirt in your whole family since the drying of the flood. I've no starch for the like of you, and let you walk on now to Killamuck.[9]

The effect is cumulative. In unshakable tradition, 'Audience broke up in disorder at the word shift' was the telegram despatched by Gregory to Yeats who was (odd though it might seem) away in Scotland at this dangerous moment. But there are divergent traditions and records. According to some scribbled notes made on headed paper of the International Literary Service Ltd (Fetter Lane, London) catcalls began when, in the third act, Christy attacked his 'resurrected' father. Some of these were political, but the most sinister demand was for the author himself: 'Bring him out and we will deal with him.'[10] Thanks to Gregory there was no other author that night but Synge, and no other male director, thanks to Yeats. There and then, Gregory sought the dramatist's permission to make further cuts in the dialogue, for implementation the following week.[11] It was too little, too late, as far as public order was concerned.

Nic Shiubhlaigh's account makes no mention of the telegram or the textual detail it highlighted – she fell out with Gregory and her memoirs are almost as neglectful of the Old Lady as of Molly Allgood. The moment in Act Three where the audience 'broke up' occurs *after* the love-scene – torrid enough in 1907 terms – between Christy and Pegeen. Local opinion has turned on Christy, once his injured but un-dead father has appeared. Something close to torture at their hands is imminent; the women offer Christy escape as a way of alienating Pegeen from him. Then, with the additional emphasis of rhyme, he declares:

CHRISTY: It's Pegeen I'm seeking only, and what'd I care if you brought me a drift of chosen females, standing in their shifts itself maybe, from this place to the Eastern World.[12]

Drift/shift ... the effect of various mnemonic devices in the play contributes powerfully to the audience's absorption into the callous story
of intended parricide, suspected larceny, accusations of blasphemy, and
ordeal by fire. The audience had never been allowed to relax; repeatedly,
its self-regard had been violated. Yet the question remains – why the word
'shift', as the final straw which led to stamping and shouting in the theatre?

A 'shift' is a chemise, that item of female underwear worn between
body and dress so as to allow the latter to move rather than cling rigidly
to the body. While a later pathology of fashion would condemn 'clingy'
clothing, it seems that the freedom of movement permitted by wearing a
'shift' was more provocative in 1907, at least to a city audience keen
both to preserve its rural modesty and to defend its new sophistication.
Nevertheless, as a provocation to riot, 'shift' is a poor enough word. But
the source of the offence lay back in the 1890s, when this audience, or
the new public which it represented in the Abbey's pits and stalls, was
undergoing its formative trauma. The occasion had been the defence
of, but more dramatically, the destruction of C. S. Parnell, the Synges'
neighbour in Wicklow and more recently the Uncrowned King of Ireland.
After the crisis of citation in the divorce courts as Mrs O'Shea's lover, the
hunted and hounded leader had suffered the indignity of having a 'shift'
thrown in his face – or, in another version of the potent myth – had been
discovered with a lady's shift in his cab. Unwittingly, Synge's choice of
one word had revived a bad conscience to self-defensive fury – 'Audience
Broke up at Freudian Slip'.

With this in mind, one can read the all-Synge Abbey programme of 26
January 1907 as a steadily mounting assault on Catholic Ireland's unsteady
confidence. The pure cottage interior of old Maurya has been replaced by
a kitchen serving also as commercial premises; the surnameless antiquity
of Bartley and Cathleen is now complicated by the competing claims of
Flahertys, Mahons and Quins; the purity of death-by-drowning mush-
rooms into assault and battery by loy, rope and burning sod. Instead of
stoical resignation, tinged with biblical allusion, we hear whingeing and
bullying. Far from preserving rural Ireland for comic resolution, Synge
throws in a dozen recognisable place-names, and even invokes a town-
crier. Perturbed by Pegeen's less than pious tongue, unable to accept that
an Irish household would take in a frightened murderer, and subliminally
reminded of their own hounding to death of Parnell (as now Christy is
hounded), the audience broke up at the word 'shift'. They became a crowd
'arguing and fighting with itself' and finally taking to the streets in 'an
ugly mood'.[13]

It was in the wake of this explosion that the author made his way homewards, unable to speak to his fiancée, the focal point of so much vilification during the disturbances. Synge's courage, in travelling alone by tram or train out to Kingstown after the show, is remarkable. Bearing in mind the explicit threats made in the theatre, he could have chosen security in the Nassau Hotel, where Gregory usually put up during her Dublin visits. He preferred to go back to where his mother and Florence Ross waited in Glendalough House. Sunday brought some relief, though a reply from Yeats in Scotland required him to meet Gregory in the course of the day.

Strange though it may seem, in the middle of this artistic and political crisis, Synge reassured Molly that, if he got an opportunity, he would tell Gregory 'about *us*'. Perhaps he assumed, as others did, that *The Playboy* would be taken off, in the face of dangerous public disapproval, and that an unexpected week of privacy would open up for leading actress and author alike. Yeats, however, had different ideas. At Professor Grierson's home in Aberdeen, he had spent Synge's opening night expatiating on the growing importance of Sinn Féin, the need for conflict with the Catholic Church, and the power of the new play whose premiere he had ostentatiously missed.

Back in Dublin by Monday, he sat with Synge to watch a repeat performance of Saturday night's disturbance, identifying to his own satisfaction forty or so men who made the play inaudible. These were disciples of Arthur Griffith, whose hostility to *In the Shadow of the Glen* had done so much to dig a trench between politics and the theatre.[14] Yeats defended the play in terms of legitimate dramatic exaggeration, adding the barbed comment that 'the people who formed the opposition had no books in their houses'. Synge was becoming grist to Yeats's campaign against the new middle class, even though the dramatist remained more or less silent during the exchanges. That day's *Freeman's Journal* condemned Synge's 'unmitigated, protracted libel upon Irish peasant men and, worse still, upon Irish peasant girlhood'. His language was 'barbarous jargon . . . elaborate and incessant cursings . . .' which placed the characters beyond salvation. 'Redeeming features may be found in the dregs of society. Mr Synge's dramatis personae stand apart in complete and forbidding isolation.' Anonymous letter-writers-to-the-editor weighed in. Whereas the paper's reviewer appeared unaware that the character played by Molly Allgood was named Pegeen (he referred with absurd formality to 'Margaret' throughout the review), 'A Western Girl' attributed to Sara Allgood 'a word indicating an essential item of female attire which the lady would probably never utter in ordinary circumstances even to herself'.[15] In the face of such ignorant hostility in the most popular organ of the press, the Abbey were resolved to see *The Playboy* through the originally scheduled week-long run. Other reviews on Monday 28 January had been less extreme, though none was positive.

The performance of that evening brought renewed trouble, thanks to the forty Griffithites and others, some of whom apparently booed in Gaelic. The source of these objections is difficult to pinpoint if the journalistic details are to be trusted – 'What would not be tolerated in America will not be allowed here.' One male member of the audience tried to turn the tables on native protestations of innocence by shouting 'What about Mullinahone and the witch burning?' only to get 'very emphatic execrations' in return.[16] All of this took place before the end of the first act. It was Willie Fay, rather than Yeats or Synge, who now faced the second-night audience with their sticks and their threats to pull down the curtain themselves. Determined to carry on with the performance, he called for police protection. According to the *Irish Independent*, Synge and Gregory decided to dismiss the police, aware that nothing was to be gained with an ultra-nationalist audience by relying on the batons of the British state. Twenty minutes of chaos followed, before the curtain was lowered at the end of the act.

There had been calls for the author, including one or two demands for someone to 'Kill the Author'.[17] At this juncture, Synge (who was suffering from flu and the hoarseness which always accompanied it in his case) and Lady Gregory entered the auditorium, with the former taking a seat near the orchestra pit. He told a journalist that he simply could not speak and, when the audience clamoured for him, he was forced to leave. The players doggedly acted out the last inaudible act, and *The Playboy* had survived his second public appearance in Dublin.

Interest abroad in these events is indicated by the presence of a journalist from the International Literary Service. The local press was not universally hostile. The *Independent* reported Synge's determination to see out the week-long run in the name of 'the liberty of art'. The *Irish Times* grudgingly found a degree of 'remorseless truth' in the play. The *Dublin Evening Mail*, a paper circulating mainly in Protestant circles, detected organised political motivation among the protesters. It was this factor, paradoxically, which held the cast together. Whereas rehearsals had been interrupted by some players' complaint about Synge's language, the ferocious singing of Sinn Féin songs during the early performances reinforced a professional determination not to capitulate. This solidarity was not shared by the inveterate diarist Holloway who, on the Tuesday morning, witnessed the company's response to the opposition. His timidity was shared by Francis Sheehy Skeffington, a pacifist later murdered by a British officer: Skeffington's letter to the *Irish Times* argued a case for artistic freedom provided 'Mr Synge will not again subject Mr Fay and his company to such an ordeal'.[18]

By now Yeats was present, but strangely distant. He conducted his defence of the theatre mainly through newspaper interviews, though he did from mid-week onward harangue the audience on a number of occasions. His comments verged at times on the flippant; the journalist covering for Fetter Lane, reporting him as declaring: 'there was one person at least who would come the gainer out of the tumult – it would no doubt sell an extra edition of Mr Synge's book.' Here Yeats appears to have lost sight of the ailing dramatist, and taken a pot-shot at George Roberts, publisher of the play. The crisis was becoming shapeless. On Tuesday, a young drunk played a waltz on the piano even before *Riders* was performed; chastised, he resumed his seat and the one-acter passed off well. Someone played a toy trumpet. A nephew of Lady Gregory's was arrested for drunkenly singing the British national anthem and assaulting a policeman; another nephew, Hugh Lane, acted as a kind of steward for the police, identifying troublemakers in the audience.

Tuesday night's performance had led to the greatest commotion, with the police clearing the theatre, while Trinity students lined up outside to sing (soberly, we may suppose) the national anthem by way of further provocation. The crowd, singing rival songs, moved along towards Eden Quay and the river, growing in numbers as it did. At least one ringleader was arrested, but the police dispersed the crowd without quite resorting to a baton-charge. Synge's route to the railway station covered some of the same ground.

The episode involving Geoffrey Gough, Gregory's nephew and neighbour on the Clare–Galway border, indicates that the police were not solely committed to fisticuffs with Sinn Féin. Gough may well have been drunk, but in the Gregory version of things he had gone to the Abbey 'to try to maintain order in the theatre, which he helped to do; but on his way home was unfortunately pitched upon by the police & arrested, & unluckily hit a policeman in the excitement of the moment.' Robert Gregory was keen to dismiss rumours that the term 'blackguard' was used by a magistrate in the subsequent court hearing, but his explanation only serves to confirm the vast gulf between the Abbey's regular audience and some of its well-placed supporters. Robert Gregory thanked Lord Gough for some excellent shooting at Lough Cutra and, and having done his bit to quell his mother's troublesome rioters, was on his way back to London.[19]

The author made two specific contributions to 'the debate'. Following the mêlée of Monday 28 January, the *Dublin Evening Mail* secured an interview in which he was reported as saying various things he later felt obliged to correct in a letter to the *Irish Times*. In the interview – during which the lights failed – he said he didn't 'care a rap' about the protests, intending to see the week out come what might. What the journalist catches is Synge's nervous excitement, his breaking off to speak to an Abbey attendant, his snapping of his fingers, the precision of his phras-ing – 'Exactly so.' When he wrote to the *Irish Times*, Synge made weightier remarks about the characters of Shylock and Alceste in Shakespeare and Molière, and emphasised that there were 'several sides to "The Playboy"'. But he also acknowledged 'the patience and courtesy of the interviewer'.[20]

Yeats's master-stroke was to be a public debate. Having missed the opening night through his long-standing commitment to lecture in Aber-deen, he was determined to mark the close of the run with some positive seizing of the occasion. Newspaper coverage had been particularly sharp in writing up his inability to reply when challenged in Gaelic: the National Poet's reliance on the 'Northern Police Court' made good copy. This latter detail referred to Yeats's appearance in court to give evidence against Patrick Columb [sic] and Pearse Beaslai. The older man was the father of Padraic Colum, Synge's friend and walking-companion, the other a rising journalist.[21] Young Colum published a dignified letter in the *Freeman's Journal*, defending his father whom he felt had been wrongly treated as 'the member of a gang'.

On 31 January, the *Irish Times* carried a highly intelligent letter from Ellen Duncan, linking the *Playboy* riots to the scandal provoked by Édouard Manet's painting *Olympia* in 1865, the year of Yeats's birth. Duncan (1850–1937), who had already previewed the play in *The Speaker* (London), founded the Dublin United Arts Club later in 1907, and in 1914 became the first curator of the city's Municipal Gallery of Modern Art.[22] While she neatly observed the strong resemblance of Synge's *audience* to the stage-Irish caricatures it deplored, she also advanced a penetrating analysis of the play's central weakness (as she saw it). In her view, 'the underlying psychological idea – the stimulating effect of hero worship, following on a lifetime of suppression – is not sufficiently brought out.' She found *The Playboy* inferior to *The Well of the Saints* and *Riders to the Sea*, and regarded the theatre's handling of the situation as 'extra-ordinary'.[23]

On the same day, the *Dublin Evening Mail* carried a letter of the same import, signed 'La Linge' (French for linen, a teasing reference to the offending shifts). With this correspondent, the art-historical analogy involved not Manet but the Dutch painter Adrian van Ostade whose 'rugged actuality' was contrasted satirically with eighteenth-century French rococo prettiness. Sinn Féin, the writer suggested, had not an artist within its narrow ranks, but 'a peasant painted to its specification would be an idyllic thing, à la Watteau'. If Synge had any ambitions to win the Sinn Féin 'howlers' to his side all he had to do was portray the Irish peasant as a flawless demigod, 'using language as reticent as that of a Bishop when denouncing an editor who dares to think'. Indeed, it might be better to leave words out altogether and produce pure mime – 'the artistes thinking carefully pruned thoughts in Gaelic'. Whoever La Linge was, s/he could turn the stock conflict of Artist vs. Public into dangerous channels.[24]

With public discussion taking this kind of direction, it behoved Yeats to draw his allies together. A debate, chaired by P. D. Kenny (1864–1944), took place on Monday 4 February in the theatre which had seen so much wild improvisation the previous week. Unlike the newspaper columns, this forum effectively limited participants to two options – support of the play or opposition. Synge was too ill to attend, and in any case thought the event mistaken. According to Lady Gregory, the protesters were so vehement they 'wouldn't even let their own speakers be well heard'. W. J. Lawrence spoke critically of the decision to maintain the week-long run. Sheehy Skeffington and Frank Cruise O'Brien deplored the introduction of the police. All of this was predictable. But a Kerry 'medical', a friend of James Joyce's according to Roy Foster, threatened to open up hidden wounds.

Daniel Sheehan introduced himself as 'a peasant who knew peasants' and also a medical student. He 'had never seen the doctrine of the survival of the fittest treated with such living force as by Mr Synge'. More particularly, the play was about 'sexual melancholia'. Sheehan spoke so frankly about the frustrations of people in rural areas that 'many ladies, whose countenances plainly indicated intense feelings of astonishment and pain, rose and left the place'. Marriage laws were partly to blame, and Synge had usefully drawn attention to the country's plight. Shawneen Keogh, the Kerry 'medical' diagnosed, was a 'Koch's disease man'.[25] Sheehan was followed by Mark Ryan, a London-based doctor, an ally of Maud Gonne's in the days when Synge had explored extreme nationalism, and almost certainly a member of the Irish Republican Brotherhood.

According to Lady Gregory, Ryan supported the company fairly well.

At about this juncture, Ellen Duncan sent up her name, offering to speak. The chairman, known familiarly as 'Pat', declined to call her on the grounds that he did not want to see her insulted. Even some of the Abbey's opponents were showing signs of disgust at their camp-followers' behaviour. When John Butler Yeats spoke, he ironically praised the island of saints and scholars – adding 'plaster saints' in case his point was missed.[26]

Both Synge and Gregory were against the idea of a public debate, Synge observing that 'our opponents are low ruffians not men of intellect and honesty with whom we can reason'.[27] With Sheehan of Kerry on his side, Yeats may have wondered if his allies were not just as dangerous to the cause of artistic self-sufficiency. His father's anti-Catholic sneer – the papers thought it so – did not help. But when, in immaculate evening clothes, he reminded his hostile audience that he was the author of *Cathleen ni Houlihan*, the point gained him a respectful hearing. He had played the Green card. Mary Maguire 'never witnessed a human being fight as Yeats fought that night'.[28] His speech was reprinted in *The Arrow*, including the detail in which he claimed a measure of credit for *The Playboy*. After all, he had preceded Synge to Aran and had heard the tale of a man, who had killed his father, sheltered by the community. (It was suggested to Yeats that he might kill his own father, whose 'plaster saints' jibe he later wove into a celebration of the night, 'Beautiful Lofty Things'.)

With his bravado, Yeats had undercut Synge's position which had been to present *The Playboy* in terms of dramatic genre rather than social realism. Arguments about tuberculosis (or Koch's disease) were unlikely to displace the rhetoric of the 'safe house' where men of spirit were protected by the folk from the iniquitous 'polis'. Ellen Duncan's shrewd observation, to the effect that Synge had not really gone to the bottom of this psychological problem, was at the same time brushed aside. Privately, Yeats boasted that the riots had been 'the first real defeat of the mob here and may be the start of a party of intellect, in the arts, at any rate'.[29] This line won him the support of Ezra Pound when that rioter arrived from the Western world. But at a price demanded instantly. Synge had been associated in the public mind with a line of anti-Catholic prejudice thought distinctive of the Yeats family. Two years later, when Synge was dying, no Catholic priest would heed Molly's pleadings. In February 1907, he had already been manipulated to fit Yeats's grand view of Irish reality.

Further evidence of Yeats's exposed position was neatly encapsulated on the title-page of *The Abbey Row*, a pamphlet published by Maunsel's.

It was 'Not edited by W. B. Yeats'. Here the line of defence adopted by Synge's supporters was insufficiently elevated to win the poet's approval. Emphasising the word which prompted the telegram to Aberdeen, one of the best items in the collection began:

> Oh, no, we never mention it, its name is never heard -
> New Ireland sets its face against the once familiar word.
> They take me to the Gaelic League where men wear kilts, and yet
> The simple word of childhood's days I'm bidden to forget!
>
> They tell me no one says it now, but yet to give me ease -
> If I must speak they bid me use a word that rhymes with 'sneeze'.
> But, oh! their cold permission my spirits cannot lift -
> I only want the dear old word, the one that ends in 'ift'.[30]

– and proceeded in the same style for another two verses. The final signature, 'S', may have been designed to suggest Synge's authorship, but only as a further provocative gesture to public and poet alike. The author was Susan Mitchell.

Some very meticulous calculations have been made in an effort to establish how many people were active in the disturbances. Measuring the night's takings against the theatre's full capacity (*circa* 560), Professors Hogan and Kilroy have proved that only about eighty seats were sold for the rowdy Monday night. On the Tuesday, there were somewhere in the region of two hundred, and at midweek, a near capacity crowd of about 420. The opening night had been fully booked, including complementary allocations. From this, a pattern emerges – determined but limited disruption by a small proportion of the audience at the premiere; a poor attendance at the next performance, which was more thoroughly disrupted by a very small contingent; and then a gradual recovery of interest by all sections with some disruption (as we have seen) caused by the play's supporters as well as its detractors. These figures point to the notion of planned demonstration, and also put into perspective various claims on the support of public opinion.[31]

One of the vexing features of the *Playboy* disputes was the claim of each side that the other represented a kind of modern decadence. The militant separatist Patrick Pearse, who modified his views of Synge later, saw in the *The Playboy* what he called a 'gospel of animalism'. (Gospels meant a lot to Pearse, even those he denounced.) This came close to the accusation of decadence which always hovered round Synge's ears, with his alleged morbidity. But the new play did not just revel in sex and violence, it staged a thoroughly contemporary Ireland albeit disguised as rural Mayo. Munster newspapers, museums in Dublin, bigamists in Ulster – the whole country was dragged into 'the dungpit of the yard'. If the setting was vastly remote, why is a town-crier heard in Act Three, why is a local doctor invoked, why are coasters and ferries referred to?

Synge's nephew, Hutchie, put his finger on a transference of setting, ill-absorbed into *The Playboy*. In a notebook/diary poignantly written up in a Dublin mental hospital, he wrote: 'it was the annual gathering of tinkers to the Wicklow [town] regatta at the beginning of August in 1902 which brought to Synge ... a form of English in which he could really express himself.' Or perhaps it was the races on the strand at Arklow, or the roads of rural County Wicklow. Just as Hutchie's insights recover the shadowy presence of 'the east of Ireland' in his uncle's celebrated play of the western world, and constitute a kind of family legend, so too the characters in Michael James Flaherty's licensed-to-sell-beer-wine-and-spirits household deconstruct the mirage of a primitivist Gaeldom – with riotous consequences. Rumours of the 'mad Mulrannies', invoked in the opening moments of *The Playboy*, in no cruel way anticipate Hutchie's fate. But perhaps they ghost the dramatist's fears for his own sanity back in his Parisian den.

Gossip is true intelligence in this play, and the locals' observations about California and Africa point up not just their ignorance but their vulnerability to 'news', world events, the bustle of contemporary communications and movements. What laps on the sands which the girls run across at low tide to reach Christy Mahon is not Atlantic seepage, but the filthy modern tide which Yeats denounced and Magee (with Joyce) strove to understand instead. It is in the face of these factors – and Synge had carefully noted the impact of returned 'Yanks' when he toured Mayo for the *Manchester Guardian* – that the Gaelic myth sought to defend the purity of western Irish women.

A counter-myth was ready to hand, mirror-like. John Ross, a judge, congratulated Gregory and her colleagues in the Abbey. 'You have earned the gratitude of the whole community. You are the only people who have had the pluck to stand up against this organised intimidation in Dublin.'[32] Indicating that battle-lines had previously been drawn between new forces of obscurantism and the upholders of individual freedom, Ross's comment not only anticipates the trouble which would arise over Seán O'Casey's *The Plough and the Stars* in 1926, but implies a state of semi-permanent conflict which would later erupt on other issues – abortion, birth control, censorship, divorce – with a tiny liberal, aristocratic or upper-middle-class minority holding the last ditch against organised intolerance. In this prophetic view, at once accurate and partisan, the *Playboy* riots inaugurated a tradition of controversy which persisted well into the 1970s, and perhaps even to the Miss X case of 1992.

According to Yeats in 1907, and to some extent Gregory also, the Irish Edwardian public had degenerated into societies and clubs, had surrendered its mental life to newspapers and journalists. For Yeats, the events of these days fed into his growing hatred of democracy. Ezra Pound would shortly take up the cudgels in the same cause, using the dead Synge as a platform. It was middle-class society, with its neatly ordered opinions and shrewdly calculated values, which constituted decadence. While the author of *The Playboy* had in practice often called for more democracy in running the Abbey, at least democracy in little matters, Yeats chose to set up Synge as an aristocrat rejected by the ignorant mob.

These irreconcilable attempts to impose the charge of 'modernity' on each other brought little consolation to the warring factions. Yet the central device, or structuring figure, of the row is present in the play itself – which is a comic exploration of the mysteries and pitfalls of representation. The mirror Christy uses to study his own face has been repeatedly interpreted by critics keen to link it to Joyce's 'cracked looking glass of a servant' in *Ulysses*, to Wilde's less plebeian imagery, and finally to the Shakespearean holding the mirror up to nature. When the *Evening Mail* interviewer put the question to Synge about Shakespeare and the mirror, he had responded negatively and emphatically.

But his mirror is at the heart of the play, hidden by Christy's back when the girls try to press eggs and a boiled chicken ('Feel the fat of that breast, Mister') on him. Synge's use of it is characteristically deft, and unconsciously loaded with anthropological implication. In a subsistence culture like that of Atlantic Ireland in the nineteenth century, mirrors had little aesthetic significance, either as to personal beauty or artistic purpose: Christy's emergent vanity is nicely caught. Fragile, often broken, they were the remains of a wedding gift in the distant past or became symbolic of aspirations for the future. Carefully invoked as tokens of coming good fortune, other domestic objects in *The Playboy* also play a significant role in bringing together Synge's knowledge of his country's history and his uncanny dramatic skill. The second act of *The Playboy* opens, like the first, with a list. To Pegeen's shopping for a trousseau is now added Christy's admiring inventory of the kitchen's treasures –

CHRISTY [*to himself, counting jugs on dresser*] Half a hundred beyond. Ten there.
   A score that's above. Eighty jugs. Six cups and a broken one. Two plates. A power
   of glasses. Bottles, a school-master'd be hard set to count...[33]

Given the author's economy in recording what he had done, seen or
read, it is not possible to document anything like a provable source for
such moments in the play. For the theatregoer, the point is the lyrical
stasis induced by Christy's enumeration of his beloved's possessions. This
will in turn prove to be deeply ironic, but the dramatic effect is brilliant.
Nevertheless, Synge was a thorough workman not a magically inspired
genius. In Asenath Nicholson's *Annals of the Famine in Ireland* (1851) he
would have found – in my view, *did* find – just such a list, compiled by a
Donegal schoolmaster in the course of writing to the Lord Lieutenant.
Supplicating on behalf of 4,000 or more residents in the parish of West
Tullaghobegly, Patrick M'Kye had detailed: 'One cart ... No swine, hogs
or pigs, Twenty-seven geese, Three turkeys, Two feather beds ... Eight
brass candle sticks, No looking glasses above 3d in price, No boot, no
spurs ...' etc. In a succeeding paragraph, it is recorded that 'None of their
either married or unmarried women can afford more than one shift ...'[34]
The appearance of the word 'shift', here signifying a degree of apparel
which would afford decency in otherwise degraded circumstances, surely
confirms the suspicion that Synge in writing not only *Riders to the Sea*
but *The Playboy* also drew on the American missionary's account of the
hungry 1840s. Those who clamoured against Synge's alleged insult to the
west were unaware how thoroughly he had imbibed the poignancy of its
greatest trauma.

From distant Rome, Joyce joined in the affray. He hinted that Synge
might have been drinking more than usual, and warned of attempts
(predictably by Sinn Féin and *The Leader*) to 'find out *all* about Synge's
life in Paris'. While this may only reflect Joyce's justified cynicism on the
topic of motivation in the cultural nationalist press, he went on to observe
that this 'will be nice' for Lady Gregory. Given that Joyce, like Synge, had
enjoyed good relations with her, there are no grounds for reading his
letter as directing cynicism at her. On the contrary, in his Joycean way, he
is expressing sympathy with her for the pain which muck-raking into
Synge's Parisian past will induce. He looks forward – again in a characteristically embittered yet sympathetic way – to having Synge cited as
his 'master' when *Dubliners* will finally appear.[35]

Though Joyce's friend from Kerry had specified a Darwinian subplot
as the valuable and provocative aspect of the play, a more influential

analysis reverted to pathology. When Yeats came to 'write up' Synge after his death he dwelled on the death of mid-nineteenth-century politics and the taking hold of a very different culture. 'As I stood there watching, knowing well that I saw the dissolution of a school of patriotism that held sway over my youth, Synge came and stood beside me, and said, "A young doctor has just told me that he can hardly keep himself from jumping on to a seat, and pointing out in that howling mob those whom he is treating for venereal disease." '[36]

Who Synge's acquaintance was, has never been established. Perhaps it was Daniel Sheehan who is known to have been present, but who was not yet a qualified doctor. Or Coppinger, whom Joyce later mentioned. Or Wright who had examined Synge in May 1899. Other candidates would include Oliver St Gogarty, Alfred Parsons and the younger Charles Ball. Though the question of venereal disease will arise again – not to contaminate Synge – the identity of the doctor is less important than Yeats's general diagnosis: something rotten in the state of Ireland, which Synge (a wounded surgeon, if ever there was one) had skewered.

One of the best-known consequences of the riots is Synge's 'The Curse: To a Sister of an Enemy of the Author's Who Disapproved of "The Playboy".' On 25 and 26 March, he wrote to Molly about the poem, half-afraid to pass it on, half-distracted by another he was writing about Molly herself and not her censorious sister, Peggy Callender. More than injured artistic pride was at stake here, almost an element of vindicative prophecy. Peggy's drunken husband, Tom, later contracted syphilis from a prostitute, and carelessly infected her. Lady Gregory, fearing that the Synge family would now destroy the poem, copied it for Yeats.[37]

The trouble did not subside, though the after-shocks took different forms. Judge Ross wrote an obliging letter to Gregory, praising the Abbey, which was printed as a flyer in the name of a cause loftier than propaganda: 'Before its establishment there was an evil spirit apparent in our theatres calculated to stimulate national vanity and partisan hatred. All this is changed, the people have been taught to tolerate the representation of themselves as they are, and love higher artistic ideals.'[38] This patronising of the masses did not endear the Abbey to a newly politicised public, especially among semi-prosperous emigrants. Productions of The Playboy in America stirred up further opposition. 'In New York, a currant cake and a watch were flung, the owner of the watch claiming it at the stage door afterwards.'[39] But Synge had loyal supporters in the States, among them the lawyer John Quinn, and Francis Hackett, literary editor of the Chicago Evening Post. Hackett had visited the Abbey in August 1907, to refuel his distinctive brand of cultural nationalism and anticlericalism. Synge joined his party in the audience, which included the Yeatses (father and son), and C. B. Loomis.[40] *For and Against the Playboy and the Irish Players*, a pamphlet sponsored by two Irishmen with addresses on Broadway, reproduced in decidedly sympathetic terms a debate which had taken place at the premises of the Knights of Columbus in January 1911. Irish-American opinion was not unanimously hostile to Synge.

In Cork, trouble recurred in August 1910. Nevertheless, the self-styled Athens of the South also provided a defender of Synge. At the local Literary and Scientific Society, Daniel Corkery (1878–1964) celebrated an unspotted escapist who 'carries us away from the dreary intercourse of daily life, gives us holiday where there are fresh winds, and seagull's wings'. Unfortunately, this idyllic reading is based on the conviction that Synge was too sane to bother with problems of heredity, 'the bug bear of modern literature'.[41]

CHAPTER 20

'Sorrow's Sauce for Every Kiss'

And surely a man shall see that the noblest works and foundations have
proceeded from childless men; which have sought to express the images
of their minds, where those of their bodies have failed.

Francis Bacon[1]

The riots revealed something dysfunctional in the links between Ireland
and what aspired to be its national theatre. Though the protesters were
relatively small in number, the larger and more inchoate body of opinion
was of the same mind. No longer could the leaders of the Revival assume
that a little education of public taste would cure all ills. No longer could
the general mass of citizenry dismiss Yeats and his associates as dreamers
and mystics. Reality was at issue.

Synge kept apart from the hurly-burly of the *Playboy* arguments. Searching criticism of its dramatic structure and psychological coherence had
been made by Padraic Colum and Ellen Duncan whose personal goodwill
could not be doubted. Within the Abbey, his fellow directors had expressed disquiet about its verbal 'excesses'. While Gregory and Yeats had
insisted on performing the play for its full week-long run, neither had
been particularly helpful in the days before the premiere. Molly stood
firm. While he wrestled with lingering fever and headaches, she attended
to his needs, looking for books and writing 'little notes'. He counselled
her diplomatically when she pressed for advice about the progress of her
career. She had played the lead in 'the biggest play of the season', and
could take satisfaction from that. He seemed to take greater pleasure in
sales of his new play than in its stage success, two hundred copies within
a week.[2] A persistent cough irritated his affections. Inside a few days he
signed letters to her as 'Your old T[ramp]' or 'With infinite love'. The
excitement of a visit frightened him, and Molly scolded when he cancelled
her plans. Unstable emotion, often found in victims of sustained fever,
surged through brief communications. 'I am dreadfully weak, I have a
sharp headache and the sweat is runing [sic] down my face with the
exertion of writing these few lines. That is only natural of course, as I

have had no solid food [for three days]. I feel otherwise wonderfully better.'[3] The household oppressed him, with his mother bedridden, and Robert dropping in and out in a way which frustrated Molly's arrival. Her own condition continued to cause anxiety. She was well enough to walk in Glen Dhu with friends from the theatre, despite his ill-disguised misgivings. Yet she needed to consult Henry Swanzy, an eye-specialist and former pupil of Rathmines School.

By 8 March 1907, JMS was 'as happy as the Lord God'. Just as Dr Wright had pronounced the glandular swellings of 1899 free of 'serious symptoms', so now another unmentionable condition was discounted. 'This is the third time they have tried to find the tubercular microbes in me and they have always failed utterly so if Peggy [Callender, Molly's married sister] says again that I am tubercular you may tell her to HOLD HER GOB!'[4] Much relieved, Synge looked forward to another English tour. He felt, however, that he should avoid Annie Horniman who had so deplored his conduct with Molly on an earlier tour. He conceded that the third act of *The Playboy* still needed 'pulling together'.[5]

As Kathleen Synge recovered her health, she began to think about a possible wedding. The domestic hardship awaiting the two lovers appalled her, but she acknowledged that her son was entitled to a measure of happiness, while she could not provide a home indefinitely. When Charles Frohman arrived in the spring of 1907 with a view to managing an Abbey programme in the United States, Synge lamented that 'if there is any money made out of the tour I shant get much of it.'[6] His feelings hardened a few days later, when Willie Fay and his wife turned up at Glendalough House with all the backstage news – Frohman had only been shown one of Synge's plays as against five or six by Gregory and a similar number by Yeats. He was disposed to withhold his work from both the English and American tours, complaining pointedly about Gregory's attitude.[7]

At the same time, he recognised how Molly's career was blossoming at the Abbey and congratulated her on playing in W. S. Blunt's *Fand*. Frohman's interest in taking plays to America prefigured the negotiations about publishing Synge's works after his death in 1909. He appreciated that the American manager might be 'genuinely afraid' of staging his work 'for fear of making a row with the Irish Americans'; in those circumstances, he even conceded that he would 'have no cause to be annoyed with the directors'. But if 'the tour is going largely for the cultivated University audiences it is a very different matter' – Yale University and its publishing house on the one hand, and the Hibernians on the other.[8]

Shuttling between home and his doctor's rooms in Dublin, and fitting in occasional walks with Molly, Synge felt distanced from the theatre where he was regarded as the most approachable and sympathetic of the directors. He recognised that he was tied to it by Molly's presence, otherwise he might be 'inclined to clear away to Paris and let them make it a Yeats–Gregory show in name as well as in deed'. This was not a serious proposition – ill-health argued otherwise – and he quickly conceded that Gregory and Yeats 'have both been very kind to me at times and I owe them a great deal'.[9] Publicly Synge had been Olympian, his behaviour during the *Playboy* riots dignified to a fault. Privately, after the play had closed, his correspondence with Molly lost some of its earlier bathos, while manifesting a growing sense of resignation. His mother regarded him as decidedly bad-tempered, and worried about his future with a bad-tempered wife. He commented philosophically, 'If only she knew!'

Towards the end of the month, he sketched out ideas for a new play. Revising his plan, he thought he would 'make the old woman be the mother of the man the saints [sic] killed, instead of his own mother'.[10] Nothing like this scenario has been found among Synge's papers; given his fondness for cumulative rewriting, a culling of the papers is suspected. As he considered using the old woman – 'she might be a heathen' – as 'a sort of jeering chorus', it is clear that he was considering a historical or proto-historical setting, with Christianity presented in uneasy coexistence with an earlier dispensation. He may have had Yeats's narrative poem, 'The Wanderings of Oisin', in mind though literature in Gaelic is rich in such confrontations between the new and old world-views. The story of the Children of Lir, which he had studied in Gaelic, concludes with the advent of Christianity. Synge's intentions in late March 1907 looked to a less benign dénouement. A murderous saint would blend Christy Mahon with the harsh miracle-worker of *The Well of the Saints*.

Molly's position was improving daily. Her ailing, affable lover confided in her about a possible new play, and Peggy Callender resumed sisterly relations after her latest outburst. Synge's well-known poem – 'To a Sister of an Enemy of the Author's' – emerged during his excursions with Molly. He thought 'small affairs' and squabbles good material for poetry, though what seems 'pure gold' in the heat of composition could turn out 'poor stuff after all'. For a man who defied the world when it came to drama, who resisted experienced actors and directors such as the Fays and Lady Gregory, Synge lacked confidence in his poetry to a striking degree. He wanted someone who could tell him 'when – if ever – my verses are good. That is a thing I cannot do for myself and I've got to find out.'[11]

Drama, in contrast, gave objectification to his experience of conflict and misunderstanding; his characters cannot be reduced to some source in his personal life. The comic and ironic turns of plot transformed what was taken from the raw. The great love-scene in *The Playboy* between Pegeen and Christy invokes the legendary associations of the Nephin Mountains, which Ned Synge could see from the Pratts' house at Enniscoe, but in the play land agents feature only in the list of likely victims the hero has killed. 'Poetry talk', on the other hand, continued to bother the author whenever he tried his hand at rhyme and metre. With the exception of a very small number of ballad-like poems – 'Danny' and 'The 'Mergency Man', and of course, the early and crude 'Ballad of a Pauper' – Synge's poems cling to a notion of sincerity which is almost naive. Ending up some undistinguished lines for Molly, he attempts a tight, enigmatic couplet:

> Heavy riddles lie in this
> Sorrow's sauce for every kiss![12]

Perhaps, as he admitted, that wanted seeing to. The riddles are not so much concealed with skill as abandoned with regret. The poem's larger fault or – rather – significant feature, lies in its final line where sorrow and the sexual embrace are linked through allusion to a Gaelic proverb, 'Hunger is the best sauce'. Whereas the proverb commends wise simplicity – those who want food need nothing to titillate the palate – Synge's epigram concedes that a kiss is improved by sorrows which precede it. While the lines of 26 March never amounted to much, they add a little weight to the view that unhappiness played a positive role in the affair with Molly – at least for him!

The Abbey actors could be trusted to fuel his anxieties. Despite all he and Molly had endured, his illness in late 1906 and the public trials of *The Playboy* in early 1907, he still suspected the company she kept. The idea that she should go walking (or even cycling) so far south as Glendalough robbed him of sleep. It was 'of course *impossible* that [she] should go off that way with those four louts. Mac would certainly be drunk coming home.' (Mac was Francis Quinton McDonnell who acted under the name Arthur Sinclair and eventually became Molly's second husband.) Ambrose Power flirted with the irascible Peggy Callender, no staunch friend of *The Playboy*'s author. The trip was outrageous on many grounds – Molly was associating with unsteady young men, the young men in question were particularly offensive to her beloved, and finally

Glendalough (though he never quite articulated this fear) lay too close to the once hereditary lands of his fathers. Synge resorted to blackmail – Molly had made him so 'very wretched and very unwell' that he must visit his doctor the next day. But 'in any case come to me on Sunday as usual, dearest love, and comfort me again'.[13]

In the course of editing his letters to Molly, Ann Saddlemyer established that unusually late development of the menstrual cycle formed the basis of the young woman's difficulties to which Synge had responded sympathetically. But his fears that she might become an invalid – she was just twenty at the time – appear exaggerated. In the course of a single letter he could curse himself for taking her on long walks, inquire if she did not make too much of her period pains, and seek to ensure that Sally Allgood did not reveal their intentions to the Abbey company. Three times in 1907, he and Molly postponed what were reasonably definite plans to marry. More than adequate grounds for these delays can be listed – differences of class and religious background, her youth, his continuing ill-health, their relative poverty. But as with the long saga of telling Kathleen Synge about their relationship, too many reasons for postponement are cited. In April, the doctor's advice that he should once again have swollen glands removed from his neck led to one such decision, though no operation took place until September. April was a busy month for Synge; despite his illness, Gregory and Yeats were away in Italy with Robert Gregory, leaving him in charge of the theatre. He was keen to organise his own holidays with Molly, and this required delicate negotiations with her sister and others who might club together for a collective summer holiday. Anything could be planned in advance, except the wedding.

For example, there were plans to stage *The Playboy* in Edinburgh. Holbrook Jackson (author of *The Eighteen-Nineties*) had written a positive review. Henri Lebeau, champion of *The Well of the Saints*, wrote to congratulate his hero on the new play. Inquiries about translation rights came from Prague. Synge was able to resume cycling and, despite an 'unsightly lump in my lug' (his neck glands), he ventured out to an International Exhibition in Ballsbridge. Post-colonialist admirers of *The Playboy* may note that 'A bit of the war-song the niggers were singing was exactly like some of the keens on Aran.'[14]

As far as work was concerned, the first six months of 1907 had been difficult. He managed articles for *The Shanachie* and was encouraged by the *Manchester Guardian's* interest in publishing more. *The Aran Islands* was selling steadily. In retrospect, Synge appears to have reached the crest of a wave with *The Playboy*, which remains his best-known and best-liked play. When he told his doctor in May about plans for a wedding, Alfred Parsons replied, 'Well you're a great sportsman to go and get married before you've made your name!'[15] What Synge had not made was an adequate income. He was also caught between the ability to earn by writing articles at home and his inability to settle on a new dramatic project. Slowly gathering material for a book on Wicklow, he advised Molly about keeping a journal. 'The public are very ignorant about the inner side of the smaller theatrical life, and very curious about it, so such articles would be sure to go.' Concealed behind this commercial proposition was his perpetual anxiety about what his 'little madcap' got up to. 'I am glad you seem lonesome.'[16]

His relations with the Abbey improved. Even Annie Horniman had written friendly letters to him, and Molly was instructed to be steadily polite. 'One gets into the way of wearing a sort of mask after a while, which is a rather needful trick.' While she was away, he made inquiries with Jack Yeats about a holiday in Devon from where he could travel up to London and meet Molly. Little disasters at home – a burst tyre while cycling, a sharp east wind – led to outbreaks of localised ill-health, a sore leg and a cold in the eyes, as if his body was issuing casual reports from a deeper source of illness as yet dormant. These setbacks rekindled a more comprehensive melancholy: 'I used to sit over my sparks of fire long ago in Paris picturing glen after glen in my mind, and river after river – there are rivers like the Annamoe that I fished in till I knew every stone and eddy – and then one goes on to see a time when the rivers will be there and the thrushes, and we'll be dead surely.'[17]

In this self-consciously nostalgic mood, Synge was inclined to forget the changes in Wicklow and its improved communications with the capital city. He was still the gentleman's son pursuing the sports and recreations of his endangered class. While Annamoe and Glendalough usually lay beyond the reach of Molly's colleagues, more northerly parts of the county were increasingly accessible. It was a habit with them to gather after ten o'clock Mass in Dublin's pro-cathedral for a Sunday excursion. The 'gentlemen' – including Padraic Colum, the Fay brothers, Seamus O'Sullivan and George Roberts – paid for the 'ladies' – Máire Garvey, Máire Nic Shiubhlaigh and the Allgoods. The tram (horse-drawn in the early days) bore them to Rathfarnham. Routes of varying lengths then led onwards by way of the Two Rock or Three Rock mountains, the Hell Fire Club, or Sugar Loaf. They sang as they went, and lived off the country by getting something to eat from friendly cottagers. Sometimes they went twenty or thirty miles and came home by the Bray train, passing through Glenageary in carriages which Synge in Glendalough House could hear rattling past St Paul's Church. The talk was rich, covering topics 'from pitch and toss to manslaughter'.[18]

In the years when all of Europe was discovering the pleasures of country walking, he sought to preserve a more solitary relationship with the out-of-doors. Instead of opening up the countryside to energetic town-dwellers, he tried to reinvent the countryman's assumed intimacy with nature. But the facts of modernisation, however scaled down for pre-independent Ireland, cried out against it. The trams, the trains, the tourists all intruded on his privacy under heaven. When the Allgood sisters took a room in Glencree they were rudely awoken (literally) to discover that their host used it to hide contraband tobacco. And when Sally on the same occasion climbed the mountainside to study her part in *Measure for Measure*, she was startled by Americans in a limousine who were equally startled to find an Irish peasant reading Shakespeare.

Synge's comedy was dipped in the same intelligent gall. His jealousy symbolised the difference of manners growing up between the people who acted in the Abbey and those who directed it. Difference there had long been, but a new confidence was gradually taking hold of what Mrs Synge still saw as the lower orders. These were not all drunken rioters such as had disrupted *The Playboy*. Molly's rising up out of a quayside furniture shop was only one example of a cultural resurgence which affected many ordinary people who did not necessarily pack doctrinaire nationalism in their kitbag. Her deceptions tortured him, not because he believed her unfaithful in some carnal fashion but – simply – because he could not understand. He was deceived more than she deceived. When he told her she would never understand why he felt ten years older than he did the previous week, he inverted the truth. He was racing into middle age as an explanation of what he could not confront.[19]

Yet in his doggedly fair way he admitted that, like anyone else, he too told lies in small trivial matters to 'outside people'. His changeling did not remain constant to his image of her. Touring to Glasgow and Cambridge involved breaks which no amount of tiffing and making-up could disguise. When Molly spent money, Synge pointed out that they had been planning to marry in July. He could resort to hackneyed explanations: 'I am very nervous, very highly-strung … if I was not I couldn't be a writer.' Within twenty-four hours he switched to grandiosity: 'Your letter … has rolled the stone off my grave at last.' Whatever prompted this piece of Messianism, he undertook to burn the letter as requested. Plans to meet in London were secretly made, each of them to stay in separate 'digs'.[20]

He was taking more interest in less intimate friendship. The prospect of some days with Jack Yeats in Devon brought a flush of excitement, and he reminisced with a London cousin about contacts inside the family – 'glad to see Percy at Bertha's in the winter'.[21] His account of Uncle Alec's lingering reputation in the Aran Islands suggests that he was familiar with the dossier of letters chronicling the vicissitudes of missionary life and catch-as-catch-can sea-fishing. While Molly headed towards Oxford with the Company, Synge took the boat for Devon. He had not 'given up the idea of being married in the summer. But we shall have to see how our money stands. I have not got my Doctor's bill yet.'

The journey was serialised in letters to Molly. A deftly placed break in one letter mutely hinted that they might come home together by ... WHITE'S HOTEL WEXFORD – the formal address doing duty as a proposal to stay in the same accommodation. But he split a new pair of trousers 'in the gable end', unconsciously imitating an accident which had befallen 'Mac' in the ladies' dressing-room at the Abbey. That was more likely to amuse Molly than his account of Jack Yeats and his wife, Cottie (Mary Cottenham). They seemed 'a very happy couple after eleven years of it, and they must be comfortably off as everything is very nice in a simple way'. In London, he put up in Handel Street, despite his earlier complaints about the noise from other guests, and found it necessary to write to praise her performance in *In the Shadow of the Glen*. There wasn't 'much use going behind the scenes the place is so cramped and crowded'. When she had two shows a day, he occupied himself at the House of Commons, in a delegation visiting Stephen Gwynn, the Nationalist MP, literary critic, and fellow philanthropist of Mrs Humphry Ward. Delegations did not include actresses, nor was Molly present when Synge and Yeats supped with Lord Dunraven.[22]

More than differences of class disturbed their London days. 'I must talk to you and I will not say anything to upset you before your shows,' he wrote from his lodgings on Friday 14 June. 'I nearly fainted yesterday when I got back to my room, my dispair [sic] was so intense.' Though he felt ill, he was committed to visiting Masefield in Greenwich, whose household had its own anxieties.[23] Less than a week later, they were back in Dublin, thinking of holidays. Though he consulted the doctor about his lungs, and was advised to get his glands removed, the familiarity of Glendalough House reassured him. Elkin Mathews sent a cheque for £3 11s 3d which went into the holiday fund. In arrangements which might or might not include Sally

Allgood and others from the company, the proposal was to take summer accommodation at Lough Bray, in north Wicklow.

This address covered two contrasting houses. Occupied in 1907 by a gamekeeper and his wife (the McGuirks), the smaller stood on the road-side leading from Glencree towards Sally Gap. Here Molly spent what time she could. Less than half a mile away on the northern shore of Lower Lough Bray, Synge occupied a stylish abode far from the primitive stone hut in which Nora Burke of *In the Shadow of the Glen* had plotted to abandon her impotent husband. To this dwelling (more gentleman's shooting lodge than cottage) the redoubtable Lady Powerscourt had retired in 1833 to refuel her evangelical zeal after the conference at which 'Pestalozzi' Synge had presided. It was, she averred, 'a little fishing cottage over a lake embraced in high mountains, of majestic, threatening appearance, seeming to defy the approach of any evil to the children of the Most High . . . a lone spot, three miles from Powerscourt.'[24] Synge described the place in not dissimilar terms, though his alienation produces not spiritual renewal but aesthetic anxiety. 'There is a dense white fog around the cottage, and we seem to be shut away from any habitation. All round behind the hills there is a moan and rumble of thunder coming nearer, at times with a fierce and sudden crash. The bracken has a nearly painful green in the strangeness of the light.'[25]

In 'Glencree' – an essay never published in his lifetime – Synge once again identifies with the outcast or self-outcast. Whereas Theodosia (Viscountess Powerscourt) in 1833 reported her mission to the benighted Roman Catholics of this remote area, Synge (hidden in the ferns) uses the silence generated when people are away at Mass to isolate a tramp who has paused furtively to wash his shirt in a mountain stream:

Before he was quite out of sight the first groups of people on their way home from the chapel began to appear on the paths round the hill, and I could hear the jolting of heavy outside cars. By his act of primitive cleanness this man seemed to have lifted himself also into the mood of the sky, and the indescribable half-plaintive atmosphere of the autumn Sundays of Wicklow. I could not pity him. The cottage men with their humour and simplicity and the grey farm-houses they live in have gained in a real sense – 'Infinite riches in a little room', while the tramp has chosen a life of penury with a world for habitation.[26]

Lough Bray Cottage retained a larch grove which Synge and Molly called the Trees of Jerusalem. These were to be among the happiest days of Synge's life, spent in what was spiritually his *Heimat* but in the company of the difficult woman he loved, whose origins were so very different. 'A Landlord's Garden in County Wicklow', with its ironic tribute to past dignities at Castle Kevin, appeared in the *Manchester Guardian* on 1 July; *The Aran Islands* had been published in April; London, Oxford and Cambridge had witnessed *The Playboy* without commotion. It felt like a season of hope.

Ill-health did disrupt these halcyon days, but the immediate victim was Molly rather than John. The 'dispair' of London had arisen from her irregular and heavy periods. Some time before 26 June, she had become alarmed and, on the advice of her own physician, consulted Arthur Barry, gynaecologist at the National Maternity Hospital in Holles Street, Dublin. In a demonstration of the smallness of Dublin's professional life, Molly's doctor had indirectly participated in the treatment of her lover's unspecified illness – Swanzy had been instrumental in bringing Margaret Huxley to Dublin back in 1883.[27]

The specialist's written response to Molly's menstrual problems was reassuring. The extent to which she and Synge discussed this temporary crisis may be gauged from the fact that a draft reply to Barry survives in Synge's hand – though in Molly's voice.[28] Nor is there any basis for speculation on the topic of an unwanted pregnancy, or even a fear of pregnancy which turned out to be unwarranted. Synge discussed Molly's condition with his mother who, like Dr Barry, had reassuring things to say. It is inconceivable that, in discussion with Kathleen Synge, he could have admitted sexual intercourse let alone a fruitful consequence. Nor, as a man capable of the most resilient silence, would he have lied to her. There is scarcely more positive proof of the couple's unconsummated relationship, even if it is proof based on lack of evidence. Mrs Synge disapproved of anything suggestive of his sharing the same roof with Molly. It was she who redirected John Synge to the grander 'cottage' where 'Pestalozzi' Synge's spiritual sister had retreated from the world.

If anything, it was Synge who maintained concern about Molly's health rather than Molly herself. He repeatedly advised her against strenuous exercise, and this included travelling out from Dublin to join him at one of the cottages near Lough Bray. Did he attune his mind to the disrupted rhythms of her body during the early summer months of 1907? In the eyes of many, his letters would appear remarkably frank. 'Remember if you are quite normal this time ... your day will be Saturday.' And about three days later, 'If I get well again and if you get over your period all right you will be able to come up for some days at least.'[29] But the frank specification of her period, not often a topic of Irish uxorious concern, is counterbalanced by an emphasis on his own ill-health.

Not surprisingly, he is worried about the impact of her condition on their future as man and wife – 'You have escaped once, and now you want to break the doctors [sic] orders and risk your career and the happiness of our married life!' None of the surviving letters reflect a desire to have children, just as there is no evidence of consummated sex: parenthood does not arise. Synge was expert, often unconsciously so, in turning one theme into another. At Lough Bray, he fears for her safety on the exposed route she must walk if she is to join him, but then curiously implicates himself who signed many letters as her 'Old Tramp':

Oh it is cruel of you to make me so unspeakably anxious. I'll have to go off now and sit on the mountain-road half the day to look out for you as the place is full of soldiers and queer tramps that have come about the [army] camp.[30]

Molly stuck by her man, to his bitter end. But their associates are curiously reluctant to comment on the relationship. During the summer of 1907, Francis Hackett (1883–1962), later a distinguished novelist, visited the Abbey and met Synge.[31] Hackett, together with his brother and the lawyer John Quinn, worked without stint to advance Synge's cause both before and after his death. In private, Hackett explicitly praised the sexual quality of Synge's imagination, but veered away from any commentary on Molly. A man of forthright opinions, hostile to clerical influence, he can hardly be thought of as simply conventional in this discretion. Women were equally silent on the topic of Molly Allgood.

Mary Colum's *Life and the Dream* (1947) is a neglected source of intelligent commentary on the Irish Literary Movement. A loyal admirer of Synge's who reviewed his posthumously published *Works* in the *Irish Review*, she recorded carefully the mysterious rumours which circulated about him in 1907 – without casting any light on what the mystery was. It is clear that she admired not only the writer but the man himself, 'who had the most sensitive face of all the writers' attached to the movement. Like Hackett, much of her life was spent in America, free from the constraints of Dublin opinion. Yet she never once mentions Molly Allgood in her detailed account of the Abbey, its playwrights and players.[32] Something akin to the dense white fog round Mrs McGuirk's cottage absorbs the young, wilful actress in the memoirs of her contemporaries.

Matters naturally altered between them as his health declined and she grew confident in her profession. He became more paternal, even as he expressed impatience to see her. The books he recommended included

Swift's *Journal to Stella*, the very paradigm of a correspondence between ageing writer and bright young woman. In the National Gallery in Merrion Square, he approved Titian's magnificent portrait of Baldassare Castiglione, but emphasised pictures of Swift and Stella also. 'I wondered how *we'll* look when we're stuck up there!'[33] To Molly on tour in Galway, he transmitted a poem with a marginal note:

There's snow in every street	I wonder if it
Where I go up and down	is right after all?
And there's no man or dog that knows	Anyhow its better.
My footsteps in the town.	Be careful of this
	MS. and maybe you'll
I know the shops and men	be able to sell it
French Jews and Russian Poles	to an American
For I go walking night and noon	collector for £20 when
To spare my sack of coals.	I'm rotten.

Then neatly secularising Swift's cathedral into a museum, he maintained the blend of morbidity and humour with the suggestion that 'This would be a nice sheet to put up in the Museum over our skulls, bye and bye when we go up to keep Swift and Stella in countinance [sic].'[34]

Synge regarded his poems as occasional pieces, and though the 'bosh' sent to Galway had been originally written in 1896 (and clearly describes Paris) they convey a poignant sense of the loneliness which persisted even within his love of Molly. Snatching moments at Lough Bray, postponing marriage, quarrelling on paper, making up, the two advanced steadily if not always in step with each other, towards their ultimate separation. For her, it was a stage in her early life which she passed through with spirit and dignity, confident that other futures lay ahead. For him, it was part of the one road chosen for him, the same road from childhood illness to Mount Jerome Cemetery.

BOOK FIVE

In the Green Room

Elpis, or Hope

If I am to stay alive, I am bound to continue to get love wrong, all the
time, but not to cease wooing, for that is my life affair, love's work.

Gillian Rose[1]

When Yeats published a memoir of his old friend in the American
magazine, *The Dial* (April 1928), the opposing frontispiece was of a
fisherman drawn by Pablo Picasso. Elsewhere in the same issue, 'John
Eglinton' reviewed a short book on the Victorian positivist thinker and
novelist, Harriet Martineau. As a tableau for the dramatist then close on
twenty years dead, a more suitably mixed effect could hardly have been
devised. The drawing shows a strong-limbed yet emaciated man carrying
a basket of fish on his head, as if to recall *Riders to the Sea*. Like Synge,
Martineau had been racked by prolonged ill-health; she had combined a
tough-minded outlook on socio-economic matters with a hatred of
slavery. Freedom of the spirit, in each case, was held in place by an
unblinking recognition of the pain inherent in all labour. Death is the last
labour.

But, most striking is Martineau's exemplification of a way of dying.
It might be called Stoic though, in the middle of the anxious nineteenth
century, defiance rather than philosophical resignation characterised
deathbed individualism. As the implications of Darwin's theories further
separated the individual from any confidence in his/her own unique
place in a divine order, so a distinctly modern attitude towards death
emerges. 'Man has created death', Yeats will write at a time when he
would assemble a pantheon of Irish dead heroes, Parnell, Kevin O'Hig-
gins, and of course Synge. In an undated entry from his diary appearing
in *The Dial* some nineteen years after it had been written, Yeats recorded
how Molly Allgood had told him that her lover 'often spoke of his
coming death'.[2]

Perhaps the unbroken sequence of tributes to Synge's ill-health which
dogged his uncertain infant steps and his manly strides made such
frankness easier. Perhaps eye-dabbing Victorian morbidity was the

matrix from which his frankness broke free, while retaining its contours. While Yeats persisted in relating Synge's death to that of Parnell and Lady Gregory – the first of these two being incapable of a philosophical thought and the second of an impious one – it makes as much sense, if not more, to place Synge in a grander tradition of those who face death articulately and bravely, the tradition of Socrates, Bruno, David Hume, Goethe, Oscar Wilde, and Gillian Rose. On the occasion of his mother's death, however, Synge's demeanour was to be less philosophical, and understandably so. It was a stage in the course of his own demise, allowing him to test-by-failing some of his resolve in the face of coming dissolution.

It is twenty years now since Susan Sontag found it advisable to preface an influential book with the observation that 'illness is not a metaphor ... the healthiest way of being ill ... is one most purified of, most resistant to, metaphoric thinking.' Referring to cancer patients specifically, she argues that they 'are lied to, not just because the disease is (or is thought to be) a death sentence, but because it is felt to be obscene – in the original meaning of the word: ill-omened, abominable, repugnant to the senses.'[3] If this is or was true in latter-day America, so much more so was it true in late Victorian and Edwardian Ireland. Given that the other fear lurking in the Synges' medicine cabinet – were Johnnie's swollen glands tubercular? – also invoked an illness associated with flushes, emotional displays and even (it was averred) excessive sexual activity, then the conventional meaning of 'obscene' might have been lip-read among witnesses to Synge's condition. His practice of retreating to Paris did little to mitigate his offence. *La Traviata* (1853) had made the point; *Ghosts* brought it permanently home by fixing upon a sexually-transmitted and hereditary disease.

Synge's attempt at a novel about nurses has been dated to 1897–8, the period of his first surgical operation.[4] In his last, uncompleted play upon which he struggled even on his deathbed, a character opts for death, uniquely in his dramatic *oeuvre*. As against the tendency to read the work as a transcription of his experience, illness in Synge must be recognised as both metaphor and actuality, which is to say that it enacts precisely what the word meant in the original Greek (*meta-phora*) which he knew – a carrying-over. As a teenager, he feared that he was the vehicle of a diseased inheritance, and that he should not perpetuate this condition by begetting children. But the documentation preserving this record is economical with details which might precisely date the onset of fear. His last days become critical for any attempt to write his life.

The fact that Synge died in a nursing home with the unusual name, Elpis, has obscured a continuity in his medical records. Elpis (from a Greek word denoting hope) was simply the Mount Street Nursing Home renamed, in which he had been treated as early as 1897. Established in 1890 by Margaret Huxley (matron of nearby Sir Patrick Dun's Hospital), with a friend of hers who acted as superintendent, and with the ubiquitous Harry Stephens, it was Dublin's first private hospital in the modern sense of the term.[5] The question of medical provision had become problematic in Victorian Dublin, with religious allegiance defining the problem. The growing prosperity of the Catholic middle class led to the establishment of hospitals in which patients were no longer indebted to the philanthropy of long-dead founders (Protestants, for the most part) in institutions instinctively regarded as part of the social and political establishment. By a counter movement, non-Catholics aimed to secure medical provision independent of the mores and values associated with papal teaching, especially in matters involving sexuality. The virtual segregation of patients into opposing denominational 'wards', which came to characterise Irish hospital build- ing for too long in this century, was not yet in place in Synge's day. But the distinctly secular nursing home in which he died had its place in a chronicle of rival provision, based on mutual suspicion in ethics.[6] It later became a convent.

In her mature years a wearer of elaborate feather hats and something of a character, Margaret Rachel Huxley (1855–1940) has been described as 'the pioneer of modern nursing in Dublin', possessing 'ability of a remarkable order'. It was she who had overseen the expansion of the Home from a single house (No. 48) in Lower Mount Street to the extensive network of rooms in Nos. 19, 20 and 21 in which her most distinguished patient died.[7] When Synge first entered what later became known as Elpis, he had recently been involved in mortgage transactions concerning two similar houses (Nos. 53 and 54 Upper Mount Street). His brother-in-law's professional acumen was busy converting such property from tenement residences into a business investment, with lucrative consequences from which Synge would never benefit. Though he died in the care of the most advanced nursing service available in the city, he also died in the shadow of those vestigial family properties which were the urban equivalent of 'A Landlord's Garden in County Wicklow', decaying, at once unfruitful and seedy. Some antici- pation of this irony must have struck him when he turned over an early draft of 'A Landlord's Garden' to sketch out a letter to his solicitors about the division of income from the Mount Street houses.[8]

If twelve years of intermittent treatment in the same institution seems routine in one whose health was always delicate, the progress of his illness was marked also by deflections and remissions. His condition, disguised by misdiagnosis or euphemistic diagnosis and a likely element of self-deception, was almost certainly malign from an early age. In November 1889, his neck glands were swollen, not to mention what Mrs Synge termed 'his groins'. Indeed his 'groins' – the seat of lust for Ben Jonson – were swollen to the point where he had to travel by tram into Dublin, unable to walk to his music lessons. When he returned from his first German expedition in June 1894, Mrs Synge was inclined to attribute mysterious lumps on his wrists to excessive piano practice.[9] At the beginning of 1897 his voice was so weak and husky he was deemed unfit for teaching or lecturing. Later 'his mother complained of his procrastination in making an appointment with his doctor'. December saw him under the knife.[10]

Eighteen months later, on 9 May 1899, Synge arrived back from Paris looking well. At the time Mrs Synge was worried about Ned's depressed state, but noted promptly that, within twenty-four hours, her returned prodigal had a bad cold. His condition deteriorated, and she was decidedly worried over the weekend of 20–21 May. On the Monday she 'got up early to see how Johnnie was, rather better, but sent Kate for Dr Wright ... Dr W. came [and] told J. to stay in bed, very feverish and face much swelled.'[11] Nevertheless, Wright assured Mrs Synge that her son 'had no serious symptoms'. To the eye of his visiting nephew, 'his face was pale and so swelled that it looked queerly lopsided'.[12] The childish ailments, aggravated by serious bouts of asthma and these disturbing juvenile swellings, came under scrutiny of many doctors.

A father (W. B. B. Scriven) and son (George Scriven) had already attended to his infant needs, augmented by Dr Henry Oulton. A local physician, Wright, was also summoned on the occasion just described. The Stephens dossier is niggardly in further identifying Dr Wright, a point which will become significant when final assessment of Synge's fatal illness is considered. Samuel Synge is even more discreet on the topic of doctors; while pointing out that the Scrivens were relatives, Sam was unable to go further than allude to another doctor 'whose name I forget'.[13] But, if Wright was or became Mrs Synge's regular doctor, then nothing more than the conventional provision expected by solid middle-class families is indicated. If he was a specialist, even an apprentice one, then the area of Wright's specialism will be of interest. Consultants were only sought in 1897 when Synge was first operated upon, and in the event of recurrences.

Of these John Benignus Lyons, the medical historian, has unfailingly good things to say. Wallace Beatty (1853–1923) was Canadian-born, Trinity-educated, attached to the Adelaide Hospital in Dublin, a mid-Victorian citadel of Protestant self-protection in a realm where Catholic values were being asserted in new hospitals run by orders of nuns. Charles Bent Ball (1851–1916) was attached to Sir Patrick Dun's Hospital, an older establishment than the Adelaide; he also held the Regius Chair of Surgery in Trinity and his brother (Sir Robert Stawell Ball) presided as Astronomer Royal in Ireland. Sons of Robert Ball (1802–57, naturalist), the Balls were pillars (if the solecism can be tolerated) of the professional establishment, practitioners of science and liberal culture. Like the Jolys, and like several Synges in the generation of John's nephews, these were members of a historically distinct intelligentsia. Europe's collapse into war in August 1914, or the outbreak of republican violence at Easter 1916, or the renewal of internecine strife in Ireland during 1919 – these events mark the end of a brief era, that of Edwardian–Georgian Ireland. Synge's death in March 1909 was an augury, his unfinished *Deirdre* a dramatic prophecy.

Charles (later Sir Charles) Ball worked with Alfred Parsons (1865–1952), a brilliant diagnostician. Parsons was personally known to J. B. Lyons, whose recent essays in medical biography are particularly illuminating in the cases of the Wilde and Synge families. Therein lies a continuity of professional commentary at once valuable and discreet. At the time, August 1907, a crucial diagnosis ('cancer') was uttered aloud on the adult Synge – too late, as the utterer realised – by the literary surgeon, Oliver Gogarty. Even then the full truth about his condition may have been kept from Synge.[14]

Why should this have been? After all, the dramatist in him possessed immense mental robustness; he was less likely to panic at news of serious illness than many others. His nearest sibling in the family, Sam with whom he had grown up, was a qualified doctor. But the fact that Synge had entered his teenage years while his brother studied medicine only complicates the pattern of knowledge and delay which appears to mark the patient's own response to his recurring ill-health. Sam, it must be admitted, was abroad for most of John's maturity; his advice, sought and given on at least one occasion, does not survive. In Paris, one of Synge's close friends had been the Dublin-born doctor, James Cree. Cree was to die young, and in any case an ointment he had prescribed proved useless.

Closer to home, Harry Stephens, Mrs Synge's redoubtable business manager and since 1884 Annie Synge's somewhat cavalier husband, was now part-owner of the Mount Street Nursing Home; Sam was back on leave for two years from June 1904 onwards, during which time he took a further medical qualification at Trinity College.[15] In his last illness, the world-renowned dramatist was trammelled in family networks and indebted to relatives.

The litany of illnesses is repetitive (like all litanies) and bewildering in its detail. Asthma (particularly when he was with his family in County Wicklow), dental decay, chickenpox, abscesses, loss of hair, swollen wrists, swollen glands, influenza – are recurrent burdens, with Hodgkin's disease playing the Devil's part. Family correspondence establishes beyond all doubt a constancy of concern about the child's health. From a different perspective, Lyons has marshalled the facts in an essay which takes its title suggestively from one of Synge's abortive compositions – 'Etude morbide'.[16] The medical historian commences with the year 1897, concentrating on the adult patient. A different kind of authority can be found in a short essay written by Synge himself shortly after the first of his operations in Elpis. Though some of the details may be assumed to be fictitious – Nurse Smith, for example – 'Under Ether' provides a vivid account of his sensations, and to an extent his behaviour, during his descent into unconsciousness, and after.

To its comico-stoic details can be added the conscientious visits he received from his relatives – brother-in-law Harry calling on Sunday, the day after Synge's first operation, and mother on Wednesday 15 December 1897. Harry Stephens as first visitor was both acting head man of the family, in the absence of the patient's brothers, and doubling up in his proprietorial role at Elpis. If a zone of informed confidentiality actually embraced John Synge, to let him know particulars of his real condition in health, then Harry remained central to it. He and Synge may have been close on a generation apart in age – fifteen years, to be precise – but they had more in common than had the patient with his siblings, including Harry's wife, Annie. History, which in this case amounts to Yeats, has not been fair to Harry Stephens. If anyone in the family knew of Synge's cancer, he did; and if anyone was well-placed to judge whether the patient should be informed, he was. Without rival in the family, Harry was a man of the world.

In all, Synge spent eleven days in the nursing home, returning to Kingstown in time for Christmas. The bill, amounting to £8 5s 0d, was promptly paid at his own insistence though, in the days following, Mrs

Synge felt she 'ought to have waited and showed it to Harry as he might have got it reduced …'[17] Other bills followed, to be received with equal gratitude. Synge's own account of his first operation for cervical adenitis (not yet revealed to him or perhaps to anyone as cancered) includes hallucinations and momentary delusions ('I am an initiated mystic … I could rend the groundwork of your souls …') of which hashish-smoking Yeats might have been jealous. The essay's final sentence anticipates a powerful motif in the *The Playboy of the Western World*, that of a death necessary for life – 'The impression was very strong on me that I had died the preceding day and come to life again, and this impression has never changed.'[18]

Conscience-bound even under ether, Synge had also feared that he came close to divulging the secrets of his earlier life:

Clouds of luminous mist were swirling round me, through which heads broke only at intervals. I felt I was talking of a lady I had known years before, and sudden terror seized me that I should spread forth all the secrets of my life. I could not be silent. The name was on my lips. With wild horror I screamed:

'Oh, no, I won't!'

'No, I won't!'

'No, I won't!'

'Oh, no, I won't!'

'No, I won't!'

'No, I won't!'

using the sullen rhythm that forms in one's head during a railway journey.[19]

As biographical evidence, 'Under Ether' deserves cautious attention. In Synge's lifetime it remained out of sight, to be included in the 1910 (posthumous) *Collected Works* and silently removed from the 1911 edition. For the moment we will pause on an issue which has detained us before – the implementation, in seemingly straightforward autobiographical fragments, of local tactics which are recognisably those of fiction. Not only is Nurse Smith a palpable renaming, but so is Doctor Batby – Synge had consulted Dr Wallace *Beatty* who arranged for surgery under Charles *Ball.* More significant is the incident of wild horror, for it is not clear from the context what it was that Synge repeatedly screamed he wouldn't do. Do the words refer to his desperate efforts not to name the lady of former years in the presence of the surgeons and nurses, not to 'spread forth all the secrets' of his earlier emotional life? Or, by a more radical but strictly justifiable second interpretation, do these words record his side of an exchange with the lady in question, all those years ago? (In December 1897, Synge was still only twenty-six). Are they the involuntary assertion of sexual self-denial?

An examination of the 'original' essay provokes further questions. What survives in Trinity College, Dublin, is a typescript with some slight emendations in Synge's own hand. The evidence indicates that the author carefully revised it from an earlier version, and it may indicate also that another hand has been at work in shaping what has come down to us as the published text. In relation to the lady of former years, the scrupulous reader will notice that Synge's phrase 'I have mentioned before' has been altered by him to 'I had known years before'; clearly an earlier text (or a longer text, from which 'Under Ether' was excerpted) dealt with this person in some other regard.

Another significant and related alteration – from 'the lady' to 'a lady' – deserves attention in assessing the essay as biographical evidence. The change strongly suggests that the relationship was sufficiently distinctive to require (in his revising eye) a more diffused and less individuated reference. As revision is likely to have occurred with some view of ultimate publication, the question of Synge's assumed readership arises. Written for his eyes only, 'Under Ether' was under no obligation to identify or conceal the lady. Perhaps her real name has also dropped from the text in the course of revision. In this light, the interpretation offered above – that Synge reports memories of what he feared might have been a near-confession of some act of self-denial – is, if anything, rendered more plausible.

Finally, the typescript is made up of sixteen pages cut in various odd sizes, some being mere strips carrying only three lines of type. Here is the most palpable evidence of a drastic reduction in the length of the essay, even if the wielder of scissors can never be identified either as Synge or as some other covert editor.[20] A swooping upward curve of the mutilated paper after the last words allows for the suspicion that these had not always been the last words on the line. In keeping with the character of his surviving papers as a whole, 'Under Ether' smells of amputation or absence. The editors of 1910–11 both included and excluded it, like an unloved relative.

The immediate consequences of Synge's first surgery did not reassure his mother, who inscribed in her final diary summary for the year a terse 'John not well ...' On 5 January 1898, she advised Robert that his youngest brother looked somewhat better, a state of affairs which made her if anything more anxious as it increased the likelihood of his returning to Paris. Life for Synge was a pattern of echo and release. Though it has been accepted that the operation of 1897 led to a quasi-remission of almost ten years, when he was leaving Dublin for Paris in October 1900, Mrs Synge was able to report that her youngest was anxious about the return of an enlarged gland not, apparently, in precisely the same position as before but 'back pretty far' on his neck. At the end of the following April, he was 'poorly' and had to beg money from home in order to get back to Kingstown. In the summer of 1901, even thirteen-year-old Edward Stephens was aware of Uncle John's swellings, while Mrs Synge was divided between relief at his putting on weight and persistent anxiety about 'the very large gland which is terribly disfiguring to him'.[21] Synge delayed his return from France that year until Robert, who had returned from South America with his family, had moved out of their mother's house in Crosthwaite Park. He was not open to scrutiny.

'Worn and weary and disfigured' had been Synge's own self-description to her *circa* April 1901.[22] However, the description survives only in Mrs Synge's transmission of it to Sam in China. And this poses a question of a very technical yet pressing kind – why have all of Synge's letters to his family, before January 1903 when he was approaching his thirty-second birthday, disappeared?[23] We know for certain that his declaration of political disaffiliation from inherited values, and his Parisian commitment to socialism, is not among his mother's papers. We note in addition that his account of disfigurement and ill-health, also reported from the safe remoteness of Paris, does not survive, whereas the voluminous correspondence of Kathleen and her conventional, undistinguished sons has been assiduously preserved with its recurrent, anxiety-ridden yet imprecise précis of what was wrong with Johnnie. Do these topics – ideological and socio-medical – identify the very reasons for the disappearance of the letters in which Synge raised them with his family?

For the biographer, evidence of serious illness is a peculiarly difficult problem in that it is properly the concern of non-literary specialists while it is also a topic of profoundly subjective comment by friends and family, nearest and dearest, gossip and prophet of doom. Kathleen was both a mother and a saint, one who read these distressing symptoms not only as pain inflicted upon her beloved youngest child but also as part of God's inscrutable plan. Her letters to Robert and Sam keep us informed of John's condition but our ultimate sense of this is also filtered through the subject's own taciturnity, the notions of decorum governing family correspondence, professional etiquette among surgeons, and the propensity of Kathleen Synge to see God's hand on the sinner's neck.

In any case, there were sustained bouts of coughing, attacks of asthma, and various kinds of recurrent fever. Synge himself joked on the serial-cum-publishing timetable of his ailments when, in the middle of the *Playboy* troubles, he wrote to Lady Gregory complaining of a 'second edition of influenza'.[24] Thus, when the aftermath of *The Playboy* found Synge in mid-1907 suffering from pains in the legs and back, together with the familiar swelling of his neck glands, no diagnosis could simply ignore the events of the previous ten years. By this point, Samuel Synge and his wife had returned to the Chinese mission fields after two years on furlough. J. B. Lyons assumes that there was a conference between Synge's reverend-doctor brother and Alfred Parsons in which Sam would 'have been told all there was to tell about his brother's malady'.[25] Against the publicly available evidence, Sam later denied that cancer was the cause of his brother's death.[26]

If indeed cancer was already known to be about its lethal business, was a diagnostician like Parsons likely to tell? Was the kindly Sam the sort of person to whom distressing, even scandalous, news could be entrusted? The family was headed up by several less than helpful figures. There was Robert as eldest son (but he had been away in Argentina until 1900); there was Sam as spiritual and medical adviser (he was also away and more apprehensive than authoritative); and there was the busy, conventional, reliable interloper Harry Stephens, perhaps never wholly trusted even by those who relied on him. Stephens's usefulness casts its own suspicion on the general absence of Ned Synge from accounts of Johnnie's illness; the second eldest son rarely features. Long a widow, ageing and soon to make her own pact with Elpis, Kathleen Synge still presided over a family which never released John Synge from its anxious care.

Less than a year after Sam's departure, John was back in the nursing home awaiting more surgery on his neck. Controversy over *The Playboy* certainly aggravated his general condition, not least because both his mother and sister mutely shared the hostile views of the rioters. Florence Ross, who was home on leave and staying at Silchester House, went with the family on holiday to Tomriland in Wicklow. Her enlightened and liberal attitude to the theatre, dancing and other unsaintly activities helped to mend matters in the household. In the event, Synge did not join the holiday party, but took independent accommodation at Lough

Bray Cottage from 28 June for a few weeks, setting himself up for the uneasy interlude with Molly.

Different parties give differing testimony to the state of Synge's health in 1907. For Yeats, a decidedly partisan commentator, the Irish public's rejection of his theatre's greatest play cruelly accelerated, if it did not actually cause, its author's death two years later. Harry Stephens, closer to the confidence of Synge's doctors than anyone else, tends to pinpoint Mrs Synge's death at the end of 1908 as the fatal prompt. Edward Stephens records that the English poet, John Masefield, saw in his friend 'a dying man clutching at life, and clutching most wildly at violent life, as the sick man does ...' – this was in response to Synge's showing him the poem, 'Danny', in London in early June 1907. To the nephew-biographer, the poem's relish of assault and battery was to be explained in quite other terms – 'John shared with his brothers ... a tough quality so much part of their nature that they employed it without modifying the quiet demeanour that was usual in their home.'[27] Here, surely, family traits are imposed rather than observed.

But the symptoms which gave rise to concern were unmistakable and their import inescapable. When Synge and Molly returned to Dublin on 4 August after their rural idyll, his health was undeniably poor. He thought that his glands were getting even larger. Asthma, a constant slight fever, and a nagging cough, further reduced his vitality. Plans for a trip to Brittany were quietly abandoned. Though Lebeau was greatly disappointed, he had often wondered why Synge was 'delaying over and over so much to get rid of those glands'.[28] Now, instead of taking the air in rural France, he entered the nursing home – by this date, officially known as Elpis – for a two-week period, 13–26 September. On the eve of surgery, his letter to Molly skittered between unconvincing optimism – 'I feel wonderfully gay!' – and exhortations of bravery – 'a certain amount of wretchedness is good for people when they're young – I wouldn't be half as nice as I am if I hadn't been through fire and water!!!' Six days after surgery, Molly had not yet seen him, while to Lady Gregory, Synge was prepared to admit that the operation had been 'a rather severe one as it turned out'. Yeats was still at Coole Park, in remote Galway. When he finally travelled to Dublin to see his fellow director, he was tickled by the rumour that, as Synge came out from under the ether, 'his first words, to the great delight of the doctor, who knows his plays, were, "May God damn the English, they can't even swear without vulgarity".'[29]

Edward Stephens's great dossier of fact and opinion gives the impression that this second operation, which took place in Lower Mount Street on Saturday 14 September 1907, went well. Facilities had been improved under Margaret Huxley's management, with the installation of a lift and a proper operating theatre. New techniques of anaesthesia reduced the delirium experienced ten years earlier, though Stephens was informed that his uncle 'heard voices saying that the operation had been successful'. (This might be deemed a piece of post-operational self-deception or an attempt by the surgeons to reassure the patient.) The following day Robert, the first family visitor, brought back a good report; after all, 'as the swelled glands that had occasioned the operation had been next the spot from which others had been removed and no second operation had been necessary for almost ten years, neither John nor his relations thought that the disorder ... might manifest itself in other parts.'[30]

Young Stephens called with a book and found his uncle in good spirits. Etiquette forbade Molly from visiting Synge in his hospital bed, but she went to see him on his return home. They spoke of their coming marriage and his plans for a new kind of play, based on myth rather than peasant life. But Lyons gives a quite different account of the prognosis before and after September 1907:

The diseased glands if viewed by an inexpert microscopist might appear as baffling as an abstract painting until the pleomorphic cellular infiltration was pointed to by a pathologist and explained as a disorderly assembly of cells, varied in size and shape, replacing the normal, stolid lymphocytes; an apparently purposeless usurpation by large cells with blistered nuclei, by pink eosinophils, by mononuclear cells with indented nuclei and by giant cells with many large nuclei ... a sinister, morbid extravaganza to delight some Des Esseintes of the laboratory for whom a plasma cell is no less beautiful than a topaz, who sees disease and distress objectively as the tax exacted by nature for the infinite wonders inherent in protoplasm, a dreadful excrescence governed by its own laws and periodicities.[31]

This lyric passage is not so much typical of J. B. Lyons's style of medical history as it is indicative of a mode of writing conventionally applied to the topic of the dead Synge – the high style. Yeats also favoured elaborate imagery in discussing his friend's mortality. The thing eluded direct representation, being as reticent as Synge himself. When he travelled to Kerry in October to consolidate his recuperation, asthma resumed its assault, robbing him of breath and speech. The cough which racked him at night arose from a chest in which the conditions later imagined by

Professor Lyons were already taking hold; it persisted. He persisted in smoking. Back unexpectedly soon in Kingstown, he was less depressed than might have been anticipated, having bought a rustic chair, the first item of furniture for the home he planned to set up with Molly – perhaps even before Christmas. On Sunday 27 October, his fiancée sat down for the first time for a Synge family meal.

Florence Ross was in Dublin in late October or early November. His niece, Ada, was also expected to visit, in lieu of her brother who was ill.[32] Synge was trying to work on *Deirdre*, avoiding unnecessary engagements and excursions. Nevertheless, on 12 November he attended a lecture at Alexandra College by Laurence Binyon (1869–1943) on oriental art, probably in the company of Edward Adderley Stopford.[33] A carefully nurtured belief that he was related to Lafcadio Hearn, through the Stephens family, provided a justification for his interest in Japanese culture. In his own paradoxical way, Synge had converted the west of Ireland into an orientalist theme, and now *Deirdre* was leading him to even stranger things.

Tumultuous 1907 was drawing to an inconclusive close. Synge's own health was parlous, Molly's a matter of concern at least to him. Financially *The Playboy* augured extremely well, especially as John Quinn in New York was to arrange a copyright edition of the plays and to buy the *Playboy* manuscript. Caution was still required in Dublin. When he spotted advertisements for relatively cheap housing in the *Irish Times*, he got Molly to respond: inquiries from an address such as Glendalough House would elicit no concessions or discounts. In the theatre, Synge thought it necessary to explain Molly's regular unpunctuality in a semi-formal letter to Yeats as co-director which ended with a plea for greater consultation in the company as a whole – 'I am all for more democracy *in details*.' When some swelling recurred in his neck, he arranged to see Parsons on 2 December, who made him nervous. But at a check-up on 21 December, 'The doctor says I'm all right' – or so he wrote to Molly.[34]

The year ended with a judicious letter to his cousin, Edward, in Surrey announcing his imminent marriage to Molly – who 'is both Papist and Protestant, having been baptised into both churches in her infancy' – but asking that the matter be regarded as confidential for the moment – 'it may come off very soon, but owing to my health and finances it is a little uncertain.'[35] Edward, who married a fellow artist named Moloney in 1908, was sympathetic. After the Christmas holiday, which the lovers spent separately in their respective homes, Molly took tea at Glendalough House with her future mother-in-law on 2 January 1908. The following day Synge reported five degrees of frost outside his window and berated her for not wearing warm enough clothes. His solicitude reads like transference.

First, her minor ailments and distresses are easier to bear than his increasing pains and tumours. So attention is concentrated on the former as a means of repressing a terror which might otherwise get out of hand. But, secondly and more particularly, there are occasions when the lover focuses his attention on her reproductive system – her periods or any irregularity which occurs. This pinpoints a transference of concern specifically on to the functioning of her reproductive system through which both of them might perpetuate themselves as parents. Such material is generally inferred rather than excavated in the letters, though on occasion it breaks the surface abruptly. More often, certain opacities in the letters are suddenly illuminated in this regard; having offered to advance money for warmer clothes, John postscripts urgently – 'Remember this is quite serious you know what will *happen* next week ...' [his emphasis].[36]

In the early months of 1908, 'the prospects of an early marriage grew darker' as Andrew Carpenter has aptly phrased it. Nevertheless, the couple decided on a flat at 47 York Road, Rathmines, in which to prepare a future home. As an indication of how readily Florence Ross accepted news of her childhood sweetheart's approaching marriage, she presented him with a double bed on indefinite loan. Other furnishings included the *sugán* chair bought in Kerry the previous autumn, and various items provided by Mrs Synge who took some consolation in the nearness of John's intended home. Rathmines, however, is much closer to the thirteen granite steps of Orwell Park than to Kingstown; Synge's plans were, if anything, to take him nearer to his childhood.[37] The move was effected on 23 January, with Edward Stephens acting as chief assistant.

Synge was due at the Abbey that night, and he proposed walking into Dublin. In Harcourt Street uncle and nephew decided to visit the new gallery sponsored by Sir Hugh Lane, Lady Gregory's nephew. The author of *The Playboy*, politely saluted by the doorman as a recognised celebrity, proceeded to tour the nineteen-year-old round the pictures, commenting particularly on Antonio Mancini's portraits. Yeats, in 'The Municipal Gallery Revisited', later incorporated the high praise Edward Stephens is likely to have been the first to hear:

Mancini's portrait of Augusta Gregory,
'Greatest since Rembrandt,' according to John Synge;
A great ebullient portrait certainly;
But where is the brush that could show anything
Of all that pride and that humility?
And I am in despair that time may bring
Approved patterns of women or of men
But not that selfsame excellence again.[38]

Time was already inducing despair, less grandly than the poet was to suggest thirty years later. Two days after her son had left home, Mrs Synge recorded in her diary how she had consulted two doctors who agreed that she required further examination, and how she had written to inform Sam and Robert. Johnnie would be told when he next called in. He was busy with theatre problems, he was trying to entertain one of the Von Eickens who had travelled from Germany at the end of 1907. (Molly was inclined to be jealous though the visitor was near fifty.) He was able to joke with Yeats about astrological interference with his hot-water bottle, causing it to burst. He rebutted Stephen MacKenna's satirical comments on his new lodgings – 'you will be opening a bank-account at the Bank of Ireland one of these days . . . you will join the Y.M.C.A.; there is danger in RATHMINES . . .'[39]

Several months later, after Mrs Synge had undergone a medical ordeal of her own, Synge was making one of his regular visits to Glendalough House:

When she went out to meet him at the door she was shocked by his pallor . . . After lunch, she took John up to her bedroom and there he told her the news that he had held back in order to save her for as long as was possible from distress and anxiety. He had been growing steadily worse, and lying awake until three in the morning with pains in his stomach and back. He had been twice to Dr Parsons, but his mother said he had borne the pain too long in a lonely lodging with no proper food. John said that the doctor had found a small lump in his side . . .[40]

So, on 30 April 1908, Synge again entered Elpis for what was *not* to be the last time. At the beginning of the month, he had received a cheque from Fred Sutton & Co. (Harry Stephens's firm of solicitors) enclosing cheques for £819 14s 7d, deriving from his interest in Nos. 53 and 54 Upper Mount Street. With £800 of this described as principal – the interest was paid late – it would appear that Synge was realising this asset. Harry advised placing the money on deposit, as if his brother-in-law was preparing for major expenditure in due course – marriage, surgery, travel, death.[41] A hasty note to Molly a few days before entering Elpis failed to disguise the fact that his illness was now discussed at the Abbey – 'Dont be uneasy about me. Henderson told *me* about six times that I had a tumour, but he knows about as much about it as a tom cat.'[42] On 4 May – the day before Charles Ball was due to operate – Synge wrote to Yeats about his 'papers' – the mocking quotation marks are his own. He was concerned about what might happen 'under the operation or after it'. Early 'stuff' should not get into print. But, he went on contradictorily, he did not want his 'bad things printed rashly – especially a morbid thing about a mad fiddler in Paris' which he hated. This left open the possibility of printing these things in a way which was not rash, and also confirmed his preservation of the 'Etude morbide', the pseudo-diary of the man who believes himself to suffer from a disease 'he is really without'.[43] Illness, and the fear of it, went back ten years or more in Synge's case; he preserved the literary evidence of it, and did not wholly prohibit publication.

On the same day, he also wrote two letters to Molly. In one, he asked her to visit him at four in the afternoon; the other (hardly longer) reads in its entirety:

My Dearest Love,
This is a mere line for you, my poor child, in case anything goes wrong with me tomorrow, to bid you good-bye and ask you to be brave and good, and not to forget the good times we've had and the beautiful things we've seen togethe[r]
Your old Friend.[44]

The first went straight to his fiancée, the second was directed to the Abbey, 'to be sent in cover in case of death'. Perhaps the latter can be read as the deeply-thought resolve of a man keen to minimise the pain his death would give; perhaps, however, it may alternately be read as revealing the gaps between youth and age, relative ignorance and all-too-personally-felt experience, even between dearest love and old friendship. Eloquence and truthfulness could scarcely harmonise in these circumstances, but somehow both appear to be in short measure, as if each were deferring to the claims of the other.

The surgeons' findings were equally depressing. The tumour was judged inoperable, yet Synge remained two months in Elpis, finally

moving to his sister's house on 6 July. Molly had packed up his things in
the York Road flat as early as 25 May, partly because Mrs Synge was bound
for Wicklow, and partly in acknowledgement that he would not be able
to look after himself. Meanwhile, he also remained in the dark as to his
precise condition. Or did he? To Molly he kept up a familiar tone of wary
cheerfulness, so that by mid-May he had assured her he was 'over the
worst' though obliged 'to stay very quiet indeed'.[45] She herself had been
ill. What with her complicated career in the theatre where he remained a
director even in his sickbed, conditions were very far from ideal for a full
exchange of confidences. Did she but know it, the second letter of 4 May
was stowed away not far from the green-room door where he had been
in the habit of waiting for her. Mrs Synge had written to Robert on 12
May frankly declaring that 'Ball had no hope of our dear boy's life . . . the
tumour or abscess is still there as it cannot be removed . . . He has no idea
he was in danger . . .'[46] She had been given the news confidentially by
Parsons on 5 May.

Yeats was in touch with Quinn in New York, expressing grave concern
about their friend's condition. During their correspondence, Arthur
Symons (who had encouraged both Synge and Joyce) suffered a complete
mental breakdown. Yeats could not be precise about the cause of Synge's
illness, and Quinn's belief that no one in such a condition should be asked
to run a theatre did not result in any clarifying specification of the trouble
borne by 'a man with a lurking disease in his system, or with the devilish
little disease germs conducting a combat battle with the healthy germs
. . .' On the positive side, George Roberts of Maunsel and Co. had travelled
to New York with a view to arranging publication of Synge's plays by
Dutton & Co.[47] By the following month, cancer had featured in New York
rumours of Synge's plight, some of these circulating through the Catholic
presbytery of St Brendan's parish. Quinn offered the patient in Elpis the
services of a stenographer so that *Deirdre* might be finished.[48] But then,
in September 1908, Symons's collapse in Bologna distracted both men
from the seemingly less urgent case of Synge. Symons had been sexually
precocious on a grand scale, and the worst was feared. 'Too much woman,
I suppose,' mused Quinn a day or two before Christmas.[49]

Staying at Silchester House in July, Synge had been able to entertain
Molly at his sister's invitation. She travelled out on Friday afternoon, 10
July 1908, despite her back troubles and medical appointments. He affably
acknowledged that she had been 'so good' during the visit, but he could
not get round to writing 'a particularly intimate and tender note' because
of the pressure of business correspondence. What he did write was to say

that she could be 'very nice – when you like'. While Annie was agreeable in letting Molly visit, the prospect of a tennis party required him to disappear from view – unless the weather spoiled everything. He was unable to walk further than the path which led from the back of the Stephens's garden, round the parish church next door, and in by the front drive. Florence called, on her way to Greystones. Pains and aches alarmed and annoyed him. Molly continued to attend Dr Barry, with Mabel Dickinson (born 1875), a 'medical gymnast and masseuse' but also Yeats's mistress, for company. To Quinn, Synge conceded that 'a heavy illness, and two months confinement make a curious break in one's life', this perhaps a more realistic acknowledgement of how things stood than the melancholia he turned on and off for Molly. From San Francisco, Agnes Tobin had inquired about his health, progress on *Deirdre*, and about a 'Miracle Play' which eludes identification. Summer dragged on, he grew weary of 'this perpetual garden' and 'got a hankering to go up and stay a couple of weeks at Lough Bray' – a wholly impractical undertaking.[50]

The nursing home and surgeon did not furnish accounts until the autumn, with Ball writing disingenuously that he was glad to hear the patient was 'so well. As requested I beg to name a fee of 55 guineas.' The Elpis account for sixty-six days' residence, the exploratory operation, and many newspapers, came to £37 6s 6d. Acknowledging receipt of payment on 5 October, Huxley joined with Ball in perpetuating a deception – 'I am very pleased to hear you have made steady progress towards recovery & hope your foreign travels will be of great help to you.'[51] On the same day, Stopford wrote inviting him to lunch, but the card had to be forwarded to Oberwerth.

Synge maintained an unofficial and highly unorthodox line of communication with the medical world: correspondence with one of the nurses who took care of him in 1908. Apart from the robust cordiality of her advice to him – 'you want a good shaking & indeed I would enjoy giving it to you' – what remains significant is the woman's playfully variable signatures in writing to her former patient. She is 'The little black dot' or 'Dot', or even on one risqué occasion 'Molly'. These tributes to Synge's success in making friends across boundaries of class, professional etiquette and gender, were not wholly concealed from the small band of inmates in Elpis. One postcard sent from London, and signed 'D–t', was addressed to Synge in Elpis just a few days before his death: the picture was of a snarling kitten, with the Suffragette slogan below, 'I Want My Vote'.[52]

But death had chosen to harvest the Synges, mother and son, in the natural order of sowing. Kathleen Synge had been only in her early thirties when Johnnie was born in 1871; in widowhood she was remarkable in her fortitude and robustness of soul and body. By the beginning of 1908, however, she was approaching seventy, and her health had begun to fail. She reluctantly acknowledged Molly Allgood as her youngest son's fiancée, perhaps consoling herself that, even in allying himself to a Roman Catholic, he was likely to find some domestic stability for the years following her death. The acceptance of another woman as part of John's emotional world coincided unhappily with a realisation of her own mortality. At the end of January, Dr Beatty took a serious view of the swelling in Mrs Synge's groin. The necessary operation was performed in Elpis, after some days' delay in finding a room; doubtless her son-in-law's influence speeded up the process. Edward Stephens records that, many years later, he was told that his grandmother's illness was 'in some ways similar to that from which John was suffering' – both had forms of cancer.[53]

She made plans for another summer holiday at humble Tomriland. Victorian families were far less disposed to discuss ill-health with outsiders than the survivors of the Great War and the beneficiaries of subsequent medical advance. This was especially true of cancer victims; Gogarty, according to Yeats, believed that Synge's family were kept in the dark as to the nature of his illness – 'they do that because people would fear it as hereditary.'[54] The Synges were prone positively to assume each other's well-being in their silence. This did not prevent Mrs Synge on one occasion from relaying a message about heavy menstrual bleeding to Molly Allgood through her son.[55] 'Exogamous' medical conditions could be mentioned with a startling lack of embarrassment. It was when illness seemed to 'run in the family' that a complex of hereditarian anxieties – some medical, some economic – might be provoked into activity.

The correlation of disease in parent and child recalled their shared frailty in the days immediately following Johnnie's birth. And those days had been darkened further by the sudden death of John Hatch Synge a few days before the son's first birthday, prompting the young Synge to write in the privacy of his notebooks:

Without knowing, or, as far as I can remember, hearing anything about doctrines of heredity I surmised that unhealthy parents should have unhealthy children ... Therefore, I said, I am unhealthy, and if I marry I will have unhealthy children ... so I will never marry.[56]

Claiming that he was 'between thirteen and fifteen' when he came to this conclusion, Synge in effect dates it to the onset of puberty. His fastidious avoidance of the word 'fourteen', however, and his fussy distinction between what he knew and what he heard (and an equally odd qualifying of what he didn't know or hear with the phrase 'as far as I can remember') might be taken as evidence of an anxious protection of the exact circumstances in which he linked his 'unhealthy' father to his own oath of celibacy. Now, as he prepared for marriage, his surviving parent was to succumb to a disease very similar in its major symptoms to his own illness. On 11 September, Doctors Beatty and Wright conferred in Glendalough House and confirmed the seriousness of her condition. Nevertheless, in the first week of October 1908, Synge departed rather suddenly for a four-week trip to Germany, on the pretext that to see the Von Eickens would 'set him up' for the winter.

Before setting out, he had handed over a manuscript collection of poems to Yeats, including one very recent piece inspired by a conversation with Molly. In it, he anticipated an unattended funeral, but rearranged the roles to be played by the chief actors in his personal drama:

> I asked if I got sick and died would you
> With my black funeral go walking too,
> If you'd stand close to hear them talk and pray
> While I'm let down in that steep bank of clay.
> And, No, you said, for if you saw a crew
> Of living idiots, pressing round that new
> Oak-Coffin – they alive, I dead beneath
> That board – you'd rave and rend them with your teeth.[57]

Communicating this tough-minded poem to his fiancée on Friday 2 October, in a letter which also listed his recent medical expenses, Synge still expected to see her in Dublin within a few days. On 6 October, however, he took the SS Leinster to Holyhead on the first leg of a tiring journey through London to the Continent.

Indigent as ever, he had made no advance booking, and three hotels turned him away before he succeeded in putting up for the first night in a boarding house. Next day he divided his time between sitting on a chair in Hyde Park and taking refreshment in an Express Tea Shop he and Molly had used the previous year. The price of a stamp worried him. Due to leave by train at 8.35 p.m., Synge's last day in the imperial capital was one of petty anxieties.[58] The guest-house at Oberwerth offered refuge and strength.

At first Annie Stephens kept her brother informed of their mother's condition, while Molly and he exchanged tiffy letters in the best lovers' tradition. He was pleased to be back with the Von Eicken sisters, though he noted with some exaggeration that they were getting old – 'Gorse', the youngest, was about forty-five. He walked the streets, wrapped in a greatcoat and carrying a stick out of necessity. Much of the time he sat exhausted near the river taking some pleasure from the endless life of boats. 'Now a big tug with two funnels is coming up & towing a string of <big> barges ... nearly a quarter of a mile long – two little fellows with mops are leaning over the edge of the tug washing her sides.' When the weather relented, he sat under the acacia trees, or on the Von Eicken balcony. Gossip helped, but not much. The eight sisters had heard from a Dublin friend, a Mrs Vanston, that he was engaged to an actress. So he swore to Molly, 'I'll never go abroad again without you, Nish!'[59]

In Dublin, Molly was prepared to visit her future mother-in-law in the nursing home, but Synge advised her that the time for such visits had passed – 'she is so ill I dont [sic] suppose they would even tell her you'd been there.'[60] Her decline and death were marked by progressive exhaustion, though a congenital skin disease, asthma, and chronic diar-rhoea are the officially recorded causes of death. What, one might wonder, did Synge think of his own absence at this juncture? On the evening before adding this advice, he had begun what he hoped would be a long cheerful letter to Molly, only to have its mood shattered the following day. News that Kathleen Synge had died at home reached him by telegram on Monday 26 October.[61] Robert informed him that the funeral would take place the following Thursday adding, however, 'dont come unless strong enough for journey'.[62] Synge evidently replied promptly and in some detail, for his brother sent a second telegram: 'you ought not to come[.] in that case funeral wednesday'. But no alterations to the burial plans were made, and Kathleen was interred in Mount Jerome on 29 October.

In the event, her youngest son stayed on in Koblenz for a week, missing the interment by ten days. Either Sir Robert Matheson or his son Robert (or both) was among the attendance and it is difficult to believe that Cherrie, though married in South Africa, did not send her condolences.[63] In less than six months, John Synge would join his mother in the same suburban limited-liability burial-ground, far from the landed estates and the parish churchyards. No 'ancestor was rector there/Long years ago.'[64]

Given that advice on visiting Elpis was redundant, Synge's response was to bring the two women in his life directly together in his mind, expressing sorrow at his fiancée's absence now that he had only her to live for. His mother, he thought, was '73 or 74' – family records suggest that she was in fact several years younger, and the registration of her death specified sixty-eight. In keeping with this image of her, he recalled her as less than robust yet desiring that she 'would rather die with all her faculties still clear than drag on into real old age'.[65] Molly naturally wrote in return to console him, but her 'little letter' which was 'an inexpressible comfort' to him has disappeared with all her side of their correspondence.

Synge certainly thought a good deal about his mother before he finally left Koblenz on 5 November. He tried to think happily about her 'as ... she would have wished'. At some point on his journey home, 'the sun rose over low boggy tracts and arms of sea' and he resolved that he and Molly in their life together 'must often get up early and see the sun rise'.[66] Low spirits and plans for the future, the dead mother and the wilful beloved alternated in his thoughts. The courageous bereaved mother of *Riders to the Sea* and the self-liberating wife of *In the Shadow of the Glen* are eclipsed in these moments of melancholy. Some apprehension of his literary friends' condescending attitude breaks through. 'People like Yeats who sneer at old fashioned goodness and steadiness in women seem to want to rob the world of what is most sacred in it. I cannot tell you how unspeakably sacred her memory seems to me.' Sacred was not a word Kathleen Synge would have tolerated in casual use, as her son well knew in choosing to repeat it in these tributes to her. Her death following treatment in the nursing home in which he himself had often been treated, and for a disease (as he must have known by this time) so close to his own, struck his being with a deadly impact. 'It makes me rage when I think of the people who go on as if art and literature and writing were the first things in the world. There is nothing so great and sacred as what is most simple in life.' Here Synge comes close to a renunciation of the Muse in favour of Molly as substitute Mother. 'I hope you'll be as good to me as she was ...'[67]

The day after he set out from Germany, Ned wrote to Robert in terms which starkly record the parlous state of their youngest brother's finances. They agreed that he should live on in what had been their mother's house, with a servant Bridget housekeeping under Annie Stephens's supervision. Provisions would continue to be bought from the same shops used by Mrs Synge, that is, on credit: at the end of the month, it was proposed, 'if J. has no funds', Ned would foot the bills out of the balance of £50 which

Robert had advanced for his mother's needs. There is no mention of Molly or marriage.[68] But down at Greystones, Aunt Harriet (Mrs Dobbs, Kathleen's sister) wrote inviting Synge and his 'friend' to visit, but making clear her limited emotional commitment to Molly – 'Your dear Mother was glad to have her out to see her, and you, and for her sake, and for your sake, I would like to be friendly with her.'[69]

Meanwhile, the lawyers were losing no time. Within two days of his arrival at Glendalough House where his mother had died and where he must struggle to live – 'very dreary coming back to this empty house' – Annie Stephens told him about his expectations under the will. He was to get a £1,500 share (at 5 per cent) out of the property, together with whatever in the way of 'carpets, saucepans [,] linen etc etc' he might need in due course for his married quarters. His own death threw its shadow back on to the letter in which he reported his inheritance to Molly – 'The £1500 is I think really mine, not for my life only, so I will have that to leave you.' And he continued in a grammatical tense which almost accelerates into his own death – 'Otherwise I should have had to save closely.'[70] By 17 November, he had 'belly-ache' . . . and rheumatism in both back and neck.

The diagnosis of Hodgkin's disease (defined by Thomas Hodgkin in 1832) may have been made as early as 1897; certainly it was clear to Gogarty ten years later in August 1907 when he advised Synge in the street to have his swollen glands removed. Uncertainty as to the precise date of diagnosis is complicated by the codes of decorum practised by doctors in the late Victorian period. According to J. B. Lyons, Synge was sympathetically deceived by Doctors Beatty and Ball. 'Their patient had no dependents, no fortune to dispose of, no major responsibility to burden him. He might remain well for a decade.'[71] If this accorded with the time-honoured maxim, *Guérir quelquefois, soulager souvent, mais conforter toujours* [To heal sometimes, to soothe often, but always to comfort], the maxim did not accord with the spirit of Synge's plays. From the almost forensic counting of stitches in *Riders to the Sea* through to Deirdre's impulsive joining her lover in the grave, the drama celebrates a decisive confrontation with grim reality.

Intelligent, the brother of a qualified doctor, the brother-in-law of a partner in Elpis Nursing Home, was Synge on the topic of his illness what the French call *complaisant*? Did he prefer to be kept in ignorance of his actual condition, despite the recurrence of disturbing symptoms? The sexual register of the French adjective is apt, for Synge explicitly linked his illness – whatever it might be – to questions of marriage and procreation.

While anxiety at the onset of puberty is common enough, Synge had recorded that, between the ages of thirteen and fifteen, he explicitly associated his condition with his dead father. (Quite when he engaged in the act of recording is difficult to estimate, and so the claim of a teenage crisis remains vague.) The youngest son of a father who died more or less unseen was prone to fear that what racked his own young body had earlier destroyed its progenitor. The anxiety finds literary expression at an early stage. The close rewriting of inherited syphilis as a heliotropically approved marriage, which constitutes his reading of Ibsen in *When the Moon Has Set*, clearly indicates that the theme preoccupied the dramatist, if not the ordinary man who sat down to breakfast. And *When the Moon Has Set* continued to preoccupy Synge long after its aesthetic weakness was evident to all.

There is, then, this possibility to contend with – that John Synge avoided a decisive confrontation with his diseased body because it might have transformed itself into a family scandal. The theory requires the indulgence of many fantasies – that, for example, John Hatch Synge did not die of smallpox as duly certified but of something less mentionable, that young Synge's doctors and his brother-in-law colluded in concealing a morally reprehensible diagnosis rather than a merely fatal one, that the clumsy excisions inflicted by Stephen MacKenna on his friend's letters did indeed conceal a scandal and not just a sensitivity. But the theory is also backed up by some undeniable factors – Synge's mature recording of his teenage oath of celibacy, and his unchallenged reputation for sexual restraint. If Sam, as his daughter-in-law has suggested, chose to write for publication those innocuous *Letters to My Daughter* because 'he was a scientist and wished to dispel speculation & rumours', what, *circa* 1930, could these rumours of the dead Synge have been?[72] Did they echo some fear expressed unguardedly by the dramatist himself, albeit in contradiction of the facts?

In Paris, as he had explained with some amusement to the saintly Cherrie Matheson, he was regarded as a saint. The question is – did he ever have sexual intercourse with Molly? For if he did, then we must assume that he had reassured himself on the issue of inherited venereal infection. In this particular light, his relationship with Molly falls into two phases – before and after the death of Kathleen Synge. His mother's death from cancer left him only five months of life, during which the impossibility of marriage, like the impossibility of completing *Deirdre*, gradually bore in upon him. His own weakness of body, intensifying almost daily in its pervasive agony and distress, must be acknowledged as the major cause. But, read more systematically within the family context, the death of Kathleen from a cancer akin to that which was killing him, reawakened the issue of unhealthy parents and offspring who should not marry.

Before contemplating the downward spiral of pain, courage, despair and oblivion which it was Synge's wretched fate to enter for the long months and weeks following his mother's death, we should confront an issue seemingly ignored by other biographers. Were John and Molly both virgin lovers? The record of his jealousy and her provocative behaviour has already been established, in which differences of age, class, and religious background have been recognised as obstacles to a spontaneous relationship. When they met in 1905, he was thirty-four or -five; she was nineteen, legally a minor, whose father was dead. Early chroniclers of their romance were obliged by decorum – itself deriving from the close family ties linking Edward Stephens to his subject – from speculating on the question of sexual consummation. Free in this regard, David Kiely describes the two as 'passionate lovers', draws attention to the way in which John and Molly contrived to spend part of the summer of 1907 in cottages less than a mile apart in Glencree, a pleasant valley in north County Wicklow. But he declines to discuss whether Synge ever knew Molly in the biblical sense.

The issue is probably undecidable at this remove. But the components of a decision can be briefly listed. Nothing we know of Synge's earlier life proves that he had lost his virginity. Nothing of his fears about Molly's admirers crystallises as an accusation of infidelity on her part during their love-affair, though his fears persisted. When he died, she was twenty-one, an age at which even an actress – immoral profession though it was in the eyes of many – might yet retain her virginity. Within two years of his death, she married an English critic and went on to bear him two children. Molly most times behaved in a manner which suggested that she felt positively about married life. On the other hand Synge, after his mother's death, did not press that they should take their engagement to the logical point of marriage which would have legitimised any sexual consummation. Synge's solicitude on the issue of Molly's late periods is also consistent with a knowledge that he (at least) had done nothing which might interrupt her menstruation. Gogarty, who was himself a patient in Elpis late in 1908, characterised Synge by obscurely alluding to 'impotence of fancied power'.[73]

After the autumn of 1908, his physical capacity for such a consummation may have been in rapid decline while, ironically, the death of his mother eased the financial and social difficulties involved in marriage. There is no logical reason to see any such sexual decline as causally linked to Kathleen Synge, yet psychologically he did tend to reassign certain emotional roles in his life from her to Molly in a manner which cannot have advanced the prospect of consummated marriage. If his mother's death had suggested renewed caution in the matter of an unhealthy child's subsequent marriage, then Synge's failure to fulfil his promise to Molly is explained. Though he possessed all the formal requirements for making her his bride – freedom from parental interference, a small but adequate income, and a genuine and intense concern for her well-being and reputation, the fact remains that John Synge did *not* marry Molly Allgood in the several months remaining to him after his mother's death.

CHAPTER 22

Ulster Will Fight!

In and out of the dreary trenches
Trudging cheerily under the stars
I make for myself little poems
Delicate as a flock of doves.

Richard Aldington[1]

The accelerated one-sidedness of Synge's dialogues with Hope converged with his work on a play which looks back to his own earliest attempts at drama, while it also confronts the inevitable ending of his own life. Of all the plays, *Deirdre of the Sorrows* is the easiest to place in biographical terms. Incompletely revised at the time of his death, it reflects not only a Yeatsian theatrical idiom but also the day-to-day intimacies of Synge's engagement to Molly, for whom he was writing the title role. These factors liberate the play from the secretive processes which had led to *Riders* or even *The Playboy.* Synge was not only writing for the Abbey – which had not been in existence during his apprenticeship – he was a director of the Company whose players he knew thoroughly, employing mythic materials with which they were familiar from their work with Yeats.

Synge had struggled with the tale of the Children of Lir while still an undergraduate. In Aran in 1900 (or possibly 1901), he turned to translating the tale of the Sons of Uisneach; fifty-seven leaves survive of this first encounter with the source of the *Deirdre* plot.[2] For in its Gaelic original form, the story of Deirdre's fatal love for Naisi was (like the Children of Lir) a prose epic, not drama. It had been rhymed by the eminent Victorian, Samuel Ferguson, in a version recently classified as a subtle exercise in political ecumenics, reconciling the warring parties of olden times as an example to the factions of the nineteenth century. Like Russell (in 1901) and Yeats (1906), Synge was concerned to render the story in a fully dramatic form.[3] *Deirdre of the Sorrows* was the great undertaking after *The Playboy,* and also a major change of direction. He was at work by 5 September 1907; typescripts, for a formal reading if not for trial rehearsal, were prepared in November 1907.[4] The identification of its theme with his dying months is generally true, but a reconsideration of the point at which his life began its decline has already indicated that *The Playboy* itself lies on the graveside of a rising and falling arc.

Deirdre has continued to give lovers of Synge's drama considerable difficulties. For some, the unfinished play constitutes an experiment beyond the 'peasant dramas', a bold move cruelly frustrated by the author's death. An alternative explanation locates the play's origins in the same condition which gave rise to his death. Sympathetic critics have hedged their bets. Prior to the publication of *When the Moon Has Set*, the contrast between *Deirdre* and its known predecessors in the canon encouraged such an isolation of the last play. But Synge's first full-length play contains much that recurs in his last.[5] The notion of progression, steady or otherwise, is not adequate to the facts of Synge's writing life as we know them. In several ways, *Deirdre* marks a reversion, in style, in substance, and in its larger orientation.

It would be easy to list features adapted, consciously or otherwise, from *When the Moon Has Set*. Foremost is the invocation of sun and moon in the solemnised union of two lovers – Eileen and Colm at the end of the early play, Deirdre and Naisi in the opening act of the last. That the common source can probably be assigned to *The Golden Bough* does little to diminish the significance of Synge's return to the theme.[6] But whereas the earlier play finally displaces the beliefs inherited by Colm and diligently practised by Sister Eileen, in *Deirdre* the declaration which weds the lovers – 'By the sun and moon and the whole earth' – is presented as veritably the orthodox creed of that remote period.[7]

Veritably, but not wholly. Employing an idiom modified from the successful plays, Synge has his saga-folk ejaculate, 'The gods help the lot of us . . .' or 'The gods save you, Deirdre'.[8] These phrases are recognisable adaptations of late-nineteenth-century Hiberno-English, and the concentration of them in the first act may have been intended to reassure audiences that the idiom of Martin Doul and Christy Mahon had not been lost in Synge's recourse to a pre-Christian Ireland. By the same token, however, they undermine any notion of sun- and moon-worship as the natural orthodoxy of Conchubor's court. They are only pluralistic reformulations of a familiar Christian vocabulary. The language of *Deirdre*, like that of the early play, is riven by religious friction.

Synge was well aware of the difficulties thrown up by attempts to write historical fiction or drama. 'Now it is impossible to use our own language or feeling with perfect sincerity for personages we know to have been different from ourselves.' Having coolly approved Walter Scott's novels of the Scottish wars, he proceeded without ceremony to dismiss other work from the same hand – 'any one who is familiar with Elizabethan writings will not tolerate Kenilworth ... To us now *as readers* the old literature itself is so priceless we look with disgust at imitations of it.'[9] Does this draft essay of March 1907 – written two months after the *Playboy* riots – prophetically condemn the play with which Synge sought to move beyond his great achievement?

In his own critical opinion, he acknowledged the present as in itself historically conditioned. Even if 'the soul of the people' is not conceptually rigorous, it is clear that he is averting to the oral traditions of Jacobite sentiment and activity as providing a sustained and sustaining continuum, in contrast to the boundary line which divides Spenser and Sidney from Walter Scott and Harrison Ainsworth. These reflections are highly relevant to *Deirdre*, a play whose heroine has been tutored to regard her fate, not just as something which is conditioned by prophecy but which is determined by it. Prophecy, we might remember, had figured prominently in the early deliberations of the Brethren at Powerscourt and retained its place in Mrs Synge's interpretations of the Bible. When Synge translated Andrew Mac Curtin's Gaelic text of *The Fate of the Children of Uisneach*, he discovered the fatal prediction of Deirdre's impact on Naisi and his brothers already in place. When he came to write the play, his preferred verb was neither 'prophesied' nor 'predicted', but 'foretold'. The king inquires of an old retainer, 'Does she know the troubles are foretold?' The answer would suggest that the young woman has paid little heed to such matters. A few moments later, however, when Deirdre introduces herself to Naisi, she pointedly asks him, 'Do many know what is foretold, that Deirdre will be the ruin of the Sons of Usna, and have a little grave by herself, and a story will be told forever?' The self-dramatisation, neatly effected in her use of her own name and in the inverting and projection of 'foretold' as 'told forever', promptly indicates that this is a tragedy of self-fulfilling prophecy. Deirdre exists under two kinds of compulsion – that an aged king is determined to 'have' her, and that she features in a predicted catastrophe for the Sons of Usna. Opting for the second, she not only acts to substantiate the prediction but also to engross herself in the final killings. Her decision to flee with Naisi to Alban is thus less an escape from Conchubor's rheumatic embrace and more a fusion of choice and fatalism, action and inertia. In this sense, the larger plot fits the odd discrepancies of idiom and the more sinister divergences of religious invocation. Deirdre's is to be a modern tragedy, despite the brocade and the approximated Gaelic nomenclature. She is closer to Hardy's tragic women than to any other dramatic character in the Anglo-Irish repertoire.[10]

The story of Deirdre is part of the Ulster cycle of sagas, and one could no more relocate it in Wicklow than shift King Arthur to Cumberland. Synge's family connections in Ulster were a great deal less immediate than was the case with Glanmore Castle or even Aran. His brothers holidayed with Traill cousins in Antrim; Ned Synge had long sojourned in Cavan. Synge himself had paid brief visits to both Cavan and Donegal, fishing with his brother Bob in May 1905, for example.[11] Minor incidents of family lore hardly compared to the groundswell of social unrest in Ulster. For, in the months after the *Playboy* riots, a major dock strike occurred in Belfast, followed by a police mutiny. Rioting on the Falls Road in mid-August 1907 was suppressed by regular troops. All this occurred within a longer process of political upheaval, commencing at least as early as the resistance to Home Rule in 1886 and reaching a peak with the Solemn League and Covenant of 1912. Amid the Ulster turmoil of 1907, when Synge was working towards his last play, two publications might be noted – the papal decree, *Ne temere*, of 2 August, and the first instalment of Patrick Pearse's 'In First-Century Ireland' in *An Claidheamh Solais*. Writing *Deirdre*, Synge lived into the dawning of a new era, one in which sectarian and linguistic issues were to prove even more contentious than they had been in the past.

Ulster contributed distinctively to the cultural nationalism now best known through the southern-based initiatives of Pearse and the others who would be executed in 1916. Bulmer Hobson's *Brian of Banba* (1905) anticipated *Deirdre of the Sorrows* in a number of respects, but it was Hobson's founding of a local boys' organisation which provides the more important link with Synge's new preoccupations. Extended on a national scale in 1909 (the year of Synge's death) under the name, Na Fianna Eireann, the movement adapted some of the ideas underpinning Baden-Powell's scouts association (founded the previous year) to nationalist rather than imperialist goals. While B.-P. 'boy scouts' were trained in reconnaissance and the woods of Berkshire echoed to codes and calls later heard on the Western Front, Na Fianna moved more directly to train young Irishmen for conflict. The aligning of nature with human conflict – an indirect product of applied Darwinism – implied the eclipse of those civic virtues and institutions so sedulously built up throughout centuries of 'western civilisation'. The tightly-knit brotherhood of warriors who dedicate themselves to Deirdre may descend from the Ulster cycle. But the 'stranger fighters'[12] who oppose them realign the antique to contemporary Britain, Ireland and Germany.

Before 1907, the conventions regarding marriage between Protestants and Catholics had generally led to the sons of such marriages following the allegiance of the father, while daughters adhered to their mother's Church. *Ne temere* imposed strict obligations on the Catholic partner to ensure that all children were baptized Catholics and raised within that faith. For Molly Allgood and John Synge, the new rules compounded the difficulties arising from their differences in age, social standing, and professional activity. While Synge might be complacent about his future children's religious education – knowing they would have access to his own tolerance – his mother would scarcely applaud her next batch of grandchildren being spirited into the papist confessional. With *Ne temere* faintly audible in the background, *Deirdre of the Sorrows* moves away from the mythological past towards the contentious present.

A major change occurs between the courtship of Naisi and Deirdre and that of Christy and Pegeen in the previous play. *The Playboy of the Western World* certainly did not lack passion, but this had involved a slow-paced scene of declaration and response, rhythmically sensitive and controlled, matched later by a scene of violence and renunciation equally formal in its structure. Sexual beauty in *The Playboy* is engendered in figures of speech, imaginative projection, and the mirroring of one character's desire in another. Sexual beauty, in contrast, in *Deirdre* is preordained. In 1902, Yeats wrote of Deirdre as 'some mild modern housewife but for her prophetic vision'.[13] Here he mocked Ibsen but failed to persuade Gregory that Deirdre's children were integral to the story. One must note the striking childlessness of Synge's play also. The second act brings to an end a seven-year-long period which Naisi and Deirdre have passed blissfully in the woods of Alban. And just as the two plays differ in their conception of love, so do they differ in their representation of violence.

The undercurrent of violence, felt even in the play's evocation of arcadian security, parallels the absence of children: both speak of a truncated future, broken succession, and an end to human generation. Yeats touches on the theme when he notes that, in Gregory's prose version, 'women indeed, with their lamentations ... for fallen roof trees and lost wealth, give the stories their most beautiful sentences'.[14] The roof tree recurs in a poem of Yeats's addressed to the social revolution of Edwardian Ireland, 'Upon a House Shaken by the Land Agitation'. Lost wealth was a topic Synge had more right to than Yeats. Instead, Synge's play explores historical anachronism in a different connection.

In Act Two, Fergus says benignly enough to Deirdre, 'Let you come this day for there's no place but Ireland where the Gael can have peace always.' The propagation of a linguistic type – the Gael – as an entire cultural collectivity was to be a hallmark of Patrick Pearse's nationalism. At this level, we hear Synge responding to a new cultural argument, very different from the Celticist tonalities of *The Well of the Saints*. When other characters use such terms as Britain, Orion or Saxon, the play's hybrid nomenclature becomes obvious, for such English-language words are arranged side by side with Alban, Fedlimid, and Slieve Fuadh. Indeed, *Deirdre* is a difficult text to *speak*, for it inconsistently anglicises some Gaelic name-elements and preserves others more or less as they were found in the source material. In this connection, Synge's preoccupation with historical *fiction* in March 1907 deserves reconsideration; likewise his emphasis on the role of the *reader* in adjudicating between Elizabethan literature and its modern imitation. Did Synge – however briefly – consider writing a novel based on the Sons of Uisneach? Deeply attached as he now was to Molly, the obligation to write for the stage was absolute. In any case, the play echoes them in the relative ages of Conchubor and Deirdre, the self-dramatisation of the actress/heroine, childlessness, and the obsession with coming death.

Synge's expression of a critical opinion was a rare enough event. On his decision to use saga material for his last play, the draft of a letter to his friend MacKenna is highly revealing – 'I do not believe in the possibility of "a purely fantastic, unmodern, ideal, breezy, springdayish, Cuchulainoid National Theatre" . . .'[15] That was written in late January 1904, with Yeats's *The Shadowy Waters* in mind. If the initial presentation of Naisi and his brothers looks and sounds like a capitulation to the breezy Cuchulainoid stereotype, the blood-soaked conclusion serves to underline the play's deeply critical perspective.

Several early stage directions point up an insouciance which does not exclude threats of violence. Laughter had certainly been present in the source material, but in Synge's hands it takes on more sinister overtones. When Naisi enters the hut where Deirdre and Lavarcham are staying in the woods, he does so 'hilariously, shaking rain from his clothes'. When he drinks a toast, again he does so 'hilariously'. These unspoken signals do little to cancel the implication of the brothers' words when they demand entrance – 'Open the door, or we will burst it.'[16] Synge's insistence had fallen on difficult, even impossible, matters – on negotiations between our feelings and those of 'personages we know to have been different from ourselves'.[17] For the play cannot be taken as if it were some report miraculously despatched from the remote past, an e-mail from Emain; it is a point of multiple exchanges between versions of the past, rival conceptions of theatre, and conflicting political urgencies.

Writing at the end of the twentieth century, I find it difficult to read Conchubor's inquiry in Act One, 'Does she know the troubles are fore-told?' without consideration of the Troubles which have agitated Ulster for the last thirty years or more, troubles which (in the marital/sexual area) were exacerbated by the legacy of the papal decree.[18] Of course, the king's words are delivered in the compacted grammar of Synge's classic style. Rendered back into standard English, Conchubor's question would be 'Does she know the troubles which are foretold?' – with a clearer indication that it is the substance of the prediction which concerns him rather than its mere inscription in Deirdre's mind. In such details, Synge remains a highly political dramatist, though not perhaps of the persuasion generally attributed to him. The band of three, the Sons of Uisneach, rove through the woods of Slieve Fuadh in a way which cannot evade interpretation. It would be anachronistic to regard them as a trio of Provisional IRA in training – 'You're great boys taking a welcome where it isn't given ...'[19] But neither do they magically represent Iron Age inhab-itants of the island known now as Ireland.

Nevertheless, Deirdre articulates a prophetic future which also reports the firing of Conchubor's wooden halls:

I see the flames of Emain starting upward in the dark night, and because of me there will be weasels and wild cats crying on a lonely wall where there were queens and armies, and red gold, the way there will be a story told of a ruined city and a raving king and a woman will be young forever.[20]

This is the consequence of Deirdre's initial escape from Conchubor's oppressive insistence on marriage. Self-determined to undertake vol-untarily something which is pre-determined anyhow, she has greatly extended the scale of the catastrophe. But the cunning of Conchubor's digging a new grave behind a tent, together with the stagecraft of its alternate display and concealment, touches on more contemporary matters than saga and less local concerns than the Abbey Theatre's antique style. The closing moments of Verdi's *Rigoletto* (1851) and, even more to the point, the pervasive erotic treachery of Puccini's *Tosca* (1900) suggest that Synge's play was reaching out towards a more comprehensive under-standing of modern violence than its sources allowed.[21]

At the height of the fighting in Act Three, a soldier warns his king of the comprehensive disaster about to occur – 'Emain is in flames, Fergus has come back and is setting fire to the world. Come up Conchubor, or your state will be destroyed.'[22] The second sentence rightly translates the Gaelic noun 'domhan' as 'world' while managing also to convey the nuance of difference between the two words. Whereas 'domhan' can connote 'everything', 'all about you', 'the entire caboodle', the English phrase 'setting fire to the world' acquires in translation a more grandiose tonality, almost a cosmic range of reference. In contrast, the precision of 'your state will be destroyed' points up the anachronistic presence of so modern a political concept as the 'state' in a play set in the Iron Age. Some nationalist historians strove to legitimise the latter-day campaign for Irish independence by seeking to show that an earlier, unified nation had been destroyed by the Norman invasions of the eleventh century. Alice Stopford Green's *The Making of Ireland and its Undoing* (1908), which appeared while Synge was still working on *Deirdre*, was one of these.

These discords of phrasing, between 'setting fire to the world' and 'your state … destroyed', might be explained in terms of the play's unfinished status, blemishes which Synge, had he lived, would have removed. On the other hand, occurring in such close proximity to each other they cannot have gone unnoticed. It may be more helpful to see an intention to distinguish this new play from what had been Synge's expressed desire for *The Well of the Saints* – 'a monochrome painting, all in shades of one colour'.[23] He felt strongly that his main obstacle in pushing the play towards completion was the need for a grotesque dimension.

This he attempted by introducing a character named Owen into the second act, a spy who precipitously kills himself having revealed that Naisi had killed his (Owen's) father. Grotesque though some of this may succeed in being, the playwright remained thoroughly dissatisfied. Owen, who has suffered from pre-Christian asthma, joins the list of male characters in the play who resemble Synge himself in a detail undetectable to all but the initiated. As sinister prankster, as something close to a eunuch (in his address to Deirdre) and finally as impetuous suicide, he breaks up the heroic alignment inherited from the original source. Significant also is the divergence from a source-tale known to Synge, in which Deirdre kills herself by leaping from Eoghan/Owen's chariot.[24] If the latter issue is unlikely to excite theatregoers, it adds to the investment of private feeling in Owen. In an undeveloped way, he becomes in the playwright's dying hands what scholars of Greek tragedy call a *pharmakos*, or scapegoat.

Perhaps this is to pay too much attention to a character whose role had not been finalised when the pen slipped from the author's hand. But the instability of Owen also points up the instability of the individual self in a dramatis personae regimented according to corporative principles. It is not simply that Conchubor is identified with 'the state' of Ulster, and that Naisi, Ardan and Ainnle are members of what Victorian translators of the Ulster Cycle termed the Red Branch Knights; the drive towards identity in corporative membership is an active and accumulating motif, reaching its critical moment when the Sons of Usna are treacherously attacked by 'the strange fighters' in the wood. Here again, Synge's cultivation of a phrase which has not entirely been translated into English exemplifies another of those highly localised details in the dialogue where he creates a momentary effect of de-familiarisation.

Who are 'the strange fighters'? In terms of a reconstruction focused on a generalised historical retrospect, one might simply call them foreign mercenaries, a class of soldier not unknown in pre-modern Irish history. Synge, however, is not engaged in an amalgam of re-presentations for which such a gloss might be helpful. What is required is a linguistic rather than archaeological precision in analysing this detail. The linguistic difference between a fighter and a soldier or warrior lies in the difference between implied status and actual engagement. To fight is to fight some-body; grammatically, the verb is keen to move on from an intransitive to a transitive role, to get to grips, to force others to be fighters also, to effect a merger of identities by violence. Though Naisi was the first to use the term, Deirdre takes it up in her prophetic account of the world after the catastrophe. The fighters are a de-familiarised version of what the Red Branch had been, a professional troop pledged to a cause. In the early twentieth century, percipience in this regard orients the play not towards the Celtic past but towards a contemporary European phenomenon.

The coincidence of Synge's dying efforts to finish *Deirdre* with the foundation of British imperialist and Irish nationalist scout movements has already been noted. Far from suggesting Hobson's Fianna as any direct source for Synge's rival woodland brotherhoods, I would point to the relative autonomy of the political and literary discourses. The phe-nomenon certainly reached well beyond the British Isles, being best known through the German word, *Wandervogel,* figuratively used to describe hikers and nature-lovers but implicating a youth movement or *Bund* which will have the gravest political consequences. It is important not to confuse the early stages of such a movement with its pathological 'maturity', important also not to extrapolate giddily from an Irish dra-matic reference to a Germanic ideology.[25] In October 1908, the dying Synge found the 'inconceivably wonderful' Rhineland inspirational. There his breath sounded 'like a foghorn', and 'knocking about in the woods' promised to advance work on *Deirdre*.[26] These apprehensions of the artist and doomed invalid remain deeply personal. Nevertheless, it is hardly too much to say that Naisi's hilarity and threat to burst down Deirdre's door has given rise to a very modern phenomenon – we will encounter them as Auxiliaries, Irregulars, Specials; and then under other more up-to-date names.

But this is to run too far ahead. In 1899 the American satirist-cum-sociologist Thorstein Veblen published *The Theory of the Leisure Class* in which he related successive stages of Western civilisation and explored the interdependence of 'pecuniary' and 'predatory' employments or occupations. In a chapter called 'The Conservation of Archaic Traits', he observed (without bothering to cite argument or evidence) that 'the discipline of the pecuniary employments acts to conserve and to cultivate certain of the predatory aptitudes and the predatory animus.' Given the multiple ways in which Synge's play sets up temporary associations between his own condition and – successively – Conchubor, Naisi, Owen, and Naisi once more, and proceeds in an awareness of Molly as the actress for whom the part of Deirdre was written, then it would be careless to forget that his original intention was to call his play, 'The Sons of Usna'. While it would be crass to identify the brothers Naisi, Ardan and Ainnle with the Synge brothers, there is an argument to be heard in which that code (cautiously expressed) should be tested against Veblen's thesis.

Leaving aside Sam (committed to his long career in China), we have found Synge's brothers gratefully if somewhat shamefacedly established in the pecuniary employments. Where they might once have hoped for landed status in their own right, they had settled for lesser ways of reinserting themselves into the land system, albeit on a salaried basis. The case is straightforward with Ned Synge, the land agent; with Bob, we have to watch him return from the Argentinean ranches and commence his efforts to repossess Glanmore Castle as a personal retirement home. There is a shrewd comment in the Greene/Stephens biography – 'Robert Synge ... seems to have spent most of his life while in Ireland with a fishing rod in his hands'.[27] The leisure interests of the pecuniary class were sublimated predatory acts – fishing, hunting, shooting.

The modern anachronisms of *Deirdre of the Sorrows* do not stand in contrast with the idyllic seven years of 'throwing a line for salmon, or watching for the run of hares' in Alban.[28] These years have been neither an exile in the manner of Duke Senior's banishment to the Green World of Shakespeare's *As You Like It*, nor have they been a period of undifferentiated, fruitful love. On the contrary, so thoroughly vacant have they been that only the announcement of their end can be presented on-stage, together with ill-disguised endeavours to advance the action by returning all concerned forthwith to Ulster. Far from echoing the quasi-paradisal accounts of nature to be found in Early Irish poetry, in all their unreflective alleged directness, the details we gain of woodland and river are mere notations. If we were to define the general mood of those Alban years, perhaps *restless tedium* would serve as a summary term. Act Two of *Deirdre* is anxious to quit the domain of enforced leisure and routine endearment. There is an appetite for tragedy in the characters, which is unclassical, modern and, to an extent, sentimental.

In 'Science as a Vocation' (1918), Max Weber compares the world of antiquity with that of the late-nineteenth century. Modern pluralism is not peaceful coexistence, as liberals might wish to think. It is a Homeric battlefield in which 'different gods struggle with one and other, now and for all times to come. We live as did the ancients when their world was not disenchanted of its gods and demons, only we live in a different sense. As Hellenic man at times sacrificed to Aphrodite and at other times to Apollo, and, above all, as everybody sacrificed to the gods of his city, so do we still nowadays, only the bearing of man has been disenchanted and denuded of its mystical but inwardly genuine plasticity. Fate, and certainly not "science", holds sway over these gods and their struggles.'[29]

Though it does little to make the play more convincing on-stage, this perspective alters the questions we bring to it. The competing religious invocations now emerge as a compensating double substitution for the loss of that Christian faith which had – all too stiffly – upheld Sister Eileen for most of *When the Moon Has Set*. But the absence of this faith, the consequent devastation or desacralisation wreaked upon the world of nature and of human relations, is admitted in the peremptory bonding of Naisi and Deirdre, in the unrepresentableness of their barren sojourn in Alban, and (climactically) in the work of 'the strange fighters'.

Deirdre of the Sorrows is an epitaph and a prophecy. More than once the author inscribes his own fate into it. But the play succeeds in looking beyond Synge's own lifetime, into an era when his story is told for ever and where he is perennially young. This is the future we now inhabit, where 'heritage' has replaced history, and cultural life is timetabled according to launchings and commemorations. It has been, by the same token, an era of terrorism and manipulated fate, with a literary jargon of Terrible Beauty liberally deployed. Those who have argued that the Anglo-

Irish Renaissance was neglectful of Ulster, preferring to look west or south and to base itself in Dublin rather than Belfast, might find in a revived *Deirdre* evidence to the contrary. This was the play with which he was locked in battle, entering Elpis for the last time.

CHAPTER 23

'All Is Over. Huxley' (March 1909)

I have no religion. I am an Irish Protestant.

Oscar Wilde[1]

During the crisis of May 1908, Yeats had begun to write of Synge in the past tense, when referring to 'the death of his imagination'.[2] Other modes of vital activity were also in terminal decline. Sexual excitation would have been in abeyance for months due to general weakness. Even earlier, he had cancelled a holiday, being 'in a state of absolute physical weakness, and probably moral weakness, too'.[3] Yet he continued to live in the drab house where his mother had died, close to his sister and brother-in-law in all but understanding.

Synge was to be at once crowded and abandoned by loved ones in the final months of his trial. Bits of money came through but these were as wearisome as Lebeau's inquiries about work in Ireland.[4] When John Quinn in New York heard how gravely ill Synge had become, he was – according to the elder Yeats – 'like a raging lunatic', inveighing against the Yeatses, gentle George Russell and all of Ireland.[5] Synge's death was a defining experience for his generation and that of his immediate elders. Family, friends, and latter-day critics have identified in Synge an epitome of death – and yet also found it nigh impossible to characterise this death. To borrow a phrase from Rilke's haunting account of a moribund gentility, 'He was dying his own hard death'[6] – so exclusively his own that none could know it except as gossip.

As with Gogarty, the knowing doctor, Augusta Gregory and Yeats were under no illusion as to Synge's bodily state in mid-1908. A telegram from Yeats to Quinn near the end of May 1908 – 'No immediate danger, slightly better' – gave little comfort. George Roberts had confided that Yeats and Gregory were 'keeping the serious condition of Synge's illness quiet' but the lawyer could not deduce what their good reason might be. 'Anything may be a tumor, but if it is cancerous then it is bad.'[7] In June he suggested that the invalid might recover his spirits in New York, an invitation Synge frankly turned down – 'I'm afraid it would hardly be the thing for me.'[8]

On 2 February 1909, he entered Elpis for the last time. At some point in the preceding days, he had called on Stephen MacKenna and his wife to say goodbye; 'You will never see me again.' At least this is how Yeats subsequently recorded the matter. Maud Gonne had not realised Gregory had been 'dangerously ill', but 'I have a different impression about poor Synge'.[9] Synge himself had written to Molly on 1 February, conveying the impression of a man in need of rest and a few novels by George Eliot; he signed off as 'Your Old Tramp'. He was to write only one other, equally brief, letter – to Lolly Yeats at the Cuala Press about arrangements for his book of poems.[10] Molly visited almost daily, though an Abbey tour removed her from Dublin for a week in mid-February. Gregory was in Coole, recovering from a cerebral haemorrhage, and Yeats was running hither and thither. The family attended dutifully.

The final departure from Glendalough House had been watched in frightened awe by his nephew to whom the dying man said, in business-like fashion, that 'he would like to show me where he had left his papers'. Synge put a travelling rug on his shoulders for warmth when the two went upstairs to where he kept manuscripts and letters in an old painted wardrobe. These were turned over, transferred from hand to hand, laid aside for a last time. Robert arrived with a cab, and the brothers departed for Elpis, a hour's drive away on the edge of Georgian Dublin. Up to the last moment, there was talk of his staying in lodgings near the nursing home, presumably for economy's sake. Typescripts of the Wicklow and Kerry essays, together with the latest state of *Deirdre of the Sorrows*, were taken in the hope that the patient would be able to work.[11]

Installed in Elpis by mid-afternoon, Synge was now on the outer rim of life, facing the void. Two days later, his brother and sister began to pack up the contents of the house, paying off the maids and leaving only one older servant (Mary Tyndal) as a kind of caretaker. They had read the signs and saw no likelihood of their brother's return. By Saturday, Charles Ball had decided against surgery. A week later, on Saturday 13 February, Synge signed the will which Harry Stephens had drawn up on his implicit instructions. 'That evening he said farewell to Molly who was going with the other members of the Abbey company to Manchester to play for a week at the Gaiety Theatre.'[12] According to Stephens, the wonderful reception given to Synge's plays in Manchester was 'the greatest comfort' to him during the lonely week in Elpis when Molly was away.

The *Manchester Guardian* printed three enthusiastic reviews by Padraic Colum.

Several weeks of failing life remained. Molly resumed her daily visits, travelling out by tram from the theatre. At the beginning of March, Synge told Yeats that she had been compelled to see a doctor, so poor a housekeeper was Mrs Allgood. On 9 March, Molly was only allowed to stay for ten minutes. By St Patrick's Day, she could visit only on alternate days.[13] Yeats also called frequently. At the Abbey, Joseph Holloway was able to supplement their decorous accounts of the patient from a private source of his own. A Miss Kitty Clinch, known to Holloway's niece Eileen, was a patient in the next room to Synge; from her, he learned that the Catholic nurse in attendance prayed for her patient when she went to Mass. This spiritual thoughtfulness across formidable divides of opinion, feeling, and habit Synge discussed with a smile even in his mortal distress. On 10 March, two weeks before the end, Holloway knew there was no hope: 'the poor fellow' was suffering from what the inveterate first-nighter called 'internal causes'. The next day Eileen saw Synge in a corridor, pale and emaciated in his dressing gown; she only recognised him when he turned into the room she knew to be his.[14]

Yeats also had a spy in the camp, an invented Owen to match Synge's, or rather a minor enemy round whom he could concentrate his reflections on Synge's death, even though this involved a certain shuffling of dates in Yeats's memory. Maurice Joy (1884–1944) was a fool from Kerry who had acquired an English accent. But Yeats's animosity against Joy went beyond such limited follies: 'To be operated on at the same time as Synge struck one as sheer insolence.' Many people had inquired more earnestly about the younger man than about the author of *The Playboy*. Yeats could stand it no longer and burst out with, 'I hope he'll die . . .' Two weeks after Yeats mentioned this, Synge wrote the poem beginning 'I asked if I got sick and died . . .' Or so Yeats liked to believe, despite the obvious evidence that the poem was written for Molly.[15]

As Yeats relates the incident – suppressing Joy's name for greater contempt – it is stitched into the liturgical brocade of his response to the final crisis. He reported the grim facts of Synge's condition to Gregory down at Coole – 'the various lumps in his side' (6 March), 'looked very very ill' (8 March) – but he was also working on a quite different level of observation in which his friend's decaying body was less central than his own crystallising mind. To his lover Mabel Dickinson, he had confided as early as May 1908 that his attitude towards Synge might persuade her that he had 'no heart'. Yeats's cornucopia of emotions included a shrewd sense of his own ability to suppress emotion – or even to exploit it without further emotion.

Yeats had spent most of December 1908 in Paris, taking French lessons and seeing Maud Gonne. The journal which he commenced on his return opens with two addresses – Abbey Theatre Dublin and 18 Woburn Buildings, Euston Road, London' – as if to underline the lack of an Irish home base. It was not until 31 January 1909 that he mentioned Synge, having visited him at Glendalough House and found him ill. He was staying at the Nassau Hotel, and news of his friend's return to Elpis may not have reached him promptly. By 6 February – four days later – he could write of 'Synge dying at this moment'. Yet a poem ('A Friend's Illness') he was working on at the time refers to Gregory not Synge. The complex emotional bonds between the two older Abbey directors, with Gregory sometimes cast as a protective mother and sometimes as an undeclared lover, cut into the flesh of Yeats's natural concern for his younger associate.

He was preoccupied with the state of Irish public opinion – it was grossly 'excited into an active state of democratic envy and jealousy' – and he dwelt on the pervasiveness of 'ill-breeding' in thought, manners, and behaviour. A frequent companion during this period was one Edward Evans whose bible classes Yeats (however improbably) was attending. He also delved into his own pedigree to sketch a seventeenth-century coat of arms in his journal. Amid these emblematical distractions, Synge does not capture his attention until 5 March when Yeats received a progress report on *Deirdre*. Synge 'spoke of his work this winter doubtfully, thought it not very good, seemed only certain of his third Act'. Yeats declined to ask more questions for fear that he might be (accurately) detected in trying to establish whether 'another could complete his work if he died'. Silence fell on the question of Synge until 23 March when Molly Allgood reported that the home had ceased to give its patient food. He was about to die.[16]

At some point during these final days, Margaret Huxley sent for a minister of religion whom Synge consented to see. To judge by accounts of her own funeral many years later, her religious views were of a decidedly liberal kind, as befitted a niece of T. H. Huxley. Given Holloway's omission of a name, no Catholic priest can have been involved. Molly had sought frantically for a priest who would agree to say Mass for Synge's recovery – but in vain. In view of Edward Stephens's silence, we can conclude that Church of Ireland clergy from the parish of Glenageary were not involved.

It seems that Synge and his unknown clerical visitor spoke about 'the weather and such-like topics'.[17]

Robert saw him on Monday 22 March, two days before the end. His nephew, and loyal chronicler, saw him the following day. Stephens's account does indicate that Robert delegated that day's duties to him, notably to bring some champagne and a special corkscrew which Harry Stephens owned, allowing small quantities to be drained off for a feeble patient. The young man was shown to a new room – no. 31 instead of 29 – to which his uncle had been moved the same day, 'a sunny back room from which there was a view across house-tops to the hills'.[18] These were the hills of Johnnie Synge's childhood, visible from Newtown Little and the end of Orwell Park, the hills he learned to walk in, the hills which stretched down to Wicklow and the once ancestral estates where strange creeds had been nurtured.

I was shocked by the change in John's appearance since the last time I saw him but, as a student of twenty, I . . . did not fully understand how near he was to death. At first he was too weak to talk; but the nurse screwed the tap into the cork of the bottle I had brought and gave him some champagne, and then he seemed a little brighter. He asked me whether I had heard any blackbirds singing yet: I said that I had heard thrushes but had not heard any blackbirds. For a few minutes I chatted to him about home and college interests and left without understanding that I would not see him again.[19]

Others did see him before he died at 5.30 the next morning. There were nurses in attendance, and Margaret Huxley must be assumed to have been on the premises now that the end was so close. When her telegram – 'All is over. Huxley.' – was delivered to Silchester House on the morning of 24 March, Harry Stephens had not yet left for work in Dublin. The time, therefore, was probably not much after 8.00 a.m., suggesting that she had been on the spot to set matters in motion personally. Yet registration of the death did not occur until 15 April, when the cause was given as cancer of the bowel, '15 months certified'.[20]

At 8.00 a.m., a group from the Abbey arrived at Elpis to see the corpse. This included Molly who, at twenty-one, can scarcely have had any prior confrontation with death face to face. Body-washer and layer-out had worked without stint in the few hours available, but the ravages of advanced and extensive cancer could not be concealed. She had probably seen him the previous day, yet the dead man as object shocked her, as Holloway (who may have been present) recorded. Quite who else attended is unknown, though the delegation must have included other men and women, the women to support Molly and the men to make the whole grisly business acceptable to the nursing home.[21]

Stephens, who had taken in the telegram, cycled to Robert Synge's home (where he arrived at 9.00 a.m.), and then on to Edward's, by now certainly in residence. The eldest brother proceeded into Dublin, where he met the ever reliable Harry Stephens in his office, and then travelled out to the southern suburb of Harolds Cross where some members of the family had been buried in Mount Jerome, a large modern cemetery. Back in 1895 Aunt Jane had been interred in a multiple-burial grave – oddly, given that she was not married. On her legacy, Johnnie had set up for a while in Paris. But she had been even more generous in her lifetime to Sam, who had bought the grave in recognition of her funding of his education for holy orders. Now it was soon established that the sceptical dramatist should join her, rather than be taken to any of the traditional Synge burial grounds in Wicklow. Given that Sam was on the other side of the globe, no last-minute consultation can have taken place: evidently arrangements for the burial had been agreed in 1906 while the elder brothers were all at home.

Though 'the day was a stormy, "wuthering" day',[22] the two Stephens boys were sent next to Glendalough House where they found Mary Tyndal absorbed in preparations for receiving the body. Having known Johnnie since he was an infant, she now cleared 'a fine strong table' for the coffin; no slip-ups of the kind which add poignancy to Riders to the Sea were to be permitted. Letters remained unopened, including one with a cheque for 19s 1d, royalties on sales of The Well of the Saints.[23] The body was transported by Waller's undertaking firm from Elpis to Glendalough House late in the evening of Synge's death.

It had proved too late for Yeats and Synge to see each other. And when Yeats did learn of Synge's death, he noticed with a dry professional eye that Molly 'began repeating over & over "what shall I do, what shall I do," with the movement her body has in [The Gaol Gate]'.[24]

The brutal fact eluded comprehension. Synge's death occurred not so much within a chronology of events as within a composition of memories. The striking feature of Yeats's position vis-à-vis Synge is that the writing comes after the event, as a calculated configuration of the dead dramatist. The enterprise is launched punctually on 24 March:

Synge is dead. In the early morning he said to the nurse, 'It is no use fighting death any longer', and he turned over and died. I called at the Hospital this afternoon and asked the assistant matron if he knew he was dying. She answered, 'He may have known it for weeks, but he would not have said so to anyone. He would have no fuss. He was like that.' She added, with emotion in her voice, 'We were devoted to him.'[25]

The funeral took place on 26 March. Two further days passed before Yeats resumed his journal, with a confidence not evident before. 'On the morning when I heard of his death a heavy storm was blowing and I doubt not when he died that it had well begun.' Support for this mystic synchronising of natural disaster and human death took a mellower form: 'my sister Lolly said to my other sister at breakfast, "I think it will be all right with Synge, for last night I saw a galley struggling with a storm and then it shot into calm and bright sunlight and I heard the keel grate on the shore." ' In recollection, Yeats emphasised Synge's disciplined personality – 'almost as proud of his old blood as of his genius.' And then, 'He knew how to hate.' This was not Quinn's view, who 'never heard him utter any word of bitterness about any Irishman'.[26]

This dramatic construction of the dead Synge proceeds in a series of writings by Yeats, from the private journal, through 'Synge and the Ireland of his Time' (1910) to the tactical release of some journal material as 'The Death of Synge' (1928), and then to the measured but oddly remote evocation of 'John Synge' in one of the last great poems, 'The Municipal Gallery Revisited' (1937). The formality of the process, together with what Yeats himself recognised as a degree of cold-bloodedness, stands in contrast to the swirl of immediate tributes, depreciations, and gossipy notes. According to Kitty Clinch nearby, Synge 'kept murmuring "God have mercy on me, God forgive me" in his delirium just before death'. This may reflect the desire of believing Catholics to believe that Synge died close to, if not within, the true Church; yet Miss Clinch's version of the last words is plausible. The same source suggests that Synge's favourite nurse sprinkled him with Holy Water as he lost consciousness. Stephens comes no nearer to endorsing a deathbed conversion, or change of mind, than to record that Synge 'read the Bible regularly during the closing days of his life and that he kept it in brown paper lest his reading a religious book should provoke comment'.[27] Holloway's emotional intelligence may have been limited, but his account of Synge begging the doctor 'to do something for him like he did before' rings truer than Yeats's textbook stoicism.

Holloway suggests a gulf between the dying man and his family. 'His people used to call to enquire, but never went up to see him. Every day he used to ask were any of his *affectionate* relatives there that day.' It is true that Annie Stephens was temporarily away in County Cork when the end came, looking after her daughter who was an asthma victim (like Synge himself).[28] Stephens makes it clear that from 2 February onwards, Robert or one of the Stephenses saw him 'from day to day'. Even Annie, with her own domestic anxieties, had made a point of writing to Molly, following a visit on 16 February. On that occasion she unquestionably saw her brother and did not merely call to the door of the nursing home. Far from avoiding Elpis, Robert was himself a patient there for several days, leaving on 15 March with the manuscript of *Deirdre of the Sorrows* which his brother had given him, or which had been passed to him.[29] In Yeats's account of things, nobody but Molly was allowed admission in the last week or so.[30] If there is a gap in the duty rota, then the missing person is Ned Synge, who later in the year began to make difficulties over translation rights and other legal issues. As Ned lived at Sandycove, no further from Dublin than Kingstown, it may be suspected that he was out of town – for whatever reason – during Synge's dying days. Yet it was he who attested Synge's death for the cemetery authorities.

At the Abbey, Synge's long-expected death set in motion various rituals of commemoration and respect. Performances were suspended for the remainder of the week. On Thursday 25 March, the day intervening between death and burial, Yeats and Henderson (the secretary) called to pay their respects to Robert Synge – 'a queer looking man in black clothes that did not fit, very pious I believe, & I think by his manner hating us all'[31] – adding an unwelcome request that a death-mask should be made by the sculptor, Oliver Sheppard.[32] But this, Robert declared to be quite impossible: the coffin had been closed and he refused point-blank to open it. Not only did the predictable reluctance of a family to whom publicity and appearance was painful rule out such a scheme, but the dreadful change which had come over his brother's features made a likeness unobtainable. After the delegation had left, Robert wrote to his brother in China, enclosing a cutting about John from the day's *Irish Times*.

At half past eight on the Friday, the three Stephens men – Harry, and his sons – slipped out of Silchester House by way of the garden and a path which ran alongside St Paul's but not through the church grounds. It seemed a fitting approach to the funeral of a man who hid his bible-reading under brown paper. No service was conducted in Glenageary parish, though the rector joined the mourners at Glendalough House where Robert Synge and Edward Synge (with his two sons and his brother-in-law, Victor Price) waited. William ('The Judge') Ormsby – Harry Stephens's shooting companion of old – brought the number up to nine. No women of the family participated, and no neighbours. The party dispersed according to their rank into three or four mourning carriages, which stood behind the tall hearse and its four black horses waiting on Adelaide Road. As chief mourner Robert was in charge, instructing Waller's men when to enter the house for the coffin and when to start the journey westward.

The cortege left Kingstown for Mount Jerome, taking well over an hour. At the high iron gates of the cemetery, facing across Kimmage Road to the railings of a small public park, 'a group of those who had known John as a writer and as a director of the National Theatre Society joined the procession . . . up the main avenue to the chapel.' It was half past ten. This chapel served in place of a parish church and there the Rev. Edmund Robinson (one of the rectory Robinsons from Delgany) read the Book of Common Prayer's Order for the Burial of the Dead. From thence to the graveside. After the interment, Yeats was seen wandering like a lost body among the tombstones. That evening he and his sister, Lily, went late to the Abbey and found the company sitting in silence in the green room, 'all the men together and opposite them in the big chair the poor girl, shrunken, broken and exhausted, but very brave and calm'. Sally Allgood was with her sister, whose main concern was how she should answer all the letters she had received.[33]

Next day the chief mourners were listed as the Synge brothers Edward and Robert – Sam in China was not mentioned – and two nephews. These latter included Hutchie, but not Ned Stephens who may have been deemed too young to count. His version of the event arranges the scene into two mutually exclusive groups. By 'friends' is meant those companions of silent J. M. Synge who worked in the theatre or who in some other way collaborated in his art. Molly stayed away, grieving in private, but her sisters Sara and Annie were present, signifying how tantalisingly close Synge had come to bridging the gap between family and friends. The list is predictable enough – Yeats, George Roberts of Maunsel, Thomas MacDonagh (executed later for his part in the Easter Rising), the actor Seamus O'Conghaile, W. K. Magee, essayist, and so forth.[34]

But who were H. F. Saphius, E. M. Saphius, and F. E. Saphius? In the best traditions of Irish newspapers, these exotic names misrepresent the other side of Synge's family – Harry Stephens, Ned Stephens, Frank

Edmund Stephens. And why did Molly Allgood stay away? The previous day Yeats already knew that she would not attend – 'dazed with grief'.[35] She had promised Synge not to mix with the fools and hypocrites by his grave, but no such commitment could be regarded as binding. On the other hand, having watched over her lover's dying and seen his body after death in Elpis, she may have been too distraught for the public formality of a funeral. Or was she already distancing herself from a love which had been ill-fated, Deirdre-like, under the stars?

Even the tributes and memories arising within his theatrical circle generated conflict. Annie Horniman had sent daffodils unaware, pre-sumably, that her hectoring letters on yellow paper had made Synge unable to see a daffodil without anger. Nor was this an unobserved irony: the thought of her unconsciously-repeated offence struck Yeats as he walked back from the grave towards Harolds Cross, the wiser for having stumbled among the dead.[36] Closer to home, Lady Gregory's summation may have been written with a view to pleasing Yeats, but its lack of warmth is unmistakable: 'we cant say, & dont want to say what was true, he was ungracious to his fellow-workers, authors & actors, ready in accepting praise, grudging in giving it . . .'[37]

Announcements and obituaries appeared in many papers. That in *The Times* of London was later excerpted in *The Irish Book Lover*. The *Manchester Guardian*'s long tribute was reprinted in Dublin's *Freeman's Journal*: 'He had at his command an instrument of incomparable fineness and range in the language which he learned from the common people among whom he lived.' G. H. Mair anonymously continued, 'He would listen to the talk of the peasant girls through a chink in the floor of his sitting room,' and thereby harrowed the ground for sustained assaults on Synge's innate decency. In America, Francis Hackett wrote a half-column in the Chicago *Evening Post*. The old Fenian, John Devoy, contributed a half-tribute, complaining about regional pronunciation and mis-representations of it in *The Playboy*, to the *Gaelic American*.[38]

Though Molly held her place in the Abbey's corps of players, and helped to assemble an actable *Deirdre*, she was not allowed to hold centre-stage in the afterlife of her lover. Yet some great or nearly great persons sought to console her. Arthur Symons, who had reached the Aran Islands before Synge and outlived him by nearly forty years, wrote in June, 'You who mourn him must realise that his name will remain among those writers whose names survive death, and remain: Triumph.' Yeats's wreath in Mount Jerome had carried a quotation from Proclus: 'The lonely returns to the lonely, the divine to Divinity.'

Certainly Synge's death eluded the city in which he was born. Henderson of the Abbey, whom Yeats likened to a 'grasshopper in the hedge, and is a burden', called it a funeral small but select. At the United Arts Club, Casimir Markievicz ' "spoke like a gentleman" about all WBY had done for the dead dramatist'.[39] Writing from Paris the following Monday, Maud Gonne referred vaguely to Synge's 'awful illness' and ran on to opine that an invalid's life would have been terrible for him.[40] Yeats vituperated in the privacy of his journal about 'idiot' enemies at the graveside – 'Lawrence who against all regulations rushed up to the dressing-rooms after the *Playboy* to tell the actors they should not have played in so "disgraceful a play" ...'[41] But there was another side to Yeats's rhetoric, an aspect no less combative in its metaphysical terminology.

The transition is begun in Entry 124 of the journal where a discussion with Harry Stephens over the impact of the *Playboy* riots on Synge's health is reported as the prelude to a meditation on the 'drifting, silent man, full of hidden passion' whose 'physical weakness increased this impression'. Then Yeats shifts tone and rhythm to recall the scenes of rioting in 1907; this is Entry 125 in its entirety:

On the night of the *Playboy* trouble he said to me, 'So-and-so,' naming a friend of his, a young doctor, 'says, "It is all I can do to keep myself from jumping up on a seat and pointing out among the howling men in the pit those whom I am treating for venereal diseases." '[42]

Then, under the heading 'Celebrations', Yeats strikes a wholly new note:

i

He was one of those unmoving souls in whom there is a perpetual 'Last Day', a perpetual trumpeting and coming to judgment.

ii

He did not speak to men and women, asking judgment of them as lesser writers do; but, knowing himself a part of judgment, he was silent.

iii

We pity the living and not such dead as he. He has gone upward out of his ailing body into the heroical fountains. We are parched by time.

iv

He had no need of our sympathies and so kept hid from all but all the knowledge of his soon-coming death, and was cheerful to the very end, even joking some few

hours before he died. It was as though we and the things about us died away from
him and not he from us.[43]

    This is Synge processed, as it were, in Yeats's occult metaphysical system.
The result is a figuration – not unlike the Parnell of Yeats's poems in the
1930s – quite distinct from the man whom others knew in the life. One
consequence of this is the use of the dead Synge by Ezra Pound (and,
more discreetly in the early stages, by Yeats himself) as a scourge upon
the back of 'democratic' critics, the sort

> now growing up
> All out of shape from toe to top,
> Their unremembering hearts and heads
> Base-born products of base beds.[44]

In short, the dead Synge is recruited to Yeats's avant-garde totalitarianism,
his death declared more admirable than the lives of others.

Ninety years later, we look back at the painful events of March 1909
through a mythology broadcast through Yeats's autobiographies and
poems, his system of terroristic philosophy called *A Vision*, in all of which
Synge is commended. There was not room, as Gregory admitted, for a
mixed opinion of Synge in which his silence might be termed arrogance
or vanity. Entry 124 of the 1909 journal had ended: 'neither Lady Gregory
nor I know what he thought of our work – he had the most perfect
modesty and simplicity in daily intercourse. With him, self-assertion of
any kind was impossible. The external self, the mask, the persona, was a
shadow; character was all.'[45]

    But what character? It is an inevitable conclusion of Yeats's thinking
that Synge's character is/was unknowable. In one way, this device neatly
overcame the difficulty which the impresario faced in recommending a
figure whom others should, but could not, emulate. Yet Synge's self
remained more unfinished than inscrutable; the critical point had been
passed some time in 1907 or early 1908, between the high achievement of
The Well of the Saints and the over-achieving of *The Playboy*. Even in so
short a life, it is possible to detect an early phase and to recognise in it
qualities progressively eroded in the later phase. To the best of my knowledge nobody has tried to read Synge's drama in the light of György
Lukács' theories of tragedy. But, in an essay written the year after Synge's
death, the Hungarian had declared that 'The dying heroes of tragedy . . .

are dead a long time before they actually die.'[46] It is in this sense that Synge's life relates to his work, not as source to outcome, but as a self-sacrificing example. The dramatist asked his defiant heroes – Martin Doul and Christy Mahon – to attempt nothing he did not have to undergo daily in his own self.

CHAPTER 24

The Last Will and the
WORKS of 1910

IRENA: We see the irreparable only when –
[*She breaks off.*]
PROFESSOR RUBEK [*With an inquiring look*]: When –?
IRENA: When we dead wake.

Henrik Ibsen[1]

Writing in mid-April, John Quinn puzzlingly compared the death of one Irish writer and the collapse of an English one. 'After all, Synge is better off and made a better end than poor Symons is making.' A few months earlier, Yeats had provided a lengthy account of the latter's condition, underscoring the absence of all hope with a cryptic allusion to *La Faustin* (1882) by Edmond de Goncourt: 'Paralysis also. In fact all Goncourt's lovers died of it in that novel. And they were not assisted by the desolating ignorance of the nursery.'[2] The death of a virginal Synge and the survival of decadent Symons – he recovered tolerably well and lived until 1945 – does more than highlight the peculiar uncertainties of medical diagnosis in each case. The subject of a biography is always missing, and in this sense Synge is typical rather than exceptional – even if his position within the family and his personal reticence underscore his status as missing subject.

In the wake of his death, some friends of Synge's were certainly anxious to record their reaction. Henri Lebeau, who had written from Canada, had returned to Paris only to learn from the *Manchester Guardian* that his friend was dead. 'It was a great shock to me,' he wrote to Richard Best, 'I had been exchanging letters with Synge ever since I first left Ireland for the last time in the summer [of] 1905 ... by losing Synge something which was deeply rooted in [my] own sensitiveness has departed ...' In characteristically energetic fashion, he had 'intended to write extensively' about both the life and the works but this would have necessitated 'to meet Synge again, to revive old memories ...'[3]

As early as May 1908, Quinn in New York was preparing the ground for the Elder Yeats to write a commemorative note. What survives of the resulting composition includes John B. Yeats's insistence that Synge had 'respected all the commandments even the much abused seventh', and his daughter Lily Yeats's belief that Synge's illness remained 'a mystery to his doctors, it was a tumor of the same nature as the swelling on his neck, not cancer'.[4] But John B. Yeats in exile was not easily regimented, even to honour someone he greatly admired. His younger son Jack proved more amenable. In New York's *Evening Sun* of 20 July 1909, the artist of *The Aran Islands* commemorated its author, as a walker, a talker, and a listener to talk. While this might seem an exotic place to publish a tribute to Synge, one of the *Sun's* editors had been at school with Willie Yeats.[5]

A month earlier, when Symons wrote to Molly in kindly terms of consolation, he was already certified insane in a private London mental home. Her own life lay before her in potential disarray, and in the event she did not remain long with the Abbey Company. The man she married on 15 July 1911 (in Chelsea) has received little or not attention in Ireland where he is habitually referred to as a journalist, if at all. But George Herbert Mair (1887–1926) did much to consolidate Synge's reputation in the period immediately after his death. A self-professed Scot (though born in Co. Durham) and a graduate of Aberdeen, Mair had arrived in Christ Church to take Firsts in English Literature and History. Some people thought him conceited, but Gilbert Murray did not find him 'noticeably so'. Murray, who had also moved from Scotland to Oxford, noted Mair's 'somewhat weak health' in what may have been a euphemistic tribute to the young man's capacity for alcohol. Scott of the *Manchester Guardian* was in search of a young leader-writer, and sought advice from Liberal sympathisers in various Oxford colleges. Mair had some journalistic experience, mainly on the *Aberdeen Free Press*, described himself as a liberal individualist, possessed 'an astonishing knowledge and understanding of literature, and what is no bad gift – knows how to show it'.[6] Here was a more formidable rival for Molly's affections than the local acting genius, Arthur Sinclair ('Mac'). The *Manchester Guardian* took him on at the end of 1908, not least perhaps because he was going nowhere in Oxford – All Souls had just turned him down for a fellowship. In the nick of time, he was available to cover the death of Synge.

Mair kept an odd kind of faith with Synge. Already the editor of a sixteenth-century text on *The Arte of Rhetorique*, in October 1911 he contributed a volume on modern literature to the Home University Library, a series designed for self-help students, concluding it with a judicious assessment of his wife's dead lover. Three years later, in an expanded version, Synge still featured as the climactic modern writer in English, limited in the scale of his achievement but not necessarily in its quality. Any deficiency in ideas ('if by "ideas" we mean current views on society or morality') brought him 'nearer to the great masters of drama – to Ben Jonson, to Cervantes, to Molière, even to Shakespeare himself'.[7] In one form or another, Mair's work perpetuated a positive image of Synge well into the 1960s. The contrast with Ezra Pound's opportunistic celebration in 1914 is total.

The posthumous life of J. M. Synge overlaps to a great extent with the pre-mortem difficulties of one publisher, complicated by some ill-considered interventions by members of the family. Maunsel, who duly published the four-volume *Works* in December 1910, provided a field of Armageddon on which Yeats and Joyce struggled with epigoni such as the Maunsel manager, George Roberts (1873–1953), a leading villain in Joyce's high doggerel 'Gas from a Burner'. But even before Synge's death, manoeuvres had begun on the issue of collecting his works. In November 1908, while Synge was still in Germany, a new and enterprising London firm, Sidgwick & Jackson, had begged Allan Wade – Yeats's bibliographer, visiting Dublin on theatre business – to 'go round to Maunsell's [sic], and see ... the manager, and find out what he is doing about making a collected edition of Sing's [sic] plays'.[8] Writing to Synge a month later, Sidgwick inquired about 'the collected edition of your works which Maunsel's have suggested to us'. While he may have been attempting to shift discussion from the plays alone to a larger collective project, Sidgwick was evidently under-informed about Synge's health. He added with complacent coolness, 'the last news I had of you ... was not very encouraging'.[9]

Synge's death a few months later did not bring the matter to a close. Both Roberts at Maunsel, and Ned Synge as principal executor, were approached in the following weeks, the latter being asked to approve a shilling edition of *The Well of the Saints* shortly to be staged in London. As an omen of things to come, Ned demanded to see a copy of the agreement by which Sidgwick & Jackson claimed to have rights. Defending his company against imputations of bad practice, Sidgwick quoted J. M. Synge verbatim back at his brother/executor – 'As to the little sum that is due to me from royalties, if it is too disgracefully small ... I will take it out in books from your list ...'.[10] Clearly, Ned had vetoed the proposed cheap edition, for the publishers later reported to him that the edition at 3s 6d had sold out. In this, however, they may have been more concerned to end negotiations with the executors than to stick to absolute truth for, later in the same month, they transferred a small amount of remaining Synge stock to Maunsel.[11] Characteristically, Roberts haggled about terms of payment.

Meanwhile, the Abbey Theatre was not letting the grass grow under its feet. To consolidate an international reputation which had been in large measure Synge's achievement, the Company had planned a London tour for June 1909, in which his plays would feature prominently. *The Playboy* opened at the Court Theatre on 7 June, alternating with *The Well of the Saints, In the Shadow of the Glen,* and *Riders to the Sea.* Molly Allgood starred in all four productions, a remarkably courageous and professional performance given that she was virtually the widow of their author who had written some leading parts specifically for her. With productions of *The Tinker's Wedding* (His Majesty's Theatre) in November 1909 and *Deirdre of the Sorrows* (the Court) in May 1910, the entire known canon of Synge's plays had been staged in London within just over a year of his death. In *Deirdre,* Molly's role exemplified the complex emotional force field in which these years placed her. Acting in a stage version which she had worked to establish with Yeats and Augusta Gregory, she played the title role against Arthur Sinclair's Conchubar – Sinclair whom she would marry as her second husband.

Now that copies of the will have been located, Synge's last wishes can be examined with more exactness and sympathy. We may conclude that Harry Stephens not only took down his brother-in-law's last instructions, but wrote them up in legally effective terms. (At least one of the witnesses on Saturday 13 February 1909 was a nurse in Elpis; the other, E. Harris, was not Harris the Abbey's accountant, for his initials were F. J.) In such circumstances, Harry could not also serve as executor or trustee – too much of the will had been, necessarily, his working up of Synge's oral instructions. The beneficiaries were Molly and Synge's two favourite nephews. Edward Stephens later conveyed the impression that he was *the* favourite; certainly, Hutchie features less in the surviving correspondence. Hutchie, however, was growing up in a more restricted household and Synge may have judged that the lad deserved his place of honour also. The provisions for him go some way towards justifying the nephew's claim that Synge had recognised a kindred spirit in the tearful years of 1896–7.

This is a turning-point in his biography, one which must be reached before any assessment of his 'self' is attempted. Provisions and intentions cannot be taken as one and the same thing. To interpret the dying man's wishes requires a prepared view of Synge's personality in life, and his sense of Molly's future after his death. In August it became known that his personal estate was valued at £2,362:[12]

I direct that out of the income arising from my various investments my said trustees and executors shall pay to Mary Allgood generally called Molly Allgood the sum of Eighty pounds per annum to be paid to her by equal and even half yearly or quarterly payments which ever shall be the most convenient for the term of her natural life or until she shall marry and in the event of the said Mary Allgood marrying I direct that the said annuity of Eighty pounds shall not cease but shall be reduced to the sum of fifty two pounds to be paid to her at the same time and in the same manner and I direct that the income I leave to her shall be her sole and separate estate free from the control or engagements of any husband and to be payable to her on her sole receipt And I expressly direct that she shall not have power to sell dispose of mortgage or anticipate the said life annuity of Eighty pounds or fifty two pounds if same should be reduced as aforesaid nor shall my trustees be in any way bound to acknowledge any sale alienation charge or assignment and in such event the trustees shall have liberty to withhold same from any assignee or Incumbrancer for it is my wish to provide an annual inalienable sum for her support.

Who read this will and how did they interpret it? The solicitors and executors concerned in its administration read it in the course of duty but, after its provisions were approved (30 July 1909) and set in motion, the will became publicly accessible. Though few were likely to trouble themselves in pursuit of it, the dying testator will have known that the contents of his last will could be examined. Doubtless, someone representing Molly examined it, even if she personally did not do so. Thus his determination to ensure that no future husband could get his hands on any portion of her annuity, control or exploit it, was sure to become known. Viewed in one light, the will generously allowed for Molly's eventual marriage, though on a reduced basis. But its phrasing wholly lacks the personal touch – he might as well have been providing for a domestic servant or a distant cousin. Synge's famous reticence, and inherited propriety of expression, may be responsible for the absence of any 'my beloved Molly', 'my dear friend' or whatever. In another light, however, the will could be read as making provision (but hardly generous provision) for someone in whose reliability the testator did not place much faith. A deathbed marriage could have been organised, but wasn't. And now the will provided her – not with a lump sum which might buy a small house or finance a tour of America – but with an allowance equivalent to a housekeeper's wages.[13]

The trustees, 'my brother Edward Synge and my nephew Francis Edmund Stephens', were empowered to call in, reinvest or leave unaltered the dramatist's unspecified investments. They were also empowered 'to continue the contracts which are at present in force ... and to make new contracts and new arrangements with the present publishers or others' as administrators of the literary property. No reference was made to Yeats as a person who might advise or select. Nor is there mention of unpublished work or correspondence. A distinctive provision allowed for Frank Stephens to be paid out of the estate 'as if he were employed as a Solicitor by another person'. The income from 'property investments' and the sale of books was to be divided between 'Edward Stephens second son of my sister Annie Stephens' and 'my nephew Hutchinson Synge son of my brother Edward Synge', a provision to commence before they reached their majority, 'for their books education and advancement'. On Molly's death, the entire estate was to be divided between the two nephews already named.

Trouble was brewing even before the will was executed. Before the end of April, Yeats complained to George Russell 'that Synge's executor is a Plymouth Brother [who] regards Synge's writing with grave disapproval'. Moreover, Ned Synge (according to this redaction of the saga) 'threatens to go over all Synge's plays and to expurgate passages which he thinks are objectionable'.[14] According to Hutchie Synge, his son, the two nephews went through the manuscripts 'shortly after J.M.S.'s death'; in this long-after-the-event record, Edward Stephens had wanted to censor a sentence in the 'Vita Vecchia' where Synge had written that one character was 'enceinte' [pregnant]. While this needs to be interpreted cautiously, given Hutchie's mental condition in 1942, it does suggest that Hutchie was at an early stage acting as if he were a literary executor or trustee whereas the will named him solely as a beneficiary. He certainly behaved in such a fashion after the Great War and until his health collapsed more than a decade later.[15]

There was initial confusion because the surviving manuscripts were in Robert's hands, whereas Edward was the executor among the Synge brothers. Yeats reported to Lady Gregory that Robert had undertaken to give 'all the manuscripts' to Molly, but this may have referred to manuscripts of the unfinished *Deirdre* alone. It is clear that Molly was entrusted by the Abbey directors to deal direct with the family, for she had been given the key to a safe-drawer and told 'to lock them up there' – an arrangement which would hardly accommodate the great bulk of the entire manuscript corpus.[16] Robert was as good as his word in the matter of *Deirdre*, perhaps relieved to have Ned or Hutchie shoulder the literary responsibilities.

Initially, Hutchie may have operated as a valued assistant to his besieged father. In no time at all, Ned was being pestered by some unheard-of Dubliner who sought permission to have an Italian translation of *Riders to the Sea* staged in Trieste or thereabouts. (Then there were London productions and publishers, not to mention the irrepressible Molly.) Yeats, who was as godless (if better-connected) as this Joyce fellow, claimed to be empowered by the dead dramatist to perpetuate the works through new editions, including an edition of poems and translations. J. M. Synge would not go away. When Ned, from his summer retreat in a County Louth rectory, required from Joyce a specific indication of 'how often & at what fee' his Italian friends proposed to stage the translation of *Riders to the Sea*, he was only doing his duty by the financial beneficiaries of the will he was charged to execute. On the other hand, such insistence was to have the effect of controlling and restricting the proliferation of 'objectional' material.

While he was dying Synge had been concerned to set his papers in order, and especially attentive to the sorting-out of poems and translations for a Cuala Press edition. The *Deirdre* play – Lolly Yeats claimed to have devised the title ultimately used – posed quite distinct problems for the executors. But these discrete bodies of text could not be allowed to obscure the possibilities of bringing together a collective edition, in which prose, drama, and poetry would feature. The will expressly authorised new contracts. Commercially, there was much to be gained from Synge's death. Ideologically, an unprecedented opportunity arose for Yeats to make a pre-emptive strike. Somewhere in between these extreme motives, the author's relatives worried about the outcome. Yeats prepared a memorandum for the Synge estate detailing what he believed should or should not be published. Molly helped him to date individual poems and, in preparing an introduction for the Cuala edition which his sister would print, Yeats drew on that vein of marbled prose, headed 'Celebrations', which he had been developing in the Journal entries. The Introduction is dated 4 April 1909, printing began on 8 April, and Synge's *Poems and Translations* was published on 5 July 1909. The Yeatses were not happy with the result, as an example of their printing and publishing skills: somehow the material did not easily fit Lolly's Cuala format.

One characteristic stroke of Yeats's was to quote in the Introduction

'The Curse' which Synge had decided (on advice, almost certainly Molly's) to exclude. When Maunsel in 1910 included poems and translations in the second volume of the *Works*, 'The Curse' was restored to the canon. Subtitled 'To a Sister of an Enemy of the Author's who Disapproved of "The Playboy"', these eight ferocious lines exemplify the difficulties which surround the issue of Synge's life-in-his-art:

> Lord, confound this surly sister,
> Blight her brow with blotch and blister,
> Cramp her larynx, lung, and liver,
> In her guts a galling give her.
> Let her live to earn her dinners
> In Mountjoy with seedy sinners:
> Lord, this judgment quickly bring,
> And I'm your servant, J. M. Synge.[17]

As a mock-prayer, twice explicitly addressed to the Lord, these lines cannot easily be reconciled to the subtitle, 'To a Sister ...' especially when we acknowledge that their target was Peggy Callendar, Molly Allgood's married sister. Given that Synge never prepared a text of 'The Curse' for publication, the subtitle may be regarded more accurately as a record of his giving the poem to Molly. On the other hand, if Peggy is the surly sister, is there not some implication that Molly is 'an Enemy'? All in all, the confused anger of Synge's reaction to *The Playboy* crisis is awkwardly preserved in Yeats's ostentatious quotation.

In late March 1909, Yeats and Harry Stephens opened discussions about the will. Within no more than ten days of Synge's death, Yeats writes in his journal that he knows 'a year ago Synge made another will leaving Molly all his money'.[18] Yeats's knowledge of the law was not profound – he speculated that the new will might deal only with what was inherited through Kathleen Synge's will the previous autumn, and in this he was grievously wrong. Yet he came close in the journal to accusing Stephens of manipulating the dying man to make a fresh will in which Molly's inheritance would be reduced and that of the family increased.[19] Even at this late date, it seems that Molly knew nothing of the annuity (rather than lump sum) which would be Synge's legacy to her. Robert Synge (who appears to have been her preferred point of contact with the family) had said nothing to her. She had declared to Yeats on the day he recorded his conversation with Harry Stephens, 'I will spend it all, if necessary, on his work.' In this she probably relied on Synge's assurance that what came to him under his mother's will came without strings or entails – 'I will have that to leave you.' However, he had also acknowledged that he would 'not get any money for six months'.[20] While Yeats's suspicions are consistent with the facts of the will, other interpretations suggest themselves, not the least interesting being the notion that Synge had revised his opinion of Molly during his last weeks.

By mid-May Yeats had told Maud Gonne that Harry Stephens had suggested 'revising' Synge's work, a report that does not tally with his fears a month earlier of a censorious brother's (not brother-in-law's) editorial ambitions.[21] The family had still told Molly nothing yet of a new will; they were, in Yeats's view, 'a strange people'.[22] J. M. Synge was to be, in a strict sense, *sui generis* for, in total contrast to the suspicious, pious, and strange collectivity of the Synge family, the Preface to *Poems and Translations* finally evokes

a solitary, undemonstrative man, never asking pity, nor complaining, nor seeking sympathy but in this book's momentary cries: all folded up in brooding intellect, knowing nothing of new books and newspapers, reading the great masters alone: and he was but the more hated because he gave his country what it needed, an unmoved mind where there is a perpetual last day, a trumpeting, and coming up to judgment.[23]

While this hieratic style was intended to configure a posthumous Synge round whom Yeats would assemble aristocratic or (more accurately) authoritarian values, it also helped in dealing with the likes of George Roberts. More than a year later, when the two men were contending over what was to be included in a Collected Synge, Roberts complained about Yeats's appropriation of the poetic texts, after their author had agreed to have them published by Maunsel. 'I must remind you,' Roberts wrote to Yeats, about 'your action in the matter of the publication of the Poems; when Mr Synge sent you his manuscript (which he had already arranged with me to publish – for your "opinion", you held to it for the Cuala Press. Synge then came to me and said if it was a question of us OR the Cuala Press publishing them he would unhesitatingly go on with his original arrangement with us. But for your representing that your sister's press would be idle I would have looked to the interest of my own firm . . .'[24]

Certainly, Synge had signed a contract with Maunsel on 5 October 1908 – just before he left for his last trip to the Von Eickens – for a trade edition of his poems. The Yeatses, brother and sister, provided the opportunity for a limited 'small press' presentation of work which – with the exception of one very early poem – had never got into print. Whatever were Lolly Yeats's motives, Willie Yeats's attitude was focused upon larger objectives than a mere monopoly in publishing Synge's few ballads, pasquinades and translations. John Quinn secured American copyright with an edition of fifty copies, to parallel the Cuala Press's two hundred and fifty. The problem now shifted to the more public domain and the collective publication of the plays and prose writings by which Synge was known.

An agreement between Maunsel & Co. and the executors was drawn up for signature on 26 March 1910, providing for the publication of a Collected Works no later than the end of June.[25] Though this timetable proved impossible, the problems in collecting Synge were more ideological than practical. Yeats proposed to write an introduction – not referred to in the agreement – but withdrew when he discovered that his views on the proper contents of the edition did not find universal endorsement. As late as 15 October, he told Roberts that he would 'raise Cain' if the *Manchester Guardian* articles about conditions in the west of Ireland were included. Thus, while he had complained to George Russell about Synge's brother purging the works of objectionable material – no evidence that this ever happened has come to light – Yeats was seeking to exclude published work from the definitive edition, and bullying all and sundry with threats to withhold his Introduction. The work to be excluded in Yeats's scenario was precisely that which did not fit Yeats's Ideal Synge, the one who would be used to buttress an authoritarian politics of uncaring.

The latest and fullest account of Yeats's behaviour on this occasion suggests that Roberts had 'tricked Edward Stephens into agreeing to publish the *Manchester Guardian* articles'.[26] But other documentation makes it clear that Stephens played little or no part in the various negotiations and recriminations leading up to the publication of the 1910 *Works* – he was just turning twenty-one at the time, and his elder brother and cousin (not to mention Uncle Ned) were unlikely to let him have his say in the matter. On the other hand – the other hand is very active in discussion of Synge's affairs! – Stephens's subsequent political development revealed social concerns with the commonality of Irish lives in city and country, consistent with early approval of his Uncle John's articles on the Congested Districts. (He came to sympathise with Sinn Féin and especially Michael Collins's conduct of the War of Independence.)

The wishes of commercial publishers were not to intervene between Yeats and his 'one purpose alone'. Or, in the more elegant phrasing of

Yeats's biographer, 'The reception of Synge's play had become an epiphany, expressing WBY's essential recognition of himself.'[27] Roberts of Maunsel complained that the executors had not revealed the full extent of 'the mass of unpublished Mss left by the late Mr Synge. But they have handed over to us one article hitherto unpublished, and we have mutually agreed to publish it.'[28] This was probably 'Under Ether', though the eventual edition contained other previously unpublished pieces, notably 'Glencree'. Typesetting had been under way since mid-September, when Roberts had (rather ingenuously) asked Ned Synge to supply the 'Mss or original typescript of "Operations under Ether" ... merely to check the proofs by, as we are setting up from the copies kindly supplied us.'[29] If only Roberts's spelling and typing could be trusted![30] The title he refers to – the plural 'Operations...' – suggests that the essay we know as 'Under Ether' and which appeared as the final item in the final volume of the Maunsel *Works* (1910) originally dealt with more than one surgical operation. The typescript as it survives has certainly been under the scalpel, to the extent that some pages carry only a line or two of text and the last surviving line appears carved from some now lost continuing page. 'Under Ether' was dropped from the five-volume Library Edition of 1911 while 'Glencree', as we have seen, was deprived in 1910 of its final paragraph.[31] These decisions cannot be ascribed to individuals.

To Lady Gregory, Yeats complained in September that 'Roberts has deliberately deceived us both' in connection with the contents of Synge's *Works*, but a hitherto unpublished account of the affair by Máire Garvey supports Roberts – her husband, of course – as a victim of the great man's 'scandalous manner'.[32] The publisher telegraphed the poet at Coole Park on 10 October about the Introduction he had proposed, but Yeats chose to interpret the inquiry as concerned with the contents generally of the *Works*, and referred him to the executors. This not untypical incident absorbed two days and three telegrams in all.[33] Local negotiations were interrupted by various American inquiries. One cannot doubt Ned's commitment to the proper administration of his late brother's estate any more than one can ignore Roberts's recognition that the project in hand was a major undertaking, perhaps without precedent in Irish publishing. But neither man was temperamentally suited to the role thrust upon him by J. M. Synge's dying instructions. Maunsel's manager could be alarmingly inaccurate with names – Frank Stephens became Frances Stephens in one draft of a copyright statement. On the other side, Ned Synge – or Edmund, as Roberts sometimes called him – could rarely see the forest for the twigs. Of the executors generally, Roberts wrote in an angry postscript, 'they are most stubborn people to deal with and simply wont see points they dont wish to'.[34] Even Weekes, the London-based adviser from Wicklow who acted for Maunsels and who often berated Roberts for his sloppiness, advised putting 'the pistol at their heads' and urging abandonment of 'the most difficult of all things – to treat your clients as friends'.[35] Meanwhile Yale University Press, Dutton of New York, Luce of Boston, and the *Dial* magazine were pressing about American rights.

Frank Stephens played second fiddle throughout these tortuous negotiations, though Roberts took care to keep him informed, less – one suspects – out of efficiency or courtesy than from a wish to ensure that Ned Synge did not monopolise the executors' role. In preferring Ned to Robert as his executor, J. M. Synge may have had in mind the land agent's tenacity in seeing things through. But Ned had no experience whatever of such arcane matters as proof-correction codes and international copyright law. Quite apart from any personal distaste for *The Playboy* – 'the dogs itself were lapping poteen from the dung-pit of the yard' – he was more rapidly inundated with business inquiries than anyone could have reasonably expected. A translator named Simons from Amsterdam craved permission to stage *The Well of the Saints*, adding conscientiously that, although his country was not a signatory to the Berne Convention, he would not exploit the liberties this situation afforded him.[36] While Roberts helpfully relayed messages about possible American and Canadian productions of the plays, Ned worried about the impact of these on the Abbey Theatre's future tours, and in doing so further delayed an American collected edition.[37]

Yale, negotiating through James Byrne Hackett (an Irish-born senior executive), urged 'the very considerable advantage of having Synge published by such a dignified imprint as our own'. But it jumped the gun by placing an inspired 'news' story in the Chicago *Evening Post* to the effect that a complete edition would be published shortly under that imprint – Hackett's brother worked on the paper.[38] Provoked by this, the firm of Luce (based in Boston) issued the first American edition of *The Tinker's Wedding*, and with it all hopes for a multi-volume Yale complete edition virtually disappeared. Luce regarded Synge as 'an interesting and important author' but not 'commercially ... strong enough to attract a publisher for his complete edition'.[39]

By Christmas 1910, Maunsel of Dublin had issued in four handsome volumes *The Works of John M. Synge*, bound in brown linen with gilt top-edges. As a tribute to the dead dramatist, these publications conceal a terrible row between family and friends, while also making a canonical statement as to what constituted Synge's achievement. The chief combatants had been George Roberts, Harry Stephens, Ned Synge and W. B. Yeats, with others (including Lolly Yeats) active behind the lines. Yeats dealt with Stephens whom he regarded with suspicion; Roberts and Ned alternately squared up to and backed off from each other. By July 1911, stock of this edition was 'exhausted'.[40]

Roberts could be liberal with the truth. 'Our want of working capital', as he put it, was a constant worry, derailing long-term developments. An oversight in his reading of Synge's agreements with Elkin Mathews led to some panic in May 1911, when the American complete edition was still feasible. By March 1912, the *Works* had been reprinted, Maunsel being able to supply a customer direct for fifty shillings – this in preference to waiting for three guineas from a bookseller enjoying credit terms.[41] Out of the painful last days, Maunsel & Co. managed to sculpt a monument in four volumes, the first collective edition of an Irish author to be printed and published in Ireland since the eighteenth century. The *Works* had its flaws, and the manner of its emergence is not fully known. Some questions remain unanswered. An even more lavish five-volume Library Edition followed in 1911. It is exceedingly rare, and the intentions of the publishers – who kept the four-volume edition in print – remain obscure; 'Under Ether' and James Paterson's portrait of the author disappear.[42]

In November 1911, Molly – signing as Máire Mair – wrote from Drumcondra about some 'coloured pictures of Playboy', evidently intended for yet another marketing of her late lover's great comedy.[43] No more is heard of such a project until Hutchie Synge begins to assert claims as a literary executor after the conclusion of the Great War. Meanwhile, J. M. Synge's standing as a master of 'world theatre' rose and fell. In England, a 1912 production of *The Well of the Saints* at the Royal Court was satirised by Katherine Mansfield and John Middleton Murry:

Whist! woman, when I tell ye – they'll be after pulling up the curtain, and it's myself will be destroyed entirely if you do be talking in the one ear, and the music do be sounding in the other, and the actors speaking like the saints of God with fine beautiful voices on them, or like the little cherubs of heaven, maybe, and they warm with the milk of Mary.[44]

CHAPTER 25

Perpetual Judgement, 1911–1932

Every book is a protest against the loneliness that wraps itself around each of us.

John Lighton Synge[1]

In cultural terms, the Great War registered sharply with those seeking a triple-marriage – of Irish saga, the English language, and German scholarship. *Deirdre of the Sorrows*, prophetess of modern violence, had come of age. For the itinerant Lebeau in distant Buenos Aires, 'the very existence of [my] country is threatened by the most barbarous nation which ever existed'.[2] From the British Museum, the Celticist Robin Flower reported that Kuno Meyer (founder of the Dublin School of Learning) was 'very bitter against England ... if he does come to see his friends, it must be incognito'.[3] At a production of *Riders to the Sea* in May 1915, Lily Yeats observed sobbing throughout the audience. 'Death all about us – so many we hardly mention it when we meet, partly because most one meets have sons or brothers at the front.' On the far side of Europe, all of Synge's plays were reported as translated into Polish.[4]

Molly Allgood was also to find her life transformed by the 'great game' (Kipling's term) of liberal imperialism. G. H. Mair, her husband since July 1911, had political ambitions, first as a prospective parliamentary Liberal candidate and later as a quasi-secret propagandist. In January 1912, he had become the *Manchester Guardian*'s man at the House of Commons; soon he was in private correspondence with his editor about Home Rule (then thought to be within the Irish party's grasp). In mid-September 1914, while staying in Dublin, he was contacted by the Home Secretary proposing work 'in connexion with the dissemination of English news from the Foreign office'. It was a 'strictly secret & confidential post', according to Mair's unguarded letter to the *Guardian*'s editor, C. P. Scott. In the view of Elizabeth Coxhead, he was engaged in 'often dangerous secret service work'. Whatever Mair got up to during the Great War, as an unsung Richard Hannay or 'strange fighter', honours came his way. Yet the post-war depression found him in difficult circumstances, remote from Scott and (it is clear) drinking heavily – Coxhead delicately presents him as 'highly-strung and febrile, sharing some of Molly's weak-nesses'.[5] He died on 3 January 1926. A retired *Times* war correspondent, attempting to raise funds for Mair's family, insisted that any money 'must be [placed] in other hands than the children's mother'.[6] In contrast, the Synge estate more than once obliged with advance payments of her annuity. In 1927, Ned Synge allowed her to use *Riders to the Sea* as a curtain-raiser at the Royal Court Theatre, London, provided the low fees required were paid every week – 'not letting them accumulate'. They were paid promptly.[7]

The war imposed considerable strains on the publishing industry in Ireland. Supplies of paper were not always reliable. Trade was depressed. George Roberts raised the alarm in March 1916; 'having had our affairs investigated by the Auditors we find that liquidation is imminent.' In early April the Library Edition of Synge's *Collected Works* was reported 'at present out of print'. Shortly afterwards, the destruction of Maunsel's Middle Abbey Street premises and book stock in the Dublin insurrection struck another blow at the orderly dissemination of the plays, poems and travel books. Yet by October, the London wholesalers were being advised to telephone bookbinders in England for an explanation of short sup-plies.[8] And by the beginning of the following year, things were sufficiently recovered to contemplate an edition of *The Playboy*, in two thousand copies, with six coloured illustrations by the stained-glass artist, Harry Clarke, with maybe twenty black-and-white images added.[9]

Nothing came of this venture, though Clarke did create stained glass to illustrate a poem – 'Queens' – by Synge. These miniatures were com-missioned by the Rt. Hon. Laurence Waldron (1858–1923) to form a frieze in his library in Killiney. ('Larky' Waldron was a stockbroker and a gov-ernor of Belvedere College, Joyce's alma mater). The style is strongly reminiscent of Beardsley and the 1890s, serving to underline the writer's origins in the *fin de siècle* and his sustained (if concealed) attachment to decadent themes; by the same token it is strikingly at odds with Synge's text. Clarke was particularly keen on using Synge's work; a pen-and-ink drawing of 'The Mad Mulrannies' (background figures in *The Playboy*) appeared in the November 1919 issue of *The Studio*, and the original was exhibited at the Aonach Tailteann of 1924.[10]

Further efforts to project Synge's writings into the post-war market-place cannot be traced until September 1920 when an agreement was reached between the family and Maunsel's, which quickly became more of an obstacle than an aid to progress. But by the final clause, the executors reserved 'the right of authorising a biographer to quote fragments [from Synge's works] without it being incumbent on them to offer the Publisher [i.e. Maunsel] an option of publication of such biography'.[11] The same clause referred to 'any other published or unpublished works of the late J. M. Synge': no unpublished work is named or even hinted at.

The period following the Armistice amounted to a phoney peace. Though the war was over in France, Bolshevik repercussions persisted despite widespread terror. Ezra Pound, who had written of 'The Non-existence of Ireland' in the aftermath of the *Playboy* affair, now conceded that 'the Theatre, Yeats, Synge, and co. had developed a wide sympathy for Ireland, which the revolutionaries have wiped utterly away'.[12] Politics now imposed more local difficulties than those prompted by the Great War. Edward Stephens was – in whatever minor capacity as legal drafts-man – caught up in the Treaty negotiations of 1921. For this or other reasons, the initiative lay with his Uncle Ned and Ned's son (Hutchie), Stephens's fellow beneficiary under the will. There is evidence to indicate that, in the course of 1922, George Roberts tried to persuade the family to relinquish their rights (which extended under copyright until 1960) in return for some immediate advantage. He also tried to raise money by persuading Allen & Unwin to take over his stock.[13]

Perhaps the moment was badly chosen. The Free State had scarcely emerged from Civil War, and general depression gripped the economy on both sides of the Irish Sea. Nevertheless, Maunsel's manager got in touch with Macmillan of London announcing his desire to publish a limited edition of Synge's work, 'with some additional poems, a few prose pieces, a collection of letters and a biography'. That was mid-January 1923. At the same time, Roberts put a deal to Unwin in London whereby the latter would buy large numbers of books by Synge at a bargain price, but on condition that other, less lucrative titles were taken off Maunsel's hands also.[14] By mid-May Macmillan's, Yeats's principal commercial publishers, had decided against the proposed joint publication; legal issues arose from the possible division of the old United Kingdom into two copyright 'territories'. This of course occurred before Yeats's handsome tribute to Synge was made in the Nobel speech of December 1923.

But the additional material alluded to by Roberts, including a biog-raphy, was sufficient to take the project beyond the four-volume scale of 1910, and even beyond the five volumes proposed in January. Though Maunsel's man continued, 'I regret to say that Mr Synge, who is writing the biography, will not have the MS ready before September or October

...' he did not identify precisely who in the family was at work on the literary remains.[15] Given the reluctance, even hostility, of Ned and Robert to their late brother's choice of a literary career, Hutchie must be the prime suspect. After all, copyright was vested jointly in his name and that of his cousin, Edward Stephens.

The letters in question were, or included, those which – according to the South African line of inquiry established by Ronald Ayling – J. M. Synge had written to Cherrie Matheson in the 1890s (and perhaps after) and which she (now Mrs Kenneth Houghton) had affably returned to the family in the person of Hutchie Synge at the beginning of the 1920s. It is part of Houghton family tradition that he was at work on a book about his uncle, and so it seems reasonable to conclude that the biographer on whom George Roberts was relying for an autumn 1923 delivery of copy was the same man. Even commentators close to Synge appear to have been in the dark as to his early relations with Cherrie Matheson. Writing two years after the appearance of her article in the *Irish Statesman*, the poet Padraic Colum (who had been a walking-companion of Synge's) is unable to identify her by name or to allude to the nature of the relationship between her and Synge. Colum's wife is even more reticent, not only omitting Mrs Houghton but also declining so much as to name Molly Allgood in her recollections of the Abbey.[16] This state of unknowing – it may have involved a degree of polite silence, out of consideration for the family's self-image – typifies the conditions in which biography was thought to be a matter requiring diplomacy, even delicacy.

Under the will, as summarised by Hutchie for a firm of London solicitors, he and Edward Stephens were 'the two residuary legatees' while Hutchie's father and Frank Stephens were 'the two Trustees'.[17] In practice, the Stephens brothers appear to have played second and third fiddles to the Synges, father and son. Unsympathetic to Johnnie's vocation in life, Ned was none the less concerned that the plays 'had for a long time been unprocurable in London ... This breach of our agreement was one which we regarded in an especially serious light, as it not only affected our financial interests, but also my brother's memory ...'[18] His son was sequestered in Doyle's Hotel, near the old Synge estates in Wicklow, when Cherrie Matheson's reminiscences appeared. Their publication came as a surprise to the would-be biographer of J. M. Synge: 'I fancied the incidents of their relationship would be painful to her.' He had intended to treat the matter 'anonymously', adding (in a now tantalising way): 'there was sufficient to go on without asking her for further details.' Hutchie was at the disadvantage of not having read the article of 5 July 1924. Delayed 'owing to illness', he nevertheless sought Yeats's assistance in tracing Mrs Houghton in South Africa.[19]

Ned Synge was inclined to leave matters alone, perhaps because Hutchie was usefully absorbed by such responsibilities, perhaps because he was himself both ageing and not wholly in sympathy with the tinkers, the playboys and the dirty deeds. Certainly, it was the son who commissioned illustrations for a proposed de luxe edition of *The Playboy* through which Synge's reputation would be revived. 'Mr Keating prefers to have business relations with me ...', a plausible statement, given the artist's distaste for the old landed gentry Ned Synge still represented. Seán Keating's illustrations are sternly masculine, quite unlike the suggestive figures spun from Synge's texts by Harry Clarke, who had sought the commission for the Allen & Unwin limited edition.[20] A month after Cherrie Matheson's memoir had appeared, two letters written in the same hand, but signed one by Edward Synge and the other by Hutchie, are despatched to Allen & Unwin.[21] The Keating edition of *The Playboy* is their theme. Thereafter the bulk of the correspondence is conducted by the son.

At first, Hutchie is living at home in his father's house in Dundrum, not far from the Yeats sisters. Then he is planning to travel to South Africa, a factor which exerts pressure on negotiations with publishers. Sometimes he is away from Dundrum, notably at a series of addresses in North Wales which probably represent convalescent nursing homes. W. K. Magee, bitterly self-exiled at sunny Prestatyn, reported in December – 'that curious chap E. H. Synge ... is at present laid up in a hotel here ... I don't know whether he is really ill or is mainly a hypochondriac.'[22] Writing from Carrick (or Garrick) House, Deganwy, in March 1925, Hutchie himself records that he has been confined to bed for three months; in this letter the early signs of heavy, obsessive underlining appear. A few days later, he informs Allen & Unwin that his father had recently 'firmly said he would have nothing more to do with the matter' of the family's agreement with the Dublin publishers. By way of explanation, he added that Maunsel's might be wound up, 'terminated', that very day.[23]

A thread or threat of biographical activity runs throughout what Unwin called 'the most tiresome negotiations with which we have ever been confronted'.[24] First mooted in the Maunsel agreement of 1920, and then raised by Roberts in his abortive negotiations with Macmillan three years later, the question of a new Life of Synge – to replace that of Bourgeois who is never named though he was back in Ireland in 1920 – haunts all discussion of new editions, whether collected, augmented or illustrated.[25]

What is symptomatic in these ghostly allusions is uncertainty as to whether Hutchie and his father contemplated a Life which one or both of them might write or whether they were trying to anticipate and control work by some other potential biographer. Complaining of ill-health and some difficulty with his memory, Hutchie wrote from the Fitzwilliam Nursing Home in Dublin (he referred to it as simply Fitzwilliam House) concluding that any contract 'will omit any reference to a biography'. This was in response to a proposal that the likely publishers of a new edition should be guaranteed that 'no biography by too copious extracts should injure the sales of the books'.[26]

During this correspondence of autumn 1924, there are occasional references to South Africa, more specifically the Cape. Kenneth Houghton was by now a distinguished public servant, member of a Commission on Native Education in Cape Province.[27] Hutchie's trip may have been prompted by concern for his health but, additionally, it may have been linked with his interest in papers held by Cherrie Houghton. Her 'John Synge As I Knew Him' with Yeats's condescending Preface, had appeared in the same month that the *Yale Review* published some of Synge's letters to his German translator, Max Meyerfeld.[28] Quite apart from Hutchie's delicate health, there was nervousness among surviving members of J. M. Synge's generation in the family. Trying to stabilise his firm's position in the slow whirlwind of paper spinning out from Hutchie's sickbed, Roberts 'had very great difficulty in getting the Synges to sign the Agreement ...' That was on 10 June 1925, when the biographical project was again under consideration; so actively, indeed, that Hutchie could declare that 'in regard to a biography ... we wish to be free to get the best terms we can'.[29]

At the beginning of 1926, his father took over negotiations with Allen & Unwin. Things went no better. Having drawn the Society of Authors into the affair some considerable time earlier, Ned Synge now protested to those obliging arbiters: 'We object in toto! and from every point of view, both from that of my brother's memory and on financial grounds to large quantities of his works being thrown on to the shelves of the remainder booksellers, which Mr Unwin seems to contemplate as a sound business policy.' Stanley Unwin, seeking to comfort the Society's officers, observed that 'Mr Synge is still obsessed with his unfortunate experience with Messrs. Maunsel.'[30]

Less than a month later, history was about to repeat itself, with riots at the Abbey Theatre during the first production of Seán O'Casey's *The Plough and the Stars*. Macmillan of London were only too willing to become publishers of the latest Irish dramatist who, in shocking the public into states of outraged self-recognition, was truly Synge's successor. 'You have disgraced yourselves again,' Yeats shouted elegantly at the audience. In the Synge residences, the issue of how to deal with the dramatist's life and work was sinking into the oblivion of too great concern. Outsiders like Padraic Colum, who at the funeral had looked more like a character from Synge's 'peasant' plays than a colleague in the literary profession, were publishing their memoirs.[31] The situation required careful monitoring. Though Hutchie had occasionally alluded to the role of his cousin, there is no record of Edward Stephens being drawn into 'the innumerable draft contracts of one kind and another', which irritated Stanley Unwin. Even Unwin's well-intentioned efforts, as late as 1929, to build an income for the estate through Czech and other translation rights drew little but mistrust from the Edward Synges of Knockroe.[32]

Nevertheless, a special edition of *The Playboy*, with ten colour illustrations by Keating, had eventually appeared in September 1927 under the Allen & Unwin imprint. The thousand numbered copies were beautifully printed by Curwen in England, with the illustrations (signed 'Céitinn' in Gaelic, not 'Keating' in English) carefully guarded with tissue paper. The business of reviving Synge was afoot, however preciously or unsteadily. Members of the family, mindful of Hutchie's limited skill as a custodian of his uncle's reputation, felt obliged to contribute. Having returned for 'family reasons' from the Chinese missions, Sam Synge became rector of Annamoe in County Wicklow, where so many holidays had been passed. By 1922 the Irish Free State had become the temporal power, with the Church of Ireland in continuing decline as one of the rival spiritual powers. Robert Synge was busy up the road reclaiming Glanmore as an ancestral pile, corresponding with John Joly about drainage.

The Synges were back in Wicklow, but Wicklow was not back with them. Even people of their own class were changed utterly in the years since 1909. Not only had the independence movement been supported by a few distinguished individuals from the upper classes – famously the Gore-Booth sisters – but even the Republican opposition to settlement with Britain had its supporters among these families. In June 1928, when Lady Gregory drove down from Dublin to visit the Bartons, she learned of how her hosts had hidden four Republicans 'on the run' and was reminded how Erskine Childers (the Svengali of Irish Republicanism, or 'Damnable Englishman') had been arrested there and subsequently executed.[33] His body had lain in state – if such can be said of one executed by the state he helped to found – at Glendalough House, visited once or twice upon a time by the youthful Johnnie Synge. A clerical predecessor of Sam Synge's had attended Childers at his execution.

Renewed interest in Synge the dramatist had been stimulated by the Allen & Unwin edition of 1927. Seán Keating's involvement signalled a degree of rapprochement between the author of the plays which libelled the good name of Ireland and the new political order established by a sizeable portion of the same people. Keating's best-known work had encapsulated the spirit of nationalist resolution under titles – such as *The Men of the West* – which in part derived from Synge's dramatisation of allegedly characteristic 'types'. By contrast, Harry Clarke's 'Queens', and the more publically accessible 'Mad Mulrannies', showed Synge as the deviser of bare-breasted androgynous figures amongst whom poorly disguised contemporary artists peeped out.[34]

Nor was the new interest confined to Synge's homeland. On 15 March 1928, the British Broadcasting Corporation hosted a talk by the poet James Stephens who reminisced about the dramatist, then nearly twenty years dead. There is no evidence on the Synge side that Stephens – a man of very humble origins and no relation of the Harry Stephens family – ever met John Synge, eleven years his senior. Despite this lack of obvious credentials, Stephens delivered a monologue in which it was impossible to distinguish between factual reportage and imaginative sympathy. '[Synge] could assure a thirsty companion that behind a certain folding of a certain hilly track there was a well.' Or, more intrusively, 'He grew [sic] in a house that was filled with the furnitures and curiosities of strange countries.'[35] Through radio, and untrammelled creative reminiscence, there was no limit to what might become of JMS. Underscoring the popular British audience Stephens reached, the *Radio Times* published his script on 23 March.

Aware of Hutchie's tribulations, and no doubt alert also to Edward Stephens's rising star as a solicitor trusted by the new regime,[36] Archdeacon Synge (as he became) commenced his own version of J. M. Synge's life. At least that seems the soundest interpretation of a February 1928 entry in Lady Gregory's journal.[37] Unfortunately the journal itself has suffered deliberate mutilation at this point – 'page taken out' Gregory noted without explanation. As a result, her record of the memories – whether Sam's, Ned's or Robert's – trails off: 'They are very simply written . . .'[38] Later, she came close to resuming contact with Sam and his project. Some 'diaries' had been shown to Robert Barton, the archdeacon's neighbour at Glendalough House, Annamoe, a man who had signed the Treaty of 1921 and then opposed it during the ensuing Civil War. Glendalough

House – not to be confused with Kathleen Synge's semi-detached residence of the same name in Kingstown – was the 'sun-trap, in the midst of the bleakest mountain scenery' evoked by Constance Markievicz from her prison cell in the winter of 1920. On that Saturday in June 1928, when Gregory motored through gorse-lined byroads into Wicklow, the company at Bartons' included David Robinson, son of a Delgany rector but renowned as a dashing Republican comrade of the late countess. Not a gathering where Sam Synge fitted, for all that he had shown papers to their host. Bob Barton said 'there was nothing in them to print'.[39]

If these were John Synge's diaries, then indeed so laconic a publication might have provoked either indifference or mild ridicule. Perhaps the diaries in question were not the dramatist's but Sam Synge's, dating back to the period when he and Johnnie were growing up together in Rathfarnham and Greystones. Or they were Kathleen's diaries, with letters to her faraway sons. All of these lesser papers were subsequently alluded to and even quoted in *Letters to My Daughter*, published four years later, whereas *Letters* makes no reference to John Synge's own diaries, preserved in the family archive in Dundrum.

A September review of Yeats's book *The Death of Synge* in the *Irish Statesman* by Sean O'Faolain, the short-story writer, provoked a small flurry of response and counter-response. Arthur Lynch, the Boer War colonel and sometime MP, alleged a number of inaccuracies, only to be himself gently rebuked by Stephen MacKenna.[40] O'Faolain suggested consumption as cause of death, but the subsequent exchange of views was more concerned with the degree and quality of Synge's nationalism. The seventh seal on Saint John's life in Paris was breaking. And whatever Bob Barton might have made of these veterans of *fin-de-siècle* irredentism, their names linked to J. M. Synge's cannot have reassured the archdeacon.

Other members of the family had other preoccupations. Edward Stephens, his brother Frank, and their younger cousin John Lighton Synge contributed to a lavish handbook for Dublin's second Civic Week in September 1929. Frank Stephens wrote on 'The Foundations of Dublin Commerce', J. L. Synge on the mathematician W. H. Rowan. A public lecture on 'The Arran Islands' in the Irish Salon of Photography demonstrated how Synge's prose masterpiece had been absorbed into a new synthesis of Irish values.[41] Stephens served on the committee with Bulmer Hobson, J. W. Manning, Dermod O'Brien, and other lively spirits of the reviving city. A barrister by profession, he became an enthusiast for native Irish enterprise, even to the point of manufacturing his own toothpaste (trade-name, Gráinne) in the back of his office.[42]

Some time in April 1929, Sam Synge evidently sent a manuscript work of his own, or part of it, to Lady Gregory at Coole. She was in her late seventies. Naturally enough, she sent an account of the proposed book to Yeats, now sixty-three, only to receive anxious rebukes from Annamoe Rectory. 'If possibly you even made short notes of any parts, please be sure that nothing gets into print in any way.' A week later, 'Please remember that I cannot under any circumstances allow any one to publish any of the M.S. or any comments on any part of the M.S.'[43] Just a few months earlier, 'The Old Lady' had – according to legend – said 'No' to a smart and determined young dramatist called Dennis Johnston. She was in no mood for an archdeacon's fitful discretions. The first version of her reply opened haughtily, 'I did not expect from John Synge's brother the discourtesy of, for the second time, a registered envelope.'[44] This was put aside in favour of more charitable sentiments, which did not fully mature. 'I do not know to how many acquaintances or others you lent the MS. I was told by one of them the opinion given you, which was not far from that formed by me.' She concurred with Barton's view of Sam 'erring through ignorance'.[45]

The delay between February 1928 (when Lady Gregory had intimations of the archdeacon's work) and the book's final appearance in the spring of 1932 could be explained in terms of its unattractiveness to publishers. Starkly lacking any endorsement from Synge's celebrated and influential colleagues, *Letters* can hardly have excited much interest as a manuscript – the archdeacon wrote in a simple hand on cheap, lined notepaper. Furthermore, the text was patently naive, offering no comment on the plays or poems. A formidable range of authors – including Bourgeois in 1913, Masefield in 1915, and of course Yeats (1911, 1928, etc.) – elevated their subject to a level to which the fabricated *Letters* could only distantly aspire. No firm of Allen & Unwin's standing was prepared to consider publication. Maunsel, who might have taken an interest in anything about their renowned author, had ceased publishing in 1925.

Other tallies of Synge's achievement were coming into circulation. The *Dublin Magazine*, a distinguished but unradical literary journal, carried a bibliography of his publications in its last issue for 1930. Then, in 1931, Cork University Press published *Synge and Anglo-Irish Literature* by Daniel Corkery. This was not only a home-produced book, it was a brutally direct confrontation with the cultural presumptions of Synge's class, a work likely to give far more offence than satisfaction in the Synge households of Annamoe Glebe, Glanmore Castle and suburban Knockroe. Quite apart from his *a priori* hatred of the 'Protestant Ascendancy' and its cross-bred 'Anglo-Irish' literature, Professor Corkery made short work of Synge's domestic situation in boyhood – 'of course there is no intentional neglect . . .' While acknowledging the bond of love between mother and son, he concludes that Synge's upbringing was one of 'almost unguessed-at loneliness'. Then he cites Bourgeois's detection of 'an unfortunate and mysterious love affair', refers in some detail to Cherrie Matheson's *Irish Statesman* article, and proceeds to attribute Synge's conversion to the cause of Ireland as the happy consequence of his quitting it for Europe. MacKenna and Lynch are made to testify to the sufficiency of his nationalist leanings. Synge, as it were, was to become himself by ceasing to be a member of his own family.

On the topic of Synge's health, Corkery was no less frank. 'Some cancerous disease had attacked him. He went into the Elpis Private Hospital. He came out of it in May, 1908, thinking that an operation had been performed, whereas the doctors had merely closed up the wound when they saw the disease had gone too far for them.'[46] The family had not paid good money to Margaret Huxley (and Harry Stephens) for medical privacy, only then to smile upon public discussion twenty years later. To Yeats's oracular praise of the dying Synge it was possible to turn a deaf ear; after all, Yeats was a licensed genius, and Protestant, and almost a gentleman.[47] Corkery was the self-declared successor to D. P. Moran, representative of Catholic Nationalism, of the self-governing unwashed.

It is most likely then that *Synge and Anglo-Irish Literature* provoked the publication of *Letters to My Daughter*. Given the prolonged and largely fruitless negotiations between the Knockroe Synges and London publishers, coinciding with the swelling stream of incidental publications about Synge – by Cherrie Matheson, Padraic Colum, Arthur Lynch,[48] Stephen MacKenna, and always of course Yeats – the archdeacon took his timidity in his hand and arranged for publication by the Talbot Press of Dublin. He had his manuscript complete by December 1931, less than twelve months after Corkery had been feted in the *Manchester Guardian*, the *Observer*, the *Irish Press* and the *New York Times Literary Review*. It appeared before Easter of the following year, unfeted.

In its crabbed way, *Synge and Anglo-Irish Literature* had vindicated the dramatist and the man, albeit in terms which few beyond Irish Ireland could comprehend. In the view of Corkery's own latter-day apologist, much in it is simply an expansion of ideas aired in a lecture of 1910, a year after Synge's death. Written up at length as the necessary qualification for academic appointment in University College, Cork, the book of 1931 was more of a swansong than a call to arms. If the aspirant professor did indeed rehash his earlier responses to Synge and serve them up in an ultra-nationalist theoretical pot, 'Corkery qualified them in such a way that the book is usually misread as an attack on Synge and a justification of the *Playboy* rioters.'[49]

To understand *Letters to My Daughter*, one has to remember that it followed after Yeats's *Death of Synge* (1928) as well as after Corkery's stolid diatribe. Though the paternal epistolary commonplaces which are distributed between 1 July 1914 and 22 February 1928 constitute a record of some kind, the book is also remarkable for the extracts from family correspondence and diaries which intervene between the letter of 9 February 1926 to the author's daughter and that of 22 February 1928. Given that Sam Synge had transcribed these passages from his mother's papers, it is possible that this body of material featured in the dossier shown or sent to Bob Barton and Lady Gregory, and that Sam's letters (or some of them, at least) to Edith Synge may even have been fabricated to augment what Barton and Gregory had so promptly dismissed.

Alluding to Bourgeois's biography, Sam Synge presents himself as writing in November 1922: 'Your Uncle John's life has been written, as you know. I have seen the outside of the book, but have on purpose never read it. I wished not to do so until I had written to you various little things that I, his chief playmate as a boy, could remember about him.'[50] It has been said that he adopted the curious form of *Letters to My Daughter* partly in order 'to dispel speculation & rumours'. Mary Colum much earlier spoke of the 'mysterious rumors' circulating about the playwright at the time of the *Playboy* riots.[51] The record of J. M. Synge's life does not suggest a reputation vulnerable to scandalous myth or – for that matter – damaging truthful revelation. No surviving evidence challenges his own amused confession to Cherrie Matheson that, in turn-of-the-century Paris, he was regarded as a saint. No biographer has committed him- or herself to the proposition that the relationship with Molly Allgood was sexually consummated. J. B. Lyons, medical historian, is of opinion that it was not. In so far as sex in Rathmines or the rue d'Assas is concerned, there never was much chance of speculation or rumour. Finally, nothing suggests that the author of *The Playboy*, unsuspected before now, did in fact 'commit murder or a bad nasty thing, or false coining' the like of Christy Mahon in the starved imaginations of the Western World.[52]

Conclusive evidence against these charges might be found in Samuel Synge's silence on such matters. He does not even protest too much. He does not protest at all, instead providing as unremarkable an account of his brother as might be worked up for any nondescript of their class and age. It is true that he has difficulty admitting that Johnnie drank whiskey down among the people. But he does acknowledge it despite the strong feeling of Protestant evangelicals against alcohol. Political disloyalty in Paris, rather than moral laxity, might explain his desire to infantilise J. M. Synge. Even if he had thought deeply about his brother's work, the late 1920s were not the moment for decoy exercises in nursery reminiscence. The Free State was now well and truly established; nothing was to be gained by distracting attention from the love of country every-where evident in Synge's work. And, in any case, not one of his siblings or near relatives had disengaged from the new polity, taken the boat to Torquay or Tasmania. On the contrary, they had steered home to the land of their birth, Sam from China and Robert from Argentina. Ned, the most unionist of the brothers and a long-serving magistrate under the *ancien régime*, never left Irish shores, even missing the Isle of Man holiday in 1882. Irishness in Synge was never an embarrassment.

Conversion to Catholicism might have embarrassed some in the family, though Kathleen Synge just before her death reconciled herself to John-nie's going through the marriage ceremony in Molly's parish church. Her youngest son's reading of the devotional classics – Francis, Thomas, Teresa – signalled an interest in the Catholic past, unmatched by any curiosity about contemporary religious practice. But even a threatened revelation of some clandestine 'going over to Rome' could hardly have justified the labour which went into *Letters to My Daughter* more than twenty years after the suspected apostasy. And again, no evidence could have been adduced to substantiate a claim that Synge had died a Catholic, he who had virtually been reared an Open Brother.

So we must turn in dismay to the pages of Samuel Synge's compilation, searching among its harmless anecdotes and touching recitations of name and date for an unintended clue to its author's motivation. The letters were published 'for the relations and friends of the late John M. Synge who may care to see them. No one else is asked to read them.' Nor do the occasional notes cast much light on the subject – though one virtually admits the post-hoc basis of the correspondence.[53] Then, just two pages before the point at which the letters give way to extensive transcripts from Kathleen Synge's diaries, the topic of J. M. Synge's health and death is raised. 'The "Playboy" riot I do not think he very much minded. That was not the sort of thing that worried him. Nor did it make any great difference to his health. His last illness was an old trouble that he had been fighting against for years and which at last surgery could no longer overcome. Sir Charles Ball, after your Uncle John's death, very kindly wrote to me telling me particulars. It was not, however, a cancer that your Uncle John had, but another trouble.'[54] As so often happens when little is intended, much is apprehended. What *was* the sort of thing that had worried the dramatist?

It is possible that Archdeacon Synge wished to dispel in his daughter's mind the fears which sprang up at the word, cancer. Yet, that is to assume that Edith Synge was genuinely the recipient of these letters on the dates given in the printed text. That notion has been scotched, not least because she was almost invariably with her father and so hardly in need of comforting letters.[55] (She grew to be an independent woman of rigorous intellect.) In the period running up to publication of *Letters to My Daughter*, Robert Synge's wife was dying, and the cause (cancer) was unmentionable in family circles.[56] Here is a rationale for Sam's attempt to reverse a diagnosis passed on his brother at the opening of the century, but *only* in so far as his letters were intended for the family. Outside that quarter, Bourgeois as early as 1913 had gone so far as to indicate 'some sort of tumour, possibly cancer'. Corkery had been belligerently precise.[57] And Gogarty, who had diagnosed the particular cancer, was increasingly voluble. The growing reputation of Joyce's unsavoury *Ulysses* offered no balm. 'The tramper Synge is looking ... to murder you. He heard you pissed on his halldoor in Glasthule.'[58]

In publishing his letter of '3 February 1923', Sam cannot have seriously hoped to rebut the accepted diagnosis of Hodgkin's disease as the cause of his brother's death. He was himself a medical doctor. What then was he contemplating as he slipped these denying and too-revealing sentences into print? To answer such a question, one should perhaps reconsider the matter of speculation and rumour. For it is feasible that speculation fastened not on what actually killed Synge, but on the more complex and less verifiable issue of what Synge had believed (at some time or another) to be the cause of his long illness. The Diarist of the 'Etude morbide' had worried over the problem of the man who believed himself to suffer from a disease he really did not have. As late as May 1908, Synge debated with himself the fate of this manuscript – which survived him.

Four verdicts have been passed on the cause of his death on 24 March 1909. The certificate, as registered some three weeks after the event, specified cancer of the bowel, present for the previous fifteen months. In Mount Jerome Cemetery, however, the cause of death was given as 'abdomenal tumour', evidently by Ned Synge who got his brother's age wrong by one year. To bowel cancer and a tumour in the abdomen add Gogarty's August 1907 on-the-street diagnosis of Hodgkin's disease (lymphadenoma). This has generally been accepted, perhaps because nobody has ever bothered to verify it in the General Registry of Births, Marriages, and Deaths (Lombard Street).[59] The specification of 'fifteen months' in the Register of Deaths is a little odd in that the deceased had not been medically examined at the date implied (say, January 1908); it was only in May 1908 that abdominal surgery was attempted, and the inoperable tumour discovered.

In the case of Kathleen Synge, dying just five months earlier, the register and cemetery appear to record secondary causes of death, with no mention made of the malignancy diagnosed in late January 1908. Neither makes acknowledgement of anything comparable to a 'disease in some ways similar to that from which John was suffering'.[60] The issue is bedevilled by a reluctance of the public authorities to record certain causes in the Register, by the practice of doctors to specify what might be termed immediate (cardiac arrest) or secondary (asthma) causes, and by the avoidance in family discourse of naming diseases thought ill-omened as well as fatal. As Wilde's Algernon gaily noted a few years earlier, even severe chills were becoming hereditary.

Maud Gonne's prompt declaration that Synge's death had been 'the happiest thing that could have happened' may be further evidence of her indifference to the living and dying of others. In June 1909, T. W. Rolleston, who had lived close to the Synges in their Greystones days, observed to John Quinn, 'What I told you about his incurable disease turned out only too true.'[61] Joyce's casual report to his brother Stanislaus two months later that 'Synge is said to have been syphilitic, poor man' lacks any kind of authority – though it might be recalled that Joyce had been a medical student in Paris (where Gonne continued to live), and his family was not unspotted in these matters. Gonne's prediction, that for a Synge who might survive the crisis of March 1909 'an invalid's life would be so terrible', does not accord with the causes of death as usually given. On the other hand, chronic invalidism was what lay ahead for Ibsen's Osvald Alving. In January 1912, Yeats complained bitterly about defamation of the literary movement: 'One of the curious things is the lying rumours that have been put in circulation about us everywhere, one which seems to be believed as a matter of course is that Synge died of disease contracted by living an immoral life, I was told the other day that everybody knew that the story about cancer was invented to hide this.'[62] In this latter context, Sam's unconsciously Ibsenite euphemism – 'an old trouble that he had been fighting against for years' – takes on precisely the undertones the archdeacon was anxious to quell. Even if he preferred the thought of tuberculosis to the publicly registered cause of death (cancer), the raising of the topic could only give rise to uglier speculation.[63]

Undertone eludes reassuring interpretation by the young and frightened. If Synge had investigated his condition – and his brother's medical books had been to hand – then he would have found that, in two of the five cases of Hodgkin's disease reported in the *Dublin Journal of Medical Science* between January 1888 and August 1905, syphilis was implicated. One of the five was reported by W. M. A. Wright, a recent graduate of Trinity's medical school, and almost certainly the 'Dr Wright' who attended Synge in 1899.[64] The *DJMS*'s account of 'Mr H' (who lived in Ranelagh with his father) noted that, though he died of Hodgkin's disease in 1901, he had contracted syphilis six or eight years earlier. In an even later case, a doctor from the Adelaide (Sam's old training hospital) observed that 'Hodgkin's disease is, comparatively speaking, rare. Glandular enlargement, whether as a result of some of the infectious diseases or due to tubercular, syphilitic or other poisons, is very common.'[65]

Sensitivity on the question was extreme at the turn of the century. When Synge had written 'The Curse' about Molly's sister, he became aware that Peggy Callender had contracted syphilis from her husband, possibly as a drunken consequence of rows about *The Playboy*. Yet he could only wish to 'make it thoroughly wicket [sic] then it would be lovely'.[66] Nor was this reluctance a matter of personal modesty. The public records of predominantly Catholic Dublin aimed to convey the unlikely statistic that, in the year of Synge's death, no one died of venereal disease – just as no one committed suicide. The professions maintained a high degree of diplomacy, not so much hypocrites as the custodians of hypocrisy. As a Dr Smith had said when Wright read his paper, there was 'a chaotic state of confusion in the professional mind as regards lymphatic diseases'.[67] Among non-professionals, confusion might feature as obsession. The Diarist of the 1897/8 'Étude' found in reviews an 'analysis of nerve decay', he whose 'brain by some horrible decadence is grown a register for appalling things'.[68] The words might be attributed to Osvald Alving. In May 1899, Wright cleared John of 'serious symptoms'.

What Joyce's postscript of August 1909 demonstrated was a state of opinion rather than fact, a distinction of crucial importance in assessing the impact of disease on Synge's life and work. If rumour of syphilis had reached Fontenoy Street in north Dublin by late summer 1909, its source was not necessarily Continental. While the upsurge of Parisian recollections in the late 1920s may have alarmed the archdeacon, it is important to note that Joyce linked Synge's alleged cause of death to Arthur

Symons's General Paralysis of the Insane. The priest in the opening story of Joyce's *Dubliners* – a collection to which George Roberts and his legal adviser, Charles Weekes, would take exception – was not so lucky. As with the unfortunate, non-fictional Susan Pollexfen (Mrs John Butler Yeats) on 3 January 1900, the verdict on 'Father Flynn' had been General Paralysis – more specifically General Paralysis of the Insane, in his case.[69] But GPI is not only a specific consequence of syphilis in Joyce's work; it is a pervasive cultural metaphor, the General Paralysis of an Insane Society. If J. M. Synge had fears that he might cease to be, there was evidence all round him – stated, implied, or powerfully repressed – of dis-grace in death. Even if Synge could be (in some ideal biographer's ideal system) proven to have died a virgin unspotted, the nature of the disease allowed for inheritance as well as first-hand infection.

We can, I believe, dismiss syphilis as a diagnosis with respect both to congenital transmission and direct infection. In relation to the latter, the combination of Synge's recorded symptoms in pre-puberty and his unchallenged reputation for moral probity would leave little room for infection through casual intercourse – though the 'lavatory seat' anxieties of young men are difficult to dislodge. As for congenital syphilis, the route necessarily involves an infected *mother*; in the Synge family, Kathleen outlived her husband by more than thirty-five years, healthy years as far as we know until close to the end. Finally, the discrepancies between the cause of death as registered by Robert (cancer of the bowel) and by Ned (abdomenal tumour) eloquently disavow any need to 'agree a story'.

That is to speak of fact. While all of this should have been reassuring to the anxious and ailing youngest son, the fact that his mother was stricken in 1908 with symptoms similar to his own may have prompted recollection of his own childish observations and undertakings. Anxiety about his own condition is palpable in his reiterated inquiries about Molly's sexual health. There is more to go on. Opinion does not exclude the opinion of the subject about himself, and here J. M. Synge's auto-biographical fragments need to be re-examined.

The first to be considered deals with Darwin's *On the Origin of Species*:

Till then I had never doubted and never conceived that a sane and wise man or boy could doubt. I had of course heard of atheists but as vague monsters that I was unable to realize. It seemed that I was become in a moment the playfellow of Judas. Incest and parricide were but a consequence of the idea that possessed me.[70]

This incident has proved impossible to date, though we do know that

Synge finished *The Descent of Man* on 12 October 1895, when he was twenty-four, and had returned from his first trip to the Continent. In the concluding pages of Darwin's second and more alarming masterpiece, his dominant preoccupation (with non-human species, man's place in the world of nature) is pushed aside. A shockingly domestic and intimate injunction leaps out. 'Both sexes ought to refrain from marriage if in any marked degree inferior in body or mind, but such hopes are Utopian and will never be even partially realised until the laws of inheritance are thoroughly known ... all ought to refrain from marriage who cannot avoid abject poverty for their children.'[71]

Knowing that Synge read this in his early twenties, and also that his first encounter with any of Darwin's writings cannot have occurred before 1886 at the very earliest (when he was going on sixteen), then the following second passage from the fragments also deserves reconsideration:

ill health led to a curious resolution which has explained in some measure all my subsequent evolution. Without knowing, or, as far as I can remember, hearing anything about doctrines of heredity I surmised that unhealthy parents should have unhealthy children – my rabbit breeding may have put the idea into my head. Therefore, I said, I am unhealthy, and if I marry I will have unhealthy children. But I will never create beings to suffer as I am suffering, so I will never marry.[72]

Apart from the palpable terror of the youth described in this passage, its most notable feature is its post-hoc status. Yet the twenty-five-year-old (or older) man privately records that the resolution of more than ten years earlier explains all his subsequent 'evolution'. And if the passage was written (as its editor allows) as late as 1898, then Synge had already proposed marriage to Cherrie Matheson (in June 1896), and undergone the first of his Elpis operations (December 1897).

This renewed scrutiny of Synge's autobiographical jottings has the effect of prising apart three distinct factors too often run together – his loss (or lack) of religious faith, his encounter with Darwin, and his anxiety about health and heredity. There is literary evidence also. Read as a rewriting of Ibsen's *Ghosts, When the Moon Has Set* – under way by the mid-1890s – anxiously rebuts the notion of guilty inheritance from the ancestral past. It does so by systematic redistribution, replacing a father with an uncle/namesake, and associating Paris with music rather than art, drink or vice. (Synge had abandoned music as a career *before* reaching Paris.) The syphilis which breaks through in Oswald's final dementia identifies what is structurally and thematically excluded from Synge's first completed play. The last adjustment to *Deirdre* was to introduce a character with obscure origins textual and sexual: idiotic Owen 'screaming with derisive laughter', the anachronistic victim of 'the French disease' in Iron Age Alba.

Quite when Synge escaped from the belief that unhealthy parents must have unhealthy children, and from the resolution that he should never marry, cannot be established. To judge by his mother's letters, a peculiar crisis arose in November 1889, when he was closer to nineteen than eighteen: 'glands swelled & sore again in his groins & boils on his legs.' Casually reporting her son's pubertal agonies, she continued, 'he hurt himself last week walking in & out & carrying his fiddle . . .'[73] That this was not the first time his 'groins' had swollen indicates something more than a pedestrian accident. Young Johnnie had every unreason to be frightened. What demands respect is the courage of a teenager or young man enduring the anxiety and extreme loneliness such a conviction imposed, whether for a period of mere months or much longer. Despite the high spirits commended by nurses almost to the last weeks of illness, his eventual non-marriage, non-begetting of children and (it is likely) non-consummation of sexual relationships are of a piece with early terror.

Early terror and final agony. Cancer of the bowel as the final cause of death is quite consistent with a previous diagnosis of Hodgkin's disease, for the latter may lead to secondary cancers in the body. Loss of hair, genital pain – the resemblances of Hodgkin-symptoms (in a frightened layman's eyes) to the popular notions of (congenital) syphilitic infection provoked the alarms and terrors which Synge only gave voice to in a retrospective on childhood and not in any direct record of his actual condition at any specific time.

In 1939, Synge's grave (originally Aunt Jane's) at Mount Jerome was reopened to receive the body of his sister-in-law, Mary Harmar; in 1951, it was opened to receive his brother Sam's remains. Certainly, he was buried amid the family.

CHAPTER 26

'A Likely Gaffer in the End of All ...'?

Those Mohicans outside the Hungry Monk in April 1996, within a last-trumpet's sound of 3 Bethel Terrace, what did they think of Christy Mahon? It seemed a fair question. They clanked on, like extras on a crowded *Tinker's Wedding* set. Synge might have clanked after them, keen to hear of cider parties, one-parent families, and the risks involved in ear-piercing. After all, he was a decent fellow, on the side of the underdog, a bit of a mystery of course, there's money behind him somehow, but – yes – a decent fellow, and with brains too.

What sort of person was Synge? *Women liked him. He never praised other people's work. He mixed well with his social inferiors. He exhausted himself in mental labour. He was a superficial reader. He was sexually inexperienced. He loved nature. Languages came easily to him. He was preoccupied with his own illness.* Each of these statements is true, but inadequate. Though they tot up important characteristics, they come to nothing like John Synge. As we no longer assume that each human being organises him or herself round some thing-like essential inner core, dynamic or contemplative, machine or spirit, the question needs to be rephrased.

What were the crucial moments in Synge's life? *The death of his father in 1872. His rejection by Cherrie Matheson. The diagnosis of Hodgkin's disease. Giving up music. Wrapping a bible in brown paper. Reading Darwin. The journey to Aran. Reading Molly Allgood's first letter. Meeting James Joyce.* This list approximates to a primitive biography more readily than the first list outlined a character portrait. But the order in which events are considered profoundly affects our view of the life. If it could be proved that Synge bought his ticket for Galway ten days before his interview with Mrs Matheson, the cause-and-effect interpretation generally advanced would be jeopardised. But if we knew more about Barbara Conneely or the Société Fraternelle, Synge would be altered also.

Are we then left adrift on some inflatable 'lilo-of-choice', among innumerable versions of Synge bobbing on the heated pool of post-modernism, none claiming to be any truer than the next? The desire to know a historical character appears to be illicit nowadays, a species of bad manners. Yet Francis Hackett, who met him in 1907, characterised Synge and his work in unambiguous terms: 'A red thread of sex goes through all the plays, like a melody through a Wagner opera, and sex in Synge is the pride of the peacock and the lust of the goat. He is natural man, without any of the bothersome metaphysics that tease Yeats. He has much more the serene temperament of a painter, only painters haven't vibration as a rule, and all of Synge's plays have vibration, like the pulse in the body.'[1]

Rather unexpectedly this anticipates D. H. Lawrence, while also repeating the comparison between Synge's work and the visual arts which had cropped up more than once in the *Playboy* controversy. What one person sees of another's personality is usually a combination of things or qualities, not a single defining characteristic. And so, while we may feel confident that John Synge was good company, he was also shy; he liked children but for a long period forswore parenthood and marriage. He was precocious and pretty obtuse; he had iron self-control and blubbed in some of his letters. This is more like a character portrayal, and not simply in its contrariness. Synge's character was problematic, and there were rare moments when he signalled this.

One occurs in his treatment of Pater's *Renaissance*. Responding to the chapter on the school of Giorgione (*c*.1477–1510), Synge wrote a 'criticism' of it with unusual care and an odd word or two: 'What is this song or picture or book, this enjoying [sic] personality presented in life or in a book to ME?'[2] I don't think this constitutes either an assertion of confident, philistine personality or an instance of that influence on young men which Pater claimed to fear in his own work. (The final chapter of *The Renaissance* was said to have encouraged homosexuality.) What we have here is a critique of the Paterian aesthetic moment, with its emphasis on immediate sensuous experience and on art untrammelled by ethical or historical considerations. Under Synge's gaze, it has been turned inside-out to become a quizzical assertion, made by the necessary other partner in any notion of the aesthetic moment – the sentient self. While Pater secretly longs to be an artwork experienced by suitable art-lovers, Synge's little rewriting insists on the relative autonomy of both subject and object. His apparently unintentional phrase – 'this enjoying personality' – pinpoints the indulgent introspection of what Pater had presented as an approach to art.

Synge's unedited notebooks are so fragmentary that it is unwise to piece together a Syngean outlook. At the end of his so-called 'Autobiography', the dramatist offers a definition of human identity which doubles as a statement on religious belief. 'A cycle of experience is the only definite unity, and when all has been passed through, and every joy and pain has been resolved in one passion of relief, the only rest that can follow is in the dissolution of the person.'[3] This complements what John Eglinton meant when he wrote: 'Synge was more than an episode in Yeats's history: he was a disturbing event, which brought Yeats back from the abstract to the personal.'[4] In other words, Synge generated a sense of personality in Yeats, who by all accounts was badly in need of such a boost.

In this sense, Synge now looks very like the catalyst which T. S. Eliot invoked in his 'Impersonal Theory of Poetry', that piece of finely filiated platinum introduced into a chamber containing oxygen and sulphur dioxide. While Eliot's later ideological excesses are to be deplored, the intelligence which pervades 'Tradition and the Individual Talent' should not be ignored. If his distinction between 'the man who suffers and the mind which creates' gives offence today, this does not annul the fact of Synge and Eliot as contemporaries, responding in different but comparable ways to the crisis of Western culture in the decades before August 1914 (and, in the case of Eliot, those following that date, also).[5]

Eliot would hardly approve of an alliance between his Impersonality Theory and the 'genetic structuralism' of the maverick Marxist, Lucien Goldmann. Nevertheless, in the case of a tragic dramatist like Synge, whose approach to genre was so delicately informed by historical problems, the implications of Goldmann's Hidden God (Le Dieu caché, 1959) deserve attention even here where the priority should remain biographical. Basing his sociology of literature and belief on a close examination of Jean Racine's plays and the Pensées of Blaise Pascal, Goldmann argued that a homology could be discerned between the forms of literature and the contradictions inherent in specific seventeenth-century French social groups (e.g., la noblesse de robe and the Jansenists). The question worth posing here is this: Can Synge's drama be interpreted as the cultural 'equivalent' of a subdivision of Irish Protestantism, in the overlapping aftermath of Disestablishment and the penultimate crisis of landlordism? While the issue cannot be pursued here, it is clear that the anti-territorialist basis of the Brethren's organisation and their anti-clerical liturgical practices come once more into play, not only as unconscious precursors to certain themes in Synge's drama, but also as unexpected preludes to national political change.[6]

This historical placing serves to remind us that, if the personality of

J. M. Synge remains inscrutable to a degree, his career lies open to view. Of some early trial pieces Nicholas Grene has justly written: 'What is most significant is that Synge wrote them at the age of twenty-three, rather than fifteen.'[7] That delayed start, attributable to a love of music or a poor education or a lack of literary confidence, artificially compresses the mature work into an astonishingly brief period between late 1903 and his death in March 1909. It should be now clear that the best of the plays have roots in earlier experience, echoing their author's reading and reflection as well as his more celebrated travels. The delay in seeing *The Aran Islands* into print deprived Synge of an achievement in prose at a time when his confidence might have been boosted, his vital energies recharged, and his outlook on life and his country preserved more sweetly. As it was, the great prose work (issued finally in April 1907) got ensnared in the *Playboy* controversies. Thereafter Synge never managed to compile the Wicklow book he intended.

In short, after writing *The Playboy* Synge's resources were in steady and irreversible decline. Personally, I do not think the riots can be blamed for hastening his end as some, anxious to exploit his death, have declared. Nor can we see Kathleen Synge's death as anything more than the formality of a 'final blow'. The truth is that *The Playboy* itself is part of the decline, not its major cause. It is not simply that Ellen Duncan had put her finger on an unconvincing aspect of the play – something might have been done to rectify a minor structural weakness, an issue of psychology rather than dramatic art. Compared to *The Well of the Saints*, the play of 1907 lacked concentration and intensity; it was episodic – brilliantly so – but episodic where the earlier full-length play had traced a single, richly embroidered line through ironic exposition, reversal, and visionary renewal.

The rapid succession of one-act plays in 1903/4, the marginalised experiment of *The Tinker's Wedding*, the Celtic and the comic in two full-length plays produced within two years, and the dogged weaving of tragic *Deirdre* deserves some final consideration. Such an achievement cannot be written off, nor written up, as the frenzied energy of a man on the brink of the grave. Synge's oddly constituted timetable of life led to his responding to a series of cultural upheavals as if they were occurring almost simultaneously, whereas for others these events were assignable to year after separate year. *Riders to the Sea* brought together images of loss at sea, the Great Famine and (Tom Paulin has suggested) commemoration of 1798. *In the Shadow of the Glen* echoed Ibsen, recalled the steady procession of emigrants from Ireland, and touched dangerously on topics of madness and illicit sexuality. *The Well of the Saints* brought together

Nietzsche and a Celticising strategy of self-renewal in the Church of Ireland: it also blasphemed. *The Playboy* disinterred Parnell, insulted Irish family values, and appeared to celebrate murder by staging calculated violence. Finally, there is *Deirdre of the Sorrows*, a love-play highlighting treachery and internecine war, a costume drama prophesying guerrilla days and dirty tricks. By the time it was staged, however, the public had turned to commemorate rather than eviscerate J. M. Synge. Privately, Yeats thought it 'a rather loosely jointed rather monotonous play with some moments of magnificent tragedy'. Publicly, it 'went finely and was even a financial success'.[8] Yet in the half-dozen years – less – of his career, Synge moved from one sensitive issue to another, a wounded surgeon probing the body politic and spiritual.

Whatever about Eliot's doctrine of separate powers, Synge's health cannot be separated from the mind which suspects. Here too one encounters a double timetable – of Synge's illness as a relatively objective condition, and Synge's anxiety about illness as a form of retribution or shame. And here we touch on the most unsatisfactory of all Synge's complicated works, *When the Moon Has Set*. Yet his undertaking to un-write Ibsen's *Ghosts* cannot be deciphered as an autobiographical confession of syphilitic infection, even though there is other evidence pointing to Synge's concern about heredity, insanity, and pollution. What Sigmund Freud's English translators call syphilidophobia may in Synge's case have outlasted the brief period of conscious fear (which I associate with the decision to consult Dr W. M. A. Wright in May 1899), and then merged with the debilitating effects of Hodgkin's disease from which Synge eventually died. For Freud, the irrational and intense fear of contracting (or already having) a venereal disease functions as a disguised fear of castration – a classic Freudian doctrine less useful in this context than an appreciation of Synge's powerfully inhibited instinct towards sexual consummation.

The sexuality which Francis Hackett heard as the dominant melody in all Synge's drama was, according to this line of argument, a compensation. In conflict with this, at least one member of the family has told me that she has no doubts about Synge's sexual activity in Paris: it conformed, she believes, with the conventional behaviour of young middle-class men at the turn of the century. He had some recourse to prostitutes, and probably a more personal and extended relationship with at least one woman who cannot now be identified among his friends there. Though this interpretation runs against his own declaration that he was regarded as 'a saint' by his Parisian acquaintances and a pagan by his family circle, it does not rule out two chastely maintained love-affairs closer to home.

These were not without their complexities. Synge's relationship with Florence Ross may have been a childhood infatuation between cousins, but it was exacerbated and even 'traumatised' by his encounter with Darwin. What might have been a mildly perturbing intellectual challenge prompted fear-laden thoughts of incest and parricide – prompted guilt. Characteristically, records of this Darwinian discovery are vague as to dates and locations. But the episode strongly resembles what Freud calls *Nachträglichkeit,* an event ordinary enough in itself which triggers the intensification of some earlier episode which was (until the second) also ordinary enough. The same process has been detected in Synge's encounter with death in 1901–2. It is greatly to the credit of Synge and Ross that they came to be warm friends in adult life. This does not diminish the significance of bereaved days spent in Blackburne's woods as reactivated on the day dead Darwin delivered his tardy message about evolution.

Though once again the documentation fails to be specific, this day of blinding enlightenment may well have found the adult John Synge socialising with his Matheson neighbours. If Cherrie Matheson has been rescued from her former reputation as ultra-pious philistine it remains the case that, as far as sexual gratification is concerned, she was unquestionably a strict dweller within the ten commandments. According to Hutchie Synge, her letters were nothing resembling those of a lover, virgin or otherwise – and he was uniquely placed to know, having read them before he destroyed them.

On John Synge's side there was prolonged 'signification of excitement', not to forget several proposals of marriage. The trauma of Florence/Darwin continued to 'vibrate' (Hackett's term). So, what if the proposals to Cherrie were made precisely in the knowledge that there had been no sexual overtures between these non-cousins and, additionally, in the confidence that well-rehearsed differences of religious belief ruled out any chance of his being accepted as suitor? In this scenario, the journey to Aran was not a reaction against disappointment in Crosthwaite Park but a heroically maintained self-abnegation, which included the proposal to Cherrie, culminated symbolically on the cliffs near Kilronan and – this is crucial – extended into the writing of *The Aran Islands* in which the abnegation is itself negated. Here, indeed, is Nietzschean overcoming of the self. Within this demanding regime, Synge's repeated admiration for the physical beauty of island women recorded in notebook passages of unmistakable sexual implication, is significant precisely because it remains generalised implication, never getting beyond (at most) a quasi-

indiscreet naming of (some) Barbara, a compound figure at once ancestral, aboriginal, and (twice) infant-dead.

Cherrie's refusal of his offers of marriage became a strong thread in the
tapestry of Synge's work. Six years elapse between the rejection of May
1898 and his meeting with Molly Allgood in late 1904. His annual shuttling
between Paris and Kingstown provided for independent sexual experience
after the *café-concerts* or rare excursions to the Moulin Rouge. But there
is no proof, unless a confident understanding of what young men got up
to in those days constitutes such evidence. The women whom Synge
undoubtedly met and knew in Germany, France and Italy – Thérèse
Beydon, the Von Eicken sisters, Margaret Hardon, Marie Zdanowska –
were in one crucial regard very similar to the young Englishwomen he
met and liked in Castle Kevin. Like Rosie Calthrop, they were all believers
and (with the exception of the Polish Catholic) Protestants. If Synge was
able to unburden himself to some of them (notably Vaneska von Eicken),
it was precisely because they were cut from the same cloth as the burden.

Molly certainly came from different cloth. Unmistakably a daughter of
lower-middle-class Catholic Dublin, she gave little indication of a deep
attachment to any beliefs of a religious kind, though she went to Mass
and looked forward to marriage in her parish church. Her most striking
characteristic, within the economics of Synge's emotional system, was her
age – or rather her youth. Eighteen at the time they first met, Molly was
his virgin love. A lively contrast to the bourgeois conventionalism of
Cherrie Matheson, she neatly recreated Florence Ross's innocence. My
conviction is that Synge never took steps to alter that state, either because
it was precisely what he valued in Molly and/or because he was (after the
renewed onset of Hodgkin's) not able to do otherwise. Within a psycho-
cultural analysis, Molly was just the girl for Synge because she functioned
to advance that abnegation which had its double-origins with
Florence/Darwin, which developed a ritual and a pattern in hopeless love
for Cherrie, and which found a local habitation and a name on the Aran
Islands.

Unlike Florence, Cherrie and most of the Continental women whom
he knew, Molly brought him beyond the laager of evangelical Protestantism. The fact that she had a (dead) Orangeman father enhanced
her role as Eurydice to Synge's Orpheus. It also allowed for a redistribution
of duties between them as to who led who out of who's 'Other' world.
She was primarily 'the Other' in that she was near plebeian and Catholic.
Yet what she provided in that social and cultural sense was made available
to him – more extensively and with a clearer mythopoeic fertility – in

Aran, Kerry and Mayo. Synge's travels were the outer map of his inner life. As Irish Catholicism, even Gaelic-speaking Catholicism, had been the object of his forebears' spiritual concern, his radical and liberating initiatives in the literary movement doubled up as compulsive repetition.

Molly was his virgin love. But their associates maintained a strange silence about her, just as they hinted at mysterious rumours about him. Writing more than ten years after Molly's death, Elizabeth Coxhead found it 'very hard to credit' that she had been in love with Synge and believed that, in the undeniable shock which his death inflicted on her, relief at her escape and remorse at feeling such relief played a large part.[9] She was flirtatious to a degree which differences of class could not adequately explain for him. Later she drank heavily, and may have begun to do so while he was alive. Her marriages were unhappy, the second one a tragic-comic attempt at her own version of compulsive repetition – she married Mac, whom Synge always viewed as a rival. Synge's will is cast in the formal legal terminology one would expect from the drafting pen of Harry Stephens: no 'beloveds' or 'my dears' escort Molly's name as beneficiary. The annuity provided for her was substantial, given the limited assets available to Synge, but it was hedged round with caution. Perhaps, as disease launched its final assault and Molly planned an English tour, the scales protecting every lover's eyes were lowered from Synge's.

In his last months J. M. Synge did not prove to be a likely gaffer. Christy Mahon's achievement had been hard won, but it carries within it no authorial allusion to himself as 'gaffer' – a leader or boss – nor 'gaffer' as an affectionate contraction of grandfather, great progenitor. On the contrary, the mercurial Christy takes over from Synge and replaces him: one notes a loss of subtlety both in *The Playboy* itself and in the final unfinished *Deirdre*. The gaffer had exited in 1905, a beggar renewed in his blindness, a leader of his blind woman, potent in words and dreams. Synge's revision of the third act of *The Well of the Saints* in the spring of 1908 was his final, deftest act.

In December 1912, Yeats met 'some woman' at John Masefield's in Greenwich and entered into dispute about the dead dramatist.

She then said, 'Did you know Synge?'

'Yes,' I said.

'But no [sic] him well I mean,' she said.

I saw that I was interfearing [sic] with a popular conception founded probably on the new realist conceptions of a genius, as a drunk Calvanist [sic].[10]

Some who knew Synge complained of his arrogant reticence. But in the kindly words of James Stephens, 'his approach to knowledge was – to be silent'.[11]

The Brethren: Origins and Beliefs

With Some Notes on the Matheson Family

In the late 1820s, a young Irish Churchman of highly respectable background found himself ministering in a district of County Wicklow some eight or so miles to the north of Roundwood. John Nelson Darby (1800–82) had few enough parishioners, but Theodosia Wingfield (1800–36) Lady Powerscourt was keenly supportive of the Church of Ireland's evangelical wing.[1] Two distinctive, not wholly divergent, accounts of Darby's circle accentuate the importance of different focal points – the Powerscourt Estate with the nearby church at Calary, and Trinity College, Dublin.

In the city, four men came together through their common dissatisfaction with the worldliness of the Established Church – John Gifford Bellett (1795–1864), Edward Cronin (1801–82), J. N. Darby, and Anthony Norman Groves (1795–1853). The last-named, a dentist with a practice in Exeter, had enrolled in Trinity specifically for its climate of evangelical piety. Cronin, who had been a Catholic and was training to be a doctor, came from Cork. Bellett was a barrister, and Darby (as we have said) was already embarked on a clerical career. In the winter of 1827/8, the nucleus of this group had met for prayers in a house in Fitzwilliam Square. Later in 1828, Darby published *The Nature and Unity of the Church of Christ* in which differences with the Established Church were clearly discernible, and the following year the group recruited the support of Lord Congleton who assisted them in renting premises in Aungier Street, Dublin.[2]

Darby's territorial base as a 'parochial' clergyman lay well south of the city, across the Wicklow border on the edge of the mountain road which leads from Enniskerry to Roundwood. In Powerscourt House, her ladyship encouraged prayer meetings at which Darby spoke, sometimes for hours on end, to his band of followers. Among the stated or unstated objects of their theological animus was the Established Church, its worldly engagements, its ordination of a clerical 'class' distinct from the laity, and a host of fine points of church doctrine upon which the saints hoped to dance. These differences emerged gradually, but the larger background of 'Darbyite' meetings in Wicklow and Fitzwilliam Square was the political crisis which resulted in the concession of Catholic Emancipation in 1829. Though the general impression of this branch of Protestant evangelicalism has discerned a strong anti-Catholic element, there was some common ground in the Catholic demand for a breakdown of the Established Church's hegemony and in the Darbyite condemnation of worldliness.[3] In at least one rural area, Castlecomer, County Kilkenny, 'undenominational Protestants' (as Brethren sometimes chose to style themselves) preferred burial in the public authority (predominantly Catholic) graveyard, rather than to lie in death with scions of the Established Protestant Church of Ireland. This unlikely convergence of feeling should be borne in mind when J. M. Synge's emotional commitments, first to Cherrie Matheson and later to Molly Allgood, are discussed. Considered historically, his choices did not draw him towards two contrasting ideological 'positions', but raised in repeated form the same interrogation of the Church in which he was brought up.

Throughout the 1830s, the Establishment maintained an unsuccessful defence of its tithe income (levied on a largely Catholic population), and in these disturbed years Darby effectively seceded from the Church of Ireland and withdrew to Plymouth (where there were sympathisers). But Brethrenism did not disappear from Ireland.[4] Much of the credit for keeping the flame alive can be assigned to forebears of J. M. Synge. The early Dublin meetings were held at No. 8 Fitzwilliam Square, home of Francis Synge Hutchinson (1802–33), the son of the Rev. Sir Samuel Synge [Hutchinson] Bt.[5] The Powerscourt meetings were chaired by John 'Pestalozzi' Synge, with his brother Edward Synge often in attendance.

J. B. Stoney's account of the Powerscourt group provides much of the detail.[6] The generally accepted 'founder', Darby, gives the dates 24–8 September 1832 for the second Powerscourt conference, indicating also that the Rev. Robert Daly presided as he had done at the first event (4–7 October 1831). In a more recent history, John Synge is credited with chairing a five-day conference on unfulfilled prophecy, held at Powerscourt on 23 to 27 September 1833, and with introducing William Rhind to the movement. While living at Buckridge House, Teignmouth in Devon, Synge had employed Henry Craik (1805–66, another founding Brother) as tutor to his two eldest sons (i.e., the dramatist's uncles).[7] Earlier, John Synge had published a dissuasive against secession, 'A Call to the Converted': As It Relates to Members of the Church of England (London: [1831]). This mixture of caution and eccentricity had long characterised his dealings with the public. During his phase of enthusiasm for the educational theories of Johann Heinrich Pestalozzi (1746–1827), he was anxious to reassure Irish readers that the motive behind the Switzer's innovatory systems was strictly biblical.[8]

These patrons of the early Brethren in their urban and rural gatherings – Francis Synge Hutchinson and John 'Pestalozzi' Synge – were first cousins. Their Synge fathers had married Hatch sisters, Dorothy and Elizabeth. Amidst this febrile piety, the seventy-year-old Francis Synge (formerly an MP) died in 1831, obliging his son ('Pestalozzi') to return to Glanmore Castle. But during the mid-1820s, John 'Pestalozzi' Synge was master of Roundwood, and both properties remained in the family's possession for a further two decades.[9] While the ownership of estates can be established with a reasonable degree of precision through public records and deposited family papers, membership of a church is a less exactly determined matter.

Darby could have reasserted his priestly status within the Church of Ireland simply by acknowledging the Thirty-Nine Articles, but did not do so. It is highly unlikely that any of the early-nineteenth-century Synges publicly denied their affiliation to the Established Church, even while they chaired and cheered at Brethren meetings. It was not that membership of the Brethren was beneath them socially; on the contrary, Darby admitted that his 'passed for an aristocratic movement'.[10] This was strikingly true in Wicklow. Not only the Synges of Roundwood and Glanmore but – more impressive – Lady Powerscourt and John Vesey Parnell (later Lord Congleton) lent substance to this belief, with the Truells of Clonmannon adding their support from the solid gentry. The bond between property and Church, which can be specified in various concepts of land and parish and tithe, was targeted in some of the more radical of Brethren doctrines.

It is no easy matter to establish what these doctrines amount to. First, members of the Brethren insist that only the Bible provides all that is required for salvation. That merely leaves the problem of interpretation, and two thousand years of dispute. Then, among Exclusive Brethren, there is a marked reluctance to have any commerce with those who are not already saved. Without an identifiable clerical body, and without training colleges or libraries, Brethrenism is an elusive set of beliefs to authenticate or interrogate. Over a period of a century-and-a-half, shifts of emphasis have taken place; schisms and expulsions have occurred, indicating acute disagreement among members.[11]

The Brethren were and are separatists. By separatism here is meant not simply a programme to disassociate the Church from the State – as would eventually occur in 1869 with Disestablishment – but a more radical social and personal commitment to separation from unbelievers. Here the clinching biblical text was 2 Corinthians 6:17 – 'Wherefore come out from among them, and be ye separate, saith the Lord, and touch not the unclean thing; and I will receive you.' In due course, Darby's followers were to apply this injunction even to their own brethren. In more strictly ecclesiological terms, the fundamental idea of Brethrenism is 'the ruination of the Church', an idea which can be traced directly back to Lady Powerscourt, Darby and the early Irish phase. Because there is/was no possibility of the Church rescuing itself from its entanglement with the State, with secular, mercenary, and unspiritual forces, it is/was essential for 'the saints' to 'come out of' such corruption and cleave to themselves only. The rationale for this latter piece of unctuous self-interest is to be found in the Calvinism underpinning the Brethren which (as it happens) had long been influential in the Church of Ireland: if some are predestined to be saved, why should they loiter (Christ-like) among sinners, wine-bibbers, and the like?

Within this separated community, no warrant existed for a distinct ministry: each individual might prophesy and pray according as s/he is inspired, a position sanctioned in 1 Corinthians. Charismatic worship, according to which the meeting appointed no preacher or prayer leader but waited for the Spirit to move someone, featured in Brethrenism, but it was not common in the early Dublin meetings. Some of these notions were hardly original with the Brethren; 'the priesthood of all believers' had long been a widespread notion among small sects; and prophecy, in which Lady Powerscourt was expert enough to perturb her otherwise compliant rector, had characterised millennialism from the early days of the Reformation. McPhail quotes a seventeenth-century catalogue of errors for discrete details of what becomes a more cohesive body of belief two hundred years later. Centrally he identifies the notion: 'That there is now no Church of Christ upon the earth ... The saints as pilgrims do wander as in a Temple of Smoak, not able to find religion, and therefore should not plant it by gathering or building a pretended supposed House, but should wait on the coming of the Spirit.'[12] Logically consistent with their 'faith alone' position is the characteristic of Brethren that '[in] the fervour of their worship of Christ they seem to have feared to face the full implications of [h]is humanity ... some held that [h]e died, not by the crucifixion, but by a voluntary act independent of the cross.'[13] No half-orthodox Protestant could hold to such a view.

The millennial excitement of the English Civil War period is worlds away from Crosthwaite Park, even if the Temple lands in County Wicklow had come to that family (and thence to Hatches and Synges) as a direct result of the conflict between King and Parliament. What had threatened a social revolution at Putney or Bedford in the 1640s could hardly be identified with the decorum of Fitzwilliam Square. Nevertheless, the organisational – or anti-organisational – base of Brethrenism had profound implications for a state church. The Rev. Sir Samuel [Synge] Hutchinson, Bt, and the Rev. Doctor Robert Traill may have been evangelicals of differing stripes, but neither was under any illusion as to the embattled situation of the Church of Ireland, grossly outnumbered by Catholics and embarrassed by the opulence of some among its own prelates. While Darby became something of an autocrat after he 'led out' the Exclusive Brethren from the larger body in 1848, the greater danger to established churches came from the democratic and outwardly undemarcated movement founded in Dublin at the end of the 1820s and the beginning of the '30s. Because they abjured all notions of a formal church organisation, they felt little compulsion to leave the particular church or parish community into which they had been born. This was particularly the case among early Anglican attenders at the Brethren's meetings, as distinct from former Nonconformists; the pattern persisted in Ireland in a way which impinged on the education of J. M. Synge.

In a biography of Synge, the most significant component of the Brethren community in Ireland is the Matheson family, neighbours in Kingstown for many years. The following account is incomplete, but may give some indication of their extent. The earliest printed evidence which I have discovered of anyone bearing the name Matheson in Ireland is *Journal of a Tour in Ireland During the Months of October and November 1835* (printed for private circulation only, London, Bentley, 1836). This is attributed to G. F. G. Matheson, in the catalogue of the University Library, Cambridge (S 488 d 83 1).

A clearer line of descent begins with: Robert Edwin Matheson (1845–1926, sometimes said to have been born in Australia) and Charles Louis Matheson (1851–1921) were the sons of Robert Nathaniel Matheson, clerk of the Privy Council, Ireland, and of his Swiss wife Victorine Jossevel who had been married in Kent on 13 September 1842. Both sons were educated at the Rathmines School, Dublin.

In January 1866 at 'York St Church Dublin', Robert married Cherrie M. Hardy who died in 1911; they had one son and four daughters – i) Victoria Charlotte, born 10 December 1866, who married Henry Courtney and had no children; ii) Cherie Marie Louise, born 12 October 1870, who in 1902 married Kenneth Houghton whom she bore two children; iii) Helen

Constance, born 30 September 1876, who married Robert J. Fleming whom she bore two sons; iv) Robert Nathaniel, born 30 September 1879, who married Norah Kathleen Ormsby on 1 December 1915 and had five children; v) Winifrid Clare, born 27 September 1881, who remained unmarried.

Charles married Elinor Tuthill and they had two sons and three daughters – i) Arthur (born 1878); ii and iii) Eileen and Mary (twins born 1880); iv) Vera (born 1884); and v) Freddie (born 1892).

Notes

ABBREVIATIONS

Persons

ES	Edward Synge (1859–1939), brother
JMS	Edmund John Millington Synge (1871–1909)
KS	Kathleen Synge, née Traill (1840–1908), mother
RAS	Robert Anthony Synge (1858–1943), brother
SS	Samuel Synge (1867–1951), brother
JJ	John Joly (1857–1933), family friend
MA	Molly Allgood (1887–1952), fiancée
WBY	William Butler Yeats (1865–1939), poet and playwright

Manuscripts

NLI	National Library of Ireland
TCD	Trinity College, Dublin
Stephens	Edward Millington Stephens's manuscript (MS with the appropriate call number) or typescript (TS with the appropriate call number) biography of his uncle, J. M. Synge, preserved in TCD
BL	British Library
NYPL	New York Public Library

Printed Sources

CW I	J. M. Synge, *Collected Works*, Volume I: *Poems* (edited by Robin Skelton). London: Oxford University Press, 1962.
CW II	J. M. Synge, *Collected Works*, Volume II: *Prose* (edited by Alan Price). London: Oxford University Press, 1966.
CW III	J. M. Synge, *Collected Works*, Volume III: *Plays, Book I* (edited by Ann Saddlemyer). London: Oxford University Press, 1968.
CW IV	J. M. Synge, *Collected Works*, Volume IV: *Plays, Book II* (edited by Ann Saddlemyer). London: Oxford University Press, 1968.
Letters I	Ann Saddlemyer (ed.), *The Collected Letters of John Millington Synge*, Volume One: *1871–1907*. Oxford: Clarendon Press, 1983.
Letters II	Ann Saddlemyer (ed.), *The Collected Letters of John Millington Synge*, Volume Two: *1907–1909*. Oxford: Clarendon Press, 1984.
Daughter	Samuel Synge, *Letters to My Daughter; Memories of John Millington Synge*. Dublin: Talbot Press [1932].
My Uncle	Andrew Carpenter (ed.), *My Uncle John: Edward Stephens's Life of J. M. Synge*. London: Oxford University Press, 1974.
G & S	David H. Greene and Edward M. Stephens, *J. M. Synge 1871–1909*. New York: Macmillan, 1959.

G & S II   David H. Greene and Edward M. Stephens, *J. M. Synge 1871–1909* (revised edition). New York/London: New York University Press, 1989.

CHAPTER 1: **The Former Lives of J. M. Synge**

1 T. E. Hulme, 'Bergson's Theory of Art' in *Speculations* (London: Routledge, 1960), p. 152.

2 The gift – a copy of *Birdie and Her Dog; With Other Natural History Stories* (London: Partridge, 1876) – is inscribed 'E. John M. Synge / from his kind friend Mr Joly 25th December 1877' (TCD MS 6214). See also JJ to Annie Stephens (née Synge) 27/11/1932 (TCD MS 6178).

3 'Murthering Irish. His image, wandering, he met, I mine. I met a fool i' the forest.' James Joyce, *Ulysses*, ed. Jeri Johnson (Oxford: World's Classics, 1993), pp. 191–2. Synge's friend, Stephen MacKenna, lived at Clamart for a period.

4 See an anonymous note in *Plays* (London: Allen & Unwin, 1932) where it is claimed that the form, John M. Synge, was first introduced by the Cuala Press in the posthumous *Poems and Translations* (1909), in violation of the dramatist's insistence on representing two forenames by their initials only.

5 Introducing a selection of eighteenth-century letters written by one of the bishop Synges, the historian M.-L. Legg suggests that the naming incident may date to the reign of Elizabeth rather than Henry VIII; see M.-L. Legg (ed.), *The Synge Letters: Bishop Edward Synge to His Daughter Alicia, Roscommon to Dublin, 1746–1752* (Dublin: Lilliput Press, 1996), p. xxxvii n9. The Latin phrase may be translated: 'he is so named because he was a canon' (i.e., one who sang the offices).

6 John Lighton Synge (1897–1995) was a Fellow of the Royal Society; his daughter Cathleen Morawetz (born 1923) is professor of mathematics at New York University.

7 See TCD MS 6220, esp. MS 6220/45: KS to RAS, 31/12/1888.

8 ES to JJ, 8/8/1881, TCD (Joly Papers) MS 2312/464 f. 2.

9 See John Joly, *Reminiscences and Anticipations* (London: Fisher Unwin, 1920).

10 See Maurice Bourgeois, *John Millington Synge and the Irish Theatre* (2nd edn; New York/London: Blom, 1968), pp. 16 n3, 86 n4 etc. Pound's 'John Synge and the Habits of Criticism' is discussed in Chapter 16 below. For information on E. H. Synge's health, I am grateful to Cathleen Morawetz (9/7/1998).

11 Conversation with Stephens's daughter, Mrs Ann Porter, 2/12/1996.

12 George Roberts (for Maunsel) to Macmillan's, 24/5/1923 (University of Reading).

13 In a letter to the present writer (1/9/1996), Mrs Margaret Synge suggested that no originals of the *Letters* ever existed, that SS had found the device of addressing synthetic letters to his daughter 'a convenient format for conveying fact to the public'. Mrs Ann Porter (née Stephens) in a letter of 27/9/1996 concurred, adding that 'feelings must have been running high' when her father was effectively put in charge of the surviving papers.

14 TCD (Joly Papers) MS 2312/621, SS to JJ, 18/4/1932.

15 Samuel Beckett to Thomas MacGreevy, 19/7/1959: quoted in James Knowlson, *Damned to Fame: the Life of Samuel Beckett* (London: Bloomsbury, 1996), p. 794 n128.

16 The term comes from Frantz Fanon's *The Wretched of the Earth* (1961) where it describes a radical reorientation of allegiances by one whose origins lie with the oppressor but who decisively sides with the oppressed in an anti-colonial struggle for liberation. The applicability of Fanon's Algerian thesis to Ireland has been the focus of much contention.

17 Ann Saddlemyer, 'In Search of the Unknown Synge', Masaru Sekine (ed.), *Irish Writers and Society at Large* (Gerrards Cross: Smythe, 1985), p. 196.

18 G & S II, p. xv.

19 Ibid., p. xi; see pp. 58 ff. for Greene's comments on the depredations wreaked on Synge's papers by various members of the family, without reference to SS.

20 For the early Japanese interest, see two letters in the University of Reading archive collection: Allen & Unwin to Maunsel & Co., 26/5/1923 (copy), and Allen & Unwin to Edward Hutchinson Synge, 19/3/1925 (copy).

21 In Hiberno-English, the surname Mahon can be pronounced either to emphasise two syllables or virtually to render it as a hononym of the word, 'man'.

22 Henri Lebeau to JMS, 16/2/1909, quoted in Stephens MS 6197/4806.

23 Information provided by Professor Cathleen Morawetz, May 1998.

24 JMS to Stephen MacKenna, 23/2/1908, see *CW II*, p. 348 n1.

CHAPTER 2: *Fin-de-Siècle* Beginnings

1 Max Nordau, *Degeneration*, trans. from the 2nd German edn (London, Heinemann, 1895), p. vii.

2 TCD MS 4414, entry for 1/9/93.

3 TCD MS 6216 (typescript copy of KS's diary), entry for 10/1/1901.

4 Thomas Jordan, 'Is Conscience a Product of Evolution?', *Irish Ecclesiastical Gazette*, 3 March 1883, p. 179. The article was responding to the implications of Charles Darwin's and Herbert Spencer's thought. Since July 1869, the Church of Ireland was not a state establishment. On the other hand, the growth of Unionism in the 1880s and after provided an alternative bond between political and theological loyalties, and additionally incorporated the traditionally dissenting Churches.

5 Nordau, *Degeneration*, p. 2.

6 Figures taken from Mary E. Daly, *Dublin, the Deposed Capital: a Social and Economic History* (Cork: Cork University Press, 1984).

7 When the present writer visited the graveyard on 17 July 1996, a human skull was visible under one of the Famine headstones, doubtless disturbed by foxes or rabbits. Traill's diary for the years 1832–8 has been privately printed (1975) by R. Synge Harbord; the manuscript is TCD MS 8413.

8 See Christopher Morash (ed.), *The Hungry Voice: the Poetry of the Irish Famine*. (Dublin: Irish Academic Press, 1989), pp. 245–8. The location of the seat – which suggestively repeats the well-attested 'Synge's Seat' on Aran – was pointed out to me by Mary Mackey of Schull, who informed me that local tradition held that Synge had sometimes met one of his female cousins at this place.

9 Statistics derived from W. E. Vaughan and A. J. Fitzpatrick (eds), *Irish Historical Statistics: Population 1821–1971* (Dublin: Royal Irish Academy, 1978). Pre-Famine census figures lack the reliability of those from 1851 onwards.

10 Ralph S. Brooke, *Recollections of the Irish Church* (London: Macmillan, 1877), p. 33. *Faithful Unto Death: a Memoir of William Graeme Rhind* (London: Yapp, [1863?]), p. 42. The anonymous memoirist is quoting an account of *c*.1833–5. Moral agents were employed by some landlords with the double – probably self-cancelling – intention of bridging the gap between proprietor and tenant and inculcating the values of evangelical Protestantism to the lower orders.

11 *My Uncle*, p. 11.

12 In the 1830s, W. G. Rhind had combined evangelical preaching and the encouragement of cottage industry on the Synge estate, but severe injuries sustained in a house fire forced him to abandon his good works and return to Britain in 1838. For his account of 'seventy families employed in knitting, spinning, weaving etc', see *Faithful Unto Death*, p. 41.

13 Though John Hatch Synge (Jack) was the youngest son by his father's first marriage, there was a second family (widow and very young family) in 1845 who disappear from the frame of reference. Provision for them may well have strained the resources of the heir as he attempted to recover Glanmore Castle.

14 'The corncrake was heard at Rathmines, for the first time this year, on 15 May' *Rathmines School Magazine*, vol. 3 (1874), p. 119.

15 Daly, *Dublin*, pp. 153 and 159.

16 Glasnamullen was one of just two townlands in the electoral division which had a total population of 254; see Ken Hannigan, 'Wicklow Before and After the Famine', in Ken Hannigan and William Nolan (eds), *Wicklow: History and Society* (Dublin: Geography Publications, 1994), p. 816.

17 See TCD (Joly Papers) MS 2312/498–499, ES to JJ, 5 and 10/5/1882.

18 TCD (Joly Papers) MS 2312/482, ES to JJ, 4/2/1882; MS 2312/485, ES to JJ, undated.

19 TCD MS 6220/12, KS to RAS, 2/4/1888.

20 See Stephens MS 6197/4525 dealing with JMS's alarm at the moral risks MA was exposed to.

21 Quoted by R. F. Foster, *W. B. Yeats: a Life*, Vol. 1: *The Apprentice Mage* (Oxford/New York: Oxford University Press, 1997), p. 512.

22 *CW II*, p. 53.

23 G. B. Shaw, 'A Note on Irish Nationalism', *New Statesman*, 12 July 1913 (an Irish supplement), p. 2.

24 *CW IV*, p. 79. In fairness to Pegeen's contention, we should perhaps note that the President of France between 1873 and 1879 was Marshal MacMahon (1808–93) who had helped to suppress the Commune of Paris in 1871.

25 In 1907, JMS sent MA *Tess of the d'Urbervilles*, hardly a sensitive choice given that it recounts a young girl's betrayal by her socially superior lover; see JMS to MA, 14/5/1907, *Letters I*, p. 345.

26 TCD (Joly Papers) MS 2312/494. ES, writing from Kingscourt in Cavan, to JJ in Rathmines, and citing his mother's account of an assault which had occurred near Orwell Park.

27 Francis Galton, *Hereditary Genius: an Inquiry into Its Laws and Consequences* (London: Macmillan, 1869), p. 336. As Galton was Darwin's cousin, his theories of intellectual family are self-ratifying.

28 See W. J. Corbet, 'Is the Increase of Insanity Real or Only "Apparent"?', *Westminster Review*, May 1897, pp. 539–50. A regular contributor to the *Westminster* and the *Fortnightly*, Corbet's knowledge of the Irish administration of insanity was equalled by his hereditarian diagnosis.

29 R. F. Foster, *Paddy and Mr Punch* (London: Penguin, 1995), p. 53. For the same writer's more detailed comments on Brethrenism among the Parnells, see his *Charles Stewart Parnell: the Man and His Family* (Hassocks: Harvester Press, 1976), pp. 12–13 etc.

30 See Christopher Harvie's neglected *The Centre of Things* (London: Unwin, 1991) on Cazamian.

31 *CW IV*, pp. 59 and 75.

32 For the background, see Paul Bew, *Conflict and Conciliation in Ireland 1890–1910: Parnellites and Radical Agrarians* (Oxford: Clarendon Press, 1987).

33 Preface to *Poems and Translations* (dated December 1908); see *CW I*, p. xxxvi.

34 Robert Baldick (ed. and trans.), *Pages from the Goncourt Journal* (Oxford: Oxford University Press, 1978), p. 17. The journal was originally published between 1887 and 1896 in nine volumes.

35 Perhaps it is with Victorian historians themselves – notably W. E. H. Lecky (1838–1903) and the younger J. B. Bury (1861–1927) – that one might ultimately find the beginnings of an answer. See also W. J. McCormack, *Sheridan Le Fanu* (3rd edn; Stroud: Sutton, 1997).

36 ES was reading *Dombey and Son*, evidently for the first time, in 1882; despite the novel's powerful critique of money ethics, he was determined to extract rents which he conceded were high from his mother's tenants in County Galway, and to pursue similar claims in King's County. See TCD (Joly Papers) MS 2312/479–483, ES to JJ, 15/1/1882 to 10/2/1882.

37 TCD (Joly Papers) MS 2312/585a, KS to JJ, 18/4/1879.

CHAPTER 3: The Banality of Good

1 William Allingham, 'Four Ducks on a Pond', in Geoffrey Taylor (ed.), *Irish Poets of the Nineteenth Century* (London: Routledge, 1951), p. 53.

2 *Daughter*, p. 7. Three of the Synges' children died in infancy; the dramatist was thus the fifth surviving child, the fourth son.

3 According to the records of the Church Missionary Society, SS and his wife resigned from the China mission in 1914 (the date these letters allegedly begin) 'for family reasons (MS annotation in the *Register of Missionaries . . . from 1804 to 1904*, as preserved in the CMS, London).

4 A series of articles in the *Dublin Journal of Medical Science*, appearing between January 1872 and 1875, dealt with the smallpox epidemic of which J. H. Synge was a victim: for an overview, see Thomas W. Grimshaw, 'On the Prevalence of Small-pox in Dublin', DJMS, vol. 65 (June 1878), pp. 490–508. See Entry 5 in the Register of Deaths (District of Rathfarnham, Dublin South) for 1872. The entry was made on the same day by 'Mary Jane McNeill, present at death, 4 Holles Street, Dublin'. This last address was a nurses' residence. The famous Holles Street Maternity Hospital, scene of 'The Oxen of the Sun' episode in Joyce's *Ulysses*, had not yet been built.

5 TCD (Joly Papers) MS 2312/582, KS to JJ, 16/4/1878.

6 Ibid.; MS 2312/584, KS to JJ.

7 Ibid., MS 2312/580, KS to JJ, 22/4/1878.

8 The Rev. John Plunkett Joly (1826–58) died – like Synge's father – within a year of his youngest child's birth. JJ's mother (the German-born countess Julia Anna Maria Georgina di Lusi, 1827–86) was a nervous invalid, to the extent that he was invited to spend Christmas with the Synges, e.g. in 1881 when JMS was ten; see TCD (Joly Papers) MS 2312/596.

9 'Mr and Mrs Synge lived first at No. 1, and afterwards at No. 4, Hatch Street, one of the wide residential streets made through John Hatch's property . . . Here were born Mrs Synge's two elder sons Robert and Edward, and Annie, her only daughter to survive infancy' (Stephens TS, vol. 1, p. 134). The couple moved to Newtown Villas about nine years after their marriage in 1856.

10 TCD (Joly Papers) MS 2312/441, ES to JJ, 3/2/1880; and MS 2312/449, ES to JJ, 5/11/1880.

11 *CW II*, p. 6.

12 *Daughter*, p. 33. ES's spelling as an undergraduate was at least equally bad.

13 The Castle came into the possession of the Blackburne family in 1850. The owner in the 1880s was Edward Blackburne, a barrister like the late John Hatch Synge but (as a QC and the son of a former Lord Chancellor) one more distinguished in the profession than Synge's father had ever been.

14 TCD MS 2312/417, ES to JJ, 19/10/[1877].

15 *CW II*, p. 12.

16 Ibid., p. 5; Padraic Colum, *The Road Round Ireland* (New York: Macmillan, 1926), p. 365.

17 *Daughter*, p. 38.

18 See *CW II*, p. 3 ('For three days a south wind has been blowing over Paris . . .') Edward Stephens accepted that the notebook now classified as MS 4382 was used to preserve 'a short autobiographical sketch' (TS, vol. 1, p. 152), but he also notes that 'some pages have been torn out, evidently by John himself' and that Synge 'slightly distorted his story to disguise personalities' (pp. 152–3).

19 *CW II*, p. 4. The allusion to Dante successfully eludes identification.

20 TCD MS 4424 (1). Florence wrote from No. 1 Brookhill Avenue.

21 TCD MS 4369.

22 See Declan Kiberd, *Inventing Ireland* (London: Cape, 1995), pp. 176–7.

23 TCD MS 6220/18, KS to RAS, 7/5/1888.

24 See TCD (Joly Papers) MS 2312/424, ES to JJ, 31/12/1878, for details of a New Year holiday at Ballylough in Antrim; and MS 23/14/444–5, 27 and 31/3/1880 for visits to Clonmannon. RAS was involved on both occasions.

25 *Daughter*, p. 25. For the Landseer and other pictures, see ibid., pp. 100–1.

26 Ibid., p. 77.

27 Ibid., p. 76.

28 TCD MS 4370 f. 8v (see also 'I saw a pair of sandpipers near the river 23rd April' – f. 9; 'I heard a grey wagtail singing to day the 30th of April' – f. 9v, etc.). More than a dozen such emphasised passages occur in the first 17ff. of the notebook. Much of the remainder, ff. 18–51, is given over to the detailed observations recorded in ink, with occasional accounts of meetings attended. It seems likely that the inking-over of very early entries was prompted by greater success in recording complex observations.

29 Ibid., f. 20v.

30 Ibid., f. 33 r and v.

31 Ibid., f. 43. Perhaps it is not entirely clear whether JMS transcribed verbatim one exchange of views, in which case the 'I' refers to Kane, or (more likely) concluded with his own findings.

32 Elias Tardy (died 1888 aged 71) was rector of Augharamullen, and thus a neighbour of ES at Kingscourt; his son Thomas Joseph Hill Tardy (1849–1901) was rector of nearby Magheracloone. See TCD (Joly Papers) MS 2312/555, ES to JJ, 11/7/1883.

33 TCD MS 4370 f. 43v–44. Alfred Cort Haddon (1855–1940) was professor of zoology at the Royal College of Science, Dublin, 1880–1901. He led several important expeditions to New Guinea and Sarawak and was elected an FRS in 1899.

34 TCD MS 6220/28, KS to RAS, 21/7/1888, writing from Greystones, County Wicklow.

35 TCD MS 6221 f. 7, KS to SS, 8/11/1896. Also TCD MS 6220/49, KS to RAS, 18/3/1889. In the latter, she refers to a room in No. 22 Trinity College 'where the Christian students meet for prayer meetings etc.'. Noting two recent conversions, she continues, 'It is a great comfort & encouragement to us in our prayers for Johnnie to see God's wonderful grace & mercy.'

36 *CW II*, pp. 10–11. The passage quoted was assembled from two sources in Synge's surviving MSS. Carpenter, in *My Uncle* (p. 36) identifies the passage in Darwin's *On the Origin of Species* (London: Murray, 1859), p. 479. In fact, Darwin's argument at this point is rather more complicated, invoking, not evolution by name, but natural selection (p. 478), and 'inheritance or community of descent' (p. 479). 'The natural system is a genealogical arrangement . . .' (ibid.). The prominence of terms, more usually found in discussion of human characteristics, properties, and families, brings these pages close to Synge's immediate domestic concerns. It may be worth noting that Synge's recollection of the passage more closely parallels the account of the Natural History Museum display case (in his contretemps with Edward Stephens in 1902) than Darwin's actual words.

37 F. Burkhardt and S. Smith (eds.), *Correspondence of Charles Darwin* (London: vol. 3, p. 2; see Adrian Desmond and James Moore, *Darwin* (London: Penguin, 1992), pp. 314–15.

38 TCD MS 4379 f. 83v. Raymond Williams, in *Problems in Materialism and Culture* (London: Verso, 1980), argues that Darwinism had an implicit social theory from the outset, in that it drew on Thomas Malthus's study of the relationship between population and resources (pp. 86–102).

39 TCD MS 4416 20/9/1895.

40 Ibid., 30/9/1895.

41 If Synge was writing in excited reverie, he could well have merged the landscape of Killiney with that of Wicklow where he holidayed (sometimes with Cherrie included in the party).

42 Stephens TS, vol. 1, p. 158, identifies her as Anne Traill and gives a date of 23 August 1882.

43 *CW II*, p. 7.

44 Ibid., p. 8. KS's younger brothers Robert (1843–1916) and Edmund (1847–1923) Traill had emigrated to Argentina in 1868. The cousins who broke up John Synge's idyll were most likely Robert Traill's sons, Robert (1871–1947) and his younger brother, John – Robert Traill junior being John Synge's exact contemporary. JMS's reference to a 'girl of my own age' remains inscrutable, as Edmund Traill's children were all younger.

45 Ibid., pp. 6–7.

46 Ibid., p. 8.

47 Ibid., p. 9.

48 TCD MS 6200/24, A. H. Synge to J. H. Synge [November 1857].

49 See, in particular, *The Triumph of Grace; or Scriptural Proofs that God Will Exempt His People from the Judgment which Shall Condemn the World* (London: Hunt, [1863?]). This repeats what is more or less Brethren doctrine on several crucial points; it denounces the notion of sacraments – 'of pagan origin' (p. 85) – and laments the failure of the Reformation. See also *Hymns for Public and Social Worship Selected by Rev. Alexander H. Synge* (Ipswich: Hunt, 1862).

50 John Hatch Synge did not die until 13 April 1872, yet Kathleen was appointed on 9 April to be administrator of her brother-in-law's will – four days before his death, the future dramatist's father's death from smallpox was taken as inevitable. As Uncle Edward's provision (£200) for Johnnie was not to be be paid until twelve months had elapsed, it brought no immediate relief for the mother of six. See TCD MS 6199/3 for Edward Stephens's notes on this will.

51 *CW II*, p. 4. The evangelical wing of the Church of Ireland has always been close to doctrinal Calvinism, and Synge's phrase is ambiguous. The 'Five Points' of Calvinism are – i) Predestination; ii) Particular Redemption of a certain chosen number; iii) Original Sin; iv) Irresistible Grace, or the effectual calling of the Elect; and v) the Final Perseverance of the Elect.

CHAPTER 4: **The Encumbered Present**

1 Edmund Gosse, *Father and Son: a Study of Two Temperaments* (London: Penguin, 1986), p. 71.

2 See William Murphy, *Prodigal Son: the Life of John Butler Yeats (1839–1922)* (Ithaca/London: Cornell, University Press, 1978).

3 In 1928, RAS consulted JJ about drainage in the grounds surrounding Glanmore Castle. His repossession of a property once owned by his father's eldest brother was overshadowed by his wife's terminal illness and what he saw as the sorrowful state of politics in the Irish Free State; see TCD (Joly Papers) MS 2312/614, RAS to JJ, 14/6/1928. Harry Stephens looked after Glanmore during some of RAS's absences, caused by his wife's illness (letter of Ann Porter to the present writer, 17/4/1998).

4 For a longer account, see P. C. Williams, 'Pestalozzi John: a Study of the Life and Educational Work of John Synge' (Trinity College, Dublin (Ph. D.), 1965).

5 J. H. Synge graduated BA from Trinity College, Dublin, in 1844; he was admitted to the Irish bar in 1847. Evidence of his personality comes indirectly – 'Sam cant help being slow. He is very like his dear father in that as well as other things ...' TCD MS 6220/7, KS to RAS, 28/2/1888.

6 See TCD MS 6199/9 for notes made by Edward Stephens. In the lease of 1855, John Hatch Synge featured as 'the devisee of the late Elizabeth Synge', i.e., the daughter of John Hatch MP who married Francis Synge. That is, she was John Hatch Synge's grandmother, through whom Hatch property came direct to the dramatist's father.

7 *My Uncle* includes a transcript from the Traill family Bible, giving her date of birth as 25 March 1838 – see p. 13. But in November 1908, her age at death was given as 68, which would give a birth date of 1840, and consequently her age on marriage in January 1856 would have been only 15 years and 10 months. The latter seems unlikely.

8 Edward Stephens gives the date as 18 January; *The Family of Synge* (ed. K. Synge) prefers 15 January. The marriage settlement was dated 17 January, and registered 19 January; see Dublin Registry of Deeds, 1856:2:163. It can be safely assumed that the settlement was legally established before the wedding ceremony; hence the couple married on 18 January 1856.

9 *My Uncle*, p. 17. No. 1 Hatch Street is a smaller property than its neighbours because it forms part of a corner house; a move from it would have been a predictable development for the newlyweds.

10 Dublin Registry of Deeds 1864:1:18–30. The houses in question were Nos. 5–14 and Nos. 21–23 Hatch Street; i.e., they did not include the two briefly occupied by the Synges after their wedding.

11 In a letter written from Ipswich simply dated 'Sat. Dec 11', Rev. A. H. Synge inquired of the future dramatist's father, 'How are you getting on in the Farm – has it done well this past year? beef & mutton hold terrible prices for the eaters butter 1/7 per lb & often hard to buy. & what does the Law fetch?' (TCD MS 6200/65). This indicates that John Hatch Synge did draw on his Galway properties (or on Glanmore) for an income linked to crops as well as rent.

12 The saga of KS's struggle with her tenant on Brackloon is chronicled in TCD MS 6220.

13 See Dublin Registry of Deeds, 1866:10:231. The Grand Canal formed a half-circle round the southern half of the city, lying outside a previously acknowledged boundary, the Circular Road. It was crossed by Leeson Street at a junction beyond which residential Dublin was developing in the middle of the century.

14 Dublin Registry of Deeds, 1869:20:70 (re. Ely Place). Charles Rankin, who was in No. 1 Newtown Villas in 1880, held it on a lease of thirty-one years at £65 p.a. If J. H. Synge had been paying a similar annual sum ten years earlier, it amounted to less than half the income from Ely Place.

15 *My Uncle*, p. 22. The description of the Orwell Park houses as small is hardly objective, and may be based on a comparison with Mrs Traill's previous Monkstown residence.

16 Or were there hereditary associations? An undated set of documents preserved in NLI include 'A Map of the River Dodder between Mr Wilkinson & Mr Synge's Grounds' and a copy of arbitration in favour of Synge and his wife, and 'the Rev. Saml Synge Esq & wife' in a boundary dispute with Abraham Wilkinson. As this Samuel Synge changed his name to Hutchinson in 1813, the dispute can be dated to the very early nineteenth century. The presence of both Synges in this conflict with their neighbour strongly suggests that the property (on the south bank of the Dodder near Butterfield and clearly more extensive than the map in question shows) had come to them from John Hatch, their common father-in-law. See NLI MS 8939.

17 These were William Hume Frizell (entered 1873, son of Charles Frizell of Castle Kevin); John Percival Frizell (entered 1875, also of Castle Kevin); Edmund Damyon Frizell (entered 1883, of Derrylossary.) All came from the same Wicklow locality.

18 *Rathmines School Magazine*, vol. 3 (1874), pp. 90–6. The English master was T. B. Wilson, a notable Dublin figure in later years and author of a biography of Sir William Wilde.

19 TCD (Joly Papers) MS 2312/463 and 458, ES to JJ, 6/7/1881 (writing from Kells, County Meath) and 6/4/1881 (from Hull, Lincolnshire). (Cf. 'The old chap that receives the rents for me in Sunderland was most civil & showed me all over the town & came with me to New Castle . . .' (6/4/1881).)

20 TCD (Joly Papers) MS 2312/477 and 552, ES to JJ, 8/1/1882 and 27/6/1883.

21 KS to RAS [16 April 1888], quoted in *My Uncle*, p. 42; see TCD MS 6220/15.

22 *Daughter,* p. 53; see also pp. 50, 52, 56.

23 Ibid., p. 44. Joly (1857–1933) was professor of geology at Trinity College, Dublin, from 1887 to 1933; elected a Fellow of the Royal Society in 1892, and a Fellow of his college in 1919.

24 TCD MS 2312/452, ES to JJ, 9/11/1880.

25 *CW II*, pp. 5–6; ellipses as in the published text.

26 *Daughter,* p. 49. See Stephens TS, p. 295, for a reference to JMS selling pigeons and rabbits.

27 TCD (Joly Papers) MS 2312/605 and 610, RAS to JJ, 8/1/1882 and 19/2/1882.

28 TCD MS 6220/13, KS to RAS, 5/4/1888.

29 Dublin Registry of Deeds 1883: 28:183; 33:148; 51:122; 1884: 3:82. The sums were £827 18s 9d and £1,430 1s 11d; the dates 1873 and 1875 respectively. I do not suggest that Dobbs had given these sums outright but that he had advanced them on (untraced) securities.

30 TCD MS 6220/11, KS to RAS, 27/3/1888.

31 TCD MS 6220/23, KS to RAS, 10/6/1888.

32 See TCD MS 2312/409 etc. for repeated references to the young men's social activities together.

33 TCD MS 2312/416, ES to JJ, *c.* August 1877.

34 The painter Richard Holmes Hearn (died 1890) was a friend of Millet's, and wrote on Jean Paul Laurens. For details of the Hearn/Stephens household, see Paul Murray, *A Fantastic Journey: the Life and Literature of Lafcadio Hearn* (Sandgate: Japan Library, 1993), pp. 218–20. See also Lilo Stephens, 'Lafcadio Hearn and His Relations in Dublin', *Eigo seinen,* 1, May 1973, pp. 38–9.

35 Dublin Registry of Deeds 1884:15:20; the trustees were her brother, Edward, and Dr Henry William Oulton, of Lower Gardiner Street.

36 *My Uncle,* p. 31.

37 To judge from his correspondence, ES took up his post in the summer of 1881, that is, right at the onset of the Land War. In August, he wrote: 'I am [an] object of observation ... I am spoken of as the new agent & looked on me [sic] whith [sic] some misgiving. Keep an eye to see if the envelopes ever look as if they were opened ... mine are just the ones that would interest them ...' ES to JJ, from the Pratt Arms Hotel, Kingscourt, Cavan, 5/8/1881. TCD (Joly Papers) MS 2312/445 f. 2.

38 SS to RAS, quoted in Stephens MS, TCD MS 6192/1182. See also CMS archives in the University of Birmingham Library, especially G1/CHI/O – 1897 (items 160, 214 and 299).

39 Dublin Registry of Deeds 1885:43:15. The John Synge in question was John 'Pestalozzi' Synge (1788–1845) under whom the Glanmore estate collapsed; the archbishop in 1838 was Richard Whately (1787–1863), though the transaction resulted from legal changes which permitted the Church of Ireland to sell endowed property after the Tithe War.

40 Dublin Registry of Deeds 1896:42:232. The leases are dated 25/3/1830 and 27/4/1830.

41 Dublin Registry of Deeds 1908:27:76. In the period *c.*1878–90, No. 53 Upper Mount Street was occupied by John V. Cassidy; the immediate lessor was Marcus Moses, who later changed his name to Marcus Lingard. No. 54 was occupied by Albert Meldon, the immediate lessor being John W. Browne. Each house was valued at £90 p.a. By *c.*1904, the rateable valuation had dropped to £60 p.a.

42 JMS to Fred Sutton & Co. [? 9 April 1908], *Letters II,* p. 147.

43 See NLI 16 G 17 (52) for a 'Map of Leeson Street and proposed Avenues leading therefrom ...' submitted to the Commissioners by the estate of Francis Synge in July 1829. The map shows an adjoining holding in the name of Francis Synge's brother, the Rev. Samuel Synge (1756–1846).

44 Dublin Registry of Deeds 1898:10:122.

45 James Joyce, *Dubliners,* ed. Terence Brown (London: Penguin, 1992), pp. 35–42. Jimmy Doyle, son of the prosperous Catholic merchant, had been educated (like Synge) at Trinity College, Dublin.

46 The Norwegian origin is recorded in a note on the obverse of a family portrait, now

hanging in Ballylough House, County Antrim. I have also drawn on a manuscript family
history in the possession of Richard Traill, of Ballylough. See Hugh Marwick, *Merchant
Lairds of Long Ago, Being Studies of Orkney Life and Conditions in the Early Eighteenth
Century* (Kirkwall: Macintosh, 1936).

CHAPTER 5: **Grey Stones and Plymouth Brethren**

1 A. M. Toplady, author of this well-known hymn and a graduate of Trinity College, Dublin,
   also wrote *The Historical Proof of the Doctrinal Calvinism of the Church of England* (1774).
2 John Ferrar, *A View of ... Dublin ... with a Tour to Bellevue* (Dublin, 1796). Robert Fraser,
   General View of ... the County of Wicklow (Dublin, 1801).
3 G. N. Wright, *Guide to Wicklow* (2nd edn., Dublin, 1827); Samuel Lewis, *Topographical
   Dictionary of Ireland* (1837).
4 Details of church-building are taken from Séamus Ó Saothraí, *Greystones Presbyterian
   Church 1887–1987 and the Kilpeddar Witness from 1851* (Greystones, privately printed,
   [1987]); see p. 19. The Church of Ireland building was enlarged in 1875, 1888, and 1898.
5 The Brethren's original meeting-place was at Kenmare Terrace. A small group at first, they
   began to build Ebenezer Hall on Hillside Road by their own labours in 1907.
6 Ó Saothraí, *Greystones*, p. 22.
7 Formally, there was no Greystones Masonic Lodge before 1911. There is no evidence that
   any of the Synges were members; on 19/5/1892 JMS spent 4s 3d at a masonic bazaar in
   Dublin.
8 James Price (ES's father-in-law) was elected a vestryman for the coming year, with
   Cathcart Dobbs as honorary secretary (see lecture-script by James Scannel in the public
   library, Greystones).
9 See KS's diary, quoted in *Daughter*, p. 179; unfortunately no venue is given, but it is likely
   that the concert in question took place at Knockeeven, home of the Price family; Stephens
   TS, p. 299.
10 George A. Birmingham, *Pleasant Places* (London/Toronto: Heinemann, 1934), p. 60.
11 Ibid., pp. 65–6. TCD MS 4415 14/8/1894 records a visit by JMS to the Bartons' house.
12 G & S, p. 19. ES was employed as land agent on the Pratts' Cabra Castle estate (*c.*8,000
   acres) in Cavan; he also serviced Joseph Pratt's 18,000 acres (mainly of bog and mountain)
   in Mayo. The latter was centred on Enniscoe House, built *c.*1790 but only passing into
   Pratt possession in 1834.
13 TCD MS 6220/7, KS to RAS: KS's diary, cited in part in *Daughter*, p. 191.
14 *Daughter*, p. 22.
15 TCD (Joly Papers) MS 2312/577, KS to JJ, 4 August 1877.
16 TCD (Joly Papers) MS 2312/430, ES to JJ, 28/6/1879.
17 TCD (Joly Papers) MS 2312/590, KS to JJ, 10/7/1879.
18 *Daughter*, p. 53.
19 *My Uncle*, p. 34; *Letters I*, p. xix.
20 TCD (Joly Papers) MS 2312/507, ES to JJ, 23/7/1882.
21 *My Uncle*, p. 30.
22 TCD (Joly Papers) MS 2312/511, ES to JJ, 8/8/1882.
23 Ibid., MS 2312/513, ES to JJ, 5/9/1882.
24 Ibid., MS 2312/539, ES to JJ, 22/2/1883.
25 Ibid., MS 2312/562, ES to JJ, 7/10/1883.
26 *My Uncle*, p. 20. Editha Truell died 21/1/1919. Her second husband, Theodore Webber
   Gardiner died eight days later, aged 80; both are buried in Nun's Cross.
27 R. F. Foster, *Charles Stewart Parnell: the Man and His Family* (Hassocks: Harvester, 1976),
   p. 129.

28 See Judith Flannery, *Christ Church, Delgany, 1789–1990* (n.p. *c.*1990), p. 139.

29 George Russell to John Quinn, 27/4/1909; see G & S, pp. 59–60. The rumour started with WBY.

30 These also included Westview 1, Trafalgar House, Bushfield House, and 'Stanley Terrace, next door to the shop'; see *Daughter*, p. 91. Within a summer, it was sometimes necessary to move from one abode to another.

31 Stephens TS, p. 291.

32 Quoted in ibid., p. 293. Mrs Traill was staying in a different house.

33 *Freeman's Journal*, 23 July 1887.

34 TCD MS 6220/22, KS to RAS, 1/6/1888.

35 TCD MS 6220/24, KS to RAS, 16/6/1888.

36 See *Irish Builder*, vol. 31 (1889), pp. 296–7. Jackson (1840–1917) was MP for North Leeds and a great commercial patron. Dobbs died in 1914 aged 78.

37 *Daughter*, p. 178.

38 *My Uncle*, p. 20.

39 See W. Blair Neatby's article in *The Protestant Dictionary* (London: Harrison Trust, 1933).

40 TCD (Joly Papers) MS 2312/468. ES to JJ, 10/8/1881. There were seven Matheson girls in all, the daughters of two brothers. If there is anything in ES's jibe, then the 'good catch' was probably Victoria Matheson, eldest sister of JMS's beloved Cherrie. (See Appendix for details of the family.)

41 It is not clear whether Mrs Robert or Mrs Charles Matheson should be identified as Annie Stephens's visitor. (See TCD MS 6220/2, KS to RAS, 24/1/1888.)

42 *My Uncle*, pp. 20, 3.

43 See entries for 13–20/8/1889 in KS's diary, as given in *Daughter*, p. 183.

44 *My Uncle*, p. 52; *Daughter*, p. 78; for the essay (written post-1903 and first published in July 1907), see *CW II*, pp. 230–3; the essay never specifies an exact location for the garden, accomplishing a synthesis of various recollections within a distinctly literary structure.

45 *My Uncle*, pp. 52–3. In March 1888, Dowse had expressed surprise that JMS read William Paley and Samuel Butler; these sound but hardly fervent Anglican authors were probably deployed to keep local evangelicals at bay while he prepared to go up to Trinity; see TCD MS 6220/11, KS to RAS, 27/3/1888. Having gained his purpose, JMS dropped his orthodox reading and faced down the curate.

46 Ibid., p. 45; see Mary C. King, *The Drama of J. M. Synge* (London: Fourth Estate, 1985), pp. 2–3, 7, 19 etc.

47 *Daughter*, p. 60; *My Uncle*, pp. 34, 66. Aunt Jane also spoke of her brother's work in Aran.

48 See WBY, Preface to the first edition of *The Well of the Saints* in *CW III*, p. 63.

49 TCD MS 6220/5, KS to RAS, 14/2/1888. No. 44 Harcourt Street was James Price's Dublin house.

50 TCD MS 6220/15, KS to RAS, 16/4/1888.

51 TCD MS 6220/5, KS to RAS.

52 The townland of Knockroe consisted of 260 acres of land, plus 26 acres of water. In 1856, J. H. Synge held all but three acres of this; after his death in 1872, McDonagh acquired a lease.

53 TCD MS 6220/7, KS to RAS, 28/2/1888.

54 After 1872, Brackloon was divided into two lots, J. H. Synge having held the entire townland (364 acres) from the Bishop of Tuam. Baylee acquired a lease on 278 acres after 1872.

55 TCD MS 6220/7, KS to RAS, 28/2/1888. KS played the piano, JMS the violin.

56 TCD MS 6220/15, KS to RAS, 16/4/1888.

57 Ibid.

CHAPTER 6: **The Stay-at-Home Student**

1 WBY, 'The Academic Class and the Agrarian Revolution' (1899), reprinted in *Uncollected Prose*, vol. 2, ed. J. P. Frayne and Colton Johnson (London: Macmillan, 1975), p. 152.

2 In June 1888, Charles W. Baylee agreed to give up the farm because his brother had decided to vacate Mount Baylee in Clare and return to Canada. All of this suggests that the Baylees were far from being the hapless tenants of conventional representations of the Land War.

3 TCD MS 6220/18, KS to RAS, 7/5/1888. Lissie had committed herself to supporting a young relative who planned to emigrate, and did not become a patron of the Synge boys. KS did not wholly approve of her anyway – 'she dines early & <u>calls</u> it lunch.'

4 The undergraduate body was exclusively male, though a system of external examinations was already in existence in 1888, by means of which women could acquire qualifications from the college.

5 Charles Henry Miller, MA (1886) officially was assistant to the registrar of university electors, living in Glenageary, close to the Synges and Stephenses (from October 1890) in Crosthwaite Park.

6 G & S, p. 18 etc.

7 Richard Pine and Charles Acton (eds), *To Talent Alone: The Royal Irish Academy of Music 1848–1998* (Dublin: Gill & Macmillan, 1998), pp. 2–7–209. For a more extended commentary, see Ann Saddlemyer, 'Synge's Soundscape', *Irish University Review*, vol. 22, no. 1 (Spring 1992), pp. 55–68.

8 Harry White, *The Keeper's Recital: Music and Cultural History in Ireland, 1770–1970* (Cork: Cork University Press), 1998. p. 7.

9 TCD MS 6220/6, KS to RAS, 22/2/1888.

10 TCD MS 6220/22, KS to RAS, 1/6/1888.

11 James Joyce, *A Portrait of the Artist as a Young Man*, ed. Seamus Deane (London: Penguin, 1992), p. 194.

12 Posnett coined the term 'comparative literature' for a book published in New York in 1886. For an account of the academic background, see W. J. Mc Cormack, *From Burke to Beckett: Ascendancy, Tradition and Betrayal in Literary History* (Cork: Cork University Press, 1994), pp. 206–12.

13 See *Letters I*, p. 85.

14 *My Uncle*, pp. 53–4.

15 Samuel Synge took his MB and B.Chem. degrees in 1895, his MA and MD in 1904. He was ordained a deacon in 1896, a priest in 1903. From 1896 to 1914 he worked for the Church Missionary Society in China.

16 Edward Stephens goes out of his way to record that a search for adjoining houses in Kingstown was jointly led by KS and her daughter (Mrs Stephens), involving the ladies visiting a local estate agent on 28 June 1890, an undertaking which suggests that matters were not being left in Harry Stephens's hands, able lawyer though he was (*My Uncle*, pp. 56–7).

17 See *My Uncle*, p. 57. Jane Synge was the unmarried sister of the dramatist's father, and she lived with the Stephenses until her death – that is, with her niece rather than with her sister-in-law (Kathleen Synge).

18 Ibid., p. 58.

19 TCD MS 4373 f. 25.

20 Ibid., f. 29v.

21 *CW IV*, p. 143.

22 *Daughter*, p. 33.

23 G & S, p. 28; TCD MS 4413, 16/3/1892.

24 TCD MS 4413, 17/3/1892. 'Baile' restores the Gaelic spelling of place-names beginning Bally . . ., etc. 'Kind sir' was a form of salutation Synge noted among the humble and weak.

25 Ibid., 21/3/1892. According to Stephens, Synge read *The Children of Lir* in a bilingual edition published *c*.1882 by the Society for the Preservation of the Irish Language (*My Uncle*, p. 67).

26 Ibid., 16/4/1892.

27 Ibid., 17/4/1892.

28 *Rathmines School Magazine*, vol. 3 (1874), pp. 52–4; *Blue, White and Blue Christmas Annual* 1872, pp. 59–63. The author of 'A Story of Lugnaquilla' was W. Pakenham Walsh, whose sources included local tradition as well as romantic fiction clichés.

29 See TCD MS 4393, esp. ff. 35–49.

30 'Autobiography', *CW II*, p. 13.

31 See Chapter 9 for discussion of *When the Moon Has Set*; see *CW III*, pp. 215–17 for the fragments.

32 Among the authors Synge was reading in the spring of 1892 were J. R. Froude, George Petrie, Richard Pococke, and Edward Wakefield.

33 The description of Holt is Musgrave's; see *Memoirs of the Different Rebellions in Ireland*, 4th edn., with an introduction by David Dickson (Fort Wayne: Round Tower Books, 1995), p. 289 n1. Holt was a tenant farmer who had occasionally acted for the county authorities as a kind of bounty hunter; his position in 1798 was determined largely by his non-engagement in the Orange Order. For Holt's service under Francis Synge, see Stephens TS, vol. 1, p. 37.

34 TCD MS 4413, 13/6, 14/6, 27/6, 28/6 (all 1892).

35 See John D'Alton, *Memoirs of the Archbishops of Dublin* (Dublin, 1838) and G. H. Orpen in the *Journal of the Royal Society of Antiquaries of Ireland*, vol. 38 (*c*.1908), p. 17 etc. Also James Lydon, 'A Land of War' in Art Cosgrove (ed.), *A New History of Ireland*, vol. II, *Mediaeval Ireland 1169–1534* (Oxford: Clarendon Press, 1987), esp. pp. 256–63.

36 *My Uncle*, p. 72. Margaret Sutton of Calary Tavern married Thomas Evans of Greystones; depopulation of the mountain particularly reduced the Protestant community.

37 Ibid., pp. 71–7, esp. p. 73.

38 To be exact, Synge 'Finished text of Musgraves Irish Rebellions & Appendix 1–10' on 20/4/1892. The list of 'Protestants massacred in . . . Wicklow' occurs in Appendix 16; it seems unlikely that he would have abandoned this reading at so late a point.

39 Stephens TS, vol. 1, p. 40. Thomas Hugo died 9/7/1809 and was buried in Derrylossary churchyard; members of the family were still living in the district in the 1880s and '90s. Ambrose Weekes was married to 'Frances Mary Weekes alias Stephens', as her tombstone puts it. She had died in 1793, aged 60. Though her husband is buried with her, no date of death is given in his case. Part of the Hugo property came into the possession of the Bartons, whom the young J. M. Synge visited: see p. 66, etc. Memories of Weekes's murderous activities survived until as recently as 1938: see the archives of the Department of Irish Folklore (University College, Dublin), Schools Manuscripts no. 918 (County Wicklow), testimony of Desmond Fitzgerald, aged 14, of Moneystown.

40 Charles Boycott (1832–97) had been an agent in Mayo with whom the Land League refused to have any truck, and who had been forced to recruit labourers, members of the Orange Order, from Ulster in order to salvage his harvests in 1880.

41 Stephens and his latter-day editor distinguished between 'the Golden Belt' and the Plateau (see *My Uncle*, pp. 3–13 etc.). This is an economic distinction, though the colourful terminology derives from Sir Jonah Barrington, a shrewd if extravagant commentator on Irish affairs after 1798. Geographers emphasise the division between east and west Wicklow, effected by Lughnaquilla Mountain, while historians stress the late creation of Wicklow as a county and the incoherence of its component parts.

42 *My Uncle*, p. 70. The Frizells had held Castle Kevin since the eighteenth century. Harding (or Hardin, as his gravestone has it) died 23/8/1911, aged 73, and is buried in Derrylossary.

43 Ibid., p. 75.

44 Ibid., p. 79.

45 TCD MS 4373 f. 12. See G. T. Stokes, *Ireland and the Celtic Church* (3rd edn; London: Hodder, 1892), p. 52 etc. The work had first appeared in 1886. Stephens assumes that Synge's reading was focused solely on this book, by which Stokes was best known. The diary (13 July 1892) indicates that Synge also bought Stokes's *Ireland and the Anglo-Norman Church* (1888). As the rental of Castle Kevin was finalised on 14 July (*My Uncle*, p. 70), Synge's choice of new reading prepared him for a house deriving its name from the Anglo-Norman church.

46 TCD MS 4413, 28/7/1892; 29/7/1892.

47 For the Avoca trip ('3 & 1/4 hours "going" '), see TCD MS 4413, 3/9/1892; for a walk to Lough Nahanagan 'and then across the mountain to Glendalough', see TCD MS 4413, 7/9/1892. See also 'Caught 17 trout in C. Kevin stream' (TCD MS 4413, 6/9/1892), etc.

48 TCD MS 4413, 29/9/1892; for the list of Synge's reading in 1892, see ibid. ff. 136–7; G & S, p. 33.

49 See the summary prefacing the TCD catalogue of Synge's correspondence. His subjects were: algebra and arithmetic, astronomy, English composition, ethics, Euclid, Greek, languages (i.e., Gaelic and Hebrew), Latin, logic, mathematical physics, mechanics, and trigonometry.

50 KS's diary; see *Daughter*, p. 193.

CHAPTER 7: **Escaping Home Rule in Germany (1893–4)**

1 Charles Darwin, *On the Origin of Species* (London: Murray, 1859), p. 422.

2 Richard Pine and Charles Acton (eds), *To Talent Alone: the Royal Irish Academy of Music 1848–1998* (Dublin: Gill & Macmillan, 1998), pp. 207–8.

3 TCD MS 4414: 2/1, 31/1 4/1, 5/1, 6/1, 9/1, 10/1, 14/1, 16/1 18/1, 19/1, 23/1 30/1 (all 1893).

4 Ibid., 26/1/93, 9/1/93. On 14/2/93 he began to arrange the work for string orchestra.

5 Ibid., 21/4/93.

6 Stephens TS, vol. 1, p. 594.

7 Richard Ellmann regarded Joyce's fictitious singer as based on Olive Kennedy who had sung with Joyce in 1902. See his *James Joyce* (2nd edn.; Oxford: Oxford University Press, 1983), p. 365.

8 Stephens TS, vol. 1, pp. 594–5.

9 TCD MS 4414, 1/1/93.

10 Ibid., 8/1/93; see Declan Kiberd, *Synge and the Irish Language* (Dublin: Gill & Macmillan, 1993), pp. 23–4, for an account of Synge's orthographic and grammatical errors in these infrequent Gaelic entries.

11 TCD MS 4414, 23/1/93. He was still reading Taylor on 24/2/93 ('Isaac Taylor's "Mind in Form" ') and on 8/3/93 ('Isaac Taylor's Modern Movements') in *Ultimate Civilization and Other Essays* (London: Bell & Daldy, 1860).

12 The opening words of Flavius Josephus's *Jewish Wars*, as translated by Robert Traill (and edited by Isaac Taylor); see *The Works of Josephus* (London, Houlston & Stoneman, 1847), vol. 1, p. 31.

13 Edmund Gosse, *Father and Son* (London: Penguin, 1986), p. 94. Published anonymously in 1907, this provides a vivid account of a Plymouth Brethren childhood in the 1850s.

14 Taylor, *Ultimate Civilization*, 1860, p. 81.

15 Isaac Taylor, 'The Meaning of Terms – Rise of the Malign Emotions', in *Fanaticism* (London, 1833), p. 24.

16 Ibid., pp. 299–300.

17 Ibid., p. 355.

18 Quoted in *Daughter*, p. 193.

19 Taylor, 'The Meaning of Terms', p. 355. See G & S, p. 12.

20 Quoted in G & S, p. 11.

21 See H. Stuart Hughes, *Consciousness and Society: the Reorientation of European Thought 1890–1930* (Brighton: Harvester Press, 1979), pp. 37–9.

22 Francis Galton, *Hereditary Genius: an Inquiry into its Laws and Consequences* (London: Macmillan, 1869), pp. 190–1. The 1892 edition added a prefatory chapter stressing 'race' as a neglected factor.

23 Ibid., pp. 265, 276.

24 'The Vagrants of Wicklow' in *CW II*, p. 202. The editor dates the writing of this piece to 1901–2, though it was not published until 1906.

25 Galton, *Hereditary Genius*, pp. 367 and 367–8. For Darwin on pangenesis, see Adrian Desmond and James Moore, *Darwin* (London: Penguin, 1992), pp. 531–2.

26 Synge to an unknown correspondent, translation as given in *Letters 1*, p. 29. The MS is a draft, for which the editor has provided a likely date and provenance – Wicklow, mid-July 1895.

27 See Francis Galton, *Finger Prints* (1893) and *Finger Print Directory* (1895).

28 Quoted in G & S, p. 37.

29 Richard Wagner, *Beethoven*, trans. Edward Dannreuther (London: Reeves, 1880), p. 61.

30 Ibid., p. 125.

31 See TCD MS 4424 (3), Mary H. Synge to JMS, 6 May 1893. (She thought his age disqualified him.)

32 See TCD MS 4377 (account book) and MS 4414 (diary for 1893).

33 JMS to MA, 25/10/1908; *Letters II*, p. 215.

34 See TCD MS 4377, entry for 7 February 1894.

35 Quoted in G & S II, p. 41.

36 JMS to the Von Eicken family [2 February 1894], *Letters I*, p. 9 (original in German).

37 See Ann Saddlemyer's notes in *Letters I*, p. 8.

38 The text given is basically *CW I*, pp. 8–9, though I have added some full-stop punctuation for clarity.

39 See *CW III*, pp. 181–2 for an English translation commissioned by Stephens while working on the biography of his uncle. See also TCD MS 4415, 23/4/1894.

40 Taylor, 'The Meaning of Terms', p. 355.

CHAPTER 8: *Dämmerung; or,* Wicklow Revisited

1 Quoted in *Personal Recollections of the Right Rev. Robert Daly ... at Powerscourt and Waterford* (Dublin: Herbert, 1872), p. 17.

2 The best critic of this play – usually known as *When the Moon Has Set* – is Mary C. King; see her edition (with commentary) of the two-act version published as a special number of *Long Room*, no. 24/25 (1982), and her *The Drama of J. M. Synge* (London: Fourth Estate, 1985), esp. pp. 160–77.

3 For the conflate version of *When the Moon Has Set*, see *CW III*, pp. 153–7; on the letters, etc., see *Letters 1*, p. xvi.

4 'Saw old a mhournín sitting in by her fire very picturesque', TCD MS 4414, 16/7/1893.

5 *My Uncle*, p. 123.

6 Charles Frizell held about 260 acres in fee, most of it woodland plantation *c.*1865. Henry Harding held 47 acres from Frizell *c.*1877 onwards. For the Harding family in the 1790s, see Ruán O'Donnell, *The Rebellion in Wicklow, 1798* (Dublin: Irish Academic Press, 1998), pp. 51, 242.

7 Ambrose Weekes died (apparently by his own hand) and was buried in Derrylossary churchyard, where a half-submerged tombstone commemorates him and his wife and

son. The latter, William Sutton Weekes of Castle Kevin, died 2 February 1846. No date is given for Ambrose Weekes's death. The name of Ambrose Manning (buried in Rathdrum 7/10/1857, aged 27), like that of William Sutton Weekes, suggests a high degree of intermarriage between these local families.

8 All quoted material in this paragraph is to be found in NLI MSS 9876–9910.
9 See Desmond Fitzgerald's report (School MS 918, p. 77) in the archives of the Department of Irish Folklore, University College, Dublin.
10 TCD MS 4389 ff. 37–8.
11 Constance Gore-Booth to Eva Gore-Booth, 8/12/1920; see *Prison Letters of Countess Markievicz* (London: Longmans, 1934), p. 257.
12 *CW II*, p. 221; for Synge's divergence from his original notes, see Nicholas Grene, 'Synge and Wicklow', in Ken Hannigan and William Nolan (eds), *Wicklow: History and Society* (Dublin: Geography Publications, 1994), p. 702.
13 *My Uncle*, p. 5.
14 No diary for 1901 survives; Grene's calculations are based on the Stephens MS.
15 NLI MS 11,333. The *Dublin Mercury* of 10–12/8/1769 briefly reported how a gentleman in County Wicklow shot himself; a formal death notice reads: 'Suddenly at Roundwood, co. Wicklow, Mr M'Cracken, formerly an eminent peruke-maker of this city.'
16 Wills (proven 1769 and 1771) indicate M'Cracken had property in more than one county.
17 NLI MS 11,984. See also *The Charter of the Royal Canal Company* (Dublin: Chambers, 1789), p. ii; *Report of the Committee Appointed by the Royal Canal Company 12th June 1793* (n.p. n.d.), p. [1]; Ruth Delany, *Ireland's Royal Canal, 1789–1992* (Dublin: Lilliput Press, 1992), pp. 24–5, 200–1.
18 See Appendix 7 in Peter O'Shaughnessy (ed.), *Rebellion in Wicklow: General Joseph Holt's Personal Account of 1798* (Dublin: Four Courts Press, 1998), p. 167. The Synge family tree (privately published in 1937) gives no indication of a Synge/Stewart marriage; it also neglects the traceable ancestors of John Hatch MP. In matters of class, the genealogist operates as a tree surgeon.
19 KS to RAS, January 1890, quoted in Stephens MS.
20 *CW II*, pp. 189–92. Synge alters both the location and date of the incident, in keeping with his practice with essays based on real-life experience and involving individuals still alive at the time of publication. He also omits all reference to Harry Stephens, presenting himself as the sole protagonist.
21 For Holt's relations with Francis Synge, see O'Shaughnessy, *Rebellion in Wicklow*, p. 36 and esp. p. 146 which cites Isaac Butt's 1838 account of Holt's friendship with gentry and the loose sexual morality of his entourage. For the Harneys' ghostly cottage, see Nicholas Grene, 'Synge and Wicklow', p. 709.
22 Grene, 'Synge and Wicklow', p. 710. By the 1950s, when the present writer was living between Aughrim and Ballinaclash, the Harneys had themselves become a topic of folklore.
23 Notebook 39 of E. H. Synge, entry dated 15 July 1942; from a copy made for his brother J. L. Synge, now in the possession of Cathleen Morawetz (née Synge), New York.
24 Corbet's publications include twelve articles in the *Fortnightly Review* and *Westminster Review* between 1893 and 1906.
25 This is a notebook, now NLI MS 11,995, inscribed 'from the Hatch Papers Glanmore 1902' (f. 1).
26 Quoted from Stephens MS in Grene, 'Synge and Wicklow', p. 696. A network of intermarriages linked Darbys, Droughts and Graveses, and (in one case) a Graves and a Synge. The unfortunate Drought may have been 'family' to some slight degree. He was also probably related to Captain Richard Reynell Drought (of Ballinavoola, Glenealy), vice-chairman of Rathdrum Union in the 1880s.
27 *CW II*, p. 232.

28 Ibid., pp. 122–4. It is not clear what celebrations are referred to. Parnell's funeral had, of course, taken place in 1891 long before JMS had gone to the west. The unveiling of 'the Chief's' statue did not take place till 1911, two years after JMS's death. The allusion may be more generically to centenary commemorations of the United Irishmen rebellion.

29 *G & S I*, p. 4.

30 King, *Drama*, pp. 38–9.

31 TCD MS 4389, f. 6.

32 Ibid., ff. 9–11.

33 Ibid., f. 13.

34 Mary King (ed.), 'When the Moon Has Set', *Long Room*, nos. 24/25 (1982), p. 17.

35 King (ed.), 'When the Moon Has Set', p. 35; ellipses as in the original.

36 Daniel J. Casey, 'John Millington Synge: A Life Apart', in Edward A. Kopper, Jr. (ed.), *A J. M. Synge Literary Companion* (New York: Greenwood Press, 1988), pp. 2, 1.

37 King (ed.), 'When the Moon Has Set', p. 11; see Friedrich Nietzsche, *The Birth of Tragedy [and The Genealogy of Morals]*, trans. Francis Golffing (New York: Doubleday, 1956), p. 99.

38 *My Uncle*, p. 20.

39 For variant readings, see notes to Saddlemyer's text of the one-act version in *CW III*, pp. 156–76.

CHAPTER 9: **French Leave (1896–1903)**

1 James Joyce, *Ulysses*, ed. Jeri Johnson (Oxford: World's Classics, 1993), p. 192.

2 SS to Baring-Gould, 2/4/1897, CMS archives, University of Birmingham Library.

3 See *Mercy and Truth*, vol. 3 (1899), p. 219.

4 Ibid., vol. 1 (1897), pp. 95, 295; vol. 2 (1898), pp. 18, 118.

5 See SS to ? Crosby, 5/10/1897 (copy) in CMS archives, University of Birmingham Library.

6 See 'A Coasting Trip on the T.C.D.' (by Mary Synge), *Mercy and Truth*, vol. 7 (1903), pp. 235–8, 269–72; and 'Six Months' Work in Fu-Ning Hospital' (by Marcus Mackenzie), vol. 6 (1902), p. 331.

7 Mackenzie, 'Six Months' Work', p. 329.

8 *Letters I*, pp. 18–21, esp. Saddlemyer's notes.

9 G & S, p. 49.

10 Preserved in the Carl A. Kroch Library, Cornell University Library, Ithaca, New York.

11 See Toni O'Brien Johnson, *Synge: The Medieval and the Grotesque* (Gerrards Cross: Smythe, 1982), pp. 6–7.

12 *My Uncle*, p. 92.

13 TCD MS 4416, 18/6/1895; Maurice Bourgeois, *John Millington Synge and the Irish Theatre* (2nd edn.; New York: Blom, 1968), p. 263.

14 See Stephens MS 6192/1526. These incidents occurred in the rue d'Assas.

15 'if you need any information about the Celtic language or about our accent, I am at your disposal' (Saddlemyer's translation); see *Letters I*, p. 23.

16 The family history of Du Maurier's heroine is remarkably detailed; see *Trilby* (Oxford: Oxford University Press, 1995), pp. 36–7.

17 TCD MS 4417.

18 Bourgeois *John Millington Synge*, p. 38.

19 'The Demonstrations in Rome, By an Eye Witness', *Irish Times*, 16/3/1896, may draw on his report.

20 JMS to Francisco Morosini, [24/3/1896, draft], *Letters I*, pp. 36–7.

21 JMS to Thérèse Beydon [c.23/2/1896, draft], ibid., p. 35.

22 JMS to Thérèse Beydon [c.29/5/1896, draft], ibid., p. 37.

23 *My Uncle*, p. 97.

24 For the description of the scene, see TCD MS 4382 f. 11v.

25 On his health at this point, see JMS to Thérèse Beydon [*c*.10/6/1896, draft], *Letters I*, p. 38.

26 Information supplied by his daughter, Mrs Ann Porter.

27 See n. 51 below, for an account of this source and the caution required in interpreting it.

28 G & S, p. 62.

29 JMS to Maud Gonne [16/4/1897, draft], *Letters I*, p. 47.

30 The quotation comes from a letter of KS to RAS; see G & S, p. 63.

31 WBY, *Essays and Introductions* (London: Macmillan, 1961), p. 298.

32 Samuel Hearne (1745–92), whose *Journey from the Prince of Wales Fort* was published in
    Dublin in 1796; see Charles Darwin, *The Descent of Man* (London: Murray, 1871), vol. 2,
    p. 327.

33 See PRO: CO 904/18 (Dublin Castle List of Suspects) where he is also listed as a member
    of the Irish Republican Brotherhood. Lynch married Annie (daughter of the Rev. John
    D. Powell) in 1895.

34 Arthur Lynch, *Ireland's Vital Hour* (London: Stanley Paul, 1915), p. 107. John Quinn also
    remarked on Synge's 'large head, square jaws [and] wide mouth', though he remembered
    him as a 'soft-spoken man': J. Quinn to F. J. Gregg, 1/4/1909, NYPL, MSS Division.

35 See *CW IV*, p. 71. For Lynch's trial, see PRO: DPP 4/36 (also DPP 1/7). It is sometimes
    claimed that Mayo-born John MacBride was Synge's model for this conceit. However,
    Synge and Lynch were friends whereas no evidence suggests that Synge knew MacBride,
    who was a domestic sadist.

36 Arthur Lynch, *My Life Story* (London: Long, 1924), p.150.

37 NLI: Best Papers. Quotations (ff. 3 and 8) from a typescript identified as MacKenna's
    work through its reference to a walking-stick, described as his in Padraic Colum's *The
    Road Round Ireland* (New York: Macmillan, 1926).

38 On the meeting with Le Braz, see G & S, p. 64.

39 See Stephen MacKenna, 'Synge', *Irish Statesman*, 3/11/1928, p. 170; also MacKenna's
    typescript in the Best Papers (NLI), f. 15. He reports the story of Synge's participation in
    the Kruger reception, by which he probably means no more than participation as an
    onlooker on the pavement.

40 Arthur Lynch, 'Synge', *Irish Statesman*, 20/10/1928, p. 131.

41 Stephen MacKenna, 'Synge', ibid., 3/11/1928, p. 170.

42 I am grateful to Liam Breatnach for this story. *L'Irlande Libre* (no. 4, avril 1898, p. 4) was
    liberal enough to reprint an article from *Libre Parole* (an anti-Semitic paper) in which
    Wilde is cited as a victim of hypocritical British justice – the nature of his crime was not
    of course specified in the organ of exile nationalism.

43 Mary Colum, *Life and the Dream* (London: Macmillan, 1947), pp. 111, 121, etc.

44 Bourgeois, *John Millington Synge*, p. 47. Two translations of *Intentions* appeared in 1905;
    neither seems to be the work of Cugnier or Synge.

45 See Jane Haville Desmarais, *The Beardsley Industry: the Critical Reception in England and
    France from 1893 to 1914* (London: Ashgate, 1998), p. 42 etc.

46 TCD MS 4419, 25/3/1898 and 9/4/1898.

47 As his diary for 12/6/1899 notes a 'Letter from the Green One', received while he was in
    Wicklow, this exciting theory can be laid aside (see TCD MS 4420).

48 See *Toulouse-Lautrec* (London: South Bank Centre/Paris: Réunion des musées nationaux,
    1992), pp. 310–36.

49 I owe this point to Christopher Prendergast, speaking on Radio 3 in January 1999. For
    Opisso's picture, see D. M. Chapman Huston, *The Lamp of Memory* (London: Skeffington,
    1949), p. 149.

50 These phrases/objects occur respectively in *When the Moon Has Set, Riders to the Sea, In
    the Shadow of the Glen, The Aran Islands, Deirdre of the Sorrows*, and *The Playboy*.

51 Material quoted is taken from a typescript prepared by John Lighton Synge, consisting of extracts from his brother's Notebook 39. A note by J. L. Synge, below the paragraph on the occult, reads: 'Here one scents the insanity of E. H. S. [i.e. at the time of writing, 1942], but in a factual setting.'

52 John Quinn to F. J. Gregg, 1/4/1909, NYPL, MSS Division.

53 L'Irlande Libre, no. 1 (Mai 1897), p. 4.

54 G & S, p. 67.

55 See Letters I, p. [41] where the editor quotes this phrase, without providing a source.

56 My Uncle, p. 108.

57 D. S. Neff, 'Synge, Spinoza, and The Well of the Saints', ANQ, vol. 2, no. 4 (1989), pp. 138–45.

58 Ibid., pp. 112–14. Hope Rea was an art historian who published popular guides to Tuscan art, etc. She later developed an interest in the supernatural.

59 'Etude', CW II, p. 27.

60 Ibid., p. 35.

61 Footnote text to 'Etude morbide', ibid., p. 25.

62 'Etude', CW II, pp. 28–9.

63 Ibid., p. 29. Here Synge indicates an awareness of the controversy about insanity and heredity which ran through the Westminster Review and Fortnightly Review in the 1890s and after.

64 JMS to WBY, 4/5/1908, Letters II, p. 155.

65 See Mary King, The Drama of J. M. Synge (London: Fourth Estate, 1985), p. 163, etc. Pater's celebrated essay 'The School of Giorgione' appeared in the Fortnightly Review in October 1877, and was later incorporated into The Renaissance.

66 See Desmarais, Beardsley Industry, for a discussion of musical analogies in criticism.

67 'I believe that the four painters who have had, and still have, the most influence, such as it is, on the ordinary Protestant Christian mind, are Carlo Dolci, Guercino, Benjamin West, and John Martin', John Ruskin, The Stones of Venice (London: Allen, 1896), vol. 1, p. 161.

68 In its clumsy way, the 'Vita' searches for that unity of culture which WBY later sought in the Quattrocentro and fascism. Cf. Ruskin's Dante, 'the central man of all the world', ibid., vol. 2, p. 207.

69 CW II, p. 19.

70 Ibid., p. 23.

71 Quoted from the transcript of E. H. Synge's Notebook 39; I have capitalised the initial letter of each line, as the typist had economically run two verse lines together with a slash mark between them.

72 CW II, p. 24.

73 TCD MS 6218 (typescript copy of KS's diary), 22/11/1899.

74 See chapter 11 for C. Matheson's memoir.

75 CW II, pp. 19–20.

76 Daughter, pp. 161–2.

CHAPTER 10: 'Give Me the Sun'

1 Introduction to Henrietta Frances Lord's translation (2nd edn.) of Henrik Ibsen, Ghosts (London: Griffith, 1890), p. vii.

2 See W. D. Howells to Edmund Gosse, 24/2/1889, Transatlantic Dialogue: Selected American Correspondence of Edmund Gosse (Austin: University of Texas Press, 1965), pp. 212–13.

3 Preface to The Playboy, CW IV, p. [53].

4 Ghosts was first produced in Germany – privately – in 1886. See Michael Meyer, Henrik

Ibsen: The Farewell to Poetry 1864–1882 (London: Hart-Davis, 1971), p. 298. Meyer quotes a German actor who referred pointedly to 'Wilhelm Lange's terrible translation' of *Pillars of Society*; see Meyer, pp. 243–3. Lange was also responsible for the translation of *A Doll's House* which bore the title *Nora*. Synge's approaches to Ibsen were not calculated to reveal the subtlety of the Norwegian texts.

Among English translations, note Mrs Henrietta Frances Lord's *Nora* in 1882 and her *Ghosts* in 1885 (reissued 1890); Archer's *Pillars of Society* and *Ghosts* in 1888, his *A Doll's House* in 1889; in 1890 Mrs Lord's *Nora* appeared in a second revised edition, followed by her *Ghosts*; a popular edition of Archer's *A Doll's House* appeared in 1892, rivalled by a further issuing of Mrs Lord's *Nora*. In 1893 Mrs Lord's *Nora* was again reissued. Details from Vera Ingunn Moe, *Deutscher Naturalismus und ausländische Literatur* (Frankfurt: Lang, 1983) and Michael Egan, *Ibsen: the Critical Heritage* (London: Routledge, 1972).

5 TCD MS 4419, 00/3/1898; see also Ann Saddlemyer's comment in her Introduction to *CW III*, p. xii.

6 Karl Beckson, *Arthur Symons: a Life* (Oxford: Clarendon Press, 1987), p. 224. The play was not published until 1917, that is, eight years after Symons's nervous breakdown.

7 Michael Holroyd, in the Introduction to G. B. Shaw, *Major Critical Essays* (London: Penguin, 1986), p. 11. 'On 16 December [1891, Shaw] wrote to his fellow Fabian Sydney Olivier criticizing the opposition to Parnell from within the Fabian Society; and that same day he decided to publish 'The Quintessence . , .'

8 For an account which might suggest the need for a comparison with Ireland, see Magnus Nodtvedt, *Rebirth of Norway's Peasantry* (Tacoma: Pacific Lutheran University Press, 1965).

9 James Joyce, *Stephen Hero*, ed. Theodore Spencer (London: Granada, 1977), p. 42.

10 In the play, these three correspond with the orphanage built to honour Captain Alving's memory (cf. the Young Men's Christian Association, of Anglophone countries), venereal disease as finally revealed in Osvald, and tuberculosis (the other great fear of nineteenth-century families). For Synge and Joyce's sharing the membership card of a French equivalent of the YMCA, see Chapter 9 above.

11 Joyce, *Stephen Hero*, p. 51.

12 Quoted in WBY, *Memoirs*, ed. Denis Donoghue (London: Macmillan, 1972), p. 204.

13 See his poetic version of Ibsen's *Brand* (London: Penguin, 1996).

14 For some acute remarks on symbolic acts and elements in the play, see Mary King, *The Drama of J. M. Synge* (London: Fourth Estate, 1985), p. 174, etc.

15 The use of the word as a euphemism for pregnant survived in certain circles in Ireland well into the 1960s: a young married woman, visiting relatives of her husband's who were Plymouth Brethren, was requested to keep her coat buttoned up because they knew her to be 'enceinte'.

16 'The Quintessence of Ibsenism' in Shaw, *Major Critical Essays*, p. 92; 'Preface to *The Tinker's Wedding*', *CW IV*, p. [3].

17 *CW III*, pp. 165, 161.

18 *Wicklow Newsletter*, 28/9/1901 and 5/10/1901.

19 Mary King (ed.), 'When the Moon Has Set', *Long Room*, nos. 24/25 (1982), p. 35.

20 King, *The Drama*, p. 164.

21 King (ed.), 'When the Moon Has Set', p. 33.

22 *CW III*, pp. 172–3. The text cited here is an editorial composite and, for the sake of simplicity, marks distinguishing the various manuscript sources have been omitted.

23 On this point, see John Northam, *Ibsen: A Critical Study* (Cambridge: Cambridge University Press 1973), p. 77, etc. Where Ibsen's Regina aspires to use a discourse more socially elevated than that to which she has been born, Synge's Mary Costello is occasionally able to recover a refined speech of which she has been deprived in her humiliation.

24 See *CW I*, p. 14, where the editor gives the poem the title, 'Execration'.

25 *CW III*, p. 177.

26 Henrik Ibsen, *Ghosts and Other Plays*, trans. Peter Watts (London: Penguin, 1964), pp. 101–2.

27 See Théodore Zeldin, *Ambition and Love* (Oxford: Oxford University Press, 1979), p. 304.

28 Colm: 'Do you remember?' Eileen: 'Not clearly.' (King (ed.), 'When the Moon Has Set', p. 23).

29 *CW III*, p. 177.

30 See Ernesto Caroli (ed.), *Fonti Francescane* (Padova: Edizione Messaggero, 1990), p. 178.

31 Eileen Matheson (born 1880) was the eldest daughter (with her twin Mary) of Charles Louis Matheson; Vera, Eileen's sister, was born in 1884; see Appendix below.

32 *CW III*, p. 177.

33 TCD MS 4422, 26/1/1903, and 27/1/1903. Archer's translation of *When We Dead Awaken* was produced at the Imperial Theatre, 25–26 January 1903.

CHAPTER 11: **First Love?**

1 Mary Doul in *The Well of the Saints*, Act Three; see *CW III*, p. 133.

2 This colourful detail is provided by Ronald Ayling in 'Synge's First Love: Some South African Aspects', *Modern Drama* (February 1964), p. 457.

3 Edmund Gosse, *Father and Son* (London: Penguin, 1986), pp. 45–6. Ann Thwaite denies the Irish sojourn and makes no comment as to why the claim was made (*Edmund Gosse: a Literary Landscape 1849–1928*, London: Secker, 1984, p. 14). Though Gosse 'fictionalised' some aspects of his background and experience, Ireland was a likely place in which his mother made contact with people of a Brethrenish disposition.

4 'I was unlike others of my generation in one thing only. I am very religious, and deprived by Huxley and Tyndall, whom I detested, of the simple-minded religion of my childhood, I had made a new religion, almost an infallible Church of poetic tradition, of a fardel of stories, and of personages, and of emotions, inseparable from their first expression, passed on from generation to generation by poets and painters with some help from philosophers and theologians.' (WBY, *Autobiographies*, London: Macmillan, 1979), pp. 115–16).

5 See TCD MS 4378 f. 55r (upside down). The notebook has been dated to 1895–6, but these entries may be later. Synge's study of Frazer in relation to Christianity is confirmed by his linking Proserpine and 'eating the god'.

6 See article in the *Irish Ecclesiastical Gazette*, vol. 19, no. 223 (1 October 1877), p. 316. Merrion Hall, converted into the Davenport Hotel in the mid-1990s, had been established in the 1860s, through the munificence of Henry Bewley, a Quaker who had attached himself to Brethren meetings.

7 *Irish Ecclesiastical Gazette*, 27 June 1885, p. 554.

8 They were first published by Ann Saddlemyer (ed.) as *Letters to Molly: John Millington Synge to Maire O'Neill 1906–1909* (Cambridge, MA: Belknap Press, 1971). Molly's letters to Synge were apparently destroyed by his family after his death. See also Ayling, 'Synge's First Love', p. 456.

9 G & S, p. 38; Ayling, 'Synge's First Love', p. 451.

10 See also *Special Report on Surnames in Ireland* (Dublin: HMSO, 1909), and – in a different mode – *The Name of the Beast* (Dublin: Thom, 1897). Doubtless, underlings did much of the work on his statistics, but he seems to have been unique among holders of his office in sponsoring them.

11 I derive Matheson's authorship from the *Dictionary Catalogue of the New York Public Library*.

12 *My Uncle*, p. 89.

13 Cherrie's presence can also be inferred from her friendship with Florence Ross who lived with the Synges at this point.

14 Her account of the incident is different. 'While he was playing he lost himself absolutely in the music, and once or twice he groaned while playing. His small nephew, who was in the room, said when he had finished: "Uncle Johnnie, why did you make that noise." He turned to me with a look of agony on his face. "Oh, did I," he said, and picked up his violin and quickly left the room. I did not see him again for hours.' 'John Synge As I Knew Him', *Irish Statesman*, 5 July 1924, pp. 532–4, reprinted in E. H. Mikhail (ed.), *J. M. Synge: Interviews and Recollections* (London: Macmillan, 1977), p. 4.

15 *My Uncle*, pp. 89–90.

16 'If I remember rightly, your Uncle John very often started for abroad earlier in the winter than January' *Daughter*, p. 96.

17 *My Uncle*, p. 93.

18 TCD MS 4416, entries for 16/11/95, 22/11/95 and 30/11/95. In these entries, Synge uses Cherrie Matheson's initials to identify her, and not the literary pseudonym, Scherma. See also Quentin Bell, *Victorian Painters* (London: Routledge, 1967), p. 79.

19 Between 1898 and 1902, Cherrie Matheson exhibited close on twenty pictures at the Dublin Sketching Club, and at least one at the Water Colour Society of Ireland. From their titles, it is clear that she spent time at Arcachon and Pau (in France), at Glengarriff (in Cork) and in the Scottish Highlands. While some titles indicate the conventionality of her work (*The Silver Lining*, 1902), others share common ground with Synge – e.g., *Out of the Mists* (1899) and *In the Fair, Pau, France* (1901). Her pictures fetched from one to five guineas. See Ann M. Stewart, *Irish Art Societies and Sketching Clubs: Index of Exhibitors 1870–1980* (Dublin: Four Courts Press), (1985). II, 495.

20 See TCD MS 4116, entries for 4th, 10th, 11th, 12th, 14th, 22nd and 29th December 1895, these mainly in German and using the name Scherma which is noted (10/12/1895) as an alias.

21 *My Uncle*, p. 94.

22 See Andrew Carpenter's Introduction (esp. p. ix) to *My Uncle*.

23 Ibid., p. 94.

24 The entry appears in German in TCD MS 4416. Stephens's habit of translating foreign-language entries, and presenting them as if Synge had made them in English, masks the difficulty of deciphering them.

25 The 'Plan for a Play' is printed in *CW III*, pp. 181–2.

26 *My Uncle*, p. 97. But see TCD MS 4417 where the entry appears in German, though Synge is in Italy. From this and other instances, it seems clear that Scherma is regarded as a literary or foreign-language personality, while C.M. is admitted into English-language record-keeping. But see below, for evidence in relation to the 1898 proposal of marriage.

27 JMS to Thérèse Beydon (draft) [*c.*23/2/1896], *Letters I*, p. 35.

28 Quotation from E. H. Synge's Notebook 39, as transcribed by J. L. Synge.

29 WBY, 'A Memory of Synge' in Mikhail (ed.), *J. M. Synge*, p. 1.

30 Matheson, 'John Synge as I Knew Him', in Ibid., p. 6.

31 WBY prefaced Matheson's memoir in the *Irish Statesman* with 'A Memory of Synge', thereby depriving her of any priority in the matter. 'I do not know why I have not crossed out that allusion to *Dana*,' he declared, 'except that it might give pleasure to *Dana*'s embittered editor.' Of the two editors, the socialist Ryan (1876–1913) was dead by 1924, so WBY's desire to suppress references was aimed at John Eglinton (pseudonym of William Kirkpatrick Magee).

32 *My Uncle*, pp. 99–100.

33 Stephens (*My Uncle*, p. 100) quotes KS's diary for 21 May 1896.

34 See *My Uncle*, p. 90, for his acknowledgement of Annie Stephens as a source.

35 Ibid., pp. 100–1.

36 See Canon Leslie's [typescript] succession lists for the diocese of Glendalough, preserved in the library of the Representative Church Body, Dublin.

37 Ayling, 'Synge's First Love', pp. 458–9.

38 Matheson 'John Synge As I Knew Him', in Mikhail (ed.), *J. M. Synge*, p. 4; *My Uncle*, p. 104.

39 In the 1860s, Sir Benjamin Lee Guinness (1798–1868) restored St Patrick's Cathedral at a cost of £150,000. A decade later, the other Protestant cathedral in Dublin (Christ Church) was rescued from the indignity of housing butchers' stalls through the munificence of Henry Roe.

40 *My Uncle*, pp. 104–5.

41 TCD MS 6221, ff. 1–2, KS to SS, 22/10/1896.

42 Ibid., f. 3, KS to SS, 25–27/10/1896.

43 Ibid., f. 5, KS to SS, 8/11/1896. Mrs Matheson's maiden name was Cherrie M. Hardy; it is likely that her mother-in-law was responsible for *An Awakening and a Crisis: being a Translation of Two Articles on the Reform Movement in Italy ... translated Mrs Matheson, late of Achany and the Lewis, and revised by Signor Dalla Vecchia* (London: Thynne, 1908). The commitment of Brethren in the UK to evangelisation on the Continent had begun with Darby's Swiss travels in the 1830s. Alternatively, the author was Annie Matheson (of Woking, Surrey) who wrote (as one 'of the offending faith') to *The Times* on 18 April 1904, deploring the anti-Jewish pogrom in Limerick.

44 Matheson, 'John Synge As I Knew Him' in Mikhail (ed.), *J. M. Synge*, p. 5.

45 *My Uncle*, pp. 115–16. The relevant diary entries in TCD MS 4419 are less detailed – 'Vu Scherma à Dublin au Musée' (4/5/98) and 'Interview avec Mde. M.' (6/5/98). It is clear that Stephens's interpretation relies on family sources rather than his uncle's surviving diaries. Between the conversation with Mrs Matheson on the Friday and his departure for Galway on Monday, Synge met Stephen MacKenna in Dublin (Saturday, 7/5/98).

46 Matheson, 'John Synge As I Knew Him', in Mikhail (ed.), *J. M. Synge*, p. 5.

47 The magazine, edited by the Jesuit Father Thomas Finlay, ran from 1894 to 1911.

48 Matheson, 'John Synge As I Knew Him', in Mikhail (ed.), *J. M. Synge*, p. 5.

49 Ibid., p. 5. Given the lapse of time between the conversation and the memoir, we can ignore the recommendation to *read* Lady Gregory's plays, which would require a date at which a quantity of her dramatic work was in print; Synge's allusion was as likely to productions as to publications.

50 The play was as much Gregory's work as WBY's, under whose name alone it was produced in 1902.

51 In Joyce's *Ulysses*, a fictionalised John Eglinton remarks, 'Synge has promised me an article for *Dana* too' (London: Penguin, 1993, p. 185), thus confirming his positive attitude towards the journal.

52 Thomas Mann, *Doctor Faustus*, trans. H. T. Lowe-Porter (Harmondsworth: Penguin, 1968), p. 399.

53 *The Autobiography of Johann Wolfgang von Goethe*, trans. John Oxenford (Chicago: University of Chicago Press, 1974), vol. 2, p. 423.

54 Matheson, 'John Synge As I Knew Him', in Mikhail (ed.), *J. M. Synge*, p. 5.

55 Samuel Beckett, *Murphy* (London: Calder, 1963), p. 7. (The novel was first published in 1938.)

56 Ibid., p. 36.

57 *CW III*, pp. 25–7. There is an ironic antecedent for this use of the cup, in *When the Moon Has Set*. In Act Two, Eileen signals her willingness to listen to Colm's reverie by covering his cup with a saucer.

CHAPTER 12: **Dreaming of Captain Dreyfus on Inis Meáin**

1 Arthur Symons, 'The Isles of Aran', *The Savoy*, no. 8 (December 1896), pp. 75–6.

2 Arthur Symons, reviewing Alfred Jarry's play, *Ubu Roi* (1896), quoted by R. F. Foster, *W. B. Yeats: a Life*, vol. 1: *The Apprentice Mage* (Oxford/New York: Oxford University Press, 1997), p. 173.

3 Symons, 'The Isles of Aran', p. 82.

4 Arthur Symons, 'A Causerie – From a Castle in Ireland', *The Savoy*, no. 6 (October 1896), p. 94.

5 Toni O'Brien Johnson, *Synge: the Medieval and the Grotesque* (Gerrards Cross: Smythe, 1982), p. 6; *My Uncle*, p. 114.

6 See the Introduction to Nicholas Grene's edition of J. M. Synge, *The Well of the Saints* (Washington: Catholic University of America Press, 1982), p. 2.

7 TCD MS 6200/17, A. H. Synge to J. H. Synge, 9/3/1852.

8 See Paul F. Bootheroyd, 'The Reverend Alexander Hamilton Synge in the Aran Islands', *Cahiers Irlandais* (1983).

9 TCD MS 6200/24, A. H. Synge to J. H. Synge.

10 *Suffolk Mercury*, 16 and 23 March 1872. According to the obituary, J. H. Synge attended the funeral on 16 March; WBY to Augusta Gregory, 11/1/1907, quoted in Foster, *W. B. Yeats*, p. 357.

11 TCD MS 6200/22, A. H. Synge to J. H. Synge, 22/10/1857. The cleric in question was R. F. Spencer; Stopford Augustus Brooke (1832–1916) became a minor contributor to the Irish Literary Revival, mainly as an anthologist.

12 TCD MS 930b/540, JMS to Isabel Synge, 29/5/1907. *The Aran Islands* was published *c.*28 April.

13 JMS to Augusta Gregory, 1/7/1898, *Letters I*, p. 48; TCD MS 4385 f. 40.

14 WBY to JMS [early January 1897], Ann Saddlemyer (ed.), *Theatre Business: the Correspondence of the First Abbey Theatre Directors: William Butler Yeats, Lady Gregory, and J. M. Synge* (Gerrards Cross: Smythe, 1982), pp. 25–6; JMS to Maud Gonne [6 April 1897], *Letters I*, pp. 47–8.

15 WBY to JMS, 21/6/[1898], Saddlemyer (ed.), *Theatre Business*, p. 27.

16 Foster, *W. B. Yeats*, p. 172.

17 Seaton F. Milligan, *Cruise to Galway and the Western Isles* (n.p.), p. 3.

18 TCD MS 4419, 10/5/1898.

19 When Elizabeth Frances Digby died *c.*1894, the inheritors included the daughter of a Digby–St Lawrence marriage who was sister-in-law to Lord Ardilaun (Arthur Edward Guinness). Stephens's firm, Fred Sutton & Co., acted for Arthur Guinness, the brewing company.

20 TCD MS 4385, ff. 55–7. This passage occurs relatively late, and is immediately followed by a matter-of-fact account of kelp-making, a quasi-industrial process involving the burning of seaweed.

21 Friedrich Nietzsche, *The Birth of Tragedy [and The Genealogy of Morals]*, trans. Francis Golffing (New York: Doubleday, 1956), p. 45.

22 TCD MS 4379, f. 85: see Mary King, *The Drama of J. M. Synge* (London: Fourth Estate, 1985), p. 105, for a discussion of this in connection with *The Well of the Saints*.

23 JMS, *The Aran Islands*, ed. Tim Robinson (London: Penguin, 1992), p. 5. (For this chapter, I have deviated from my practice of citing the standard 4-vol. *Collected Works* because of Robinson's exceptional knowledge of the terrain and his well-informed linguistic commentary.

24 Actually, what had excited Synge was William Stokes, *Life and Labours in Art and Archaeology of George Petrie* (London, 1885).

25 *The Aran Islands*, p. 6.

26 Ibid., p. 7.

27 Ibid., p. 10.

28 Ibid., pp. 10–12. Robinson identifies the site of Máirtín ó Conghaile's recitations as Clochán na Carraige, 19 feet long, 8 feet high, with a tiny window at one end (p. 139).

29 Ibid., p. 12. 'Dark' here means blind, a usage in Hiberno-English which Synge further exploits in *The Well of the Saints* where the blind beggars have the 'surname' Doul (= Gaelic 'dall').

30 *My Uncle*, p. 118.

31 TCD MS 4419 [20]/5/1898.

32 Tim Robinson, *Stones of Aran* (Dublin: Lilliput Press, 1995), p. 158.

33 *My Uncle*, p. 119.

34 W. L. Micks, *The Congested Districts Board for Ireland from 1891 to 1923* (Dublin: Eason, 1925), pp. 63, 41–2.

35 *The Aran Islands*, p. 12.

36 TCD MS 4393.

37 *The Aran Islands*, pp. 13–14.

38 Quoted by Alan Price in *CW II*, p. 54.

39 TCD MS 4385, quoted by Price in *CW II*, p. 54.

40 *The Aran Islands*, pp. 30–2, 50.

41 For Synge's original record of the story, see TCD MS 4385 f. 62 etc.

42 *The Aran Islands*, p. 143, n23. See also Robinson's *Stones of Aran*, pp. 160–3, for a longer account of the Digby interest in Aran.

43 Ibid., pp. 44–5.

44 'Hamlet' in Frank Kermode (ed.), *Selected Prose of T. S. Eliot* (London: Faber, 1975), p. 48.

45 Nietzsche, *Birth of Tragedy*, p. 103.

46 TCD MS 4419, 25/6/1898, 26/6/1898.

47 *My Uncle*, p. 124.

48 TCD MS 4420, 12/1/1899, 18/1/1899.

49 *My Uncle*, p. 127.

50 Ibid., p. 130. Some years later, JMS allegedly took up the topic again with her: 'I think your vision is coming true, but never in a church …' SS had an ever more elaborate version of the same incident in which his sister-in-law had a six-part vision climaxing with JMS 'kneeling in St Paul's Cathedral at worship'. *Daughter*, p. 113.

51 *My Uncle*, p. 131. See also W. J. McCormack, 'Setting and Ideology: with Reference to the Fiction of Maria Edgeworth', in Otto Rauchbauer (ed.) *Ancestral Voices: the Big House in Anglo-Irish Literature* (Dublin: Lilliput Press, 1992), pp. 33–60.

52 *The Aran Islands*, pp. 28–9.

53 Ibid., pp. 60–1.

54 Ibid., p. 63. For a discussion which emphasises how bitterly the Dreyfus Affair divided France, but not along any simple left/right axis, see George Steiner, *No Passion Spent: Essays 1978–1996* (London: Faber, 1996), pp. 224–7.

55 TCD MS 4385 ff. 37–8.

56 *The Aran Islands*, p. 66.

57 Ibid., pp. 70–1.

58 Ibid., pp. 74–6.

59 Ibid., p. 95.

60 Ibid., pp. 95–6.

61 TCD MS 4384 f. 47v. See Chapter 14 below for speculation as to whom the woman may have seen.

62 *The Aran Islands*, p. 88. Pampooties were a distinctive form of island footwear.

63 Ibid., p. 87.

64 Ibid., pp. 94–5.

65	WBY to JMS [1/12/1901], John Kelly and Ronald Schuchard (eds), *The Collected Letters of W. B. Yeats*, vol. III (Oxford: Clarendon Press, 1994), p. 130.

CHAPTER 13: **Travelling at Nightfall**

1	Juvenal, *Satires*, X, 22. (A traveller with empty pockets will sing in the thief's face.)
2	*CW I*, p. 62. The four lines, which Skelton entitled, 'Abroad', were written in Koblenz in late 1908.
3	See *Crossmolina Parish: An Historical Survey (c.*1981).
4	See TCD MSS 4396 and 4406, the latter datable more precisely to July 1907.
5	*CW II*, p. 196.
6	TCD MS 6218 (typescript of KS's diary), 30/7/1899.
7	Ibid., numerous entries for July 1899, also 20/11/1899.
8	Ibid., 26/7/1900, 25/8/1900.
9	Declan Kiberd, *Synge and the Irish Language* (Dublin: Gill & Macmillan, 1993), p. 238. Strictly speaking 'Gaeltacht' is a term conceived only after 1921.
10	'In West Kerry', *CW II*, p. 240.
11	Ibid., p. 239.
12	Ibid., p. 252.
13	Ibid., p. 251.
14	Ibid., p. 255.
15	Ibid., pp. 249, 263.
16	Ibid., pp. 251, 262, 275.
17	Ibid., p. 258.
18	TCD MS 4379 f. 46.
19	'The Vagrants of Wicklow', *CW II*, p. 202.
20	John Rylands Library, University of Manchester, MS 126/66, C. P. Scott to JMS, 26/5/1905 (draft), quoted in Bruce Arnold, *Jack Yeats* (London: Yale University Press, 1998), p. 134.
21	JMS to Stephen MacKenna, 30/5/1905, *Letters I*, p. 111.
22	For a detailed account of Synge's business relations with this firm, see James G. Nelson, *Elkin Mathews: Publisher to Yeats, Joyce, Pound* (Madison: University of Wisconsin Press, 1989).
23	Arnold, *Jack Yeats*, p. 136.
24	'From Galway to Gorumna', *CW II*, pp. 286, 287.
25	'Among the Relief Works', *CW II*, p. 296.
26	'The Kelp Makers', *CW II*, p. 307.
27	JMS to KS, [*c.*16]/6/1905, *Letters I*, p. 113.
28	Jack Yeats, 'A Letter about J. M. Synge', *CW II*, p. [401]; the letter originally appeared in the New York *Evening Sun* of 20/7/1909.
29	See Seán Noone, *Where the Sun Sets: Ballycroy, Belmullet, Kilcommon and Kiltane, County Mayo* (Naas: Leinster Leader, 1991), pp. 117 and 189.
30	'The Smaller Peasant Proprietors', *CW II*, p. 323.
31	JMS to Stephen MacKenna 13/7/1905, *Letters I*, pp. 116–17. The League was founded by William O'Brien (1852–1928) in 1898.
32	Quotations from JMS to Stephen MacKenna, 9/4/1907, *Letters I*, p. 330.
33	'Can We Go Back into Our Mother's Womb? A Letter to the Gaelic League, By A Hedge Schoolmaster', *CW II*, pp. 399–400. Again, as with the 'Autobiography', the editor of *CW II* has chosen to create a synthetic text. Though much of what is printed can be found in Synge's handwriting in one notebook or another, there is a suspiciously high proportion of WBY's hate-words in this short piece, together with praise of Yeatsian heroes. Synge never sent it to the papers (G & S, p. 262).

34 JMS to Augusta Gregory, 11/9/1904, *Letters I*, p. 93–4.
35 TCD MS 4379 ff. 46–7.
36 JMS to Stephen MacKenna, 13/7/1905, *Letters I*, p. 116.
37 John Butler Yeats to W. B. Yeats [September 1907]; quoted in Arnold, *Jack Yeats*, p. 148.

CHAPTER 14: **A Month in the County: August 1901**

1 Seamus Heaney, 'Glanmore Sonnets' [IV], *Field Work* (London: Faber, 1979), p. 38.
2 'A Landlord's Garden in County Wicklow', *CW II*, p. 230.
3 *My Uncle*, p. 146. For incidental detail in this and the previous paragraph, see TCD MS 6218, 18/6/1901, 21/6/1901, 12/7/1901, 20/7/1901, 9/8/1901.
4 Thomas Synge's existence is established through *Griffith's Valuations*; his name does not appear in the family tree, not even in the annotated copy in the Society of Genealogists' library, London.
5 Costello is buried in Derrylossary churchyard, close to the Barton and Childers graves.
6 *CW II*, pp. 209–10.
7 *Wicklow People*, 17/8/1901, p. 7.
8 Ibid., 7/9/1901, p. 5.
9 *Wicklow Newsletter*, 17/5/1902.
10 Sigmund Freud and Joseph Breuer, *Studies on Hysteria* (London: Penguin, 1974), pp. 186–201. The 'auxiliary moment' is discussed in relation to two cases, but 'Katharina' is the more compelling, as we now know that the girl was sexually attacked by her father, not, as Freud pretended, her uncle. The significance of this concept (in German, *Nachträglichkeit*) was established by Jacques Lacan.
11 *CW III*, p. 41.

CHAPTER 15: **The Year 1902 and the One-Act Plays**

1 Fredric Jameson, *Signatures of the Visible* (London: Routledge, 1992), p. 1.
2 TCD MS 4421, 19/1/1902.
3 Ibid., 21/1/1902; TCD MS 6218, 23/1/1902, 8/2/1902; MS 4421, 22/1/1902, 24/1/1902.
4 JMS to Augusta Gregory, 22/2/ [1902], *Letters I*, p. 53; TCD MS 4421, 16/2/1902.
5 JMS to Augusta Gregory, 22/2/[1902], *Letters I*, p. 53; TCD MS 4421, 12/4/1902, 19/4/1902.
6 William Coleman (Sr.) died on 20/1/1900, aged 92; his wife lived on for a further twelve years. An advertisement in the *Wicklow Newsletter* of 31/8/1901 establishes that William Coleman (Jr. died 1918 aged 64) held Tomriland under lease from Mrs Editha Gardiner of Glanmore.
7 TCD MS 6218 (typed copy of KS's diary) entries for 10/4/1902, 14/4/1902, 24/4/1902, 10/5/1902, 20/5/1902; JMS to Stephen MacKenna [12/6/1902], *Letters I*, p. 57.
8 TCD MS 6218, entries for 22/7/1902, 23/7/1902.
9 *CW IV* p. 152. TCD MS 6218, entries for 23/7/1902, 30/7/1902, 4/9/1902.
10 *My Uncle*, p. [53].
11 TCD MS 4393 f. 10v.
12 Ibid., f. 23r.
13 See N. Grene, 'Synge and Wicklow', in Ken Hannigan and William Noland (eds), *Wicklow: History and Society*, (Dublin: Geography Publications, 1994), p. 697. In her declining years, KS had an occasional companion, Miss Massey, who can hardly have been her former maid.
14 *My Uncle*, p. 151.
15 *CW III*, p. 39.

16 The plays included WBY's *The Pot of Broth*, and *Eilis agus an Bhean Deirce* by Peadar Mac Fhionnlaich; the production was overseen by the Fay brothers on 4 December 1902.

17 *My Uncle*, pp. 154–5.

18 WBY to James Joyce [2/11/1902], John Kelly and Ronald Schuchard (eds), *The Collected Letters of W. B. Yeats*, vol. III (Oxford: Clarendon Press, 1994), p. 242.

19 Even *In the Shadow of the Glen* may harbour a detail or two of Aran legend; notably that of the premature confining of Dr Stoney, the island doctor given to excessive drinking. His rescuer from burial alive had helped to carry the coffin, with the Rev. William Kilbride in attendance.

20 O. St J. Gogarty, *As I Was Going Down Sackville Street* (London: Rich & Cowan, 1937), p. 289.

21 *Riders to the Sea*, *CW III*, p. 15.

22 Asenath Nicholson, *Annals of the Famine in Ireland* (Dublin: Lilliput Press, 1998), p. 188.

23 Ibid., p. 104.

24 This detail of the thread was transmitted to Grene by a neighbour, Thomas O'Neill of Ballinaclash, demonstrating the tenacity of folk memory over three-quarters of a century, but note the same details in the *Wicklow Newsletter* of 31/8/1901.

25 *My Uncle*, pp. 161–3. Stephens explains Rosie's non-attendance as a gesture of respect for KS. But a stage production of *Riders to the Sea* (which JMS had discussed with her repeatedly) might have been an ordeal for a woman recently bereaved – her fiancé had died suddenly.

26 See *CW II*, p. 211n.

27 Karl Beckson, *Arthur Symons: A Life* (Oxford: Clarendon Press, 1987), p. 225.

28 Máire Nic Shiubhlaigh, *The Splendid Years* (Dublin: Duffy, 1955), p. 55. (Translation added by the present writer.)

29 But see the ethnographical work on Aran by Browne and Haddon, quoted in n. 40–41 below, where Barbara names 29 women of 570 surveyed.

30 TCD MS 4384 f. 53.

31 For the death of Barbara Synge (1790–2) on 19 May, see the annotated copy of *The Family of Synge* at the Society of Genealogists, London. For the later death, see TCD MS 6218, 27/10/1901: Cicely Barbara Aileen Synge (1899–1901), died at Kilmainham Wood, Meath, of enteritis.

32 No other dramatic project was unnamed, and JMS's diary for 3 February 1903 provided this title. See *CW III*, pp. 206–7, for the text and editorial head-note.

33 *My Uncle*, p. 143; TCD MS 6218, 4/9/1903.

34 *My Uncle*, p. 134, quoting Annie Stephens.

35 See TCD MS 6218, 8/12/1899, 22/5/1900, 23/10/1900, 3/1/1901, 5/2/1901, 14/4/1902. The incident at Delgany occurred on 1 June 1899.

36 See TCD MS 6218, 25/11/1902, 25/12/1902.

37 WBY to JMS [1/12/1901], Yeats, *Letters III*, ed. Kelly and Schuchard, p. 130. *The Aran Islands* was rejected by Grant Richards, A. H. Bullen, Alfred Nutt, T. Fisher Unwin, and Elkin Mathews.

38 See Declan Kiberd, *Synge and the Irish Language* (Dublin: Gill & Macmillan, 1993), pp. 65–6.

39 See *CW III*, p. 206.

40 For an excerpt, see Breandán and Ruairí Ó hEithir, *An Aran Reader* (Dublin: Lilliput Press, 1991), pp. 5–58. The original appeared in PRIA in 1893.

41 Browne and Haddon, in ibid., p. 51.

42 See Tim Robinson's Introduction to his edition of J. M. Synge, *The Aran Islands* (London: Penguin, 1992), p. xxxv; also Tomás Ó Máille, *An Ghaoth Aniar* (Baithe Atha Cliath, 1920).

43 The attack took place on the night of 6 October 1894; see James Carney, *The Playboy and the Yellow Lady* (Dublin: Poolbeg, 1986).

44 '*If* the idea had occurred to me I could and would just as readily [have] written the thing, as it stands, without the Lynchehaun case or the Aran case' JMS to S. MacKenna [?17/4/1907], *Letters I*, p. 333.

CHAPTER 16: Too Many Impresarios

1 Jack Yeats, 'A Letter About J. M. Synge', *Evening Sun* (New York), 20/7/1909; see *CW II*, p. 401.

2 Symons, 'A Causerie – From a Castle in Ireland', *The Savoy*, no. 6 (October, 1896), p. 95.

3 Denis Donoghue, *William Butler Yeats* (New York: Ecco Press, 1988), pp. 11–33.

4 JMS to KS [17/1/1903], *Letters I*, p. 65.

5 Ibid.

6 JMS to KS, 21/1/1903, *Letters I*, p. 67.

7 Samuel Beckett, *Disjecta* (London: Calder, 1997). The passage comes from a review of Thomas MacGreevey's book about Jack Yeats.

8 For details of De Basterot, see James Pethica's annotations in *Lady Gregory's Diaries 1892– 1902* (Gerrards Cross: Smythe, 1996), p. 17 etc.

9 The date was September 1897: see Pethica (ed.), *Lady Gregory's Diaries*, p. 152.

10 JMS to A. Gregory, 1/7/1898, *Letters I*, p. 48.

11 JMS to A. Gregory [? 30/4/1902), *Letters I*, p. 55.

12 'An Epic of Ulster', *CW II*, p. 367.

13 JMS to KS, 21/1/1903, cited in Richard Ellmann, *James Joyce* (new edn; Oxford: Oxford University Press, 1983), p. 125, citing a copy provided to him by David Greene: see also *Letters I*, p. 66–7.

14 Herbert Gorman, *James Joyce* (New York: Farrar & Rinehart, 1939), pp. 101–2.

15 James Joyce to Forrest Reid, 1/8/1918, Joyce, *Letters I*, ed. Stuart Gilbert (London: Faber, 1957), p. 117.

16 Carla Marengo Vaglio, '*Giacomo Joyce* and the *Vita Nuova*', in Franca Ruggieri (ed.), *Joyce Studies in Italy*, vol. 5 (1998), pp. 81–106.

17 Ellmann, *James Joyce*, pp. 160–1.

18 The most recent account is Adrian Frazier, *Behind the Scenes: Yeats, Horniman, and the Struggle for the Abbey Theatre* (Berkeley: University of California Press, 1990).

19 James Joyce, *Poems and Exiles*, ed. J. C. C. Mays (London: Penguin, 1992), p. 104.

20 A. E. F. Horniman to JMS, 26/5/1904; see *Letters I*, pp. 68–9.

21 J. Quinn to F. J. Gregg, 1/4/1909, NYPL, MSS Division; see also B. L. Reid, *The Man from New York: John Quinn and His Friends* (New York: Oxford University Press, 1968), pp. 30–1.

22 Terry Eagleton, *Crazy John and the Bishop and Other Essays on Irish Culture* (Cork: Cork University Press, 1998), pp. 249–72, esp. pp. 257–8.

23 Bastien von Helmholz [i.e. Ezra Pound], 'John Synge and the Habits of Criticism', *The Egoist*, 2/2/1914, pp. 53–4.

24 James Stephens to the *New Age*, 18 March 1915; see *Letters of James Stephens*, ed. Richard J. Finneran (London: Macmillan, 1974), p. 155.

25 From *Riders to the Sea* and *Deirdre of the Sorrows* (Act Three); see *CW III*, p. 17, and *CW IV*, p. 261.

26 Quoted by Peter Jones in the Introduction to *Imagist Poetry* (London: Penguin, 1972), p. 28.

27 See 'A Few Don'ts by an Imagiste' in ibid., p. 132.

28 May Sinclair, *The Egoist*, 1 June 1915.

29 James Joyce to Elkin Mathews, 12/7/1909, Joyce, *Letters I*, pp. 66–7.

30 James Joyce to Stanislaus Joyce, 4/8/1909, Joyce, *Letters II*, ed. Richard Ellmann (London: Faber, 1957), p. 231.

31 ES to James Joyce, 23/8/1909, Carl A. Kroch Library, Cornell University. Also a notebook of Hutchie Synge, from a copy made by his brother, J. L. Synge.

32 James Joyce to Stanislaus Joyce, 2/9/1909, Joyce, *Letters II*, p. 244. ES had been consulting the Society of Authors about the proposition to let the 'Italian Grand Guigol [sic] Company' produce a translation of the play; see BL Add. MS 56830 f. 75, letter of 25/8/1909.

CHAPTER 17: **A Tragic Miracle, 1905**

1 Friedrich Nietzsche, *The Birth of Tragedy* [*and The Genealogy of Morals*], [trans. Francis Golffing] (New York: Doubleday, 1956), pp. 59–60.

2 TCD MS 6218 (copy of KS's diary), 1/2/1903, 13/5/1903, 21/5/1903, 3/6/1903, 24/6/1903.

3 Ibid., 8/8/1903.

4 See also Chapter 7, 'Varieties of Celticism', in Mc Cormack, *From Burke to Beckett: Ascendancy, Tradition and Betrayal in Literary History* (Cork: Cork University Press, 1994), pp. 224–56.

5 See H. Zimmer, *The Celtic Church in Britain and Ireland*, trans. A. Meyer (London: Nutt, 1902); James D. Heron, *The Celtic Church in Ireland* (London: Service & Paton, 1898); G. T. Stokes, *Ireland and the Celtic Church* (London: Hodder & Stoughton, 1888). For concern with this topic in the contentious province of Ulster, see T. W. Roe, *The Church of Ireland Before the Reformation* (Enniskillen, 1845; 2nd edn Belfast, 1866).

6 Quoted in *CW III*, pp. 262–3.

7 Ibid., p. 71.

8 Ibid., p. 87. Ballinatone lies south of Greenane (where the main action of the play takes place).

9 *Letters I*, p. 76. The circumstances of the letter's composition and delivery (if it was ever sent to MacKenna) are unclear: JMS may have intended to use part of its argument for a public statement, along the lines of 'Can We Go Back into Our Mother's Womb?' written in the aftermath of the *Playboy* controversy three years later. See Ann Saddlemyer (ed.), 'Synge to MacKenna: the Mature Years', *Massachusetts Review*, vol. 5, no. 2 (Winter 1964), pp. 275–95.

10 See Gertrude Schoepperle, 'John Synge and his "Old French Farce"', *North American Review*, no. 214 (1921), pp. 504–13.

11 See *CW III*, p. 262, for a list of extant manuscripts/typescripts; see also N. Grene, *The Synge Manuscripts in the Library of Trinity College, Dublin* (Dublin: Dolmen Press, 1971), pp. 26–7.

12 *CW III*, p. 79.

13 See ibid., p. 90.

14 For these sites, see Geraldine Lynch, 'The Holy Wells of County Wicklow', in Ken Hannigan and William Nolan (eds), *Wicklow: History and Society* (Dublin: Geography Publications, 1994), pp. 625–48. For Synge ownership of Glasnamullen, see p. 661. The careful geography of *The Well of the Saints* is discussed in Mc Cormack, *Burke to Beckett*, pp. 244–7.

15 *CW III*, p. 91.

16 Ibid., p. 97.

17 Ibid., p. 123.

18 Alan Price, *Synge and Anglo-Irish Drama* (London: Methuen, 1961), p. 138.

19 *CW III*, p. 125. This is a colloquial use of antiphrasis where 'mend' implies its opposite, 'destroy'.

20 Ibid., p. 135.

21 Mc Cormack, *Burke to Beckett*, pp. 249–50.

22 *CW III*, pp. 77, 97. The allusion to murder links JMS's play to a forgotten Abbey production, *The Eyes of the Blind*, by Winifred Letts (1882–1972, aka Mrs W. H. M. Verschoyle), produced in April 1907. This lost play revolved around 'a murder on a Wicklow bog' (Robert Hogan and James Kilroy, *The Abbey Theatre: The Years of Synge, 1905–1909* (Dublin: Dolmen Press, 1978), p. 175).

23 *CW III*, p. 149.

24 Ibid., p. 151.

25 See Hogan and Kilroy (eds), *Abbey Theatre*, pp. 16–17.

26 See ibid., pp. 19–22.

27 See ibid., pp. 21–2.

28 WBY to JMS, 21/8[1904] from Coole Park; see Ann Saddlemyer (ed.), *Theatre Business: the Correspondence of the First Abbey Theatre Directors: William Butler Yeats, Lady Gregory and J. M. Synge* (Gerrards Cross: Smythe, 1982), p. 60.

29 TCD Synge Correspondence, Item 646, H. Lebeau to JMS, 26/3/[1905].

30 Henri Lebeau et J. & J. Tharaud, 'Moines de l'Athos', *Cahiers de la quizaine* (ser. 5, no. 7), 1904, pp. 39–45.

31 NLI Best Papers, MS 11,001 (19) i, H. Lebeau to R. I. Best, 14/6/1905.

32 For a brief account, see John Rodgers, *Mary Ward Settlement (Late Passmore Edwards Settlement): A History 1891–1931* (London: Mary Ward Settlement, 1931). Presided over by the anti-suffragette Mrs Humphry Ward (1851–1920), the Settlement (founded in 1897) brought together the legacy of English Unitarian theology, the philanthropy of John Passmore Edwards (1823–1911), and the newer values and needs of London University colleges in nearby Bloomsbury.

33 TCD Synge Correspondence, Item 167, H. Lebeau to JMS, 20/5/[1905].

34 Lebeau's article appeared in what proved to be the final (no. 12) issue of *Dana*, dated April 1905. However, most Irish periodicals escape from the printer's clutch later than the date they carry.

35 R. W. Lynd, 'The Nation and the Man of Letters', *Dana*, no. 12 (April 1905), pp. 371–6.

36 George Moore, *Hail and Farewell*, ed. Richard Cave (Gerrards Cross: Smythe, 1976), p. 553.

37 *Letters I*, pp. 84–7.

38 TCD Synge Correspondence, Item 647, H. Lebeau to JMS, 9/12/[1905].

39 Ibid., Item 294, H. Lebeau to JMS, 13/1/1907.

40 Ibid., Item 328, H. Lebeau to JMS, 3/5/1907.

41 Ibid., Item 362, H. Lebeau to JMS, 14/8/1907.

42 Ibid., Item 367, H. Lebeau to JMS, 28/8/1907; Item 372, H. Lebeau to JMS, September 1907.

43 JMS to MA, 24/11/1907, *Letters II*, pp. 85–6.

44 TCD Synge Correspondence, Item 416, H. Lebeau to JMS, 26/2/1908.

45 JMS to Stephen MacKenna, 30/5/1905, *Letters I*, p. 111.

46 Charles Taylor, *Sources of the Self: the Making of the Modern Identity* (Cambridge: Cambridge University Press, 1989), p. 443.

CHAPTER 18: **Enter Molly, Centre-Stage**

1 WBY, 'A Prayer for My Daughter', *Yeats's Poems*, ed. A. Norman Jeffares and Warwick Gould (London: Macmillan, 1989), p. 295.

2 Elizabeth Coxhead, *Daughters of Erin* (London: Secker & Warburg, 1965), p. 177.

3 Ibid., p. 179n.

4 JMS to A. Gregory [9/6/1906], *Letters I*, p. 170.

5 JMS to MA, 3/9/1906; [14/7/1907], ibid., p. 201.

6 See Ann Saddlemyer's Introduction to *Letters to Molly: John Millington Synge to Maire O'Neill 1906–1909* (Cambridge, MA: Belknap Press, 1971), p. xix.

7 Charles Weekes, Sr., had premises at 27 Essex Quay. C. A. Weekes was at school with WBY.

8 A. Gregory and WBY to JMS, 21/8/[1904], Yeats, *Letters*, vol. III, ed. John Kelly and Ronald Schuchard (Oxford: Clarendon Press, 1994), pp. 637–8; though signed by both, it is clear from the opening sentence that the letter was dictated by WBY to Gregory; see p. 596 for the 11/5/1904 letter to A. E. F. Horniman.

9 JMS to MA 19/7/[1906] and 20/7/1906, *Letters I*, pp. 177–80.

10 JMS to MA [20/7/1906], 27/7/[1906]; [28/7/1906]; 7/8/1906, ibid., pp. 180, 182, 186.

11 JMS to MA [17/8/1906], ibid., pp. 190–1.

12 JMS to MA, undated enclosure with [27/8/1906], ibid., pp. 193–4.

13 See f. 14 of Gregory's notebook devoted to an essay on JMS (NYPL, MSS Division). 'But when he thought of the actual stage he could not see any possible side wings for that "wide windy corner of high distant hills". He had also talked of the return of the father being at the very door of the chapel where Christy was to wed Pegeen; but in the end all took place within the one cottage room.'

14 JMS to MA, [30/8/1906], [1/9/1906], [8/9/1906], [6/9/1906], *Letters I*, pp. 198–9, 203, 202.

15 Saddlemyer (ed.), *Letters to Molly*, p. xiii.

16 JMS to MA [22/9/1906], *Letters I*, p. 207.

17 JMS to A. Gregory [29/9/1906], ibid., pp. 209–10. The London-based priest was probably Gerard O'Donovan, also a novelist, who worked in Toynbee Hall, an urban mission based in Whitechapel. For the Synge family's links with such philanthropy, see pp. 0000 above.

18 JMS to MA [16/10/1906], ibid., pp. 217–18.

19 JMS to MA [18/10/1906], ibid., p. 218. See also J. B. Lyons, *What Did I Die Of? The Deaths of Parnell, Wilde, Synge and Other Literary Pathologies* (Dublin: Lilliput press, 1991), p. 151.

20 JMS to MA [19/10/1906], *Letters I*, p. 219.

21 JMS to MA [21/10/1906], Saddlemyer (ed.), *Letters to Molly*, p. 40; 18/8/1907, p. 180.

22 JMS to MA [25/10/1906], ibid., p. 42.

23 JMS to MA, 1/11/[1906], ibid., p. 45.

24 JMS to MA [undated], ibid., p. 182; 10/9/1907, ibid., p. 193.

25 JMS to MA [19/11/1906], *Letters I*, p. 238.

26 JMS to MA, Saddlemyer (ed.), *Letters to Molly* [18/11/1906], [19/11/1906], p. 55; [20/11/1906], *Letters I*, pp. 236–8.

27 JMS to MA [22/11/1906], *Letters I*, p. 239.

28 JMS to MA [23/11/1906], ibid.

29 JMS to MA [23/11/1906], Saddlemyer (ed.), *Letters to Molly*, p. 57.

30 JMS to MA [24/11/1906], *Letters I*, p. 241.

31 JMS to MA [29/11/1906], Saddlemyer (ed.), *Letters to Molly*, pp. 60–1.

32 JMS to MA [30/11/1906], ibid., p. 64; 1/12/[1906], ibid., pp. 65–6.

33 JMS to MA, 2/12/1906, ibid., p. 67.

34 JMS to MA [7/12/1906], ibid., p. 72.

35 Frank Newbolt, 'The Etchings of E. M. Synge, A.R.E.', *The Studio*, vol. 60 (1913), pp. 101, 98, 104. Synge's London gallery issued the *Catalogue of a Memorial Exhibition of Original Etchings* (1906).

36 JMS to MA [10/12/1906], Saddlemyer (ed.), *Letters to Molly*, p. 74; [13/12/1906], p. 77.

37 JMS to MA, 19/12/1906, *Letters I*, p. 264.

38 JMS to MA, 27/12/1906, Saddlemyer (ed.), *Letters to Molly*, p. 81.

39 Maurice Bourgeois, *John Millington Synge and the Irish Theatre*. (2nd edn New York: Blom, 1968), pp. 148–9; for the actor's comment, see Robert Hogan and James Kilroy (eds), *The Abbey Theatre: the Years of Synge, 1905–9* (Dublin: Dolmen Press, 1978), p. 123.

40 JMS to WBY, 11/1/1907, gives terms proposed by Synge and Gregory; see *Letters I*, p. 282.

41 Ann Saddlemyer (ed.), *Theatre Business: the Correspondence of the First Abbey Theatre Directors: William Butler Yeats, Lady Gregory and J. M. Synge* (Gerrards Cross: Smythe, 1982), p. 205. I am grateful to Warwick Gould for his comments on WBY's movements.

42 JMS to MA, 27/1/1907, *Letters I*, p. 285.

43 Máire Nic Shiubhlaigh, *The Splendid Years* (Dublin: Duffy, 1955), p. 81.

44 JMS to MA, 31/1/1907, *Letters I*, p. 287.

45 JMS to MA [11/2/1907], ibid., p. 293.

46 JMS to MA [19/2/1907], ibid., p. 298.

47 JMS to MA [22/2/1907, and postscript of 23/2/1907], ibid., p. 301.

CHAPTER 19: **Edwardian Winter, 1907**

1 Terry Eagleton, *Heathcliff and the Great Hunger* (London: Verso, 1995), p. 307.

2 *CW II*, p. [53].

3 G & S II, pp. 252–3.

4 *CW IV*, p. 54.

5 Ibid., pp. 67–73.

6 Ibid., p. 89.

7 Máire Nic Shiubhlaigh, *The Splendid Years* (Dublin: Duffy, 1955), p. 83.

8 Mary Colum, *Life and the Dream* (London: Macmillan, 1947), p. 137.

9 *CW IV*, p. 105.

10 Three leaves, (a fourth is missing) in the Berg Collection, NYPL. These notes may record a conversation with Sara Allgood, with whose papers they are preserved.

11 See f. 15 of a notebook (Forster-Murphy Collection, NYPL) in which Gregory wrote a memoir of Synge for her grand-daughters.

12 *CW IV*, p. 167.

13 Nic Shiubhlaigh, *The Splendid Years*, p. 83.

14 JMS to MA, 27/1/1907, *Letters I*, p. 285; R. F. Foster, *W. B. Yeats: a Life*, vol. 1: *The Apprentice Mage* (Oxford/New York: Oxford University Press, 1997), p. 360.

15 Extensive material culled from press reports of the riots can be found in James Kilroy, *The 'Playboy' Riots* (Dublin: Dolmen Press, 1971) and Robert Hogan and James Kilroy, *The Abbey Theatre: the Years of Synge, 1905–1909* (Dublin: Dolmen Press, 1978, esp. pp. 123–71).

16 *Freeman's Journal*, 29/1/1907; quoted in Kilroy, *'Playboy' Riots*, p. 15.

17 *Irish Independent*, 29/1/1907; quoted in Kilroy, *'Playboy' Riots*, p. 17.

18 *Irish Times*, 12/1/1907; quoted in Kilroy, *'Playboy' Riots*, p. 22.

19 Undated letter from Robert Gregory to Hugh, Viscount Gough, Berg Collection, NYPL.

20 JMS to the *Irish Times* [30/1/1907], *Letters I*, p. 286.

21 For extensive extracts from the court reports, see Hogan and Kilroy, *Years of Synge*, pp. 132–8; for Padraic Colum's letter, see Kilroy, *'Playboy' Riots*, pp. 53–4.

22 In this role, she later corresponded with Michael Collins, Augusta Gregory and WBY in connection with Hugh Lane's contested bequest of Impressionist paintings; see papers in the Berg Collection, NYPL.

23 *Irish Times*, 31/1/1907; quoted in full in Kilroy, *'Playboy' Riots*, pp. 55–6.

24 *Dublin Evening Mail*, 31/1/1907; quoted in full in Kilroy, *'Playboy' Riots*, pp. 54–5.

25 Foster, *Yeats*; for a press report of Sheehan's contribution, see Kilroy, *'Playboy' Riots*, p. 86.

26 See A. Gregory to JMS, [5/2/1907], Ann Saddlemyer (ed.), *Theatre Business: the Correspondence of the First Abbey Theatre Directors: William Butler Yeats, Lady Gregory and J. M. Synge* (Gerrards Cross: Smythe, 1982), pp. 210–14.

27 JMS to MA, [5/2/1907], *Letters I*, p. 289.

28 Colum, *Life and the Dream*, p. 139.

29 WBY to John Quinn, 18/2/1907, quoted in Saddlemyer (ed.), *Theatre Business*, p. 211n.

30 *The Abbey Row, Not edited by W. B. Yeats* (Dublin: printed by Maunsel, 1907), p. 10.
31 See Hogan and Kilroy, *Years of Synge*, p. 144.
32 Reported by Robert Gregory in a letter to Hugh Gough, Berg Collection, NYPL.
33 *CW IV*, p. [95].
34 Asenath Nicholson, *Annals of the Famine in Ireland* (Dublin: Lilliput Press, 1998), pp. 66–7.
35 See James Joyce to Stanislaus Joyce [?1/2/1907] and 11/2/1907, Joyce, *Letters II*, ed. Richard Ellmann (London: Faber, 1957), pp. 209, 211.
36 WBY, 'J. M. Synge and the Ireland of His Time', in *Essays and Introductions* (London: Macmillan, 1961), p. 312.
37 See WBY, *Memoirs*, ed. Denis Donoghue (London: Macmillan, 1972), p. 202.
38 Dated 16/1/1910; quotation from printed copies in the Berg Collection, NYPL.
39 WBY, 'The Bounty of Sweden', in *Autobiographies.* (London: Macmillan, 1979), p. 203.
40 See Francis Hackett to John Quinn, 10/8/1907, NYPL, MSS Division.
41 See Patrick Maume, *'Life that is Exile': Daniel Corkery and the Search for Irish Ireland* (Belfast: Institute of Irish Studies, 1993), p. 27. The quoted phrases derive from Corkery's lecture-notes.

CHAPTER 20: 'Sorrow's Sauce for Every Kiss'

1 'Of Parents and Children' [1625], Francis Bacon, *A Critical Edition of the Major Works*, ed. Brian Vickers (Oxford: Oxford University Press, 1996), p. 352.
2 JMS to MA [26/2/1907], *Letters I*, p. 303.
3 JMS to MA [?4/3/1907], ibid., p. 305.
4 JMS to MA [8]/3/[1907], ibid., p. 307.
5 JMS to MA 9/3/1907, ibid., p. 310.
6 JMS to MA 14/3/[1907], ibid., p. 313.
7 JMS to MA 18/3/1907, ibid., p. 316.
8 JMS to MA 19/3/1907, ibid., p. 317.
9 JMS to MA 21/3/[1907], ibid., p. 318.
10 JMS to MA 25/3/[1907], ibid., p. 320.
11 JMS to MA [26/3/1907], ibid., pp. 320–21.
12 Ibid.; see *CW I*, p. 51, for the final version of the poem.
13 JMS to MA, 29/3/[1907], *Letters I*, p. 322.
14 JMS to MA, 13/5/1907, ibid., pp. 343–4.
15 JMS to MA [15/5/1907], ibid., p. 346.
16 JMS to MA [17/5/1907], ibid., pp. 348–9.
17 JMS to MA, 22/5/1907, ibid., p. 353.
18 Sara Allgood, 'Memoirs', incomplete typescript in the Berg Collection, NYPL, see ff. 33–4.
19 JMS to MA, 23/5/1907, and postscript of the following day, *Letters I*, pp. 354–5.
20 JMS to MA, 27/5/1907 and 28/5/1907, ibid., pp. 359–60.
21 JMS to Isabella Synge, 29/5/1907, ibid., p. 361.
22 JMS to MA [30/5/1907], [3/6/1907], [11/6/1907], ibid., pp. 364, 365, 367.
23 JMS to MA [14/6/1907], ibid., pp. 367–8.
24 *Letters and Papers of the Late Theodosia A., Viscountess Powerscourt* (16th edn, London: Rouse, 1905), p. 180. See also W. J. Mc Cormack, 'The "Plymouth" Brethren?: Prolegomena to the Rewriting of J. M. Synge's Biography', *Religion and Literature*, vol. 28 nos 2/3 (Summer–Autumn 1996).
25 *CW II*, p. 235.

26 Ibid., p. 236. The quoted phrase comes from Christopher Marlowe's *The Jew of Malta* (Act One).

27 See the account of E. Savell Hicks's funeral tribute to Huxley in the *Irish Times* of 15/1/1940.

28 JMS to MA, 26/7/1907 (an annotation), *Letters II*, p. 000.

29 JMS to MA, postscript to [14/7/1907]; JMS to MA, 17/7/[1907], ibid., pp. 11 and 14.

30 JMS to MA, 17/7/[1907], ibid., pp. 13–14.

31 B. L. Reid, *The Man from New York: John Quinn and His Friends* (New York: Oxford University Press, 1968), p. 49.

32 See Mary Colum, *Life and the Dream* (London: Macmillan, 1947), pp. 108 etc.

33 JMS to MA [28/7/1908] and 30/11/1908, *Letters II*, pp. 173–4, 228.

34 JMS to MA, 14/9/1908, ibid., p. 198.

CHAPTER 21: **Elpis, or Hope**

1 Gillian Rose, *Love's Work* (London: Chatto, 1995), p. 99.

2 'The Death of Synge and Other Pages from an Old Diary', *The Dial*, vol. 84, no. 4 (April 1928), p. 280.

3 Susan Sontag, *Illness as Metaphor* (London: Allen Lane, 1979), pp. 3, 9.

4 TCD MS 4382.

5 *My Uncle*, p. 109. In 1909, the properties making up Elpis were owned by Margaret Huxley and Francis Manning. Huxley was the sixth child of William Huxley, elder brother of Thomas Henry Huxley.

6 In 1900, the governors of the Nurses' School included Margaret Huxley (Hon. Sec.), Mrs McDonnell (Richmond Hospital), C. B. Ball (Sir Patrick Dun's Hospital), Sir William Thompson (Richmond, Whitworth and Hardwick Hospitals). The School had originated in the Eye Hospital in Molesworth Street when Huxley had been in charge there.

7 T. G. Moorhead, *A Short History of Sir Patrick Dun's Hospital* (Dublin: Hodges Figgis, 1942), p. 159. Huxley had been in Dublin since at least 1884.

8 See *Letters II*, p. 147.

9 TCD MS 6220/51; KS to RAS, 11/11/1889; G & S, p. 43.

10 TCD Stephens MS 6192/1163 and 6192/1307.

11 TCD MS 6218 (copy of KS's diary), 22/5/1899.

12 TCD Stephens MS 6192/1526.

13 *Daughter*, pp. 122–3.

14 G & S quote (p. 273n) a letter written by Gogarty in old age, to the effect that he had not thought JMS's glands were (merely) tubercular and that it was consequently important to have them removed; also J. B. Lyons, *Oliver St John Gogarty: the Man of Many Talents* (Dublin: Blackwater, 1980).

15 See J. B. Lyons, *What Did I Die Of? The Deaths of Parnell, Wilde, Synge, and Other Literary Pathologies* (Dublin: Lilliput Press, 1991), p. 149.

16 'Étude Morbide: the Illness of John Millington Synge', in ibid., pp. 139–70.

17 KS to SS, 22/12/1897, quoted by Stephens in MS 6192/1319.

18 *CW II*, p. 43.

19 Ibid., p. 41.

20 TCD MS 4357.

21 *My Uncle*, pp. 113, 139, 143. See also TCD MS 6218, entry for 13/2/1901 – 'I wrote to Johnnie and answered his [letter] about the glands and sent £1: 0: 0. p[ostal] order for teeth' – and 30/4/1901.

22 JMS to KS, quoted (p. 44) in the introduction to *Letters I*.

23 Four earlier postcards to his mother (datable to 7/4/1900, 11/3/1901, ?27/2/1902 and 23/3/1902) have been preserved, one of them in the possession of Brian Boydell, composer.

It is clear that other, later, items of correspondence to his mother have also disappeared; see JMS to MA, 17/10/1907 (*Letters II*, p. 69) which refers to a letter from Kerry no longer traceable.

24 JMS to A. Gregory [26 January 1907], *Letters I*, p. 284.

25 Lyons, *What Did I Die Of?*, p. 151.

26 *Daughter*, p. 150. See pp. 415–6 below.

27 *My Uncle*, p. 192.

28 TCD Synge Correspondence, Item 367, Henri Lebeau to JMS, 28/8/1907.

29 JMS to MA, 13/9/[1907]; JMS to A. Gregory, 20/9/[1907]; and note citing WBY to John Quinn, 4/10/1907, *Letters II*, pp. 58–9.

30 *My Uncle*, p. 194.

31 Lyons, *What Did I Die Of?* pp. 157–8.

32 See JMS to MA, 9/11/1907, *Letters II*, p. 76.

33 Edward Adderley Stopford (1843–1919), one of a distinguished Anglo-Irish family of liberal views, brother of the nationalist historian, Alice Stopford Green (1847–1929). JMS had met him through his cousin, Edward M. Synge, of Byfleet, Surrey; see *Letters I*, pp. 259–60.

34 JMS to MA, 22/10/1907, 19/12/1907, 21/12/1907, *Letters II*, pp. 70, 111, 112.

35 JMS to Edward M. Synge, 31/12/1907, ibid., p. 116.

36 JMS to MA, 3/1/1908, ibid., p. 121.

37 *My Uncle*, p. 197.

38 WBY, 'The Municipal Gallery Revisited', *Yeats's Poems*, ed. A. Norman Jeffares and Warwick Gould (London: Macmillan, 1989), p. 439.

39 Stephen MacKenna to JMS, undated, quoted *Letters II*, p. 141. Stopford lived on Frankfort Terrace, just round the corner from JMS's new accommodation in York Road.

40 *My Uncle*, pp. 200–1, incorporating some of Carpenter's editorial conflations.

41 TCD Synge Correspondence, Item 425, Fred Sutton & Co. to J. M. Synge, 8/4/1908.

42 JMS to MA, undated [?25/4/1908], *Letters II*, p. 148.

43 JMS to WBY, 4/5/1908, ibid., p. 155; see *CW II*, p. 28, for the 'Étude'.

44 JMS to MA, 4/5/[1908], *Letters II*, pp. 153–4.

45 JMS to MA (undated), ibid., p. 156.

46 Quoted in ibid., p. 156.

47 John Quinn to WBY, 23/5/1908; Alan Himber (ed.), *The Letters of John Quinn to William Butler Yeats* (Epping: Bowker, 1983), pp. 114 and 117.

48 J. Quinn to WBY, 10/6/1908, ibid., p. 130. Quinn's source was Father Dennis O'Donovan.

49 J. Quinn to WBY, 20/12/1908, ibid., p. 126.

50 JMS to John Quinn, 11/7/1908; to MA, 11/7/1908, [13/7/1908], 15/7/1908, [20/7/1908]; *Letters II*, pp. 164–9.

51 TCD Synge Correspondence, Item 477, C. B. Ball to JMS, 1/10/1908, also Elpis account of 26/9/1908; Item 478, Margaret Huxley to JMS, 5/10/1908.

52 See Items 447 (7/7/1908), 453 (19/7/1908), 457 (1/8/1908, from 'Molly'), 460 (c.August 1908) and 546 (22/3/1909) in TCD Synge Correspondence.

53 *My Uncle*, p. 200; see also Lyons, *What Did I Die Of?*, p. 160.

54 WBY, *Memoirs*, ed. Denis Donoghue (London: Macmillan, 1972), p. 220.

55 Lyons, *What Did I Die Of?*, p. 153.

56 *CW II*, p. 9.

57 JMS to MA, 2/10/1908; see *Letters II*, p. 205.

58 JMS to MA, 7/10/1908, ibid., p. 206.

59 JMS to MA [9/10/1908], ibid., p. 208.

60 JMS to MA, 'Monday morning' [i.e. 26/10/1908], ibid., p. 216.

61 The death certificate states that Kathleen Synge died the previous day (a Sunday); that is, on 25 October. There is no reference to the cancer acknowledged in Stephens's comments

on the similar deaths of mother and son. (See Registry of Deaths in the District of Kingstown, Union of Rathdown, County of Dublin: Entry 467 (2/11/1908 on the information of RAS).)

62 TCD Synge Correspondence, Item 481 (telegram).
63 See Stephens MS 6197/4623 for evidence of R. Matheson.
64 'Under Ben Bulben', Peter Allt and R. K. Alspach (eds), *The Variorum Edition of the Poems of W. B. Yeats* (London: Macmillan, 1977), p. 640.
65 JMS to MA, 'Wednesday evening' [i.e. 8/10/1908], *Letters II*, p. 216.
66 JMS to MA [30/10/1908], ibid., p. 217; 25/10/1908, p. 216; 6/11/1908, p. 219.
67 JMS to MA [9/11/1908], ibid., p. 221.
68 TCD Synge Correspondence, Item 484, ES to RAS, 6/11/1908.
69 See *Letters II*, p. 226 n2.
70 JMS to MA, 9/11/1908, ibid., p. 220.
71 Lyons, *What Did I Die Of?*, p. 146.
72 Mrs Margaret Synge, of Ballinglen, to the present writer, 1/9/1996.
73 Lyons, *What Did I Die Of?*, p. 153; on Molly's menstruation, etc., see Saddlemyer's annotation of JMS to MA, 1/5/[1907], *Letters I*, p. 325; see also O. St J. Gogarty, *As I Was Going Down Sackville Street* (London: Rich & Cowan, 1937), p. 283. The obscure quotation is from Alfred Tennyson's 'A Character' (1830).

CHAPTER 22: 'Ulster Will Fight!'

1 Richard Aldington, 'Insouciance', *Complete Poems*, London: Wingate, 1948.
2 TCD MS 4,341 (a school exercise book).
3 For an authoritative account of Synge's sources, and of earlier treatments of the *Deirdre* material, see Declan Kiberd, *Synge and the Irish Language* (Dublin: Gill & Macmillan, 1993), pp. 176–95.
4 NLI: MS 29,520.
5 Mary King, *The Drama of J. M. Synge* (London: Fourth Estate, 1985), pp. 161–2.
6 James Frazer's *The Golden Bough* had begun to appear in 1890.
7 *CW IV*, p. 215.
8 Ibid., pp. 183, 189. In a less than meticulous examination, I count eight such invocations in Act One, none in Act Two, and two in Act Three. Their absence from the one act set outside Ireland is noteworthy.
9 Ibid., pp. 393–4.
10 *CW IV*, p. 209. For a further account of this 'modernism', see Katharine Worth, *The Irish Drama of Europe* (London: Athlone Press, 1978), pp. 122–4, where the influence of Maeterlinck and Wagner is discussed.
11 G & S, p. 185.
12 Lest it be thought an interference with JMS's text posthumously, by WBY or someone else, the phrase can be found in the typescript of November 1907 – NLI: MS 29,520 f. 14 (of Act Three).
13 Introduction to A. Gregory, *Cuchulain of Muirthemne* (Gerrards Cross: Smythe, 1970), p. 16.
14 WBY in the Preface to *Cuchulain*, p. 16.
15 Ann Saddlemyer (ed.), 'Synge to Mac Kenna: the Mature Years', *Massachusetts Review*, vol. 5, no. 2 (Winter 1964), pp. 279–95, esp. p. 281.
16 *CW IV*, pp. 203, 205, 203.
17 Ibid., p. 393.
18 In 1910, a Presbyterian wife was deprived of her children and deserted by her Catholic

husband for refusing to conform with the new Vatican requirements; see the *Northern Whig*, 19/11/1910.

19 *CW IV*, p. 205.
20 Ibid., p. 267.
21 Katharine Worth has compared some of Deirdre's speeches to 'arias [through which] the movement of the plot is suspended to allow a lyrical outpouring of feeling in which pain is taken up into melody and beauty'. See her *The Irish Drama of Europe*, p. 125.
22 *CW IV*, p. 259.
23 Quoted in W. M. G. Fay and Catherine Carswell, *The Fays of the Abbey Theatre* (London, Rich & Cowan, 1935), pp. 167–8.
24 See Kiberd, *Synge and the Irish Language*, pp. 179–80.
25 For the background to this movement, and its various philosophical aspects, see John McCole, *Walter Benjamin and the Antinomies of Tradition* (Ithaca/London: Cornell University Press, 1993), pp. 35–70. In the 1930s, Samuel Beckett did not fail to see links between the cult of the Red Branch in certain versions of Celtic saga and Germanic fascism; see the present writer's 'Austin Clarke: The Poet as Scapegoat of Modernism', in Patricia Coughlan and Alex Davis (eds.), *Modernism and Ireland: the Poetry of the 1930s* (Cork: Cork University Press, 1995), pp. 75–102.
26 JMS to MA, 12/10/1908, *Letters II*, p. 288.
27 G & S, p. 185.
28 *CW IV*, p. 227.
29 'Science as Vocation' is included (pp. 129–56) in Hans H. Gerth and C. Wright Mills (eds), *From Max Weber* (New York, 1958). I quote the passage as translated by Fredric Jameson, *The Ideologies of Theory: Essays 1971–1986*, vol. 2: *The Syntax of History* (London: Routledge, 1988), p. 11.

CHAPTER 23: 'All is Over. Huxley' (March 1909)

1 In conversation with Gerald Balfour.
2 WBY to Mabel Dickinson, 11/5/1908; quoted by R. F. Foster, *W. B. Yeats: a Life*, vol. 1: *The Apprentice Mage* (Oxford/New York: Oxford University Press, 1997), p. 384.
3 The words are Henri Lebeau's, paraphrasing a letter he had received from JMS; see TCD Synge Correspondence, Item 367, Lebeau to JMS, 28/8/1907.
4 E.g. £14 5s 0d 'being net amount of interest payable to you by the Hon Mrs [A. E. D.] Bligh on part of the sum of £500 which you advanced to her on foot of certain securities'. TCD Synge Correspondence, Item 522, Fred Sutton & Co. to JMS, 19/1/1909.
5 John Butler Yeats to WBY, 1/7/1908, Foster: *W. B. Yeats*, vol. 1.
6 Rainer Maria Rilke, *The Notebooks of Malte Laurids Brigge* (London: Hogarth Press, 1930), p. 15.
7 J. Quinn to F. J. Gregg, 28/5/1908, NYPL, MSS Division.
8 JMS to John Quinn, 16/6/1908. NYPL, MSS Division.
9 WBY, *Memoirs*, ed. Denis Donoghue (London: Macmillan, 1972), p. 205; Gonne to WBY, 'Samedi' [in February 1909], *The Gonne–Yeats Letters 1893–1938*, ed. Anna MacBride White and A. Norman Jeffares) (London: Hutchinson, 1992), p. 265.
10 See *Letters II*, pp. 252–3.
11 *My Uncle*, p. 208.
12 Ibid.
13 WBY to A. Gregory [9 March 1909], WBY to Florence Farr [17 March 1909], quoted from unpublished material kindly provided by John Kelly.
14 *Joseph Holloway's Abbey Theatre: a Selection from his Unpublished Journal* (Carbondale: Southern Illinois University Press, 1967), pp. 124–7.

15 WBY, *Memoirs*, ed. Denis Donoghue. A minor man of letters, Joy had been the contemporary of Synge during an earlier stay in Elpis, but was textually mobilised by Yeats for the final crisis.

16 Ibid., pp. 154, 160, 169, 177, 196, 199; but see also WBY to Gregory, 23/3/1909 – 'I am too scared in thought & sad about Synge to write more.' (Material provided by John Kelly.)

17 *Holloway's Abbey Theatre*, p. 128.

18 *My Uncle*, p. 211.

19 Ibid.

20 Ibid. The registration was effected by 'M. F. Scott Inmate 19 Lower Mount Street'; see Entry 100, Register of Deaths (District No. 4, South Dublin Union) for the second quarter of 1909.

21 *Holloway's Abbey Theatre*, p. 128 (under the date 6 July, that is, nearly five months after the event). Holloway had earlier recorded that he heard the news of Synge's death from W. J. Lawrence 'about twenty to three'.

22 From a reminiscence by Thomas MacDonagh, in *T. P.'s Weekly*, 9 April 1909, p. 469.

23 Bod. MS 52647 f. 291, FS (of Sidgwick & Jackson) to JMS, 22/3/1909.

24 W. B. Yeats to Augusta Gregory (author of *The Gail Gate*, as Yeats spelled it), [24 March 1909], quoted from unpublished material provided by John Kelly.

25 WBY, *Memoirs*, pp. 199–200.

26 Ibid., pp. 200–1; J. Quinn to F. J. Gregg, 1/4/1909, also: 'He never talked rancorously of any man with whom he differed in politics ... And more than all, I never heard him indulge in little or petty gossip about other persons in Dublin.'

27 *My Uncle*, p. 209. Holloway confirms the bible-reading, though JMS 'did not care to see minister or priest'.

28 Ibid., p. 210.

29 G & S II, p. 331.

30 WBY to A. Gregory (undated, but probably 17 March 1909), Allan Wade (ed.), *Letters of W. B. Yeats* (London: Hart-Davis, 1954), p. 526.

31 WBY to A. Gregory, [26/3/1909], unpublished material provided by John Kelly.

32 The idea may have originated with John Quinn who cabled Gregory to indicate his financial support for a monument deriving from a death-mask. However, Quinn did not learn of JMS's death until the end of the month. See J. Quinn to WBY, 16/4/1909; Alan Himber (ed.), *The Letters of John Quinn to William Butler Yeats* (Epping: Bowker, 1983), p. 130.

33 Lily Yeats's account, quoted in a document accompanying J. Quinn to F. J. Gregg, 3/4/1909, NYPL MSS Division.

34 Other names listed in the *Irish Times* included T. J. Callender (Molly's afflicted brother-in-law) and E. M. Weddall (who appears to have been attached to the Achill Island missions).

35 WBY to A. Gregory, [25/3/1909], from unpublished material provided by John Kelly.

36 Foster, *W. B. Yeats*, vol. 1, p. 400.

37 From a fragment in the Berg Collection, NYPL; see ibid., p. 401.

38 See J. Quinn to WBY, 16/4/1909; Himber (ed.), *Letters of John Quinn to William Butler Yeats*, p. 130.

39 Foster, *W. B. Yeats*, vol. 1, p. 400.

40 M. Gonne to WBY, Monday [29/3/1909], *The Gonne–Yeats Letters*, ed. White and Jeffares, p. 269.

41 WBY, *Memoirs*, pp. 200–1.

42 Ibid., p. 204. WBY in a letter to John Quinn of 18 February (i.e. less than a month later) is less dramatic: 'I wish medical etiquette permitted me to go down and stand in front of that pit and point out, among the protesters in the name of Irish virtue, the patients I am treating for venereal disease.' Quoted in B. L. Reid, *The Man from New York: John Quinn and His Friends* (New York: Oxford University Press, 1968), p. 48.

43 WBY, *Memoirs*, p. 205.

44 'Under Ben Bulben', Peter Allt and R. K. Alspach (eds), *The Variorum Edition of the Poems of W. B. Yeats* (London: Macmillan, 1977), p. 639.

45 WBY, *Memoirs*, ed. Donoghue, p. 204.

46 Georg Lukács, *Soul and Form*, trans. Anna Bostock (London: Merlin Press, 1974), p. 159.

CHAPTER 24: **The Last Will and the *WORKS* of 1910**

1 Henrik Ibsen, *Ghosts and Other Plays*, trans. Peter Watts (London: Penguin, 1964), p. 278.

2 J. Quinn to W. B. Yeats, 16/4/1909, and W. B. Yeats to J. Quinn, 12/1/1909; Alan Himber (ed.), *The Letters of John Quinn to William Butler Yeats* (Epping: Bowker, 1983), p. 132 and n5.

3 NLI: MS 11001 (19) i, Henri Lebeau to R. I. Best, 6/5/1909.

4 These excerpts are taken from a composite document sent by Quinn to F. J. Gregg of the New York *Evening Sun*, 3/4/1909 (hence the American spelling); the typescript is preserved in the MSS Division of NYPL.

5 See also Jack Yeats to Elkin Mathews, 6/9/1909, Reading MS 392 f. 899.

6 Gilbert Murray to C. P. Scott, 19/11/[1908], John Rylands Library, University of Manchester. The son of an East of Scotland fleet surgeon in the Royal Navy, Mair was born in Sunderland, Co. Durham, on 8 May 1887.

7 G. H. Mair, *Modern English Literature from Chaucer to the Present Day* (London: Williams & Norgate, 1914), p. 305. Mair's account of Synge in the various editions of this book derives in no small way from the anonymous tribute in the *Manchester Guardian*, published immediately after the dramatist's death. It is, however, significantly shorn of the passage describing Synge's confessed practice of listening to servant-girls through a chink in the floor.

8 Bod. MS 52646 ff. 37–8, Sidgwick & Jackson to Allan Wade, 19/11/1908 (copy).

9 Ibid., ff. 212–13, Sidgwick & Jackson to J. M. Synge, 19/12/1908 (copy). Sidgwick's source was John Masefield.

10 Bod. MS 52648 f. 175, Sidgwick & Jackson to Edward Synge, 27/5/1909 (copy), quoting from a letter of J. M. Synge dated 8/1/1909.

11 Ibid., f. 260, Sidgwick & Jackson to Edward Synge, 16/6/1909 (copy), and Sidgwick & Jackson to George Roberts, 24/6/1909 (copy). In July 1909, Edward Synge joined the Society of Authors in order to have professional advice in administering his brother's will: see BL Add. MS 56830 ff. 67, 72 etc.: the Society advised him about Maunsel (that is, George Roberts) whom it described as 'rapacious and difficult to deal with' (G. H. Thring to E. Synge, 21/7/1909, BL Add. MSS. 56830 f. 74). He also joined the Société des Auteurs et Compositeurs Dramatiques and the League of British Dramatists (1933) for the same purpose.

12 See *Joseph Holloway's Abbey Theatre: A Selection from His Unpublished Journal* (Carbondale: Southern Illinois University Press, 1967), p. 129. The destruction of the Customs House during the Irish War of Independence, and of the Four Courts (with nearby buildings) during the ensuing Civil War, resulted in a vast loss of testamentary documentation, including wills. Where details of pre-1922 wills are available, they often derive (as in Synge's case) from a copy preserved in some lawyer's office.

13 On the other hand, in 1908 Vyvian Holland rented a small unfurnished flat in Kensington Palace Mansions for £75 p.a. including service.

14 George Russell to John Quinn, 27/4/1909; see Alan Denson (ed.), *Letters from AE* (London/New York: Abelard-Schuman, 1961), p. 66.

15 Details taken from a transcript made by or for John Lighton Synge, Hutchie's younger brother, kindly provided by Cathleen Morawetz, daughter of J. L. Synge. Elsewhere in the

same notebook-transcript, Hutchie expresses fears that his own notebooks might have been destroyed by his father.

16 W. B. Yeats to Augusta Gregory [2/4/1909], from unpublished material provided by John Kelly. The manuscript was in their hands by 25 April.

17 *CW I*, p. 49. The place referred to in l. 6 is Mountjoy Jail in Dublin.

18 W. B. Yeats, *Memoirs*, ed. Denis Donoghue (London: Macmillan, 1972), p. 208.

19 I have heard it said in Wicklow, almost ninety years after J. M. Synge's death, that the financial difficulties of the family were not unrelated to Harry Stephens's handling of their affairs, this without any implication of incompetence on his part.

20 JMS to MA, 9/11/1908, *Letters II*, p. 220.

21 See M. Gonne to W. B. Yeats [London, May, 1909], *The Gonne–Yeats Letters 1893–1938*, ed. Anna MacBride White and A. Norman Jeffares (London: Hutchinson, 1992), pp. 270–1.

22 WBY, *Memoirs*, p. 208.

23 W. B. Yeats [untitled Introduction] in J. M. Synge, *Poems and Translations* (Churchtown: Cuala Press, 1909), p. [xiv].

24 George Roberts to Yeats, 18/10/1910, quoted by Robin Skelton in *CWs I*, p. xvii.

25 See copies preserved in George Roberts's papers, NLI MS 13272 (1).

26 R. F. Foster, *Yeats; a Life*, vol. 1: *The Apprentice Mage* (Oxford/New York: Oxford University Press, 1997), p. 604 n198, citing W. B. Yeats to Joseph Hone, 3/10/1910 (Berg Collection, NYPL).

27 Ibid., p. 419.

28 NLI: MS 13272 (2), George Roberts to Charles Weekes, 3/11/1910 (copy).

29 NLI: MS 13272 (1), George Roberts to Edward Synge, 19/9/1910 (copy).

30 While advising Roberts on complicated negotiations with American publishers, Weekes had complained, 'I am surprised at any respectable house giving you much attention. Your typing is the worst I have ever seen.' NLI: MS 13272 (4), Charles Weekes to George Roberts, 6/2/1911 (copy).

31 For a description of the 'Under Ether' manuscript, see p. 344 above; for 'Glencree', see p. 219 ff.

32 NLI MS 8320, quoted by Foster, *W. B. Yeats*, vol. 1, p. 607 n82.

33 TCD Synge Correspondence, Item 563.

34 NLI: MS 13272 (4), George Roberts to Charles Weekes, 2/2/1911 (copy).

35 NLI: MS 13272 (1) annotation to George Roberts to Charles Weekes, 13/9/1910 (copy) and Weekes to Roberts, 27/10/1910 (copy).

36 Reported in NLI: MS 13272 (1), George Roberts to Edward Synge, 20/7/1910 (copy).

37 See NLI: 13272 (7), undated draft of letter to Edward Synge, probably c.May 1911.

38 NLI: 13272 (3) James Byrne Hackett to George Roberts, 24/2/1911 (Hackett and Roberts were personally acquainted). Chicago *Evening Post*, 24/2/1911.

39 NLI: MS 13272 (4), John W. Luce to George Roberts, 23/2/1911 (copy).

40 NLI: MS 13272 (7), George Roberts to E. Golding Bright, 3/7/1911 (copy).

41 See NLI: MS 13272 (7), various documents and copies of agreements. Also NLI: MS 13272 (15), Mollie Roberts to George Roberts, 6/3/1912.

42 For a brief but unsatisfactory description of the 1910/1911 editions, see *CW II*, pp. xii–xiii.

43 TCD Synge Correspondence, Item 570, Máire Mair to 'Mr Synge', 17/11/1911.

44 'Jack & Jill Attend the Theatre', *Rhythm* (August 1912), p. 120.

CHAPTER 25: Perpetual Judgement, 1911–32

1 J. L. Synge, *Kandalman's Krim: a Realistic Fantasy* (London: Cape, 1957), p. 11.

2 I am grateful to Cathleen Morawetz for a reconstruction (9/7/1998) of her uncle's

movements after March 1909. For the Buenos Aires letter, see NLI: MS 11001 (19) i, Lebeau to R. I. Best, 26/7/1915.

3   NLI: MS 11000 (22), Robin Flower to R. I. Best, 13/11/1914.

4   Lily Yeats to John Quinn, 4/5/1915, quoted in B. L. Reid, *The Man from New York: John Quinn and His Friends* (New York: Oxford University Press, 1968), p. 217. John Middleton Murry to Katherine Mansfield [24/3/1915], *The Letters of John Middleton Murry to Katherine Mansfield* (Auckland: Hutchinson, 1983), p. 50. The translator claiming this achievement was Florian Sobieniski.

5   Elizabeth Coxhead, *Daughters of Erin* (London: Secker & Warburg, 1965), p. 207.

6   G. H. Mair to C. P. Scott, 14/9/1914; Col. Linnie James to C. P. Scott, 19/1/1926, John Rylands Library, University of Manchester. The Home Secretary in 1914 was Reginald McKenna (1863–1943).

7   BL Add. MS 63447.

8   Data drawn from papers in the University of Reading archives: Roberts to Allen & Unwin (11/3/1916); memo from Maunsel to Allen & Unwin (5/4/1916); undated letter (envelope postmarked 9/5/1916), and Maunsel to Allen & Unwin (11/10/1916).

9   Ibid., Maunsel to Stanley Unwin, 15/1/1917.

10   See JMS [and Harry Clarke], *Queens* (Mountrath: Dolmen Press, 1986); also Nicola Gordon Bowe, *The Life and Work of Harry Clarke* (Dublin: Irish Academic Press, 1989), pp. 78–9.

11   Univ. Reading archives: copy of a Memorandum of Agreement, dated 18/9/1920.

12   Ezra Pound to John Quinn, 15/11/1918; Timothy Materer (ed.), *The Selected Letters of Ezra Pound to John Quinn 1915–1924* (Durham, NC: Duke University Press, 1991), p. 169.

13   Univ. Reading archives: E. H. Synge to Allen & Unwin, 7/1/1924; Roberts to Allen & Unwin, 8/4/1922 and 12/4/1922.

14   Ibid.: a typed 'Report of Mr Roberts Call 25.1.23' in the Allen & Unwin file.

15   Ibid.: see three letters from Maunsel to Macmillan on this topic, 20/1/1923 to 25/5/1923.

16   Padraic Colum, *The Road Round Ireland* (New York: Macmillan, 1926), pp. 357–8. Mary Colum, *Life and the Dream* (London: Macmillan, 1947).

17   Univ. Reading archives: see Allen & Unwin to G & G. Keith, 23/4/1925, quoting E. H. Synge.

18   Ibid.: 4-page, undated draft to Maunsel & Roberts, filed with correspondence of May 1924. See also Allen & Unwin to E. H. Synge, 1/4/1925: 'our persistent protests at the insufficiency of the Supplies of the Synge publication in London...'

19   TCD Synge Correspondence, Item 575, E. H. Synge to W. B. Yeats, 17/7/1924.

20   Bowe, *Harry Clarke*, p. 201.

21   Univ. Reading archives: Edward Synge to Allen & Unwin, and E. H. Synge to Allen & Unwin – both 30/8/1924.

22   NLI: MS 11,001 (27) ii, W. K. Magee to R. I. Best, 21/12/1924.

23   Univ. Reading archives: E. H. Synge to Allen & Unwin, 27/3/1925 and 31/3/1925.

24   Ibid.: Allen & Unwin to E. H. Synge, 25/11/1925.

25   Early in October 1920 Maurice Bourgeois was arrested by British troops while travelling back to Dublin from Glenamalure (and the cottage in which *In the Shadow of the Glen* was set) with Constance Markievicz and Sean MacBride; see Maud Gonne to W. B. Yeats (n. d.), (*The Gonne–Yeats Letters 1893–1938*) ed. Anna MacBride White and A. Norman Jeffares (London: Hutchinson, 1992), pp. 413–4. According to Robert Brennan (1881–1964), later an important Irish diplomat, Bourgeois was acting as 'an agent for the French Government [whose] mission was to observe the Irish scene in the interests of France ... the memory of 1916 still rankled ...' (Robert Brennan, *Allegiance* (Dublin: Browne & Nolan, 1950), p. 274.)

26   Univ. Reading archives: E. H. Synge to Allen & Unwin, 13/10/1924; Allen & Unwin to E. H. Synge, 29/9/1924. The Fitzwilliam Nursing Home occupied two houses in Upper Pembroke Street, with the painter Sarah Purser living next door. The street was a continuation of

Hatch Street, part of the great development raised by Hutchie's ancestor, John Hatch, in more prosperous and easygoing days.

27 Ronald Ayling, 'Synge's First Love: Some South African Aspects', *Modern Drama* (February 1964), p. 460.

28 It is clear from Edward Synge's correspondence with the Society of Authors that the executors had no advance notice of the *Yale Review* publication of Synge's letters: see BL Add. MS 63447 ff. 112–14.

29 George Roberts to Allen & Unwin, 10/6/1925; E. H. Synge to Allen & Unwin, 4/4/1925 (from Carrick House, Deganwy). Though E. H. Synge gives the address as Carrick House, this is more likely Garrick House, a boarding establishment run by Eugenia Mary Jones. While it was not registered as a nursing home, it may well have taken in convalescents as did many similar establishments on the North Wales coast. I am grateful to Elizabeth Burns of St Asaph for this information.

30 Univ. Reading archives: G. H. Thring (Society of Authors) to Allen & Unwin, 8/1/1926; Allen & Unwin to Society of Authors, 13/1/1926. See also BL Add. MS. 63447 ff. 169–71 etc.

31 E.g. Padraic Colum's 'Memories of John M. Synge', *Literary Review* (New York), 4 June 1921.

32 Univ. Reading archives: Allen & Unwin to E. H. Synge, 15/1/1925. On the issue of translation rights, see Allen & Unwin to E. H. Synge, 8/4/1929, and the reply from E. Synge of 11/4/1929. By this date, it may be that Hutchie was no longer able to conduct business. For his suburban residence Ned had appropriated the name of one of the Galway townlands owned by his father, J. H. Synge.

33 Childers was court-martialled and shot in November 1922. See Augusta Gregory, *Journals*, vol. 2, ed. D. J. Murphy (Gerrards Cross: Smythe, 1987), p. 282, for comments on her visit to Wicklow.

34 See Bowe, *Harry Clarke*, pp. 72–8, for an extended description of the panels, framed between a prologue and epilogue in elaborate 'Japonisme', perhaps a tribute to Synge's interest in his distant cousin, Lafcadio Hearn.

35 James Stephens, 'Reminiscences of J. M. Synge', in Lloyd Frankenberg (ed.), *James, Seumas & Jacques: Unpublished Writings of James Stephens* (London: Macmillan, 1964), pp. 57–8.

36 According to the British Library, Stephens was responsible for the Dublin Civic Week handbook (1929).

37 Gregory, *Journals*, vol. 2, p. 234: 'leisure gave me time to read through the notes – memories of Synge – written by his older brother (for his daughter) which another brother, Archdeacon Synge, had sent me some time ago.' Logically, this suggests that either Ned or Robert Synge had written 'for his daughter', with Sam merely an intermediary.

38 Ibid.

39 Ibid., p. 282.

40 See Sean O'Faolain, 'Literature and Life: Yeats on Synge', *Irish Statesman*, 29/9/1928, pp. 71–2; Arthur Lynch, 'Synge', *Irish Statesman*, 20/10/1928, p. 131; Stephen MacKenna, 'Synge', *Irish Statesman*, 3/11/1928, pp. 169–70.

41 See pp. 6–7 for E. M. Stephens's Preface, pp. 29–37 for J. L. Synge on Hamilton Rowan, and pp. 38–41 for Frank Stephens on the history of commerce in Dublin.

42 Information from a family source.

43 Samuel Synge to Augusta Gregory, 30/4/1929 and 8/5/1929: Berg Collection, NYPL.

44 Augusta Gregory to Samuel Synge, 9/5/1929 (cancelled and unsent), Berg Collection, NYPL.

45 Augusta Gregory to Samuel Synge (undated), Berg Collection, NYPL. See also Gregory, *Journals*, vol. 2, ed. Murphy, pp. 434, 437–8.

46 Daniel Corkery, *Synge and Anglo-Irish Literature* (Cork: Cork University Press, 1931), pp. 46, 57–8, 63.

47 For a splendid class analysis of Yeats during the years of his collaboration with Synge, see two letters from Violet Martin to Edith Somerville, in Gifford Lewis (ed.), *The Selected Letters of Somerville and Ross* (London: Faber, 1989), pp. 240, 252 etc.

48 Prior to his letter in the *Irish Statesman* of 20/10/1928, Lynch had referred to Synge in *My Life Story* (London: Long, 1924), pp. 121, 148–50.

49 Patrick Maume, *'Life that is Exile': Daniel Corkery and the Search for Irish Ireland* (Belfast: Institute of Irish Studies, 1993), p. 113.

50 *Daughter*, p. 131.

51 Mrs Margaret Synge to the present writer, 1/9/1996. See also Mary Colum, *Life and the Dream*, p. 136. Mrs Colum had begun to publish her memoirs in 1928.

52 *CW IV* p. 71.

53 *Daughter*, pp. 5, 114.

54 Ibid., p. 150.

55 A point made in essence by Mrs Margaret Synge in the letter to the present writer already cited.

56 I am grateful to Cathleen Morawetz for this information (9/7/1998). Mrs Mary (Blakiston) Synge (1861–1930) died on 5/10/1930.

57 Maurice Bourgeois, *John Millington Synge and the Irish Theatre* (2nd edn; New York: Blom, 1968), p. 234; Corkery, *Synge and Anglo-Irish Literature*, p. 63 (relying on Bourgeois).

58 James Joyce, *Ulysses* ed. Jeri Johnson (Oxford: World's Classics, 1993), p. 191. Glasthule was a lower-middle-class area immediately north of Glendalough House, a considerable pressure on its respectability.

59 For a 'table showing deaths from various diseases' in the year of Synge's death, see Charles A. Cameron, *Report Upon the State of Public Health and the Sanitary Work Performed in Dublin During the Year 1909* (Dublin: Sealy, Bryers and Walker, 1910), p. 37.

60 *My Uncle*, p. 200.

61 T. W. Rolleston to John Quinn, 16/6/1907, NYPL, MSS Division.

62 W. B. Yeats to Augusta Gregory, 11 January 1912; from unpublished material provided by John Kelly. On 25 November 1911, Yeats had seen G. B. Shaw 'about a certain matter for the Synges'.

63 Some thoughts on the nineteenth-century encounter with alcoholism, syphilis, and TB are provided in Thomas Dormandy, *The White Death: a History of Tuberculosis* (London: Hambleton Press, 1999), pp. 61–2 etc.

64 See Stephens MS 6192/1526. Also the excerpts from Mrs Synge's diary in *Daughter*, p. 224, 'sent Kate for Dr W ... Dr W. came told J. to stay in bed very feverish and face much swelled' (22/5/1899).

65 George Peacocke, 'Hodgkin's Disease Occurring in Twins', *Dublin Journal of Medical Science*, vol. 120 (August 1905), pp. 85–9.

66 JMS to MA, [28/3/1907], *Letters I*, p. 321.

67 William M. A. Wright, 'Case of Lymphadenoma', *Dublin Journal of Medical Science*, vol. 85 (February 1888), pp. 106–10.

68 *CW II*, p. 29.

69 I am grateful to Professor J. S. Kelly for information about the stated cause of Mrs Yeats's death; see Yeats *Collected Letters*, vol. II, ed. W. Gould, J. Kelly and D. Toomey (Oxford: Clarendon Press, 1997), p. 485. Her sister, Agnes Pollexfen, suffered from manic psychosis and was committed for years to an asylum; see R. F. Foster, *W. B. Yeats: a Life*, vol. 1: *The Apprentice Mage* (Oxford/New York: Oxford University Press, 1997), p. 155.

70 *CW II*, pp. 10–11 where the reference is to nothing more precise than 'a book of Darwin's'. For 'Incest and parricide, thy father's murderer', see Act Two, Scene One of Dryden and Lee's *Oedipus* (1679).

71 Charles Darwin, *The Descent of Man* (London: Murray, 1871), vol. 2, p. 403.

72 *CW II*, p. 9.

73 TCD MS 6220/51, KS to Robert Synge, 11/11/1889.

CHAPTER 26: 'A Likely Gaffer in the End of All...'?

1 Francis Hackett to John Quinn, 26/6/[1911], NYPL, MSS Division.
2 TCD MS 4378 f. 26r.
3 *CW II*, p. 14.
4 [W. K. Magee], John Eglinton, *Irish Literary Portraits* (London: Macmillan, 1935), p. 27.
5 Frank Kermode (ed.), *Selected Prose of T. S. Eliot* (London: Faber, 1975), pp. 40–1.
6 See Lucien Goldmann, *The Hidden God: a Study of Tragic Vision in the* Pensées *of Pascal and the Tragedies of Racine*, trans. P. Thody (London: Routledge, 1964). Synge's peculiar resistance to individualisation might be reconsidered in the light of Goldmann's concept of transindividuality (see esp. Goldmann, *Method in the Sociology of Literature* (Oxford: Blackwell, 1980), pp. 91–110).
7 In the Introduction to *The Synge Manuscripts in the Library of Trinity College, Dublin* (Dublin: Dolmen Press, 1971), p. 10.
8 WBY to A. E. F. Horniman, 15/1/1910; and WBY to Allan Wade, 3/2/1910; from unpublished material provided by John Kelly.
9 Elizabeth Coxhead, *Daughters of Erin* (London: Secker and Warburg, 1965), pp. 187, 193.
10 WBY to August Gregory [15/12/1912]; from unpublished material provided by John Kelly.
11 James Stephens, 'Reminiscences of J. M. Synge', p. 57.

APPENDIX: **The Brethren: Origins and Beliefs**

1 See Robert Daly (ed.), *Letters and Papers by the Late Theodosia A., Viscountess Powerscourt* (3rd edn; Dublin: Curry, 1839).
2 See Andrew Miller, *The Brethren: A Brief Sketch of Their Origin, Progress and Testimony* (London: Morrill [1879]), pp. 9, 12–13, 21. Peter L. Embley, 'The Early Development of the Plymouth Brethren' in Bryan R. Wilson (ed.), *Patterns of Sectarianism* (London: Heinemann, 1967), pp. 213–43.
3 For the anti-Catholic aspect, see R. J. M'Ghee's anonymous pamphlet, *The Priest and His Dog: to the Roman Catholics of Powerscourt* (1832).
4 *Chief Men Among the Brethren* includes at least ten little-known Irishmen – Henry Bewley (1814–76), F. C. Bland (1826–94), the 5th Earl of Carrick (1835–1901), the 8th Earl of Cavan (1815–87), John Marsden Code (1805–73), William Talbot Crosbie (1817–99), Sir Edward Denny (1796–1889), Richard J. Mahoney (1827–92), and James Butler Stoney (1814–97). In addition to the ten Irish 'chief men among the Brethren', one can list Sir Richard O'Donnell of Newport House, County Mayo. And given that a whole tribe of Stoneys became Darbyites, the suspicion arises that the laudanum-taking Dr James Johnson Stoney, who served in the Aran Islands from 1858 to 1869 with a fine record of mischievous anti-sectarianism, may have been a renegade Brother.
5 'The group moved significantly toward the formation of a sect when in November Hutchinson, a layman, became the first among them to conduct a communion service independent of the prayer-book.' See Hutchinson in *The Blackwell Dictionary of Evangelical Biography* (Oxford: Blackwell, 1995).
6 Quoted in W. B. Neatby, *A History of the Plymouth Brethren* (London: Hodder, 1901), p. 39.
7 F. R. Coad, *A History of the Brethren Movement* (Exeter: Paternoster Press, 1968), pp. 36, 45, etc.
8 *A Biographical Sketch of the Struggles of Pestalozzi to Establish His System ... by an Irish*

Traveller [i.e. John Synge (Dublin: Folds, 1815), pp. xvi–xvii. See also T. C. F. Stunt, 'John Synge and the Early Brethren', *Christian Brethren Research*, no. 28 (1976), pp. 39–59.

9 Lewis's *Topographical Dictionary* (1837) gives the proprietor of Roundwood as John Gower.

10 See Neatby, *Plymouth Brethren*, p. 42. Darby acquired his middle name from his godfather, the victor at Trafalgar.

11 For a specifically Irish analysis, see G. S. McPhail, 'The History and Doctrines of the Plymouth Brethren', typescript preserved in the library of the Representative Church Body, Dublin.

12 See Thomas Edwards, *Gangreana: A Catalogue of Errors* (1646).

13 See W. B. Neatby's article in *The Protestant Dictionary* (London: Harrison Trust, 1933).

Acknowledgements

I wish to acknowledge gratefully the permission of The Board of Trinity College (Dublin) to quote from the Synge Papers in their possession. I also acknowledge The John M. Synge Trust in the same regard.

Poetry, prose, and unpublished correspondence of W. B. Yeats are quoted by kind permission of Anne Yeats and Michael Yeats, and A. P. Watt, London.

No work of research is independent of the institutions which preserve manuscript and other sources. I happily acknowledge the co-operation of the British Library, Brotherton Library (University of Leeds), Cornell University Library, John Rylands Library (University of Manchester), Lincoln's Inn Library (London), National Gallery of Ireland, National Library of Ireland, New York Public Library, Public Record Office (Kew), Registry of Deeds (Dublin), Society of Genealogists (London), Stirling Library (Yale University), Trinity College, Dublin (Library), University of Birmingham Library (Church Missionary Society archives), University College, Dublin (Dept. of Folklore), University College, London.

A number of individuals assisted with advice or information – Cathal Dallat Sr., David Lammey, the late Denis Stephens, Pamela and Richard Traill (Antrim); Michael Simpson, Tom Staley (Austin, Texas); Tim O'Sullivan (Cahirciveen); Joyce MacCormack (Carlisle); Richard Barrett, Charles Benson, Ciaran Brady, Liam Breatnach, Nuala Butler, Andrew Carpenter, Guy French, Paddy Gillan, James Hamilton, Fred Hanna, Helen Hewson, N. F. Lowe, Gerry Lyne, J. B. Lyons, Sheelagh McCormack, Simon McCormack, Derek Mahon, Jane Maxwell, Bernard Meehan, Catherine Murphy, Felicity O'Mahony, Stuart O Seanóir, Andrew Pierce, Kathleen Pendiville, Hilary Pyle, Raymond Refaussé, Patrick Scanlon, Philip Shields, Alex Ward (Dublin); Bill Johnsen (East Lancing); Mary and Proinsias Ó Drisceoil (Kilkenny); Bernard Reymond (Lausanne); Malcolm Barry, Helen Carr, Howard Caygill, Angela Darwin, Rebecca Dawson, Warwick Gould, Kirstie Hall, Jane Haville, Guy Holborn, Hilary Laurie, Maria Macdonald, Fiona Macintosh, Cath McKenzie, Ken Osborne, Len Platt, Deirdre Toomey, John Wyse-Jackson (London); Steve

Crook, Rodney Phillips (New York); Conor Carville, Roy Foster, Selina Guinness, Colin Harris, Claire Hutton, George Huxley, John Kelly (Oxford); Rolf and Magda Loeber (Pittsburg); Mike Butt, Brian Ryder (Reading); Mary Mackey (Schull); Marjorie, Eleanor and Nicholas Grene, Chris Halliday, Geoff and Mary King, Hillary O'Kelly, David Rose (Wicklow); Joan Powell (Winchester); Pamela Hatfield and Joe Spence (Windsor); Jenny Scott (Woking).

I am particularly grateful to Cathleen Morawetz (née Synge) in New York, Ann Porter (née Stephens) and Mrs Margaret Synge in Wicklow; and to Pamela and Richard Traill in Antrim for advice and guidance on matters of family history. My interpretation of the lives of their kith and kin cannot have given pleasure in every case, and I want warmly to acknowledge their willingness to let me explore potentially painful lines of inquiry. Phyllis Matheson (Dublin) provided valuable information about her kinswoman, Cherrie Matheson. John Kelly (Oxford) generously gave me access to unpublished portions of the W. B. Yeats correspondence bearing on the poet's relations with Synge. In Dublin Paddy Gillan solved innumerable last-minute problems through diligent and prompt research – for which relief, much thanks. At a late, crucial point, Conor Carville, Paddy Gillen, and Simon Mc Cormack joined me in a day-long expedition into Wicklow in successful search of elusive evidence. It was for such moments, under bright threatening Wicklow skies, that I undertook the biography in the first place.

Index